CONTEXTUALIZING ACTS

SBL
Society of Biblical Literature

Symposium Series

Christopher R. Matthews,
Editor

Number 20

CONTEXTUALIZING ACTS
Lukan Narrative and Greco-Roman Discourse

CONTEXTUALIZING ACTS
Lukan Narrative and
Greco-Roman Discourse

Edited by
Todd Penner and Caroline Vander Stichele

Society of Biblical Literature
Atlanta

CONTEXTUALIZING ACTS
Lukan Narrative and Greco-Roman Discourse

Copyright © 2003 by the Society of Biblical Literature

All rights reserved. No part of this work may be reproduced or transmitted in any form or by any means, electronic or mechanical, including photocopying and recording, or by means of any information storage or retrieval system, except as may be expressly permitted by the 1976 Copyright Act or in writing from the publisher. Requests for permission should be addressed in writing to the Rights and Permissions Office, Society of Biblical Literature, 825 Houston Mill Road, Atlanta, GA 30329 USA.

Cover photo of the leaf of Papyrus 46 containing 2 Cor. 11:33–12:9 courtesy of the Papyrology Collection, Graduate Library, University of Michigan.

Library of Congress Cataloging-in-Publication Data

Contextualizing Acts : Lukan narrative and Greco-Roman discourse / edited by Todd C. Penner and Caroline Vander Stichele.
    p. cm. — (Society of Biblical Literature symposium series ; no. 20)
Includes bibliographical references and indexes.
ISBN 1-58983-080-6 (pbk. : alk. paper)
    1. Bible. N.T. Acts—Socio-rhetorical criticism—Congresses. I. Penner, Todd C. II. Vander Stichele, Caroline. III. Series: Symposium series (Society of Biblical Literature) ; no. 20.
BS2625.52 .C66 2003
226.6'06—dc22   2003019716

        1 10 09 08 07 06 05 04 03   5 4 3 2 1

Printed in the United States of America on acid-free, recycled paper
conforming to ANSI/NISO Z39.48-1992 (R1997) and ISO 9706:1994
standards for paper permanence.

Ἀγνώστῳ θεῷ

Acts 17:23

CONTENTS

Acknowledgments ix

Abbreviations xi

Contextualizing Acts
    Todd Penner 1

From History to Rhetoric and Back: Assessing New Trends
    in Acts Studies
    Joseph B. Tyson 23

Luke and the *Progymnasmata*: A Preliminary Investigation
    into the Preliminary Exercises
    Mikeal C. Parsons 43

Civilizing Discourse: Acts, Declamation, and the Rhetoric
    of the *Polis*
    Todd Penner 65

The Trial Scene in the Greek Novels and in Acts
    Saundra Schwartz 105

ΜΕΤΑΒΟΛΗ ΠΟΛΙΤΕΙΩΝ—Jesus as Founder of the Church
    in Luke-Acts: Form and Function
    David L. Balch 139

Paul's Farewell to the Ephesian Elders and Hector's Farewell
    to Andromache: A Strategic Imitation of Homer's *Iliad*
    Dennis R. MacDonald 189

Cultural Divides and Dual Realities: A Greco-Roman
    Context for Acts 14
    Amy L. Wordelman 205

Roman Propaganda and Christian Identity in the Worldview
of Luke-Acts
Gary Gilbert 233

History or Story in Acts—A Middle Way? The "We" Passages,
Historical Intertexture, and Oral History
Samuel Byrskog 257

The Jerusalem Community in Acts: Mythmaking and the
Sociorhetorical Functions of a Lukan Setting
Milton Moreland 285

Gender and Genre: Acts in/of Interpretation
Caroline Vander Stichele..311

Bibliography of Primary Sources..331

Bibliography of Modern Authors 335

Index of Primary Sources 379

Index of Modern Authors 400

Contributors 407

Acknowledgments

Most of the essays in this volume were originally presented as papers in the session "Recent Approaches to Acts," held at two separate International meetings of the Society of Biblical Literature: Rome (2001) and Berlin (2002). These two sessions are part of a larger session, "Whence and Whither? Methodology and the Future of Biblical Studies," which is dedicated to the examination of methodology in the field of biblical studies and is organized and run by the editors of this volume. Both sessions on Acts proved to be stimulating and engaging encounters, and we are grateful to the participants for reworking their presentations for publication. The contributors to this volume have all been wonderful to work with, and we are most grateful for their interest in and efforts for this project. We regret that Loveday Alexander, who presented in the Berlin session, was not able to participate in this volume, but those interested in her essay "Acts and the Ancient Reader" will find a version of it in her forthcoming publication on Acts with T&T Clark.

With respect to the ISBL meetings, we are appreciative of the help and support offered by the coordinators, especially Matthew Collins and Kristin De Troyer, both of whom were formative for the initiation of the "Whence and Whither" unit the year prior in Capetown, South Africa. Moreover, without travel funds provided by our respective institutions, the wonderful opportunities afforded by the ISBL meetings would have been lost. We are therefore indebted both to Austin College, which provided generous support through the Sid Richardson Foundation, and to the Amsterdam School of Cultural Analysis (ASCA) of the University of Amsterdam. Further support for Todd Penner's travel and research time (part of which was devoted to work on this volume) was provided by a Wabash Center for Teaching and Learning in Theology and Religion Summer Fellowship and a Junior Scholar Grant from the Southwest Commission on Religious Studies (SWCRS). Support for the work of junior scholars through organizations such as these is an encouragement and a true relief.

In terms of the production of this volume, help has come from many quarters. Gayle Bowers, Lindy Olsen, Michele Kennerly, Leah Gilliam, Jason Carl, and Amber Childress of Austin College were helpful with various editing and other practical matters. Special thanks goes to Ann Melton, who, as a student intern in the Department of Religion at Austin College, provided a truly Herculean labor in the final "hours" of this project—this volume is much better for her efforts. Thanks also to Michele Kennerly and Jacqueline Klassen for assistance with the indexing of this volume. We would also like to express gratitude to our colleagues and administrators for their support of this project. At Austin College, Dean Michael Imhoff, as well as Deans Dan Setterberg and Bernice Melvin, have been supportive of the time and effort that have gone into this volume and did what they could to make this endeavor possible. Further, Steve Stell, the chair of the Department of Religion and Philosophy, has been an ideal colleague, mentor, and friend over the past few years—his irrepressible generosity and unyielding support is, in a word, extraordinary. Finally, Carol Daeley deserves special recognition for her patience in the midst of the repeated misfortune of finding her print jobs queued behind the ones for this volume—she showed great restraint, throwing only the gentlest and most artful of verbal jabs in the process. At the University of Amsterdam, Jan Willem van Henten and Athalya Brenner have offered support and encouragement at various stages of this project and have also helped to furnish a pleasant and stimulating collegial working environment.

Practically speaking, this volume would not have seen the light of day had it not been for the initial expression of interest and encouragement by Christopher Matthews, the Symposium Series editor. Chris played a significant role in giving shape to this volume early on, and we are grateful for his keen editing eye (which saved us from *numerous* oversights) and delightful wit—it was a pleasure working with this "Rider on the Storm." Further, the manuscript benefited from the extensive, skillful labor of Bob Buller, Production Associate for SBL. We are grateful for the energy and time he invested in this project. Finally, Rex Matthews, SBL Editorial Director, was most helpful at various stages of this project—we are grateful to him for his encouragement with and input into this project.

Three more acknowledgments are in order. First, both the ISBL meetings and the production of this volume in particular have taken up a significant amount of energy and time. We are grateful to our spouses—Jacqueline Klassen and Jan Jans—for putting up with time away and time otherwise engaged. It would have been difficult if not impossible to complete this project without their moral support and patience. Second, the influence of our teachers has been formative in stimulating our initial interests in, shaping our perspectives on, and situating our approaches to the book of Acts. We would thus especially like to acknowledge Larry Hurtado of the University of Edinburgh; Carl Holladay, Luke Johnson, Vernon Robbins, and Hendrik Boers of Emory University; and Joël Delobel of the University of Leuven, who were outstanding pedagogues and mentors. Finally, recognition should also go to that mysterious figure from the past, the one we have come to call "Luke," one of many strangers of early Christianity who readily whets the appetite for knowing the unknown as well as the unknowable.

Abbreviations

Primary Sources

Aelius Aristides
   Or.   *Orationes / Orations*
Appian
   Bell. civ.   *Bella civilia / Civil Wars*
   Hist. rom.   *Historia romana / Roman History*
Apuleius
   Metam.   *Metamorphoses / The Golden Ass*
Aristotle
   Poet.   *Poetica / Poetics*
   Pol.   *Politica / Politics*
   Rhet.   *Rhetorica / Rhetoric*
   Top.   *Topica / Topics*
Arrian
   Anab.   *Anabasis of Alexander*
Augustine
   Conf.   *Confessions*
Cicero
   Att.   *Epistulae ad Atticum / Letters to Atticus*
   De or.   *De oratore / On the Orator*
   Inv.   *De inventione rhetorica / On Invention*
   Leg.   *De legibus / On the Laws*
   Off.   *De officiis / On Duties*
   Rep.   *De republica / On the Republic*
   Corp. herm.   *Corpus hermeticum*
Dio Chrysostom
   Or.   *Orationes / Oration*
Dionysius
   Ant. or.   *De antiquis oratoribus / The Ancient Orators*
   Ant. rom.   *Antiquitates romanae / Roman Antiquities*
   Isocr.   *De Isocrate / On Isocrates*
   Lys.   *De Lysia / On Lysias*
   Thuc.   *De Thucydide / On Thucydides*

Eusebius
   Hist. eccl.   *Historia ecclesiastica / Ecclesiastical History*
Hesiod
   Theog.   *Theogonia / Theogony*
Homer
   Il.   *Ilias / Iliad*
   Od.   *Odyssea / Odyssey*
Horace
   Carm.   *Carmina / Odes*
Ignatius
   Eph.   *To the Ephesians*
   Magn.   *To the Magnesians*
   Rom.   *To the Romans*
Isocrates
   Nic.   *Nicocles*
Josephus
   Ant.   *Antiquitates judaicae / Jewish Antiquties*
   C. Ap.   *Contra Apionem / Against Apion*
   War   *Bellum judaicum / Jewish War*
Justin Martyr
   1 Apol.   *1 Apology*
Libanius
   Or.   *Orationes / Oration*
Lucan
   Bell. civ.   *Bellum civile / Civil War*
Lucian
   Hist.   *Historia / How to Write History*
Minucius Felix
   Oct.   *Octavius*
Origen
   Cels.   *Contra Celsum / Against Celsus*
Ovid
   Fast.   *Fasti*
   Metam.   *Metamorphoses*
Pausanias
   Descr.   *Graeciae description / Description of Greece*
Philo
   Legat.   *Legatio ad Gaium / On the Embassy to Gaius*
Plato
   Ep.   *Epistulae / Letters*
   Phaedr.   *Phaedrus*
   Pol.   *Politicus / Statesman*
   Resp.   *Respublica / Republic*

Soph.	*Sophista* / *Sophist*
Symp.	*Symposium*
Pliny the Elder	
Nat.	*Naturalis historia* / *Natural History*
Pliny the Younger	
Ep.	*Epistulae* / *Letters*
Pan.	*Panegyricus*
Plutarch	
Adul. amic.	*Quomodo adulator ab amico internoscatur* / *How to Tell a Flatterer from a Friend*
Ant.	*Antonius* / *Life of Antony*
Comp. Lyc. Num.	*Comparatio Lycurgi et Numae* / *Comparison of Lycurgus and Numa*
Comp. Thes. Rom.	*Comparatio Thesei et Romuli* / *Comparison of Theseus and Romulus*
Lyc.	*Lycurgus* / *Life of Lycurgus*
Num.	*Numa* / *Life of Numa*
Princ. iner.	*Ad principem ineruditum* / *To an Uneducated Ruler*
Rom.	*Romulus* / *Life of Romulus*
Thes.	*Theseus* / *Life of Theseus*
Polycarp	
Pol. Phil.	*To the Philippians*
Quintilian	
Inst.	*Institutio oratoria* / *The Orator's Education*
RG	*Res Gestae Divi Augusti*
Rhet. Alex.	*Rhetorica ad Alexandrum*
Rhet. Her.	*Rhetorica ad Herennium*
Seneca	
Apoc.	*Apocolocyntosis*
Ep.	*Epistulae* / *Letters*
Statius	
Silv.	*Silvae*
Strabo	
Geogr.	*Geographica* / *Geography*
Suetonius	
Aug.	*De Vita Caesarum: Divus Augustus*
Jul.	*De Vita Caesarum: Divus Julius*
Nero	*De Vita Caesarum: Nero*
Vesp.	*De Vita Caesarum: Divus Vespasianus*
Tacitus	
Agr.	*Agricola*
Ann.	*Annales* / *Annals*

Tertullian
    Adv. Jud.   *Adversus Judaeos / Against the Jews*
Vergil
    Aen.   *Aeneis / Aeneid*
    Ecl.   *Eclogues*
Xenophon
    Hell.   *Hellenica*
    Lac.   *Respublica Lacedaemoniorum / The Constitution of the of the Lacedaemonians* (Spartans)

Secondary Sources

AB	Anchor Bible
AGJU	Arbeiten zur Geschichte des antiken Judentums und des Urchristentums
AnBib	Analecta biblica
ANF	*The Ante-Nicene Fathers.* Translated by A. Roberts and J. Donaldson. 1885–87. 10 vols. Repr., Peabody, Mass.: Hendrickson, 1994.
ANRW	*Aufstieg und Niedergang der römischen Welt: Geschichte und Kultur Roms im Spiegel der neueren Forschung.* Edited by H. Temporini and W. Haase. Berlin, 1972–.
ASA	American Sociological Association
BETL	Bibliotheca ephemeridum theologicarum lovaniensium
Bib	*Biblica*
BibInt	Biblical Interpretation
BMCR	*Bryn Mawr Classical Review*
BN	*Biblische Notizen*
BZNW	Beihefte zur Zeitschrift für die neutestamentliche Wissenschaft und die Kunde der älteren Kirche
CA	*Classical Antiquity*
CBQ	*Catholic Biblical Quarterly*
CIL	*Corpus Inscriptionum Latinarum.* 1863–
ClassBul	*Classical Bulletin*
CJ	*Classical Journal*
ConBNT	Coniectanea neotestamentica or Coniectanea biblica: New Testament Series
CQ	*Classical Quarterly*
EH	Europäische Hochschulschriften
ESEC	Emory Studies in Early Christianity
ETL	*Ephemerides theologicae lovanienses*
FCNTECW	Feminist Companion to the New Testament and Early Christian Writings

FGH	*Die Fragmente der griechischen Historiker.* Edited by F. Jacoby. Leiden: Brill, 1954–64.
FRLANT	Forschungen zur Religion und Literatur des Alten und Neuen Testaments
GBS	Guides to Biblical Scholarship
GR	*Greece and Rome*
GTA	Göttinger theologischer Arbeiten
HDR	Harvard Dissertations in Religion
HNT	Handbuch zum Neuen Testament
HTKNT	Herders theologischer Kommentar zum Neuen Testament
HTR	*Harvard Theological Review*
IBS	*Irish Biblical Studies*
ICC	International Critical Commentary
IFT	Introductions in Feminist Theology
ILS	*Inscriptiones latinae selectae.* Edited by Hermann Dessau. Berlin: Weidmann, 1892–1916.
JAAR	*Journal of the American Academy of Religion*
JAC	Jahrbuch für Antike und Christentum
JBL	*Journal of Biblical Literature*
JHS	*Journal of Hellenic Studies*
JJS	*Journal of Jewish Studies*
JR	*Journal of Religion*
JRS	*Journal of Roman Studies*
JSJSup	Journal for the Study of Judaism in the Persian, Hellenistic, and Roman Periods Supplement Series
JSNT	*Journal for the Study of the New Testament*
JSNTSup	Journal for the Study of the New Testament Supplement Series
JSOTSup	Journal for the Study of the Old Testament Supplement Series
JSPSup	Journal for the Study of the Pseudepigrapha Supplement Series
JTS	*Journal of Theological Studies*
KEK	Kritisch-exegetischer Kommentar über das Neue Testament (Meyer-Kommentar)
LCL	Loeb Classical Library
LEC	Library of Early Christianity
LS	*Louvain Studies*
MH	*Museum helveticum*
MJS	Münsteraner Judaistische Studien
MnSup	Mnemosyne, biliotheca classica Batava, Supplement
NIB	*New Interpreter's Bible.* Edited by L. E. Keck. 12 vols. Nashville: Abingdon, 1994–2002.

NICNT	New International Commentary on the New Testament
NovT	*Novum Testamentum*
NovTSup	Supplements to Novum Testamentum
NS	new series
NTS	*New Testament Studies*
PRSt	*Perspectives in Religious Studies*
PW	Pauly, A. F. *Paulys Realencyclopädie der classischen Altertumswissenschaft*. New edition by G. Wissowa. 49 vols. Munich: Druckenmüller, 1980.
RAC	*Reallexikon für Antike und Christentum*. Edited by T. Kluser et al. Stuttgart: Hiersemann, 1950–.
RB	*Revue biblique*
RG	Rhetores graeci
RelSRev	*Religious Studies Review*
SAC	Studies in Antiquity and Christianity
SANT	Studien zum Alten und Neuen Testaments
SB	Sources bibliques
SBLDS	Society of Biblical Literature Dissertation Series
SBLEJL	Society of Biblical Literature Early Judaism and Its Literature
SBLMS	Society of Biblical Literature Monograph Series
SBLRBS	Society of Biblical Literature Resources for Biblical Study
SBLSP	Society of Biblical Literature Seminar Papers
SBLSymS	Society of Biblical Literature Symposium Series
SBLTT	Society of Biblical Literature Texts and Translations
SBLWGRW	Society of Biblical Literature Writings from the Greco-Roman World
SBS	Stuttgarter Bibelstudien
SCJ	Studies in Christianity and Judaism; Etudes sur le Christianisme et le Judaisme
SEÅ	*Svensk exegetisk arsbok*
SEG	Supplementum epigraphicum Graecum, 1923–.
SemeiaSt	Semeia Studies
SJLA	Studies in Judaism in Late Antiquity
SNTSMS	Society for New Testament Studies Monograph Series
SP	Sacra pagina
SR	*Studies in Religion*
SSEJC	Studies in Scripture in Early Judaism and Christianity
SSN	Studia semitica neerlandica
StPB	Studia post-biblica
SUNT	Studien zur Umwelt des Neuen Testaments
TANZ	Texte und Arbeiten zum neutestamentlichen Zeitalter
TLG	*Thesaurus Linguae Graecae* (CD-ROM E), 1972–.
TynBul	*Tyndale Bulletin*

TZ	*Theologische Zeitschrift*
VCSup	Supplements to Vigiliae Christianae
WMANT	Wissenchaftliche Monographien zum Alten und Neuen Testament
WUNT	Wissenschaftliche Untersuchungen zum Neuen Testament
YCS	Yale Classical Studies
ZBK	Zürcher Bibelkommentare
ZNW	*Zeitschrift für die neutestamentliche Wissenschaft und die Kunde der älteren Kirche*

**All quotations from ancient Greek and Latin writers, unless otherwise noted, are from the Loeb Classical Library.

CONTEXTUALIZING ACTS

Todd Penner

Paula Fredriksen has recently and aptly observed that "once method determines our perspective on our sources, *how* we see is really what we get."[1] The early Christian book of Acts serves as an interesting test case for this conclusion, as the various methods used and results obtained from well over a century of study illustrate the widespread diversity of interpretive strategies for reading Lukan narrative. That Richard Pervo's *Profit with Delight* should have been published at about the same time as the third edition of F. F. Bruce's classic commentary on Acts is a testament to the rather strong *Tendenz* of particular trajectories of scholarship—often with seemingly little dialogue going on between them.[2] These are two very different approaches to and appreciations of Lukan narrative strategies, and there are many more that could be added, which offer significantly different appraisals of the genre and setting of the text.

While readers of this volume no doubt will already be inclined toward—perhaps already entrenched in—their own particular reading strategies, it is still worth engaging issues of methodology in the study of Acts. This volume in many respect aims at this lofty goal. At the same time, there is an underlying commitment already in place: whatever particular—if not sometimes from certain viewpoints also peculiar—method and reading strategy one adopts, it will clearly and inevitably involve situating Lukan narrative within the literary, social, and cultural world of antiquity. This volume is committed to exploring this particular *Tendenz,* although the precise manner of that investigation is purposely varied and open-ended.

---

[1] Paula Fredriksen, *Jesus of Nazareth, King of the Jews: A Jewish Life and the Emergence of Christianity* (New York: Knopf, 1999), 7.

[2] Richard I. Pervo, *Profit with Delight: The Literary Genre of the Acts of the Apostles* (Philadelphia: Fortress, 1987); Frederick F. Bruce, *The Book of Acts* (3d ed.; NICNT; Grand Rapids: Eerdmans, 1988).

Predecessors

Anyone even remotely familiar with the study of Luke-Acts knows how much attention has been paid to the prologue of the Gospel. It is here that Luke sets out his stated goal of presenting a narrative of early Christianity that is in some way situated in the context of *other* narratives that have come before. Scholars have been particularly interested in the way that Luke intends to differentiate his narrative from those of his predecessors, as the point of difference is also one of identity. The argument has been made—and probably correctly so—that we can learn much about Luke-Acts by beginning first with the writer's own self-conscious assertions about his methods and interests, even if we have to give careful attention to the various nuances of these. It is probably fitting that a collection of essays devoted to the study of Lukan narrative should begin in a similar vein. Much can be learned by comparison, and it may thus prove helpful for situating the essays compiled herein to give some shape to past scholarship, so that the structural cohesion—the narrative *dianoia*—of this current project comes into sharper focus.

If one looks back over the past fifteen years, the place to start, not just chronologically but also in some sense methodologically, is with *The Social World of Luke-Acts: Models for Interpretation*.[3] In this seminal collection scholars such as Bruce Malina, Jerome Neyrey, Richard Rohrbaugh, Dennis Oakman, John Pilch, John Elliott, and Vernon Robbins took a dramatic and decisive turn toward the use of social-scientific and anthropological models to analyze Lukan narrative. Arising out of The Context Group, originally formed to work against the increasing specialization in the field of biblical studies and to promote a more holistic and inclusive approach to the study of biblical texts, the writers in this volume explore the relevance of ancient models of honor/shame and patron/client; dyadic personalities; deviance theory; urban and countryside relations and tensions; function of body zones in healing narratives; ritual theory; and the place of purity in the symbolic world of Luke-Acts.

This work followed closely upon the ground-breaking monograph by Philip Esler, *Community and Gospel in Luke-Acts*,[4] which was one of the first major studies systematically to apply social-science methodology to an analysis of the Lukan narrative. Esler argues that Luke-Acts should be

---

[3] Jerome Neyrey, ed., *The Social World of Luke-Acts: Models for Interpretation* (Peabody, Mass.: Hendrickson, 1991).

[4] Philip F. Esler, *Community and Gospel in Luke-Acts: The Social and Political Motivations of Lucan Theology* (SNTSMS 57; Cambridge: Cambridge University Press, 1987).

read as a legitimization of a sectarian movement that was under social and political pressures from the Roman world. His work was, however, still somewhat tied to historical reconstructions lying behind Luke-Acts and resonated with more traditional methodologies, a legacy of redaction-critical concerns still fairly prominent in the 1980s. The studies in *The Social World of Luke-Acts,* to the contrary, moved beyond these former approaches in a significant way, focusing much more on the application of social-science methodology to the narrative of Luke-Acts and integrating sociological and social-cultural analysis with literary criticism.[5] This collection as a whole still stands as not only one of the more important studies in the field of Luke-Acts scholarship but also as one of the more notable applications as a whole of social-science methods to New Testament analysis.

Just two years later, in 1993, the first volume of what is rightly regarded as one of the more elaborate research undertakings in New Testament scholarship of the past decade was published: *The Book of Acts in Its First Century Setting* (five volumes of the planned six-volume set have thus far appeared).[6] This work is essentially the perpetuation, updating, and partial reconceptualization of the classic work edited by Frederick J. Foakes Jackson and Kirsopp Lake, *The Beginnings of Christianity: The Acts of the Apostles,* published in five volumes between 1920 and 1933.[7] The published five volumes of Winter's project have as their express purpose to explore the historical context of the book of Acts, providing more broadly conceived historical-critical assessments of the wide range of literary, social, cultural, political, and geographical horizons for understanding the narrative of Acts as a reflection of the realities of its early settings in life. This framework for situating Acts is still fairly traditional—very much in

---

[5] Vernon K. Robbins's study, "The Social Location of the Implied Author of Luke-Acts," in Neyrey, *Social World of Luke-Acts,* 305–32, is one of the essays that achieved this aim of holism in interpretation rather well; he combines social-world analysis with social-science interpretation, followed with literary-critical observations that focus on the *implied* author (cf. idem, "Luke-Acts: A Mixed Population Seeks a Home in the Roman Empire," in *Images of Empire* [ed. L. Alexander; JSOTSup 122; Sheffield: Sheffield Academic Press, 1991], 202–21). One can perceive *in nuce* here what would later flower into his more self-consciously designated sociorhetorical method of textual interpretation (see especially his *The Tapestry of Early Christian Discourse: Rhetoric, Society and Ideology* [London: Routledge, 1996]).

[6] Bruce W. Winter, ed., *The Book of Acts in Its First Century Setting* (5 vols.; Grand Rapids: Eerdmans, 1993–96).

[7] Frederick J. Foakes Jackson and Kirsopp Lake, eds., *The Beginnings of Christianity: The Acts of the Apostles* (5 vols.; London: Macmillan, 1920–33; repr., Grand Rapids: Baker, 1979).

line, in fact, with the direction of the earlier *Beginnings of Christianity*. The first volume sets this up clearly, since ancient historiography forms the sole focus of genre engagement.[8] The fact that alternative historical subgenres are considered, though not, for example, the ancient novel or epic, might suggest (at least implicitly) that the project editors connect the truth quality of Acts to its generic specificity as ancient *historia*, although the actual contributors are probably of varied opinion on this matter. The one essay that engages something of the novelistic persuasion, Richard Bauckham's "The *Acts of Paul* as a Sequel to Acts," does so only to bolster the more assured historical grounding of the book of Acts, continuing the traditional and firm delineation between ancient novels—including here Christian apocryphal Acts—and what we find in the canon.[9] It is thus evident that there are tensions in the first volume: some scholars are much more tied to traditional historical questions, while others are clearly interested in moving beyond to the analysis of narrative function. These different models are not explicitly interwoven in the volume let alone the series, and this represents a curious but perhaps telling phenomenon.

In 1996, the year in which volume 5 of Winter's series appeared,[10] Ben Witherington edited a collection entitled *History, Literature and Society in the Book of Acts*.[11] This collection is noteworthy in large part because of its

---

[8] Bruce W. Winter and Andrew D. Clarke, eds., *The Book of Acts in Its Ancient Literary Setting* (vol. 1 of *The Book of Acts in Its First Century Setting*; Grand Rapids: Eerdmans, 1993).

[9] Richard Bauckham, "The *Acts of Paul* as a Sequel to Acts," in Winter and Clarke, *Book of Acts in Its Ancient Literary Setting*, 105–52. One of the more innovative and intriguing studies in this volume is Loveday Alexander's "Acts and Ancient Intellectual Biography" (31–63), where she moves beyond her earlier, more formalistic study (*The Preface to Luke's Gospel: Literary Convention and Social Context in Luke 1.1–4 and Acts 1.1* [SNTSMS 78; Cambridge: Cambridge University Press, 1993], originally submitted as her doctoral dissertation in 1978) to explore the paradigmatic narrative function of Socrates for the construction of the Acts narrative. A similar emphasis on narrative function can be found in David Peterson's "The Motif of Fulfillment and the Purpose of Luke-Acts" (83–104), as well as in F. Scott Spencer's "Acts and the Modern Literary Approaches" (381–414), which lays out the development of narrative readings and their importance for Acts studies. Also noteworthy is Philip E. Satterthwaite's study, "Acts against the Background of Classical Rhetoric" (337–79), especially his emphasis on the importance of *secondary rhetoric* (i.e., the use of oratorical rhetorical skills for prose composition) for Lukan narrative analysis (343).

[10] Irina Levinskaya, *The Book of Acts in Its Diaspora Setting* (vol. 5 of *The Book of Acts in Its First Century Setting*; Grand Rapids: Eerdmans, 1996).

[11] Ben Witherington, ed., *History, Literature, and Society in the Book of Acts* (Cambridge: Cambridge University Press, 1996).

eclectic character. While there is some older[12] as well as newer[13] ground covered, most striking is the overall framework given to the collection.[14] It is clearly Witherington's own agenda as editor to solidify the historical—and by this an element of historicity—in the Acts account. This comes to the forefront most clearly in his contribution paralleling Acts and the Gospel, using the lessons from the latter for implying compositional procedures for the former.[15] Witherington is committed not only to solidifying the use of sources by Luke in Acts but also to affirming their fundamental reliability. The fact that he sees it as necessary to add a (corrective?) addendum to the classicist W. James McCoy's essay dealing with historiography and Thucydides,[16] the latter of which does not fully support

---

[12] E.g., Loveday Alexander continues her questioning of the preface to Luke-Acts, examining how it does not match up to the generic expectations for a work of Hellenistic historiography ("The Preface to Acts and the Historians," 73–103); Charles Talbert returns to his argument that Acts represents the literary form of *bios* ("The Acts of the Apostles: Monograph or *Bios?*" 58–72); and David P. Moessner ("The 'Script' of the Scriptures in the Acts of the Apostles: Suffering as God's 'Plan' (Βουλή) for the 'Release of Sins,'" 218–50) revisits the methodology of his earlier study (*Lord of the Banquet: The Literary and Theological Significance of the Lukan Travel Narrative* (Minneapolis: Fortress, 1989; repr., Harrisburg, Pa.: Trinity Press International, 1998), focusing on the way in which the writer of Acts has utilized Israel's Scripture to plot the framework in which Jesus' suffering and God's plan are worked out in Acts.

[13] E.g., Jerome Neyrey, "Luke's Social Location of Paul: Cultural Anthropology and the Status of Paul in Acts" (251–79), focuses on the presentation of Paul in Acts in terms of his high social status; and Bill Arnold, "Luke's Characterizing Use of the Old Testament in the Book of Acts" (300–323), offers an interesting investigation of the way in which Luke uses Hebrew Bible citations to characterize the main apostles in the narrative.

[14] Richard Bauckham's two contributions are illustrative in this respect. These essays follow his typically elaborate and sophisticated argumentation, developing the exegetical basis for James's speech in Acts 15 and deciphering the distinctively Christian tradition in the kerygmatic summaries of Acts ("James and Gentiles [Acts 15.13–21]," 154–84; idem, "Kerygmatic Summaries in the Speeches of Acts," 185–217). In both instances Bauckham, although a believer in the creative power of early Christian transmission (see esp. his fascinating study, *Jude and the Relatives of Jesus in the Early Church* [Edinburgh: T&T Clark, 1990]), still invests a significant amount of faith in the use of tradition by Luke, and it seems to be an important assumption that Luke did not maintain free reign over his sources.

[15] Ben Witherington, "Editing the Good News: Some Synoptic Lessons for the Study of Acts," 324–47; cf. idem, "Finding Its Niche: The Historical and Rhetorical Species of Acts," in *SBL Seminar Papers, 1996* (SBLSP 35; Atlanta: Scholars Press, 1996), 67–97.

[16] Ben Witherington, Addendum to "In the Shadow of Thucydides," by W. James McCoy (23–32).

Witherington's own positivistic understanding of Thucydidean *historia*, suggests that this is a major *Tendenz* of the collected volume.[17] Nonetheless, the varied nature of the approaches in this volume, including the diversity in the understanding and assessment of tradition itself, signals a particular creative energy that the book of Acts still elicits on the contemporary biblical scene.

Two years later I. Howard Marshall and David Peterson's *Witness to the Gospel: The Theology of Acts* appeared.[18] The contributors to this large volume cover pretty much the entire gamut of Lukan theology in Acts, focusing on particular themes and/or textual units. As a whole this volume stands as a seminal contribution to the analysis of Lukan theology, but tensions exist here as well. On the one hand, many of the contributors to the collection are fairly clear on the fact that they are dealing with the Lukan portrayal, arrangement, and/or depiction of themes and events.[19] In other essays, however, Lukan theology is often (inadvertently?) fused with historical realities.[20]

---

[17] These emphases stand in sharp contrast to the writers who go out of their way to suggest both generically (Talbert, "Acts of the Apostles") and narratively (Neyrey, "Luke's Social Location of Paul") that the move to historicity is not so simple in the case of Acts. Craig Hill ("Acts 6.1–8.4: Division or Diversity?" 129–53), although still emphasizing the presence of some tradition in Acts 6:1–8:4, is overall skeptical with respect to the traditional and/or source nature of the speech of Stephen and the surrounding narrative. In the preface, though, Witherington clearly assumes that the various essays represent different but complementary approaches to Acts. This is not at all clear, however. In fact, it may well be argued that many of these methods of analysis presume conflicting and sometimes competing models for interpretation, not to mention the utilization of different definitions and meanings for the common vocabulary of interpretation (esp. concepts such as tradition and history).

[18] I. Howard Marshall and David Peterson, eds., *Witness to the Gospel: The Theology of Acts* (Grand Rapids: Eerdmans, 1998). This collection was to have been the original sixth volume of *The Book of Acts in Its First Century Setting* (as indicated by the list of forthcoming titles in the series on the dustjackets of the earlier volumes). By the time the fifth volume of 1996 was published (Levinskaya, *Book of Acts in Its Diaspora Setting*), the Marshall and Peterson volume had been replaced by one entitled *The Book of Acts in Its Theological Setting* (ed. Bruce W. Winter), which is still forthcoming with Eerdmans some seven years later.

[19] E.g., John Nolland, "Salvation-History and Eschatology" (63–81); Joel Green, "Salvation to the End of the Earth: God as Saviour in the Acts of the Apostles" (83–106); Christoph Stenschke, "The Need for Salvation" (125–44); and Andrew C. Clark, "The Role of the Apostles" (169–90), the latter of whom is especially cautious in referring throughout his essay to the Lukan "representation" and "conception" in the portrait of the disciples.

[20] E.g., Heinz-Werner Neudorfer, working on the speech of Stephen, seems to move rather effortlessly between tradition, redaction, and history, making little

In this respect Brian Capper's essay is the most methodologically reflective and for this reason one of the more important ones in the volume. Capper originally wrote an essay on the community of goods in Jerusalem for the fourth volume of *The Book of Acts in Its First Century Setting,* which had a significant focus on the historical dimensions of the accounts.[21] In this later essay he returns to this same topic but now analyzes the sociocultural, conceptual, and literary backgrounds,[22] arguing that at the point that Luke is no longer indebted to his literary paradigms the reader has reached the historical tradition. This formulation aptly summarizes the overall commitment of the volume: there is a historical core to Acts, although what it is and how to retrieve it receives a variety of responses.

One year later, in 1999, one of the more important (and certainly more influential) collections on Luke-Acts in the past fifteen years was published: *Jesus and the Heritage of Israel: Luke's Narrative Claim upon Israel's Legacy.*[23] In the conclusion, David Moessner and David Tiede herald the representative direction reflected in the volume as a sea change in interpretation. The volume concludes with the expression of the following sentiment: "Amid a sea change of interpretation, the quest for the theology of Luke-Acts becomes again a vital narrative, rhetorical, hermeneutical, and historical enterprise."[24] The dramatic change touted herein is that Luke composed a narrative using Israel's Scriptures, which were reconfigured to persuade the reader toward the particular argumentative ends Luke had in view.[25] The

---

distinction between these quite different aspects ("The Speech of Stephen," 275–94). Elsewhere, and more subtly, in David Peterson's study of worship among the early Christians ("The Worship of the New Community," 373–95) and Brad Blue's examination of Jewish worship and its role in Acts ("The Influence of Jewish Worship on Luke's Presentation of the Early Church," 473–97), it is not always easy to discern when Luke qua writer is in view, when the historical early church is, or when they have both been amalgamated together.

[21] Brian Capper, "The Palestinian Context of Community of Goods," in *The Book of Acts in Its Palestinian Setting* (ed. R. Bauckham; vol. 4 of *The Book of Acts in Its First Century Setting;* Grand Rapids: Eerdmans, 1995), 323–56.

[22] Brian Capper, "Reciprocity and the Ethic of Acts," in Marshall and Peterson, *Witness to the Gospel,* 499–518.

[23] David P. Moessner, ed., *Jesus and the Heritage of Israel: Luke's Narrative Claim upon Israel's Legacy* (Harrisburg, Pa.: Trinity Press International, 1999).

[24] David P. Moessner and David L. Tiede, "Conclusion: 'And Some Were Persuaded...,'" 368 (cf. 358, 360).

[25] Although not cited in the volume, Nils A. Dahl's classic article, "The Story of Abraham in Luke-Acts," in *Studies in Luke-Acts* (ed. L. Keck and J. L. Martyn; Minneapolis: Fortress, 1966), 139–58, offered some initial suggestions in this direction in terms of understanding the Lukan reconfiguration of the Hebrew Bible toward Christian argumentative ends.

collection makes an especially significant contribution in detailing the function of narrative in ancient historiography, with particular appeal to the meaning and purpose of the Lukan prologue.[26] One of the critical emphases that arises as a result is that the sequence of the narrative of Luke-Acts is an essential component of Lukan rhetorical/literary strategy. Thus, literary artistry is at the heart of the theory and practice of ancient historiographical composition.

In the same year that Moessner's volume was published, Joseph Verheyden edited a sizeable collection of essays entitled *The Unity of Luke-Acts*,[27] which (re)visits the question that Richard Pervo and Mikeal Parsons had earlier placed in sharp relief: Do the Gospel and the second volume really (or must they of necessity) form a unified composition?[28] The essays in this volume are diverse, but there is also an overarching consistency in terms of the emphasis on narrative and theological readings of Luke-Acts. This is evidently in line with the intention of the volume: to focus on the literary and theological links that prove unity of authorship, unity of purpose, and unity of theological conception, demonstrating the connections between the Gospel and Acts.[29] However, it is also noteworthy in terms of what is

---

[26] David Moessner contributes a major essay examining how the narrative sequence relates to the function of reader persuasion ("The Appeal and Power of Poetics [Luke 1:1–4]: Luke's Superior Credentials [παρηκολουθηκότι], Narrative Sequence [καθεξῆς], and Firmness of Understanding [ἡ ἀσφάλεια] for the Reader," 84–123), while Darryl D. Schmidt ("Rhetorical Influences and Genre: Luke's Preface and the Rhetoric of Hellenistic Historiography," 27–60), Vernon K. Robbins ("The Claims of the Prologues and Greco-Roman Rhetoric: The Prefaces to Luke and Acts in Light of Greco-Roman Rhetorical Strategies," 63–83), and David L. Balch, ("ἀκριβῶς ... γράψαι (Luke 1:3): To Write the Full History of God's Receiving All Nations," 229–50) further the discussion of the rhetorical function of the prologue, particularly as it relates to the sequence of the narratives that follow and to the literary relationship between the Gospel and Acts.

[27] Joseph Verheyden, ed., *The Unity of Luke-Acts* (BETL 142; Leuven: Leuven University Press, 1999).

[28] Mikeal C. Parsons and Richard I. Pervo, *Rethinking the Unity of Luke and Acts* (Minneapolis: Fortress, 1993). Cf. the comments on Parsons and Pervo by Joseph Verheyden, "The Unity of Luke-Acts: What Are We Up To?" in Verheyden, *Unity of Luke-Acts,* 5–7.

[29] See, e.g., Robert L. Brawley "Abrahamic Covenant Traditions and the Characterization of God in Luke-Acts" (109–32); Loveday Alexander, "Reading Luke-Acts from Back to Front" (419–46); Michael Bachmann, "Die Stephanusepisode [Apg 6,1–8,3]: Ihre Bedeutung für die lukanische Sicht des Jerusalemischen Tempels und des Judentums" (545–62); and Peter J. Tomson, "Gamaliel's Counsel and the Apologetic Strategy of Luke-Acts" (585–604), all of which maintain consistency with the volume's stated aim.

fundamentally missing in these essays. For instance, the collection, despite its massive size, employs relatively little social-world or social-science analysis, and only a few of the essays make use of a Greco-Roman cultural framework for understanding Lukan discourse.[30] Overall, aside from extensive engagement with Hebrew Bible texts and their reconfiguration in Acts, the reflection on Lukan theology and discourse is articulated in fundamentally non-(anti-?)Greco-Roman categories.[31]

METHODOLOGIES

Specific trajectories that surface in these recent works have shifted the questions related to Acts from previous discussions, preparing the way for studies such as this one.[32] One might think particularly of those collections and studies that have focused on social-world analysis, coupled with both rhetorical and social-science investigations. Moreover, literary approaches to Luke-Acts have increasingly become fused with the reading strategies derived from more traditional approaches.[33] Perhaps when one looks on the current scene, particularly the essays collected in this volume, one should first and foremost highlight this aspect of fusion that has taken place: literary analysis has largely been coupled with other means of exploration, evoking new insights in the process.

Further, a number of studies have refocused attention on Lukan narrative as embodying ancient literary strategy.[34] Here the accent has clearly

---

[30] One notable exception is Albert Denaux's fine contribution, "The Theme of Divine Visits and Human (In)hospitality in Luke-Acts: Its Old Testament and Graeco-Roman Antecedents" (255–79).

[31] In this respect, *The Unity of Luke-Acts* can be set alongside *Witness to the Gospel*, since both offer a predominantly theologized (i.e., Christian) understanding and assessment of Lukan discourse. This differs in some respects from the approaches in the other volumes, which tend to emphasize the importance of the Greco-Roman materials for understanding the framing and content of the Lukan narrative.

[32] Other collections could have been discussed here as well. Worth noting are especially the following: Petri Luomanen, ed., *Luke-Acts: Scandinavian Perspectives* (Publications of the Finnish Exegetical Society 54; Göttingen: Vandenhoeck & Ruprecht, 1991); Richard P. Thompson and Thomas E. Phillips, eds., *Literary Studies in Luke-Acts: Essays in Honor of Joseph B. Tyson* (Macon, Ga.: Mercer University Press, 1998); and Christopher M. Tuckett, ed., *Luke's Literary Achievement: Collected Essays* (JSNTSup 116; Sheffield: Sheffield Academic Press, 1995).

[33] This shift was given significant stimulus by the work of Robert Tannehill, *The Narrative Unity of Luke-Acts: A Literary Interpretation* (2 vols.; Minneapolis: Fortress, 1986–90).

[34] This is especially the case with the studies in *Jesus and the Heritage of Israel* and to a lesser extent those in *History, Literature and Society in the Book of Acts*,

fallen on reassessing the narrative rhetorical strategies that a writer such as Luke was trained to utilize. The focus is also clearly on genre-related questions in these studies: one understands and appreciates Luke's aims as a reflection of the literary ethos of antiquity. Although less attention is paid to explicit formal discussions of genre, the underlying form-critical impulse can still be perceived, even if fleetingly: Luke's literary paradigms and narrative techniques reveal (impel?) his particular argumentative narrative strategies. The importance of genre in the current debate should thus not be underestimated—it has quite literally dominated Luke-Acts scholarship over the past twenty years. Although Martin Dibelius long ago seemed to push these issues to their limit, today they are gaining fresh momentum under the premise that the elusive key to the Lukan text still lies in its generic identification. Perhaps this is not quite yet the sea change that is heralded by Moessner and Tiede. Still, one cannot deny that the direction has been set for future research and that interaction with and engagement of the agenda set particularly by *Jesus and the Heritage of Israel* will be one of the challenges for future scholarship on Acts.

These broader reflections, then, bring us to the issue of method. While one could comment on the diversity and proliferation of methodologies in the study of Acts over the past fifteen years, one is struck more by the explicit lack of methodological reflection that has accompanied all of this voluminous research. We are often assured that our diverse individual methods are not in conflict, that they are somehow all resolved in the end.[35] However, even a cursory reading of recent Acts studies would challenge this premise: there is much now being done on Acts that is simply incompatible with other particular methodological frameworks. If Acts is in fact to be understood and read like an ancient novel, then this emphasis fundamentally (re)shapes how one thinks about sources and redaction. If, however, one affirms that Acts is a form of ancient *historia,* then one has to decide what kind of history it is, in order to discern the particular kind of reading strategy that is thereby evoked. One has then to establish the connection between *historia* and history/historicity as

---

regardless of how this emphasis might be conceived by the individual contributors to these volumes.

[35] Mark A. Powell, *What Are They Saying about Acts?* (New York: Paulist, 1992), concludes his fine survey of the various issues by offering a mediating observation with respect to the diversity of viewpoints: "most of the disagreements occur within parameters that define areas of consensus" (108). Verheyden, in his introductory essay to *The Unity of Luke-Acts* ("Unity of Luke-Acts," 52), (re)assures the reader that narrative analyses "on important points often only seem to confirm to a large degree the results of sound redaction-critical investigations."

well. In this sense, the assessment by Fredriksen at the outset of this essay is particularly pertinent for the current study of Acts—our methods do indeed determine our results.[36]

One can, of course, also raise the critical question as to why we prefer certain methods over others. It is interesting in this respect that the collections discussed above have strong tendencies in specific directions. There is, for example, a predominant emphasis on the genre of historiography. There are a few exceptions represented in these collections, but clearly these are not the majority view. While not all scholars represented would share the same position on what it means to label Acts as historiography (i.e., in terms of issues related to historicity), it is noteworthy that the *Sitz im Leben* of Acts in its first-century context has largely been articulated in two specific directions: (1) from a literary perspective there has been a focus on comparisons with ancient historical compositions; (2) from a historical perspective there has been a major stress on reconstructing the broader outlines of the sociohistorical world of the first century. These foci are not to be devalued in and of themselves, since they have been and will continue to be worthwhile scholarly avenues of pursuit. It is important to note, however, that these foci are traditional in their orientation, as historical-critical methodology has been significantly engaged (and invested) in these two primary enterprises. One must also acknowledge that there is a particular epistemological commitment grounded in this framework: there is something about history and something about theology that is implicitly inscribed in this process. One might think more broadly in terms of an incarnational commitment of historical criticism: that divine elements (however defined or articulated) happen in human history, that there really were events "fulfilled among us." Thus, recent Acts study still reflects, at least in part, a commitment to this older theohistorical paradigm of interpretation, although some of the previous articulations have taken on a different shape in the ensuing years.

There is, naturally, nothing wrong with or objectionable about this situation; neither the ties with past historical-critical scholarship nor the presence of ideological and theological convictions embedded in our methodologies are problematic per se. Rather, my point is to suggest that the guild of biblical studies commits to particular paradigms that are then quite expectedly and thoroughly reinforced in the guild. Thus, the delineation of Acts as a piece of ancient *historia* says something about personal

---

[36] Hans Georg Gadamer's *Truth and Method* (trans. J. Weinsheimer and D. G. Marshall; 2d ed.; New York: Continuum, 1993) is still foundational in this respect, demonstrating the sociocultural and philosophical limitations of our methods and results, especially in the study of texts.

commitments to both Acts and history; it means something to designate early Christian texts in this manner. The resistance to reading Acts as a novel or epic—in part because of the undeniable aura of fictionality that surrounds those genres—suggests that specific theological and ideological commitments shape the kinds of questions we ask and the methods we practice.

While the particular commitment to the historical nature of Acts may be fairly self-evident in the practice of the guild, other similar types of commitments are much more subtle in nature. For instance, the evident tendency in the collections noted above to immerse Acts in its Jewish theological context (and that as defined largely by Hebrew Bible tradition) and to engage Acts in its historical context purely in terms of the history and society of empire and the imperial literature of history demonstrates a particular protectionism of the biblical texts that can hardly be denied. The studies cited above demonstrate a pattern of focusing on Lukan theology in terms of an explicitly developed Christian discourse based on interpretations of the reconfigured traditions from the Hebrew Bible in the New Testament and/or in terms of the discourse of Greco-Roman historiography or the sociocultural sphere of a safely constructed Roman Empire. These are comfortable areas for framing the discursive practice for interpreting Acts. However, one must also realize in this respect the conditionedness of the guild itself. On the one hand, those studying the New Testament and early Christian literature have largely belonged to Christian communities. Within those contexts Jewish background—particularly the Hebrew Bible—has been accepted (indeed appropriated) as something suitable and safe. Genesis or Isaiah is much more comfortable as the underlying tradition for Acts than, say, Plato or Vergil.[37]

---

[37] An interesting and related issue is scholars' use of the category/concept tradition. For instance, Earl J. Richard, *Acts 6–8:4: The Author's Method of Composition* (SBLDS 41; Missoula, Mont.: Scholars Press, 1978), makes a strong case for the free, creative hand of Luke in Stephen's speech and the surrounding narrative (278, 307), yet he still insists on referring to tradition in terms of discrete material ranging from the Septuagint to the story of Jesus (286, 288–89, 291–92, 297–98, 300, 305–9, 311). This represents a fascinating tension in the work of contemporary Luke-Acts scholars. Moreover, the Hebrew Bible (even if in Greek) or the Jesus tradition also seems to provide a buffer of sorts, insulating Acts from the broader Greco-Roman sociocultural world. These trends are not new, as the category Hellenistic Judaism, especially in the *Religionsgeschichtliche Schule*, originally provided a form of protection for earliest Christianity, which was alleged to have taken over the Greco-Roman ethos through this (already) hellenized Jewish mediator/medium. This emphasis should give contemporary scholars pause, however, since there is much going on in these categorizations and methods that relates to cultural and societal prejudice. For initial explorations in this direction, see Shawn Kelly, *Racializing Jesus: Race, Ideology and the Formation of Biblical Scholarship* (New York: Routledge, 2002).

In this same way, the stress on the Hebrew Bible as the primary context for Lukan theological analysis involves an ideological commitment different from that associated with examining the relationship of Acts to ancient historiography, but they both relate in some way to larger ideological convictions situated in the discipline. Moreover, at the same time one would be absolutely remiss in this context not to point out that there was a revolution in scholarship starting in the mid-1960s that reacted against the older *Religionsgeschichtliche Schule*'s focus on seemingly everything *but* the Hebrew Bible. The Shoah was the significant factor in this shift: biblical critics were forced to reevaluate what role biblical scholarship itself played in that devastating and horrific event of the twentieth century. This challenge to post–World War II scholarship continues to bear significant fruit.[38] We should not, however, lose sight of the shape that the New Testament discipline more generally, and Acts studies in particular, has taken as a result. More important, regardless of the reasons for and the legitimacy of this shift, it is worthwhile questioning the degree and extent to which this current approach fits comfortably with the ideological and theological agendas of current biblical scholarship in its manifest forms.

The scholarship of the past fifteen years evidenced in the predecessors delineated above has been significant and in many cases also groundbreaking. The burgeoning of social-scientific analysis, wedded to literary, rhetorical, and social-world analysis, has yielded valuable results. More fundamentally, this fusion of methods has pushed some of the traditional modes of analysis in fresh directions and, in the process, opened up significant avenues for engagement with Acts. Still, awareness of the limitations of our framing methodologies is a helpful starting place for beginning to push the boundaries of research into new regions and to generate different questions in the process, perhaps ultimately resulting in new(er) paradigms for interpretation. The current volume does not make a claim to represent any new paradigm as such. Rather, it in some ways represents a culmination of the processes of interpretation that have preceded it. Perhaps what makes the collection distinctive in its own right is the deliberate multiplicity of approaches cultivated herein, which nonetheless coalesce around a relatively defined common core of themes and in some cases assumptions as well. These are worth noting briefly so as to provide a more orderly accounting of the contents to follow.

---

[38] See, most recently, Todd Linafelt, ed., *A Shadow of Glory: Reading the New Testament after the Holocaust* (New York: Routledge, 2002); and Tania Oldenhage, *Parables for Our Time: Rereading New Testament Scholarship after the Holocaust* (New York: Oxford University Press, 2002).

TENDENZEN

If one is set on invoking particular *topoi* related to the study of Luke-Acts, then obviously a discussion of this particular collection's *Tendenzen* is paramount. Not all contributors to this volume will agree on all of the issues. Some of them, for example, have stronger commitments to the historicity of Acts than others. There is thus at one level no unified voice—no unified vision—present in this collection. I think it is important to put that on the table at the outset rather than to impose a harmonizing framework on the essays. At the same time, there is a certain intentionality about this current collection in terms of how it took shape and what it includes, as well as a particular unifying factor that occurs as the pieces coalesce into a collected whole. While the essays are of course written individually, they now exist as a unified phenomenon, and trends from one inevitably seep into another. It is this larger, naturally evolving vision of this collection as an entity in its own right—independent in some sense from the personal commitments of the individual authors—that I want to lay out in what follows. It is true, of course, that as the interpreter of this collection my own sense will no doubt prevail more than I intend (or even know). If Samuel Byrskog were to write this introduction I have no doubt it would look significantly different in both aim and scope. Having said that, I must concur with him that "scholarship is a cultural phenomenon." To this end, then, we might do best by admitting this fact—this conditionedness—of our attempts at interpretation and move on.

As one reads this volume it becomes readily apparent, as Joseph Tyson aptly notes in his contribution, that there is a particular sociorhetorical spirit that pervades throughout. It is no coincidence that Vernon Robbins is cited in many of the essays. In some sense, however, even without the specific invocation of Robbins, one can observe that the predilection for fusing historical, literary, rhetorical, social-scientific, and social-world analysis in more recent scholarship has had a significant impact on the research conducted by the contributors here.[39] All the studies in this volume reconfigure in some way these larger emphases of the past fifteen years, pushing the boundaries of former approaches and opening up potentially new vistas for the exploration of Acts.

It should be noted at the outset that this volume intentionally promotes a mixed-genre matrix for the study of Acts. No one genre is

---

[39] Exemplary in this respect is the work on Acts by Daniel Marguerat, some of which has now been collected and translated into English. See Daniel Marguerat, *The First Christian Historian: Writing the "Acts of the Apostles"* (trans. K. McKinney et al.; SNTSMS 121; Cambridge: Cambridge University Press, 2002).

prioritized. In fact, in many respects this collection downplays the significance of genre as a category of interpretation, so that even those scholars who use genre as an interpretive lens do so in order to move on to larger literary and cultural topics. The famous Italian classicist Gian Biagio Conte has defined the use of genre as follows: "genres are matrixes of works, to be conceived not as recipes but strategies; they act in texts not *ante rem* or *post rem* but *in re*. They are like strategies, inasmuch as they are procedures that imply a response, an addressee as an integral part of their own functioning, a precise addressee recognizable in the very form of the text."[40] At one level, such a definition is helpful, moving beyond more formalistic assessments of genre. The essays collected in Moessner's *Jesus and the Heritage of Israel* clearly reflect the utility of connecting generic identifications with particular strategies of reading such as Conte suggests. At the same time, there are also limits to this approach, insofar as some of the most important strategies for interpretation move beyond the boundaries of particular genres; sociocultural *topoi*, for example, are not genre specific.

One of the advances gained in a mixed-genre approach is precisely that it broadens appreciation of the dynamics of literary and rhetorical strategies that cannot be isolated in any one particular genre. Moreover, one gains, as a result, a more extensive sense of how genre categorization can in fact perform a limiting function in analysis, especially with respect to ancient narrative comparison: genre as a formalistic category seems to control and shape the discussion of function. There is, then, a certain tyrannizing effect that is inherent in the process of genre identification. In this collection, a mixed-genre perspective yields significantly different avenues of pursuit. One will note, for instance, an emphasis on rhetoric (Parsons, Penner), epic (MacDonald, Wordelman, Moreland), historiography and biography (Balch, Penner), novels (Schwartz), broader sociocultural *topoi* (Gilbert, Byrskog, Wordelman), as well as sociocultural processes (Moreland, Gilbert, Byrskog). As a whole, this collection suggests that broadening the application of various models for understanding and interpreting Acts will in fact push analysis in significantly new directions. At the same time, Caroline Vander Stichele's assessment in the conclusion also makes us aware of some of the more problematic cultural and gender issues related to the genre discussion.

It is important to stress that this emphasis on expanding methodology in the study of ancient texts raises another fundamental issue that strikes at the center of Conte's understanding of genre: the presumption

---

[40] Gian Biagio Conte, *Genres and Readers: Lucretius, Love Elegy, Pliny's Encyclopedia* (trans. G. W. Most; Baltimore: Johns Hopkins University Press, 1994), 112.

of a textually determined reader. Loveday Alexander has been experimenting for some time with a broader conception of reception history for Acts in its ancient context, illustrating the utility of reading Acts from multiple literary and sociorhetorical locations in antiquity.[41] The question can be raised as to what degree the constructed audience of Acts has performed the same function as the constructed genre in terms of limiting meaning and analysis.[42] Therefore, when we think of the context of Acts, alongside a complex literary and cultural matrix in which Luke writes, we must also envision a complex readership. This volume pushes this particular emphasis in fairly strategic ways, as all of the essays collected here make pointed contributions to our understanding of Acts from diverse generic fields and from differing implied reading audiences. In fact, a more holistic appreciation of author, genre, and audience emerges from the collective totality arising from multiple representations of the ancient world (a task only approximated in initial ways in this volume). These elements were generally truncated in past historical-critical study so as to form rather artificial skeletal remains of the more vivacious and vibrant realities. Traditional historical criticism in some sense failed at this juncture: it imagined it could reconstruct a world that in fact is un(re)constructable (because it is not fully knowable) in its wholeness and entirety. Thus far, Acts scholarship has largely focused on small parts of Luke's macro context, but the possibilities are quite literally endless.

---

[41] See esp. Loveday Alexander, "Marathon or Jericho? Reading Acts in Dialogue with Biblical and Greek Historiography," in *Auguries: The Jubilee Volume of the Sheffield Department of Biblical Studies* (ed. D. J. A. Clines and S. D. Moore; JSOTSup 269; Sheffield: Sheffield Academic Press, 1998), 92–125; idem, "Narrative Maps: Reflections on the Toponymy of Acts," in *The Bible in Human Society: Essays in Honour of John Rogerson* (ed. M. D. Carroll R. et al.; JSOTSup 200; Sheffield: Sheffield Academic Press, 1995), 17–57; idem, "'In Journeying Often:' Voyaging in the Acts of the Apostles and in Greek Romance," in Tuckett, *Luke's Literary Achievement*, 17–49; and idem, "Fact, Fiction and the Genre of Acts," *NTS* 44 (1998): 380–99.

[42] In his classic essay, "What Is an Author?" Michel Foucault addresses the way in which the concept of author, despite claims that this character allows for the proliferation of meaning in a text, in point of fact is used as an ideological product to limit such expansion and multiplication of meaning. With respect to the discussion here, the concept of genre has a similar limiting affect on meaning, as does, one might note, the notion of reader. While the principle of an implied reader is helpful for the analysis of a text such as Acts, there is also a sense in which this category represents another means of restraining multivalency and the multiplicity of meaning signification possible within the ancient world. See Michel Foucault, "What Is an Author?" in *The Foucault Reader* (ed. P. Rabinow; New York: Pantheon, 1984), 101–20. I thank my colleague Jim Gray for drawing my attention to this essay.

The broadening of a generic model also raises the issue of the expansion of methodologies. In some sense, the response to the problem of the cultural limitedness that Byrskog draws to our attention is in fact to expand our models, allowing them to intermix and cross-fertilize. We should not lose sight of the fact that our own guiding methods are highly relativistic and culturally bound. Byrskog's contribution is so important in this respect, since his work arises from a context quite different from the North American scene that has generated the majority of the studies in this volume. Byrskog thus reminds us of the culturedness of our own approaches, but he also challenges us to revisit age-old questions (i.e., sources in Acts) from some newer angles of investigation. The quest to dispense with the history behind the text, which Tyson observes as one major thread through some of the essays in this collection, is also to be situated emphatically within a North American context. Moreover, in a similar vein, Wordelman's essay, bringing postcolonial insights to bear on the interpretation of a specific Lukan narrative, demonstrates the profound influence of our cultural biases in interpretation, and Vander Stichele's conclusion does much the same from the perspective of a gender-critical analysis. In the end, our texts have much less to do with shaping our methods than the guilds and cultures out of which we come.

In line with the broadening of perspectives in this volume, the emphasis on social formation (Moreland) and oral history (Byrskog) should be viewed as part of more recent attempts to rethink the function of the material in Acts. While Moreland focuses on the present use of the text (i.e., in the time of the author), Byrskog emphasizes the pastness in the present of the material, attempting to understand the processes in a different direction. It is no secret that Moreland and Byrskog have fundamentally different commitments to history and its intersection with Acts. I will not try to harmonize them in this respect. I think, however, that their fundamental commitment to the study of the relationship of texts to the identity of author and reader/eyewitness demonstrates a strong *Tendenz* in this volume as a whole. There are profoundly human social processes operative in a text such as Acts, and we have been highly neglectful in theoretically addressing and conceptually analyzing these phenomena. Schwartz's contribution, although admittedly in quite a different vein, similarly stresses this aspect in terms of her analysis of the function of trial narratives, particularly their reflection and refraction of the identity of a Greek East under a Roman imperial gaze. Further, both Penner and Parsons emphasize educational processes as critical in the development of literary and rhetorical skill and the promotion of sociocultural values in antiquity. The contributions by Gilbert, Wordelman, MacDonald, and Balch similarly affirm the dynamic life processes that are embedded in our literary representations. Finally, Tyson and Vander Stichele raise these same issues in their essays, but with respect to the contemporary guild. Overall, then, there is a fairly strong humanist trend in these observations and approaches, irrespective of the particular theological and ideological commitments of the individual contributors. Fundamental in all of this, as Moreland reminds us, is individual and group identity formation—and the subject of study is both part of that process as well as its product.

At this stage, where we begin to probe more deeply into the richness of our texts as constituent elements of first-century human processes, it is worth highlighting another dominant theme in this volume: Lukan narrative argumentation. Almost all the essays make some claim to laying bare the dynamics and modalities of the Lukan argumentative process as it unfolds in narrative. Argument serves the ends of much larger agendas, which themselves are deeply grounded in human reasoning and sociocultural processes of the first- and second-century Mediterranean worlds. The move away from simply identifying patterns to exploring Lukan function and imaging in the text is thus a significant move forward in this context.

The essays in this volume also evidence a strong tendency to move rapidly into the Greco-Roman world, ranging far afield in a manner reminiscent of earlier *Religionsgeschichtliche Schule* study. From the *progymnasmata*, to declamatory exercises, to epic traditions, to imperial discourse, to the portrayal of founding figures—it is apparent that widely diverse and divergent fields are being explored here. Moreover, this collection is intentionally meant to be illustrative, not exhaustive. While the religious context is not represented in this collection per se, this does not signal any deliberate intention in the organization of the volume; it is simply another avenue to be explored alongside the ones here. Of course, from the perspective of the older *Religionsgeschichtliche Schule* the lack of an explicitly religious focus would indeed seem strange. It was, after all, a history of *religions* school of investigation that deliberately set out to analyze the early Christian texts, traditions, themes, and social processes within the religious world of antiquity. I consider these collected essays in some sense to signal the birthing of a new *Religionsgeschichtliche Schule* in terms of fundamental method and broad conceptualization, but it is one in which an explicit religious connection may in fact prove to be less essential. This may seem unusual in some ways, but we might well ask whether or not the Protestant-Catholic debates that permeated the largely Protestant study in the history of religions school did not, in some sense, also generate and project a perception of our ancient texts and their communities that was more religious than it really ought to have been.[43]

---

[43] On the way in which the Protestant polemic against Catholicism played out in the study of the ancient world, see Jonathan Z. Smith, *Drudgery Divine: On the*

If this volume is at all revealing, then the shift to the civic and political realm that seems to surface throughout many of the essays might suggest several different things: early Christianity was immersed in sociocultural and civic-political contexts to a greater degree than has generally been recognized; religious themes are more clearly sociopolitical in their orientation than has previously been realized; and our own modern interest in politics and culture has resulted in the (re)creation of early Christianity in this new(er) image and in light of more recent debates. Whatever the case may be (and these options need not be mutually exclusive), this shift toward pedagogical, sociocultural, and political orientations in the study of Acts is striking. Moreover, if one were to do a search on the word "theology" in this volume, one would in fact find that, despite the predominance of phrases such as "Lukan theology" in other collections and studies, it is almost nonexistent here (and this was not in any way an intentional aim of this volume at the outset). This is not to suggest that one could not find correlative elements in this collection, but the predominant perception (or implication) seems to be that Lukan theology is in many respects indistinguishable from the sociocultural topics as they are reconfigured in Lukan narrative argumentation. Perhaps not all the contributors would agree that this in fact constitutes the larger concept of theology in the study of Acts, but the practice reflected in this volume very much places the stress on the full participation of Lukan discourse in its ancient contexts and settings.

Finally, I would be remiss if I did not dwell for a brief moment on the fairly blatant adjectival description "Greco-Roman" (understood here to encapsulate both the shared and distinctive Greek and Roman elements of the ancient world) that defines the contextualization of Lukan discourse explored in this collection. Indeed, the title of this volume adamantly commits to examining Acts in its Greco-Roman discursive context. While this was, again, not a planned aim of this volume, the reader who takes even a casual glance at the primary source citation index will likely be struck by just how few references there are to Hebrew Bible writings. The Jewish writer Josephus is represented, but in the end Greek and Roman writers predominate. Tyson and Vander Stichele quite justifiably raise this as a concern. I am not sure this is something that needs to be defended at this point in time, but it does require further consideration and reflection. It may indicate a shift in some sectors of the guild; it may also be a corrective of sorts to the predilections of previous scholarship. The answers to these and related questions will ultimately be clearer further down the road.

Comparison of Early Christianities and the Religions of Late Antiquity (Chicago: University of Chicago Press, 1990).

For the moment, it is worth noting that, although no contributor to this volume probably would deny the profound influence of Jewish tradition on Acts, reading Acts in its first-century context may mean also rereading that Jewish tradition in this same light. In other words, as we move outward into the Greco-Roman world we are perhaps seeing a reconfiguration of not only Christianity but its Jewish counterpart/context as well. There might well exist a symbiotic relationship here largely unexplored or ignored so far. As Moessner and Tiede note, "to view Luke as an interpreter of Israel is by no means to underestimate the Hellenistic environment of his project. The volumes are redolent with the tropes and *topoi* of Hellenism and the Hellenistic Judaism of the Mediterranean basin."[44] However, although much recent scholarship has focused on demonstrating the continuity between early Christianity and Judaism,[45] including extensive analysis of the Lukan use of Hebrew Scripture and tradition,[46] the continuity of first-century Judaism and Christianity might more profitably be assessed and studied in terms of their shared continuity with the larger Greco-Roman world in which they "lived, moved, and had their being." We may find, in the end, that such a shift in focus need not imply that the Jewish story meant less to Luke but rather that Luke infused the story of Israel with meaning precisely in and through his reconfiguration of it in a context steeped in the rhetorical training, language, literature, culture, and society of the Greek and Roman worlds.

The implications of this approach to Acts are fairly profound if still not yet fully perceived or adequately articulated. It includes not least a reevaluation of our own protective tactics in assessing Lukan rhetorical strategies and the delineation of the contours of Lukan theology/ideology. As an organic whole, the essays in this volume suggest that to understand Acts (as fully as we possibly can) there must be a renewed fervor to let it all go, to allow the Lukan narrative to take the plunge into the vitality (and,

---

[44] Moessner and Tiede, "Conclusion," 365.

[45] In this connection current scholars are indebted to the work of Joseph Tyson, who has dedicated a good portion of his career to the exploration of the relationship of Luke-Acts to Judaism. His most recent contribution addresses this issue in the history of scholarship: *Luke, Judaism, and the Scholars: Critical Approaches to Luke-Acts* (Columbia: University of South Carolina Press, 1999).

[46] See the recent and exhaustive study by Dietrich Rusam, *Das Alte Testament bei Lukas* (BZNW 112; Berlin: de Gruyter, 2003); as well as Moessner, *Lord of the Banquet*; Luke T. Johnson, *Septuagintal Midrash in the Speeches of Acts* (Milwaukee: Marquette University Press, 2002); Robert L. Brawley, *Text to Text Pours Forth Speech: Voices of Scripture in Luke-Acts* (Bloomington: Indiana University Press, 1995); and Craig A. Evans and James A. Sanders, *Luke and Scripture: The Function of Sacred Tradition in Luke-Acts* (Minneapolis: Fortress, 1993).

to be sure, also sometimes the depravity) of its ancient context. Although explored here in a preliminary way, such a baptism has yet to take place in the study of early Christian texts and history.[47]

---

[47] I would like to express my appreciation to Vernon Robbins and Greg Bloomquist, who read an earlier version of this chapter and offered helpful feedback; to Caroline Vander Stichele for her critical and substantive engagement over these issues and this piece; and to Scot McKnight for his encouraging words in the process. Finally, special thanks goes to Hendrik Boers for the stimulating sessions in New Testament Theology at Emory. He may well not agree with all that is written here, but he provided the inspiration.

From History to Rhetoric and Back: Assessing New Trends in Acts Studies

Joseph B. Tyson

Critical research on the Acts of the Apostles has never been carried out in an intellectual or cultural vacuum, so it is instructive to project a consideration of changes in the study of Acts against a wide background. These changes may be seen as parts of the major transformations that took place in both biblical and nonbiblical studies in the latter half of the twentieth century.

This essay will examine and assess some of the recent critical scholarship on Acts as a stage in the history of scholarship and in terms of its potential for advancing our understanding of the world in which Acts was written. It is generally assumed that critical biblical scholarship, including the study of Acts, was predominantly historical until the latter half of the twentieth century. From that time to the present, we have seen the development of scores of newer methodological approaches, most of them disavowing any interest in the history reflected in the New Testament texts. This essay does not intend to treat all of these approaches but rather to concentrate primarily on certain critical methods as represented in this volume. It is, however, unclear how these methods should be categorized. They fall broadly under the umbrella of literary studies, but they might more narrowly be designated as rhetorical studies. Although some of the scholars mentioned here may not see themselves as rhetorical critics, the label is useful in pulling together those approaches that concentrate on the strategies of persuasion to be found in Greco-Roman literature and in Acts. These studies take many forms: some explore relationships with other ancient writings (intertextuality), others express an interest in the social context associated with the author and audience of Acts (sociorhetorical criticism), and still others attempt to identify the ancient genre that would include Acts (genre criticism). Of course, there is a good deal of overlap among these types of study, and a single author may employ more than one approach. For purposes of this essay, I will use the term rhetorical criticism as inclusive of all of the above-named approaches.

Walter Wink sharpened the discussion of methodology when, in 1973, he wrote that the historical-critical method as used in biblical criticism was bankrupt.[1] Drawing on the private business sector, he used the metaphor of bankruptcy not to refer to a business without assets but to a business that fell short of its goal and required new management. Wink wrote,

> Biblical criticism has produced an inventory of thousands of studies on every question which has seemed amenable to its methods, with a host of additional possibilities still before it. It has a method which has proven itself in earlier historical periods to be capable of remarkable achievements. It has in its employ hundreds of competent, trained technicians. Biblical criticism is not bankrupt because it has run out of things to say or new ground to explore. It is bankrupt solely because it is incapable of achieving what most of its practitioners considered its purpose to be: so to interpret the Scriptures that the past becomes alive and illumines our present with new possibilities for personal and social transformation.[2]

Wink's analysis appears to suffer from two misjudgments. First, he has misjudged the purpose of historical biblical criticism. His understanding is given away in the title to his book, *The Bible in Human Transformation*. Although many interpreters have expected their studies to illumine the present, at least some of the giants in our discipline were primarily interested in learning what light the Bible might shed on the past, not the present. To be sure, their research was carried on within their own historical contexts, and we know that these contexts affected their judgments. Contemporary scholars know that pure objectivity is impossible, but it is simplistic to say that the purpose of biblical study is to support a goal that might be called "human transformation." Second, there is a further misjudgment in categorizing past biblical scholarship as strictly historical-critical. I will return to this criticism further on in this essay.

Despite these fundamental flaws, Wink successfully called attention to some of the causes of the decline of historical criticism. Primary among them was the critique of objectivity, which affected both biblical and non-biblical studies in the latter half of the twentieth century. If it is true that historians are unable to distance themselves sufficiently from their own time to understand the past, and if it is true that we all approach the past from limited perspectives, then where can we confidently turn for certainty about the past? It then becomes difficult both to accept any single historical approach and to adjudicate among a variety of diverse approaches.

---

[1] Walter Wink, *The Bible in Human Transformation: Toward a New Paradigm for Biblical Study* (Philadelphia: Fortress, 1973).
[2] Ibid., 1–2.

Wink, of course, was not alone in claiming that we have lost confidence in historical studies. Almost all of us became convinced that all human beings, critics included, carry with them their unexamined presuppositions and that objectivity is an elusive goal.

The critique of objectivity has a long history, an examination of which would take us too far afield from our present purpose. However, it is worthwhile to observe one of its results in biblical studies: methodological proliferation. This proliferation results in part from a diminishing confidence in historical criticism and is justified by the critique of objectivity. If no single perspective may be privileged, who is to say what perspectives are to be excluded? Newer, fresher examinations may indeed provide a kind of enlightenment that we have missed in the past. Coming out of feminist, Afrocentric, cross-cultural, and postcolonial biblical approaches, these interpretations have produced important new insights. Nevertheless, the proliferation is noteworthy.[3]

Many of the proponents of these methods see themselves as providing a corrective to an earlier historical-critical method, which is said to have enjoyed hegemony among biblical scholars for about two centuries. Although this judgment about the dominance of historical criticism is largely correct, there are some important exceptions that should not be neglected. In what follows, I will concentrate on two scholars who played major roles in the development of the historical-critical study of Acts but who also devoted a good deal of attention to nonhistorical matters.

From History

The beginning of the critical study of Acts was not unlike that of the study of the New Testament generally. It was motivated by questions of historicity and characterized by attempts either to affirm or to deny the actuality of events described in the book. Ferdinand Christian Baur, one of the pioneers in the critical study of Acts, distinguished between historicity and history, and this distinction had a major bearing on his work. A. J. Mattill has shown how Baur was influenced by the work of Matthias

---

[3] Recent discussions of method bear this out. For instance, Steven L. McKenzie and Stephen R. Haynes include essays on fourteen critical methods, but theirs is an attempt to simplify. Richard N. and R. Kendall Soulen have entries on no fewer than thirty-five. See Steven L. McKenzie and Stephen R. Haynes, eds., *To Each Its Own Meaning: An Introduction to Biblical Criticisms and Their Application* (rev. ed.; Louisville: Westminster John Knox, 1999); and Richard N. Soulen and R. Kendall Soulen, *Handbook of Biblical Criticism* (3d ed.; Louisville: Westminster John Knox, 2001).

Schneckenburger on Acts.[4] Baur considered the work of Schneckenburger, who had been his student, as a watershed in the history of New Testament scholarship. In his review, however, Baur observed that scholarship could not remain where Schneckenburger had left it. He wrote, "We must either go backward from the aim stated by the author or go forward beyond that aim to further investigations of the historical character of Acts."[5] What Baur means by "the historical character of Acts" is of great interest.

Following suggestions of Baur himself, Schneckenburger had produced a detailed study of the extensive parallels in Acts between Peter and Paul. The two perform similar miracles, experience life-changing visions, deliver apologetic and evangelistic speeches, and undergo imprisonments followed by remarkable releases. In content, some of Peter's speeches sound like Paul. In his speech to the household of Cornelius, Peter states: "I truly understand that God shows no partiality, but in every nation anyone who fears him and does what is right is acceptable to him" (Acts 10:34-35 NRSV). After Peter has reported to the other apostles in Jerusalem about his vision and experience with Cornelius, they all are led to say, "Then God has given even to the Gentiles the repentance that leads to life" (11:18). Finally, in the meeting of the apostles, with Paul present, Peter affirms, "We believe that we will be saved through the grace of the Lord Jesus, just as they will" (15:11).

In contrast, the speeches of Paul, with one exception, do not sound like the Paul of the letters. The exception is in Paul's speech at Pisidian Antioch, where he announces that forgiveness of sins is available through Jesus Christ and that "everyone who believes is set free from all those sins from which you could not be freed by the law of Moses" (13:39).[6] Here Paul sounds like the author of Romans and Galatians. Elsewhere in Acts, however, the themes of the Lukan Paul are fundamentally Jewish, more specifically Pharisaic. The Lukan Paul stresses monotheism, creation, and resurrection. Most important, there is a great deal of stress on his observance of Torah. In his apologetic speeches in Acts 21–26, Paul repeatedly denies that he has done or taught anything contrary to the laws of Moses or the traditions of his people. Precisely to avoid suspicion that he has taught such contrary practices, Paul is counseled by James to pay the

---

[4] See A. J. Mattill, "The Purpose of Acts: Schneckenburger Reconsidered," in *Apostolic History and the Gospel: Biblical and Historical Essays Presented to F. F. Bruce on His Sixtieth Birthday* (ed. W. W. Gasque and R. P. Martin; Grand Rapids: Eerdmans, 1970), 108–22. See also Matthias Schneckenburger, *Über den Zweck der Apostelgeschichte* (Bern: Fischer, 1841).

[5] Quoted by Mattill, "Purpose of Acts," 112.

[6] Note, however, that even here the language is not characteristically Pauline.

expenses of four men who have taken on Nazarite vows (21:17–26). Paul is quite willing to do this, and in his defense speeches that follow his arrest he stresses his connection with Jews and identifies himself with the party of the Pharisees (23:6; 26:5). It is made clear in Paul's appearance before the Sanhedrin that his belief in resurrection is distinctively Pharisaic and, consequently, fundamentally Jewish (23:8).

Schneckenburger's study is notable for its emphasis on the text and its literary strategies. Further, he does not ask if the text is historically reliable but rather what these literary parallels mean for the understanding of Luke's text. To shift the focus in this way has drastic consequences, as Baur recognized. He was impressed that Schneckenburger had contested the historical purpose of the author of Acts, and he saw this as a signal of release from concern with its alleged historicity. Baur is here reflecting the context in which he had previously been immersed, one in which the historicity of Acts was either assumed or questioned. What does it mean, however, to be released from these concerns?

Clearly this does not mean that Baur and his school are no longer concerned with history. The reconstruction of early Christianity as a kind of battleground between Petrine and Pauline Christianity is evidence that history is the issue. What really happened in the early decades after Jesus is a matter of genuine concern. However, what Schneckenburger and Baur introduced was a new way of going about historical reconstruction, a method we call *Tendenzkritik,* in which documents such as Acts are examined for their ideology, their emphases, and their theology—and attention to these literary devices has a bearing on the historical reconstruction. For Baur, the parallelization of Peter and Paul means that the author of Acts is attempting to bring competing parties together. Acts is a consensus document, intended to heal a serious division.[7] I do not think it is an oversimplification to say that Baur wants to move away from examining the episodes in Acts, asking if they really happened, if they rest on reliable early traditions, or if there are some historical kernels embedded within them. Instead, he wants to know about the author. He wants to discover the historical context within which the author wrote and then to determine what bearing this might have not only on the history narrated in the particular text but

---

[7] Baur did not publish a commentary on Acts, but his treatment is to be found in a number of essays and articles. His most extensive study of Acts is in *Paul, the Apostle of Jesus Christ, His Life and Work, His Epistles and His Doctrine: A Contribution to a Critical History of Primitive Christianity* (trans. A. Menzies; 2 vols.; London: Williams & Norgate, 1876). The English is a translation of the second German edition edited by Eduard Zeller (1866–67). See also Ferdinand Christian Baur, *The Church History of the First Three Centuries* (trans. A. Menzies; 3 vols.; London: Williams & Norgate, 1878), vol. 1. The first German edition was published in 1853.

also on the history reflected by the text. In later terminology, we may say that Baur was interested in the text both as window and as mirror. Baur is certainly not to be considered an early literary critic of Acts, but it is notable that, even at this early stage of historical criticism, attention to certain literary qualities of the text is not absent and that questions about authorial intent and examinations of literary devices are germane to the broader historical quest.

About a century later we may see a similar methodological mix in the five-volume *Beginnings of Christianity,* edited by Frederick J. Foakes Jackson and Kirsopp Lake, and more particularly in a number of studies by Henry J. Cadbury in these volumes and elsewhere.[8] The indisputable purpose of *Beginnings* is a historical one, as is stated with clarity in the preface to volume 1. The editors assumed that the Synoptic Problem had been resolved and that this solution could contribute to historical study: "The great literary achievement of the last fifty years of New Testament scholarship was the discovery and the general solution of the synoptic problem. It is the task of this generation to translate these results into the language of the historian; to show how literary complexities and contradictions reveal the growth of thought and the rise of institutions."[9] It is of interest to note that source criticism and literary criticism are, by implication, equated, and it is quite clear that the function of literary criticism, however defined, is to support the study of history. Nevertheless, the five volumes of *Beginnings of Christianity* devote a good deal of attention to literary matters. Volume 2 has a great deal of material on the "Composition and Purpose of Acts," including an essay entitled "The Greek and Jewish Traditions of Writing History," by Cadbury and the editors.[10] This volume also contains an appendix by Cadbury on the preface of Luke that has exercised a formative influence on contemporary literary and rhetorical criticism.[11]

Cadbury's *Style and Literary Method of Luke* (1920) and *The Making of Luke-Acts* (1927) are remarkable for the attention they pay to literary matters.[12] The former volume is well-known for Cadbury's destruction of William Hobart's argument supporting the identification of the author of

---

[8] See Frederick J. Foakes Jackson and Kirsopp Lake, eds., *The Beginnings of Christianity: The Acts of the Apostles* (5 vols.; London: Macmillan, 1920–33; repr., Grand Rapids: Baker, 1979).

[9] Ibid., 1:vii.

[10] Ibid., 2:7–29.

[11] Ibid., 2:489–510.

[12] See Henry J. Cadbury, *The Style and Literary Method of Luke* (Cambridge: Harvard University Press, 1920); idem, *The Making of Luke-Acts* (2d ed.; London: SPCK, 1958; repr., Peabody, Mass.: Hendrickson, 1999).

Luke-Acts as a physician.[13] In this volume Cadbury devoted a great deal of attention to the Lukan vocabulary generally as well as to the alleged medical language. On the latter, Cadbury claimed that, if Hobart was right, Luke should exhibit a greater tendency to use medical terms than do other cultivated writers of his time. However, Cadbury's comparison of Luke with the nonmedical but cultivated Lucian showed that the two writers used much the same vocabulary with about the same frequency.

In *The Making of Luke-Acts,* Cadbury examined the factors in the composition of the two-volume work: the motives and forms in the transmission of material as well as the sources, language, and genre of the writing. He also called attention to the author's use of popular forms: his inclusion of speeches, letters, and literary formulas. Cadbury emphasized the popular character of the writing and, probably influenced by Karl Ludwig Schmidt, hesitated to classify Luke-Acts in terms of classical forms.[14] He concluded that Luke-Acts comes closer to history than to any other classification, but he maintained that Luke was really a transmitter of popular tradition. He wrote, "[Luke's] efforts at literary form only bring into sharper outline the incurably unliterary character of his materials."[15]

It is interesting to note that in *The Making of Luke-Acts* Cadbury only turns to questions of the historicity of Acts in his last chapter, where he also treats the identity of the author. Recognizing that many readers might have expected him to treat the subject of historical accuracy earlier, he defends his procedure:

> Prior to the question of its truth we have set the question of its genesis. It may be confidently claimed that this order of procedure often throws light on the question of historicity, and perhaps more often gives the question of historicity a less insistent place in our thoughts. It is desirable to approach historical records in this sequence and with this distinction. We should inquire what the author thought took place before we ask what took place. We should ask why the author narrates it as he does before we ask whether it is true as he narrates it. The study of the making of a book is a prerequisite to its evaluation.[16]

---

[13] See William K. Hobart, *The Medical Language of St. Luke* (Dublin: Figgis, 1882). It is notable that Adolf von Harnack followed Hobart's lead in identifying Luke as a physician. See his *Luke the Physician: The Author of the Third Gospel and the Acts of the Apostles* (trans. J. R. Wilkinson; New Testament Studies 1; London: Williams & Norgate, 1908).

[14] See Karl Ludwig Schmidt, *The Place of the Gospels in the General History of Literature* (trans. B. R. McCane; Columbia: University of South Carolina Press, 2002). The original German edition was published in 1923.

[15] Cadbury, *Making of Luke-Acts,* 134.

[16] Ibid., 362.

Cadbury thus stands as a colossus, with one foot on each shore. Firmly rooted in the historical-critical study of Acts, he nevertheless devotes significant attention to issues that still occupy biblical scholars working decades later.

The point of this brief foray into the past is to show that, despite the hegemony of historical criticism in the study of Acts, concern with literary matters has not been absent. The critique of earlier criticism that makes it into a one-dimensional enterprise that neglected the literary qualities of the texts is inaccurate. Granted, of course, some of our forebears did examine the literary qualities of early Christian texts, but they employed such literary study to support their historical research. A Cadbury might insist that literary study should precede historical inquiry, but even he would not neglect the latter.

To Rhetoric

The intellectual and cultural patterns of the late twentieth century, briefly alluded to above, have set the historical context for biblical studies generally and for the study of Acts specifically. It is no coincidence that many of us began to turn toward literary studies of Acts within a context of diminishing confidence in historical study and that, as a result, methodological proliferation was encouraged. We began to experiment with narrative, reader-response, genre, and rhetorical criticism. It is plausible to suggest that literary and rhetorical critics of the New Testament expressed a sense of freedom from the domination of historical criticism, not so much by relocating their perspectives, as some other critics did, but by turning attention to hitherto neglected aspects of the texts they had long studied. Furthermore, such critics found it possible to make use of literary theory as practiced outside the biblical disciplines and could legitimately claim that their approach to biblical texts was in no way privileged but was the same as that used in the study of other ancient writings. Literary-critical studies of the New Testament have burgeoned in recent years, and critics have produced a library of books from which we can learn a great deal.

Rhetorical criticism, examples of which appear in this volume, emerged from within the broader category of literary criticism. The shift from historical to literary and then to rhetorical criticism, although not without precedents, has been dramatic but by no means universal. We did not suddenly wake up one morning and corporately decide to abandon historical-critical studies. A perusal of any recent issue of *New Testament Abstracts* shows that historical criticism is alive and well. The monumental publication, *The Book of Acts in its First Century Setting*, which appeared from 1993 to 1996, contains, alongside several examples of the newer approaches, a number of essays whose chief concern is the historical accuracy of Acts.[17]

The use of rhetorical criticism as a specific method of biblical study, at least with respect to the American study of the Hebrew Bible, probably started with James Muilenburg's presidential address to the Society of Biblical Literature on 18 December 1968.[18] Muilenburg used this occasion to challenge the Society to go beyond form criticism, which, he noted, was bound to generalize and thus to neglect the unique, unrepeatable, and particular aspects of a literary formulation. He said,

> What I am interested in, above all, is in understanding the nature of Hebrew literary composition, in exhibiting the structural patterns that are employed for the fashioning of a literary unit, whether in poetry or in prose, and in discerning the many and various devices by which the predications are formulated and ordered into a unified whole. Such an enterprise I should describe as rhetoric and the methodology as rhetorical criticism.[19]

From the perspective of classical studies, George Kennedy addressed similar issues in 1984 and applied them specifically to the New Testament.[20] He noted Muilenburg's address as well as the commentary on Galatians by Hans Dieter Betz but protested that no rigorous method had yet been applied to biblical studies.[21] Kennedy contended that the study of rhetoric was to be distinguished from literary criticism, which he took to be a study of the language of the Bible understood from our time. He also insisted that rhetorical criticism is much more than the study of style. He defined rhetoric as

> that quality in discourse by which a speaker or writer seeks to accomplish his purpose. Choice and arrangement of words are one of the techniques employed, but what is known in rhetorical theory as "invention"—the treatment of the subject matter, the use of evidence, the argumentation, and the control of emotion—is often of greater importance and is central to rhetorical theory as understood by Greeks and Romans.[22]

---

[17] See Bruce W. Winter, ed., *The Book of Acts in Its First Century Setting* (5 vols.; Grand Rapids: Eerdmans, 1993–96).

[18] For the published form of the address, see James Muilenburg, "Form Criticism and Beyond," *JBL* 88 (1969): 1–18.

[19] Ibid., 8.

[20] George A. Kennedy, *New Testament Interpretation through Rhetorical Criticism* (Chapel Hill: University of North Carolina Press, 1984).

[21] Hans Dieter Betz, *Galatians: A Commentary on Paul's Letter to the Churches in Galatia* (Hermeneia; Philadelphia: Fortress, 1979).

[22] Kennedy, *New Testament Interpretation*, 3.

Kennedy proceeded to outline the major features for the practice of rhetorical criticism and included a chapter on the speeches in Acts.[23]

In the last decade of the twentieth century, a flood of monographs and articles making use of aspects of rhetorical criticism and applying them to Acts appeared.[24] Fortunately, most scholars who engaged in rhetorical criticism were already familiar with a wide range of Greek and Latin literature, or they quickly became familiar with it and were able to help the rest of us see similarities in the use of rhetorical devices and parallels in the employment of *topoi*. We learned to distinguish between judicial, deliberative, and epideictic speech and sometimes to identify these kinds of speech in Greek literature and in Acts.

Although the contributions to the present volume exhibit a good deal of diversity, most of them may fairly be classified as rhetorical-critical. Todd Penner is willing to call his approach historical-critical, but it is evident that he has something in mind that does not easily fit under this rubric.[25] Indeed, his approach, as well as that of many of the other authors represented here, constitutes a dramatic shift when seen over against earlier critical methods. As a specific method, it is best to regard Penner's approach as a special kind of rhetorical criticism and to refer to it as sociorhetorical criticism. This method may be described by citing a number of characteristic emphases to be found in these newer studies of Acts.

The most notable feature exhibited here is an apparent disinterest in the historical reliability of Acts. Samuel Byrskog, who is the exception in this respect among the contributors to this volume, suggests that this lack of interest is a uniquely American phenomenon.[26] Penner is the one contributor to make this claim explicit: "one is no longer interested primarily (or even at all) in the historicity of the material in Acts but rather

---

[23] Kennedy acknowledges that, for the most part, the rhetoric of Paul in Acts differs from that in the epistles. However, the speech of Paul to the elders of Ephesus (Acts 20:18–35) "is the first in Acts that seems based on direct knowledge by the narrator, and the only speech really evocative of Paul's personal style, though simplified for use in an historiographic work" (ibid., 139). Kennedy assumes that Timothy was the source for this speech as well as for the information in the "we" sections.

[24] For important collections of essays, see Duane F. Watson, ed., *Persuasive Artistry: Studies in New Testament Rhetoric in Honor of George A. Kennedy* (JSNTSup 50; Sheffield: Sheffield Academic Press, 1991); Stanley E. Porter and Dennis L. Stamps, eds., *The Rhetorical Interpretation of Scripture: Essays from the 1996 Malibu Conference* (JSNTSup 180; Sheffield: Sheffield Academic Press, 1999).

[25] Todd Penner, "Civilizing Discourse: Acts, Declamation, and the Rhetoric of the *Polis*," in this volume.

[26] Samuel Byrskog, "History or Story in Acts—A Middle Way? The We Passages, Historical Intertexture and Oral History," in this volume.

in examining the only thing Acts can really yield in the end: a window to Luke's sociocultural world."[27] One is reminded of Baur's announcement that future scholarship need not be concerned with historicity. However, whereas Baur's disinterest in the historical reliability of Acts led to an examination of theological tendencies and their historical implications, rhetorical criticism has led recent scholars to learn as much as possible about the persuasive strategies to be found within the text.

Sociorhetorical criticism goes beyond an interest in the rhetorical strategies of the text and examines the social context within which the text was written. Vernon Robbins in particular has emphasized the social context of Acts and other early Christian documents.[28] Robbins regards sociorhetorical criticism as an integrative approach: "One of the most notable contributions of socio-rhetorical criticism is to bring literary criticism ... social-scientific criticism ... postmodern criticism ... and theological criticism ... together into an integrated approach to interpretation."[29] A major aspect of sociorhetorical criticism is that it not only looks within the text for its rhetorical qualities but searches outside the text for possible relationships. As Robbins states, "A text is always interacting somehow with phenomena outside itself."[30] These phenomena include other texts, so intertextuality is an important area of interest in these studies. But sociorhetorical critics also include the surrounding culture, and it is here that their studies are breaking through to new and important insights about the book of Acts.

Sociorhetorical criticism of Acts has also led to a reappraisal of its literary quality and standing in the ancient world. Mikeal Parsons believes that Luke, like most ancient authors, cut his teeth on the *progymnasmata* tradition.[31] Penner, in distinction from Erich Auerbach and others, affirms that Acts could take its place with other texts that constituted the high culture of antiquity.[32] For him, Luke is an ancient historian, a designation that inspires no confidence in the historical reliability of Acts but allows us to perceive the author's purposes more clearly.

---

[27] Penner, "Civilizing Discourse," 84.

[28] See Vernon K. Robbins, *Exploring the Texture of Texts: A Guide to Socio-Rhetorical Interpretation* (Valley Forge, Pa.: Trinity Press International, 1996); idem, "Writing as a Rhetorical Act in Plutarch and the Gospels," in Watson, *Persuasive Artistry*, 142–68; and idem, "From Enthymeme to Theology in Luke 11:1–13," in *Literary Studies in Luke-Acts: Essays in Honor of Joseph B. Tyson* (ed. R. P. Thompson and T. E. Phillips; Macon, Ga.: Mercer University Press, 1998), 191–214.

[29] Robbins, *Exploring the Texture of Texts*, 1–2.

[30] Ibid., 36.

[31] Mikeal Parsons, "Luke and the *Progymnasmata*: A Preliminary Investigation into the Preliminary Exercises," in this volume.

[32] Penner, "Civilizing Discourse," 66–69.

Moreover, sociorhetorical criticism exhibits a great deal of interest in the political dimensions of the author's strategies. David Balch, drawing on Dionysius, Plutarch, and other ancient authors, understands Luke-Acts to be dealing with the foundation of and the constitution for the emerging Christian community.[33] For Penner, Acts is a history that educates Christians in the values of the movement; in addition, drawing on commonly recognized values, Acts portrays the Christian characters as uniquely embodying these values when compared to other groups. Penner writes, "It is evident that Jewish, Greek, or Roman readers would take this much away from Acts: the great civic traditions of antiquity are manifested in the narrative in the Christian community."[34] In Luke's construction of reality, the value to which everyone subscribes is embodied only in the Christians. In his contribution to this volume, Gary Gilbert compares certain Roman imperial strategies with those found in Acts.[35] Among other things, he calls attention to the list of nations in Acts 2, which he understands as a narrative strategy that places Christian claims in competition with Roman claims and substitutes Jesus for Caesar as sovereign over all people. Scholars represented here would seemingly agree that the author of Acts is engaged in making claims that compete with similar imperial claims and that Luke's rhetorical strategies are consonant with those used in the wider Greco-Roman world. In other words, Luke engaged in mythmaking, a term that Milton Moreland uses in his examination of Acts.[36] Moreland analyzes Luke's choice of Jerusalem as the place of Christian origins. He notes that there were other candidates and that diversity characterized the earliest Christian movement. Luke, however, wanted to portray the origin of the Christian movement as unified and harmonious, so he suppressed knowledge of most alternative Christian groups and pictured the leadership of the apostles as unchallenged. Moreland claims that Luke begins the story in Jerusalem in order to stress apostolic leadership and to connect the movement with the Hebrew epic.

However, not all rhetorical criticism is, strictly speaking, sociorhetorical. Some scholars who are interested in ancient strategies of persuasion focus their attention on issues of intertextuality and genre. Intertextuality is

---

[33] David L. Balch, "ΜΕΤΑΒΟΛΗ ΠΟΛΙΤΕΙΩΝ—Jesus as Founder of the Church in Luke-Acts: Form and Function," in this volume.

[34] Penner, "Civilizing Discourse," 94. See also Saundra Schwartz, "The Trial Scene in the Greek Novels and in Acts," in this volume.

[35] Gary Gilbert, "Roman Propaganda and Christian Identity in the Worldview of Luke-Acts," in this volume; idem, "The List of Nations in Acts 2: Roman Propaganda and the Lukan Response," *JBL* 121 (2002): 497–529.

[36] Milton Moreland, "The Jerusalem Community in Acts: Mythmaking and the Sociorhetorical Functions of a Lukan Setting," in this volume.

an especially important aspect of rhetorical criticism, and it is sometimes used not simply to show rhetorical similarities but also to claim that a later writer made specific use of an earlier text. Dennis MacDonald has long been calling our attention to parallels between the Homeric epics and various New Testament texts.[37] In this volume he devotes attention to the farewell speech of Paul in Acts 20:17–38 and Hector's farewell to Andromache in *Iliad* 6.[38] MacDonald intentionally goes against the prevailing view that the speech of Paul to the elders at Miletus was modeled on Jewish testamentary texts and claims that Luke had a copy of book 6 of the *Iliad* before him. MacDonald uses a number of criteria to bolster this claim: the text in question was accessible to Luke and his readers; it was often imitated; the parallels are dense; and there are distinctive traits shared in the two texts. MacDonald notes that, although the parallels are dense, the two texts do not preserve the same sequence of motifs, and, although both texts present their main characters as heroes, the definitions of heroism differ. This difference leads MacDonald to characterize Paul's speech in Acts as offering a new understanding of heroism. While Hector emphasizes valor and distinction in battle, Paul cites a saying of Jesus—"It is more blessed to give than to receive" (20:35)—as the measure of heroism. Luke thus made use of the Hector-Andromache scene in order to introduce a new interpretation of heroism.

Although Balch, in contrast to his earlier writing, here minimizes the significance of genre, genre continues to be an important issue among rhetorical critics.[39] Loveday Alexander has devoted insistent attention to the understanding of the Lukan prologues and provides us with a cogent argument about the genre of Acts.[40] She concludes that Acts provides the

---

[37] See Dennis R. MacDonald, *Christianizing Homer: The Odyssey, Plato, and the Acts of Andrew* (New York: Oxford University Press, 1994); idem, *The Homeric Epics and the Gospel of Mark* (New Haven: Yale University Press, 2000); and idem, ed., *Mimesis and Intertextuality* (Harrisburg, Pa.: Trinity Press International, 2001).

[38] Dennis R. MacDonald, "Paul's Farewell to the Ephesian Elders and Hector's Farewell to Andromache: A Strategic Imitation of Homer's *Iliad*," in this volume.

[39] Balch, "ΜΕΤΑΒΟΛΗ ΠΟΛΙΤΕΙΩΝ."

[40] See Loveday Alexander, *The Preface to Luke's Gospel: Literary Convention and Social Context in Luke 1.1–4 and Acts 1.1* (SNTSMS 78; Cambridge: Cambridge University Press, 1993); idem, "Formal Elements and Genre: Which Greco-Roman Prologues Most Closely Parallel the Lukan Prologues?" in *Jesus and the Heritage of Israel: Luke's Narrative Claim upon Israel's Legacy* (ed. D. P. Moessner; Harrisburg, Pa.: Trinity Press International, 1999), 9–26; and idem, "The Acts of the Apostles as an Apologetic Text," in *Apologetics in the Roman Empire: Pagans, Jews, and Christians* (ed. M. Edwards et al.; New York: Oxford University Press, 1999), 15–44.

reader with a number of apologetic episodes but should not itself be classified as an apology, at least not in the sense of the great second-century apologies of Justin and Athenagoras. She writes, "Generically, Luke's choice of vehicle brings him closer to the world of 'popular' narrative and pamphlet than to the 'higher' forms of rhetorical discourse which were adopted by the later apologists: closer, let us say, to the novels, the martyrologies, the idealized philosophical biographies, or even the *Acts of the Pagan Martyrs,* than to *Against Apion.*"[41]

An important contribution to the discussion of the genre of Acts has more recently been provided by Marianne Palmer Bonz.[42] Palmer Bonz rejects the classification of Luke-Acts as historiography. The purpose of Luke-Acts, she believes, is to create a myth of Christian origins, similar to Virgil's *Aeneid,* a frequently imitated epic of Roman origins:

> Above all, Luke appears to have been inspired by Virgil in his presentation of the church as the natural and, indeed, the only legitimate successor to ancient Israel. Seizing upon the divine origins of the Trojan people, long established in legend, Virgil's epic extends those claims to encompass Rome and its inhabitants. The promise of ancient Troy reaches its fulfillment in the creation of the Roman people, just as, in Luke's narrative, the promise of ancient Israel reaches its fulfillment in the establishment and growth of the new community of believers.[43]

Other aspects of rhetorical criticism might profitably be included here, but perhaps what we have is enough to demonstrate the interests embodied in this scholarship, its distinction from earlier scholarship, and some of its results. Although individual scholars may move off in different directions, what ties them together is an interest in the persuasive strategies to be found in ancient Greco-Roman literature and Acts.

And Back?

The caption above is intended to convey a degree of uncertainty as well as to provide an opportunity to explore a question about where we may be headed. My question is this: Do the kinds of studies represented in this volume and elsewhere provide us with the possibility of raising once again certain historical questions? I will approach this issue indirectly by way of a few comments intended to initiate consideration of the

---

[41] Alexander, "Acts of the Apostles," 44.

[42] See Marianne Palmer Bonz, *The Past as Legacy: Luke-Acts and Ancient Epic* (Minneapolis: Fortress, 2000).

[43] Ibid., 192–93. Cf. Moreland's essay in this volume.

possibilities of and problems with the kinds of studies we classify as rhetorical, specifically those called sociorhetorical.

Despite the inevitable differences in individual application, the distinctive feature of rhetorical criticism is the attention devoted to the ancient literary scene and the awareness of rhetorical strategies employed by ancient authors, the educational system that stressed the development of rhetorical skills, the pervasive influence of Greek and Latin epics, and the political power of narratives. If earlier scholars primarily asked questions about the historicity of the episodes in Acts, rhetorical critics are mainly asking questions about the ways in which this text relates to ancient Greco-Roman literature and the strategies used to construct social and political reality.

Probably the most exciting contribution of these studies is their ability to describe the literary world in which the author of Acts lived and to draw significant inferences from this description. Contributions in this volume show that, although the author of Acts was interested in topics and events that rarely occupied the attention of major writers, he nevertheless was well educated and probably comfortable in elite society, familiar with the classics of Greek and Latin literature, and competent in producing persuasive narrative. The intended readers would enjoy a similar location, possessing the ability to appreciate persuasive narrative if not to produce it. If this is correct and if Luke-Acts is, at least in part, intended for an audience of believers, then we have learned a great deal about the social status of a significant group of Christians, although their specific time and place may remain indeterminate. Above all, the studies represented here insist on understanding the text of Acts as something that works within the ancient world in ways similar to the ways in which other examples of ancient literature worked. They take seriously the fact that Luke-Acts was written in Greek by an author who presupposed an audience that spoke and read the Greek language and had a wide familiarity with epic literature, an ability to hear echoes from well-known texts, and an appreciation for a carefully presented argument.

There are, however, some voices that caution us against an exaggerated appraisal of Luke's work. Loveday Alexander, for example, resists a classification of Luke at the topmost rung of the literary ladder.[44] Although Richard Pervo describes his method as making use of form criticism rather than rhetorical criticism, he would come to a similar conclusion as Alexander regarding the social location of Luke's audience. He calls attention to the entertaining value of adventure and travel narratives and identifies Acts as a form of ancient popular literature, a genre that would also include the

---

[44] Alexander, "Acts of the Apostles."

apocryphal Acts.[45] These observations suggest that we might profitably look again at Karl Ludwig Schmidt's contention that the Gospels represent a kind of writing that he designated as *Kleinliteratur*.[46] Schmidt would presuppose an audience for the Gospels and Acts that might not approach the elevated level that seems to be implied by some of the studies in this volume. Perhaps Luke's greatest drawback is the attention he paid to persons and places that were not considered to be of great significance. Whatever might be the outcome of a reexamination of Schmidt's categorization of the Gospels as *Kleinliteratur,* the studies here have shown that the author of Acts would probably have been welcome to attend a gathering of the best-known authors of his day, even if he might have been slightly uncomfortable.

Recognition of the Greco-Roman context of the author and audience of Acts not only leads to a new appreciation of Luke's world but also raises a serious question. Characteristically, New Testament scholarship has emulated a pendulum, swinging back and forth between an emphasis on the Jewish context for various New Testament texts and a stress on the Greco-Roman context. The history of this tendency is well known and need not be repeated here. Nevertheless, some warning is in order. Clearly, a kind of scholarship that emphasizes the compatibility of Acts with Greco-Roman rhetoric will observe things about Acts that have been neglected before. It will find similarities with literature that are more appropriate than those heretofore noted. Inevitably, its stress will be on the Greco-Roman context for Acts.

While expressing great appreciation for the scholarship represented by rhetorical criticism, I nevertheless take note of the fact that we now seem to be neglecting the other major context in which Christianity arose and in which the author of Acts appears to have a great interest: the Jewish context. While Acts appears to be at home in the Greco-Roman world, its author devotes significant attention to Jews and Judaism. There may be various ways of explaining this degree of attention, but its presence in the text cannot be doubted. The major characters in Acts are Jews; the message they preach is expressed as the fulfillment of the Hebrew scriptures; the origin of the movement is located at the heart of the Jewish nation; Jewish rituals continue among Christian converts; and so forth. Paul argues vigorously that his own beliefs are in total harmony not only with the Hebrew scriptures but also with Pharisaic Judaism. To be sure, Acts pays significant attention to Jewish opposition to the Pauline preaching and

---

[45] Richard I. Pervo, *Profit with Delight: The Literary Genre of the Acts of the Apostles* (Philadelphia: Fortress, 1987).

[46] Schmidt, *Place of the Gospels.*

frequently contrasts it with the positive response of Gentile audiences. Yet most remarkable is the amount of attention this author devotes to the Jewish response, even in contrast to the more positive Gentile response. The richness of description of Jews and Judaism contrasts with the lack of description regarding Gentiles. Acts begins and ends with Jews. The first scene is set in Jerusalem and the last in Rome, but both deal with Jewish concerns. In Acts 1, Jesus orders the apostles to remain in Jerusalem (1:4), and they ask about the restoration of the kingdom to Israel (1:6). The last major scene of Acts is set in Rome but is devoted to meetings of Paul with Jews—meetings that issue in his solemn announcement addressed to these Jews: "Let it be known to you, then, that this salvation of God has been sent to the Gentiles; they will listen" (28:28). While vigorous controversies about the function of Acts 28:28 within the Lukan corpus are well known among scholars of Acts,[47] my point here is not to continue the debate about this verse's meaning. Rather, I want merely to point out that the author of Acts, despite his Greco-Roman training and his immersion in that literary world, has an interest—one may almost say an obsession—with things Jewish. Neglect of this dimension among modern scholars, including those interested in the rhetorical aspects of Acts, constitutes a serious deficiency that I hope will soon be corrected.[48]

Finally, I want to say a word about the historical dimensions of the newer studies of Acts, especially those we call sociorhetorical. Rhetorical critics frequently celebrate a freedom from historicity, a term that I understand to signify questions about the historical accuracy of Acts. More than a century and a half ago Baur also took pleasure in freedom from historicity, but, as we know, with him historicity and history were not the same; one could have an interest in the historical dimensions of Acts without raising questions about its accuracy. When I ask if we are moving back to history, I do not ask about historicity but rather about the historical and social context within which Acts was written and first heard or read. If it

---

[47] See Joseph B. Tyson, ed., *Luke-Acts and the Jewish People: Eight Critical Perspectives* (Minneapolis: Augsburg, 1988); idem, *Luke, Judaism, and the Scholars: Critical Approaches to Luke-Acts* (Columbia: University of South Carolina Press, 1999).

[48] George Kennedy was aware of the necessity to include attention to Jewish rhetorical devices in studying New Testament literature (Kennedy, *New Testament Interpretation,* 12). Palmer Bonz also gave a good amount of attention to Luke's involvement with Israel in her book, *The Past as Legacy.* Moreland similarly stresses the significance of Jerusalem for Luke in his contribution in this volume. In a different way, Amy Wordelman has been seriously attentive to the role of anti-Judaism in Acts and has taken this motif to a new level (see her "Cultural Divides and Dual Realities: A Greco-Roman Context for Acts 14," in this volume).

is the case that our author was a part of a literary world that prized rhetorical skills, what does the publication of Acts suggest to us about this world? Where does it fit in terms of what we know about the political, social, economic, even ideological and intellectual dimensions of this world?

In this connection, one may even ask about chronology: Does attention to the rhetorical aspects of this text help us to locate Acts chronologically? In the long run, it will not suffice to associate Acts with an indeterminate Greco-Roman world; eventually we will need to be more precise. In his contribution to this volume, Milton Moreland, perhaps unintentionally, displays the need to work seriously at the question of chronology. He shows how important it is to understand the context within which Acts was written, and he cautions against seeking to find this context in the narrative time of the text. In mythmaking, he says, there is always a gap between "the group's setting and the narrative world it creates."[49] Moreland thus calls attention to two things: the distance between the world within the text of Acts and the actual world of the author, and the importance of finding a viable context for the writing of Acts. Moreland assumes a first-century date for Acts, but he also maintains that Acts is an apology—not for Christianity generally but for a particular type of Christianity. While Moreland's Acts sees itself lined up with the apostles, the Hebrew epic, and Jerusalem Christianity, Moreland does not pursue the question of when such an apology was thought to be necessary. Elsewhere I have considered the likelihood that Acts was written in the early second century at a time when Marcion challenged precisely the alignments that Moreland calls to our attention.[50] Whether or not one agrees with this dating, it will be helpful for rhetorical critics, especially sociorhetorical critics, to devote serious attention to the question of the date of Acts. If we can narrow the possibilities for the date when Acts first appeared, we ought to be in good position to make even more precise observations about its literary, social, and political contexts.

To ask about a return to history is not to encourage a revival of historical criticism as we once knew it or a return to questions about the historical accuracy of early Christian texts. It is, rather, to encourage the application of what we have learned about Acts and Greco-Roman literature toward the exploration of the world that we can glimpse through Luke's window.

---

[49] Moreland, " Jerusalem Community in Acts," 298.

[50] At the Acts Seminar (Santa Rosa, Calif., 19 October 2002) both Richard I. Pervo and I presented papers in which we pursued the possibility of dating the composition of Acts in the first quarter of the second century (see "The Date of Acts: A Reconsideration" [Tyson] and "Dating Acts" [Pervo], forthcoming in *Forum*).

Conclusion

By way of summary, I call attention to four points. First, although earlier critical studies of Acts were dominated by historical concerns, attention to literary aspects of the text was not absent. It is, of course, accurate to refer to this period in the history of scholarship on Acts as characterized by historical criticism in the limited sense of the phrase. Debates about the historical accuracy of episodes as reported in Acts and of the book as a whole have been seemingly endless. However, this picture should not be overdrawn to the neglect of certain literary questions raised by scholars such as Ferdinand Christian Baur and Henry J. Cadbury. It is probable that Baur and Cadbury would not be satisfied with the present results of sociorhetorical criticism, but neither would they have been dismissive of its concerns and methods.

Second, rhetorical studies of Acts have given us a greater appreciation for the relationship of Luke to a rich Greco-Roman literary heritage, which he must have shared with an intended audience. We have learned to think of the author of Acts as a recipient of a good Greco-Roman education and as an author aware of the persuasive power of literature. His interest in geographical locations of minor significance and in persons lacking in social prominence may have tended to diminish his significance in the Greco-Roman literary world, but his connection with this world is still visible to us.

Third, despite the many contributions of this scholarship, there is a tendency to neglect the seemingly obsessive concern this author had with Jews and Judaism. It is inevitable that a form of criticism that focuses attention on persuasive strategies and literary devices drawn from the Greco-Roman world would tend to interpret the author of Acts within that world and hence confine him to it. However, as stated above, Luke's interests may have tended to separate him from the first class of Greco-Roman writers. Among other interests, Luke's concern with Jews and Judaism would have been cited by leading authors of his day as evidence that, despite his training and rhetorical competence, he had not achieved the highest status as a writer. Although some rhetorical critics have called attention to Luke's concern with Jews and Judaism, much more needs to be done. Is it simply that he chose to write about the rise of a movement that was somehow connected with Judaism, or is there something more at work here? I for one would like to see questions of this sort addressed by sociorhetorical critics.

Finally, studies of Acts that stress the sociorhetorical aspects of the text have the potential for shedding light on the historical context of the author and his intended audience and so to turn our attention back to historical, even chronological, issues. This is not to say that we should return to questions of the historical accuracy of Acts but rather that we should continue to explore the social, political, and historical contexts within which the book was written. Ernst Haenchen wrote that Acts "had no 'life-situation' in the Church at all."[51] He meant this for the first century. Although Haenchen presumed that Acts was written in the first century, he was perplexed that it did not find an audience until after the time of Justin Martyr in the second century. Sociorhetorical critics might well examine some issues raised by Haenchen's claims. Is it likely that authors write to unknown or nonextant audiences? Or is it more likely that they write to and for audiences that they know very well? Explorations of questions such as these should provide a firmer grounding than we now have for dating the Acts of the Apostles and for describing its social location.

---

[51] Ernst Haenchen, *The Acts of the Apostles: A Commentary* (trans. B. Noble et al.; Philadelphia: Westminster, 1971), 9.

Luke and the *Progymnasmata:* A Preliminary Investigation into the Preliminary Exercises

Mikeal C. Parsons

Since George Kennedy's brief chapter on Acts in *New Testament Interpretation through Rhetorical Criticism,* a flurry of rhetorical analyses of the speeches in Acts has appeared.[1] Though these works have marked differences in detail, the cumulative effect of these studies (noting in various speeches, especially by Paul, the use of major components of rhetorical

---

[1] George A. Kennedy, "The Speeches in Acts," in *New Testament Interpretation through Rhetorical Criticism* (Chapel Hill: University of North Carolina Press, 1984), 114–40. See also Clifton C. Black, "The Rhetorical Form of the Hellenistic Jewish and Early Christian Sermon: A Response to Lawrence Wills," *HTR* 81 (1988): 1–8; Robert Morgenthaler, *Lukas und Quintilian: Rhetorik als Erzählkunst* (Zürich: Gotthelf, 1993); Jerome Neyrey, "The Forensic Defense Speech and Paul's Trial Speeches in Acts 22–26: Form and Function," in *Luke-Acts: New Perspectives from the Society of Biblical Literature Seminar* (ed. C. H. Talbert; New York: Crossroad, 1984), 210–24; Philip E. Satterthwaite, "Acts against the Background of Classical Rhetoric," in *The Book of Acts in Its Ancient Literary Setting* (ed. B. W. Winter and A. D. Clarke; vol. 1 of *The Book of Acts in Its First Century Setting;* Grand Rapids: Eerdmans, 1993), 337–79; Marion L. Soards, "The Speeches in Acts in Relation to Other Pertinent Ancient Literature," *ETL* 70 (1994): 65–90; idem, *The Speeches in Acts: Their Content, Context, and Concerns* (Louisville: Westminster John Knox, 1994); Fred Veltman, "The Defense Speeches of Paul in Acts," in *Perspectives on Luke-Acts* (ed. C. H. Talbert; Macon, Ga.: Mercer University Press, 1978), 243–56; Duane F. Watson, "Paul's Speech to the Ephesian Elders (Acts 20.17–38): Epideictic Rhetoric of Farewell," in *Persuasive Artistry: Studies in New Testament Rhetoric in Honor of George A. Kennedy* (ed. D. F. Watson; JSNTSup 50; Sheffield: Sheffield Academic Press, 1990), 184–208; Bruce Winter, "The Importance of the *Captatio Benevolentiae* in the Speeches of Tertullus and Paul in Acts 24:1–21," *JTS* 42 (1991): 505–31; idem, "Official Proceedings and the Forensic Speeches in Acts 24–26," in Winter and Clarke, *Book of Acts in Its Ancient Literary Setting,* 305–36; Dean Zweck, "The *Exordium* of the Areopagus Speech, Acts 17.22, 23," *NTS* (1989): 94–103; and now also, Derek Hogan, "Paul's Defense: A Comparison of the Forensic Speeches in Acts, *Callirhoe,* and *Leucippe and Clitophon,*" *PRSt* 29 (2002): 73–87.

speech, especially judicial), in my opinion, has been to demonstrate that the author of Acts was familiar with the devices and strategies of ancient rhetoric as practiced during the Hellenistic period.[2]

Nonetheless, with some notable exceptions scholars have been reluctant to apply these insights to the Gospel of Luke and the narrative portions of Acts, refusing in effect to follow the pioneering work of Robert O. P. Taylor's *Groundwork for the Gospels,* published in 1946.[3] One reason for hesitation has been the recognition that the rhetorical handbook tradition represented by Cicero, Quintilian, and others is aimed at training orators for declamation; that is, their focus is on delivering oral speeches, not on writing narratives. This reading of the handbooks, of course, misses the point that these writers generously quote examples from various Greek and Latin epics, histories, poetry, and the like. Still, the reluctance is understandable.

If, however, these other studies of the speeches in Acts do show that Luke was more than competent in the handbook tradition, then it would be fair to conclude also that he would have cut his rhetorical teeth, as it were, on the *progymnasmata* tradition. The *progymnasmata* were "handbooks that outlined 'preliminary exercises' designed to introduce students who had completed basic grammar and literary studies to the fundamentals of rhetoric that they would then put to use in composing speeches and prose."[4] As such, these graded series of exercises were probably intended to facilitate the transition from grammar school to the more advanced study of rhetoric.[5]

---

[2] Satterthwaite concludes: "At point after point Acts can be shown to operate according to conventions similar to those outlined in classical rhetorical treatises" ("Acts against the Background," 378). Furthermore, I suggest, given the ambient rhetorical context of antiquity, that Luke's authorial audience, while likely unable themselves to reproduce these rhetorical devices in composition, were nevertheless able to respond to their effects.

[3] Robert O. P. Taylor, *Groundwork for the Gospels, with Some Collected Papers* (Oxford: Blackwell, 1946). I find persuasive Taylor's rationale that as a Hellenic citizen the "Christian was bound to pursue the art of pleading, both in his own defense and in the work of persuading others.... It was only natural that he should use the methods in vogue. And in the work of the Rhetores, we have an exposition of their methods" (75).

[4] Willi Braun, *Feasting and Social Rhetoric in Luke 14* (SNTSMS 85; Cambridge: Cambridge University Press, 1995), 146.

[5] Quintilian, in fact, refers to the preliminary exercises as part of the educational curriculum of young boys (*Inst.* 1.9). On the role of rhetoric in the educational curricula of antiquity, the standard works remain Stanley F. Bonner, *Education in Ancient Rome* (Berkeley and Los Angeles: University of California Press, 1977); Donald L. Clark, *Rhetoric in Greco-Roman Education* (New York:

Four of these *progymnasmata* from the first to fifth centuries C.E. have survived (see table on page 63).[6] What is important about these writings is that some of the exercises in the *progymnasmata* are clearly intended to embrace both written and oral forms of communication. For example, in his chapter "On the Education of Young Students," Aelius Theon, the author of the earliest extant *progymnasmata,* remarks:

> So then, I have presented these things, not thinking that they are all suitable for all beginners, but in order that we might know that training in the exercises is absolutely necessary, not only for those who are going to be orators, but also if anyone wishes to practice the art of poets or prose-writers [λογοποιῶν], or any other writers. These things are, in effect, the foundation of every form of discourse.[7]

Thus, though the rhetorical handbooks and the *progymnasmata* often address the same topics, the *progymnasmata,* aimed as they are at equipping young students with the building blocks of communication, both

---

Columbia University Press, 1957); and Henri I. Marrou, *A History of Education in Antiquity* (trans. G. Lamb; New York: Sheed & Ward, 1956).

[6] In addition to the text of Aelius Theon (cited below), other surviving *progymnasmata* include those by Hermogenes of Tarsus (second century; critical edition in *Hermogenes Opera* [ed. H. Rabe; RG 6; Leipzig: Teubner, 1913], 1–27; English translation in Charles S. Baldwin, *Medieval Rhetoric and Poetic [to 1400] Interpreted from Representative Works* [New York: Macmillan, 1928], 23–38); Aphthonius of Antioch (fourth century; critical edition in *Aphthonii Progymnasmata* [ed. H. Rabe; RG 10; Leipzig: Teubner, 1926], 1–51; English translation in Ray E. Nadeau, "The *Progymnasmata* of Aphthonius in translation," *Speech Monographs* 19 [1952]: 264–85; an online translation of Aphthonius by Malcolm Heath of the Classics Department at the University of Leeds may be found at www.leeds.ac.uk/classics/resources/rhetoric/index.htm); Nicolaus of Myra (fifth century; critical edition in *Nicolai Progymnasmata* [ed. J. Felten; RG 11; Leizpig: Teubner, 1913]; no English translation available). English translations of, introductions to, and notes about Theon, Hermogenes, Aphthonius, and Nicolaus (along with selections from some others) may be found in George A. Kennedy, ed. and trans., *Progymnasmata: Greek Textbooks of Prose Composition and Rhetoric* [SBLWGRW 10; Atlanta: Society of Biblical Literature, 2003]). A fifth document, a commentary on Aphthonius's *Progymnasmata* attributed to John of Sardis, is available in the Teubner edition, *Ioannis Sardiani Commentarium in Aphthonii Progymnasmata* (ed. H. Rabe; RG 15; Leipzig: Teubner, 1928).

[7] 70.24–30; Patillon, 15 (see n. 10). James R. Butts, "The *Progymnasmata* of Theon: A New Text with Translation and Commentary" (Ph.D. diss., Claremont Graduate School, 1986), 187 n. 36, rightly observes: "This statement is clear evidence that T[heon] understood the *progymnasmata* as providing instruction for literary activity ranging far beyond the technical parameters of rhetoric."

written and oral, serve as a kind of filter for the handbooks to sift out what comments might be more appropriate for written communication.

Taking this one step further, George Kennedy has commented on the significance of these rhetorical training manuals for early Christian texts:

> The curriculum described in these works, featuring a series of set exercises of increasing difficulty, was the source of facility in written and oral expression for many persons and training for speech in public life.... Not only the secular literature of the Greeks and Romans, but *the writings of early Christians beginning with the gospels* and continuing through the patristic age, and of some Jewish writers as well, *were molded by the habits of thinking and writing learned in schools.*[8]

If the last part of Kennedy's comment is true, and if, among the Gospel writers, Luke at least was familiar with rhetorical exercises similar to those discussed by Theon and others, then a thoroughgoing investigation into the rhetorical conventions of Luke is warranted.[9] It is important to tease out the implications of this for understanding the impact of Luke's writings upon his authorial audience, who presumably also knew how to respond appropriately (if unconsciously) to the effects of persuasive rhetoric. Particular focus will thus be placed on illuminating our understanding of how Luke told his story, that is, the rhetorical strategies and literary conventions he employed, including how these might have been understood by his audience.

Our arguments about Luke's knowledge of the rhetorical devices preserved in the *progymnasmata* tradition are drawn primarily from the *Progymnasmata* of Aelius Theon of Alexandria (ca. 50–100 C.E.), the earliest extant textbook and the only one roughly contemporary to Luke.[10] I am

---

[8] Kennedy, *Progymnasmata*, ix (emphasis added). Some might wish to quibble with Kennedy and argue that the influence of the *progymnasmata* on early Christian writings began even earlier with Paul.

[9] As recently as 1994, Duane Watson was able to write, "a thorough and balanced assessment of the rhetoric of the Gospels has yet to be written" (Duane F. Watson and Alan J. Hauser, eds., *Rhetorical Criticism of the Bible: A Comprehensive Bibliography with Notes on History and Method* [BibInt 4; Leiden: Brill, 1994], 115).

[10] I have used the critical edition of the Greek text (along with a French translation) found in Michel Patillon and Giancarlo Bolognesi, eds. and trans., *Aelius Théon: Progymnasmata* (Paris: Belles Lettres, 1997). The Patillon text has replaced Leonard Spengel, ed., *Rhetores Graeci* (3 vols.; Leipzig: Teubner, 1854–56), 2:59–130, as the standard critical edition. Patillon, with the aid of Bolognesi, has reconstructed five chapters (13–17) from the Armenian manuscripts that were missing from the Greek texts. For text and translation of Theon, see also Butts, "*Progymnasmata* of Theon."

not, of course, suggesting any kind of literary dependence between Luke and Theon, but rather that Theon's text conveniently represents the kind of rhetorical exercises practiced in the first century, many of which, in fact, had been practiced as early as the first or second centuries B.C.E.[11] Thus, I assume that most (but not necessarily all) of what Theon says about these rhetorical exercises was not unique to Theon. This assumption is buttressed by occasional appeal to the discussions in the rhetorical handbook tradition, which, while discussing specifically rhetorical speech, are remarkably similar to a number of Theon's points. Further, in terms of its basic structure, the extant Greek manuscripts preserve twelve chapters, while the Armenian versions add another five. The first two chapters consist of a brief preface, summarizing the contents that follow, and also add a philosophical passage "On the Education of the Young." Finally, Theon's presentation is unique among the extant *progymnasmata* both in its form of address (it is directed to the teacher and not the students) and in its order and number of exercises.[12]

For the sake of space, I will deal only with the first three of Theon's topics—chreia, fable, and narrative—concentrating particularly on the third topic, narrative.[13] I will conclude with some observations about the exegetical implications of the rudimentary exercise of grammatical inflection, which Theon commends for practice on chreia, fable, and narrative. The goal of this all-too-brief study is to entice others to consider the virtues of

---

It should be noted that both Patillon and Butts have rearranged the chapters in Theon to reflect what they believe to be Theon's original order of presentation. They have also inserted "On Refutation and Confirmation," a separate chapter in all extant Greek manuscripts, into the chapter "On the Narrative," again restoring what is believed to have been the original order. Hence, when I cite Theon, I have employed the Spengel numbering system (which is still the standard), supplementing it with the page number where the text can be found in the Patillon edition. For a thorough treatment of the author, text, versions, and critical editions, see Patillon, *Aelius Théon,* vii–clvi, as well as Butts, "*Progymnasmata* of Theon," 7–95. While I have consulted the translations of Patillon, Kennedy, and Butts, unless otherwise noted I am responsible for all the translations of Theon, based on the Patillon critical edition.

[11] Butts, "*Progymnasmata* of Theon," 7. Theon himself acknowledges that others had written on the subject of preliminary exercises (1.15–16) and can even refer (1.18) to "traditional exercises" (ἤδη παραδεδομένοις γυμνάσμασιν).

[12] The chart on page 63 conveniently summarizes the differences (modified from Kennedy, *Progymnasmata,* xiii).

[13] I have elsewhere catalogued some brief suggestions about how other *progymnasmata* topics might inform our reading of Luke, with some notation on studies already exploring these various subjects. See Mikeal C. Parsons, *Luke: Storyteller, Interpreter, and Evangelist* (Peabody, Mass.: Hendrickson, forthcoming).

the study of the *progymnasmata* in their own right and for their potential contribution to our understanding of Luke and Acts.

On Chreia

Theon defines the chreia as "a brief assertion or an action revealing shrewdness" (96.19–20; Patillon, 18) that in the exercise can be expanded or compressed (101.4–5; Patillon, 24). After discussing the general categories of chreia (verbal, descriptive of an action, or mixed [97.11–99.12; Patillon, 18–21]), Theon lists the species of a chreia. Of these, the most significant for our purposes is the enthymeme. Theon illustrates the enthymeme with the following example: "Socrates the philosopher, when a certain Apollodorus said that the Athenians had condemned him to death unjustly, laughed and said, 'Do you wish that they had done so justly?' It is necessary for us to add a proposition that it is better to be condemned unjustly than justly, which seems to have been omitted in the chreia, but is potentially clear" (99.34–100.3; Patillon, 22). Theon's example reflects the general view that an enthymeme is an assertion expressed as a syllogism in which one of the premises or rationales is omitted.

The chreia or anecdote has surely received the most attention from biblical scholars.[14] Earlier works tended to limit their discussion to an isolated chreia and its elaboration through expansion or compression in the narrative immediately following the anecdote.[15] Vernon Robbins, who has

---

[14] Prominent among that literature is the work by Burton Mack and Vernon Robbins, esp. Burton L. Mack and Vernon K. Robbins, *Patterns of Persuasion in the Gospels* (Sonoma, Calif.: Polebridge, 1989); Burton L. Mack, *Rhetoric and the New Testament* (GBS; Minneapolis: Fortress, 1990); Vernon K. Robbins, *The Tapestry of Early Christian Discourse: Rhetoric, Society, and Ideology* (London: Routledge, 1996); idem, *Exploring the Texture of Texts: A Guide to Socio-Rhetorical Interpretation* (Philadelphia: Trinity Press International, 1996). This interest in the chreia tradition has led also to the collection and publication of the chreia exercises of prominent *progymnasmata*; see Ronald F. Hock and Edward N. O'Neil, eds. and trans., *The Chreia in Ancient Rhetoric: The Progymnasmata* (SBLTT 27; Atlanta: Scholars Press, 1986); idem, *The Chreia and Ancient Rhetoric: Classroom Exercises* (SBLWGRW 2; Atlanta: Society of Biblical Literature, 2002). On studies particular to the Gospel of Luke or with significant sections devoted to Luke, see Klaus Berger, "Hellenistische Gattungen im Neuen Testament," *ANRW* 2.25.2:1031–432; Braun, *Feasting and Social Rhetoric;* William R. Farmer, "Notes on a Literary and Form-Critical Analysis of Some of the Synoptic Material Peculiar to Luke," *NTS* 8 (1961–62): 301–16; and Roland Meynet, *L'Évangile selon saint Luc: Analyse rhétorique* (2 vols.; Paris: Cerf, 1988).

[15] Richard B. Vinson, "A Comparative Study of Enthymemes in the Synoptic Gospels," in Watson, *Persuasive Artistry,* 119–41; Wilhelm H. Wuellner, "The Rhetorical Genre of Jesus' Sermon in Luke 12.1–13.9," in Watson, *Persuasive Artistry,* 93–118.

explored the *progymnasmata* in relation to the New Testament perhaps more than any other biblical scholar,[16] has recently moved the discussion to a new level in his examination of Luke 11:1–13, and especially the Lord's Prayer in 11:2–4, from the perspective of the progymnastic elaboration of the chreia.[17] Robbins gives a careful and richly textured discussion of Luke 11:4 within what he calls the "enthymemic network of reasoning" related to Jesus' earlier saying, "Forgive, and you will be forgiven" (Luke 6:37–38). Robbins demonstrates that Luke 11:5–8 and 9–10 serve as further elaborations on the theme of forgiveness in the Lord's Prayer.

Furthermore, Robbins notes both similarities and differences between Luke and the *progymnasmata,* demonstrating that there was no compulsion for writers to follow the exercises slavishly. For example, rather than having a well-articulated rationale follow the chreia as the Hermorgenean *Progymnasmata* suggests, Robbins points out that the Lord's Prayer, which he treats as an abbreviated (rather than expanded) chreia, itself contains a supporting premise: "Forgive us our sins, for we ourselves forgive every one indebted to us." The enthymemic network reaches its conclusion in 11:13, which defines the topic as "the heavenly Father's giving of the Holy Spirit in contexts where people pray the prayer Jesus taught his disciples."[18] While it is impossible to do justice in a few brief sentences to Robbins's complex argument, let me assert that his work here (and elsewhere) demonstrates the fruitfulness of looking to the *progymnasmata* for clues to the rhetorical strategies Luke employed in communicating his story, a story that, given the rhetoric in the air of his day, his audience would no doubt have understood with all its rhetorical subtleties.

On Fables

If the chreia tradition is a well-furrowed field in biblical studies, the second topic of the *progymnasmata,* the fable, is relatively untouched. This is somewhat surprising, since Theon's definition of the fable as "a fictitious

---

[16] In addition to the works cited above, see Vernon K. Robbins, "The Woman Who Touched Jesus' Garments: Socio-Rhetorical Analysis of the Synoptic Accounts," *NTS* 33 (1987): 502–15; idem, "Progymnastic Rhetorical Composition and Pre-Gospel Traditions: A New Approach," in *The Synoptic Gospels: Source Criticism and the New Literary Criticism* (ed. C. Focant; BETL 110; Leuven: Leuven University Press, 1993), 111–47; and idem, "Introduction: Using Rhetorical Discussions of the Chreia to Interpret Pronouncement Stories," *Semeia* 64 (1994): vii–xvii.

[17] Vernon K. Robbins, "From Enthymeme to Theology in Luke 11:1–13," in *Literary Studies in Luke-Acts: Essays in Honor of Joseph B. Tyson* (ed. R. P. Thompson and T. E. Phillips; Macon, Ga.: Mercer University Press, 1998), 191–214.

[18] Robbins, "From Enthymeme to Theology," 214.

story which depicts or images truth" (72.28; Patillon, 30) sounds like a typical, rough and ready definition many would use to describe Jesus' parables. To be sure, studies such as those of Mary Ann Beavis have effectively explored some of Jesus' parables in light of Aesop's fables,[19] but no one to my knowledge has given more than a cursory look at the *progymnasmata* in this light. However, if the authorial audience of Luke might have heard Jesus' stories also as fictitious stories imaging truth, comparison to the preliminary exercises might prove worthwhile. I cite one example.

At one point Theon notes, "It may be possible for one fable to have several conclusions (or morals), if we take a start from each of the matters in the fable" (75.28–31). When read in light of this comment, the parable of the Dishonest Steward in Luke 16 takes on new dimensions. The relation of the parable proper (16:1–8a) to the material immediately following (16:8b–13) has long vexed interpreters. C. H. Dodd called 16:8–13 "notes for three separate sermons on the parable as text."[20] Fitzmyer concludes that the applications of the parable found in 16:8–9, 10–12, and 13 "undoubtedly stem from different settings."[21] On the contrary, if Luke and his audience were accustomed to a fable or parable having more than one conclusion or interpretation or moral, it is highly unlikely that anything about the literary shape of this parable would have given the authorial audience any reason to question its rhetorical unity.[22] Far from a clear sign of redactional disruption and separate social settings, according to the *progymnasmata* a conclusion with multiple interpretations or applications was a conventional and acceptable way to end a fictitious story imaging truth.[23]

---

[19] See especially Mary Ann Beavis, "Parable and Fable: Synoptic Parables and Greco-Roman Fables Compared," *CBQ* 52 (1990): 473–98; and idem, "Ancient Slavery as an Interpretive Context for the New Testament Servant Parables with Special Reference to the Unjust Steward (Luke 16:1–8)," *JBL* 111 (1992): 37–54.

[20] Charles H. Dodd, *The Parables of the Kingdom* (rev. ed.; New York: Scribner, 1961), 17.

[21] Joseph A. Fitzmyer, *The Gospel according to Luke* (2 vols.; AB 28–28A; New York: Doubleday, 1981–85), 2:1105. Charles H. Talbert, *Reading Luke: A Literary and Theological Commentary on the Third Gospel* (New York: Crossroad, 1982), 153, comes closer to acknowledging the unity of the interpretations by noting that they are held together by a "complex web of interlocking devices."

[22] In that sense, Craig Blomberg's attempt to see each of the interpretations as reflecting the point of view of one of the characters in the parables is closer to Theon's account than most modern interpreters are (see his *Interpreting the Parables* [Downers Grove, Ill.: InterVarsity Press, 1990], 165–66).

[23] Though beyond the parameters of this essay, which are limited to the final form of the Lukan writings, one cannot help but wonder, especially if the historical Jesus was also a rhetorical Jesus, whether or not such complex elaborations on a fable could not in fact have gone back to Jesus himself.

On Narrative

Theon's comments about narrative seem to be the most intriguing in their potential for understanding Luke's rhetorical strategies.[24] In his chapter "On the Narrative," Theon defines a *narrative* (here διήγημα) as "an explanatory account of matters, which have occurred or as if they have occurred" (78.16–17; Patillon, 38). In his first reference to the topic, Theon used the term διήγησις to describe the elementary exercise of narration: "For the one who has expressed well and in varied ways a narrative or a fable will also compose a history well" (60.3–4; Patillon, 2).[25] The term διήγησις is also the word Luke uses in his preface to describe the attempts of others and, by comparison, his own account of "the events fulfilled among us." While commentators have rightly explored the occurrences of this term in various historiographical writings, we should not neglect the rhetorical connotations altogether. As Theon asserts: "The virtues of a narrative are three in number: clarity, conciseness, and plausibility (or persuasiveness); above all, if it is possible, the narrative should have all the desirable qualities" (79.20–22; Patillon 40). Let us look briefly, then, at these three virtues in light of Luke's writing.

CLARITY

According to Theon, the first virtue—clarity—is achieved in one way through the arrangement (τάξις) of the subject: "Guard also against confusing the times and the order of the events.... For nothing confuses the thought more than these things" (80.26–29; Patillon, 41). Inadvertently confusing the order of events, of which he disapproves, is clearly distinguished by Theon from the elementary exercise of intentionally "rearranging the order of events" (87.13; Patillon, 50), of which he approves. Theon later comments:

> We shall, however, rearrange the order in many [Armenian: five] ways. For it is possible, beginning with the middle to run back to the beginning,

---

[24] On Theon's chapter on narrative and its relevance for New Testament study, see also Vernon K. Robbins, "Narrative in Ancient Rhetoric and Rhetoric in Ancient Narrative," *SBL Seminar Papers 1996* (SBLSP 35; Atlanta: Scholars Press, 1996), 368–84.

[25] Theon generally appears to use the terms διήγησις and διήγημα interchangeably (see 60.3–11; Patillon, 2), while other writers, such as Hermogenes (4.9–15), distinguish between the two, arguing that διήγημα refers to the elementary exercise and that διήγησις is equivalent to the "statement of facts" portion of a speech (*narratto*). To further complicate matters, when Theon does seem to distinguish between the two terms it is in direct opposition to Hermogenes's distinction (e.g., for Theon διήγησις refers to the elementary exercise of story writing, and διήγημα is the "statement of facts" part of a speech [cf. 60.5; Patillon, 2]).

then to come back to the final portions—as Homer has done in his *Odyssey*.... It is also permissible, beginning with the end, to go on to the middle, and thus to come back to the beginning—as Herodotus teaches us in his third book.... Furthermore, it is possible, beginning with the middle, to go on to the end, then to conclude with the beginning. And again, it is possible, beginning with the end, to return to the beginning and to conclude with the middle events. And it is also possible, beginning with the first things, to shift to the final parts and to stop with the middle. So much for the rearrangement of order. (86.9–87.13; Patillon, 48–50)

From the examples in Homer and Herodotus, it is clear that this transposition often occurred in shorter pericopae within the narrative. Not all later rhetorical treatises agreed with this practice of transposing the order of events, especially those associated with judicial speeches that may have revolved around preserving the exact sequence of events (cf. *Rhet. Alex.* 30.28–31; *Rhet. Her.* 1.9.15). In support of this procedure, however, Quintilian writes: "Neither do I agree with those who assert that the order of our narrative should always follow the actual order of events, but I have a preference for adopting the order that I consider most suitable" (*Inst.* 4.2.83).[26]

Luke is likewise concerned with the presentation of events in the narrative. He claims that after he has thoroughly investigated everything, he will write in order (καθεξῆς; Luke 1:3). What exactly does Luke mean by this term? Our first clue comes in Luke's use of the word καθεξῆς elsewhere in his writings (Luke 8:1; Acts 3:24; 11:4; 18:23). Of those occurrences, surely the most significant is the use of the term in Acts 11:4. When the Jerusalem church heard about Peter's associations with Gentiles, they sent an envoy to question him about these events. The narrator notes that Peter began to explain in order or step by step (καθεξῆς). The modern reader expecting the story to be told in chronological sequence will be surprised to hear that Peter begins by reversing the order of the presentation of the visions: his own vision precedes that of Cornelius (cf. Acts 10). However, the word καθεξῆς has little to do with chronological or linear order. Rather, Peter (and in a larger sense the narrator) is seeking to present the events in a manner that his audience will find convincing.[27] For Luke, then, καθεξῆς

---

[26] The Latin text reads: "Nam ne iis quidem accedo, qui semper eo putant ordine, quo quid actum sit, esse narrandum, sed eo malo narrare, qui expedit." Quintilian is, of course, writing about what is considered appropriate for the order of the statement of facts in a speech. My translation is intended to underscore the similarity with Theon.

[27] Robert C. Tannehill, *The Narrative Unity of Luke-Acts: A Literary Interpretation* (2 vols.; Minneapolis: Fortress, 1986–90), 2:144, observes: "Peter presents the narrative 'in order' (11:4). The order is a narrative order, but it is not the same as the order of events in chapter 10. Peter begins not with Cornelius' vision but with

here has rather everything to do with a rhetorically persuasive presentation that displays the virtue of clarity. That was what Peter was attempting to do in Acts 11, and it is what Luke purports to do in his preface as well as throughout the rest of his narrative.[28]

CONCISENESS

Turning next to conciseness, Theon states: "Likewise the narrative is concise in its content and its style. For conciseness is communication that signifies that which is the most essential of the matters, neither adding that which is not necessary nor taking away that which is necessary according to the content and the style" (83.15–19; Patillon, 45).[29] Theon advises the avoidance of synonyms (since they make the sentence needlessly long), the use of words instead of phrases where appropriate (say "he died" rather than "he departed from this life"), simple words rather than compound ones, and shorter rather than longer words (84.5–17; Patillon 46). Three further comments are necessary. First, Theon clearly warns against sacrificing clarity for conciseness and credibility in expression (79.21–24; Patillon, 40; 84.17–18; Patillon, 46). Second, Theon concedes that writing history (here he uses the term ἱστορία)[30] may of necessity take longer than speaking a narrative, since in writing one may need to narrate the protagonist's ancestry, prior events, and the like (see 83.25–84.10; Patillon, 45–46). Finally, what Theon says here about conciseness has to be balanced with his rather extensive treatment in his introduction about the virtues of the paraphrase, wherein one says the same thing well a second or more times (see 62.10–64.25; Patillon, 4–7; cf. also ch. 15 on "Paraphrases" in the Armenian versions; Patillon, 107–8).[31]

---

his own vision.... A sequence of events led Peter to change his mind. Now his audience is being led through the same sequence so that they can appreciate and share Peter's new insight."

[28] Other signs of clarity have to do with matters of style, namely, avoiding poetic and coined words and tropes, archaisms, foreign words, and homonyms (cf. 81.8–10; Patillon, 42). See also Theon on clarity in the fable (76.31–35; Patillon 36).

[29] Brevity is also a topic of discussion in the handbook tradition (see *Rhet. Alex.* 84.17–18; Cicero, *Inv.* 1.28; *Rhet. Her.* 1.14).

[30] While it is clear that Theon views ἱστορία as the combination of narratives (60.6; Patillon, 2), it is not clear whether Theon thinks exclusively in terms of historiography. Certainly ἱστορία includes historiography, but it does not seem to be limited to it. After reviewing all the occurrences of ἱστορία (60.4, 6; 67.4; 70.3, 6, 12; 77.15; 80.17; 81.2, 7; 83.25, 31; 87.23; 91.15; 121.2; 122.30; 123.1; conveniently indexed by Patillon, 199), the general distinction rather seems to be between prose writing and poetry (see esp. 123.1).

[31] While Theon here spends much space discussing the paraphrasing of one author by another, he does also mention, quite positively it seems, Demosthenes,

With these caveats in mind, we turn to Luke. Since there is no comparative material for Acts, we will limit our comments to the Gospel. We begin by acknowledging that Luke's Gospel rivals Matthew's for the longest text. Surely Luke was no slavish follower of the *progymnasmata*'s call for conciseness! With a closer examination, however, some interesting points emerge. In his chapter on "Length" in *The Tendencies in the Synoptic Tradition*, E. P. Sanders examines the phenomenon of relative length among the Synoptics.[32] Sanders concludes that these developments cannot be charted dogmatically in such a way as to fix the flow of information (and thus definitively solve the Synoptic Problem), since developments flow in both directions (the pericopae become both longer and shorter, more and less detailed, more and less Semitic). Nonetheless he finds that when Mark and Luke are compared, Luke is shorter than Mark more times than Mark is shorter than Luke.[33] This finding is rather remarkable given the fact that the whole of Luke is approximately 50 percent longer than the whole of Mark.

Thus, while Luke has the tendency in Acts to repeat material (ascension, Paul's Damascus road experience, conversion of Cornelius), in Luke there is a tendency toward conciseness, which, given the Third Gospel's overall length, is a bit surprising.[34] Not only does Luke eliminate whole

---

who not only transferred material from one speech to another but even repeated material within a single speech (64.1; Patillon, 6–7).

[32] E. P. Sanders, *The Tendencies of the Synoptic Tradition* (SNTSMS 9; Cambridge: Cambridge University Press, 1969), 69–82. Sanders analyzed the texts in seven different categories: (1) Old Testament quotations in one Gospel but not the others; (2) speeches longer in one than in the others; (3) speeches present in one but not the others; (4) dialogues in one but not the others; (5) scenes and events in one but not the others; (6) actions in one but not the others; and (7) differences in length within the same pericope.

[33] According to A. M. Honoré ("A Statistical Study of the Synoptic Problem," *NovT* 10 [1968]: 95–147), there are eighty-four pericopae in the triple-tradition material. In those pericopae (see chart on 96), Mark uses 8,630 words, compared to Luke's 7,884 words (cf. Matthew with 8,336). In addition, there are six pericopae in common between Mark and Luke not found in Matthew (ibid., 139). In those passages, Mark uses 357 words, compared to Luke's 274 words.

[34] This observation was made long ago by Henry J. Cadbury, who after detailing repetition as one the tendencies of Lukan style (especially in Acts), observed: "In contrast to this prolixity in Acts [repetition], the apparent tendency in Luke to avoid parallel scenes must be mentioned. The Gospel, if we may assume that it used Mark, not only omits the second of Mark's accounts of feeding the multitude, but appears to cancel his account of Jesus in his home town (Mark 6:1–6), and of his anointing by a woman (Mark 14:39), and perhaps other sayings or scenes in Mark by introducing, before he comes to these scenes, independent

scenes from Mark (e.g., the second feeding story), at times he eliminates seemingly unnecessary phrases (see Theon above). For example, Luke has replaced Mark's temporal introduction in Luke 1:32 ("When evening came, when the sun set") with the more concise phrase "When the sun was setting." Sanders concludes, "In the case of Matthew, I think the title of abbreviator is unjustified, although it may be applied to Luke with more justice."[35] Further exploration of Luke's abbreviations in light of the *progymnasmata* is therefore in order.

PLAUSIBILITY/PERSUASIVENESS

According to Theon, "for the narrative to be credible/plausible, one must use words that are suitable for the persons and the subject matters and the places and the occasions/contexts; in the case of the subject matters those that are plausible and naturally follow from one another. One should briefly add the causes of things to the narration and say what is unbelievable in a believable way" (84.19–24; Patillon, 46).[36] Let us consider in light of these comments Luke 5:1–11, the call of the first disciples and the miraculous draught of fish.[37] Leaving aside the difficult issue of the relationship of this story to John 21:1–14,[38] we might consider the story in relationship to Mark's version of the call of the first disciples (1:16–20). A number of commentators have argued that inserting the miraculous catch of fish just before the call of the disciples provides a psychologically plausible account for why these fishermen would have left everything to follow Jesus.[39] Rather than seek a *psychological* reason for the change, however, the *progymnasmata*, along with the rhetorical handbooks (Quintilian, *Inst.*

---

versions (Luke 4:16–30; 7:36–50, etc.) Matthew on the contrary appears to repeat passages from Mark a second time" ("Four Features of Lucan Style," in *Studies in Luke-Acts* [ed. L. E. Keck and J. L. Martyn; Nashville: Abingdon, 1966], 89).

[35] Sanders, *Tendencies of the Synoptic Tradition*, 87.

[36] Theon evidently considered plausibility/persuasiveness (πιθανός and its cognates) as the key element in narrative: "For it is always necessary to keep what is plausible in a narrative; for this is its best quality" (79.28–29; Patillon, 40). On plausibility, see also Quintilian, *Inst.* 4.2.32; *Rhet. Alex.* 30.1–4; Cicero, *Inv.* 1.21.29–30). Cf. Theon's comments on plausibility/persuasiveness in the fable; 76.35–77.9.

[37] I am indebted to the work of my student Derek Hogan for much of what follows. He and the other students in my doctoral seminar entitled "Luke and Rhetoric" (fall 1999) provided the initial stimulus for this investigation.

[38] See Raymond Brown, *The Gospel according to John* (2 vols.; AB 29–29A; New York: Doubleday, 1966–70), 2:1090.

[39] Fitzmyer, *Gospel according to Luke*, 1:563; R. Alan Culpepper, "Luke," *NIB* 9:116.

4.2.32; Cicero, *Inv.* 1.21.29–30), may provide the context for understanding the Lukan version as an example of rhetorical plausibility.

In the Markan version of the story, Jesus has hardly begun his ministry when he sees two pairs of brothers fishing. He calls these (presumably) complete strangers, who inexplicably follow without hearing his teaching or witnessing his miraculous power. The rendering of the story sounds somewhat far-fetched, and perhaps Mark intends it so. Nonetheless, Luke makes changes in the story to "tell the unbelievable in a believable way." Among the healings that precede the call of Simon is the healing of Simon's mother-in-law. The audience is led to believe Simon knows of her miraculous recovery. This fact makes more understandable Simon's willingness both to allow Jesus on board his boat and to teach from it. Simon, in Luke, is not welcoming a stranger on board but acknowledging the holy man who had already healed a family member.

While we may view Luke's redaction as a distortion of Mark's rhetoric, no longer does it seem implausible that these fishermen would leave everything to follow Jesus. The audience would have little difficulty in believing that the fishermen follow Jesus.[40] Theon's comments on plausibility suggest that the audience would have conceived of this plausibility in rhetorical terms, however much those of us living in the early twenty-first century might wish to speak of this plausibility in psychological terms. Finally, I would contend that mining the comments on narrative in the *progymnasmata* might give exegetical assistance at other points in understanding the literary conventions employed elsewhere in the Lukan narratives.

On Inflection

Every beginning language student is aware that Greek is a highly inflected language, but, in light of the *progymnasmata,* the significance of that fact for interpretation has not been fully appreciated. Inflecting the main subject or topic (κλίσις) was one of the first exercises taught to beginning students of elementary rhetoric and, since the exercise focused on the rhetorical function of inflection, provided a transition from the study of grammar to the study of rhetoric. Theon gives a rather full description of how such inflection is to take place in his discussions of the chreia and fable, referring back to it also in his treatment of narrative (85.29–31; Patillon, 48). In his chapter "On Fables," Theon asserts:

---

[40] In a sense, this scene also provides the plausibility for the call of Levi later in this same chapter, which, following Mark very closely, has Levi follow immediately and presumably without any prior relationship with Jesus.

Fables should be inflected, like chreia, in different grammatical numbers and oblique cases.... The original grammatical construction must not always be maintained as though by some necessary law, but one should introduce some things and use a mixture (of constructions); for example, start with one case and change in what follows to another, for this variety is very pleasing. (74.24–35; Patillon, 33; cf. also 101.10–103.2)

Quintilian also comments briefly on the use of inflection as a rhetorical device.[41] Following a discussion of the effects of repetition, he suggests: "Other effects may be obtained by the graduation or contrast of clauses, by the elegant inversion of words, by arguments drawn from opposites, asyndeton, paraleipsis, correction, exclamation, meiosis, the employment of a word in different cases (*in multis casibus*), moods and tenses" (*Inst.* 9.1.34). Elsewhere he likewise asserts:

At times the cases and genders of the words repeated may be varied, as in "Great is the toil of speaking, and great the task, etc."; a similar instance is found in Rutilius, but in a long period. I therefore merely cite the beginnings of the clauses. *Pater hic tuus? patrem nunc appellas? patris tui filius es?* [Is this your father? Do you still call him father? Are you your father's son?] This figure may also be effected solely by change of cases, a proceeding which the Greeks call πολύπτωτον.[42]

The feature that Theon calls κλίσις, Quintilian refers to as πολύπτωτον, but the phenomenon seems to be the same. Inflection was more than just an ornamental figure of style designed to please the aesthetic tastes of the audience. In fact, Quintilian included inflection in his discussion of figures of thought, a "class of figure, which does not merely depend on the form of the language for its effect, but lends both charm and force to the thought as well" (9.3.28).[43] The function of inflection was thus for emphasis (see 9.3.67) and to attract the audience's attention to the subject under discussion (9.3.27).

---

[41] Aristotle also commented briefly on πτῶσις, as he called it (*Poet.* 1457A; *Rhet.* 1.7.27; 2.23.2; and esp. 3.9.9), but he used the term generally to refer to similar forms of words whether nouns, verbs, adjectives, or adverbs. See also *Rhet. Her.* 4.22.30–31, the writer of which, like Quintilian, views πολύπτωτον as a form of paronomasia.

[42] *Inst.* 9.3.37. The Latin text reads: "Interim variatur casibus haec et generibus retractatio: Magnus est dicendi labor, magna res et cetera; et apud Rutilium longa περιόδῳ, sed haec initia sententiarum sunt: Pater hic tuus? Patrem nunc appellas? Patris tui filius es? Fit casibus modo hoc schema, quod πολύπτωτον vocant."

[43] The Latin text reads: "genus, quod non tantum in ratione positum est loquendi, sed ipsi sensibus cum gratiam tum etiam vires accommodat."

Any student of elementary rhetoric would have been accustomed to inflecting the main topic or subject of a chreia, fable, or narrative, and presumably an ancient audience would have been naturally, almost instinctively, able to identify the main subject by hearing the topic inflected in the various cases of the Greek noun. If true and if Luke were the student of rhetoric that I think him to have been, then we might expect Luke to have used this inflection convention to provide rhetorical markers as to the topic or subject of various parts of the Lukan narrative. Let us test this hypothesis by exploring whether a topic is ever so inflected in Luke and Acts. Since speeches in Acts and parables in Luke, in addition to the narrator's prose, are the major forms of communication in Luke-Acts, it would be reasonable to expect to find examples of inflected subjects in these three kinds of communication.[44]

SPEECHES IN ACTS

We might first examine the speeches of the Lukan Paul, since, as we already noted, previous studies have demonstrated that Paul in Acts is fully aware of and deftly employs the various components of deliberative, epideictic, and especially juridical speech in various addresses in Acts. When we turn to Paul's Areopagus speech, we find in fact that the five occurrences of God or θεός are inflected in four cases within a matter of a few verses: 17:23 (dative); 17:24 (nominative); 17:27 (accusative); 17:29 (genitive); 17:30 (nominative). This inflection would suggest that the topic of Paul's Areopagus speech was God, a not so surprising fact, since this speech is well known for its lack of an explicit christological formula.

We find a similar pattern in Paul's speech before Agrippa, where again, θεός is inflected in four cases: Acts 26:6 (genitive); 26:8 (nominative); 26:18 (accusative); 26:20 (accusative); 26:22 (genitive); 26:29 (dative). Interestingly, it is only after Agrippa accuses Paul of being "mad with much learning" that Paul finishes his inflection by using θεός in the dative case, ironically confirming for the authorial audience at least the second half of Agrippa's claim that Paul has much learning, or at least enough to know how grammatically to inflect the subject of his speech. That God, not Christ, is the subject of the defense speech is somewhat more surprising than the case with the Areopagus speech, given the various claims regarding the christological climax of Paul's defense.[45]

---

[44] I have limited my examples to instances where the term under consideration has been inflected in the four main cases (nominative, genitive, dative, and accusative) within a reasonably short and well-marked narrative unit, one that would presumably be recognizable to an attentive audience.

[45] See esp. Robert O'Toole, *Acts 26: The Christological Climax of Paul's Defense Speech (Ac22,1–26,32)* (AnBib 78; Rome: Pontifical Biblical Institute, 1978). The

PARABLES IN LUKE

Among the parables in Luke, the last parable in Luke 15 proves a fascinating case. The parable in Luke 15:11–32 has long been known in English as the parable of the Prodigal Son, and this is probably still the most popular title of the story. No less prominent a figure than Joachim Jeremias, however, in his classic study of the parables, suggested that Luke 15 is more aptly described as a "parable of the Father's Love."[46] Even Jeremias's judgment could not derail the tide of subsequent interpreters, many of whom still see the parable as predominately about the prodigal younger brother. Joel Green's comments are characteristic: "as important as the father is to this parable, center stage belongs to the younger son."[47]

Does the grammar of inflection help us understand better how an ancient audience may have heard this parable? The term *son* occurs eight times in Luke 15:11–32, once in the accusative plural (15:11) and seven times in the nominative singular in reference to the prodigal (15:13, 19, 21 [2x], 24, 25, 30). We might reasonably expect that the subject of a parable or story would occur most frequently in the nominative case; however, if we take seriously the role of grammatical inflection in the educational system of late antiquity, then we might not be surprised to learn that not only does the word "father" occur twelve times in the parable, but it also appears in all five cases at least once and in four cases, including the vocative (a rarity in Luke), at least twice: nominative (15:20, 22, 27, 28); genitive (15:17); dative (15:12, 29); accusative (15:18, 20); vocative (15:12, 18, 21). The conclusion seems irresistible that an ancient audience, which was conditioned (even unconsciously) upon hearing an inflected word to identify that term as the subject of the story at hand, would have naturally understood that the subject of the parable was a father and his love.

---

pattern is not limited to Paul's speeches. For example, a similar pattern emerges in Stephen's speech in Acts 7. Stephen uses the word θεός seventeen times in the chapter, twelve times in the nominative (7:2, 6, 7, 9, 17, 25, 32 [2x], 35, 37, 42, 45), three times in the genitive (7:43, 46, 56), and once each in the dative (7:20) and accusative (7:40). Again, that God is the subject of Stephen's rehearsal of Israel's holy history is really not surprising, but the inflection of θεός, along with the fact that θεός is the last word in the speech proper, provides grammatical and textual moorings for this theological conclusion.

[46] Joachim Jeremias, *The Parables of Jesus* (trans. S. H. Hooke; 2d ed.; New York: Scribner, 1972), 128.

[47] Joel B. Green, *The Gospel of Luke* (NICNT; Grand Rapids: Eerdmans, 1997), 578.

"FIRST-LEVEL" NARRATION[48]

Finally, the narrator uses this same strategy. I cite two examples.[49] The first four occurrences of "people" (λάος) in Luke 1 are found in four different cases: 1:10 (genitive); 1:17 (accusative); 1:21 (nominative); 1:68 (dative). Since, with one notable exception (Acts 15:14), all occurrences of λάος in Luke and Acts refer to the Jewish people, this phenomenon perhaps gives grammatical and rhetorical underpinning to the importance Luke assigns to the Jewish setting of the birth of Jesus in the infancy narrative.

In Acts 9, which records the conversion/call of Saul, the term "disciple" occurs six times in four cases, in both singular and plural: 9:1 (accusative plural); 9:10 (nominative singular); 9:19 (genitive plural); 9:25 (nominative plural); and 9:26 (dative plural and nominative singular). Again the inflection functions rhetorically to signal to the audience that whatever else the call/conversion of Paul may be about, it is in the first instance a narrative about the role of the disciples, the Christian community, in that call. This emphasis all but drops out in Paul's subsequent retellings of the event in Acts 22 and 26.[50]

---

[48] This is the term Robert Funk uses to describe the narrator's telling of the story as opposed to second-level narration, such as a character's speech (second-level narration; e.g., Jesus or Paul), or third-level narration, such as the report of a character's speech in a second-level narration (e.g., the prodigal son's speech before his father). See Robert Funk, *Poetics of Biblical Narrative* (Sonoma, Calif.: Polebridge, 1988), 30–34.

[49] If one takes Theon's comment at 74.24–25 to suggest inflecting the subject in only the oblique cases (genitive, dative, accusative), then another interesting pattern emerges. Only in Acts 12 and 28 do we find the narrator inflecting θεός in the oblique cases. In Acts 12, we find 12:5 (accusative); 12:22 (genitive); 12:23 (dative); and 12:24 (genitive). In one instance θεός is used to refer to "a god," not Yahweh God specifically (12:2). In Acts 28, we find θεός inflected again only in the oblique cases: 28:6 (accusative); 28:15 (dative); 28:23 (genitive); and 28:31 (genitive), with one reference in 28:6 to "a god." It is God in Acts 12 and not Herod or Peter, and God in Acts 28 and not Paul, who is so inflected and thus presumably the subject of each respective passage. Furthermore, θεός occurs in the last verse of each chapter. Not only is this observation significant for the interpretation of each passage, but it also may provide the textual and rhetorical markers for the overall structure of Acts. Many scholars take 13:1 with its shift to Paul and the Gentile mission to mark the beginning of a major new section in Acts. If our analysis of the inflection is correct, the audience (familiar with the telling and retelling of the story and upon retrospective patterning) would have been prepared for such a major shift by the rhetorical markers left by the oblique inflection of God.

[50] Equally important may be the emphasis on "Lord" (κυριός) in Acts 9. The word occurs in the nominative (9:10, 11, 17), genitive (9:1, 28, 31), accusative (9:27, 35, 42), and vocative (9:5, 10, 13), but not in the dative.

Any conclusion we reach about the possible rhetorical function of inflection in Luke and Acts remains tentative until we can do a more exhaustive analysis of the text and rule out counterexamples (for example, the full inflection of terms incidental to the main topic of the story being told). We should not be alarmed that Luke does not use inflection to mark the subject of every story. Quintilian rightly warned that these figures are only effective "if the figures are not excessive in number nor all of the same type or combined or closely packed, since economy in their use, no less than variety, will prevent the hearer from being surfeited" (*Inst.* 9.3.27).

We should also not view the use of inflection as a particularly elegant rhetorical device; it was, after all, one of the first exercises practiced by the beginning student of rhetoric, who quickly passed on to more challenging exercises.[51] In fact, Quintilian recognized that inflection and other figures like it "derive something of their charm from their very resemblance to blemishes, just as a trace of bitterness in food will sometimes tickle the palate" (*Inst.* 9.3.27).[52] However, its ordinary nature might argue for its effectiveness as a rhetorical device in signaling the importance of the inflected term for understanding the narrative in which it is couched. Certainly this seems to be the effect for which Theon hoped. In one of the chapters on "Listening to What Is Read," preserved only in the Armenian versions, Theon comments: "In listening, the most important thing is to give frank and friendly attention to the speaker. Then the student should recall the subject of the writing, identify the main points and the arrangement, finally recall also the better passages" (Patillon, 105–6).[53] At the least the practice of inflection deserves further study both as it was practiced in the ancient world and as it may have been employed in Luke and Acts.

Conclusion

One of the most exciting and productive advances in New Testament studies in the past twenty years has been the various explorations of the

---

[51] Nicolaus 4.18–19, for example, suggests that more advanced students could skip the exercise of grammatical inflection and move on to elaborating, condensing, refuting, or confirming.

[52] The author of *Rhetorica ad Herennium*, who also cautions that πολύπτωτον is to be used sparingly, considers πολύπτωτον to be merely an ornament of style, more appropriate for entertainment (or at best epideictic speech) than for juridical speech and is less charitable than Quintilian about its aesthetic value (*Rhet. Her.* 4.22.32).

[53] At this point I am relying on Kennedy's English translation (*Progymnasmata*, 69) of Patillon's French translation of the Armenian version of a lost Greek text. As such, as Kennedy rightly observes, these sections "would be of dubious relevance for detailed interpretation." Still, my general conclusion seems warranted.

literary features of the Gospels. These holistic readings of texts, often dubbed narrative criticism, represented a new approach to the historical-critical methods of form and redaction criticism that had dominated Gospel studies in the previous generation. The literary model adapted by biblical critics was shaped and forged by secular theorists reading nineteenth- and twentieth-century novels, and thus one of the most common and forceful critiques leveled at narrative criticism has been that it is inappropriate and certainly anachronistic to impose this model on first-century texts, which do not share the literary conventions and social settings of the modern novel. For those of us still interested in the first or early reception of the final form of the Gospels, this criticism has a nagging relevance.[54] I would submit, based in part on this preliminary investigation into the preliminary exercises, that the *progymnasmata* and the rhetorical traditions, conventions, and strategies that they represent contribute immeasurably to the development of a literary model that might make sense of the rhetorical conventions and strategies used by Luke and that we may do so under the conviction that knowing more about *how* Luke told his stories will shed further light on *what* these stories are about.

---

[54] Currently I am actually interested in three periods of reception history: the aural reception of the final form of the text by the first or authorial audience, the visual reception of the text by religious viewers in Renaissance and Baroque Italy, and the electronic reception of the text by modern culture.

Order of Treatment of Progymnasmata in Extant Treatises[55]				
Exercise	Theon (first C.E.)	Hermogenes (second C.E.)	Aphthonius (fourth C.E.)	Nicolaus (fifth C.E.)
Fable	2	1	1	1
Narrative	3	2	2	2
Chreia	1	3	3	3
Maxim	1[56]	4	4	4
Refutation	3	5	5	5
Confirmation	3[57]	5	6	5
Common-Place	4	6	7	6
Encomium	7	7	8	7
Invective	7	—	9	7
Comparison	8	8	10	8
Speech-in-Character	6	9	11	9
Ekphrasis	5	10	12	10
Thesis	9	11	13	11
Law	10	12	14	12

---

[55] This chart is modified from Kennedy, *Progymnasmata*, xiii.
[56] Treated as a form of the chreia.
[57] Refutation and confirmation are discussed by Theon in connection with narrative.

Civilizing Discourse: Acts, Declamation, and the Rhetoric of the *Polis*

Todd Penner

In the second chapter of his seminal *Mimesis: The Representation of Reality in Western Literature,* Erich Auerbach undertakes an analysis of Peter's denial in Mark's Gospel. He intends to use this incident as an example of the way in which early Christian literature—predominantly the writings of the New Testament—depicts reality in fundamentally different ways than the Roman writers Tacitus and Petronius. Auerbach is struck by the contrast between the Roman literary tradition and the narratives of the biblical writers, particularly the way in which the latter's literary world is infused with rather ordinary and mundane characters. At the same time, these characters are embroiled in the dynamism that, in his mind, reflected the unfolding spiritual forces of Christianity.[1] Auerbach explains the remarkable difference between the vantage point of these two worlds—the Roman and Christian—by the fact that both Tacitus and Petronius "look down from above."[2] In doing so he clearly sides with the tradition that regards the New Testament as reflecting the world and values of the lower classes, belonging not to the literature of high culture in antiquity but reflecting a

---

[*] An earlier draft of this essay was presented in the "Socio-Rhetorical Seminar" at the SNTS Annual Meeting in Montreal, Canada (August, 2001). I am grateful to Vernon K. Robbins for his invitation to prepare this piece for that occasion as well as to Samuel Byrskog for providing a stimulating and engaging response. Wiard Popkes, Margaret MacDonald, and Vernon Robbins also offered helpful comments on this occasion. Austin College provided generous support for travel to this conference through the Sid Richardson Foundation. Caroline Vander Stichele supplied invaluable feedback on various versions of this essay, and Lindy Olsen and Michele Kennerly were kind enough to give it a read with their critical eyes. David Balch provided a further opportunity for engagement over this piece in a doctoral colloquium at Brite Divinity School. His comments were both gracious and incisive.

[1] Erich Auerbach, *Mimesis: The Representation of Reality in Western Literature* (trans. W. R. Trask; Princeton: Princeton University Press, 1953), 43–44, 47.

[2] Ibid., 46.

perspective from below. Adolf Deissmann expressed this perception in now-classic terms: "Even when Christianity had risen from the workshop and the cottage to the palace and the schools of learning, it did not desert the workshop and the cottage. The living roots of Christianity remained in their native soil—the lower ranks of society."[3]

It is perhaps not surprising that Auerbach was able to characterize the New Testament writings so simplistically, as texts resisting the "spirit of rhetoric," since their subject matter could not easily be accounted for within the existing genres with which he was working.[4] Moreover, he considered the New Testament writings to have neither "survey and rational disposition, nor artistic purpose." This character was thought to be the result, more or less, of the writers being "profoundly stirred individuals" who presumably were too involved with the immediacy of their expression (and experience) to be able to gain the distance needed for rhetorical elaboration.[5]

ACCULTURATING ACTS

It is not my interest here to tackle Auerbach's basic framework for understanding early Christian writings or his particular assessment of early Christian religion and society. Rather, his view makes clear just how drastically the landscape has shifted in recent times. The so-called radical differences between the literature of the New Testament and its Greek and Roman counterparts have (been) collapsed significantly in the ensuing years since Auerbach wrote. Recent works on Acts illustrate this shift, as this early Christian book has been categorized as belonging to all the major genres of ancient literature: novel,[6] epic,[7] biography,[8] and

---

[3] Adolf Deissmann, *Light from the Ancient East: The New Testament Illustrated by Recently Discovered Texts of the Graeco-Roman World* (trans. L. R. M. Strachan; London: Hodder & Stoughton, 1910), 404.

[4] Auerbach, *Mimesis,* 45. Admittedly, Auerbach was working with a narrow base for this generic comparison (i.e., his high texts of antiquity were Roman and selected from a particularly small socioeconomic class of writers; the Greek East may have provided a better place to begin).

[5] Ibid., 47.

[6] Richard I. Pervo, *Profit with Delight: The Literary Genre of the Acts of the Apostles* (Philadelphia: Fortress, 1987); Susan M. Praeder, "Luke-Acts and the Ancient Novel," *SBL Seminar Papers, 1981* (SBLSP 20; Chico, Calif.: Scholars Press, 1981), 269–92.

[7] Marriane Palmer Bonz, *The Past as Legacy: Luke-Acts and Ancient Epic* (Minneapolis: Fortress, 2000); Thomas L. Brodie, "Luke the Literary Interpreter: Luke-Acts as a Systematic Rewriting and Updating of the Elijah-Elisha Narrative in 1 and 2 Kings" (Ph.D. diss., Pontifical University of St. Thomas Aquinas [Rome], 1981).

[8] Charles H. Talbert, *Literary Patterns, Theological Themes and the Genre of Luke-Acts* (SBLMS 20; Missoula, Mont.: Scholars Press, 1974), esp. 125–39; idem, "The

history.⁹ Extensive connections between Lukan narrative composition and ancient rhetorical theory and practice have been drawn out as well.¹⁰ Thus, while the content and style of a book such as Acts may still be distinct on certain levels when compared to Tacitus, Livy, or Dionysius of Halicarnassus, on many fronts it is now perceived as fully consonant with the so-called high culture of antiquity.

This assertion should not come as a surprise, since the building blocks of writing and speaking in antiquity were situated in the primary educational training. The *progymnasmata,* for instance, which contain the elementary

---

Acts of the Apostles: Monograph or *Bios?*" in *History, Literature and Society in the Book of Acts* (ed. B. Witherington; Cambridge: Cambridge University Press, 1996), 58–72; Loveday Alexander, "Acts and Ancient Intellectual Biography," in *The Book of Acts in Its Ancient Literary Setting* (ed. B. W. Winter and A. D. Clarke; vol. 1 of *The Book of Acts in Its First Century Setting;* Grand Rapids: Eerdmans, 1993), 31–63; and Vernon K. Robbins, "Prefaces in Greco-Roman Biographies and Luke-Acts," *SBL Seminar Papers, 1978* (2 vols.; SBLSP 14; Missoula, Mont.: Scholars Press, 1978), 2:193–207.

⁹ As historical monograph, Darryl W. Palmer, "Acts and the Ancient Historical Monograph," in Winter and Clarke, *Book of Acts in Its Ancient Literary Setting,* 1–29, and Eckhard Plümacher, "Die Apostelgeschichte als historische Monographie," in *Les Actes des Apôtres: Traditions, rédaction, théologie* (ed. J. Kremer; BETL 48; Leuven: Leuven University Press, 1979), 457–66; as political historiography, David L. Balch, "Comments on the Genre and a Political Theme of Luke-Acts: A Preliminary Comparison of Two Hellenistic Historians," *SBL Seminar Papers, 1989* (SBLSP 28; Atlanta: Scholars Press, 1989), 343–61; as general/universal historiography, David E. Aune, *The New Testament in Its Literary Environment* (LEC 8; Philadelphia: Westminster, 1987), 138–41; as apologetic historiography, Gregory E. Sterling, *Historiography and Self-Definition: Josephos, Luke-Acts and Apologetic Historiography* (NovTSup 64; Leiden: Brill, 1992); as institutional historiography, Hubert Cancik, "The History of Culture, Religion and Institutions in Ancient Historiography: Philological Observations Concerning Luke's History," *JBL* 116 (1997): 673–95; as biblical/typological history, Daryl D. Schmidt, "The Historiography of Acts: Deuteronomistic or Hellenistic?" *SBL Seminar Papers, 1985* (SBLSP 24; Atlanta: Scholars Press, 1985), 417–27; and Brian S. Rosner, "Acts and Biblical History," in Winter and Clarke, *Book of Acts in Its Ancient Literary Setting,* 65–82; as historical hagiography, Craig A. Evans, "Luke and the Rewritten Bible: Aspects of Lukan Hagiography," in *The Pseudepigrapha and Early Biblical Interpretation* (ed. J. H. Charlesworth and C. A. Evans; JSPSup 14; SSEJC 2; Sheffield: Sheffield Academic Press, 1993), 170–201; and as *sui generis* kerygmatic history, Fearghus Ó Fearghail, *The Introduction to Luke-Acts: A Study of the Role of Lk 1,1–4,44 in the Composition of Luke's Two-Volume Work* (AnBib 126; Rome: Pontifical Biblical Institute, 1991), 173–80.

¹⁰ See esp. Robert Morgenthaler, *Lukas und Quintilian: Rhetorik als Erzählkunst* (Zürich: Gotthelf, 1993); Philip E. Satterthwaite, "Acts against the Background of Classical Rhetoric," in Winter and Clarke, *Book of Acts in Its Ancient Literary Setting,* 337–79.

exercises for the rhetorical curriculum, had pervasive impact beyond just the composition of speeches.[11] The wide-ranging application of the core curriculum was acknowledged and even promoted by Aelius Theon, who composed one of the earliest extant copies of these rhetorical training manuals:

> So then, these subjects I have set forth not because I think that they are all suitable to every beginner, but in order that we might see that practice in the exercises is absolutely necessary, not only for those who intend to be orators, but also if someone wants to be a poet or prose-writer [λογοποιός] or if he wants to acquire facility with some other form of writing. For these exercises are, so to speak, the foundation stones for every form of writing [θεμέλια τῆς τῶν λόγων ἰδέας].[12]

Moreover, exercises such as developing speech-in-character were thought to be useful for everyday life and the inculcation of virtuous character (Theon, 1.40–42, 47–48). This emphasis is a clear manifestation of what scholars such as Vernon K. Robbins have characterized as a rhetorical culture, wherein one must conceptualize rhetoric beyond merely its formal categories and roles, appreciating its complex interconnections and fusion with all acts of speaking, writing, and artistic expression.[13] One might add

---

[11] On the *progymnasmata,* see the recent discussions by Ronald F. Hock, "Homer in Greco-Roman Education," in *Mimesis and Intertextuality in Antiquity and Christianity* (ed. D. R. MacDonald; Harrisburg, Pa.: Trinity Press International, 2001), 70–76; Ruth Webb, "The *Progymnasmata* as Practice," in *Education in Greek and Roman Antiquity* (ed. Y. L. Too; Leiden: Brill, 2001), 289–316; Raffaela Cribiore, *Gymnastics of the Mind: Greek Education in Hellenistic and Roman Egypt* (Princeton: Princeton University Press, 2001), 221–30; and the essay by Mikeal Parsons in this volume. The *progymnasmata* have recently been collected in George A. Kennedy, ed. and trans., *Progymnasmata: Greek Textbooks of Prose Composition and Rhetoric* (SBLWGRW 10; Atlanta: Society of Biblical Literature, 2003). See also the standard work by Ronald F. Hock and Edward N. O'Neil, eds. and trans., *The Chreia in Ancient Rhetoric: The Progymnasmata* (SBLTT 27; Atlanta: Scholars Press, 1986); idem, *The Chreia and Ancient Rhetoric: Classroom Exercises* (SBLWGRW 2; Atlanta: Society of Biblical Literature, 2002).

[12] Theon 2.138–143 (cf. 1.43–47); translated by James R. Butts, "The *Progymnasmata* of Theon: A New Text with Translation and Commentary" (Ph.D. diss., Claremont Graduate School, 1986).

[13] See Vernon K. Robbins, "Progymnastic Rhetorical Composition and Pre-Gospel Traditions: A New Approach," in *Synoptic Gospels: Source Criticism and the New Literary Criticism* (ed. C. Focant; BETL 110; Leuven: Leuven University Press, 1993), 110; idem, "Writing as a Rhetorical Act in Plutarch and the Gospels," in *Persuasive Artistry: Studies in New Testament Rhetoric in Honor of George A. Kennedy* (ed. D. F. Watson; JSNTSup 50; Sheffield: Sheffield Academic Press,

that this configuration takes place within a cultural and social matrix preoccupied with constructing and sustaining identity and character, wherein invention and elaboration are critical for the identification and legitimization of individuals and groups.[14]

If we take this insight seriously, New Testament discourse cannot be abandoned where Auerbach left it. Rather, it needs to be reclaimed fully as a product of the literary and cultural currents of antiquity, not simply in terms of its formal qualities, but also with respect to its representation—or, more aptly, construction—of reality. The specific goals of a sociorhetorical study of the New Testament directly respond to this pressing need, recalibrating our understanding of early Christian discourse by stressing the manifest ways in which the rhetorical ethos of antiquity imbues—at least to a large extent and in many sectors—writing and reading in the ancient world. Despite his high degree of literary sensitivity, Auerbach was fundamentally misleading in his suggestion that the differences between the New Testament writings and the high literature of the Roman period were situated primarily in content and form. Indeed, there are such differences. However, the underlying function of the language and the rhetorical substratum upon which the New Testament builds is the lifeblood of all Greco-Roman literature and much more essential in establishing congruity than is subject matter and style in and of itself. Once this foundation is acknowledged, it is possible to examine the way in which the New Testament imbibes in many respects the same cultural and literary spirit as its Greco-Roman counterparts.

The book of Acts provides an excellent example of the profit gained by reexamining this aspect in more detail. In particular, it is worth pursuing how one might as a result more fully appreciate the nature and character of Lukan discourse in its larger sociocultural context. A social and cultural construction that starts from the rhetorical strategies, language, and *topoi* of the text may provide a better point of departure for situating a text such as Acts (its writer and readers) than more traditional approaches based on interpretations of individual, specific passages. Some of these more traditional assessments frame the text of Luke-Acts by a completely different set of questions than those necessarily generated by the larger discourse of the text itself. Moreover, this (re)framing is not always so innocent: Christian

---

1991), 145–49; Brandon B. Scott and Margaret E. Dean, "A Sound Mapping of the Sermon on the Mount," in *Treasures New and Old: Contributions to Matthean Studies* (ed. D. R. Baur and M. A. Powell; SBLSymS 1; Atlanta: Scholars Press, 1996), 311–15; Bryan P. Reardon, *The Form of the Greek Romance* (Princeton: Princeton University Press, 1991), 86–88; and Christopher Pelling, *Literary Texts and the Greek Historian* (New York: Routledge, 2000), 1–17.

[14] See further, Milton Moreland's essay in this volume.

tradition has had a vested interest in making Christian discourse appear to be fundamentally different from its surrounding environment in pivotal respects. Garry Trompf, for instance, has recently characterized Luke's audience as follows: "His mixed readership is, as we can detect, steadily educated into the otherwise unnatural, peculiar patterns of the Christians' behavior—behavior that will seem mad ... unless viewed as a necessary witness to the nations in the light of eschatology."[15] For Trompf this framework sets Lukan discourse over and against Roman exploitation and military dominance.[16] However, numerous parallels can be found between this so-called "unnatural" and "peculiar" Christian language of character and the world of domination and exploitation out of which it comes. We should be careful not to be lulled into a false sense of security that the language of Christian texts is somehow more humane and gentle; radical discourses that revalue power relationships are themselves not politically and socially innocent, since the strategies used to undermine a dominant structure in many respects use the same coercive and manipulative power to do so.[17]

While obviously there are a variety of different strategies for deciphering Lukan literary and cultural codes that move beyond the traditional

---

[15] Garry W. Trompf, *Early Christian Historiography: Narratives of Retributive Justice* (New York: Continuum, 2000), 72.

[16] The interest in separation, of course, manifests itself in a variety of different ways and from within varying agendas. For instance, after examining the major theme of Jesus' death and its significance in Luke-Acts, David Seeley remarks "Luke is ... enchanted by players and stage rather than by the ideas of which they may be emblematic" (*Deconstructing the New Testament* [BibInt 5; Leiden: Brill, 1994], 102). This cuts to the heart of the Lukan project in Seeley's mind, undermining the salvific language and from there the integrity of Lukan religious discourse. However, does not this deconstruction rather point the finger at the modern interpreter? Are we not the ones who have assumed that Luke has a particular theological agenda—and then the ones who hold him accountable to it? One might well argue that in fact "players and stages" was the critical feature that Luke was highlighting in his narrative composition and that we are the ones who made it into (expected?) something different.

[17] Early Christian literary processes and products cannot be excluded from this larger sociocultural context, and this presents a serious challenge to those who want to affirm that the New Testament, with its center of piety and humility (even death on a cross!), could somehow be immune and inimical to such discursive uses of power. See Stephen D. Moore, *God's Beauty Parlor and Other Queer Spaces in and around the Bible* (Stanford, Calif.: Stanford University Press, 2001), esp. 133–99; and Todd Penner and Caroline Vander Stichele, "Unveiling Paul: Gendering *Ēthos* in 1 Corinthians 11:2–16," in *Rhetoric, Ethic and Moral Persuasion in Biblical Discourse* (ed. T. H. Olbricht and A. Eriksson; Harrisburg, Pa.: Trinity Press International, forthcoming).

approaches in this respect, I particularly appreciate the nuanced analysis illustrated most recently in Loveday Alexander's evaluation of Acts as an apologetic text.[18] Through an analysis of discrete narratives in terms of their larger rhetorical effect within the Lukan narrative, she moves beyond a traditional generic designation of *apologia* and outward toward a broader social and cultural characterization of Lukan interests and location in light of the function of apologetic features in relation to the narrative itself. She states, "if we are to make any progress in understanding the rhetorical strategies of this text, we must begin by paying more attention to the details of structure and surface texture."[19] There is much to be gained in this type of approach, which explores the complexity of such categories within the larger Lukan narrative structure. Noting the vagueness of the various "apologetic scenarios" in Acts,[20] Alexander advocates a more broadly conceived appreciation of the way in which defense can easily slip into propaganda.[21]

Such an approach challenges (at least implicitly) the traditional notion of Lukan purpose understood merely in terms of the goal(s) set out by (or retrojected by modern scholars onto) an individual writer from the past.[22] To begin with, given the complexity of the category itself, purpose can never be narrowed down to something singular (i.e., any writer has a multitude of intersecting and sometimes contradictory reasons for composition). Even more important, the traditional focus on purpose tends to detract from the codified social, cultural, and historical markers strewn throughout the text, which in large measure generate the multiplicity of meaning(s) residing therein. In my view, this acknowledgement represents the beginning of a renewed historical-critical enterprise that focuses on teasing out the complex and nuanced world(s)—literary and cultural—embedded in the text that are often obscured by the articulation of a specific purpose as an a priori category for investigation.

---

[18] Loveday Alexander, "The Acts of the Apostles as an Apologetic Text," in *Apologetics in the Roman Empire: Pagans, Jews, and Christians* (ed. M. Edwards et al.; New York: Oxford University Press, 1999), 15–44.

[19] Ibid., 27 (cf. 24–25).

[20] Ibid., 40.

[21] Ibid., 39, 44. On the Lukan utilization of propaganda, see Gary Gilbert's essay in this volume.

[22] As found from Matthias Schneckenburger, *Ueber den Zweck der Apostelgeschichte: Zugleich eine Ergänzung der neueren Commentare* (Bern: Fischer, 1841), to Burton S. Easton, "The Purpose of Acts," in *Early Christianity: The Purpose of Acts and Other Papers* (ed. F. C. Grant; Greenwich: Seabury, 1954), 33–118, to Charles H. Talbert, *Luke and the Gnostics: An Examination of the Lucan Purpose* (Nashville: Abingdon, 1966), to Robert L. Maddox, *The Purpose of Luke-Acts* (ed. J. Riches; Edinburgh: T&T Clark, 1982).

This has been a longer than usual introduction, but in some sense the principles set out herein are essential for situating the study that follows, where I set forth what a sociorhetorical analysis of a particular Lukan theme might look like if one attempts to draw out multiple threads of interconnectivity between the world constructed in Acts and the sociocultural world that exists without. Beyond that, the focus of this study is on the world as *ideally* constructed in the literature of antiquity—as opposed to the world constructed by historical sociology and anthropology (not that the ideal and the real are fundamentally disconnected as such). Still, while focusing on the ideals and the representation thereof, it is also important to keep in view that these ideals are grounded in the civic life of the *polis,* which is the theme of this essay: Lukan discourse in its civic context. This study thus begins with a brief assessment of the discourse of ancient historiography itself. Elsewhere I have explored the literary impact of this model for Acts;[23] here I expand that earlier work by stressing the intersection of culture and text, situating Luke's discourse more fully within the sphere of the *polis.* This *Tendenz* represents an important shift in orientation regarding Lukan narrative, as it links the meaning of Acts inextricably with the topography of Luke's rhetorical landscape. In order to explore the outer edges of Lukan narrative composition, then, I move on to a discussion of the practice of ancient declamation, assessing how Lukan narrative composition might strike the modern reader differently if one were to use a variant lens of interpretation. The particular focus of declamation is the life and law of the *polis,* and it is worth considering the degree to which themes in Acts might take on new life and meaning within this civic rhetorical context. Finally, I return to the methodological issues raised in the introduction in order to expand the directions implicit in the former with concluding observations on the nature of the enterprise proposed here.

The Historian as Citizen

Although Luke appears to don the mantle of an ancient historian in the composition of Acts,[24] oversimplified suggestions or tacit assumptions that

---

[23] Todd Penner, "In Praise of Christian Origins: Stephen and the Hellenists in Lukan Apologetic Historiography" (Ph.D. diss., Emory University, 2000), forthcoming with T&T Clark (2004).

[24] I do not presume to address this large question in this short study, but see the pertinent discussion in Eckhard Plümacher, *Lukas als hellenistischer Schriftsteller: Studien zur Apostelgeschichte* (SUNT 9; Göttingen: Vandenhoeck & Ruprecht, 1972); Martin Hengel, *Acts and the History of Earliest Christianity* (trans. J. Bowden; Philadelphia: Fortress, 1979); Willem C. van Unnik, "Luke's Second Book and the

the appellation "historian" means something about historical accuracy and veracity in presentation are misguided.[25] Rather, one needs to proceed from this observation to an examination of what precisely *historia* in antiquity is. More accurately, it is important to assess how individual ancient writers understood their role and function in the process of historical composition.[26]

There is, perhaps surprisingly, sufficient agreement among ancient writers over the nature of this particular task. To begin with, *historia* educated citizens in the ethos and the values of the city-state. The historian, like the orator, was interested in establishing and demarcating the life, experience, and character of the citizen and did so by providing models for imitation and reflection. Cicero summarizes this feature most elegantly: "As history, which bears witness to the passing of the ages, sheds light upon reality, gives life to recollection and guidance to human existence, and brings tidings of ancient days, whose voice, but the orator's, can entrust her to immortality?" (*De or.* 2.36; cf. *Leg.* 1.2.5). Although articulated in evidently elaborated phraseology, with an over-the-top impassioned tone, the basic thrust coheres completely with Thucydides' more sober assessment:

> Whoever shall wish to have a clear view both of the events which have happened and of those which will some day, in all human probability,

---

Rules of Hellenistic Historiography," in Kremer, *Actes des Apôtres,* 37–60; Colin J. Hemer, *The Book of Acts in the Setting of Hellenistic History* (ed. C. H. Gempf; WUNT 49; Tübingen: Mohr Siebeck, 1989; repr., Winona Lake, Ind.: Eisenbrauns, 1990); Claus-Jürgen Thornton, *Der Zeuge des Zeugen: Lukas als Historiker der Paulusreisen* (WUNT 56; Tübingen: Mohr Siebeck, 1991); Sterling, *Historiography and Self-Definition;* F. F. Bruce, "The Acts of the Apostles: Historical Record or Theological Reconstruction," *ANRW* 2.25.3:2569–603; and Jacob Jervell, "The Future of the Past: Luke's Vision of Salvation History and its Bearing on His Writing of History," in Witherington, *History, Literature and Society,* 104–26.

[25] A position seemingly proffered by Ben Witherington, "Editing the Good News: Some Synoptic Lessons for the Study of Acts," in Witherington, *History, Literature and Society,* 324–47; idem, "Finding Its Niche: The Historical and Rhetorical Species of Acts," *SBL Seminar Papers, 1996* (SBLSP 35; Atlanta: Scholars Press, 1996), 67–97. This is also the basic framework of the study by Charles W. Fornara, *The Nature of History in Ancient Greece and Rome* (Berkeley and Los Angeles: University of California Press, 1983).

[26] For further discussion of the following and related issues, see Penner, "In Praise of Christian Origins"; idem, "Early Christian Heroes and Lukan Narrative: Stephen and the Hellenists in Ancient Historiographical Perspective," in *Persuasion and Performance: Rhetoric and Reality in Early Christian Discourses* (ed. W. Braun; SCJ; Waterloo, Ont.: Wilfrid Laurier Press, forthcoming).

happen again in the same or similar way—for those to adjudge my history profitable will be enough for me. And indeed, it has been composed, not as a prize-essay to be heard for the moment, but as a possession for all time. (1.22.2–4)

Both Cicero and Thucydides make the same essential point: the writing of *historia* is about bringing the past to bear on the present, albeit implicitly, by composing narratives that highlight the particular features of human) by which is usually meant civic/political) existence. These features are thought to be static, normative, and hence universal (see Polybius 15.36.8).

Although it may seem to the modern reader looking back onto the ancient scene that there were fundamental divisions between the respective tasks of the orator and the historian, the rhetoric distinguishing them was often based on degrees of alleged excess in composition. Historians would compose narratives about events (real or imagined) to further their political, civic, and sociocultural agendas; orators would address the assembly (real or imagined) to the same end. In other words, there is much less of a divide on these issues than we are used to postulating, and the emphasis on difference in form (and some respective content) has detracted from the remarkable similarity in function, including the adoption of similar strategies of composition and persuasion.

The element that comes to the fore in much of this discussion, at least implicitly, is an emphasis on *paideia,* particularly ideas on the proper strategy to be adopted for inculcating civic and cultural virtue. Differences with respect to views on process and product are evidence for variations on the sociocultural topics deeply embedded in this larger shared discourse. When one looks at oratory and historical composition side by side, one clearly notices a debate about the nature of *paideia* itself. It is thus worth touching on the larger issues involved from the side of historical composition.

While there is much more to highlight about *historia* than just its pedagogical purpose, this important feature closely links *historia* with other ancient narrative compositions. In particular, ancient writers were particularly concerned to apply the language, the action, and the exchange thereof in the *polis* to their composition of narratives for everlasting benefit. In this framework the charges levied against other historians by Polybius and Lucian regarding the focus on the present (what those historians who curry the favor of the masses do) as opposed to the future (the proper duty of the civic-minded historian) become signifiers for different strategies of pedagogy and varying sociocultural values.[27]

---

[27] Cf. Polybius 2.56.7–10; 3.48.8–9; 12.25b.1–4; 12.25i.9; 15.36.1–7; Strabo, *Geogr.* 2.6.3; Cicero, *Leg.* 1.1.5; Lucian, *Hist.* 8–9, 38, 41, 61. This holds true, of course, only to the extent that these facets are to be taken as real descriptions of difference at

The aforementioned *progymnasmata* make this pedagogical connection more explicit, insofar as the primary rhetorical education taught the student to view all ancient narratives as models to be imitated or material for the composer's own literary and/or oral production (cf. Theon 2.145–149).

Since *paideia* was the path to citizenship, the discourse of *historia* was itself the language of the *polis*. In this context, the historian was called upon to speak frankly and boldly, to possess *parrēsia*.[28] This premiere virtue of citizenship was precisely the one that the historian was to exhibit, making the narrative a reflection of his own character,[29] itself a subject worthy of imitation. Of course, at the same time, as with all discourse(s) in the *polis,* the exchanges between the historians themselves illustrate that raw grasping for power and prestige that was the lifeblood of the ancient *polis*.[30] The so-called historiographical critiques by Polybius and Lucian

---

all! Indeed, from within the perspective on ancient historiography developed here, the various so-called descriptive categories of past and present, inferior and superior, true and false, being a flatterer, friend, and/or foe, in many respects all come to function rhetorically to denigrate the other, helping to establish one historian's narrative as primary over and against another, and, as a result, are highly unreliable as actual signifiers. On the debates and the literary *topoi* utilized, see further John Marincola, *Authority and Tradition in Ancient Historiography* (Cambridge: Cambridge University Press, 1997), 34–43.

[28] Diodorus Siculus makes this connection evident: "the frank language [παρρησία] of history should of set purpose be employed for the improvement of society" (31.15.1; cf. 15.1.1; Plutarch, *Adul. amic.* 55, 66).

[29] As Dionysius notes, "a man's words are the images of his mind" (*Ant. rom.* 1.1.3). The importance of bodily comportment in oratory (see Erik Gunderson, *Staging Masculinity: The Rhetoric of Performance in the Roman World* [Ann Arbor: University of Michigan Press, 2000], 89) is here transposed into the style and literary comportment of the historian's text. On this connection of body and speech as a reflection of civic and political identity, see Anthony Corbeill, "Political Movement: Walking and Ideology in Republican Rome," in *The Roman Gaze: Vision, Power, and the Body* (ed. D. Fredrick; Baltimore: Johns Hopkins University Press, 2002), 182–215. Epictetus's statement about a hairless male demonstrates the importance of correlating physical composure with one's ability to fulfill one's duties as a citizen, including the all-important task of providing a model for imitation: "Shall we make a man like you a citizen of Corinth, and perchance a warden of the city, or a superintendent of ephebi, or general, or superintendent of the games? Well, and when you have married are you going to pluck out your hairs? For whom and to what end? And when you have begotten boys, are you going to introduce them into the body of citizens as plucked creatures too? A fine citizen and senator and orator!" (Epictetus 3.1.27–35).

[30] This larger environment of grappling for social, cultural, and political power is not only intrinsically connected to the educative process and the various literary

(noted above) relate precisely to the discourse of the city, carried out in that context by the orator. In the end, however, the rhetoric aside, orators and historians (frequently they were one and the same) were going about the same essential task.³¹ Where the biggest division lay, it seems, was in the debate over whether one ought to appeal to the popular masses, who, enthralled with *mythoi*, were instructed more inadvertently (Isocrates, *Nic.* 2.48–49), or whether the discourse aligned with the elite, the aristocracy, or the oligarchy should prevail in the inculturating process.³² Such debates

---

and speech acts that were nurtured and shaped in that context, but this environment also produced a sharp, socially gendered, masculine edge to/in the process. See esp. Amy Richlin, "Gender and Rhetoric: Producing Manhood in the Schools," in *Roman Eloquence: Rhetoric in Society and Literature* (ed. W. J. Dominik; London: Routledge, 1997), 90–110; Tim Whitmarsh, *Greek Literature and the Roman Empire: The Politics of Imitation* (New York: Oxford University Press, 2001), 90–130; Maud Gleason, *Making Men: Sophists and Self-Presentation in Ancient Rome* (Princeton: Princeton University Press, 1995); Gunderson, *Staging Masculinity*; and A. M. Keith, *Engendering Rome: Women in Latin Epic* (Roman Literature and Its Contexts; Cambridge: Cambridge University Press, 2000), 8–35.

³¹ In terms of the actual product, when the rhetorical handbooks do make a distinction between the two tasks, it generally comes down to length (i.e., there is no fundamental distinction). For instance, Aphthonius states: "Narrative [*diegema*] ... differs from narration [*diegesis*] as does a poem from an entire poetical work" (Aphthonius 2; translation from Patricia P. Matsen, Philip Rollinson, and Marion Sousa, eds., *Readings from Classical Rhetoric* [Carbondale: Southern Illinois University Press, 1990]). In other words, the *diegema* is simply a shorter, self-contained unit of a longer narrative work, which itself combines a series of episodes. Lucian similarly comments, "For all the body of the history is simply a long narrative [διήγησις]. So let it be adorned with the virtues proper to narrative" (*Hist.* 55). Cf. Samuel Byrskog, *Story as History—History as Story: The Gospel Tradition in the Context of Ancient Oral History* (WUNT 123; Tübingen: Mohr Siebeck, 2000; repr., Leiden; Brill, 2002), 203.

³² As Isocrates notes, "you ought not to judge what things are worthy or what men are wise by the standard of pleasure, but to appraise them in the light of conduct that is useful; especially, since the teachers of philosophy ... are all agreed ... that the well-educated man must, as the result of his training in whatever discipline, show ability to deliberate and decide" (*Nic.* 2.50–52). See Claude Calame, "The Rhetoric of *Muthos* and *Logos*: Forms of Figurative Discourse," in *From Myth to Reason? Studies in the Development of Greek Thought* (ed. R. Buxton; New York: Oxford University Press, 1999), 128–29; and the essay by David L. Balch in this volume (esp. his comments focusing on Asian versus Attic historiographies [150–54]). The following comments by Plutarch are worth citing in this context, since they set up the rhetorically constructed dichotomy between the two positions quite well: "on the one side are truthfulness, love for what is honorable, and power to reason, and on the other side irrationality, love of falsehood, and the emotional element; the

were formative for the *polis* itself, and the extant literature more or less reflects this same conflict, which is immersed, it seems, in fluctuating social structures and cultural values, rather than in the oft-touted high-minded ideals of particular writers of antiquity.

However, it is too simplistic to leave it at this. *Historia* was not only *paideia,* a pedagogical strategy for inculcating the life of the city in its citizens; it also inscribed the city itself in narrative.[33] As such it provided advice for those who made decisions, models to imitate in the deliberation process, and more extensive exemplars for the ongoing civic life of the *polis*.[34] *Historia* was *polis,* though not necessarily the city as it was but as it was idealized, mythologized, and immortalized.[35] It is thus no surprise

---

friend is always found on the better side as a counsel and advocate, trying after the manner of a physician, to foster the growth of what is sound and to preserve it; but the flatterer takes his place on the side of the emotional and irrational, and this he excites and tickles and wheedles, and tries to divorce from the reasoning powers by contriving for it divers low forms of pleasurable enjoyment" (Plutarch, *Adul. amic.* 61).

[33] For a similar view with respect to epic, see Yun Lee Too, *The Idea of Ancient Literary Criticism* (New York: Oxford University Press, 1998), 60–61.

[34] See, e.g., the remarks by Arius Didymus concerning the activities of the wise man: "[he] takes part in politics ... he makes laws and educates his fellow men; furthermore, it is fitting for the worthwhile to write down what is able to benefit those who happen upon their writings" (11b; Arthur J. Pomeroy, ed. and trans., *Arius Didymus: Epitome of Stoic Ethics* [SBLTT 44; Atlanta: Scholars Press, 1999]). The historian wants, as Polybius notes, to instruct (διδάχαι) and convince (πεῖσαι) those serious learners (φιλομαθοῦντας), conferring on them benefit (διὰ τὴν ὠφέλειαν τῶν φιλομαθούντων) (Polybius 2.56.11; cf. 1.1.2; 12.25b.1–4; 12.25e.6–7; 12.25g.2–3; 12.25i.6; Livy, *Preface* 9; Tacitus, *Ann.* 3.65; Lucian, *Hist.* 37). In this respect, the words of Pericles in the famous Thucydidean funeral oration are insructive: "For we alone regard the man who takes no part in public affairs, not as one who minds his own business, but as good for nothing; and we Athenians decide public questions for ourselves or at least endeavour to arrive at a sound understanding of them, in the belief that it is not debate that is a hindrance to action, but rather not to be instructed by debate before the time comes for action. For in truth we have this point also of superiority over other men, to be most daring in action and yet at the same time most given to reflection upon the ventures we mean to undertake" (2.40.3).

[35] See further Ron Cameron, "Alternate Beginnings—Different Ends: Eusebius, Thomas, and the Construction of Christian Origins," in *Religious Propaganda and Missionary Competition in the New Testament World: Essays Honoring Dieter Georgi* (ed. L. Borman et al.; NovTSup 74; Leiden: Brill, 1994), 501–25; Palmer Bonz, *Past as Legacy;* and esp. Milton Moreland, "Jerusalem Imagined: Rethinking Earliest Christian Claims to the Hebrew Epic" (Ph.D. diss., Claremont Graduate University, 1999), as well as Moreland's essay in this volume.

that Diodorus Siculus describes *historia* as the "prophetess of truth" and the "mother-city of philosophy" (1.2.2). The two prongs of civic life, the religious and the civic/moral, are thus interconnected in historical composition. Indeed, if there be any doubt, Diodorus goes on to maintain that *historia* "contributes to the power of speech, and a nobler thing than that may not easily be found. For it is this that makes the Greeks superior to the barbarians, and the educated to the uneducated" (1.2.5–6).

This power of speech is what delimits the civilized from the uncivilized. Still, we find *historia* itself not only contributing to rhetorical prowess but also in fact mapping the structures of power through its words and graphic images. *Historia* thus embodies the *polis* in narrative. This is not the real, gritty *polis* as it exists in all times and places, but the kind that exists in the philosophy of the Greeks and the epic of the Romans.[36] While the friend of the city ought never to be an obsequious flatterer, overlooking serious faults and problematic issues, he should also never be a malicious slanderer (as Herodotus was described by Plutarch) who represents the city as it actually was in history (flawed, feeble, and fickle). Most important, like the guardians of Plato's *Republic,* the historians are to remain moderate and balanced, refraining from succumbing to the passions or detracting from the true pursuit of citizenship.[37] The truth and hence value of the *polis* can only exist in the mythic, albeit realistic and probable, landscape that the *polis* itself shapes and controls. The boundaries and structures of the latter are embedded thoroughly in and reinscribed dramatically by the structures and function of historical discourse. Therein the historian is but the servant of the *polis* and the guardian of true philosophy, with its constructed politics and values as the basis of civic identity and life. All of these features, finally, have their roots in the primary education of the educated elite male, making these patterns pervasive, potent, and persuasive in the world that gave rise to earliest Christianity.

Deliberating Acts

Once this rhetorical *ethos* and sociopolitical structure of *historia* in antiquity comes to the forefront, Acts as a whole appears in sharper focus. In terms of its construction of origins, Acts has been shown to possess

---

[36] One should nuance this emphasis, however, by noting that to view "*polis*-ideology as a glorifying, unproblematic praise of the city" (Pelling, *Literary Texts,* 178) is too simplistic; the engagement of the city in *historia,* despite the insistence on the ideal, is more complex and tempered than this (the stated purpose can be achieved not infrequently through negative characterizations).

[37] Too, *Idea of Ancient Literary Criticism,* 64.

considerable ideological force, and recent studies devoted to the exploration of Lukan poetics have reinforced this emphasis through the analysis and description of the literary (and ideological) agendas associated with historical composition in antiquity.[38] Indeed, it is only once we recognize that Acts functions within the general framework of *historia* as outlined above that serious analysis of the numerous interlocking codes for and structures of Lukan discourse in Acts can commence. Given the particular argument developed thus far, this analysis should begin with an assessment of the Lukan narrative reconfiguration of the rhetoric of the *polis* in Acts.

SPEECH AND NARRATIVE IN ACTS

The speeches in Acts have received a significant amount of attention in past scholarship, not in small measure due to the impetus of Dibelius's energetic explorations of their function and character in the book. It was in the speeches, he argued, that Luke's pastoral voice was most clearly heard, the surest basis for his creativity as a writer.[39] Assessment of the speeches

---

[38] See esp. David P. Moessner, "The Appeal and Power of Poetics (Luke 1:1–4): Luke's Superior Credentials (παρηκολουθηκότι), Narrative Sequence (καθεξῆς), and Firmness of Understanding (ἡ ἀσφάλεια) for the Reader," in *Jesus and the Heritage of Israel: Luke's Narrative Claim upon Israel's Legacy* (ed. D. P. Moessner; Harrisburg, Pa.: Trinity Press International, 1999), 84–123; idem, "'Eyewitnesses,' 'Informed Contemporaries,' and 'Unknowing Inquirers': Josephus' Criteria for Authentic Historiography and the Meaning of ΠΑΡΑΚΟΛΟΥΘΕΩ," *NovT* 38 (1996): 105–22; idem, "The Lukan Prologues in the Light of Ancient Narrative Hermeneutics: Παρηκολουθηκότι and the Credentialed Author," in *The Unity of Luke-Acts* (ed. J. Verheyden; BETL 142; Leuven: Leuven University Press, 1999), 399–417; idem, "Dionysius's Narrative 'Arrangement' (οἰκονομία) as the Hermeneutical Key to Luke's Re-Vision of the 'Many,'" in *Paul, Luke and the Graeco-Roman World: Essays in Honour of Alexander J. M. Wedderburn* (ed. A. Christophersen et al.; JSNTSup 217; Sheffield: Sheffield Academic Press, 2002), 149–64; Darryl D. Schmidt, "Rhetorical Influences and Genre: Luke's Preface and the Rhetoric of Hellenistic Historiography," in Moessner, *Jesus and the Heritage of Israel*, 27–60; and David L. Balch, "ἀκριβῶς ... γράψαι (Luke 1:3): To Write the Full History of God's Receiving All Nations," in Moessner, *Jesus and the Heritage of Israel*, 229–50.

[39] Martin Dibelius, *Studies in the Acts of the Apostles* (ed. H. Greeven; London: SCM, 1956), esp. 138–40, 164–66, 178–80, 183–85; see also Henry J. Cadbury, "The Speeches in Acts," in *The Beginnings of Christianity: The Acts of the Apostles* (ed. F. J. Foakes Jackson and K. Lake; 5 vols.; London: Macmillan, 1920–33; repr., Grand Rapids: Baker, 1979), 5:426–27; and the earlier assessment of Paul Wendland, *Die Hellenistisch-Römische Kultur in ihren Beziehungen zu Judentum und Christentum* (HNT 1/2; Tübingen: Mohr Siebeck, 1912), 331. Max Wilcox, "A Foreward to the Study of the Speeches in Acts," in *Christianity, Judaism and other Greco-Roman Cults: Studies for Morton Smith at Sixty* (ed. J. Neusner; 4 vols.; SJLA 12; Leiden: Brill, 1975), 1:206, traces this formulation back to Albert Eichorn (1810).

has frequently followed the lines set forth by Dibelius, analyzing the speeches for their contribution to Lukan narrative *dianoia*,[40] with some attention paid also to the general role of speeches in ancient historiography.[41] While earlier assessments along this line were significantly invested in source-critical questions,[42] more recent investigations have focused rather on the theological themes, scriptural connections, and the larger Lukan narrative context.[43] However, it should come as no surprise to those familiar with Lukan scholarship that the study of the relationship of speech to its narrative context has received much less attention. There are a variety of reasons for this lack of focus, the most important being that earlier scholars such as Dibelius were rather conservative in their assessment of the historical character of the narrative portions of Acts.[44] Since Lukan creativity was seen to rest primarily in the speeches, there was considerable free-ranging analysis of the speeches themselves; however, the narrative context remained largely disconnected from that assessment. Elsewhere I have made the argument that speech and narrative have to be viewed in tandem, both equal expressions of the writer's creative historical craft.[45] More often

---

[40] The concept of *dianoia* comes from Aristotle: "the parts in which, through speech, [actors] demonstrate something or declare their views" (*Poet.* 1450A). At one level this relates to *speech-in-character* as developed in the rhetorical handbooks, but it also has a broader function relating to the poetic logic of any larger narrative presentation. See Mary W. Blundell, "*Ēthos* and *Dianoia* Reconsidered," in *Essays on Aristotle's Poetics* (ed. A. O. Rorty; Princeton: Princeton University Press, 1992), 155–75; and Moessner, "Dionysius's Narrative 'Arrangement,'" 152–53.

[41] Earle Hilgert, "Speeches in Acts and Hellenistic Canons of Historiography and Rhetoric," in *Good News in History: Essays in Honor of Bo Reicke* (ed. E. L. Miller; Atlanta: Scholars Press, 1993), 83–109; Eckhard Plümacher, "The Mission Speeches in Acts and Dionysius of Halicarnassus," in Moessner, *Jesus and the Heritage of Israel*, 251–66.

[42] See, e.g., Ulrich Wilckens, *Die Missionsreden der Apostelgeschichte: Form- und Traditionsgeschichtliche Untersuchungen* (3d ed.; WMANT 5; Neukirchen-Vluyn: Neukirchener, 1974).

[43] Marion L. Soards, *The Speeches in Acts: Their Content, Context, and Concerns* (Louisville: Westminster John Knox, 1994); Luke T. Johnson, *Septugintal Midrash in the Speeches of Acts* (Milwaukee: Marquette University Press, 2002).

[44] One must keep in mind that for Dibelius, after all, Luke was still the traveling companion of Paul (*Studies in the Acts of the Apostles*, 136).

[45] Todd Penner, "Narrative as Persuasion: Epideictic Rhetoric and Scribal Amplification in the Stephen Episode in Acts," *SBL Seminar Papers, 1996*, 352–67. Alexander similarly notes, "The formal distinction between speech and narrative is largely deconstructed by Luke himself, in that the speeches he gives to his characters constantly refer back to narrative, repeat narrative, and reinforce and interpret narrative" ("Acts of the Apostles as an Apologetic Text," 40).

than not, however, scholarship has continued to keep these two features of Lukan composition fairly distinct. This will continue as long as we presume that Luke's creativity is centered in the speeches, while in the narrative portions of Acts he is much more constrained by the "facts" of his story.

In this light, the high ratio of speech to narrative in Acts seems particularly significant. When compared with other ancient histories, biographies, and novels, Luke is shown to have much more speech in relation to narrative.[46] In fact, the closer one examines Acts, the more the book looks like an extended series of speeches punctuated with shorter narrative scenes that serve to contextualize them. One way to explain or at least elucidate this phenomenon in Acts is to point to the role of declamation in ancient rhetorical training. While I do not suggest that Acts itself is simply a series of declamations, the declamatory exercises may supply a critical first step in examining the sociorhetorical nature of Acts, providing a heuristic tool for analysis. Indeed, with respect to speech composition in ancient historiography, one cannot overlook the central role that the fictions of narrative setting and speech associated with declamatory composition must have played: it was in the speeches, after all, that the historian waxed eloquent in the character of a historical personage.[47]

---

[46] G. H. R. Horsley, "Speeches and Dialogue in Acts," *NTS* 32 (1986): 612–13.

[47] Debate exists in both classical and biblical studies as to the place of historical accuracy in the speeches attributed to historical personages by historians. Some scholars are adamant that accuracy in reporting was a main concern of the ancient historian; see A. B. Bosworth, *From Arrian to Alexander: Studies in Historical Interpretation* (New York: Oxford University Press, 1988), 94–96; Simon Hornblower, *Thucydides* (London: Duckworth, 1987), 45–72; Fornara, *Nature of History*, 142–68; Stanley E. Porter, "Thucydides 1.22.1 and Speeches in Acts: Is There a Thucydidean View?" *NovT* 32 (1990): 141–42; and Antony E. Raubitschek, "The Speech of the Athenians at Sparta," in *The Speeches in Thucydides* (ed. P. A. Stadter; Chapel Hill: University of North Carolina Press, 1973), 47. Other scholars are more moderate in their commitment to accuracy as the goal of speech writing in ancient historiography (see Byrskog, *Story as History*, 211–12; and Pelling, *Literary Texts*, 112–22). It is telling, in this regard, that ancient literary critics assessed the speeches in historiography based on their perceived plausibility rather than on their likelihood of connection to actual historical events. (In terms of historical depiction there is, in fact, a close connection in the ancient mindset between the *ought* and the *is*.) Dionysius, for example, critiques Thucydides' speech between the Athenians and the Melians for being implausible in characterization and thus contributing to an unconvincing narrative revealing that his operating premise was that Thucydides had composed the speech himself (*Thuc.* 37–42; cf. Kenneth S. Sacks, "Rhetoric and Speeches in Hellenistic Historiography," *Athenaeum* 64 [1986]: 383–95; Harold W. Attridge, *The Interpretation of Biblical History in the* Antiquitates Judaicae *of Flavius Josephus* [HDR 7; Missoula, Mont.: Scholars Press, 1976], 54–55).

Further, given the political and civic contexts of historiography established earlier in this essay, it is worth stressing the overt rhetorical construction of citizenship in speech composition. The characters embody for the reader (either positively or negatively) the array of appropriate and moderate responses demanded of individuals in the *polis*. At one level, then, speeches in historical works were indebted to the rhetorical tradition at its core. At the same time, Acts provides a somewhat special case in that the relationship of narrative to speech is peculiar in Luke's second volume, at least when compared to other ancient histories. While there are some narratives that are not followed by long speeches, many Lukan narratives in fact seem to function much like the opening narratives in classic declamation: they are brief and their primary objective seems to be to contextualize the argument of the impending address. Since past scholarship has frequently taken the narrative and speech in isolation from each other, the integral connection between the two has often been overlooked; as a result, the implication for Lukan composition has also gone unexamined.

The speech of Stephen in Acts provides an interesting example. Scholars have long been puzzled by the perceived failure of the speech to address the charges leveled against Stephen in the narrative. Dibelius aptly sums up the majority view on this enigma:

> The irrelevance of most of this speech has for long been the real problem of exegesis. It is, indeed, impossible to find a connection between the account of the history of Israel to the time of Moses (7:2–19) and the accusation against Stephen: nor is any accusation against the Jews, which would furnish the historical foundation for the attack at the end of the speech, found at all in this section. Even in that section of the speech which deals with Moses, the speaker does not defend himself; nor does he make any positive counter-charge against his enemies.[48]

I disagree with Loveday Alexander's assessment ("Marathon or Jericho? Reading Acts in Dialogue with Biblical and Greek Historiography," in *Auguries: The Jubilee Volume of the Sheffield Department of Biblical Studies* [ed. D. J. A. Clines and S. D. Moore; JSOTSup 269; Sheffield: Sheffield Academic Press, 1998], 98) that this point by Dionysius is irrelevant for analysis of historiographical praxis because Dionysius was here writing as a rhetorician. I think it is precisely as a rhetorician (who was also a foremost historian!) that we need to take Dionysius's comments seriously for the study of historical composition and expectation (see further, Penner, "In Praise of Christian Origins," 192–386).

[48] Dibelius, *Studies in the Acts of the Apostles,* 167. See the similar and more recent assessment by Jacob Jervell, *Die Apostelgeschichte* (17th ed.; KEK 3; Göttingen: Vandenhoeck & Ruprecht, 1998), 248–50; and Alexander, "Acts of the Apostles as an Apologetic Text," 40, who observes that the precise nature of and response to charges in most of the accusatory scenes in Acts are difficult to decipher fully.

I have argued elsewhere that Dibelius missed the point: the speech of Acts 7 represents a counteraccusation against the Jewish leaders and opponents of Acts 6:7–15.[49] Given the importance of *synkrisis* in ancient narrative composition,[50] not surprisingly Stephen's speech moves away from a strict judicial response to a more complex epideictic speech of praise and blame against the Jewish leaders. Nonetheless, while scholars have frequently made various arguments about the historical core or *fundamentum* of this martyrdom narrative,[51] the larger issue of how the narrative serves to set up the speech has received less attention.[52] As in

---

[49] Penner, "Narrative as Persuasion," 359. See also George A. Kennedy, *New Testament Interpretation through Rhetorical Criticism* (Chapel Hill: University of North Carolina Press, 1984), 121–22; Soards, *Speeches in Acts,* 58; Harold A. Brehm, "Vindicating the Rejected One: Stephen's Speech as Critique of the Jewish Leaders," in *Early Christian Interpretation of the Scriptures of Israel: Investigations and Proposals* (ed. C. A. Evans and J. A. Sanders; JSNTSup 148; SSEJC 5; Sheffield: Sheffield Academic Press, 1997), 266–99; and Robert G. Hall, *Revealed Histories: Techniques for Ancient Jewish and Christian Historiography* (JSPSup 6; Sheffield: Sheffield Academic Press, 1991), 195.

[50] The term *synkrisis* is used here in the Aristotelian sense: *synkrisis* "is concerned with things that are closely related and about which we discuss which we ought preferably to support.... if one or more points of superiority can be shown, the mind will agree that whichever of the two alternatives is actually superior is the more worthy of choice" (Aristotle, *Top.* 3.1.6–12; cf. Theon 10). The comparative aspect Aristotle refers to here was utilized widely and substantively in the process of ancient literary composition. See Daniel Marguerat, "Luc-Actes: Une Unité à Construire," in Verheyden, *Unity of Luke-Acts,* 70–74; Andrew C. Clark, *Parallel Lives: The Relation of Paul to the Apostles in the Lucan Perspective* (Carlisle: Paternoster, 2001), 84–88; William W. Batstone,"The Antithesis of Virtue: Sallust's *Synkrisis* and the Crisis of the Late Republic," *CA* 7 (1988): 1–29; and esp. Timothy E. Duff, *Plutarch's Lives: Exploring Virtue and Vice* (New York: Oxford University Press, 1999), 243–86.

[51] On the debate between ordered trial or mob lynching, see C. K. Barrett, *A Critical and Exegetical Commentary on the Acts of the Apostles* (2 vols.; ICC; Edinburgh: T&T Clark, 1994–98), 1:319–22, 380–81; Craig C. Hill, *Hellenists and Hebrews: Reappraising Division within the Early Church* (Minneapolis: Fortress, 1992), 29–31; Ernst Haenchen, *The Acts of the Apostles: A Commentary* (trans. B. Noble et al.; Philadelphia: Westminster, 1971), 273–74; and Christoph Burchard, *Der dreizehnte Zeuge: Traditions- und kompositions-geschichtliche Untersuchungen zu Lukas' Darstellung der Frühzeit des Paulus* (FRLANT 103; Göttingen: Vandenhoeck & Ruprecht, 1970), 28–31.

[52] In some more recent scholarship, however, attempts have been made to rectify this lack. See, among others, Joachim Jeska, *Die Geschichte Israels in der Sicht des Lukas: Apg 7,2b–53 und 13,17–25 im Kontext antik-jüdischer Summarien der Geschichte Israels* (FRLANT 195; Göttingen: Vandenhoeck & Ruprecht, 2001),

the case of ancient declamation, the narrative of Stephen that precedes his oration in Acts 7 functions to provide the legal issues that are directly addressed in the speech itself. In this case, the narrative establishes a range of legal terminology and concerns (6:11, 14) that the speech will elaborate upon in some detail. Similarly, the narrative that follows the address (7:54–8:1) functions to underscore the accuracy of Stephen's characterization in his speech.

It is in this context that the practice of declamation can be particularly useful for understanding Lukan narrative invention. As one approaches the composition and function of a speech such as Acts 7 in terms of the practice of declaiming, the creative task of composing speeches placed in the mouth of a fictional character or a famous individual from the past comes to the fore. While this does not in and of itself change anything fundamental regarding the general thrust of the speeches in Acts, it does shift our understanding of the narrative settings for Luke's speeches. Rather than considering the narrative as the primary historical *fundamentum* of Luke's text, it might be better to view much of it as simply setting the stage for what is for Luke qua historian a much more critical element: the speeches, wherein the narrative characters are shown persuading, deliberating, debating, and assessing the essential issues surrounding Christian civic discourse and community. In this case, one is no longer interested primarily (or even at all) in the historicity of the material in Acts but rather in examining the only thing Acts can really yield in the end: a window to Luke's sociocultural world. It is to this larger rhetorical context for the study of Acts that I now turn.

ACTS AND THE ART OF DECLAMATION

Ancient declamation was a further developed, more advanced form of the exercises of the *progymnasmata*. Many of these elementary exercises themselves formed the basis of and were also more fully refined in the practice of declamation.[53] The surviving examples are usually separated into two categories: *controversia* and *suasoria*.[54] In both cases the speech

---

189–213; Gregory E. Sterling, "'Opening the Scriptures': The Legitimation of the Jewish Diaspora and the Early Christian Mission," in Moessner, *Jesus and the Heritage of Israel*, 199–225; and Delbert L. Wiens, *Stephen's Sermon and the Structure of Luke-Acts* (N. Richland Hills, Tex.: BIBAL, 1995).

[53] Donald A. Russell, *Greek Declamation* (Cambridge: Cambridge University Press, 1983), 10–11, 71. Cf. Webb, "*Progymnasmata* as Practice," 303–7; Cribiore, *Gymnastics of the Mind*, 231.

[54] On the history and use of these terms, see Stanley F. Bonner, *Roman Declamations in the Late Republic and Early Empire* (Berkeley and Los Angeles: University of California Press, 1949), 1–26. See also Robert A. Kaster, "Controlling

is a one-sided, structured argumentative piece (cf. Quintilian, *Inst.* 2.4.41). In *controversia* the character is involved in an issue of law, usually some wrangling over a particular legal interpretation or case. The narrative opening often consists of some rather contorted situation that the speaker then unravels. The following example from Libanius is typical: "There was a rumor that a father was seducing his son's wife. The father proposed a law that it should be permitted to kill one's own son without trial. The son now proposes a law to allow adulterers to be killed without a trial" (*Or.* 39).[55] *Suasoria*, by contrast, were prime examples of deliberative rhetoric, wherein the speaker seeks to persuade the audience toward a particular course of action. Again, as with the first case, there is usually a specific situation provided upon which the speaker's comments are based. Libanius, for instance, offers an interesting example in which he has Demosthenes attempt to persuade the people of Athens to remove the alter of mercy (*Or.* 22). While possibly loosely based on some historical reminiscences,[56] the actual narrative of Demosthenes taking refuge at the alter of mercy for protection against Philip of Macedon is a fiction. The people hand Demosthenes over, and thereupon he comes back to argue in a somewhat sarcastic manner that the altar of mercy ought to be done away with because it obviously meant nothing to the Athenians in the first place. Thus, by using various fictional settings, some liberally grounded in history and mythology, others freely invented by the declaimer, the rhetorician is able to create a speech that responds explicitly to the issue raised in the narrative, in the process of which various devices of the *progymnasmata* are employed, from the thesis and speech-in-character to the use of *topoi* and extensive descriptions (*ekphrasis*).

Scholars often portray declamations as discrete literary products, easily disconnected from the range of ancient literary activities,[57] but this

---

Reason: Declamation in Rhetorical Education at Rome," in Too, *Education in Greek and Roman Antiquity,* 317–37; Joy Connolly, "Mastering Corruption: Constructions of Identity in Roman Oratory," in *Women and Slaves in Greco-Roman Culture* (ed. S. R. Joshel and S. Murnaghan; London: Routledge, 1998), esp. 145–49; D. H. Berry and Malcolm Heath, "Oratory and Rhetoric," in *Handbook of Classical Rhetoric in the Hellenistic Period 330 B.C.–A.D. 400* (ed. S. E. Porter; Leiden: Brill, 1997), esp. 406–19; and Cribiore, *Gymnastics of the Mind,* 232–38.

[55] Trans. by Donald A. Russell, *Libanius: Imaginary Speeches* (London: Duckworth, 1996).

[56] Ibid., 93.

[57] Russell, for instance, argues for a more limited influence of declamatory practice over and against Seneca's own more sweeping application (*Greek Declamation,* 2–3). Since declamation cannot be separated totally from the larger rhetorical exercises, it can admittedly be difficult to determine influence precisely.

seems to be a rather simplistic view (see Quintilian, *Inst.* 2.10.2). Ancient (but also modern) rhetorical classifications are always post facto and therefore have difficulty accounting for the multitude of ways in which language and thought are permeated with strategies and patterns created and sustained by the basic learning blocks of Greco-Roman education, including how those blocks themselves are similarly generated out of a larger ethos. Only when we come to this recognition can we appreciate how texts such as the Gospels and Acts can at once comprise fiction and at the same time be compositions of *historia*.[58]

With respect to Acts, then, it is entirely possible that Luke has been shaped in his compositional technique and motivation by the processes that underlie the art of declamation, especially since we are thinking in terms of the broader sociorhetorical ethos that such practices elicit. First of all, there are many similarities between Acts and the declamatory examples in terms of form, content, and function, and it is at least worth considering whether there is not an implicit (if not explicit) correlation here, providing some insight into Luke's literary and rhetorical models. Second, the relationship of shorter narratives to longer speeches is an interesting parallel and may suggest the broader influence of declamatory structures and reasonings on Luke's composition. Moreover, it is tempting to view the speeches as constructed precisely to respond to fictive narrative settings in Acts, the latter of which are fundamental for Luke's larger project primarily insofar as they set the context for the speeches. Further, the use of various literary and argumentative *topoi,* the frequent deployment of speech-in-character, and the significant stress on characterization and description indicate that Acts draws on the same fundamental building blocks as the declamatory examples. Finally, there is one more element that should be noted: the primary focus of declamation is on two

---

Anne E. Orentzel, "Declamation in the Age of Pliny," *ClassBul* 54 (1978): 65–68, makes the case for reassessing the significance and extent of declamation in the Roman principate.

[58] See, e.g., the treatment of the New Testament by classicists such as Glen W. Bowersock (*Fiction as History: Nero to Julian* [Sather Classical Lectures 58; Berkeley and Los Angeles: University of California Press, 1994], 123) and David S. Potter (*Literary Texts and the Roman Historian* [New York: Routledge, 1999], 144–45), both of whom argue that early Christian narratives such as Luke-Acts are fiction in the form of history with an emphasis on verisimilitude but with little or no historical value. These scholars are essentially doing something similar to what many New Testament scholars have done (i.e., assessing *historia* generically by its correspondence to actual history), while arriving at the opposite conclusion, confusing an abstract historical form with truth and fact as well as ignoring the fact that all ancient history is more or less shaped in the same literary and cultural context as the New Testament.

major prongs of civic life: the assembly (*suasoria*) and the law courts (*controversia*). In other words, both aspects of declamation trained the citizen for major involvement in essential areas of ancient city life.[59] Indeed, the declamations seem to have much less invested in the explicit legal wranglings of the cases themselves (many of which seem strangely out of touch with real city issues and struggles) and much more riding on the navigation of the complex social roles of individuals in society through the process and product of declamation. Herein the rhetorical training provides a level of socialization through the act of declaiming, as the elite male is inculturated through speech.[60]

Declamation, then, is an imaginative form of *paideia*. In response to its apparent lack of concern with reality, Robert Kaster argues:

> It was one of the main effects of declamation to inculcate, by sheer repetition, approved values in the still impressionable minds of the next generation of the elite; that one aspect of declamation which most commended it to its culture was the reassuring ability it developed in the declaimer to respond to the most startling, novel, or extravagant circumstances by appealing to the most traditional sentiments and by marshalling the most conventionally "reasonable" arguments.[61]

In this model, Roman social order was cultivated and maintained in and through the composition of these carefully constructed, compounded narratives, attended by the detailed responses in the speeches.[62] The preoccupation in declamation with themes of disinheritance, as well as with conflict (especially between fathers and sons) over issues of duties and laws,[63] also carried with it an overt emphasis on social order and control, which made declamations popular in the early imperial period,[64]

---

[59] This is an ideal that goes back to classical Athenian practice, in which the speakers in the assembly and the law courts were not primarily professional. See Josiah Ober, "The Orators," in *The Cambridge History of Greek and Roman Political Thought* (ed. C. Rowe and M. Schofield; Cambridge: Cambridge University Press, 2000), 132–33.

[60] See the important assessment by W. Martin Bloomer, *Latinity and Literary Society at Rome* (Philadelphia: University of Pennsylvania Press, 1997), 136–42. See also Connolly, "Mastering Corruption," 148; and Kaster, "Controlling Reason," 325–26, 328, 334.

[61] Kaster, "Controlling Reason," 325.

[62] The publication of collections of declamations seems itself to have had a similar pedagogical purpose: providing material for emulation. See Lewis A. Sussman, *The Declamations of Calpurnius Flaccus* (MnSup 133; Leiden: Brill, 1994), 16–18.

[63] Berry and Heath, "Oratory and Rhetoric," 409.

[64] Sussman, *Declamations of Calpurnius Flaccus*, 4–5.

reinforcing quite well the connection Augustus made between morality and empire.⁶⁵

In this light, it is perhaps not surprising that one finds in Acts a similar focus on speeches, which can be broken down into those that present the early Christian heroes in legal settings (the various trials of Peter/John, Stephen, and Paul) and those that depict the majestic early Christian figures debating in the public forum some aspect of their polity (both to a larger audience, as in Peter's speech at Pentecost and Paul's speech at Pisidian Antioch, but also within the group itself, such as at the Jerusalem conference). This observation is important for several reasons. First, Luke deliberately portrays the early Christian characters as being involved in the two major areas of civic life, doggedly defending, detracting, deliberating, and declaiming in spectacular displays of rhetorical prowess. These Christians are thus model Greek and Roman citizens as well.⁶⁶ Second, the claim of Acts on the reader ought not to be underestimated, as we see here a prime model of imitation for the early God-lovers to follow.⁶⁷ Just as the exercise of declamation trains the rhetorician for involvement in the *polis,* the reading of Acts literally educates the reader in the act of Christian polity. Indeed, it is not entirely clear that Luke himself makes a radical distinction between the Christian polity and that of the Greeks and Romans, except in this: only the Christians in the narrative live up to the values and institutions of the civilized world; the outside characters fail miserably (i.e., Luke barbarizes the Greeks and Romans). In this regard, while scholars have rightly made much of Luke's appropriation of the Jewish

---

⁶⁵ Paul Zanker, *The Power of Images in the Age of Augustus* (trans. A. Shapiro; Ann Arbor: University of Michigan Press, 1988), 156–66; Allen Brent, *The Imperial Cult and the Development of Church Order: Concepts and Images of Authority in Paganism and Early Christianity before the Age of Cyprian* (VCSup 45; Leiden: Brill, 1999), 50–67.

⁶⁶ The connection between speech and character (*ēthos*) is essential for appreciating the larger Lukan agenda detailed in this essay. Seneca aptly demonstrates this conjunction in his recitation of the Greek proverb that a "man's speech is just like his life." He goes on to elaborate: "Wantonness in speech is proof of public luxury.... A man's ability cannot possibly be of one sort and his soul of another. If his soul be wholesome, well-ordered, serious, and restrained, his ability also is sound and sober. Conversely, when one degenerates, the other is also contaminated" (*Ep.* 114.2–3). Thus, speech by the apostles reveals not only their own sober, well-ordered character but even more so the character of the early Christianity they represent in the narrative. See further Penner and Vander Stichele, "Unveiling Paul," as well as Balch's essay in this volume (see also n. 29 above).

⁶⁷ See the fine assessment of this feature by William S. Kurz, "Narrative Models in Luke-Acts," in *Greeks, Romans, and Christians: Essays in Honor of Abraham J. Malherbe* (ed. D. L. Balch et al.; Minneapolis: Fortress, 1990), 171–89.

heritage,[68] fewer have recognized an even bolder claim on the tradition of the Greeks. This is just scratching the surface at this point, and it calls for a much more sustained investigation. For the moment, however, some thoughts on how one might proceed are offered.

SUASORIA AND CONVERSION: THE NEW CHRISTIAN *POLITEIA*

In his recent article on the Cornelius episode (Acts 10–11), Walter Wilson paves the way for a new approach to the discourse of Acts, arguing that Luke has structured the narrative of the founding of the Gentile church in terms related to the foundation narratives of colonies in the ancient world.[69] As Wilson suggests, "colonization is envisaged, like marriage, as an integrating, civilizing mechanism, one that socializes the 'other,' bringing her into a cultivated and productive state."[70] My own study of Acts 6–7 similarly focused on the integration of mixed populations in the foundation of a *politeia*.[71] David Balch has demonstrated the importance of this theme in Dionysius of Halicarnassus, showing that Luke has a sustained interest in the value of being open to foreigners as well.[72] For both Luke and Dionysius this attitude demonstrates *koinonia* and *philanthropia*, two cardinal virtues in the ancient world. This point of departure is critical because of the implications that result for our understanding of Lukan discourse. Luke appears preoccupied with presenting the Christian religion in terms of the Roman perception in which cultic practice is a part of politics (cf. Cicero, *Leg.* 2.26). This results in a Christian *politeia* that stands alongside (and, according to Luke, in many respects surpasses) the best of the Greeks and the Romans.[73] Lukan discourse in Acts is thus permeated with

---

[68] Nils A. Dahl, "The Story of Abraham in Luke-Acts," in *Studies in Luke-Acts* (ed. L. E. Keck and J. L. Martyn; Minneapolis: Fortress, 1966), 139–58.

[69] Walter T. Wilson, "Urban Legends: Acts 10:1–11:18 and the Strategies of Greco-Roman Foundation Narratives," *JBL* 120 (2001): 77–99.

[70] Ibid., 84.

[71] Penner, "In Praise of Christian Origins," 445–584.

[72] Balch, "Comments on the Genre," 354–60; see also Wilson, "Urban Legends," 90–92.

[73] This point has increasingly been made in recent treatments of Luke-Acts. See esp. Gregory E. Sterling, "'Athletes of Virtue': An Analysis of the Summaries in Acts (2:41–47; 4:32–35; 5:12–16)," *JBL* 113 (1994): 679–96; Allen Brent, "Luke-Acts and the Imperial Cult in Asia Minor," *JTS* 48 (1997): 111–38; idem, *Imperial Cult*, 73–139; Mary Rose D'Angelo, "The ANHP Question in Luke-Acts: Imperial Masculinity and the Deployment of Women in the Early Second Century," in *A Feminist Companion to Luke* (ed. A.-J. Levine with M. Blickenstaff; FCNTECW 3; Sheffield: Sheffield Academic Press, 2002), 44–69; and Gary Gilbert, "The List of Nations in Acts 2: Roman Propaganda and the Lukan Response," *JBL* 121 (2002): 497–529; as well as his essay in this volume.

political and cultural *topoi*. He deliberately presents Christianity as the model *politeia* with an exemplary constitution and leadership. Theological themes are therefore deeply embedded in, and in principle indistinguishable from, these more expansive sociocultural and political emphases.

Perhaps this fusion is best illustrated by the combination of narrative and speech in Peter's opening sermon (Acts 2), which provides an informative parallel to the *suasoria* declamatory exercise. Here Peter waxes eloquent in his deliberative rhetoric. The opening narrative sequence demonstrates the formation of the new Christian *politeia* as it is now unveiled before the totality of the Jews (people) of the Roman empire.[74] The language of Peter's speech is clearly conversionist: "call on the name of the Lord and be saved" (2:38–40). However, most intriguing is the concluding, framing narrative: after Peter's sermon, the hearers are completely overcome, and they follow the advice that they should repent and be baptized so that their sins would be forgiven and they would receive the Holy Spirit (2:38). So far this discourse seems to be typically religious in character, and not surprisingly the conclusion in 2:42 shows the converts sitting at the apostles' feet, "breaking bread, praying, and fellowshiping." Yet one cannot ignore the summary statement that follows in 2:43–47, where the converts who are saved live out in community the core values of the Christian *politeia*: sharing common property, having no need, eating food together, praising God, and displaying grace/kindness toward their fellow humans. The concluding line reads like a causal connection: as a result of this type of living, the new Christian community was rewarded with new members (2:47). In recent scholarship the emphasis in interpretation has been on the role of friendship language in the summary statements,[75] and

---

[74] The totality of representation seems to be the overall point of the listing of the nations in 2:9–11, although there are various positions on how this is achieved. See Douglas R. Edwards, *Religion and Power: Pagans, Jews, and Christians in the Greek East* (New York: Oxford University Press, 1996), 88; James M. Scott, "Luke's Geographical Horizon," in *The Book of Acts in Its Graeco-Roman Setting* (ed. D. W. J. Gill and C. Gempf; vol. 2 of *The Book of Acts in Its First Century Setting;* Grand Rapids: Eerdmans, 1994), esp. 527–30; Bruce M. Metzger, "Ancient Astrological Geography and Acts 2:9–11," in *Apostolic History and the Gospel: Biblical and Historical Essays Presented to F. F. Bruce on His Sixtieth Birthday* (ed. W. W. Gasque and R. P. Martin; Grand Rapids: Eerdmans, 1970), 123–33; and, most recently, Gilbert, "List of Nations in Acts 2," 518–24.

[75] Alan C. Mitchell, "'Greet the Friends By Name': New Testament Evidence for the Greco-Roman *Topos* on Friendship," in *Greco-Roman Perspectives on Friendship* (ed. J. T. Fitzgerald; SBLRBS 34; Atlanta: Scholars Press, 1997), esp. 236–57; idem, "The Social Function of Friendship in Acts 2:44–47 and 4:32–37," *JBL* 111 (1992): 255–72; and Jacques Dupont, *The Salvation of the Gentiles: Studies in the Acts of the Apostles* (trans. J. Keating; New York: Paulist, 1979), 85–102.

this is probably an accurate reading of Luke's presentation: the community is herein portrayed as ideal in Greco-Roman terms.[76] However, there is something more as well.

In *Contra Apionem* (2.145–146), for instance, Josephus describes the fundamental values of the Jewish constitution in almost identical terms to the summary statements in Acts: Moses' law promotes piety, *koinonia* in the community, and *philanthropia* toward humanity at large.[77] The list of cardinal virtues (*clementia, civilis, pietas,* etc.) goes far back in the literature of antiquity,[78] and evidently both Josephus and Luke are depicting their communities in line with a long-standing tradition of accepted norms and values. Moreover, both Josephus and Luke affirm that their political discourse is integrally connected to the fact that their respective laws are divinely initiated. Plutarch clarifies this implicit connection that underlies the respective Josephean and Lukan understandings of their *politeia*:

> Now justice is the aim and end of the law, but law is the work of the ruler, and the ruler is the image of God who orders all things. Such a ruler needs no Pheidias nor Polycleitus nor Myron to model him, but by his virtue he forms himself in the likeness of God and thus creates a statue most delightful of all to behold and most worthy of divinity.... with those who emulate his virtue and make themselves like unto his goodness and

---

[76] This is a theme often related to the apologetic function of the text (see Sterling, "Athletes of Virtue").

[77] See esp. the detailed study by Christine Gerber, *Ein Bild des Judentums für Nichtjuden von Flavius Josephus: Untersuchungen zu seiner Schrift* Contra Apionem (AGJU 40; Leiden: Brill, 1997); John M. G. Barclay, "Judaism in Roman Dress: Josephus' Tactics in the *Contra Apionem*," in *Internationales Josephus-Kolloquium Aarhus 1999* (ed. J. U. Kalms; MJS 6; Münster: LIT, 2000), 231–45. *Contra Apionem* 2.145–286 as a whole has many similarities with the arguments developed in Acts, especially the praise of the civic and constitutional virtue found in the community being promoted (Jewish in Josephus, Christian in Acts). In both cases, although there are deliberative features in the discourse, the larger framework is clearly epideictic in character. This accounts for why explicit charges are not fully addressed in either of the works, but rather countercharges are foisted on the constructed opposition—it is a result of the operative praise and blame rhetorical structure (see further Jan Willem van Henten and Ra'anan Abusch, "The Depiction of Jews as Typhonians and Josephus' Strategy of Refutation in *Contra Apionem*," in *Josephus' Contra Apionem: Studies in Its Character and Context* [ed. L. H. Feldman and J. R. Levison; AGJU 34; Leiden: Brill, 1996], esp. 303–9; cf. Alexander, "Acts of the Apostles as an Apologetic Text," 33–37).

[78] Helen F. North, "Canons and Hierarchies of the Cardinal Virtues in Greek and Latin Literature," in *The Classical Tradition: Literary and Historical Studies in Honor of Harry Caplan* (ed. L. Wallach; Ithaca, N.Y.: Cornell University Press, 1966), 165–83.

mercy he is well pleased and therefore causes them to prosper and gives them a share of his own equity, justice, truth, and gentleness, than which nothing is more divine. (*Princ. iner.* 781A)

For Plutarch this model issues forth in a polity based on friendship, *koinonia*, and *philanthropia*, wherein the citizens are themselves modeling the divine.[79]

One should not be surprised, of course, for this conclusion is essentially the one that Aristotle reaches in his *Politics*. The best constitution in his view was a polity based on good character, in which citizens and rulers mutually reinforced the centrality of virtues, which is the basis of happiness, according to Aristotle.[80] This is the ideal community for the ancient world; this is also the ideal embodied in Josephus's Jewish *politeia* and, not coincidentally, the new Christian community in Jerusalem as depicted in Acts. Therefore, when we see the early Christians in Acts responding to Peter's sermon by forming a community based on *koinonia*, not only worshiping God but indeed imitating the godlike virtue of mercy toward all,[81] we then know that Luke has here demarcated not only the Christian *politeia* but also in fact the Christian fulfillment of the Greek and Roman constitutional virtues. Peter's speech, then, whatever else we may say about its supposed religious content, is fundamentally a deliberative call to decide for this form of community.[82]

This portrait of early Christianity is accomplished in part by contrasting the superior *politeia* established in the narrative with the "corrupt generation" that Peter asserts as its counterpart (2:41). For instance, even a cursory reading of the Acts narrative evidences that for Luke the basic flaw

---

[79] Bruno Centrone, "Platonism and Pythagoreanism in the Early Empire," in Rowe and Schofield, *Cambridge History,* 578–81. The ideas here resonate with Epictetus's depiction of God as a good king and true father (Epictetus 1.6.40), affirming the divine patterning of human virtue in these systems of thought. Both Cicero and Seneca argue in a similar manner that in community formation (as viewed by the Stoics) the exchange of benefits in the development of community *koinonia* was fundamental to the human modeling of nature (Miriam Griffin, "Seneca and Pliny," in Rowe and Schofield, *Cambridge History,* 546–48; see also Wilson, "Urban Legends," 91–92).

[80] Christopher Rowe, "Aristotelian Constitutions," in Rowe and Schofield, *Cambridge History,* 386–87.

[81] It is noteworthy in this context of Lukan use of Greco-Roman civic *topoi* that Diodorus demarcates mercy as the hallmark of a civilized individual: "the spirits of civilized men are gripped ... most perhaps by mercy, because of the sympathy which nature has planted in us" (13.24.2).

[82] One might also think here of the connections of early Christian discourse with Roman imperial propaganda (see Gilbert's essay in this volume).

of the counterpart is the failure of both proper maintenance of constitutional order and the manifestation of civic virtue. To take just one example, the episode of Stephen's trial and martyrdom is loaded with civic themes, particularly in terms of contrasting the appropriate model of Stephen with the abhorrent behavior of Stephen's narrative Jewish opponents. They are depicted as lacking *civilis,* since they disrespect the law and tradition by falsely accusing Stephen and by killing a righteous man.[83] As Cicero states, punishment should not issue forth out of anger or malice or be controlled by the passions, otherwise it will result in injustice (*Off.* 1.89). Further, orderly decorum ought to be maintained in all aspects of life (*Off.* 1.142). However, excess and disorder go hand in hand in the Stephen narrative. The opponents, therefore, are contrasted with the character of Stephen (who essentially fulfills all the cardinal virtues), and the author elicits the debased nature of their civic character in terms of being unjust, cowardly, disorderly, and unwise (Diogenes Laertius 7.100). Indeed, while the early Christians are properly showing *pietas* toward their dead (Acts 8:2), Paul and the other opponents are trying to eradicate the Christian community (Acts 8:1, 3), further exhibiting vice by being excessive in vengeance toward the vanquished (Diodorus 13.24.4–5). Further, while the early Christian community extends mercy/charity toward all humanity (Acts 2:47), their narrative foils do not respond in kind.

This contrast is replicated throughout Acts, as various factions within the Jewish community and the Greco-Roman cities are constantly being upstaged at their own claims by the Christians. Throughout Acts we thus meet tyrants such as Herod, petty governors such as Felix, corrupt kings such as Agrippa, ineffective proconsuls such as Gallio, impotent Roman legions, treacherous Jewish councils,[84] and Jewish and Greek mobs running

---

[83] Aside from the fact that the Jewish opponents contravene Jewish law in this instance (Exod 23:7), it is also important to observe the widespread Greek and Roman belief that fair practice and administration of law was considered to be of supreme value and the manifestation of the highest virtue—wisdom. As Cicero notes, "the citizen ... will not expose anyone to hatred or disrepute by groundless charges, but he will surely cleave to justice and honour" (*Off.* 1.86; cf. 1.153–159). Diodorus similarly asserts that the fair-minded Athenian application of their just laws to the outsider represented the pinnacle of their *philanthropia* (13.25.2–3). See also Andrew Wallace-Hadrill, "*Civilis Princeps:* Between Citizen and King," *JRS* 72 (1982): 42–43.

[84] In the light of these overarching images in the Acts narrative, John Darr's proposal to (re)read the incident with Gamaliel as an ironic speech, rather than as actually supportive of the Jerusalem community, coheres with the Lukan perspective as detailed here ("Irenic or Ironic? Another Look at Gamaliel before the Sanhedrin [Acts 5:33–42]," in *Literary Studies in Luke-Acts: Essays in Honor of Joseph B. Tyson* [ed. R. P. Thompson and T. E. Phillips; Macon, Ga.: Mercer University Press, 1998], 121–39).

amok while those in power are frequently unable to establish order. It is evident that Jewish, Greek, or Roman readers would take this much away from Acts: the great civic traditions of antiquity are manifested in the narrative in the Christian community, which has God as its king (Epictetus 1.6.40), contrasted with tyrants such as Herod.[85] As Paul clearly states in the Areopagus speech, God is a king who takes care of the welfare of humans (Acts 17:25),[86] a "father to his children" (Cicero, *Rep.* 2.47), "fearing for" his subjects rather than being "afraid of" them (Plutarch, *Princ. iner.* 781E). Indeed, as one progresses through the Acts narrative, one is continually struck by the Lukan focus on order and his narrative negotiation of social and cultural conflict.

Related to this feature of the Christian manifestation of Greco-Roman ideals is the intriguing way in which ancient constitutional theory is reflected in the Acts narrative. In antiquity there was a classic debate with respect to which group or people had the best constitution. Frequently Sparta was singled out for this distinction, although there were some prominent detractors.[87] In general, those who favored the Spartan constitution did so because it was believed to combine all three forms of good government: monarchy, aristocracy, and a constitutional democracy (run by those of merit).[88] Even for Aristotle, it was deemed appropriate to have mixtures of various types of constitutions, such as democratic and oligarchic (*Pol.* 2.3.11).[89] Perhaps the most sympathetic depiction of the

---

[85] This motif is related to the larger theme of the philosopher versus tyrant confrontation that runs through Luke-Acts. See John A. Darr, *Herod the Fox: Audience Criticism and Lukan Characterization* (JSNTSup 163; Sheffield: Sheffield Academic Press, 1998), esp. 92–136; as well as O. Wesley Allen, *The Death of Herod: The Narrative and Theological Function of Retribution in Luke-Acts* (SBLDS 158; Atlanta: Scholars Press, 1997), 29–74.

[86] Cf. Paul's speech in Acts 14 (esp. 14:17), which raises similar themes. See further Dean P. Béchard, "Paul among the Rustics: The Lystran Episode (Acts 14:8–20) and Lucan Apologetic," *CBQ* 63 (2001): 99–100.

[87] Aristotle is one (*Pol.* 2.6). Earlier, however, Aristotle admits divergence in viewpoints on this matter (2.3.9–11). Cf. Josephus, *C. Ap.* 2.154, 225–231, 259, and 273.

[88] In traditional pairing (as one finds in Aristotle, for example), each of these good forms has a negative counterpart: monarchy (tyranny), aristocracy (oligarchy), constitutional democracy (democracy run by and for the poor). The basic feature that separates them is that in the negative counterpart the common good of those being ruled is not the primary motivation of the one/those ruling (cf. Aristotle, *Pol.* 3.5.1–4). See further Robert W. Wallace, "Aristotelian Politeiai and *Athenaion Politeia* 4," in *Nomodeiktes: Greek Studies in Honor of Martin Oswald* (ed. R. M. Rosen and J. Farrell; Ann Arbor: University of Michigan Press, 1993), 280–81.

[89] Rowe, "Aristotelian Constitutions," 380.

Spartan constitution is found in Xenophon's discussion. In praising the Spartan founder Lycurgus, Xenophon states that his first act as law-giver was to establish public meals (*Lac.* 5.2), something for which the Spartans and the Cretans were widely known for doing in antiquity.[90] According to Xenophon, one of Lycurgus's advances was to create mixed companies for mutual interaction between the young and the old (*Lac.* 5.5). Moreover, he "insisted on equal contributions to the food supply and on the same standard of living for all.... he made it more respectable to help one's fellows by toiling with the body than by spending money" (*Lac.* 6.3–4). Furthermore, Lycurgus's laws received the sanction of the Pythian deity at Delphi (*Lac.* 8.5). In addition, "he compelled all men at Sparta to practise all the virtues in public life" (*Lac.* 10.4). Indeed, the practice of virtue was "irresistible" in the Spartan state, being the sole requirement for citizenship (*Lac.* 10.7).[91] Closer to the time of Luke, Polybius would also reaffirm the basic outline of Xenophon's argument.[92] This reoccurring emphasis suggests that for at least some prominent writers of antiquity the pattern of the Spartan constitution, as memorialized in Hellenistic literature, was to be emulated by an emerging *politeia*.[93] Thus, alongside the theme of the combination of various forms of ruling powers, the idea of the ruler as one who cares for the welfare of all the citizens and who does not cater to one particular subgroup is understood to be a major factor in defeating the threat of civic *stasis* (Cicero, *Off.* 1.85–86; Dionysius, *Ant. rom.* 7.65.5).

Of course, one could mention many other features, but these may suffice in order to suggest that the Lukan scheme in Acts deliberately plays on

---

[90] According to Aristotle, Lycurgus's contribution was to move away from the public funding of these common meals (as in Crete) to reliance on individual aid, which he viewed as problematic since the poor suffered as a result (*Pol.* 2.6.21; but cf. 2.3.10). For more discussion on the traditions related to Lycurgus's founding of the Spartan constitution, see Balch's essay in this volume.

[91] See further Vivienne J. Gray, "Xenophon and Isocrates," in Rowe and Schofield, *Cambridge History*, 151–54.

[92] David E. Hahm, "Kings and Constitutions: Hellenistic Theories," in Rowe and Schofield, *Cambridge History*, 470–71. Polybius similarly uses Lycurgus as a famous exemplar from the past in his praise of Scipio's character (10.2.8–13). On the conception of the mixed constitution in antiquity, and especially in Polybius and Cicero, see Andrew Lintott, "The Theory of the Mixed Constitution at Rome," in *Philosophia Togata II: Plato and Aristotle at Rome* (ed. J. Barnes and M. Griffin; New York: Oxford University Press, 1997), 70–85.

[93] In this light, it is significant that Plato's Diotima describes, with seemingly great admiration, Lycurgus and Solon as "fathers" who leave behind "children." The creators of commendable constitutions thus inculcate virtue in all their offspring, which is considered an act of love and likened to the "mysteries" (*Symp.* 209c–e).

similar themes of constitutional and civic polity. The apostles can be considered to form a type of aristocracy selected by the monarch/deity.[94] The seven selected in Acts 6 represent a more democratic impulse in the narrative, as the apostles go to the people for the selection of the overseers of distributions to the widows.[95] Indeed, as with the selection of those to govern in a constitutional democracy, the seven are selected (Acts 6:5) on the basis of their merit (Acts 6:3; cf. Aristotle, *Pol.* 3.11.11; 3.12.1). This mixture of different systems of ruling in Acts seems to be deliberate, because fundamental flaws are drawn out for all the other systems displayed in the text.[96] The Greeks, Romans and Jews cannot maintain order anywhere in the empire, but the Christians, while not free from the same threats of disunity and discord, nonetheless manage to avoid disharmony and the decline of the constitution to its most deviant form (tyranny), the inevitable trajectory of every simple constitution, according to Polybius.[97]

---

[94] It is tempting in this light to view the selection of Matthias to the group of apostles as an analogy or parallel to the Roman republican and senatorial practice of selecting political duties through the drawing of lots. In this connection, the implicit emphasis on Jupiter's overseeing and approving of the Roman political structures is paralleled by the Christian God's oversight of selection to political duty in the early Christian community. See Roberta Stewart, *Public Office in Early Rome: Ritual Procedure and Political Practice* (Ann Arbor: University of Michigan Press, 1998), 37, 51; J. Rufus Fears, "The Cult of Jupiter and Roman Imperial Ideology," *ANRW* 2.17.1: 81; as well as Brent, *Imperial Cult,* 137–39, who compares the Lukan selection with the college of the *Fratres Arvales* and draws out the latter's association with imperial ideology and ritual.

[95] Luke is clearly not antidemocratic, as some scholars have suggested (e.g., Sara C. Winter, "Παρρησία in Acts," in *Friendship, Flattery, and Frankness of Speech: Studies on Friendship in the New Testament World* [ed. J. T. Fitzgerald; NovTSup 82; Leiden; Brill, 1996], 201–2).

[96] In connection with the point made earlier about the negative counter forms of government (see n. 88), it is noteworthy that the Jews tend to be portrayed as an oligarchy, while Herod is clearly depicted as a tyrant. In both cases neither are ruling for the sake of the common good. Most strikingly, the only occurrences of δῆμος in the New Testament are found in Acts (17:5; 19:30, 33; 12:22). In all instances the δῆμος (reserved for the characterization of Greek city-states) is depicted as out of control, running about in a moblike manner, with little concern for the common good.

[97] Hahm, "Kings and Constitutions," 470. This emphasis is one of the reasons why inner community discussion and debate leading toward resolution is so important in Acts (cf. 1:15–23; 6:1–6; 15:4–30; 21:18–26). When there is a hint of strife in the Christian community (such as the problem with the distributions in Acts 6:1), Luke rushes to show the Christian community responding with proper leadership and the establishment of order as a means of counteracting the threat of potential discord. It is thus unlikely, given the Lukan emphases detailed here, that the author

Having set out this larger civic context for Peter's Pentecost sermon, it is now important to stress the degree to which this speech operates in tandem with the surrounding narrative and in continuity with the larger narrative scheme of Acts. It is particularly noteworthy that we see that the present exaltation of Jesus has a corollary impact in the realm of human society in terms of empowering the early Christian community. Thus, eschatological emphases aside, there is an unmistakable focus on the emerging Christian *politeia* that is here confirmed by the miraculous signs. While Peter's speech obviously looks different from classical Greek and Roman *suasoria* examples, there are some striking similarities in function. The narrative setting of unusual speech and marvelous signs (2:1–4) is the contextual event that gives rise to the need for argumentation. The argument about the peculiar present situation is elaborated upon from Jewish Torah and reconfigured through the lens of the death-resurrection-exaltation of Jesus. The primary purpose is to identify the source of the current supernatural manifestation. The larger context, however, evidences that what is being witnessed here is much more than the spirit-inspired "drunkenness" of the early Christians; it is, rather, the emergence of the new Christian *politeia*. Peter's call for conversion in essence entails a new political order, one that models the best values of the Jews, Greeks, and Romans.[98] In this light it is not surprising that the entire speech is laced with royal imagery and that David, the biblical king par excellence, is the intertextual character that gives meaning to Jesus' exaltation.[99] For the modern reader the speech seems to be preoccupied with religious themes, but it is instructive to observe how the narrative

---

has tried to cover up more egalitarian traditions underlying the account of 6:1–6 (as Robert M. Price, *The Widow Traditions in Luke-Acts: A Feminist-Critical Scrutiny* [SBLDS 155; Atlanta: Scholars Press, 1997], 210–16, argues). Moreover, the suggestion that there is a theological conflict behind the narrative that is masked by Luke (Haenchen, *Acts of the Apostles,* 268) is also made more tenuous in this light, as there is a clear *Tendenz* throughout Acts to highlight conflicts and tensions on all levels, with those in the community being resolved and those outside being heightened. See further, Penner, "In Praise of Christian Origins," 445–584.

[98] As Balch reminds us in his essay in this volume, however, *new* for Luke also entails the phenomenon being grounded in the *old* (hence the extensive Lukan use of prophecy).

[99] Cf. the culminating royal psalm: Acts 2:34–35//Ps 110:1. In this light it is interesting to note that Peter also gives Ps 16 a messianic interpretation, which is made evident by the use of χριστός in Acts 2:31, 36. This accent further elaborates the royal nature of the speech. See David P. Moessner, "*Two* Lords 'at the Right Hand'? The Psalms and an Intertextual Reading of Peter's Pentecost Speech (Acts 2:14–36)," in Thompson and Phillips, *Literary Studies in Luke-Acts,* 228.

functions in tandem to evince a clear and precise political articulation of the empowerment explicated in the speech. Moreover, within a Christian argumentative context, what we see in both surrounding narrative and speech may be some of the first attestations of highly evocative and potent Christian political reasonings in narrative form. Peter is, from the perspective of Acts, the first Christian declaimer, evidencing forceful words in the service of artful persuasion.

In summary, in this section I have argued that if one takes seriously the narrative framing of the deliberative speeches in Acts, then one will perceive an integral link between the two. I have used the model of declamation as a way to explore what I consider to be the fictional aspects of this presentation. In particular, the so-called *suasoria* provide an excellent model for understanding the demonstrative rhetoric of Acts as it is situated within the larger epideictic framework of the macro narrative. Whether it is Peter's speech to those gathered in Jerusalem or Paul's speech to those in Athens, the fundamental connection is the mode of civic argumentation and the framing narratives that contextualize this argumentation for the reader. As we will see in the next section, these elements associated with declamation also have further resonance in the Lukan narrative, especially related to one of the central Lukan concerns: the Jewish law and its application to the inclusion of Gentiles in the new Christian *politeia*.

CONTROVERSIA AND LEGAL DISCOURSE IN ACTS

Aside from the deliberative themes predominant in Acts, one can also not ignore the aspects of judicial rhetoric characteristic of the trial-scenes and defenses. Explicit legal features, for instance, can be found in Paul's response to charges before the Jewish council, Felix, and Agrippa or in Stephen's "addressing" of the accusations of the Jewish council. In all cases the explicit judicial contexts give way to larger epideictic themes as one readily observes the heroes of early Christian history engaging those in power and prestige, overcoming the tyranny of worldly rulers in words and through their own virtuous comportment. Although a speech such as Stephen's could be considered something akin to a persuasive defense in the declamatory tradition,[100] upon closer inspection the real point of the speech is to demonstrate that Stephen was indeed powerful in word and deed. The Jewish opponents of Stephen, conversely, provide a narrative foil to the latter, demonstrating the lack of ability to control their passions, resulting in a fractious mob that becomes responsible for the death of a righteous man. The surrounding literary context confirms the praise and blame features with respect to the opposing characters of Stephen and his

---

[100] Russell, *Greek Declamation*, 49–50.

narrative adversaries. While these speeches are in part judicial defenses, they seem less connected to the more explicit legal disputations of the declamatory *controversia*.

There is at least one particular section of Acts, however, that does seem to offer a parallel to the *controversia:* the Cornelius episode that ends in the Jerusalem conference of Acts 15.[101] Beginning with the report of Peter's vision to the Jerusalem church (11:5–17) and following through to James's speech in 15:13–21, one particular feature of Jewish civic polity is the object of reflection: the mixing of Jews and Gentiles and the rules and regulations that therewith apply.[102] Cornelius's conversion thus provides the narrative framework that demands a suitable legal response from the assembly. As mentioned above, for Hellenistic historians openness to foreigners was the hallmark of a civil and just society, and the episode in Acts 15 turns on this premise. While the literary setting itself is longer than a traditional declamatory preface, the function is virtually the same: the narrative provides the particular legal issue that will be argued for or against. In this case, the legal concern strikes to the core of the identity of this newly formed *politeia:* How open ought this group to be?

---

[101] The parallel is significant in this case, since at the center of *controversia* is the proffering of a legal interpretation of the law in order to justify a position for or against a particular proposition generated from a situation of conflict (Kaster, "Controlling Reason," 325). This is precisely the scenario with respect to the admission of Cornelius and the Gentiles into the new Christian *politeia*.

[102] Mixing, in this case, readily correlates with the theme of *stasis*, which was a threat to the civic and social harmony of the *polis*. Thus, aside from the problem with the distribution to the widows in Acts 6, the larger potential threat to the stability of the Christian *politeia* by the influx of outsiders (Gentiles) is of particular concern to Luke, as evidenced by the amount of space devoted to it in Acts. Indeed, resolution of social and class conflict was a major theme across a broad spectrum of ancient literature and writers. See David L. Balch, "Rich and Poor, Proud and Humble in Luke-Acts," in *The Social World of the First Christians: Essays in Honor of Wayne A. Meeks* (ed. L. M. White and O. L. Yarbrough; Minneapolis: Fortress, 1995), 214–33; Alexander Fuks, *Social Conflict in Ancient Greece* (ed. M. Stern and M. Amit; Leiden: Brill, 1984), 66–72, 120–22, 136–37, 172–71, 177–79, 186–89; Gottfried Mader, *Josephus and the Politics of Historiography: Apologetic and Impression Management in the* Bellum Judaicum (MnSup 205; Leiden: Brill, 2000), 55–103; and Tessa Rajak, "Josephus," in Rowe and Schofield, *Cambridge History,* 594–95. Brent (*Imperial Cult,* 110–30) makes a convincing case for the predominance of the theme of *stasis* in Acts. There is a tendency in the narrative both to downplay the possibility of Christianity representing any threat of civic *stasis* for the ruling powers and to redirect such concerns onto both Jewish and Greek assemblies.

It is noteworthy in this respect that the *progymnasmata* contain a final exercise dealing with either the refutation or confirmation of a particular law, especially the introduction of a law to the assembly (Theon 12; Aphthonius 14). This comes closest to the *controversia* of declamation[103] and reveals that at least one of the emphases of ancient rhetorical education was the ability to engage and debate issues of legal relevance to the *polis*. In this light, the legal basis of the argument made in both speech and narrative in Acts, moving from new experience and revelation to appeals to law (Scripture) itself, is of particular interest. The climax of James's speech in 15:16–17 rests on an interpretation of an authoritative text (Amos 9:11–12).[104] At issue, then, is fundamentally a conflict of legally binding precedents, which the Jerusalem council attempts to (re?)negotiate, not surprisingly moving in favor of the Greek value of *philanthropia:* opening citizenship to all.

At stake in this meeting of the Christian *demos* is part of what any citizen of an ancient polity would be engaged in: deliberation of judicial themes. In fact, in Acts 15 we might catch the best glimpse into the complex literary process behind Acts, since for the source of this narrative one need go no further than Gal 2:1–10. Given the kind of free-ranging creativity I have suggested Luke has used in Acts, it would not be surprising for a historian to take the account of Paul and elaborate on it,[105] developing the themes and creating a fuller picture of what "really" happened. It is thus significant that Luke creates here his own assembly, where various voices are heard and then finally persuaded by the forceful rhetoric of James. Conflict is not denied; it is portrayed as an inevitable part of any *polis*. Moreover, the resolution of the conflict again demonstrates the superiority of the Christian *politeia* over its competitors.

---

[103] Unfortunately, the Greek version of Theon's exercises is severely truncated, with the majority of the discussion missing (Butts, "*Progymnasmata* of Theon," 538 n. 1).

[104] See further Richard Bauckham, "James and Gentiles (Acts 15.13–21)," in Witherington, *History, Literature and Society*, 154–84.

[105] See Thomas L. Brodie, "Towards Tracing the Gospels' Literary Indebtedness to the Epistles," in MacDonald, *Mimesis and Intertextuality*, 104–16; idem, "Luke's Redesigning of Paul: Corinthian Division and Reconciliation (1 Corinthians 1–5) as One Component of Jerusalem Unity (Acts 1–5)," *IBS* 17 (1995): 98–128; William O. Walker, "Acts and the Pauline Corpus Revisited: Peter's Speech at the Jerusalem Conference," in Thompson and Phillips, *Literary Studies in Luke-Acts*, 77–86; and Heikki Leppä, "Luke's Critical Use of Galatians" (Ph.D. diss., University of Helsinki, 2002). The standard objections to this position are articulated *in nuce* in Philip Vielhauer's classic essay, "On the 'Paulinism' of Acts," in Keck and Martyn, *Studies in Luke-Acts*, 33–50.

Concluding Deliberations

In this cursory treatment of some features of Lukan discourse, I have taken seriously the civic dimensions of both the historian's approach to the composition of *historia* and the embodied nature of the narrative itself in terms of its pedagogical goals. I have also taken into consideration the idea that ancient discourse and literature represent a fluid arena characterized by vitality and vivacity in the formation of argumentation and reasoning. Too often rhetorical critics have simply focused on classification and organization, rather than appreciating fully the admixture of forms and functions. I have further argued that in order to understand the literature of antiquity, especially in terms of its function, one must return to the building blocks of the educational system, particularly the *progymnasmata*—the training ground for the citizen, whether finally manifested in oratory or *historia* or yet some other form. I chose the advanced exercise of declamation as a heuristic tool for exploring these issues in more depth, particularly because declamation provides a window to the interrelation of narrative and speech, an issue of particular importance for Acts. Declamation also furnishes a fuller appreciation of the implicit civic function of rhetorical discourses, which connects with the goals of ancient historiography more generally.

As such, declamation also provides an avenue into the exploration of the civic world of Acts. It is interesting at this point to recall that declamation was, at one level, a way of affirming the social order through rational argumentation. As Joy Connolly notes, "Declamation reveals the dramatic ways in which the prosaic landscape of rhetorical pedagogy is transformed into a moralizing justification of the existing social order."[106] Reading Acts in this light is informative. First, Acts explicitly fits this mold of reassurance of the reader—with the aim, in this case, to affirm that God is behind the formation of the early Christian *politeia* as narrated in Acts and that this all comes about according to the will of this deity. As part of this agenda, the social order unfolding in the narrative is depicted by the writer to be consonant with, if not better than, the larger Greco-Roman value system. Indeed, Lukan rhetoric exploits this value system as a means to do what declamation did best: create identity in the reading/speaking community.[107] It also demonstrates for any reader in the ancient world that early

---

[106] Connolly, "Mastering Corruption," 148.

[107] As Gilbert ("List of Nations in Acts 2," 525, 527) observes: "Luke-Acts presents Jesus and the church as existing in competition with Rome and its leaders over the claim of universal authority.... Luke-Acts exploits Roman political ideology as a way to foster among its readers a clearer sense of their Christian identity and of the legitimacy of the church."

Christianity—and it alone—can reasonably respond to the social, political, and moral decay and disarray of the empire (especially as perceived from the perspective of the Greek East).

Second, the various incidents that give rise to the speeches in Acts are themselves somewhat extraordinary and larger than life, creating a narrative context in which early Christian heroes could be seen waxing eloquent on civic and religious themes (i.e., the epideictic edge of Lukan discourse). That Christians can be shown to provide reasonable and potent rhetorical responses on these diverse occasions suggests something significant about the movement herein represented: it is a legitimate and viable political and social reality on the larger Greco-Roman first-century civic landscape. At the same time, one should keep in mind that while these values are being inscribed upon the reader, the reader is also being taken in a new cultural direction through this Christian argumentation. It is not just the values of the Jews, Greeks, and Romans that Christianity sub(con)sumes in Acts; it is, rather, a Christian reconfiguration of these within their new community and narrative structure.

This last observation leads, finally, to the third point in connection with declamation: this Christian argumentation is more than merely the reinforcement of traditional cultural and political values. Rather, the purported reconfiguration promoted by the movement Luke seems to represent is moving toward the formation and promotion of a distinctively Christian culture.[108] It remains a matter of debate whether the Christian configurations of deliberation and debate in Acts can be considered radical or conventional. For example, the reconfiguration of authoritative Scripture in Acts 2 suggests a more radical perspective, while Paul's speech in Acts 17 seems much more conventional in character. However, one must keep in mind that each speech has a particular narrative audience and that the adept writer of antiquity is trained to curtail each speech-in-character to the interests and persuasive framework of a specific audience. In their respective narrative contexts, the arguments may appear much more conventional than we might anticipate from a macro analysis of Acts. Of course, the goal of Lukan argumentation—to push toward a new Christian cultural identity, embodied in an emerging *politeia* under Christ—results in a narrative poetics that no doubt would have struck many Jews, Greeks, and Romans as strange superstition. Still, as a voice articulated both in the spirit of and in reaction to dominant cultural discourses, Luke's representation of early Christianity appears at one and the same time to be both radical and conventional. Without at least some amount of the former, Christianity à la Luke-Acts offers nothing distinctive and appealing to

---

[108] See esp. the discussion by Brent, *Imperial Cult,* 101–32, 137–39.

someone in the first century, but without a healthy dose of the latter this form of Christianity could be perceived as a dangerous movement to be targeted for suppression by cultural and political forces.

Taken seriously, these observations can lead to a fundamental reorientation in our approach to Acts: Lukan discourse is fundamentally civic in nature, and the themes that predominate, as well as the pedagogical function of the narrative itself, move the reader—ancient and modern—in this direction.[109] This emphasis means that, while Acts may be understood as an apologetic text, its forceful discourse is not simply seeking to achieve outer-group authorization or to provide in-group legitimization but goes further to foster and promote a universalistic and totalizing claim on the reading audience. The apocalyptic framework, which Luke in principle de-eschatologizes, is rebirthed in the civic discourse perpetuated throughout the narrative, fully incarnating the concept of citizenship in the new Christian *politeia* and *oikoumene*. This Lukan achievement represents a grandiose and bold vision, one that establishes a polity that not only manifests all the virtues dreamed of in the philosophical and political texts of antiquity but also actualizes those in history, which here means nothing more or less than the Lukan narrative *in toto*.

The payoff for the study of Acts can be summarized as follows. On the one hand, it may involve moving beyond the (search for) sources behind the text. Acts is, finally, important for what it actually represents: a creative and innovative mythology of the formation and expansion of the Christian *politeia*. The historical kernel is really quite beside the point for Lukan *historia*. Moreover, we miss the essential contours of the Lukan discursive project in the process. On the other hand, looking at the civic dimensions of this early Christian rhetoric may open new vistas in understanding the self-perception of at least some early Christians. These vistas may also aid in establishing the more evident ethico-political connections between Luke and Paul, for instance,[110] and perhaps also lead to a reappraisal of the sociorhetorical dynamics reflected in post-Pauline texts such as Colossians, Ephesians, and the Pastorals, which share this same civic/political concern and framework. Finally, the move toward a fuller appreciation of

---

[109] This brings Acts in line with the larger discussion in the philosophical schools of the Hellenistic period, in which ethico-political discourse was dominant. See esp. Troels Engberg-Pedersen, "The Hellenistic Öffentlichkeit: Philosophy as a Social Force in the Greco-Roman Empire," in *Recruitment, Conquest, and Conflict: Strategies in Judaism, Early Christianity, and the Greco-Roman World* (ed. P. Borgen et al.; ESEC 6; Atlanta: Scholars Press, 1998), 33–34.

[110] With respect to Paul, see esp. the recent study by Bruno Blumenfeld, *The Political Paul: Justice, Democracy and Kingship in a Hellenistic Framework* (JSNTSup 210; Sheffield: Sheffield Academic Press, 2002).

the literary artistry and rhetorical sophistication of Luke's work takes us beyond the limits of traditional historical-critical approaches to Acts. In this process we will learn much from examining more fully the relationship between literature, discourse, and the pedagogical tools (such as those reflected in the *progymnasmata*) used to foster values and train individuals in the art and practice of responsible and effective citizenship. These building blocks can illuminate for us not just compositional techniques but, much more importantly, the generative matrix that shaped the minds reflected in the literature. Of course, mired as we are in the very adult world of biblical scholarship, we may have to head back to school for some additional instruction in the *paideia* of the Greco-Roman world. This should not be difficult for New Testament scholars, however, for it was, after all, (the Matthean) Jesus who, in a rather progymnastic vein, suggested that the kingdom is promised to those who are willing to become like children.

THE TRIAL SCENE IN THE GREEK NOVELS AND IN ACTS

Saundra Schwartz

The ancient novels are an important source of *comparanda* for scholars working on early Christian narrative.[1] This point has been made by Richard Pervo, who argues for reading Acts within the genre of the ancient novel in his study, *Profit with Delight*.[2] He supports his case by listing a great number of narrative elements in Acts that are also found in the ancient Greek novels. In this essay I subject one of these elements to a close, comparative analysis: the courtroom scene. The methodology employed here is derived from a typological study of the trial scenes in the Greek novels.[3] The application of this methodology to the trials in Acts offers a suggestive approach to the reading of Acts as an artful narrative and places Acts and the Greek novels within the wider legal and cultural context of the Roman Empire. The trial scenes in these texts do not necessarily tell us how the law worked in actuality, but they do reveal attitudes toward the law. They are reflections not of reality, but of *mentalité*.

Both Acts and the Greek novels lay somewhere in the gray area between historiography and poetry, between truth and lies. In his

---

[1] Demonstrated by the ongoing work of the Society of Biblical Literature Ancient Fiction and Early Christian and Jewish Narrative Group. Much of this work has been published in a volume that is now the starting point for comparative studies: Ronald F. Hock, J. Bradley Chance, and Judith Perkins, eds., *Ancient Fiction and Early Christian Narrative* (SBLSymS 6; Atlanta: Scholars Press, 1998).

[2] Richard I. Pervo, *Profit with Delight: The Literary Genre of the Acts of the Apostles* (Philadelphia: Fortress, 1987). For other studies of Acts and the Greek novels in general, see Stephen P. Schierling and Marla J. Schierling, "The Influence of the Ancient Romances on the Acts of the Apostles," *ClassBul* 54 (1978): 81–88; Susan M. Praeder, "Luke-Acts and the Ancient Novel," in *SBL Seminar Papers, 1981* (SBLSP 20; Chico, Calif.: Scholars Press, 1981), 269–92; and Loveday Alexander, "Fact, Fiction and the Genre of Acts," *NTS* 44 (1998): 380–99.

[3] Saundra Schwartz, "Courtroom Scenes in the Ancient Greek Novels" (Ph.D. diss., Columbia University, 1998). See also idem, "Clitophon the *Moichos*: Achilles Tatius and the Trial Scene in the Greek Novel," *Ancient Narrative* 1 (2000–2001): 93–113.

provocative collection of Sather lectures, *Fiction as History: Nero to Julian,* Glen Bowersock reconsiders the nature of the fact-fiction polarity. He dates the onset of this blurring of the traditional generic boundaries between truth and fiction to the reign of Nero, whose own practices as emperor began to dissolve the traditional wall between what was real and what was staged.[4] Bowersock makes the not uncontroversial argument that the flowering of Greek fiction in the empire was stimulated by the "fabulous and incredible stories ... beginning to circulate in Palestine and the Greek East."[5] One of the difficulties with this argument is the problem in distinguishing the echoes of specifically Christian material from those of the general cultural environment, a task made especially complex due to the novels' openness to a wide variety of influences.[6] The correspondence between fiction and reality is not straightforward. It is tricky, if not impossible, to "disengage nuggets of historical reality"[7] from works of fiction such as the Greek novels. Yet it is precisely because they are works of fiction that they allow us to set aside the question of how they correspond with events known from reality. We are thereby able to see more clearly the narrative techniques and artistic patterns that impose an aura of plausibility upon events that never actually happened. With the novels, then, it is possible to discuss realism without passing judgment on historical accuracy.[8]

---

[4] Glen W. Bowersock, *Fiction as History: Nero to Julian* (Sather Classical Lectures 58; Berkeley and Los Angeles: University of California Press, 1994). The issues of fictionality and historicity as they apply to the reading of Acts are addressed by Alexander, "Fact, Fiction." More generally, see the essays in Christopher Gill and Timothy P. Wiseman, eds., *Lies and Fiction in the Ancient World* (Exeter: University of Exeter Press, 1993).

[5] Bowersock, *Fiction as History,* 27.

[6] For reviews of Bowersock, see Simon Goldhill, review of George A. Kennedy, *A New History of Classical Rhetoric;* Glen W. Bowersock, *Fiction as History: Nero to Julian;* Maud A. Gleason, *Making Men: Sophists and Self-Presentation in Ancient Rome;* and John Poulakos, *Sophistical Rhetoric in Classical Greece, BMCR* 6 (1995): 350–63; Keith Hopkins, "Past Alternative" (review of Glen W. Bowersock, *Fiction as History: Nero to Julian*), *Times Literary Supplement* (16 February 1996): 29; and Simon Swain, review of Glen W. Bowersock, *Fiction as History: Nero to Julian, JRS* 86 (1996): 216–17. Hopkins and Swain are skeptical of Bowersock's argument for intensive and meaningful absorption of Christian motifs by Greco-Roman writers as early as the first and second centuries C.E. Goldhill, on the other hand, sees Bowersock's work as an invitation for further examination of the interplay of traditions in the cultural history of the Roman Empire.

[7] The expression is borrowed from Ewen L. Bowie and Stephen J. Harrison, "The Romance of the Novel," *JRS* 83 (1993): 166.

[8] On the question of verisimilitude, see David Konstan, "The Invention of Fiction," in Hock et al., *Ancient Fiction,* 3–17; John R. Morgan, "Make-Believe and

Acts and the Greek novels were evolving over roughly the same time period and among people who spoke Greek and recognized the geography of the eastern Mediterranean. Acts is most often compared to the novel of Chariton, mainly because of the chronological proximity of the two texts.[9] Chariton's *Chaereas and Callirhoe* is the earliest of the five complete novels that have survived, although fragments of other novels make it clear that other works of prose fiction had existed well before Chariton wrote his novel.[10] The precise date of Chariton's novel remains open to debate. It has been placed as early as the first century B.C.E. to as late as the middle of the second century C.E.[11] Rhetorical and lexical analyses align Chariton with authors of the first century C.E. or the beginning of the second.[12] This period coincides with the time of greatest prosperity for Aphrodisias, the city of Asia Minor that Chariton, in his proem, claims as

---

Make Believe: The Fictionality of the Greek Novels," in Gill and Wiseman, *Lies and Fiction,* 175–229; and Bryan P. Reardon, *The Form of Greek Romance* (Princeton: Princeton University Press, 1991), 46–76.

[9] For a comparative study of Chariton and Luke, as well as Josephus, see Douglas R. Edwards, *Religion and Power: Pagans, Jews, and Christians in the Greek East* (New York: Oxford University Press, 1996). For a concise discussion of other work on the subject, see idem, "Pleasurable Reading or Symbols of Power? Religious Themes and Social Context in Chariton," in Hock et al., *Ancient Fiction,* 31.

[10] The generally accepted dates for the novels are as follows: Chariton, late Hellenistic to 150 C.E.; Xenophon, mid-second to mid-third century C.E.; Achilles Tatius, 170–200 C.E.; Longus, mid-second to early-third century C.E.; and (more controversially) Heliodorus, early third or late fourth century C.E.

[11] Chariton's freedom from the extreme Atticism characteristic of the Second Sophistic has been marshaled as evidence for a composition date as early as the first century C.E.; however, stylistic criteria are a weak basis for dating, since it was entirely possible for both sophistic and nonsophistic styles to coexist. Possible evidence for a date before 62 C.E. comes from a reference to a work entitled "Callirhoe" in Persius, *Satires* 1.134; see G. P. Goold, *Chariton: Callirhoe* (LCL; Cambridge: Harvard University Press, 1995), 4–5. Arguments for dating the novel to the Flavian or Antonine periods have been based upon internal evidence, such as the depiction of Miletus, Parthia, and civic customs; see Bryan P. Reardon, "Chariton: Chaereas and Callirhoe," in *Collected Ancient Greek Novels* (ed. B. P. Reardon; Berkeley and Los Angeles: University of California Press, 1989), 17–18; Christopher P. Jones, "Le personnalité de Chariton," in *Le monde du roman grec* (ed. M. F. Baslez et al.; Paris: l'École normale supérieure, 1992), 161–67; and Marie-Françoise Baslez, "De l'histoire au roman: la Perse de Chariton," in Baslez et al., *Le monde du roman grec,* 199–212.

[12] Carlos Hernández Lara, "Rhetorical Aspects of Chariton of Aphrodisias," *Giornale italiano di filologia* 42 (1990): 267–74; and Consuelo Ruiz Montero, "Aspects of the Vocabulary of Chariton of Aphrodisias," *CQ* 41 (1991): 484–89.

his hometown.¹³ Such problems of textual chronology are familiar to scholars of early Christian texts, particularly for those of Acts. Arguments have been made to place the composition of Acts somewhere between the early 60s of the first century C.E. and the middle of the second century C.E.; evidence for a more precise date within that nine-decade window is still inconclusive.¹⁴ Given the uncertainties about chronology, utmost caution is necessary in making arguments about direction of dependency between the novels and early Christian texts. At a minimum, we can safely say they were being composed and circulated in roughly the same period and within the general context of the cities of the Greek East.¹⁵

It was during this same period of the first centuries C.E. that Roman law gradually eclipsed local legal customs. The mesh was not perfect: the redundancies and gaps created ambiguity and confusion, as Paul's legal adventures in Acts reflect. In the Greek world, some cities were free and lived under their own constitutions; others were more directly under the control of the Roman imperial government.¹⁶ The Greeks were negotiating their place in a system where a layer of Roman rulers floated above, and seeped into, local systems of power. The relationship between Romans and local elites was generally more harmonious in the Greek cities than in Judea: it was during the Flavian and Antonine periods that Greek culture fused with Roman and came to define the culture of power within the empire. This fusion involved the Greeks' reimagination of their civic communities,

---

¹³ Bowersock suggests that Chariton may have been contemporary with Antonius Diogenes, another novelist from Aphrodisias; see Bowersock, *Fiction as History*, 35–41. Cf. Douglas R. Edwards, "Defining the Web of Power in Asia Minor," *JAAR* 57 (1994): 699–718; and Gareth Schmeling, *Chariton* (Twayne's World Authors Series 295; New York: Twayne, 1974). The question of the relationship between Chariton and Xenophon of Ephesus further complicates the question. The *communis opinio* that Chariton wrote his novel before Xenophon of Ephesus has been challenged by James N. O'Sullivan, *Xenophon of Ephesus: His Compositional Technique and the Birth of the Novel* (Berlin: de Gruyter, 1995), 6–9.

¹⁴ John T. Townsend, "The Date of Luke-Acts," in *Luke-Acts: New Perspectives from the Society of Biblical Literature Seminar* (ed. C. H. Talbert; New York: Crossroad, 1984), 47–62. The arguments for the dating of Acts are surveyed in detail by Colin J. Hemer, *The Book of Acts in the Setting of Hellenistic History* (ed. C. H. Gempf; WUNT 49; Tübingen: Mohr Siebeck, 1989; repr., Winona Lake, Ind.: Eisenbrauns, 1990), 365–414.

¹⁵ Edwards, *Religion and Power*, 15–27.

¹⁶ Jean Colin, *Les villes libres de l'Orient gréco-romain et l'envoi au supplice par acclamations populaires* (Collections Latomus 82; Brussels-Berchem: Latomus, 1965); and Arnold H. M. Jones, *The Greek City from Alexander to Justinian* (Oxford: Clarendon, 1940).

which were heavily informed by the memory of a past golden age when the cities were autonomous.[17]

The Greek novels are written from the perspective of elite city-dwellers.[18] The dramatic settings look back nostalgically to a time when the Greek cities were free and autonomous. The novelists studiously avoid reference to Rome. When details drawn from the contemporary world do occur, they tend to be rather vague and served mainly to evoke a generally realistic atmosphere. How and by whom these books were read is imperfectly understood. The length of the works suggests that they would have been read silently or perhaps aloud in intimate settings.[19] One attractive hypothesis, proposed by David Konstan, is that a *paterfamilias* might have purchased a copy of a novel, which would have been quite expensive, to bring home and have read aloud as entertainment for the entire family. Stories of young people falling in love, remaining loyal in the face of threats and misfortunes, and then getting married and returning to the city would have reinforced the values of the Greek urban elite and built a sense of communal identity among their audiences.[20] The novels, then, contain an ideology that is essentially conservative, which aims to reinforce the values of a patriarchal, Greek-speaking, civic elite that followed the traditional, polytheistic religious practices of the Greco-Roman world. The ideal romances serve not only to entertain but also to reinforce the social values of the audience by presenting models of ideal behavior for an implied reader, who was meant to identify with the cultured elite (*pepaideuomenoi*).[21] In the Greek novels as in Acts, there too was profit to be had beneath a delightful veneer.

Trials in the Greek Novels

The representations of fictional trials provide an important point of comparison with the trial scenes in Acts; the comparison highlights the use of poetic techniques to lend dramatic shape to the narrative of the activities of a variety of different groups in the context of the Greco-Roman

---

[17] Simon Swain, *Hellenism and Empire: Language, Classicism, and Power in the Greek World, AD 50–250* (New York: Oxford University Press, 1996), 101–33.

[18] Suzanne Saïd, "Rural Society in the Greek Novel, or The Country Seen from the Town," in *Oxford Readings in the Greek Novel* (ed. S. Swain; New York: Oxford University Press, 1999), 83–107.

[19] Raymond J. Starr, "Reading Aloud: *Lectores* and Roman Reading," *CJ* 86 (1990–91): 337–43.

[20] David Konstan, *Sexual Symmetry: Love in the Ancient Greek Novel and Related Genres* (Princeton: Princeton University Press, 1994), 220.

[21] Swain, *Hellenism and Empire*, 101–31.

world. The courtroom scene is a particularly apt formula for the dramatization of ideology. At the center of the drama is a contest, an *agōn*, between two opponents representing opposed moral positions, with the expectation that, at a predetermined endpoint (the verdict), one contestant will win.[22] The trial scene, therefore, is a formula not only for the exposition of competing ideas but also for the valorization of the moral position implicitly supported by the text's ideology. At least this is what the expectation was: as we shall see, justice rarely is accomplished in so straightforward (and, for that matter, artless) a manner in the novels. This observation was made by the ninth-century Byzantine patriarch Photius in his synopsis of a novel by Antonius Diogenes: "In this story in particular, as in fictional works of its kind, there are two especially useful things to observe: first, that [the author] presents a wrongdoer, even if he appears to escape countless times, paying the penalty just the same; second, that he shows many guiltless people, though on the brink of great danger, being saved many times in defiance of expectations."[23] The vocabulary with which Photius distills the essence of the genre of Greek fiction reflects an underlying cognitive framework in which justice is the critical value. He defines the antagonist as "the one doing something unjust" (τὸν ἀδικήσαντά τι); the protagonists are therefore "the blameless ones" (ἀναιτίους). He correspondingly calls the resolution of the story—that is, when the villain meets his fate—"paying the penalty" (πάντως δίκην δεδωκέναι). Arguably, trials are central to the genre. As good confronts evil in an open contest, the judge's verdict provides an opportunity for the articulation of values. The description of the reactions of the internal audience draws the reader into the process of passing judgment on the characters of the narrative. The frequency of trial scenes in Greek and Latin fiction reflects the importance of rhetoric in the literary culture of the Roman Empire.[24] Novelists and at least

---

[22] The ancient rhetorical treatises borrowed from the vocabulary of athletic competition to categorize arguments. For example, the core of a case was the speaker's "stance" (στάσις); one type of rebuttal in which a defendant claimed he did nothing wrong was called the "counterhold" (ἀντίληψις); see Donald A. Russell, *Greek Declamation* (Cambridge: Cambridge University Press, 1983), 136–41.

[23] Photius, *Bibliotheca* Cod. 166 [112a]. Translation by Gerald N. Sandy, "Antonius Diogenes: *The Wonders beyond Thule*," in Reardon, *Collected Ancient Greek Novels*, 782.

[24] For trials in the Latin novels, see Petronius, *Satyrica* 108–109; and Apuleius, *Metam.* 10.6–12. Examples of possible trial scenes can be seen also in fragments of novels: e.g., in Iamblichus's *Babyloniaka* (Photius, *Bibliotheca* 94 [74b.24–30]) and in the *Antheia* fragment (col. 1; 2.15–16); see texts in Susan A. Stephens and John J. Winkler, eds., *Ancient Greek Novels: The Fragments* (Princeton: Princeton University Press, 1995), 192 (for Iamblichus), 280–83 (for *Antheia*).

some of their readers shared a taste for legal complexities, a taste informed by the era's education, where great emphasis was placed on training pupils to formulate clever arguments in far-fetched cases.[25]

For the purposes of this essay, a trial is defined as a verbal dispute between two parties, occasioned by an alleged or actual misdeed, judged by a third party who functions in an official capacity, witnessed by an audience, and entailing punishment or reward. These criteria eliminate a number of trial-like scenes, such as scenes of assemblies or other deliberations. Trials are not simple episodes, but are themselves complex (sometimes very complex) stories embedded within a larger narrative, which in turn embraces subnarratives in the form of speeches.[26]

There are thirteen trial scenes in the five extant, complete Greek novels; each of the novels has at least one (*see the list in table 1 on pages 134–35*). In the novels of Chariton and Achilles Tatius, trials are expansive and represent high points of the narratives. Heliodorus's trials represent, as does his novel as a whole, highly sophisticated narration. The final resolution of the novel is set in an exotic courtroom at the edge of the world, and a pair of trials brings together many loose narrative strands. Xenophon of Ephesus's trial is one episode among other scenes of misfortune at the hands of villains. Longus's inclusion of a single trial scene indicates that even in this idyllic novel, which seems the most removed from the reality of civic life, he could not forego a good trial scene with a pair of speeches.

The trial scene is a rich and varied *topos*—or, more accurately, a nexus of *topoi*. A composite picture of the typical trial scene emerges from the study of the trial scenes in the Greek novels. The typical trial scene is characterized by a number of common features: the accusation, the convening of the court, a pair of speeches, the spectators' reactions, a surprising twist, and the verdict. In a strict sense, the pattern of crime–arrest–punishment is not part of the unified scenic action of a courtroom trial; however, these elements are inseparable from it, as will become clear when we analyze the trials in Acts. A few general observations about each feature will suffice to illustrate the typical pattern of trials in the Greek novels.

---

[25] Such as seen in the *Controversiae* of Seneca the Elder. On the contiguity between these declamatory exercises and the situations in works of prose fiction, see Russell, *Greek Declamation,* 38; as well as Todd Penner, "Civilizing Discourse: Acts, Declamation, and the Rhetoric of the *Polis,*" in this volume.

[26] Because this essay examines how trials resonate within the larger narrative, the corpus is limited to the five Greek novels that have survived complete. In addition, because this essay is concerned with scenes rather than summaries, trials mentioned only indirectly or in passing have not been included. For narratological definitions of scene and summary, see Mieke Bal, *Narratology: Introduction to the Theory of Narrative* (2d ed.; Toronto: University of Toronto Press, 1997), 104–6.

THE CRIME

It may seem self-evident to say that a description of the crime always precedes the account of the trial; however, in contrast with some forms of contemporary courtroom drama, the suspense does not usually lie in solving whodunit mysteries but rather in seeing villains punished and heroes vindicated. Because of this focus, the audience always knows the truth before the trial begins. This foreknowledge opens a space for dramatic irony and enables readers to appreciate the ways in which the speakers in the trial manipulate the truth. The crimes that trigger trials in the novels tend to be predictably melodramatic. Sexual crimes, such as adultery and seduction, are the most common type of crime. They represent the negation of marital fidelity, a paramount principle in the moral universe of the Greek novels.[27] Kidnapping forms the central charge in two trials, and allegations of false enslavement arise in other trials.[28] Murder—attempted, actual, or merely alleged—is the other main crime in the novels.[29] The sole trial in Longus's novel (Greek trial 6) is the exception that proves the rule: consistent with his rewriting of the novel in a pastoral mode, the event triggering the trial is a mundane case of property damage. In almost all of these cases, the defendant is innocent.

THE ARREST

In eight of the scenes, there is an arrest immediately before the trial.[30] Typically, the alleged criminal is physically apprehended, then bound. Physical and verbal abuses are often part of the action. The level of violence during the arrest is a reflection of the villain's animosity to the hero and prefigures the moral contrast in the coming trial.[31] In contrast with scenes of arrest in early Christian texts, in the Greek novels the narrative time between arrest and trial is minimal.[32] When the prisoner is confined,

---

[27] Sexual crimes are found in connection with at least eight of the thirteen trial scenes (Greek trials 1, 3, 4, 5, 7, 8, 9, and 10), as well as in numerous other episodes throughout the novel that do not necessarily result in trial scenes.

[28] Kidnapping in Greek trials 2 and 13; false enslavement in 3, 7, and 8.

[29] Murder charges arise in the course of nine of thirteen trial scenes: Greek trials 1, 4, 5, 7, 8, 9, 10, 11, and 12.

[30] Greek trials 2, 5, 6, 7, 8, 9, 11, 13.

[31] The accuser may lay hands on the criminal directly (Greek trials 6, 7, 9, and 13) or have servants do it (8 and 11) but more usually gives orders for the criminal to be bound and taken away (2, 5, 7, 9, and 11). In some instances, the alleged criminal is confined either in a small room of a house (7 and 9) or in a public jail (8), and in one case given over to a guard (11).

[32] The significant exception to this is Clitophon's detention in the novel of Achilles Tatius, discussed in connection with the arrest of Peter below. For the

it is usually only for the night, until the court opens the next morning.³³ Taken out of the trial context, scenes of arrest are often indistinguishable from many other scenes in the novels where a protagonist is captured, enslaved, beaten, verbally abused, or confined.

THE ACCUSATION

In the majority of scenes (ten out of thirteen), the male protagonist of the novel is the defendant.³⁴ The only heroines to assume this role are Heliodorus's Charicleia, and Melite, a secondary female protagonist in the novel of Achilles Tatius.³⁵ On the other hand, the accusers are generally characterized as villains,³⁶ while more rarely the protagonist takes on the role of accuser.³⁷ This situation occurs in the trial of the bandit Theron for kidnapping the novel's heroine and selling her into slavery (Greek trial 2), a trial exceptional for its glorification of the public execution of a wicked villain.³⁸ In other novels, the villains are more likely to run away or kill themselves out of view of the reader. Characters who are otherwise portrayed in a neutral or positive light assume the role of villain by virtue of their opposition to the hero in a trial scene. Thus, for example, the figure of Dionysius in Chariton's novel is the protagonist in the first Babylonian trial (Greek trial 3); however, in the second trial (4) Dionysius is transformed into the antagonist by the reappearance of Chaereas, the novel's hero.³⁹ The typical trial scene thus amplifies the moral dichotomy between the protagonist and antagonist.

---

depiction of prison in Christian narrative, see Judith Perkins, "Social Geography in the *Apocryphal Acts of the Apostles*," in *Space in the Ancient Novel* (ed. M. Paschalis and S. Frangoulidis; Ancient Narrative, Supplementum 1; Groningen: Barkhuis, 2002), 125–29.

³³ As in Greek trials 7, 9, and 11.

³⁴ Greek trials 1, 4, 5, 6, 7, 8, 9, 10, 11, and 13. Note that in 9 and 10 the defendants are Cnemon and his father Aristippus, respectively. While Cnemon is technically not the main male protagonist of the novel, he functions as such in a lengthy inset narration. On Cnemon's role in the narrative, see John R. Morgan, "The Story of Knemon in Heliodoros' *Aithiopika*," *JHS* 109 (1989): 99–113.

³⁵ The female protagonists are more likely to assume a passive role, as the objects over which men contend in the trials. They are involved in trials insofar as their safety or marital status gives rise to legal actions. Cf. trials 1, 2, 3, 4, 7, 8, 12, and 13.

³⁶ Greek trials 5, 6, 7, 8, and 11.

³⁷ Greek trials 2, 3, and 12.

³⁸ The other two cases where the accuser is a protagonist are Greek trial 3, where Dionysius, a secondary hero, accuses Mithridates of attempting to seduce his wife; and Greek trial 12, where Charicleia brings a case against Hydaspes, the Ethiopian king who is her long-lost father.

³⁹ Similarly, see Greek trials 9 and 13.

THE CONVENING OF THE COURT

Descriptions of the convening and adjournment of the court serve to mark the trial scene from the rest of the narrative. Trials are set in Greek cities as well as in the courts of barbarian kings and of imperial officials.[40] Regardless of the setting, the beginning of the trial scene is formally marked by a description of how or when the court convenes, who presides over the court, what the courtroom looks like, or some other such detail. For example, Chariton exploits the proverbial opulence and rigid etiquette of the Persian court in a lavish description that serves to indicate that this courtroom will be the site of a trial grander than the previous two trials in the novel (Chariton 5.4.5–7). However, not all courtrooms are described in such detail. Often the novelists simply refer to the court by a generic term (e.g., "the next day I was brought before the demos," Heliodorus 1.13.1) and rely upon the readers to use their knowledge of how trials are supposed to work to fill in the details. A variety of legal procedures is also reflected in the novels. In general, the novelists use such details as will lend a realistic-sounding aura to the trial; upon closer scrutiny, however, historical anachronisms and imprecise terminology abound. All the novelists, to a greater or lesser degree, use a pastiche method to create a plausibly realistic courtroom.

A PAIR OF SPEECHES

Verbal debate is the centerpiece of the trial scene. Trials in the novel display an interest in speech as a means of persuasion and of revealing the truth. Because authors are able to place a speech in a detailed, circumstantial framework, there is a degree of reliability in such means of persuasion. In this respect, orations in the novel are fundamentally different from the declamations. The novelist has the power to create in the reader's mind the illusion of objective truth. Sometimes this dramatic irony highlights the hollowness of the adversary's rhetoric. For example, in Chariton's first trial in Babylon (Greek trial 3) the case resolves around a letter addressed to Callirhoe from her first husband Chaereas, who is presumed dead. Her second husband Dionysius (here the protagonist) alleges the letter was forged by the satrap Mithridates as a scheme to seduce Callirhoe. The reader knows that Chaereas is in fact alive and did in fact write the letter and therefore that Dionysius's account of Mithridates's scheme is not factually correct. That this mistake leads to judicial proceedings in the sublime court of the Persian capital

---

[40] Greek cities: Syracuse (Greek trials 1 and 2), Ephesus (7 and 8), and Athens (9 and 10). Palaces of barbarian kings: Persia (3 and 4), Ethiopia (12 and 13). Imperial officials: prefect of Egypt (5), Persian satrap of Memphis (11).

raises the stakes. The narrative presents a wonderfully self-righteous, as well as rhetorically brilliant, defense speech by Mithridates, at the climax of which he reveals Chaereas. The defendant throws the courtroom into disorder while at the same time clinching his legal victory—an impressive finale to the scene.

THE SPECTATORS' REACTIONS

The internal audience functions similarly to a chorus in Greek drama. The spectators' reactions echo and amplify the response of the ideal reader, who is expected to identify to some degree with the internal audience. Descriptions of the spectators' emotions—joy, anger, astonishment, or pity—punctuate the trial scene at key moments. A prominent theme is the public interest in private matters and the absence of matters of serious political importance from the city. For example, in Chariton's novel the city of Syracuse functions as an emotional backdrop to the drama of the family of the city's leader, Hermocrates. The assembly meets not to discuss affairs of state but to urge the marriage of the young protagonists of the novel. The heroine's death becomes a matter of the greatest civic concern, and the trial of Chaereas is portrayed as a grandiose public event. Hermocrates' authority takes precedence over the political institutions of the city, which function merely to ratify his decisions. Here, as elsewhere, the inclusion of an audience of spectators as a reactive element in the trial scenes furthers the creation of dramatic irony. The audience's emotions intensify the reader's anticipation of the revelation of what the reader already knows and so theoretically reinforces the reader's confidence in the truthfulness of the ultimate outcome of the trial and of the plot of the novel as a whole.[41]

A SURPRISING TWIST

Chance and paradox play large roles in the trials, as they do in the novels as a whole. Evidence and witnesses appear by chance at the last moment. Sometimes critical pieces of information appear not by chance but by the design of parties to the trial. The paradoxical situation of an

---

[41] The more sophisticated novelists play upon, and subvert, the reader's expectations. The strategies of the Latin novelist Apuleius are discussed in John J. Winkler, *Auctor and Actor: A Narratological Reading of Apuleius's The Golden Ass* (Berkeley and Los Angeles: University of California Press, 1985). For narratological readings of the Greek novels of Achilles Tatius and Heliodorus, see idem, "The Mendacity of Kalasiris and the Narrative Strategy of Heliodoros' *Aithiopika*," YCS 27 (1982): 93–158; and Shadi Bartsch, *Decoding the Ancient Novel: The Reader and the Role of Description in Heliodorus and Achilles Tatius* (Princeton: Princeton University Press, 1989).

innocent person who willfully confesses to a false accusation is so commonplace in the novels as to be a cliché.[42] This strategy, recognized and labeled by the Greek declaimers as the *prosangeleia,* or self-denunciation, is employed by people desperate to commit suicide. It is, as Donald Russell has aptly observed, a form of "ostentatious euthanasia."[43] The novelists do their best to maximize the shock value of such paradoxes by placing them at critical moments and by exaggerating the surprised reaction of the spectators.

THE VERDICT

The moral universe of the novels tends to be painted in black and white, and the reader is rarely in doubt as to the guilt or innocence of the parties involved in the trial scenes. Despite this, trials often result in verdicts that are contrary to what the reader knows is right. Indeed, they often confound or subvert justice and thereby perpetuate the dramatic conflict. It is not uncommon for one trial to lead to another. Many trials, for instance, form parts of extended legal actions.[44] Trials are rarely simple affairs: their very complexity is the key to their entertainment value. Other trials fail to come to a verdict because certain dilemmas are simply irresolvable.[45] In the novel of Achilles Tatius, the trials in Ephesus become so convoluted that the only way out is a pair of trials by ordeal, whereby the sexual honor of the two women on trial is vindicated. The ordeals function as a *deus ex machina,* a convenient device to bring an extremely complicated legal dilemma to a suitably spectacular ending.[46]

PUNISHMENT

If the defendant is convicted, the punishment becomes a moment of high drama. Modes of punishment are always painful and spectacular: crucifixion, burning at the stake, precipitation from a cliff, and torture. Sometimes the punishment is carried out, but more usually it is interrupted at the last moment. The more spectacular the punishment decreed, the greater the pathos of the wrongly punished defendant. Justice is instead accomplished through other means, such as miracles, religious tests, or trials in battle. For example, the hero of Xenophon's novel is falsely accused

---

[42] This occurs in Greek trials 1, 7, and 11.

[43] Russell, *Greek Declamation,* 35–36.

[44] The Babylonian trials in Chariton (Greek trials 3 and 4), the Ephesian trials in Achilles Tatius (7 and 8), and the Athenian trials in Heliodorus (9 and 10).

[45] An especially successful conundrum for prolonging a complex narrative involves the bigamous wife; see Callirhoe in Chariton (Greek trials 3 and 4), and Melite in Achilles Tatius (7 and 8).

[46] Greek trials 5, 8, 11, and 12.

of murder by a woman because he refused to become her lover. He is found guilty and sentenced to execution. Miraculously, every time the executioner ties him up to his cross, he is freed by a sudden intervention of nature (e.g., a wind blows his cross off a cliff and into a river, but the water does not harm him). Poetic justice lies outside the parameters of the law and occurs on the level of Providence or Fortune, such as when Achilles Tatius's hero is saved from public torture by a suspension in public business upon the fortuitous arrival of a sacred delegation to Artemis.

The constructed character of the novelistic trials would seem to allow a certain critical perspective on the legal system; in fact, however, the depiction of the legal system—the laws, the judges, the magistrates, the jury—is almost always neutral. This is true even in the most tyrannical of settings. In Heliodorus's novel, even when the irredeemably wicked wife of the Persian satrap falsely accuses the blameless heroine of murder, the laws of Persia are portrayed as a check on tyrannical power. Although Chariton's Persian king falls victim to his own libido, he recognizes that it interferes with his ability to perform as a reasonable judge. In the end, he sacrifices his love for her in the interest of preserving the balance of power in his kingdom. If there is ever any criticism, it is aimed at the character rather than the institution. In the larger narrative, the authority of the ruler is ultimately upheld, as the blame for injustice is deflected onto unruly subordinates. Thus, the overall *mentalité* reflected in the novels is profoundly conservative.

TRIALS IN ACTS

Before discussing similarities, it is necessary to emphasize the significant differences between the trials in the novels and those in Acts. The most significant are that the setting of Acts is contemporary and that the author assumes an openly historiographical pose. Whereas the Greek novels studiously avoid any overt reference to Rome, in Acts Roman power frames the action of the trial scenes. Many episodes, especially the trials of Paul in Acts 21–26, turn on Paul's possession of Roman citizenship; in the Greek novels, Hellenic identity serves an analogous function. Because of its contemporary setting, Acts reflects the technicalities of the Roman administration of justice more directly. There are also ideological differences between the texts. The Greek novels are driven by the ideology of mutual, heterosexual love and chastity leading to marriage; Acts is propelled forward by the evangelization of Christianity. The crimes of passion in the Greek novels (murder, adultery) are replaced by crimes against religion (blasphemy, teaching against the law of the temple, profaning the temple, introduction of an alien religion) or against the state (disturbing the peace, claiming that there is a king other than Caesar).

However, with respect to the formal construction of the narratives, the differences are not as significant as might be supposed. The criteria for the definition of a trial scene established for the Greek novels may also be fruitfully applied to Acts. In Acts, there are fourteen scenes that meet the definition of a trial scene (*see the list in table 2 on pages 136–37*). The trials in Acts fall into three groups: early, middle, and final. Trials 1–4 are set in Jerusalem and involve the apostles; they form the early group. The middle group (trials 5–9) features Paul in the Aegean. Paul is the central character in the final group (10–14) as well, which consists of the series of legal episodes in Judea. Within each group, the narratives of the trials are best understood as a sequence. As in the Greek novels, the trials form a narrative crescendo. Each trial in a series is more intense—its venue more exalted—than the previous one.

There are more individual legal scenes in Acts than there are in the five Greek novels put together. Some of these are in fact parts of larger legal action; nevertheless, it is clear that law is a predominant concern of Acts.[47] The main purpose of the trial scenes is to highlight the defendant's faith, and it is not always easy to separate adversarial from inquisitorial procedures.[48] Typically, the trial consists of an apostle being brought into court to answer charges arising as a result of his evangelical activities. The court is hostile at worst, tepid or apathetic at best. In several instances a single judge is persuaded, or almost persuaded, by the defendant's message (the council in the first trial, Gamaliel the Pharisee, the jailer in Philippi, Dionysius the Areopagite, Agrippa). In other cases, the judge is scared (the magistrates in Philippi, military tribune in Jerusalem, Felix). The spectators, when they are differentiated from the judges, tend to be characterized as a mob (ὄχλος), and almost always an angry one. They exhibit a wider range of emotions than the crowds in the Greek novels.[49] Unlike with the internal audiences in the Greek novels, in Acts the sympathies of the ideal reader are expected to be counter to the responses of at least a portion of the internal audience. As Robert Tannehill has observed, "the people are a fertile field for the Christian mission, yet, just as in the passion story, they are fickle and easily swayed by false charges."[50] Throughout Acts,

---

[47] For a brief study of the legal vocabulary in Acts, see Allison A. Trites, "The Importance of Legal Scenes and Language in the Book of Acts," *NovT* 16 (1974): 278–84.

[48] For the sake of convenience, on table 2 the person who has the authority to make a decision in the case is classified under the column heading "judge."

[49] Richard S. Ascough, "Narrative Technique and Generic Designation: Crowd Scenes in Luke-Acts and in Chariton," *CBQ* 58 (1996): 69–82; Pervo, *Profit with Delight*, 34–42.

[50] Robert C. Tannehill, *The Narrative Unity of Luke-Acts: A Literary Interpretation* (2 vols.; Minneapolis: Fortress, 1986–90), 2:60.

the variability of this *chorus,* as it were, alienates the reader from the internal audience: the text encourages the readers to view themselves as separate from the mob.

An analysis of the trials in Acts according to these criteria reveals certain details of the larger narrative structure. In the following section, the analysis of the philosophical and theological content of the speeches has been left to one side so as to emphasize the dramatic framework within which the speeches are presented.[51]

THE EARLY GROUP: TRIALS OF THE APOSTLES IN JERUSALEM

The pattern of emotional intensification can be seen clearly in the first three trials of the early group. The setting is the same for each of the three, namely, the council in Jerusalem (Sanhedrin). The narrative does not dwell upon a precise delineation of the procedures of the council in Jerusalem; rather, priests, elders, scribes, Pharisees, and Sadducees tend to form a collective mass of hostile inquisitors.[52] The trials in the Jewish courts perform a similar narrative function as the trials in barbarian courts in the Greek novels in that both are fraught with danger. The heroes' ignorance of, or in the case of Acts, active resistance to, the customs of the court places their lives in jeopardy. Despite the foreignness of the barbarian courts in the Greek novels, there is rarely an acknowledgment of linguistic differences: the barbarians speak Greek.[53] This is also the case in Acts, because the author does not acknowledge that the proceedings would have been carried on in a different language. For a Greco-Roman audience, the various officials and factions of the Sanhedrin, the high priest's role in leading the accusation, and the theological differences at issue would have marked the court in Jerusalem as exotic.

The procedure in these trials is an interrogation: the apostles are arrested and hauled before the Sanhedrin to explain themselves.[54] The charges in the first two trials are essentially the same. In the first, the charge is that the apostles "were teaching the people and proclaiming in Jesus the resurrection of the dead" (Acts 4:2). In the second, the charge is that the

---

[51] For a fuller account of the theological implications of the narrative structures in Acts, as well as their relationship with Luke's Gospel, see Charles H. Talbert, *Literary Patterns, Theological Themes, and the Genre of Luke-Acts* (SBLMS 20; Missoula, Mont.: Scholars Press, 1974); and Tannehill, *Narrative Unity of Luke-Acts.*

[52] On echoes of Jewish law in the narrative of Acts, see Stephen G. Wilson, *Luke and the Law* (SNTSMS 50; Cambridge: Cambridge University Press, 1983); and Craig L. Blomberg, "The Law in Luke-Acts," *JSNT* 22 (1984): 53–80.

[53] Heliodorus is the exception. On language in the Greek novels, see Suzanne Saïd, "Les langues du roman grec," in Baslez et al., *Le monde du roman grec,* 169–86.

[54] Tannehill (*Narrative Unity of Luke-Acts,* 2:63) has also noted this pattern.

apostles continued to teach despite the first warning and, furthermore, that they "intend to bring this man's blood upon us" (Acts 5:28). The first trial establishes the framework for the subsequent trial: it dramatizes the steadfastness of Peter and John in the face of opposition and emphasizes the persuasiveness of their message. The judges suspect that Peter and John are legitimate, but they fear the masses. What makes the message so persuasive is that Peter and John are uneducated (ἀγράμματοι; Acts 4:13). The author emphasizes the cultural gulf between the defendants and the judges, while at the same time reflecting a suspicion of cleverness. This is seen in the Greek novels as well; for example, in Chariton's first Babylonian trial (Greek trial 3) Dionysius the Ionian Greek is out of his element in the Persian court, while his opponent, the lustful barbarian satrap Mithridates, presents an overly clever speech. Acts repeatedly uses a narrative technique whereby the private deliberations of the court are presented to the reader; this does not appear as often in the novelistic trials, where the judges rarely speak in *oratio recta,* except to declare the verdict.[55] At the end of the first trial in Acts, the court sends the apostles off with a warning.

The interval between the first and second trials creates an opportunity in the narrative to juxtapose an alternative model of justice: the scene in Acts 5 when Peter confronts Ananias and his wife Sapphira about withholding part of their donation to the church. Peter intuits the truth and confronts Ananias, whereupon Ananias falls down and dies. Peter then confronts Ananias's wife, and the same thing happens, with the result that everyone is afraid. This scene establishes that God is working through Peter; Peter acts not under his own authority but merely serves as a conduit for divine justice.

The trial of the apostles in Jerusalem (Acts trial 2) is a reiteration and intensification of the trial of Peter and John.[56] The defendants are now the apostles as a group, and they are not identified by name. This time the element of the arrest is reduplicated: the apostles are arrested once and freed by an angel, so the arrest is repeated and thus intensified. The judging body now includes not only the officials, who constitute the Sanhedrin

---

[55] Cf. Acts trial 2, where the Sanhedrin sends the apostles outside of the court while they discuss the case. In Acts trial 10, the military tribune interrogates Paul in the barracks. Similarly, in trial 12, Felix summons Paul for a private discussion with him and his wife, while in trial 14 the narrative presents a letter in which Festus explains to Agrippa that he does not understand the charges against Paul. In Chariton's novel, the thoughts of the Persian king are presented in the narrative, but they are external to the trial scene proper. For example, he reflects upon the case when he reads Pharnaces' petition and discusses it with his councilors (Chariton 4.6.5–6). Between the two trials, the king ponders what to do both privately (6.1.8–12) and with his chief eunuch (6.3).

[56] Tannehill, *Narrative Unity of Luke-Acts,* 2:64, 74–77.

(Acts 4:5; τοὺς ἄρχοντας καὶ τοὺς πρεσβυτέρους καὶ τοὺς γραμματεῖς ἐν Ἰερουσαλήμ), but also the senate of Israel (Acts 5:21; τὸ συνέδριον καὶ πᾶσαν τὴν γερουσίαν τῶν υἱῶν Ἰσραήλ). Chariton uses a similar device in his Syracusan trials: the first trial (Greek trial 1) takes place before the citizen assembly, the second before an assembly of men and women. In the first trial, Chaereas is acquitted for homicide on the grounds that Chaereas did not kill Callirhoe intentionally. The second trial in Syracuse, that of the pirate Theron, almost ends with another acquittal, but thanks to a last-minute recognition of Theron as the true culprit by one of the onlookers the trial instead culminates in an execution witnessed by the entire city.

The effect of this pattern is to create a steady intensification of the issues at hand, all the while heightening the reader's anticipation for the moment when the truth—the guilt of Theron in Chariton's second trial—becomes known to the entire city. This use of irony can also be seen in the prelude to the second trial scene in Acts. As Tannehill notes, the description of the jailers' confusion when they find the prison empty and the lame attempts by the officers of the temple to understand what was happening is pervaded by a sense of dramatic irony (Acts 5:22–25).[57] After the apostles are found once again teaching in the temple, they are arrested and brought before the Sanhedrin. The result of this second trial is essentially the same as that of the first, but with this addition: the apostles, while again told to stop their activities, are beaten before being released.

The martyrdom of Stephen is the third in the first series of trials in Acts, and this trial brings the antagonism to a climax. While Stephen is singled out by name, his accusers are a generalized third-person plural. The impression created in this trial scene, as opposed to the previous two, is that of a single individual versus a mass of angry enemies. The narrative emphasizes Stephen's appearance: he has the "face of an angel" (Acts 6:15). Likewise, in the Greek novels, when the author wants to heighten the pathos of the trial scene, he describes the grief-stricken or fearful appearance of the litigants as they approach the court. For example, when the satrap Mithridates enters the court of the Persian king to defend himself, he appears "by no means bright and cheerful, but, as befits an accused man, pitiable."[58] The author of Acts seems to be deliberately subverting this conventional description of the defendant's fearful expression: after he delivers his speech, Stephen sees the heavens opening (Acts 7:55–56). By the time Heliodorus wrote his novel in the third or fourth century, the

---

[57] Ibid., 2:67–68. Although I would not go so far as Tannehill in seeing this as an example of burlesque, I agree that the dramatic irony adds to the heightening of the reader's anticipation for the ending of this second trial.

[58] Chariton 5.4.7: οὐ πάνυ τι λαμπρὸς οὐδὲ φαιδρός, ἀλλ᾽, ὡς ὑπεύθυνος, ἐλεεινός.

inversion of the convention may have already made its way back into the Greek novel tradition. This possibility is apparent in Greek trial 11, where Charicleia's radiant beauty proclaims her innocence as the pyre's flames magically encircle her without burning.[59]

The trial of Stephen cannot be resolved, and thus the scene devolves into violence. The Greek novelists also favored insoluble dilemmas: the second Babylonian trial in Chariton's novel (Greek trial 4) is an example. Two men have equally legitimate claims to be the husband of Callirhoe; the case cannot be settled with a simple verdict. Accordingly, Chariton cuts off the trial before it begins by introducing a new twist: a rebellion on the frontiers of the Persian Empire interrupts the trial and takes the king's attention away from finding a verdict. In the subsequent narrative, the rivalry of the two men is transposed to the field of war, where violence is ennobled. Chaereas's victory in battle, which leads to his reclaiming of his wife, is described as a glorious exploit in the mold of Alexander the Great.

In Acts, Stephen's trial is similarly insoluble. The hardening opposition of the temple authorities makes Stephen's acquittal impossible. The normal mechanisms of the court cannot effect a just verdict. Instead, the trial ends with a shocking form of mass violence that, while occasionally intimated in the Greek novels, never brings about the death of the hero.[60] Stephen's martyrdom serves a function in the narrative parallel to the ordeal in the Greek novels: it is a way to bring to an end a series of escalating trials that have no solution, while at the same time vindicating the claims of the defendant. The ending of the scene, though violent, has a paradoxically positive element: Stephen becomes a martyr. Although his death sets off a wave of persecutions, it leads to the spread of the apostles' teachings beyond Jerusalem—the motif driving the plot of Acts.[61] This ending brings the first series of trials to a dramatic close.

The arrest of Peter in Acts 12:1–25 is somewhat tangential to the sequence of trials in the early group. It contains elements of the previous trial scenes. From the previous three scenes, the reader fully expects that Peter's arrest will lead to a violent ending, perhaps even more so than

---

[59] Heliodorus 8.9.13: περιαυγάζεσθαι μόνον καὶ διοπτεύεσθαι παρέχοντος ἐπιφαιδρυνομένην ἐκ τοῦ περιαυγάσματος τὸ κάλλος καὶ οἶον ἐν πυρίνῳ θαλάμῳ νυμφευομένην. The parallels between the scene of her execution on the pyre (albeit thwarted) and deaths of martyrs are often noted; cf. *Polycarp* 16 and *Pionius* 22. See Bowersock, *Fiction as History*, 143.

[60] For example, see the end of Charicleia's trial in Heliodorus 8.9.15, where the crowd of spectators imposes itself between Charicleia and the despot Arsace, rushing toward the pyre to rescue the heroine from the flames.

[61] Tannehill, *Narrative Unity of Luke-Acts*, 2:100–101.

Stephen's martyrdom.[62] The venue is different: it is set in the court of Herod, who is portrayed as a despot, a character type that appears repeatedly in the novels. The despot is violent, disregards due process, rules by whim, and is driven by his (or her) appetites.[63] As in the first trial of the apostles (Acts trial 2), Peter is arrested, thrown in jail, and freed by an angel; this latter episode, however, represents an incomplete trial scene, as Peter successfully escapes before he can be brought to trial. After Herod's guards fail to find Peter to arrest him again, Herod summarily executes them instead. The narrative then immediately moves to a scene of Herod holding court in Caesarea. The use of the verb ἐδημηγόρει ("to make a speech"; Acts 12:21) for Herod's speech suggests that this is an address to the assembly rather than a pronouncement in a forensic court.[64] Herod's speech functions as the opening speech in a trial scene: it occupies the position in the narrative where the formula of the trial scene requires a speech of prosecution. The speech itself is presented indirectly, since the substance of what he says is less important than the circumstances. The audience praises Herod as having the voice of a god, whereupon an angel strikes Herod down. Here we see poetic, or divine, justice superimposed upon the structure of a trial scene—suddenly aborted midway through the scene.[65] The blameless apostle escapes, and the tyrant pays the penalty.

THE MIDDLE GROUP: TRIALS IN THE GREEK WORLD

The middle group of trials (Acts trials 5–9) is the most episodic and varied of the three groups of trials in Acts. Temporal phrases marking the

---

[62] On the parallelisms of this trial to Peter's earlier trial in Acts 4–5, as well as to the trial of Jesus in Luke, see ibid., 2:152–53.

[63] Examples of despots in the novels are the Persian king in Chariton's novel (ultimately reinterpreted as a benevolent king); Manto, the daughter of Habrocomes' master, in the novel of Xenophon of Ephesus; Thersander, whose name means "wild man," in the novel of Achilles Tatius; Arsace, the wife of the satrap of Memphis in Heliodorus's novel.

[64] Although the distinction between deliberative speech (δημηγορία) and forensic speech (δικανική) was deeply embedded in rhetorical thought (see Aristotle, *Rhet.* 1.1.10), in fictional narrative there is often considerable overlap.

[65] Precise parallels can be drawn between this trial and a scene preliminary to the trial of Clitophon in Achilles Tatius's novel (Greek trial 7). This is the arrest of Clitophon by Thersander, a stereotypical despot. Pervo calls this a "scathing parody" of the "sacred incarcerations" found in aretologies (*Profit with Delight*, 22). I would tentatively suggest that Achilles Tatius is using this specific scene in Acts. It is neither a parody nor a programmatic attack on Christianity as much as it is a playful pastiche. Achilles Tatius is quite capable of borrowing and playing with motifs from a wide range of texts, among them (perhaps) Christian literature (see Bowersock, *Fiction as History*, 125–26, 133).

beginning of trials are more vague than those in the early or the final group. However, the description of the legal procedures is richly textured. Paul's travels in the Aegean feature a smorgasbord of legal settings: a colony of Roman citizens (Philippi), a proconsular tribunal (Corinth), a citizen assembly in one free Greek city (Ephesus), and a venerable oligarchic council in another (Athens).[66] The charges against Paul are equally varied. In Philippi and Thessalonica Paul is charged with troublemaking. The charges are recast to make sense within a Roman context; for example, in Thessalonica (trial 6) Paul is accused of what seems to be treason, that is, claiming that there is a king other than Caesar.[67] He must address attacks about his introduction of alien deities or of illegal religious practices from polytheists, philosophers, and Jews alike (trials 5, 7, 8, and 9). A. N. Sherwin-White notes that, although the charges appear to be archaic or garbled, the procedures are in good order.[68] In all these trials Paul manages to evade the authorities. In two of them, despite being the intended target of the accusations, Paul is not present at the trial (trials 6 and 9) and other people get into trouble (Silas, Jason and his brothers; Gaius and Aristarchus; Alexander, the spokesman for the Jews in Ephesus). Many of the trials do not result in clear verdicts: Paul escapes; he is released; the case is dismissed; or the case is remanded to another venue. However, this is not dissimilar from the Greek novels, where even when the court comes back with a verdict, it is often quickly overturned by the events that follow.

The middle group of trials in Acts is quite different both from the earlier trials in Acts and from the trials in the Greek novels. In the first part of Acts, the scenes in the court in Jerusalem provide a moment for the defendant to proclaim his faith; in this second section, those moments of formal declaration of faith take place for the most part outside of the courtroom. For example, in Philippi (trial 5) a break in the proceedings creates narrative space for a scene in the prison. After an earthquake shakes the jail,

---

[66] Tannehill discusses four public-accusation type-scenes in Acts 16–19 (*Narrative Unity of Luke-Acts*, 2:201–3). These are the scenes I have identified as trials 5, 6, 8, and 9 in Acts. Tannehill omits the scene of Paul's appearance before the Areopagus. He suggests that the balance between Jewish accusers in his second and third scenes (Thessalonica and Corinth) and Gentile accusers in the first and fourth (Philippi and Corinth) "may be deliberate" (2:203). The neat symmetry is disrupted if the accusers in Philippi are Jewish, as argued by Daniel Schwartz, "The Accusation and the Accusers at Philippi (Acts 16,20–21)," *Bib* 65 (1984): 357–63.

[67] Acts 17:7: καὶ οὗτοι πάντες ἀπέναντι τῶν δογμάτων Καίσαρος πράσσουσιν βασιλέα ἕτερον λέγοντες εἶναι Ἰησοῦν.

[68] Adrian N. Sherwin-White, *Roman Society and Roman Law in the New Testament* (Oxford: Clarendon, 1963), 79–82, 96.

Paul sits with the jailer and converts him. This scene functions in lieu of a defense speech, and it is transposed to a significantly different space: the private sphere of the prison. Rather than escaping, as Peter had done, Paul remains in the prison. Ironically, the jailer, a figure who usually tends to be a servile and faceless instrument of the court in the novels, is Paul's addressee here. Paul's speech is appropriately simple and direct: "Believe and you will be saved" (16:31).

The trial of Paul in Thessalonica and his hearing before the Areopagus in Athens are two separate scenes, but from the perspective of the formula of the trial scene they form two halves of a single trial, albeit one set in two different cities. In the first (trial 6), Paul flees from Thessalonica before his accusers can arrest him. Instead, they arrest Paul's hosts, bring them to the *politarchoi* (the city magistrates in charge of dealing with foreigners) and lodge charges that are really targeted at Paul. The hosts are conditionally released from custody, and the legal action in Thessalonica is apparently finished; however, the formula of the trial scene demands that each speech in the narrative of prosecution be counterbalanced by a defense speech. This function is fulfilled by Paul's *apologia* before the Areopagus in Athens, which comes immediately after the Thessalonica episode, thus forming the second half of the trial, in which the setting shifts to a more prestigious venue. The symbolic significance of the Areopagus is the central reason for the insertion of this scene into the narrative; it seems to be, as Conzelmann has observed, a "purely literary creation."[69] Although the philosophers in Athens do not charge Paul and arrest him, their action of "haling him up to the Areopagus" is almost identical to other phrases used for arrests.[70] Such a mid-trial change of scenery is not unparalleled in the Greek novels: in the novel of Heliodorus (Greek trial 13), Charicles appeals to the assembly of Delphi to pursue Theagenes, his daughter's kidnapper. Theagenes, who also happens to be the hero of the novel, is accused *in*

---

[69] Hans Conzelmann, "The Address of Paul on the Areopagus," in *Studies in Luke-Acts: Essays Presented in Honor of Paul Schubert* (ed. L. E. Keck and J. L. Martyn; Nashville: Abingdon, 1966), 218.

[70] The formula is "seizing/grabbing [the defendant], they led/dragged him to [the judge or court], and said [accusation]." In the Areopagus trial (Acts 17:19) we find: ἐπιλαβόμενοί τε αὐτοῦ ἐπὶ τὸν Ἄρειον πάγον ἤγαγον λέγοντες. Cf. Acts 16:19–20, the arrest of Paul and Silas in Philippi: ἐπιλαβόμενοι τὸν Παῦλον καὶ τὸν Σίλαν εἵλκυσαν εἰς τὴν ἀγορὰν ἐπὶ τοὺς ἄρχοντας καὶ προσαγαγόντες αὐτοὺς τοῖς στρατηγοῖς εἶπαν; Acts 17:6, the arrest of Jason and brothers in Thessalonica: ἔσυρον Ἰάσονα καί τινας ἀδελφοὺς ἐπὶ τοὺς πολιτάρχας βοῶντες; and Acts 18:12, the arrest of Paul in Corinth: κατεπέστησαν ὁμοθυμαδὸν οἱ Ἰουδαῖοι τῷ Παύλῳ καὶ ἤγαγον αὐτὸν ἐπὶ τὸ βῆμα, λέγοντες (cf. also the similar pattern with Stephen [6:12–13; cf. 4:3] in the earlier set of trials and with Paul in the later set [21:27–30]).

absentia: by the time of the trial, he has already fled from the city. It is not until the final scene of the novel that Charicles finally catches up with Theagenes in the Ethiopian city of Meroe. Like the Areopagus in Paul's trial, the court of the Ethiopian king is presented as the most venerable and just in the world. In both Acts and in the novel of Heliodorus, this elevated courtroom is the setting for the hero's vindication: the case against Theagenes dissolves into an emotional scene of confessions, and Paul at least comes to no harm, even persuading one member of the Areopagus to convert.

In Corinth (Acts trial 8), an accusation is lodged against Paul; again he does not respond. The proconsul Gallio shuts him up before he has an opportunity to make his *apologia*. The pattern of the hero who is not allowed to speak in his defense is also seen in the Greek novels. This occurs in a type-scene that transposes the elements of a trial scene from the public to the private sphere—the stock scene of domestic discipline. Typically, the accused is a slave and is brought before the master of the household for interrogation and punishment. As in the trial scenes, in the Greek novels the accused is usually the protagonist, who has been reduced to slavery. The falsity of the accusation is a given. The accuser tells the master a tale that the reader knows is pure slander, but the master, instantly horrified by the crime, condemns the hero to a painful punishment without even hearing his defense.[71] This configuration can be transposed to the public realm. For example, Xenophon of Ephesus sets this scene in the court of the prefect of Egypt (Greek trial 5): Habrocomes is falsely accused of murder and brought before the assembly of Pelusium. They in turn send him to the prefect of Egypt, who listens to the accusations and immediately condemns Habrocomes to death by crucifixion. Ultimately, the master (or magistrate) discovers his mistake, sends for the hero, apologizes, and makes restitution to him. In the world of the novels, speech is a marker of *paideia*, the education that identified a person as a free Hellene rather than a barbarian or a slave. The formula of the mistaken punishment is built on the assumption that if only the hero is given the opportunity to open his mouth, his inherent superiority will be obvious to all and he will automatically be vindicated. Paul's trial in Corinth represents an inversion of this: in this case, the magistrate is not persuaded by the accusers, and the defendant is prohibited from speaking but is freed anyway.

---

[71] Examples are to be found in the scenes of punishment of Chaereas in the household of Mithridates (Chariton 4.2–3) and the punishment of Habrocomes in the house of Apsyrtus (Xenophon of Ephesus 2.5–10). For a detailed discussion, see Schwartz, "Courtroom Scenes in the Ancient Greek Novels," 115–27.

The last in the middle series of trials in Acts, Paul's trial in the theater in Ephesus (Acts trial 9), is literally the most spectacular. The setting accurately reflects the contemporary use of theaters as common meeting places for assemblies in the imperial period.[72] Theaters also function as a setting for trials in the Greek novels, as in the emergency meeting of the citizen assembly called to try Chaereas (Greek trial 2). Heliodorus presents a similar emergency session of the assembly of Delphi in the case of the kidnapping of Charicleia (trial 13), an account inspired by the vivid narrative of the meeting of the Athenian assembly in Demosthenes' *De Corona* (169–173). In the novels there are a number of scenes of *acclamatio*, a practice that was a feature of Greek civic life during the empire.[73] This trial is especially dangerous because the accusers, the judges (i.e., the assembly), and the spectators are fused into one large, angry mob. The hostile reaction to the abortive defense speech by Alexander indicates the futility of addressing the crowd. Thus the narrative tacitly excuses Paul for not making the obligatory defense in Ephesus.[74]

THE FINAL GROUP: TRIALS OF PAUL IN JUDEA

The final group of trial scenes in Acts returns to Jerusalem and Judea, as Paul's legal troubles and the involvement of the Roman authorities in the face of antagonism from the Jews form the central focus of the narrative.[75] After the episodic character of the previous sections, the narrative time slows down significantly in this final set of trials. Again, the narrative structures the trials in sets of increasing intensity. Reduplications as well as elisions invite the reader to make connections to previous events and to anticipate potential outcomes.

By its nature, the trial scene is a formula for suspense. Accusations and arrests create an emotionally charged atmosphere that culminates in a moment when two differing interpretations of events are pitted against one another. The expectation of a final verdict keeps the reader reading. The skillful narrator leads the readers on by continually holding out the

---

[72] Eric Csapo and William J. Slater, *The Context of Ancient Drama* (Ann Arbor: University of Michigan Press, 1995), 286, 291, 300–301; and William A. McDonald, *The Political Meeting Places of the Greeks* (Baltimore: Johns Hopkins University Press, 1943), 37–96.

[73] Clifford Ando, *Imperial Ideology and Provincial Loyalty in the Roman Empire* (Berkeley and Los Angeles: University of California Press, 2000), 199–205; Colin, *Les villes libres de l'Orient gréco-romain;* and Charlotte Roueché, "Acclamations in the Later Roman Empire: New Evidence from Aphrodisias," *JRS* 74 (1984): 181–99.

[74] For parallels to the Greek novels, see Pervo, *Profit with Delight*, 36–39.

[75] For an analysis of the legal realia of this section, see Sherwin-White, *Roman Society and Roman Law*, 48–70.

promise of closure. Extended trial scenes, therefore, are usually broken into smaller segments in order to sustain the reader's interest. Chariton stretches out the narrative of the Babylonian trials by introducing delays in which other scenes (a hunt, a beauty contest, a description of harem life) are inserted. Then, when the first trial in Babylon has stretched out beyond what the reader can bear, Chariton concludes it in such a way that the ending contains within it a new conflict for a second trial.[76]

The final part of Acts can be read in a similar vein. The mob violence in Judea has intensified since the early group of trials. It is against this background that Paul's trials unfold. The situation reiterates that of the earlier trials of the apostles, the difference being that now the Roman authorities are involved. The narrator highlights the military tribune's ignorance of the various factions in Judea. The tribune even mistakes Paul for some other criminal and thereby must order a meeting of the council and the chief priests to sort out the issues. This pattern will later be repeated in Festus's enlistment of Agrippa to help him formulate the precise charges for which Paul will be sent to Rome.

The action that sets off this sequence is an extended arrest scene (Acts trial 10). It is a preliminary phase of the subsequent trial of Paul before the Sanhedrin (trial 11). The escalating violence culminates (for the moment) in the confrontation between Paul and the high priest. It is tempting to see the priest's punching of Paul in the mouth as the model for a scene in Achilles Tatius where Thersander approaches Clitophon at the temple of Artemis to give him his summons, punches him in the nose, and cuts himself on Clitophon's teeth. As Clitophon says, "Thus my teeth avenged the honor of my nose."[77] The hero then launches into a high tragic lament against Thersander's tyrannical behavior. It is hard to interpret precisely what Achilles Tatius intended to do in this scene: some critics have read it as bad melodrama, others as sublime satire. Either way, it opens a second trial on a portentously violent note and establishes an absolute moral dichotomy between the evil accuser and innocent hero.

---

[76] Similar in this respect is Achilles Tatius's first trial scene, which has three full-length speeches, each followed by challenges to torture slaves for evidence. Clitophon is here found guilty for Leucippe's murder and is condemned to execution, but not before he is tortured for evidence. As the whips and the wheel are being rolled out, a sacred embassy to Artemis appears, temporarily suspending all punishments. As soon as Clitophon is released, Leucippe herself appears at the altar of Artemis to seek asylum, thereby mooting the entire first trial. The accuser, Thersander, argues that the punishment still stands and summons everyone back to court for a second trial, also with three speeches. In Heliodorus, the Athenian trials of Cnemon and Aristippus (Greek trials 9 and 10) are equally complex.

[77] Achilles Tatius 8.1.4: καὶ οἱ ὀδόντες ἀμύνουσι τὴν τῶν ῥινῶν ὕβριν.

This also seems to be the purpose of the detail of the priest's violence toward Paul in Acts.

The trial of Paul before the Sanhedrin (Acts trial 11) devolves into an insoluble conflict—a classic situation of *stasis*. Paul triggers the crisis by appealing to his commonality with the judges and invoking his status as "a Pharisee, the son of Pharisees" (Acts 23:6). Paul is a hero with multiple identities who uses them in order to win the judges' sympathy. Heliodorus is the only novelist to create a multicultural protagonist to rival Paul. This figure is Charicleia, a girl who is Ethiopian by birth but Greek by education. Among the trials in the Greek novels are scenes that take place in the court of a foreign king. This setting throws the Hellenic identity of the heroes into sharp relief and accentuates their helplessness. As foreigners, they are thrust into a situation in which they cannot win the judge's sympathy. At the end of the novel Charicleia must prove her true identity as the daughter of the Ethiopian king in order to prevent him from offering her as a human sacrifice (Greek trial 12). Likewise, Paul's trial before the Sanhedrin is an appeal to be recognized, but that recognition cannot take place in the context of political *stasis*.

The venue of the trial then shifts to a more important court, that of the Roman governor. The trials of Paul before the two Roman governors of Judea (Acts trials 12 and 13) are to be considered a pair, with the hearing before Festus a reduplication of that before Felix. The proceedings are more formal in this venue. This time the high priest and the elders bring along a professional speaker, the *rhētōr* Tertullus.[78] His speech is a near parody of rhetorical correctness; it contains fashionable rhetorical flourishes but ends with a somewhat flat appeal to the governor to examine the case for himself.[79] This scene finds a parallel in the novel of Achilles Tatius. In the second Ephesian trial (Greek trial 8), Thersander (the villain of the novel) hires a professional speaker (again, a *rhētōr*) named Sopater, who delivers an elaborate rhetorical speech and deploys logic designed to boggle the minds of the jury. Achilles Tatius makes fun of him for his overly clever arguments—but even more so he mocks Thersander for hiring the speaker and, in the end, completely misconstruing the *rhētōr*'s strategy, thereby bungling his own case. Likewise, Paul's speech looks straightforward and honest next to Tertullus's. Paul's statement avoids the extended

---

[78] Acts 24:1: ῥήτορος Τερτύλλου τινός. Trites ("Importance of Legal Scenes and Language," 282) observes that the noun ῥήτωρ occurs only here in Acts; the *hapax legomenon* reinforces the strongly legalistic tone of this scene.

[79] For rhetorical parallels between Tertullus's speech and classical authors, see Hans Conzelmann, *Acts of the Apostles* (ed. E. J. Epp and C. R. Matthews; trans. J. Limburg et al.; Hermeneia; Philadelphia: Fortress, 1987), 198–99.

captatio benevolentiae and goes straight to the *narratio*. He denies having done anything wrong, claiming that the case of his accusers has no merit and that the people who had originally lodged the complaint should be present to make the accusation. Each of these strategies was recognized in Greek rhetorical treatises; the last one was labeled the *paragraphikon,* or *demurrer,* whereby the defendant might claim that the trial was improper.[80] It is this argument that persuades Felix to delay the trial until the military tribune arrives.

Trials in the Greek novels demonstrate the narratological usefulness of judicial delays. Likewise, in Acts the space created by the suspension of the trial provides an opportunity for a private encounter between Paul and the governor. The presence of the governor's wife at this meeting highlights the informality of the setting. In this alternative rhetorical space, Paul discusses an alternate form of justice with the judge (Acts 24:25). Felix is almost persuaded but, instead of rendering a verdict, further stalls the trial until the arrival of his successor. The delay extends indefinitely, as trial 12 merges into 13, a hearing before Festus, Felix's successor. After extensive pretrial maneuvering, the latter scene moves quickly. The charges are vaguely described as "many serious charges that they could not prove" (Acts 25:7). Paul's defense is a simple denial that he did anything wrong. Paul's enemies try to persuade Festus to change the venue of the trial, whereupon Paul appeals to Caesar, thereby bringing the trial to a screeching halt.

The scene then shifts to the entrance of King Agrippa II and his entourage. As earlier with the tribune, Festus explains to Agrippa that he does not understand the charges. Agrippa agrees to hear the case in the final trial scene in Acts (trial 14). This scene, with its Roman audience hall and the pomp of the royal entourage, serves the same function that the Persian court serves in Chariton: it represents the pinnacle of grandeur. It is thus before this court that Paul delivers an *apologia pro sua vita* (Acts 26:1–23). This speech is the most rhetorically polished and complete of Paul's speeches in this group of trials.[81] Festus, the military man, interrupts the eloquent defense by suggesting that Paul's great learning (τὰ πολλά σε γράμματα; Acts 26:24) has caused him to devolve into madness. This comment echoes with the first trial in Acts, in which Peter and John were characterized as illiterate (ἀγράμματοι). Whereas in the council

---

[80] Russell, *Greek Declamation,* 44–63.

[81] For a formal rhetorical analysis of this speech, as well as the speeches of Paul before the Sanhedrin, Felix, and Festus, see Jerome Neyrey, "The Forensic Defense Speech and Paul's Trial Speeches in Acts 22–26: Form and Function," in Talbert, *Luke-Acts,* 210–24.

in Jerusalem the defendants' simplicity lends credibility to their message, in the Roman court it is Paul's education—his *paideia*—that impresses the local potentate but fails to persuade the more practical-minded Roman commander.

How, then, can the trials in the Greek novels help us interpret the problematic ending of Acts? In the Greek novels the ending is always that the couple get married, go back to where they belong, and fulfill the ideal of love in marriage. The there-and-then settings of the Greek novels fit with their happily-ever-after endings. However, the contemporary setting of Acts exposes this type of ending for what it is: a narrative device. There can be no neat happily-ever-after ending if the narrator means to extend the narrative into the world of the implied audience. Of course, this omission has also fueled discussion over the authorship of Acts and debates about whether the text of Acts represents a complete work or whether events prevented the author from bringing the narrative to a conclusion. God's command for Paul to go to Rome (23:11) points to an ending that lies beyond the boundaries of the narrative. Agrippa's decision to refer the matter to the emperor is instrumental in opening the narrative into the contemporary world of the text's Greco-Roman audience. On one level, Agrippa's verdict brings closure to the trials—he is the first official to declare that Paul has done nothing wrong—but Paul's own actions have made it impossible for Agrippa to bring the legal proceedings to an end. In the Greek novels, this would have been the place for a *deus ex machina*. The resolution of a case so complex—a narrative so compelling—calls for a spectacular scene. Paul's appeal to the emperor functions as the mechanism that will bring him to Rome, the place where he belongs. Rome, the center of the empire, where the power to administer justice converges in the person of the emperor, is the only venue suitable for the promised spectacle of Paul's fulfillment of the ideals of Acts.

This Janus-like ending simultaneously brings the narrative to its generic ending—the innocent hero is vindicated—while leaving the story open to a world that would have felt both realistic and extraordinary to the earliest readers of Acts in the Roman Empire. However, even in this respect Acts is not as different from the novels as might first appear. Among the extant complete Greek novels and the fragments there is a studious avoidance of any reference to Rome. This calculated refrain has been attributed to an effort among Greeks to assert the superiority, or at least the anteriority, of Greek *paideia*.[82] The ending of Acts sheds new light on this distinctive feature of Greek fiction. While the author of Acts was unafraid to point to Rome, his narrative seems to reflect a similar inhibition for too

---

[82] Swain, *Hellenism and Empire,* 109–18.

overt a depiction of the seat of imperial power. Rome is, as it were, present in its absence both in the Greek novels and in Acts. To use Rome as a setting for a contentious story might have attracted the wrong kind of attention from the imperial power and potentially undermined the intended effect of the narrative. It may have seemed better to divert the text's gaze from the center of imperial power and to keep Rome as a vanishing point outside the frame of the narrative. Although invisible, it is the center point that organizes the actions and verdicts within the provincial courtrooms on the peripheries of the empire. Rome thus lends significance to all the action of the narrative and is itself being drawn into the ideological drama.

Conclusion

In Acts and in the Greek novels we see how authors, coming from very different cultural positions, deployed the formula of the trial scene in order to sustain their narratives. The comparative study of these texts yields no clear indicators of directions of influence (if any); however, it does illustrate the pervasiveness of trials in narratives of the imperial period. By focusing on this particular type-scene—the trial scene—it is possible to see both commonalities as well as differences between the fictional narratives of the urban, Greek-speaking elite and the religious narratives of early Christians. The fact that these distinct groups not only coexisted in the empire but also deployed similar *topoi* in their narratives helps to underscore the continual process of identity formation and ideological positioning in the multicultural Roman Empire. There was no question of Rome's dominance by the time these authors wrote. The first centuries of the Common Era were a time when various peoples vied for a protected place within the power structures of the empire, positioned themselves against it, or both. Trial scenes thus dramatize these dynamics of difference.

In sensational narratives, such as one finds in the Greek novels and Acts, courtroom scenes reflect a world in which juridical processes had become entertainment for the masses. In the Roman world, trials served as public spectacles where the mechanisms of power were displayed for the benefit of the entire community. In prose fiction and in the narrative of Acts, trials are represented as competitions—*agōnes*—where the prospect of victory gives a definite degree of magnitude to the ideas articulated in a courtroom, a space consecrated, as it were, for debate. The prominence given to trials in the Greek novels and especially in Acts attests to the usefulness of this type-scene in texts driven to a lesser or greater degree by ideology. In the Greek novels the ideology is Hellenism, the assertion of the centrality of Greek *paideia* in the civilized world of the empire. In Acts the ideology is the promulgation of the teachings of an oriental sect to a wider Gentile audience. Trial scenes provide a flexible and readily intelligible formula for an articulation of ideology within narrative. The formula, founded upon the assumption that truth itself hangs in the balance, lends an air of impressiveness and momentousness to the display of ideas through speeches of individual characters. However, regardless of the specific ideology, in both the Greek novels and in Acts the readers are expected to gaze with pity, wonder, astonishment, and delight on the events displayed in the narrative—and to trust that in the end, to paraphrase Photius, the villains will pay the penalty and the heroes will be vindicated, if not in the temporal courtroom then certainly on the higher plane of poetic justice.

TABLE 1. TRIAL SCENES IN THE GREEK NOVELS

	Charge	Defendant	Accuser
1. Chaereas (Chariton 1.4–6)	murder of Callirhoe	Chaereas	Hermocrates, Callirhoe's father?
2. Theron (Chariton 3.4)	kidnapping? tomb robbery?	Theron	Chaereas?
3. Mithridates (Chariton 5.4–9)	attempted adultery, abuse of office	Mithridates	Dionysius
4. Dionysius versus Chaereas (Chariton 5.10–6.2)	claim to be legitimate husband of Callirhoe	Chaereas*	Dionysius*
5. Habrocomes (Xenophon of Ephesus 3.12–4.4)	murder of Araxus, Habrocomes' owner-cum-foster father	Habrocomes	Cyno, wife of Araxus
6. Daphnis (Longus 2.12–19)	negligence	Daphnis	Methymnean youths
7. Melite and Clitophon (Achilles Tatius 7.7–16)	adultery, then murder	Clitophon, Melite	Thersander
8. Priest and others (Achilles Tatius 8.7–15)	sacrilege and tyranny; adultery; unspecified charges	priest of Artemis; Melite; Leucippe and her father	Thersander, with the rhetor Sopater
9. Cnemon (Heliodorus 1.9–14)	attempted patricide	Cnemon	Aristippus, Cnemon's father
10. Aristippus (Heliodorus 1.14–17; 2.8–9)	murder of Demainete, Aristippus's wife	Aristippus	relatives of Demainete
11. Charicleia (Heliodorus 8.8–15)	murder of Cybele, Arsace's servant	Charicleia	Arsace
12. Hydaspes (Heliodorus 10.9–17)	planning to sacrifice a native virgin	Hydaspes, the king of Ethiopia	Charicleia
13. Theagenes (Heliodorus 4.17–21; 10.34–38)	kidnapping	Theagenes	Charicles

* The procedure is not a criminal trial but a *diadikasia*, in which two litigants present their competing claims to the judge.

The Trial Scene in the Greek Novels and in Acts 135

Setting	Judge	Spectators	Decision
agora of Syracuse	*dikastērion* empanelled by magistrates	entire *dēmos*	not guilty
Syracuse; theater	magistrates? Hermocrates? assembly?	the *dēmos*, meeting as an *ekklēsia* and including women	guilty: impalement on a cross
Babylon, a special hall in the royal palace designated as a law court	king of Persia	all of Babylon	not guilty
same as above (3)	king of Persia	people of Babylon	no formal verdict
Alexandria	assembly of Pelusians, then prefect of Egypt	unspecified onlookers	guilty
someplace in the countryside	Philetas the cowherd	villagers	not guilty
Ephesus, a *dikastērion* near the temple of Artemis	member of royal clan presiding over a jury/council of elders	unspecified public	guilty: torture, then death
same as above (7)	same as above (7)	entire *dēmos*	not guilty (?)
Athens	*dēmos* of Athens	"everybody"	guilty: exile
same as above (9)	same as above (9)	unspecified	guilty: exile and property confiscation
Memphis	Persian nobles	*dēmos* of Memphis	guilty: execution
Meroe, pavilion on the plain, near altar	Gymnosophists	Ethiopians	law changed by popular acclamation
same as above (12)	Hydaspes, the king of Ethiopia	people and army of Meroe	not guilty

Table 2. Trial Scenes in Acts

	Charge	Defendant	Accuser
1. Peter and John (4:1–22)	teaching the people and proclaiming resurrection	Peter, John	priests, captain of the temple, Sadducees
2. The apostles (5:1–42)	same as above (1)	the apostles	high priest and Sadducees
3. Stephen (6:8–7:1)	blasphemy	Stephen	synagogue members and allies, people, elders and scribes
4. Peter (12:1–25)	no charge (whim of Herod)	Peter	Herod
5. Paul/Philippi (16:16–40)	causing disturbances, introducing an alien religion	Paul, Silas	owners of slave girl exorcised by Paul
6. Thessalonica (17:5–9)	causing disturbances, claiming Jesus is king, not Caesar	Jason and brothers	Jews and gangsters
7. Paul/Areopagus (17:16–34)	inquiry about "alien divinities"	Paul	the philosophers?
8. Paul/Corinth (18:12–17)	persuading people to worship God against the law	Paul	Jews
9. Paul/Ephesus (19:23–20:1)	temple robbery and blasphemy	Paul (absent), Gaius, Aristarchus, Alexander	Demetrius the silversmith and artisans
10. Paul/Jerusalem (21:27–22:30)	teaching against temple law, bringing Greeks into and defiling temple	Paul	Jews from Asia
11. Paul/Sanhedrin (22:30–23:11)	same as above (10)	Paul	military tribune?
12. Paul/Felix (24:1–23)	disturbing the peace, profaning the temple	Paul	Ananias the high priest, elders, and Tertullus, a rhetor
13. Paul/Festus (25:1–12)	"many serious charges that they could not prove"	Paul	chief priests and Jewish leaders
14. Paul/Agrippa (25:13–26:31)	same as above (13)?	Paul	Festus?

The Trial Scene in the Greek Novels and in Acts 137

Setting	Judge	Spectators	Decision
Jerusalem, council	rulers, elders, scribes, high priest, priestly family	same as judges?	cease teaching, release
same as above (1)	council and senate of Israel, high priest as interrogator	unspecified	same as above (1), beating
same as above (1 and 2)	council, high priest as interrogator	"everyone sitting in the council"	no verdict: stoning
Jerusalem, Caesarea at Herod's tribunal	Herod	people of Tyre and Sidon	none
Philippi, agora	*archons, stratēgoi*	mob	beating with rods, then release with request to leave city
Thessalonica	*politarchoi*, then ultimately the assembly	mob	take security, release
Athens	Areopagus	?	mixed
Corinth, tribunal	Gallio, proconsul of Achaia	"everyone"	case dismissed: improper venue
Ephesus, theater	assembly, presided over by a clerk	rowdy mob = assembly, men of Ephesus	referral to another venue
Jerusalem, outside the temple, military quarters	military tribune	"the whole city," the people	referral to council
Jerusalem, council	chief priests council (orders of tribune)	Sadduccees, council, Pharisees, scribes	no verdict: referral to governor
Caesarea	Felix, Roman governor of Judea	?	case deferred indefinitely
Jerusalem, then Caesarea, tribunal	Festus, Felix's successor, with advisors	?	Paul appeals to Caesar
Caesarea, audience hall, much pomp	Agrippa, as advisor to Festus	Bernice, tribunes; leaders of city	not guilty, but referral to Caesar

ΜΕΤΑΒΟΛΗ ΠΟΛΙΤΕΙΩΝ
Jesus as Founder of the Church in Luke-Acts: Form and Function

David L. Balch

The conclusion of Acts (chs. 21–28) is often interpreted as a defense of Paul to Rome or the church, but this interpretation fails to appreciate fully the function of this material in the larger context of Luke-Acts. Rather, these chapters are directly related to the issue of whether Paul has abandoned the laws of Moses, a topic the writer of Luke-Acts displays an interest in throughout the narrative.[1] The conclusion of Luke-Acts concerns the accusation that Paul (and therefore also Jesus and the church) has abandoned the laws of Moses. When he arrives in Jerusalem, the apostles tell Paul:

> You see, brother, how many thousands there are among the Jews of those who have believed; they are all zealous for the law, and they have been told about you, that you teach all the Jews who are among the Gentiles to forsake Moses [ἀποστασίαν ... ἀπὸ Μωϋσέως], telling them not to circumcise their children or observe the customs [μηδὲ τοῖς ἔθεσιν περιπατεῖν]. (Acts 21:21)

The author is repeating similar accusations that had been made against Stephen:

---

* I thank Todd Penner and Caroline Vander Stichele both for inviting this paper (Society of Biblical Literature International Meeting, July 2002, Berlin) and for editing that improved the clarity and substance of the published paper. Erich Gruen, David Aune, and Clare K. Rothschild gave early critiques, for which I am grateful.

[1] David L. Balch, "Paul in Acts: '... You Teach All the Jews ... to Forsake Moses, Telling Them Not to ... Observe the Customs' (Act. 21,21)," in *Panchaia: Festschrift für Klaus Thraede* (ed. M. Wacht; JAC Ergänzungsband 22; Münster: Aschendorf, 1995), 11–23. Contrast Stanley E. Porter, *The Paul of Acts: Essays in Literary Criticism, Rhetoric, and Theology* (WUNT 115; Tübingen: Mohr Siebeck, 1999; repr., Peabody, Mass.: Hendrickson, 2001), who focuses on the modern issue of contradictions between Paul and Acts and thus neglects the function of Acts.

We have heard him speak blasphemous words against Moses and God [βλάσφημα εἰς Μωϋσῆν καὶ τὸν θεόν].... This man never ceases to speak words against this holy place and the law [κατὰ ... τοῦ νόμου]; for we have heard him say that this Jesus of Nazareth will destroy this place, and will change the customs that Moses delivered to us [καταλύσει τὸν τόπον τοῦτον καὶ ἀλλάξει τὰ ἔθη ἃ παρέδωκεν ἡμῖν Μωϋσῆς]. (Acts 6:11, 13–14)[2]

Still earlier in Luke's narrative the chief priests and crowds had brought a similar charge against Jesus himself: "He stirs up the people [ἀνασείει τὸν λαόν] by teaching throughout all Judea, from Galilee where he began even to this place" (Luke 23:5).[3] These charges thus appear to be formative for the narrative structure of Luke-Acts and the story that unfolds.

In this essay I will argue that the Lukan house churches had indeed dramatically changed Mosaic customs; further, the church differed from Jesus' own practice or was being encouraged to change by receiving foreigners into their house churches. In Greco-Roman culture, one had to argue that new practices had their origin in the ancient founder(s), in this case, Moses and Jesus. Luke argues that receiving foreigners into the people of God did not represent an abandonment of the ancient customs: it was not a change because it was predicted long ago in prophecy. This stands in contrast to the priestly stream of tradition that was opposed to Israelite mixing with foreigners.[4] Luke-Acts thus narrates the history of the people of God, claiming that God inspired prophecies that anticipate receiving these (earlier rejected) foreigners, prophecies that are renewed by Jesus and now fulfilled in the church. Hence, Luke-Acts must be understood as belonging to historical literature concerned with the changing of constitutions (μεταβολὴ πολιτειῶν).[5]

---

[2] The final Greek phrase is the equivalent of μεταβολὴ πολιτειῶν in the title of my essay, and this accusation (paired with 21:21) informs the final eight chapters of Luke-Acts.

[3] This verse indicates the three geographical sections of the Gospel and is thus Lukan redaction. See Georg Strecker, *Theology of the New Testament* (trans. M. E. Boring; Louisville: Westminster John Knox, 2000), 397, 405; Detlev Dormeyer, "Stasis-Vorwürfe gegen Juden und Christen und Rechtsbrüche in Prozessverfahren gegen sie nach Josephus' *Bellum Judaicum* und Mk 15,1–20 parr.," in *Internationales Josephus-Kolloquium Aarhus 1999* (ed. J. U. Kalms; MJS 6; Münster: LIT, 2000), 71–76.

[4] See especially Ezra 10:3, 9–15, 18–44; Neh 9:32; 13:1, 3, 23, 25, 28, 30; LXX Ps 105 [106]:35; Dan 2:43; 2 Macc 14:3, 38; Josephus, *Ant.* 4.148, 153, 159 (cf. Acts 10:28).

[5] Heinrich Ryffel, *ΜΕΤΑΒΟΛΗ ΠΟΛΙΤΕΙΩΝ: Der Wandel der Staatsverfassungen* (New York: Arno, 1973). For the centrality of the term *constitution* in Josephus, see

ΜΕΤΑΒΟΛΗ ΠΟΛΙΤΕΙΩΝ

To anticipate the direction of this essay, I will briefly summarize the broad contours of my argument. First, my research has shown that this sort of political conflict is narrated not only in histories but also in the biographies of the founders of cities/states. Therefore, I first discuss the literary genre of Luke-Acts. Drawing on the previous discussions of David Aune, Loveday Alexander, Richard Burridge, and Timothy Duff, I make brief observations on the issue of genre, arguing that biography can be political, and history in turn can be biographical. In this essay I focus primarily on the Gospel of Luke, but, in contrast to my earlier publications, I argue that the question of genre is for the most part secondary. This trajectory lays the foundation for comparing Luke-Acts with both Dionysius's history and Plutarch's biographies of founders. Moreover, in the discussion of genre I examine particular characteristics of Dionysius of Halicarnassus's and Luke's works: the former is Attic, the latter is Asian. Politically, religiously, rhetorically, and artistically, the boundary between Attic/European and Asian was fundamental in the Greco-Roman world. Second, I compare Dionysius's historiographical and Plutarch's biographical lives of Romulus and Numa (founders of Rome). I also include Plutarch's biographies of Theseus (founder of Athens) and Lycurgus (founder of Sparta). These initial comparisons enable a subsequent comparison of these histories and biographies with Luke's story of Jesus (the founder of the church). I establish sixteen similarities along with many differences, a significant reservoir of themes and values that each author varies. Third, I focus on one theme that emerges from these comparisons—founders change constitutions—and draw conclusions for Luke's apologetic denial that change has occurred. Fourth, I deal briefly with an obvious difficulty for the hypothesis that Jesus is a founder: Jesus did not establish a city or a colony with temples and the like. Finally, I comment on how Lukan Christianity relates to earlier founding figures, particularly to Moses and Romulus.

Rethinking the Significance of Genre

Luke-Acts has generally been characterized as ancient historiography. David Aune, for instance, has argued that "by itself, Luke could be classified as a type of ancient biography, but Luke was subordinated to a larger literary structure, for it belongs with Acts, and Acts cannot be forced into

---

Louis H. Feldman, *Judean Antiquities 1–4: Translation and Commentary* (vol. 3 of *Flavius Josephus: Translation and Commentary*; Leiden: Brill, 2000), xxiv–xxix. Contrast Tessa Rajak, "The *Against Apion* and the Continuities in Josephus's Political Thought," in *Understanding Josephus: Seven Perspectives* (ed. S. Mason; JSPSup 32; Sheffield: Sheffield Academic Press, 1998), 228, 242.

a biographical mold."⁶ Further, Aune has critiqued the results of Loveday Alexander, who denies that Luke's preface follows the literary conventions of historical prefaces.⁷ I will not reproduce his arguments, but he points out twelve correspondences between the *prooimion* of Plutarch's *Septem sapientium convivium,* the scientific prefaces analyzed by Alexander, and Luke 1:1–4, concluding that all of them use clichés or *topoi* with which they expected their readers to be familiar.⁸ Despite Alexander's cogent arguments, I side with Aune in this discussion: Luke should still be viewed and read as a historical work.

GENRE AND MEANING

In relation to my past publications, however, I am also shifting emphasis in the discussion of genre. A critical discussion with Erich Gruen helped me realize that the primary question is not whether the Gospel of Luke is history or biography⁹ but the use toward which history and biography are put: *both* history and biography may, depending on the author, the purpose, and the subject of the biography/history, focus on political issues and/or on particular heroes and the ethics of specific individuals. In contrast, Burridge argues that the subject of ancient biographies and of Luke's Gospel is a single person, since a high percentage of the verbs have the central character as their subject.¹⁰ Histories, he argues, do not focus on

---

⁶ David E. Aune, *The New Testament in Its Literary Environment* (LEC 8; Philadelphia: Westminster, 1987), 77–111, 116–41. Contrast Charles H. Talbert, "The Acts of the Apostles: Monograph or Bios?" in *History, Literature, and Society in the Book of Acts* (ed. B. Witherington; Cambridge: Cambridge University Press, 1996), 58–72. See Jan Radicke, ed., *Imperial and Undated Authors* (fascicle 7 of vol. 4A of *Biography;* 8 fascicles; *FGH* 4A/7; Leiden: Brill, 1999), a reference I owe to David Aune.

⁷ Loveday Alexander, *The Preface to Luke's Gospel: Literary Convention and Social Context in Luke 1.1–4 and Acts 1.1* (SNTSMS 78; Cambridge: Cambridge University Press, 1993).

⁸ David E. Aune, "Luke 1:1–4: Historical or Scientific Prooimion?" in *Paul, Luke and the Graeco-Roman World: Essays in Honour of Alexander J. M. Wedderburn* (ed. A. Christophersen et al.; JSNTSup 217; Sheffield: Sheffield Academic Press, 2002), 138–48. Cf. David L. Balch, "ἀκριβῶς ... γράψαι (Luke 1:3): To Write the *Full* History of God's Receiving All Nations," in *Jesus and the Heritage of Israel: Luke's Narrative Claim upon Israel's Legacy* (ed. D. P. Moessner; Harrisburg, Pa.: Trinity Press International, 1999), 232–39.

⁹ I argued in previous publications that Luke-Acts is history, not biography.

¹⁰ Richard A. Burridge, *What Are the Gospels? A Comparison with Graeco-Roman Biography* (SNTSMS 70; Cambridge: Cambridge University Press, 1992), 134–35, 195–96, 242, and 256–59 (but contrast 65–69). Another question concerns the significantly greater length of historical works compared to Luke. Greco-Roman biographies are comparable to Luke in length. Most are of medium length

ΜΕΤΑΒΟΛΗ ΠΟΛΙΤΕΙΩΝ

individuals but on social, political, and religious events. Herodotus's histories, for instance, do deal with the individual kings Darius and Xerxes (books 6 and 7), but these Persians are the subject of only a few of the sentences (3.5 and 6.6 percent, respectively). In Mark, however, Jesus is the subject of 24.4 percent of the verbs, and another 20.2 percent of the sentences occur on his lips, for a total of 44.6 percent of the text. In Luke, Jesus is the subject of 17.9 percent of the verbs, and another 36.8 percent of the sentences occur on his lips, for a total of 54.7 percent.[11] Similar percentages, Burridge observes, occur in Greco-Roman biographies. Agricola, for example, is the subject of 18 percent of the verbs in Tacitus's biography, with another 4 percent occurring in his speech (chs. 33–34).[12] On the other hand, my manual count of the grammatical subject of sentences and major phrases in Dionysius's history of King Lucius Tarquinius Superbus (*Ant. rom.* 4.41–85) reveals that he is the subject in 24.7 percent of them, a higher percentage than in *Agricola,* the key biography for Burridge. Dionysius writes biographies of Rome's founding kings within his history of Rome. Nevertheless, this biographical section of Dionysius's history concerns not only the individual character Lucius Tarquinius Superbus but also the dissolution of Roman kingship and the major political change from monarchy to aristocracy, to Roman consuls. In fact, the line between history and biography is not so easily drawn, as the overlap in material is not always statistically evident.

We see something similar with respect to Plutarch. Scholars have generally assumed that Plutarch was a biographer rather than a historian.[13]

(3,500–7,500 words), although Philo's *Moses* is longer (ca. 32,000 words). Matthew has 18,305 words, Mark 11,242, and Luke 19,428 (ibid., 134–35, 195–96, 242). The historian Dionysius, however, divides the early section of his *Roman Antiquities* into "books" on seven early Roman kings: on Romulus (*Ant. rom.* 1.76–2.56, 20,763 words), Numa (2.57–76, 5,981 words), Tullus Hostilius (3.1–35, 14,764 words), Ancus Marcius (3.36–45, 2,386 words), Lucius Tarquinius Priscus (3.46–73, 7,963 words), Servius Tullius (4.1–40, 13,733 words), and Lucius Tarquinius Superbus (4.41–85, 11,870 words). Both Dionysius and Luke have composed multivolume works within which there are individual "biography(ies)" of comparable, "medium" length, but the biographies Burridge studies typically are single, not multivolume works; therefore, in this respect they are unlike Luke-Acts.

[11] Ibid., 196.

[12] Ibid., 162. Of the ten biographies he studies, Burridge seems most fascinated by Tacitus's *Agricola* (155, 189), which is also the centerpiece of Albrecht Dihle's *Die Entstehung der historischen Biographie* (Sitzungsberichte der Heidelberger Academie der Wissenschaften, Philosophisch-historische Klasse 3; Heidelberg: Universitätsverlag, 1987).

[13] Burridge, *What Are the Gospels,* 156–58 (examining Plutarch's *Cato Minor*).

Duff quotes Plutarch's introduction (*Alexander* 1.1) to his *Lives of Alexander and Caesar*, which distinguishes history from biography.[14] Duff argues, however, that it is a mistake to elevate this statement into one of generic difference in ancient thought: "The boundaries between history, political biography, and related forms of writing such as *enkomion* and the so-called historical monograph, were never clearly drawn; rather, generic differences were open to construction by individual authors in order to distinguish their work from those of rivals."[15] Plutarch can thus refer to his own work as *historia* (ἱστορία) in a broader sense. To quote Duff further:

> At the beginning of his *Lives of Theseus and Romulus*, for example, he [Plutarch] declares (1.2) "I have traversed in my writing of the *Parallel Lives* that period of time which is accessible to probable reasoning (εἰκότι λόγῳ) and forms a basis for a history of facts (ἱστορία πραγμάτων)." "I have decided", he continues, "that it would not be unreasonable to go back further to Romulus, now that we have come close to his times in our history (or *research* or *narrative:* τῇ ἱστορίᾳ)." "May it therefore be possible", he goes on a little later (*Thes.* 1.4–5), "for me to cleanse the mythic (τὸ μυθῶδες) and make it obey reason and take on the appearance of history (ἱστορίας ὄψιν)." His *own Lives of Theseus and Romulus* are, he implies, or at least, have "the appearance of", history.[16]

The Plutarchian distinction here is not between history and lives but is equivalent to a Thucydidean one between history and myth. Discussing the *Life of Alexander* and the *Life of Caesar* with which it is paired, Duff further observes that "the narration of political and military events and the analysis of the processes—especially the popular support for Caesar—which led to the establishment of monarchy at Rome, are more prominent than the revelation of character."[17] Plutarch's preface to his *Life of Alexander* thus functions to differentiate his work from other historiographical works on the same theme.[18] As Duff notes, "One of Plutarch's purposes in writing the *Lives* was to provide a political and military history of the Greek and Roman world, which can be viewed within the tradition of the 'universal histories' which set the past and destiny of Greece and Rome side by side."[19] Duff, therefore, affirms the fluidity of genre between history and

---

[14] Timothy E. Duff, *Plutarch's Lives: Exploring Virtue and Vice* (New York: Oxford University Press, 1999), 14–15.

[15] Ibid., 17.

[16] Ibid., 18. Plutarch has a difficult task; see Cicero, *Leg.* 1.3.1.

[17] Duff, *Plutarch's Lives*, 21.

[18] Ibid.

[19] Ibid., 66.

biography. Thus, the debate about genre—whether the authors are writing history or biography—is much less important in this light than the issues at stake in the argument itself. This observation then refocuses our attention on the nature of what the authors are debating/engaging in their narratives: political alternatives and/or individual character. It is in this context that I now compare Plutarch's political *Lives of Romulus and Numa* with Dionysius's political history, including also, for comparison and contrast, Plutarch's political *Lives of Theseus and Lycurgus.*

While in past articles I have suggested comparing the historian Dionysius with Luke,[20] in this essay I am shifting focus by analyzing the nature and function of the lives and history that Dionysius wrote. His purpose statements include the aims of removing erroneous impressions and substituting them with true ones concerning "who the founders of the city were, at what periods the various groups came together, and [why] ... they left their native countries" (*Ant. rom.* 1.5.1).[21] He will show too what deeds (πράξεων) they performed "by virtue of which [ἐξ ὧν] their descendants advanced to a great empire" (1.5.2). The descendants of those godlike men should choose not the most pleasant and easiest lives (βίων) but rather noble and ambitious ones (1.6.4). He also comments on the subject and form (περὶ τίνων ποιοῦμαι πραγμάτων ... καὶ ... τὸ σχῆμα; 1.7.4) of his history in *Ant. rom.* 1.8. The subject concerns ancient myths, foreign wars, and internal seditions (ἐμφυλίους στάσεις), "showing from what causes they sprang and by what methods and what arguments they were brought to an end," further elucidating all the forms of government (πολιτειῶν) "both

---

[20] David L. Balch, "Comments on the Genre and a Political Theme of Luke-Acts: A Preliminary Comparison of Two Hellenistic Historians," in *SBL Seminar Papers, 1989* (SBLSP 28; Atlanta: Scholars Press, 1989), 343–61. Aune (*New Testament in Its Literary Environment,* 84–89) distinguishes historical monographs, general history, and antiquarian history, designating Luke-Acts as general history. This distinction is rejected by Gregory E. Sterling, *Historiography and Self-Definition: Josephos, Luke-Acts and Apologetic Historiography* (NovTSup 64; Leiden: Brill, 1992), 10–11. See J. M. Alonso-Núñez, "The Emergence of Universal Historiography from the Fourth to the Second Centuries B.C.," in *Purposes of History: Studies in Greek Historiography from the Fourth to the Second Centuries B.C.* (ed. H. Verdin et al.; Studia Hellenistica 30; Leuven: n.p., 1990), 173–92, who stresses the world expanding events surrounding Alexander the Great and Augustus Caesar.

[21] The critical texts utilized for this study are as follows: *Denys d'Halicarnasse, Antiquités Romaines* (trans. V. Fromentin; Paris: Belles Lettres, 1998); Carmine Ampolo and Mario Manfredini, eds., *Plutarco, Le Vite di Teseo e di Romolo* (Milan: Mondadori, 1988); and Mario Manfredini and Luigi Piccarilli, eds., *Plutarco, Le Vite di Lucurgo e di Numa* (2d ed.; Milan: Mondadori, 1990). With respect to Plutarch, the LCL and Mondadori editions have the same chapters but different section numbers within chapters; I give the LCL section numbers in this essay.

during the monarchy and after its overthrow" (κατάλυσιν) and the best customs (ἔθη) and laws, that is, the whole life of the ancient Romans (τὸν ἀρχαῖον βίον; 1.8.1–2). This form neither resembles the works of those who make wars alone their subject[22] nor of those who treat several forms of government (ὁποῖον οἱ τὰς πολιτείας) by themselves.[23] It is also not annalistic.[24] Rather, it is a combination of these, including both political debates and philosophical speculation[25] (ἐναγωνίου τε καὶ θεωρητικῆς; 1.8.3).[26] Political debates in this framework refer to all the categories of oratory—judicial, deliberative, and epideictic—since all are involved in political life.[27]

---

[22] The most obvious example is Thucydides, whom Dionysius criticizes in his treatise *On Thucydides*.

[23] See Ryffel, *ΜΕΤΑΒΟΛΗ ΠΟΛΙΤΕΙΩΝ*, on the philosophical discussion of constitutions (also see Todd Penner's contribution in this volume). Dionysius and Josephus narrate the change of the Roman and Mosaic constitutions after the deaths of Romulus and Moses, just as Acts describes the church changing after Jesus' death. In *Ant. rom.* 4.41–85 Dionysius narrates the dissolution of the Roman monarchy and the institution of consuls. In 6.22–92 he depicts the origin of the institution of tribunes, while in 6.92–8.62 he describes plebeians attaining the right to put patricians on trial. Josephus (*Ant.* 6.31–67) narrates the change from Mosaic aristocracy to monarchy.

[24] As an example of this third form Dionysius cites Atthis's (i.e., Attica) local histories. See Felix Jacoby, *Atthis: The Local Legends of Ancient Athens* (Oxford: Clarendon, 1949). Roman historiography adhered to this annalistic form; see Mark Toher, "Augustus and the Evolution of Roman Historiography," in *Between Republic and Empire: Interpretations of Augustus and His Principate* (ed. K. A. Raaflaub and M. Toher; Berkeley and Los Angeles: University of California Press, 1990), 146; and Sterling, *Historiography and Self-Definition*, 6, 21, 26–27, 32.

[25] Dionysius is hesitant about philosophical speculation (*Ant. rom.* 1.77.3), but see 2.6.4; 20.1; 21.1 (τὸ θεωρητικὸν τῆς φιλοσοφίας); 56.6; 63.3; and note 58 below. Cf. Eralda Noè, "Ricerche su Dionigi d'Alicarnasso: la prima stasis a Roma e l'episodio di Coriolano," in *Ricerche di storiografia greca di età romana* (ed. C. Letta et al.; vol. 1 of *Ricerche di storiografia antica;* Biblioteca di studi antichi 22; Pisa: Giardini, 1979–80), 1:40, who includes not only metaphysics but also the philosophical discussion of ethics (e.g. justice and piety) among Dionysius's interests.

[26] Clemence Elizabeth Schultze, "Dionysius of Halicarnassus and His Audience," in *Past Perspectives: Studies in Greek and Roman Historical Writing* (ed. I. S. Moxon et al.; Cambridge: Cambridge University Press, 1986), 136. See Fromentin (*Denys d'Halicarnasse*, 226) for interpretation and discussion of the textual problem.

[27] See Emilio Gabba, "Political and Cultural Aspects of the Classicistic Revival in the Augustan Age," *CA* 1 (1982): 44 n. 3, who cites Dionysius, *Isocr.* 11.4 and *Lys.* 16.1–3. See also Fromentin (*Denys d'Halicarnasse*, 226); and Thomas Hidber, *Das klassizistische Manifest des Dionys von Halikarnass: Die Praefatio zu De oratoribus veteribus. Einleitung, Übersetzung, Kommentar* (Beiträge zur Altertumskunde 70; Stuttgart: Teubner, 1996), 44–56.

This statement of Dionysius's purpose raises similar questions regarding Luke: Does our author narrate myth (stories of the divine foundation of a people), war, internal seditions, customs and laws, and/or the whole life of Israel/the church?

Dionysius's history typically alternates between external and internal affairs, between war and periods of peace.[28] In 1.90.2 he promises a narrative "concerning the constitution," which some scholars see fulfilled in all the rest of the history,[29] but which I view as fulfilled in his narration of nonmilitary, internal conflicts.[30] Dionysius's use of political themes/issues is thus ambiguous. On the one hand, he differentiates political/civic from military events (e.g. *Ant. rom.* 2.7.1; 14.4; 30.1), but, on the other, political institutions function in both peace and war (2.7.2; 14.4). In *Ant. rom.* 1.8.3 Dionysius contrasts military and political events, using the category of political to refer to internal seditions, not external military wars. Both political and military events are presented in terms of conflict, which is the essential component of history, according to Dionysius.[31] In fact, however, political realities loom larger than military affairs; there is little actual analysis of the latter. When Dionysius does discuss causes of historical events, they are all internal (4.63; 5.56; 7.66).[32] Since I am comparing Dionysius and Luke, the internal focus of the former raises questions about the latter. Since Luke does not narrate warfare, does this mean that Luke-Acts is not history? Does Luke narrate internal conflicts?

Continuing this line of thought, true citizens emerge from the form of government (τὸ τῆς πολιτείας σχῆμα) that Dionysius advocates. These are contrasted with slaves, who are the product of evil institutions (*Ant. rom.* 2.3.5). Many large colonies fall into seditions, and as a result they become slaves instead of free persons. By contrast, others, sometimes few in number, are successful and grow, "due to no other cause than their form of government" (2.3.7). This particular theme is given an interesting configuration by being connected to the maintenance or rejection/change in the constitution itself. Romulus, according to Dionysius, does not initiate a new form of government but advocates keeping the one the ancestors handed down, because the traditional form has brought freedom and rule (2.4.1). Dionysius's narrative then demonstrates that this traditional form of government, (re)established by Romulus, continued for many generations and is

---

[28] Clemence Elizabeth Schultze, "Dionysius of Halicarnassus as a Historian: An Investigation of His Aims and Methods in the Antiquitates Romanae" (Ph.D. diss., Oxford University, 1980), 44, 168, 248, 269, 272.

[29] Ibid., 264.

[30] See n. 23 above.

[31] Ibid., 272.

[32] Ibid., 248.

the cause of Rome's success (e.g., 2.10.4 on patronage; 7.70.5).³³ In contrast to the Romans, the Greeks, even the favored Lacedaemonians, are perceived to have rejected and changed their customs (7.72.2, 4). Dionysius here implicitly associates virtue and vice with the embodiment of constitutional values. The steadfast maintenance of one's constitutional tradition also attests to the moral condition of the very same people/figure. Change in the tradition, in this context, suggests moral decay (cf. Seneca, *Ep.* 114.2–3).

While the theme of continuity is critical for Dionysius, a main theme of his history narrates (however inconsistently) how the Roman constitution itself developed/changed (*Ant. rom.* 5.74.2–3; 10.51.3; 55.3), sometimes by violence (2.11.2–3; 6.74.3; 8.5.4; 30.4).³⁴ Although he expresses fear of change (6.24.3), he recognizes the need for adaptation (10.51.3).³⁵ Roman harmony resulted from Romulus's excellent institutions, which during civic *stasis* however might be modified by arguments in great speeches (7.66.3).³⁶ As he notes,

> In the course of time they [Romans] contrived to raise themselves from the smallest nation to the greatest ... not only by their humane reception [φιλαν-θρώπῳ ὑποδοχῇ] of those who sought a home among them, but also by sharing the rights of citizenship with all who had been conquered by them in war ... by permitting the slaves, too, who were manumitted among them to become citizens, and by disdaining no condition of men [οὐδεμιᾶς ... ἀπαξιώσει] from whom the commonwealth might reap an advantage, but above everything else by their form of government [κόσμῳ τοῦ πολιτεύματος], which they fashioned out of their many experiences [ἐκ πολλῶν κατεστήσαντο παθημάτων], always extracting something useful from every occasion. (1.9.4)

---

³³ See John P. V. D. Balsdon, "Dionysius on Romulus: A Political Pamphlet?" *JRS* 61 (1971): 25 n. 40. Themes that Dionysius highlights are as follows: the patronate survived (2.10.4), the ban on orgiastic cults remained (2.19.2–5), and there was no divorce for five centuries (2.25.7). This generates an important question: Are practices and teaching that originated with Jesus in the Gospel continued in Acts?

³⁴ Schultze, "Dionysius of Halicarnassus as a Historian," 179, 212, 241, 247–48. Josephus too, recounting the *Letter of Aristeas,* describes Ptolemy II as interested in the Jewish law and political constitution (*Ant.* 1.10). The sacred scriptures recount surprising reversals, war, courageous deeds of generals, and political revolutions (πολιτευμάτων μεταβολαί; *Ant.* 1.13). Although he employs this *topos* in the preface, Josephus is quite reluctant to narrate such a political change from aristocracy to monarchy (*Ant.* 6.39, 83–85, 90, 262–268), because the constitution was from Moses, who cautioned against amending it (*Ant.* 4.292, 295; also 223–224, 302). Since they are traitors to God's worship and religion, Israel must confess their sin for such change (*Ant.* 6.90, 92).

³⁵ Schultze, "Dionysius of Halicarnassus as a Historian," 181.

³⁶ Ibid., 122, 128, 131, 248, 272.

The term that the LCL renders as "experiences" is ambiguous, and since conflict is always involved, these events might rather be called calamities, misfortunes, and sufferings. Romans, in this construction, learn from their hardships and adapt their constitution along the way. I conclude from this discussion that Dionysius writes a particular type of history that is most concerned about politics and morality, rather than simply praising military battles and conquests. This function of the material is critical for understanding his larger work, just as it is in the case of Plutarch's biographies.

IMPLICATIONS FOR LUKE

Based on the preceding discussion of the historian Dionysius and the biographer Plutarch, I present several theses. First, Luke shifted the discourse from Dionysius by leaving out narration of military affairs, while concentrating on political/civic ones. Alternatively, Luke chose to narrate the history/life of a type of founder who did not go to war, suggesting that, as Duff has argued, biographies too may focus on political affairs. Indeed, among the works being considered here, neither Dionysius's historical narration of Numa (*Ant. rom.* 2.57–76) nor Plutarch's biographical *Numa* contains any account of war, even though Numa was a founder/king of Rome. All this suggests that it might be more profitable to understand Luke's narrative by comparing the Gospel with Dionysius's and Plutarch's historical and biographical narrations of internal civic conflict (*stasis*) and associated changes of the constitution.

However, this raises a critical question for our investigation: How does each writer understand the role, place, and function of change in the tradition? Like Dionysius and Plutarch, Luke is centrally concerned with the political institutions of the founder. There is also a contrast, however, in that Dionysius's narrative assumes that the Romans did not abolish Romulus's political institutions, while Plutarch's narrative shows the opposite. For example, Plutarch's Numa softened Romulus's focus on war, but Numa's successor reverted to a martial society (see further below). This difference raises the question regarding how we are to understand Luke's insistence that neither Stephen nor Paul changed Moses' laws (Acts 6:11, 13–14; 21:21). Paradoxically, both Dionysius and Luke trace the development (i.e., change) of crucial political institutions, but neither is as blatant about change as is Plutarch. According to Dionysius, the founder(s) established the political institutions, but significant ones were also established later (e.g., the consuls [*Ant. rom.* 4.73–74],[37] and tribunes [6.22–92]).[38] Below I

---

[37] Ibid., 182 (i.e., a change that is not a change, but rather a change of name).

[38] See David L. Balch, "Political Friendship in the Historian Dionysius of Halicarnassus, *Roman Antiquitates*," in *Greco-Roman Perspective on Friendship* (ed.

analyze the reception of foreigners into the people of God in Acts 10–15, particularly focusing on why it is that Plutarch is different and why Dionysius and Luke-Acts are similar on the key elements surrounding this pivotal issue. This comparison, I propose, will help us understand Luke-Acts better.

In light of these issues, two further points are important for the present discussion. First, for Dionysius Greekness has no ethnic limit.[39] On the other hand, the basic division in the political/social/cultural world remains Greeks versus barbarians, a conflict promoted by Isocrates, in whose *Panegyricus* Greeks are naturally at war with barbarians (158), the latter of whom are trained for slavery (πρὸς ... τὴν δουλείαν πεπαιδευμένος; 150).[40] As a result of this long-standing conflict, one of the most powerful accusations against which Dionysius defends the Romans is that their ancestors were barbarians on whom blind fortune had bestowed the blessings of the Greeks (*Ant. rom.* 1.4.2; 2.17.3). This defense then leads him to the problematic theory that the original Romans were indeed Greeks, not barbarians,[41] a theory that later morally legitimates Roman rule, specifically Roman incursions into Greece and Asia Minor. Barbarians may thus assimilate Greekness; but if they do not, they remain inhuman beasts (1.33.4; 41.1; 42.2).

Second, Dionysius's rhetorical and historiographical programs were closely related to this defensive posture,[42] and as a result he opposes Greeks to Asians.[43] The fundamental text in this respect is Dionysius's *The Ancient Orators*.[44] In this text Dionysius outlines three stages in cultural history: (1) the classical age until Alexander; (2) the post-Alexandrian age that included a period of Asian supremacy; and (3) the Augustan classicistic revival (*Ant. or.* 1–3).[45] In this model, Alexander's expansion of Greek

---

J. T. Fitzgerald; SBLRBS 34; Atlanta: Scholars Press, 1997), 127–31; as well as idem, "Rich and Poor, Proud and Humble in Luke-Acts," in *The Social World of the First Christians: Essays in Honor of Wayne A. Meeks* (ed. L. M. White and O. L. Yarbrough; Minneapolis: Fortress, 1995), 214–33.

[39] Emilio Gabba, *Dionysius and the History of Archaic Rome* (Sather Classical Lectures 56; Berkeley and Los Angeles: University of California Press, 1991), 75, 87, 105. See *Ant. rom.* 1.89.4, where Dionysius lists the ethnic groups that have become Roman = Greek.

[40] Hidber, *Das klassizistische Manifest*, 29, 44, 74.

[41] Gabba, *Dionysius and the History*, 10–16, 87.

[42] Ibid., 4, 74.

[43] Ibid., 27–29, 35–39, 53, 191–92, 199.

[44] Ibid., 23; and Gabba, "Political and Cultural Aspects," 43. Dionysius wrote *The Ancient Orators* in his early period (Hidber, *Das klassizistische Manifest*, 11).

[45] Gabba, "Political and Cultural Aspects," 46; idem, *Dionysius and the History*, 23; and Hidber, *Das klassizistische Manifest*, 18–19.

culture beyond Hellas to barbarian countries represents a decline of the culture itself.[46]

The Attic/Asian opposition is also related to class, to the social structure within Greek cities: classical, prudent oratory is the prerogative of the upper, Greek classes, while Asian rhetoric belongs to the untutored masses.[47] Dionysius's rhetorical and historiographical support of Roman growth, of ethnic mixing in the empire, and of a mixed constitution has the political goal of legitimating the participation of Greek elites in the administration of the Roman Empire.[48] Elite Greek order is opposed to the disorder of the masses, but this opposition is dependent on the unity of the Greek elite in their support of Rome.[49] Asian values were thus considered anti-Roman and populist, emphasizing the freedom and independence represented by Mithradites' revolt.[50] Rome is a guarantor against the rebellion of the lower classes. Dionysius's rhetorical Asian opponents were, of course, Greeks, who were influential in the cities of Asia Minor. Dionysius makes this manifestly evident:

---

[46] Gabba, *Dionysius and the History*, 46.

[47] Gabba, "Political and Cultural Aspects," 47; idem, *Dionysius and the History*, 29. Appearing in Dionysius's model after the pivotal point of Actium, the Attic/Asian contrast also refers to the conflict between Octavian and Antony, which represents a fundamental conflict between Rome and Egypt. This is clearly not an ethnic distinction. Cf. Hidber, *Das klassizistische Manifest*, 42 n. 186 (citing Cassius Dio 48.30.1): Caesar's military and Roman style differs from Antony's Asiatic and Egyptian mode (also cf. Plutarch, *Ant.* 2). Christopher Pelling (*Plutarch, Life of Antony* [Cambridge: Cambridge University Press, 1988], 119) incorrectly dismisses Plutarch's reference to Antony's Asiatic lifestyle as a "mere abusive slogan applied to florid orators." The contrast between neo-Attic and neo-Pergamonic style is basic also in the art of the period (see Gabba, "Political and Cultural Aspects," 46 n. 11, for bibliography). The Pergamon altar was constructed by Eumenes II in 165 B.C.E. Karl Schefold (*Der religiöse Gehalt der antiken Kunst und die Offenbarung* [Kulturgeschichte der Antiken Welt 78; Mainz: Zabern, 1998], 334–37) observes that the Pergamon altar visually represents the gods defeating the giants, the Athenians defeating the Persians, the Pergamene kings conquering the Gauls, and Stoic order defeating Eastern Isis mysticism. Also see David L. Balch, "Paul's Portrait of Christ Crucified (Gal 3:1) in Light of Paintings and Sculptures of Suffering and Death in Pompeiian and Roman Houses," in *Early Christian Families in Context: A Cross-Disciplinary Dialogue* (ed. D. L. Balch and C. Osiek; Grand Rapids: Eerdmans, 2003), esp. 95 nn. 46–50 and 105 n. 86.

[48] Gabba, *Dionysius and the History*, 19–20, 32–35, 53–57, 64, 206, 209, as well as 214–16 (on Josephus).

[49] Ibid., 54 (on Plutarch).

[50] Ibid., 25, 36–39, 53 (*Ant. rom.* 1.4.3, against Timagenes; see Appian, *Hist. rom.* 12.48, 61–62).

In every city and in the highly civilized ones as much as any (which was the final indignity), the ancient and indigenous Attic Muse, deprived of her possessions, had lost her civic rank, while her antagonist, an upstart that had arrived only yesterday and the day before from some Asiatic death-hole [βαράθρων τῆς Ἀσίας], a Mysian or Phrygian or Carian creature [κακόν], claimed the right to rule over Greek cities, expelling her rival from public life.[51]

On the first point, Luke does not share Dionysius's ethnic/cultural prejudice. Indeed, one primary characteristic of earliest Christianity was its devaluation of ethnic distinctions between Jews and Gentiles, Greeks and barbarians (e.g., Gal 3:28; Luke 3:6; 4:26–27; Acts 2:9–11; 10:35, 43).[52] On the second point, from Dionysius's rhetorical point of view, Luke is Asian. Whether the Gospel of Luke is Asian or not does not revolve around the question whether the author was Jewish or Greek.[53] The distinction is rather geographical and social/ethical. Asia began in Asia Minor and consisted of lands geographically east of Greece and Macedonia, including, of course, Judea.[54] Luke is Asian historiography because the events of the Gospel occur in Galilee and Judea, and, further, the narrative moves from east to west, the reverse of the movement, for example, in the biographies/

---

[51] *Ant. or.* 1. Cf. Albrecht Dihle, "Der Beginn des Attizismus," *Antike und Abendland* 23 (1977): 168 n. 25 (citing Cicero, *Att.* 12.6; and Diogenes Laertius 7.189); as well as Glen W. Bowersock, "Historical Problems in Late Republican and Augustan Classicism," in *Le Classicisme à Rome aux 1ers Siècles avant et après J.-C.* (ed. H. Flashar; Entretiens sur l'antiquité classique 25; Geneva: Hardt, 1979), 70 (citing Strabo, *Geogr.* 14.1.41); and Hidber, *Das klassizistische Manifest*, 76. See also Catherine Connors, "Field and Forum: Culture and Agriculture in Roman Rhetoric," in *Roman Eloquence: Rhetoric in Society and Literature* (ed. W. J. Dominik; New York: Routledge, 1997), 84–88.

[52] I feel compelled to observe, however, that some Christians in patristic, medieval, and modern times have promoted ethnic hatred in murderously effective ways, particularly against Jews and Muslims, demonstrating disjunction with the earlier traditions.

[53] Contrast Sterling, *Historiography and Self-Definition*, 113, 134–36, 327–29.

[54] When Alexander crossed the Hellespont, he thought of himself as reenacting the actions of Agamemnon crossing onto Asian soil (Arrian, *Anab.* 1.11.5). After defeating Darius's forces, he set up the following inscription: "Alexander and the Greeks set up these spoils from the barbarians in Asia" (1.16.7). When he defeated Darius near the Cilician Gates, Alexander gave a speech presenting this as a fight of free men against slaves, Europe against Asia (2.7.4–6). Alexander is repeatedly depicted as being concerned with the *barbarians* (3.15.2–3; 23.8; 4.4.2). It is noteworthy in this respect that Josephus (*Ant.* 5.220) refers to Israel as *Asian*, while Luke represents Paul crossing the Hellespont in the opposite direction of Alexander—from Asia to Europe (Acts 16:6–10).

histories of Alexander the Great. Finally, Asian historiography was populist. Luke does not promote a militarily revolutionary viewpoint like Mithridates but rather radically revises key Isocratean and Roman social values.

In Isocratean ethics and Roman society this revision is upside down in its fundamental orientation. In contrast to Dionysius, one of whose main goals was to support political leadership in Rome by elite Greeks, Luke's Asian image of leadership involved leaders serving as slaves.[55] Thus, the early baptismal confession—"there is no longer Jew or Greek" (Gal 3:28a)—is an assertion from below: "[We] Jews [Asians, non-Europeans] are not inferior!" To take another example, in Luke's story, Peter, Jesus' disciple, declares that "God shows no partiality, but in every nation anyone who fears him and does what is right is acceptable to him" (Acts 10:34b–35). Again, in both cases these represent radical reversals of Roman and Isocratean values.

From Dionysius's perspective Luke-Acts would be Asian biography/ history. Both Dionysius's and Luke's histories concern the character of the founders of nations/peoples, the modes of life they initiate, as well as the lives and history of their successors and of the people who live according to the founders' constitutions. The founder is an ideal/mythical figure whose original constitution generates virtue and the people's growth; therefore, change represents immoral corruption. From a modern point of view, change is inevitable, often good, but from these Greco-Roman historians' point of view, the lives and events they narrate must be grounded in the character and lifestyle of the original founder(s). For Luke this means, for example, that the reception of (uncircumcised, pork-eating) pagans into the people of God, however outrageous it may have seemed to the readers of his day, must be grounded in the character and laws of Abraham and Moses. Further, these historians narrate the will of God(s) as lived virtuously by the founder and the founder's people; the founder and the way of life he institutes are more virtuous than the alternatives. From a Dionysian point of view, the God who speaks the Septuagintal—Asian barbarian—Greek of Luke 1–2 and Acts 1–12 is proclaimed in European

---

[55] E.g., see Jesus' parable, "Blessed are those slaves whom the master finds alert when he comes; truly I tell you, he will fasten his belt and have them sit down to eat [ἀνακλινεῖ], and he will come and serve them [διακονήσει αὐτοῖς]" (Luke 12:37). For further bibliography, see Carolyn Osiek and David L. Balch, *Families in the New Testament World: Households and House Churches* (Louisville: Westminster John Knox, 1997), 185–88. The basic work on these upside-down values is by Willi Braun, *Feasting and Social Rhetoric in Luke 14* (SNTSMS 85; Cambridge: Cambridge University Press, 1995). Cf. also the brief comments on Luke 12:37; 14:1–24; 22:24–30 in David L. Balch, "Commentary on Luke," *Eerdmans Commentary on the Bible* (Grand Rapids: Eerdmans, forthcoming). See further notes 51 and 54 above.

Rome! Luke-Acts represents the muddy Jordan river flowing into the imperial Tiber. Luke challenges key social and religious values narrated by Dionysius in a way similar to how Dionysius, as an apologetic historian, had praised Roman and challenged some Greek values. Simultaneously, of course, as the following section shows, Luke also acculturates his value system. Luke thus Romanizes Christianity by arguing for a multiethnic people of God.

Founders and Foundings: Comparing Greco-Roman Stories

When one reads Dionysius's history, Plutarch's biographies of founders, and Luke-Acts, many similarities (including verbal ones) emerge, and the cumulative effect of these numerous verbal similarities suggests that the works belong to a common, political kind of story (but not genre). For the purpose of brevity, I will focus on Dionysius's and Plutarch's treatment of Romulus and Numa, Plutarch's portrayal of Theseus and Lycurgus, and Luke's depiction of Jesus.[56] Without suggesting that there is a rigid pattern, I briefly list sixteen similar themes and values, keeping in mind also that the manner in which these authors narrate the themes is often quite different.

1. Beginnings. Dionysius is concerned with chronology at the beginning of his book on Romulus (*Ant. rom.* 1.74–75), as is Luke (Luke 1:5; 2:1–2). He informs us, in fact, that "there was a great dispute concerning both the time of the building of the city and the founders of it" (1.72.1), the kind of tension that Luke occasionally allows us to observe (see Acts 15:2). Both historians are concerned with "the beginning" (*Ant. rom.* 1.79.10; 80.4; 89.1; 2.11.2; 18.2; 27.3; 63.1; Luke 1:2; 3:23; 24.47; Acts 1:1, 22; 10:37; 11:15). As Dionysius notes,

> So secure was the Romans' harmony, which owed its birth [ἀρχῆς] to the regulations of Romulus, that they never in the course of six hundred and thirty years proceeded to bloodshed and mutual slaughter, though many

---

[56] For this section of the essay citations of Dionysius will be limited to *Ant. rom.* 1–2, to his stories of the five groups of Greek emigrants to Rome and the first two kings, Romulus and Numa. For Luke, the founder was no longer Moses. Indeed, even before Luke, at least one Hellenistic Jewish author (Pseudo-Hecataeus) had already replaced Moses as the founder (see Bezalel Bar-Kochva, *Pseudo-Hecataeus, "On the Jews": Legitimizing the Jewish Diaspora* [Berkeley and Los Angeles: University of California Press, 1996], 34, 57, 79, 208, 220, 229–34). Bar-Kochva (142) situates Pseudo-Hecataeus in the late second century b.c.e. Text and translation in Carl R. Holladay, ed., *Fragments from Hellenistic Jewish Authors* (4 vols.; SBLTT 20, 30, 39, 40; Chico, Calif.: Scholars Press, 1983–96), 1:277–335.

great controversies arose between the populace and their magistrates concerning public policy, as is apt to happen in all cities, whether large or small. (2.11.2)

Plutarch too is concerned with chronology (*Thes.* 12.1; 18.1; 7.4; 8.7; *Rom.* 12.1, 4–6; 15.5; 27.3; 29.7; *Lyc.* 1.1–3; 7.3; *Num.* 1.1, 4; 2.1; 3.4; 5.1; 21.4; *Comp. Lyc. Num.* 2.5). Some founding events set dates for later rituals (*Thes.* 18.1; *Rom.* 15.5): "The Roman state would not have attained to its present power, had it not been of a divine origin [θείαν ... ἀρχήν], and one which was attended by great marvels [μέγα μηδὲ παράδοξον]" (*Rom.* 8.7).

2. Portents and Divine Birth. Dionysius gives various versions of the myth of Romulus's conception. The basic storyline is that someone ravished Romulus's mother, Ilea.[57] Most writers say it was the image of a daemon: there were supernatural signs, the sudden disappearance of the sun, and darkness spreading over the sky. This god comforted the girl, commanding her not to grieve since she had been united in marriage to a divinity and would bear two sons far exceeding other men in virtue and warlike courage (*Ant. rom.* 1.77.1–2), an event that is the "work of the god" (1.78.4). Our author worries whether he ought to relate such a story, since God is incorruptible and blessed, but, on the other hand, some philosophers suppose that between the race of gods and mortals there is a third order of being, daemons, who, uniting sometimes with humans and sometimes with gods, beget the fabled race of heroes (1.77.3).[58]

Plutarch narrates similar stories (*Thes.* 2.1; 6.1–2; *Rom.* 2.3–4.3; 7.5–6; 12.5; *Comp. Thes. Rom.* 6.5; *Num.* 3.4). For example, when Romulus was

---

[57] The following involves abbreviation and rearrangement; I quote Dionysius with Luke-Acts in mind. For theories (and critique thereof) of the Indo-European hero's life pattern, see Jan N. Bremmer and Nicholas M. Horsfall, *Roman Myth and Mythography* (University of London, Institute of Classical Studies Bulletin Supplement 52; London: Institute of Classical Studies, 1987), 26–27. I am not primarily concerned here with the origin or original structure of these stories. Ampolo and Manfredini (*Plutarco,* xl) suggest that Roman consciousness of their origins intensified after 338 B.C.E., when they conquered Greek Campania, especially Naples and Cuma. Bremmer and Horsfall, *Roman Myth and Mythography,* 25–62, theorize rather that after the Romans defeated the Latins in 338 B.C.E., they adopted the foundation myth of Praeneste. See Andrea Carandini and Rosanna Cappelli, *Roma: Romolo, Remo e la fondazione della città* (Exhibition, Rome; Museo Nationale Romano; 28 June–29 October 2000; Milan: Electa, 2000).

[58] See note 24 above. Dionysius may refer here to the Platonist Xenocrates. See Clemens Zintzen, "Geister (Dämonen): c. Hellenistische und kaiserzeitliche Philosophie," *RAC* 9 (1976): 640–68, cols. 640–41; Frederick E. Brenk, "An Imperial Heritage: The Religious Spirit of Plutarch of Chaironeia," *ANRW* 2.36.1:276–84.

conceived, there was an eclipse of the sun (*Rom.* 12.5). Such stories of kings/founders are so common that Plutarch's Numa must contrast himself with Romulus: "I am of mortal birth, and I was nourished and trained by men whom you know" (*Num.* 5.3; cf. Acts 14:15).

Luke's story of Jesus' birth parallels that of Romulus. An angel prophesies to Mary regarding her son's greatness and divinity (Luke 1:26–38).[59] There is miraculous divine intervention in both histories,[60] although Luke's story differs in narrating a virginal conception. Compared to Dionysius, however, Luke reduces the number of such miraculous divine births.[61]

3. DIVINE TITLES. As a result of their genealogy and this story of divine conception, "the Romans believe them [Romulus and Remus] to have been the sons of Mars" (πεπίστευνται ... "Άρεος υἱοί; *Ant. rom.* 2.2.3). Plutarch also uses such titles (*Thes.* 20.2; 36.3; *Rom.* 4.2; *Lyc.* 1.4; 5.3; 31.3; *Num.* 5.3). Intriguingly, Pisistratus (a ruler of Athens),[62] who appealed to Theseus

---

[59] Joseph A. Fitzmyer, *The Gospel according to Luke* (2 vols.; AB 28–28A; New York: Doubleday, 1981–85), 1:89–90, 310, argues that this was added in the final editing of the Gospel.

[60] See ibid., 1:338, for an interpretation of Luke 1:35.

[61] One of Rome's ancestors, Hercules, had a divine lineage and was honored as a god (*Ant. rom.* 1.40.1, 3). Others, such as the Trojans, led by Aeneas, had Atlas, the seven stars in Pleiades, Zeus, Hermes, the nymph Hieromneme, and Aphrodite in their lineage (1.61.1–3; 62.2). Finally, Romulus's successor, Tullius Servius (the sixth king), was born of a slave woman and a divine phantom, so that he also was "superior to the race of mortals" (4.2.2). His divinity was confirmed by a transfiguration story (4.2.3–4). Just as some doubted Jesus' divine sonship (Luke 4:22), many called Tullius merely the son of a slave woman, despite stories of his being generated by a god (4.1.2–2.3; 4.6.6). A significant difference between Dionysius's narrative and Luke-Acts is that the former has seven founding kings. Luke has only one Founder, only one character without a human father. Myths such as these found in the Bible present a hermeneutical challenge to a historian such as myself, who is also a Christian theologian teaching pastors in a divinity-school context. On attempts to deal with this issue, see Rudolf Bultmann, "New Testament and Mythology," in *Kerygma and Myth: A Theological Debate* (ed. H. W. Bartsch; trans. R. H. Fuller; 2 vols.; London: SPCK, 1953), 1:1–44, in particular, as well as the larger debate in both volumes. See also James A. Sanders, *From Sacred Story to Sacred Text: Canon as Paradigm* (Philadelphia: Fortress, 1987), 6, 21, 186–91, as well as idem, *Canon and Community: A Guide to Canonical Criticism* (Philadelphia: Fortress, 1984), 43–45, 51–60.

[62] In the introduction to their edition of Plutarch, Ampolo and Manfredini (*Plutarco*, xxix–xxx) observe that the legend of Theseus was promoted either by Pisistratus (565–546 B.C.E.), who claimed to be a friend of the people, or by Clisthenes (525–524 and 508–507 B.C.E.), who made it a feature of his democratic

as a model, was allegedly responsible for an interpolation in Homer that ascribed to Theseus the title "child of God" (*Thes.* 20.2, citing *Od.* 11.631)! While Luke did not attempt to interpolate his message into the Septuagint, he did understand the ancient Scriptures as prophecies. Moreover, the angel Gabriel announces to Mary that her child will be called the Son of God (Luke 1:35; cf. 3:38 and Acts 17:28–29).[63] This ascription is related to the previous point: supernatural birth suggests the supernatural character of the founder.

4. MIRACLES. If one excludes the stories of his birth and death, Romulus performs no healing or nature miracles. Dionysius is reluctant to narrate any miracles, one of the only exceptions being the "many marvelous stories" told of the second king, Numa (*Ant. rom.* 2.60.4). The nymph Egeria visits and instructs him in the art of reigning. When people did not believe, he gave the unbelievers proof of his relationship with the daemon, as she instructed. Then Dionysius narrates a feeding miracle at which the Romans are astonished (2.60.6). He is reticent about telling this story (2.61.1) and explains it by comparing Numa to other wise men, Minos of Crete and Lycurgus of Sparta. Plutarch tells no such story. Jesus, of course, works many miracles in Luke, including a feeding miracle (Luke 9:10b–17); thus here lies another contrast with Dionysius's and Plutarch's narratives.[64] Again, supernatural deeds fill out the character of the founder as someone special, someone blessed by god(s), or someone who is divine.

5. INSTRUCTION. Romulus's grandfather had instructed him in terms of what to say about the Roman form of government, and Romulus followed his teaching (*Ant. rom.* 2.3.1; also 1.7.3; 2.4.1; 28.1). Romulus's constitution (or way of life, which is Dionysius's understanding of *Romanità*) is then presented (2.6–29).[65] Maintaining the founder's and the ethnic group's

---

reform. For the former hypothesis, Martin P. Nilsson, "Political Propaganda in Sixth Century Athens," in *Studies Presented to David Moore Robinson on His Seventieth Birthday* (2 vols.; St. Louis: Washington University, 1951–53), 2:743–48, is cited, while, for the latter, it is Karl Schefold, "Kleisthenes," *MH* 3 (1946): 59–93.

[63] Cf. Feldman, *Judean Antiquities,* 472–74 nn. 1122, 1125 (on *Ant.* 4.326), where the case is made that Josephus tried to undermine any attribution of divinity to Moses in a similar way.

[64] On the disputed place of miracles in stories of founders and divine men, see Hans Dieter Betz, "Gottmensch II: Griechisch-römische Antike u. Urchristentum," *RAC* 12 (1983): 234–312, esp. 263–70 (Plato), 248–53 (Hellenistic-Roman), 257–59 (Pythagoras), and 273–86 (biographical writings). For an alternative view, see Emilio Gabba, "True History and False History in Classical Antiquity," *JRS* 71 (1981): 50–62.

[65] See Balsdon, "Dionysius on Romulus," 25 (*Romanità*).

religious rites and social customs is central in Dionysius's presentation (*Ant. rom.* book 1.21.1–2; 25.3; 32.5; 33.1–3 [a cross-reference to 7.72.14–18]; 34.4; 39.4; 40.3–6; 67–69 [a reference to 2.66]; 71.3; 76.3; 79.8, 11; book 2.6.1; 18–22 [23.2, 4, 5, "to our day"]; 23.6; 25.7; 26–27; 28.1; 34.4; 65.4; 74.4). On the other hand, not maintaining customs is considered slanderous (*Ant. rom.* book 1.33.4; 38.2; 44.2; 89.3, 4; book 2.6.2, 3; 12.4; 14.3; 19.2, 3; 34.3). As Dionysius notes,

> the admixture [ἐπιμιξίαι] of the barbarians with the Romans, by which the city forgot many of its ancient institutions, happened at a later time [than the founding]. And it may well seem a cause of wonder ... that Rome did not become entirely barbarized after receiving the Opicans, the Marsians, the Samnites, the Tyrrhenians, the Bruttians and many thousands of Umbrians, Ligurians, Iberians and Gauls, besides innumerable other nations ... [who] differed from one another both in their language and habits [οὔτε ὁμόγλωττα οὔτε ὁμοδίαιτα]; for their very ways of life, diverse as they were and thrown into turmoil by such dissonance, might have been expected to cause many innovations in the ancient order of the city. For many others by living among barbarians have in a short time forgotten all their Greek heritage, so that they neither speak the Greek language nor observe the customs of the Greeks nor acknowledge the same gods nor have the same equitable laws (by which most of all the spirit of the Greeks differs from that of the barbarians). (1.89.3–4)

Similarly, Plutarch's founders are also teachers (*Rom.* 11.1; 13.1, 3; 22.3; 27.1; *Lyc.* 13.1, 3, 5; 14.1, 4; 15.1, 3; 18.4; 19.1, 3; 20; 21; 27.1; 28; 30.5; 31.2; *Num.* 5.4, 5; 12.1; 14.1; 15.1; 22.2, 4). Moreover, Lycurgus's constitution was adopted by Plato, Diogenes, and Zeno (*Lyc.* 31.2)—he had some worthy students! Further, Plutarch's narrative about Lycurgus's constitution is distinctive in emphasizing that it was not changed for five hundred years by his successors or by the people of Sparta, until Agis reintroduced gold and silver (*Lyc.* 27.4; 29.2–3, 4, 6; 30.1; 31.5; but see 6.4–5). Finally, Plutarch is concerned to demonstrate that the negative features cannot be traced back to the founder but are to be considered later additions. In this vein, Plutarch argues that the *krypteia*, a secret service cruel to the Helots, did not originate with Lycurgus (*Lyc.* 28).

Jesus, too, is presented as a teacher. He teaches in synagogues (Luke 4:14; 5:3; etc.) and delivers his inaugural sermon in Nazareth (4:18–21, 23–27). He also teaches in the temple (19:47), for which he is accused of stirring up the people (23:5). There are fundamental similarities and differences between Romulus's way of life in Dionysius and Jesus' teaching in Luke. The primary similarity concerns the practice of receiving foreigners into the city/house churches (*Ant. rom.* 2.15; Luke 4:19 [quoting Isa 61:2]; Acts 10:1–11:18). Here I will only observe, without arguing the case, that in the travel section in Luke (9:51–19:27) Jesus teaches future leaders of the church a way of life.[66] Both Romulus and Jesus (Dionysius and Luke) are concerned with teaching a way of life, and both maintain a degree of continuity with the past. In response to accusations, Stephen and Paul claim to be teaching and guarding the laws of Moses, even though they are introducing uncircumcised pagans into local communities of the people of God.

There are also differences, however. One might contrast the last words of the two figures to bear this point out. Romulus's final words stress his father's (Mars) values: military preparedness and courage. This is reported by Julius Ascanius in Dionysius (*Ant. rom.* 2.63.3), and Livy also states it explicitly in his own history: "declare to the Romans the will of Heaven that my Rome shall be the capital of the world; so let them cherish the art of war and let them know and teach their children that no human strength can resist Roman arms" (1.16.7). This emphasis is consistent with Dionysius's whole narrative: a patriotic *encomium* for Roman military invincibility. Whichever of Jesus' final words (e.g., Luke 22:19 or 24:46) might be compared with those of Romulus, the result would be a fundamental contrast. It is interesting in comparison with Plutarch, however, to note that the values taught by both Numa and Jesus are quite similar, as both focus on peace, justice, and one's relationship to the divine (e.g., *Num.* 8.1 and Luke 10:5).[67]

6. *Stasis.* In a response to *stasis* in his own city, Numitor (the king of Alba) founds another colony. In this context, some (particularly the youths) migrate voluntarily from Alba to this new region, which is in principle supposed to resolve *stasis* in Alba but in turn results in the *stasis* between Romulus and Remus over the founding of Rome (στάσις; *Ant. rom.* 1.85.1–2; see book 1.8.2; 24.2; 31.2; 85.2; 86.1; 87.4; book 2.3.2, 4; 6.4; 9.1; 49.4; 56.3; 57.3; 58.1). Carol Dougherty observes that such civic crisis is the first stage of ancient Greek colonization.[68] Rome is founded to prevent disturbance in Alba. Then Romulus, Rome's founder, constructs a constitution that manages *stasis*—especially controlling the relations between patricians and plebeians—in a way that would "prevent them from engaging in seditions,

---

[66] See Balch, "Commentary on Luke," on 10:1–16 and 19:11–27 (1102–4, 1123).

[67] See Konrad Glaser, "Numa," *PW* 17:1242–52, esp. 1245–46 (citing Cicero, *Rep.* 1.23–30; *De or.* 2.154; Livy 1.19; Polybius 6.56.7; and Ovid, *Metam.* 16). On Plutarch's Platonizing biography, see Glaser, "Numa," 17:1251.

[68] Carol Dougherty, *The Poetics of Colonization: From City to Text in Archaic Greece* (New York: Oxford University Press, 1993), 3–30, cited by Walter T. Wilson, "Urban Legends: Acts 10:1–11:18 and the Strategies of Greco-Roman Foundation Narratives," *JBL* 120 (2001): 77–99. On Luke 23:1, see Dormeyer, "Stasis-Vorwürfe gegen Juden und Christen."

as happens in other cities when either the magistrates mistreat the lowly [ταπεινούς], or the common people, and the needy envy those in authority" (2.9.1).

Luke-Acts is similarly concerned with *stasis*. In Luke, the chief priests and the people accuse Jesus before Pilate: "He stirs up the people [ἀνασείει τὸν λαόν] by teaching throughout all Judea, from Galilee where he began even to this place" (Luke 23:5). The question whether to admit foreigners to the house churches similarly generates *stasis* in the church in Antioch (Acts 15:2). Paul's activity causes *stasis* in Ephesus (Acts 19:40), between Pharisees and Sadducees in Jerusalem (Acts 23:7), as well as in the temple itself (Acts 23:10). One key charge against Paul before the Roman governor Felix is that he generates *stasis* among Jews throughout the world (Acts 24:5). However, at James's suggestion, Paul purifies himself and performs rituals so that "all will know that there is nothing in what they have been told about you but that you yourself observe and guard the law" (Acts 21:24b). Paul claims simply to be practicing and believing Mosaic Torah, doing nothing that should offend traditional Jews and cause riots. In this Lukan depiction, Paul has not changed Moses' constitution.

Dougherty also observes that quite typically *stasis* includes murder. I will not repeat her examples here, but it is not surprising that people die in urban disturbances, especially when potential changes to central political/religious policies are under debate. The old man Eleazar as well as a mother and her seven sons (2 Macc 6–7), Jesus (Luke 23), and Stephen (Acts 6–7) become martyrs in such civic crises.[69] The relationship to *stasis* is naturally different in each case. In Luke the founder causes it civically, resolving it internally within the community; in Dionysius the founder resolves it externally. These differences can be explained by the respective sociocultural locations of the discourses themselves. Still, *stasis* is linked to founding, and the texts are quite concerned to resolve it one way or another.

---

[69] Richard I. Pervo, *Profit with Delight: The Literary Genre of the Acts of the Apostles* (Philadelphia: Fortress, 1987), 86–114, illustrates well Acts as an entertaining, ancient adventure novel. There are action-packed stories, arrests, escapes, stonings and beatings, trials, and riots. Acts is, but is not only, entertainment; however, the author has not simply generated a plot involving conflict and death for the delight of a leisured readership. Constitutional changes and their concomitant issues were at stake in the first century C.E., which generated actual *stasis*. The seriousness of this is aptly communicated by Xenophon (*Hell.* 2.3.32): "all sorts of changes in government are attended by loss of life" (καὶ εἰσὶ μὲν δήπου πᾶσαι μεταβολαὶ πολιτειῶν θανατηφόροι; cited by Ryffel [*ΜΕΤΑΒΟΛΗ ΠΟΛΙΤΕΙΩΝ*, 50 n. 148).

ΜΕΤΑΒΟΛΗ ΠΟΛΙΤΕΙΩΝ

7. VIOLENT/SUDDEN DEATH. Romulus died suddenly; darkness rushed down out of a clear sky, and a violent storm burst, after which he was nowhere to be seen. Some writers "believe that he was caught up into heaven by his father, Mars." Others (more plausibly, according to Dionysius) say he was murdered, because he exercised his power more like a tyrant than a king (*Ant. rom.* 2.56.2–3). Nevertheless, as Dionysius notes,

> the incidents that occurred by the direction of Heaven in connection with this man's conception and death would seem to give no small authority to the view of those who make gods of mortal men and place the souls of illustrious persons in heaven. For they say that at the time when his mother was violated whether by some man or by a god, there was a total eclipse of the sun [τὸν ἥλιαν ἐκλιπεῖν] and a general darkness as in the night covered the earth, and that at his death the same thing happened. (2.56.6)

Plutarch begins his biographies of the founders of Athens and Rome observing that "neither escaped domestic misfortunes and the resentful anger of kindred, but even in their last days both are said to have come into collision with their own fellow citizens" (*Thes.* 2.2; cf. 28.2; 35.4; *Rom.* 27.3–8; *Lyc.* 1.1; 11.1; 29.4; 31.4; *Num.* 2.1; 22.1; 22.6). Lycurgus committed suicide (*Lyc.* 29.4). Plutarch observes that "of the five [kings] who came after him [Numa], the last was dethroned and grew old in exile, and of the other four, not one died a natural death. Three of them were conspired against and slain" (*Num.* 22.6).

At the death of Jesus in Mark 15:33 and Matt 27:45 mention is made of darkness coming over the whole land, a motif repeated in Luke 23:44 with the added emphasis that "the sun's light failed."[70] This addition is not to be explained by appeal to Lukan apocalyptic imagery but rather should be understood as the use of the *topos* of the Greco-Roman cosmic legitimization of the founder. Moreover, like Romulus (ἀφανῆ; 2.56.2), Jesus also disappears (Luke 24:31).[71]

The stories of Romulus's and Jesus' deaths differ in many ways, not least in their length, but one similarity is striking: the reason given for Romulus's murder is that "he released [ἄφεσιν] without common consent, contrary to custom, the hostages he had taken from the Veientes" (*Ant. rom.* 2.55.6; 56.3). In his inaugural sermon at Nazareth, Jesus informs the audience that the Lord "has sent me to proclaim release [ἄφεσιν] to the captives, to set at liberty those who are oppressed" (Isa 58:6 and 61:2, cited in

---

[70] The Greek reads τοῦ ἡλίου ἐκλιπόντος. The same noun and participle are used by Dionysius, *Ant. rom.* 2.56.6 (quoted above).

[71] Feldman, *Judean Antiquities,* 472 n. 1121 (on *Ant.* 4.326), discusses Moses' "disappearance."

Luke 4:18), a mission concerning which the resurrected Christ is still teaching the disciples (Luke 24:47).

8. EPIPHANIES. One should also note the presence of stories relating an appearance and an ascension.[72] While the Romans were in doubt whether divine providence or human treachery had been the cause of Romulus's disappearance, Julius Ascanius, who had never told a lie, said he saw Romulus departing from the city fully armed—hardly a spiritual appearance story! He was told to "announce to the Romans from me, that the genius to whom I was allotted at my birth is conducting me to the gods, now that I have finished my mortal life, and that I am Quirinus" (*Ant. rom.* 2.63.3–4; see Livy 1.16). Absolutely central for Luke, of course, is Jesus' ascension (Luke 9:51; 24:51; Acts 1:9).

Plutarch records that some Athenians honor their founder as a demigod, because "many of those who fought at Marathon against the Medes thought they saw an apparition of Theseus in arms rushing on in front of them against the barbarians" (*Thes.* 35.5; see *Num.* 2.3). He is more philosophical than Dionysius about this, however, as *Rom.* 28.6–8 in fact provides an argument against the bodily assumption of a divine founder into heaven, which is precisely the kind of story Luke is interested in relating (Luke 24:30, 39, 41–43, 51; Acts 1:9–10).

9. SENDING OUT/FOUNDING A COLONY. Typically, after civic disturbance and death, some leave to found colonies; they are "sent out" (ἀποστέλλω; *Ant. rom.* book 1.10.3; 16.1, 2; 27.3; 1.85.2; book 2.1.1; 35.4, 5; 36.2; 49.3; 50.5). Plutarch does not include the theme of sending out (*Rom.* 24.3 is the closest parallel), and herein lies an important difference between Plutarch's biographies and Dionysius's history. Plutarch's biographies of founders are not focused on their successors, while Dionysius's history and Luke-Acts are centrally concerned with those who are "sent out."[73] This point depends

---

[72] On ascension stories of Roman Caesars, see Hans-Josef Klauck, *The Religious Context of Early Christianity: A Guide to Graeco-Roman Religions* (trans. B. McNeil; Edinburgh: T&T Clark, 2000), 293, 300, 305, 309, 311 (citing Appian, *Bell. civ.* 2.148; Suetonius, *Aug.* 100.4; Seneca, *Apoc.* 1.1–2; Pliny, *Nat.* 2.18–19; *Pan.* 11.1–3; 35.4). Klauck also notes that the Caesar cult, based on the official witnesses of such ascensions, employed the plural of *euangelion* to announce the good tidings/news (328–29) and that this had a rudimentary narrative element associated with it. The verb and the plural noun *gospel* are also used by the Hellenistic Jews (cf. Philo, *Legat.* 18 and 231; and Josephus, *War* 4.618). See further, Klauck, *Religious Context of Early Christianity*, 265, 298, 328–29; and Gary Gilbert's essay in this volume.

[73] When Plutarch does have reason to mention successors (*Lyc.* 6.4–5; 30.1; *Num.* 21.1; 22.7; *Comp. Lyc. Num.* 4.6–7), the context seems to be the same as the

on comparing stories of Greek and later Roman colonization with the narrative of the early Christian foundation of the Gentile mission,[74] a comparison brilliantly introduced by Walter Wilson.[75]

There are significant differences as well. In the case of Luke-Acts, the resurrected Jesus declares the apostles to be witnesses, announcing that "repentance for the forgiveness of sins is to be proclaimed in his name to all the nations" (Luke 24:47), and these apostles—these ones "sent out"—go on to found the Jerusalem community in the opening chapters of Acts.[76] If the parallels to Dougherty's cases were exact, one would expect the church in Jerusalem to send out colonists/missionaries, but in Acts the church in Antioch rather sends out Barnabas and Paul (Acts 13:1–3; see 14:4, 14; 26:17). While Dionysius, Plutarch, and Luke-Acts often have common vocabulary (one notes particularly that apostles are "the ones sent out") in the comparisons outlined above, the term "colony" (ἀποικία, ἀποικέω) does not occur in Luke-Acts. When the church in Antioch sends out Paul and Barnabas, they establish not colonies or cities but houses (Luke 10:5; 19:9; Acts 2:46; 8:3; 11:14; 16:15, 31; 18:8; 20:20) and churches (ἐκκλησίαι; Acts 8:3; 9:31; 15:3, 41; 20:28).

10. DIVINE DIRECTION. The colonists are led or commanded by heaven (*Ant. rom.* book 1.20.1; 31.3; 34.5; 55.1; 57.4; 58.2; 59.4, 5 [parable]; 66.1; 67.1; 1.79.9; 86; book 2.5.1). Again, Dougherty observes that the colonists typically consult the oracle of Apollo at Delphi, which Wilson parallels with visions from heaven in Acts 10 (cf. the divination surrounding the selection of Matthias in Acts 1:24–26).[77]

Plutarch offers many such indications (*Thes.* 3.3–4; 25.2; *Rom.* 9.7; 14.1; 19.1; 21.2; 24.1; *Comp. Thes. Rom.* 6.5; *Lyc.* 6.1, 5; 13.6; 23.2; *Num.* 3.6; 4; 6.2; 7.2–3; 8.3–10; 10.2; 13.1; 15.4–5 (magic); *Comp. Lyc. Num.* 1.1). After

---

one raised in the first paragraph of this essay (quoting Acts 6:11, 13–14 and 21:21): Do the successors maintain the founder's laws and values?

[74] Cf. Philo, *Legat.* 147, who praises Augustus for *hellenizing* the world; see Gerhard Delling, "Philons Enkomion auf Augustus," *Klio* 54 (1972): 171–92.

[75] Wilson, "Urban Legends."

[76] In Luke-Acts, moreover, this sending out is directly connected to the heightening of conflict/*stasis*. In Acts—in a revolutionary context (Acts 5:36–37) no less—tension increases between the high priest and those who are sent out (Acts 5:17, 21, 28, 33). In the following context, Stephen is accused and stoned. A persecution begins against the church, and "all except the apostles were scattered throughout the countryside of Judea and Samaria" (Acts 8:1).

[77] For an extensive discussion of these themes in Luke-Acts and Dionysius, see John T. Squires, *The Plan of God in Luke-Acts* (SNTSMS 76; Cambridge: Cambridge University Press, 1993), esp. 103–54.

the rape of the Sabine women, for instance, the Romans go to war with their men, but the ravished daughters of the Sabines, with shouts and lamentations, as in a frenzy of possession (ἐκ θεοῦ κάτοχοι), beg their fathers to have pity on them and the children whom they have now borne, since they have been "united by the strongest ties with those whom we had most hated" (*Rom.* 19.1–3). Here the unity of the two races, a key Roman civic policy, is enabled by ecstatic possession. Luke narrates an analogous, multiethnic unity enabled by the Spirit in Acts 2. Lycurgus and Numa also have in common that "they derive their laws from a divine source" (*Comp. Lyc. Num.* 1.1), a theme that connects readily with Luke-Acts as well. For early Christian apostles, hearing God's directions or commands might refer not only to the visions of Acts 10–11 (see Acts 13:4; 16:9), as Wilson argues, but also to hearing and obeying the prophets and/or the Jesus of the Gospel (cf. Isa 61:2, quoted by Jesus in Luke 4:19, which is then preached and acted upon by Peter in Acts 10:35).

11. JOURNEYING. Those sent out wander (*Ant. rom.* book 1.4.2; 10.2; 17.2, 3; 18.1; 24.4; 34.2; 52.4; 53.3; 54.1; 58.2; 72.2, 3; book 2.1.3). Plutarch has many similar stories (*Thes.* 6.6; 26–28; 30.4; *Rom.* 1.1; *Lyc.* 1.1; 3.5; 4.3, 5–6; 27.3; 29.2, 4–5; 29.5; 30.1; 31.5). One striking difference is that after Lycurgus's death, the Spartans do not journey abroad (*Lyc.* 27.3; 29.4–5); when they do, they bring home love of gold and silver, subverting the laws of Lycurgus (*Lyc.* 30.1). The content is not the same, but Jesus' (Luke 9–19) and Paul's (Acts 13–14; 16–20) journeys are central in the Gospel and Acts.[78]

12. RECEPTION OF FOUNDER OR COLONISTS/MISSIONARIES. A pivotal question in both Dionysius and Luke-Acts concerns whether the colonists or Jesus and his witnesses will be received (*Ant. rom.* book 1.9.4; 16.3; 20.1; 50.3; 57.4; 63.2; 66.2; 73.2; 1.89.3; book 2.36.2). In Dionysius, during the first year after the fall of their city, the Trojans cross the Hellespont and land in Thrace, where they received the fugitives who kept flocking to them

---

[78] David Moessner, *Lord of the Banquet: The Literary and Theological Significance of the Lukan Travel Narrative* (Minneapolis: Fortress, 1989; repr., Harrisburg, Pa.: Trinity Press International, 1998), argues that this same travel section brings the long, unresolved journey of Israel to its intended goal. Edgar Mayer, *Die Reiseerzählung des Lukas* (Lk 9,51–19,10): *Entscheidung in der Wüste* (EH 23, Theologie 554; Frankfurt: Lang, 1996), argues that Luke's model for Jesus' journey is Israel's wandering in the wilderness. The journey motif is quite widespread, as documented for sea journeys by Charles H. Talbert and John H. Hayes, "A Theology of Sea Storms in Luke-Acts," in *SBL Seminar Papers, 1995* (SBLSP 34; Atlanta: Scholars Press, 1995), 321–36.

(1.63.2), and Rome, "though she razed her mother-city to the ground, nevertheless welcomed its citizens into her midst" (1.66.2). Plutarch manifests this same concern (*Thes.* 33.1; 36.2; *Rom.* 1.3; 7.1; 9.3; 16.2; *Num.* 15.1).

In Luke-Acts this concern is also prominent: δέχομαι occurs with a relevant meaning ten times in the Gospel (3:13; 9:5; 9:48 [4x], 53; 10:8, 10; 18:17) and three times in Acts (8:14; 11:1; 17:11); ἀποδέχομαι occurs with a relevant meaning once in the Gospel (8:40) and three times in Acts (2:41; 21:17; 28:30); ὑποδέχομαι occurs with a relevant meaning twice in Luke (10:38; 19:6) and once in Acts (17:7). Further, the verbal adjective δεκτός occurs three times, and all these instances are at critical junctures in the narrative. The first occurrence is in the programmatic sermon in Nazareth, where Jesus (Luke 4:18–19) quotes Isa 61:1–2: "The Spirit of the Lord is upon me, because he has anointed me to bring good news to the poor, to proclaim the year of God's acceptance [δεκτόν]."[79] The adjective occurs later in the same sermon (4:24), then once more in the remaining bulk of the two volumes, when Peter preaches to the Roman centurion Cornelius: "in every nation anyone who fears him and does what is right is acceptable [δεκτός] to him" (Acts 10:35). The prophecy from Isaiah that Jesus quotes in his inaugural sermon is fulfilled by God's acceptance of the pagan centurion into the people of God in Acts 10. It is not surprising, then, that the penultimate line in the whole two-volume work contains this emphasis: "He [Paul] lived there [Rome] two years at his own expense and welcomed all [ἀπεδέχετο πάντες] who came to him" (Acts 28:30), with *all* here referring to *both* Jews and Gentiles. Thus, for Luke, the theme regarding who receives the word of God is central, and I suspect that it is intended as a challenge to early Christian readers to engage whether they are in fact acting on the prophets' and Jesus' words to receive foreigners.

13. GROWTH. According to Dionysius the new colony grows (αὐξάνω; *Ant. rom.* book 1.3.1, 4; 11.3; 16.2; 23.1; 31.3; 59.5; 64.4; book 2.15–17; 32.2; 36.2, 3; 47.1; 50.1; 62.5).[80] Romulus made Rome populous by insisting that the inhabitants bring up their male children and the first born of the females; second,

> finding that many of the cities in Italy were very badly governed, both by tyrannies and by oligarchies, he undertook to welcome [ὑποδέχεσθαι] and attract to himself the fugitives from these cities.... His purpose was to increase [αὐξῆσαι] the power of the Romans and to lessen that of their

---

[79] Translation from NRSV, modifying the translation of the final phrase from Isa 61:2. Matthew 5:3 and 11:5 cite Isa 61:1, but only Luke includes Isa 61:2.

[80] Cf. Herodotus 1.58.4; Polybius 2.37.8; 2.39.11; 5.10.1. Polybius compares Rome and Athens, dismissing the latter because it did not continue to grow (6.43.2)!

neighbors (2.15.3).... When I compare the customs [ἔθη] of the Greeks with these, I find no reason to extol either those of the Lacedaemonians or of the Thebans or of the Athenians, who pride themselves most on their wisdom; all of whom jealous of their noble birth [εὐγενές] and granting citizenship to none or to very few (I say nothing of the fact that some even expelled foreigners [ξενηλατοῦντες]), not only received no advantage from this haughty attitude, but actually suffered the greatest harm because of it. Thus the Spartans after their defeat at Leuctra [371 B.C.E.], where they lost seventeen hundred men, were no longer able to restore their city to its former position after that calamity, but shamefully abandoned their supremacy. And the Thebans and the Athenians through the single disaster at Chaeronea [338 B.C.E.], were deprived by the Macedonians not only of the leadership of Greece but at the same time of the liberty they had inherited from their ancestors. But Rome ... derived from them [i.e., misfortunes] a strength even greater than she had before ... thanks to the number of her soldiers, and not, as some imagine, to the favour of Fortune.[81]

Again, Plutarch shares this value (*Rom.* 16.5; 20.1; 25.1; *Num.* 5.2, 5; 8.2; *Comp. Lyc. Num.* 4.7). In a fascinating turn, however, he contrasts Romulus's policy of growth by conquest with his successor Numa's desire to serve the gods and to teach people to honor justice and hate violence and war (*Num.* 5.5)! As king, Numa tames the Romans' warlike tempers (*Num.* 8.3).

Political policies in Athens and Jerusalem were more exclusive than in Rome,[82] but Rome's policies were astoundingly successful, which must have generated debate in other Mediterranean cities concerning what civic policies were the best. Should Greeks continue to despise barbarians, and should Jews continue to exclude Gentiles (see 1 Macc 1–4; 2 Macc 4–7)?[83] Their present policies, after all, could be seen as resulting in their loss of freedom and in their now having to pay tribute to Rome!

The early Christian impulse to grow (see αὐξάνω in Luke 12:27; 13:19; Acts 6:7; 7:17; 12:24; 19:20) by receiving foreigners into Jewish-Christian house churches was a *Romanization* of the gospel. The early church did not grow by military means (also rejected by the Roman king Numa, noted above), as did Romulus's Rome, until Constantine converted, which represented a subsequent dramatic change of constitution, reverting back to

---

[81] *Ant. rom.* 2.17.1–3. This statement is in response to Greek accusations noted earlier in 1.4.2.

[82] See Gabba, *Dionysius and the History*, 87, 103.

[83] For the spectrum of debate within Hellenistic Judaism, see David L. Balch, "Attitudes toward Foreigners in 2 Maccabees, Eupolemus, Esther, Aristeas, and Luke-Acts," in *The Early Church in Its Context: Essays in Honor of Everett Ferguson* (ed. A. J. Malherbe et al.; NovTSup 90; Leiden: Brill, 1998), 22–47.

ΜΕΤΑΒΟΛΗ ΠΟΛΙΤΕΙΩΝ

Romulus's values. In Luke's narrative, rather, the church grows by preaching—by the word. Paul preaches the Lord Jesus boldly in the synagogue in Ephesus, but since they do not believe he transfers to the lecture hall of Tyrannus (Acts 19:8-9). This pattern continues "so that all the residents of Asia, both Jews and Greeks, heard the word of the Lord [ἀκοῦσαι τὸν λόγον τοῦ κυρίου, Ἰουδαίους τε καὶ Ἕλληνας; 19:10). Paul is successful in conflict with some Jewish exorcists, so that "all residents of Ephesus, both Jews and Greeks, everyone was awestruck; and the name of the Lord Jesus was praised" (19:17). They burn their magic books, and "so the word of the Lord grew mightily [κυρίου ὁ λόγος ηὔξανεν] and prevailed" (Acts 19:20).

14. MIXING. Growth is a result of mixing (*Ant. rom.* book 1.9.2; 10.2; 19.3; 34.2; 41.1; 60.1; 64.2; 73.2; 85.4; 89.2, 3; 90.1; book 2.2.2; 30.2; 46.3). When Aeneas's wanderings ceased, he and his group—these "natives of Troy"—came to the later location of Rome "in obedience to the commands of the gods" (1.58.2). They asked forgiveness for their invasion from the local inhabitants (1.58.4) and then proceeded to make a treaty (1.59.1). Following signs that they would grow (1.59.5), they

> united [μίξαντες (mixed)] the excellence of the two races, the native and the foreign, by ties of marriage ... combining in a very brief time their customs, laws and religious ceremonies [συνενεγκάμενοι ἔθη καὶ νόμους καὶ θεῶν ἱερά], forming ties through intermarriages and becoming mingled together in the wars they jointly waged, and all calling themselves by the common name of Latins.... The nations, therefore, which came together and shared in a common life [κοινωσάμενα τοὺς βίους] and from which the Roman people derived their origin ... (Dionysius goes on to list the five groups of emigrants). (1.60.1-3)

There is repeated conflict over intermarriage, however (1.64.2; 2.30.2). For Dionysius mixing thus involves not only intermarriage but also the mixing of "language and habits/customs" (1.89.3-4).

Plutarch also repeats this theme (*Thes.* 13.3; *Rom.* 9.2; 11.1; 14.2, 6; 19.7; 20.4; 21.1; 29.3; *Comp. Thes. Rom.* 6.3-4; *Num.* 1.3; 17.1-3). Romulus sees his city filling up with aliens mixed with poor and obscure persons, so he finds means of blending them and creating fellowship: mixing and thereby uniting the two (*Rom.* 14.2, 6). Romulus's successor, Numa, mixed many Spartan customs with Roman ones, as Pythagoras had taught them to him (*Num.* 1.3). Plutarch describes Numa's means of accomplishing this mixing thus:

> [Rome] was rather divided into two tribes, and utterly refused to become united [μηδενὶ τρόπῳ μιᾶς γενέσθαι], or to blot out its diversities and differences. On the contrary, it was filled with ceaseless collision and

contentions between its component parts. Numa, therefore, aware that hard substances which will not readily mingle (τὰ φύσει δύσμικτα) may be crushed and pulverized, and then more easily mix and mingle with each other (ἀναμιγνύουσιν) ... determined to divide the entire body of the people into a greater number of divisions.... He distributed them, accordingly, by arts and trades. The remaining trades he grouped together, and made one body [ἕν] out of all who belonged to them.... And thus, at last, he banished from the city the practice of speaking and thinking of some as Sabines, and of others as Romans; or of some as subjects of Tatius, and others of Romulus, so that his division resulted in a harmonious blending of them all together [εὐαρμοστίαν καὶ ἀνάμιξιν πάντων γενέσθαι πρὸς πάντας].[84]

However, Greek policies of mixing differed from Roman ones. Romulus founded Rome, but Theseus made a metropolis (συνῴκισε; *Thes.* 2.2; *Comp. Thes. Rom.* 4.1). Theseus "settled all the residents of Attica in one city, thus making one people of one city [συνῴκισε τους τὴν Ἀττικὴν κατοικοῦντας εἰς ἓν ἄστυ, καὶ μιᾶς πόλεως ἕνα δῆμον ἀπέφηνε][85] out of those who up to that time had been scattered about and were not easily called together for the common interests of all" (*Thes.* 24.1). While Romulus united different ethnic groups, Theseus united just Greeks, which is not the same civic policy.

Luke's contemporary Josephus rejects the Roman policy described here. He gives significant space to the story of Balaam (*Ant.* 4.102–158)

---

[84] *Num.* 17.1–3. This passage is close to Acts 2, 6, and 10; contrast 2 Macc 6–7. See Balch, "Attitudes toward Foreigners," 31–32.

[85] Cf. Josephus, *Ant.* 4.200–201: "let there be one holy city ... and let there be one temple therein, and one altar.... For God is one and the Hebrew race is one." Cf. Eph 4:4–6: "there is one body and one Spirit, just as you were called to the one hope of your calling, one Lord, one faith, one baptism, one God and Father of all, who is above all and through all and in all;" and Acts 17:26a: "From one ancestor he made all nations [ἐποίησέν τε ἐξ ἑνός πᾶν ἔθνος ἀνθρώπων] to inhabit the whole earth." Ephesians and Acts denationalize the formula; there is no ethnic holy city or holy temple whether in Greece, Italy, or Judea. See Lucio Troiani, "The ΠΟΛΙΤΕΙΑ of Israel in the Graeco-Roman Age," in *Josephus and the History of the Greco-Roman Period: Essays in Memory of Morton Smith* (ed. F. Parente and J. Sievers; StPB 41; Leiden: Brill, 1994), 12, who cites Cicero, *Leg.* 2.7–22: "Unlike many peoples of the ancient world, the Romans were most generous in sharing their own citizenship with others." See further Howard H. Scullard, *From the Gracchi to Nero: A History of Rome 133 BC to AD 68* (5th ed.; London: Routledge, 1982), 2 (and the index under "citizenship"); Adrian N. Sherwin-White, *The Roman Citizenship* (Oxford: Clarendon, 1939); and John P. V. D. Balsdon, *Romans and Aliens* (Chapel Hill: University of North Carolina Press, 1979), 82–96.

ΜΕΤΑΒΟΛΗ ΠΟΛΙΤΕΙΩΝ

precisely in the context of Moses delivering his constitution and laws to Israel.[86] Balaam advises the Moabite king, Balak, to have beautiful, young Moabite women seduce Jewish boys, which will anger God (4.129–130). When the boys are "enslaved" to them (4.133), the women urge the boys, since their customs are alien to all humanity, to worship their gods (4.137–140). Zambrias then opposes Moses, calling him a tyrant (4.146, 149). Zambrias goes on to assert that he has married a foreign wife and will sacrifice to the gods he chooses (4.148–149). Phinees then kills them both (4.153, 159; cf. Num 25:1–15). Feldman observes that, while Josephus addresses primarily non-Jews in the *Antiquities,* Greek was the primary language for large numbers of Jews in Egypt, Asia Minor, Syria, and Rome, and thus Josephus may well have been directing this story against assimilation to a Jewish readership supportive of the agenda of Zambrias.[87] Zambrias's rebellion was "directed not merely against the authoritarianism of Moses, but also against the refusal of Judaism to open itself to other religious views."[88] The issue was thus intermarriage,

---

[86] Feldman, *Judean Antiquities,* xxviii. See also Louis H. Feldman, *Studies in Josephus' Rewritten Bible* (JSJSup 58; Leiden: Brill, 1998), 91–136 (on Korah and Balaam); idem, "Josephus' Biblical Paraphrase as a Commentary on Contemporary Issues," in *The Interpretation of Scripture in Early Judaism and Christianity: Studies in Language and Tradition* (ed. C. A. Evans; JSPSup 33; SSEJC 7; Sheffield: Sheffield Academic Press, 2000), 159–70, 192–96; idem, "Moses," in *Josephus's Interpretation of the Bible* (Hellenistic Culture and Society 27; Berkeley and Los Angeles: University of California Press, 1998), 390–93, 433–34, 439; as well as John R. Bartlett, *Jews in the Hellenistic World: Josephus, Aristeas, The Sibylline Oracles, Eupolemus* (Cambridge Commentaries on Writings of the Jewish and Christian World, 200 BC to AD 200 1/1; Cambridge: Cambridge University Press, 1985), 153–60.

[87] Feldman, *Judean Antiquities,* 378 n. 392 (on *Ant.* 4.131; cf. 379–85; and idem, *Studies in Josephus' Rewritten Bible,* 130, 134). This key section of Josephus on Moses' constitution is, then, deliberative rhetoric. Cf. the deliberative passage in Dionysius (*Ant. rom.* 4.24) regarding whether emancipated slaves should become citizens. See further David L. Balch, "Paul in Acts," 21. Contrast Todd Penner, "In Praise of Christian Origins: Stephen and the Hellenists in Lukan Apologetic Historiography" (Ph.D. diss., Emory University, 2000; T&T Clark, forthcoming), 433, 438, who characterizes this material as exclusively epideictic. Ulrich Wilckens, "Kerygma und Evangelium bei Lukas (Beobachtungen zu Acta 10 34–43)," *ZNW* 49 (1958): 223–37, persuasively argues that Peter's sermon is addressed to *Christians,* especially in that it outlines the Gospel of Luke and seeks to persuade Christians to accept all nations into their house churches. Hence, the sermon represents deliberative rhetoric as well.

[88] Feldman, *Judean Antiquities 1–4,* 380 n. 408 (on *Ant.* 4.140). Also Willem C. van Unnik, "Josephus' Account of the Story of Israel's Sin with Alien Women in

precisely one of the means of assimilation sponsored by the Romans, according to Dionysius.[89]

Marriage is relatively unimportant for Luke,[90] but according to Dionysius and Plutarch (e.g., *Num.* 17.1–3, quoted above) there are several means of accomplishing mixing, one of the most important of which is linguistic (cf. *Ant. rom.* 1.89.3–4). In contrast to the priestly trajectory noted earlier,[91] then, Luke's story brings diverse groups together with a linguistic focus (Acts 2:7–11).

15. CHANGING NAMES. The name of the colony may be changed (*Ant. rom.* book 1.9.3; 10.2; 25.2; 26.1; 30.3; 45.2; 53.1; 65.1; book 2.2.2; 46.2; 49.1), as Dionysius makes clear: "The Albans were a mixed nation composed of Pelasgians, of Arcadians, of Epeans ... and last of all, of the Trojans. It is probable that a barbarian element also ... was mixed with the Greek. But all these people, having lost their tribal designations, came to be called by one common name, Latins" (2.2.2). Plutarch begins his story of Romulus with various theories about the source of his name, which is also of course the source of the name of the famous city (*Rom.* 1.1–2). Lukan house churches also have a distinguishing name: "it was in Antioch that the disciples were first called Christians" (Acts 11:26).[92]

---

the Country of Midian (Num. 25.1ff.)," in *Travels in the World of the Old Testament: Studies Presented to Professor M. A. Beek* (SSN 16; Assen: Van Gorcum, 1974), 241–61.

[89] Feldman often compares Josephus with Thucydides, but less often with Dionysius, and perhaps, therefore, he fails to perceive this basic cultural conflict between Josephus's Judaism and Dionysius's Roman values. He also fails to compare Dionysius's great *stasis* in Rome (*Ant. rom.* 6.22–92) with this great sedition against Moses. Contrary to Rajak, "Josephus's Political Thought," this story indicates that Josephus's *Antiquities* addresses some of the same fundamental issues addressed in his *Against Apion*.

[90] See Osiek and Balch, *Families in the New Testament World*, 136–43. On those in early Christian house churches as fictive kin, see Joseph H. Hellerman, *The Ancient Church as Family* (Minneapolis: Fortress, 2001).

[91] In the introduction to this essay I noted the strong biblical presence of a traditional priestly opposition to mixing (see the biblical references in n. 4 above). The following example is illustrative: "They [Israel] angered the LORD at the waters of Meribah.... They did not destroy the peoples, as the LORD commanded them, but they mingled with the nations [ἐμίγησαν ἐν τοῖς ἔθνεσιν] and learned to do as they did. They served their idols, which became a snare to them" (LXX Ps 105 [106]:32–36).

[92] See Hubert Cancik, "The History of Culture, Religion, and Institutions in Ancient Historiography: Philological Observations Concerning Luke's History," *JBL* 116 (1997): 694, 697.

16. LANGUAGE. The traditional language that the ethnic group speaks is maintained or modified (*Ant. rom.* book 1.20.3; 29.3; 30.2; 33.4; 52.3; 89.3, 4; 90.1; 50.3). As just noted above, Dionysius's theory of Roman mixing includes language (*Ant. rom.* 1.89.3–4, quoted above). Since, for Dionysius, that which is Greek is virtuous and that which is barbarian is vicious, the Roman rulers of the world must be (or originally have been) Greek, and, however problematic it may be, their language (originally) was Greek. Dionysius notes,

> The language spoken by the Romans is neither utterly barbarous nor absolutely Greek, but a mixture as it were, of both, the greater part of which is Aeolic; and the only disadvantage they have experienced from their intermingling with these various nations is that they do not pronounce all their sounds properly.... For it is not merely recently ... that they have begun to live humanely; nor is it merely since they first aimed at the conquest of countries lying beyond the sea ... that they have lived like Greeks [βίον Ἕλληνα ζῶντες].[93]

Plutarch shares at least aspects of this theory. He narrates the rape of the Sabines in the context in which he gives an etymology for the Roman nuptial shout, *talasius*. It is, as Plutarch observes, close to the Greek "*talasia*, as the Greeks call 'spinning,' Italian words having not yet at that time entirely submerged the Greek" (*Rom.* 15.3).

Luke's narrative of mixing, although the author does not use this word, involves not marriage but language; this feature represents one crucial function of the Pentecost story. The Hellenistic Jewish author of the *Letter of Aristeas* had already argued that the Hebrew Bible had legitimately been translated into Greek. In Acts 2 (2:4, 8–11; cf. 10:44) God speaks and understands any and every language. There is thus not only one holy language.

At this juncture, I move away for a moment from providing literary parallels in order to explore a sociocultural value that helps us understand Luke's interests. The most striking illustration of the importance of traditional versus adaptable language usage is the Isis cult, the most widely worshiped goddess in the Roman world contemporary with the rise of Christianity.[94] I have often wondered, to put it crudely, why Isis lost and Christ won. There were surely many factors involved in this, but language was certainly crucial. The worship of Isis and Osiris was, as were

---

[93] *Ant. rom.* 1.90.1. See Hidber, *Das klassizistische Manifest*, 77.

[94] See Tran Tam Tinh, "Sarapis and Isis," in *Self-Definition in the Greco-Roman World* (vol. 3 of *Jewish and Christian Self-Definition;* ed. B. F. Meyer and E. P. Sanders; Philadelphia: Fortress, 1982), 3:102–3, 105.

all religions earlier than Alexander the Great, the religion of only one people.[95] There were many Isis religious texts, but the aretalogies were virtually the only texts translated from the native Egyptian language into Greek.[96] Plutarch attempted a hellenization of Isis,[97] but his hellenization was not accepted in Egypt. Indeed, Egyptian priests from the second to the fourth century C.E. isolated themselves.[98] This is perhaps most aptly indicated in the following example, where Hermes Trismegistos praises the power of Egyptian language and criticizes empty Greek words and philosophy:

> For my teacher Hermes often used to say ... that those who read my writings ... will think them to be quite simply and clearly written, but those who hold opposite principles to start with will say that the style is obscure and conceals the meaning. And it will be thought still more obscure in time to come, when the Greeks think fit to translate these writing from our tongue into theirs. Translation will greatly distort the sense of the writings, and cause much obscurity. Expressed in our native language, the teaching conveys its meaning clearly ... and when the Egyptian words are spoken, the force of the things signified works in them. Therefore, my King, as far as it is in your power, (and you are all-powerful), keep the teaching untranslated, in order that secrets so holy may not be revealed to Greeks, and that the Greek mode of Speech, with its ... feebleness, and showy tricks of style, may not reduce to impotence the impressive strength of the language, and the cogent force of the words. For the speech of the Greeks, my King, is devoid of power to convince; and the Greek philosophy is nothing but a noise of talk. But our speech is not mere talk; it is an utterance replete with workings.[99]

Porphyry too attempted to spiritualize Egyptian religion, arguing that Egyptian sounds had no meaning to Greeks or Romans: one can pray in any language. God is not Egyptian and does not speak Egyptian. However, Iamblichus wrote a work against Porphyry, arguing that all traditional

---

[95] Reinhold Merkelbach, *Isis regina—Zeus Sarapis: Die griechisch-ägyptische Religion nach den Quellen dargestellt* (Stuttgart: Teubner, 1995), 121–30. See also Tinh, "Sarapis and Isis," 104. The potential development from an ethnic cult to an international religion is related to the question of the origin of writing universal history; see Alonso-Núñez, "Emergence of Universal Historiography."

[96] Merkelbach, *Isis regina—Zeus Sarapis,* 214–23.

[97] Ibid., 242–51.

[98] Ibid., 309.

[99] *Corp. herm.* 16.1–2 (contrast the *Letter of Aristeas*). Translation from Walter Scott, *Hermetica: The Ancient Greek and Latin Writings Which Contain Religious or Philosophic Teachings Ascribed to Hermes Trismegistus* (2 vols.; London: Dawsons, 1968), 1:262–65 (cf. 2:437–38).

Egyptian rituals are sacrosanct and that one may not change the prayers.[100] I thus conclude that traditional Egyptian priests were a crucial cause of the decline of Isis. Isis apparently had no Egyptian apostle like the Diaspora Jew Paul. Adaptation was a contentious issue, and Hellenistic syncretism promoted expansion and growth. Therefore, just as the Hellenistic-Jewish translation of the Hebrew Bible into Greek (the Septuagint) and Josephus's (and others) hellenization of Jewish history and theology gave linguistic life to Judaism, so also Luke's Pentecost story illustrates the early Christian linguistic commitment that gave Jesus life.[101]

Dionysius, Plutarch, and Luke all reflect similar kinds of debates that were also involved in the Isis cult and its spread. How does language relate to teaching? More importantly and generally, how should change be viewed? For Luke the answer is that ethnic mixing and the proclamation of the gospel in Greek promote growth.

CONCLUSION

To summarize, there are significant similarities as well as important differences[102] between the historical and biographical foundation narratives of Dionysius, Plutarch, and Luke-Acts. Their founders have quite a number of remarkable similarities, including stories of their birth without human fathers (although Plutarch must assert that Numa was mortal). Confessions of their divinity and divine power are typical (again, excluding Numa). Their teachings and practices vary widely; for example, Lycurgus institutionalized not only male homosexual relationships but also lesbian sexual relationships, of which Plutarch disapproved. Most importantly, Romulus, Jesus, and the apostle Peter share the policy of receiving foreigners. Stories of civic conflict include the founders' violent deaths (except Numa) and disappearance, their physical appearance after death, and ascension narratives. Then some of their citizens/followers (but not the Spartans) are

---

[100] Merkelbach, *Isis regina—Zeus Sarapis,* 311–15. Roger S. Bagnall, *Egypt in Late Antiquity* (Princeton: Princeton University Press, 1993), 237, notes: "a narrow priestly cadre clung to Demotic for their literature.... The small base of persons literate in Demotic was its undoing."

[101] Translation was crucial in this endeavor, but there were other factors as well (e.g., maintaining the original language, whether in Egypt or Israel). Further, the intellectual defenses of early Jewish and Christian apologists (e.g., Philo and Origen) were brilliant. Isis seems not to have been served as well by one of her own followers.

[102] On the importance of evaluating both similarities and differences when making comparisons, see Jonathan Z. Smith, *Drudgery Divine: On the Comparison of Early Christianities and the Religions of Late Antiquity* (Chicago: University of Chicago Press, 1990).

sent out under the direction of heaven; they journey and are received by others. The new colony/*ekklēsia* grows, which is related either to the citizens' intermarriage or to the translation of Scriptures and/or missionary sermons into local languages. The group then receives a new name. Dionysius, Plutarch, and Luke often tell their stories in the same words: ἀρχή (beginning); υἱός θεοῦ (son of God); διδάσκω (teach); βασιλεία (kingdom); ἔθος (custom); νόμος (law); γλῶσσα (language); ἔθνος (ethnic group); εἷς (one); δικαιοσύνη (justice); εἰρήνη (peace); κοινωνία (common); θεός (God); ἀλλόφυλος (foreigner); στάσις (sedition); ἀποκτείνω (kill); τὸν ἥλιον ἐκλιπεῖν (eclipse of the sun); ἄφεσις (set free/forgive); ἀφανής (disappearance); ἀποστέλλω (send out); δέχομαι (receive); ταπεινός (humble); αὐξάνω (grow); ἀλλάσσω (change).[103]

Aspects of Greek and Roman teaching and practices in this respect also offer sharp contrasts with Luke. For example, attitudes toward war differ, and this difference is already illustrated in the two successive founders of Rome: Romulus and Numa. Some political policies taught authoritatively by the founder(s) are debated in the present by their successors; these are sociopolitical questions that move across political biography and/or ancient history, making generic distinctions on this basis difficult for a text such as Luke-Acts. One such continuing acrimonious political question concerns the reception of foreigners into the city or house churches. To this issue I now turn.

FOUNDERS/SUCCESSORS AND THE CHANGING OF CUSTOMS

The quantity and quality of the constitutional change that Plutarch's founders introduce provides a striking contrast to Dionysius's and Luke's founder(s). Plutarch's frank narration of change in contrast to Dionysius's insistence on continuity raises the question as to why they differ. My initial suspicion is that the difference is related to Dionysius's apologetic legitimization of Romulus and Rome, while Plutarch's stories are comparisons that are not committed to the same end. This observation would have consequences for Luke, who, like Dionysius, is committed to the narrative characters—to legitimating Jesus, Peter, Stephen, and Paul. The changes these Lukan characters introduce must somehow be justified by references to antiquity (hence the importance of the references to Moses) so as not to be perceived as new developments. The ancient order was the ideal (i.e., divine, revealed) and therefore could not be changed or improved upon.

---

[103] Ancient opponents of the Christians (e.g., Celsus) made the same observation. Origen's reply is instructive: see *Contra Celsum* (trans. H. Chadwick; 2 vols.; Cambridge: Cambridge University Press, 1953), 2:55–62.

ΜΕΤΑΒΟΛΗ ΠΟΛΙΤΕΙΩΝ 175

PLUTARCH AND CHANGING THE CONSTITUTION

Plutarch's founders change their city's/state's political constitutions. The Plutarchian emphases are helpful for our investigation in that they clarify Dionysius's and Luke's stress on continuity. It is thus worth examining Plutarch's particular options in this context.

1. Theseus gave up the kingship and instituted a democracy, with everyone having an equal share (ἰσομοιρία). It was gladly accepted by the common folk and the poor (ἰδιωτῶν καὶ πενήτων ἐνδεχομένων) but not by the powerful (δυνατοῖς; Plutarch, *Thes.* 24.2–4; see *Comp. Thes. Rom.* 2.1: μεταβολή). Having done away with their offices (καταλύσας ... ἀρχάς; *Thes.* 24.3), Theseus embittered the chief men in Athens, and even the common people felt robbed of their native homes and religions (*Thes.* 32.1; contrast 35.2–5). The result is conflict with the citizens (*Thes.* 2.2), which, along with his other deeds, brings about Theseus's banishment and death (29.2).

2. Like most who have assumed great power, Romulus became haughty; he renounced popular ways (ἐξίστατα τοῦ δημοτικοῦ) and became a monarch (παρήλλαττεν εἰς μοναρχίαν; Plutarch, *Rom.* 26.1; *Comp. Thes. Rom.* 2.1–2). On the other hand, when his grandfather died in Alba, he put that government in the hands of the people and appointed an annual ruler. Plutarch notes, "In this way he taught [ἐδίδαξε] the influential men at Rome also to seek after a form of government which was independent and without a king.... For by this time not even the so-called patricians had any share in the administration of affairs, but a name and garb of honour was all that was left them" (*Rom.* 27.1; cf. *Thes.* 24.2).[104]

3. In his treatment of Lycurgus, Plutarch notes the following:

> Returning [to Sparta], then, to a people thus disposed, he [Lycurgus] at once undertook to change the existing order of things and revolutionize the civil polity [κινεῖν καὶ μεθιστάναι τὴν πολιτείαν]. He was convinced that a partial change of the laws [κατὰ μέρος νόμων] would be of no avail whatsoever, but that he must proceed as a physician would with a patient who was debilitated and full of all sorts of diseases; he must reduce and alter [μεταβαλῶν] the existing temperament by means of drugs and purges, and introduce a new and different regimen [ἑτέρας ἄρξεται καινῆς διαίτης]. (*Lyc.* 5.2)

Lycurgus then goes to Delphi and consults the oracle, where the priestess addresses him as "beloved of the gods, and rather god than man" (*Lyc.*

---

[104] This could easily be read as Plutarch's criticism of current Roman politics.

5.3). The god (Apollo) grants him a constitution that is the best in the world. Lycurgus tries to bring the first men of Sparta to his side and to strike fear into the opposite party (ἀντιπράττοντας; *Lyc.* 5.4). He also institutes many innovations (πλειόνων καινοτομουμένων; *Lyc.* 5.6; *Comp. Lyc. Num.* 2.2: μεγάλαις κρῆσθαι μεταβολαῖς) and is so eager to establish this form of government that he obtains an oracle from Delphi, which the Spartans call a *rhetra* (*Lyc.* 6.1; 13.6; 23.2; *Comp. Lyc. Num.* 1.1). Later, after the people had distorted the sense by additions and subtractions, two kings interpolated (παρενέγραψαν) a clause that when the people adopted a distorted motion, the kings had the power to adjourn the assembly (*Lyc.* 6.4). They also persuaded the city that the god authorized this addition to the *rhetra* (τοῦ θεοῦ ταῦτα προστάσσοντος; *Lyc.* 6.5). The *rhetras* were to remain unchanged (*Lyc.* 13.1, 3), but 130 years after Lycurgus the oligarchy/monarchy was curbed by the institution of the power of the *ephors* (*Lyc.* 7.1).

Lycurgus also distributed land and even redistributed furniture among the free (*Lyc.* 8.3; 9.1). He withdrew gold and silver and ordained the use of iron money alone, which meant that no teachers of rhetoric, vagabond soothsayers, or prostitutes would set foot in the city (*Lyc.* 9.1, 3; *Comp. Lyc. Num.* 1.3). He even instituted common public meals, not allowing the wealthy to dine at home, which incensed them (*Lyc.* 10.1, 3; 11.1). His opponents sent Lycurgus running from the marketplace. He was followed by young Alcander, who hit him with a stick and blinded him in one eye (*Lyc.* 11.1). The citizens were shamed by the blood and gave Alcander over into Lycurgus's hands. Lycurgus made him minister to his needs, and, seeing his lifestyle, Alcander became one of his followers (*Lyc.* 11.3). Lycurgus's changes to the lifestyle of women are striking from both an ancient Greek and a modern point of view, giving women more freedom and authority, including the right to march naked in processions (*Lyc.* 14–15).[105] Just as there was same-sex activity among men (ἐρασταί; *Lyc.* 17.1), so there was also among the women (καὶ τῶν παρθένων ἐρᾶν τὰς καλὰς καὶ ἀγαθὰς γυναῖκας; *Lyc.* 18.4). However, Lycurgus also had limits on his openness:

> [He] did not permit them to live abroad at their pleasure and wander in strange lands, assuming foreign habits [ξενικὰ ... ἤθη] and imitating the lives [μιμήματα βίων] of peoples who were without training and lived under different forms of government [πολιτευμάτων διαφόρων; 27.3]. For along with strange people [ξένοις σώμασιν], strange doctrines must come in [ἀνάγκα λόγους ἐπεισιέναι ξένους]; and novel doctrines [λόγοι καινοί]

---

[105] This aspect was criticized by Plutarch, as the young women were unconfined and unfeminine (*Comp. Lyc. Num.* 3.3, 5).

bring novel decisions [κρίσεις καινάς], from which there must arise many feelings and resolutions which destroy the harmony [ἁρμονίαν] of the existing political order. Therefore he thought it more necessary to keep bad manners and customs from invading and filling the city than it was to keep out infectious diseases. (*Lyc.* 27.4)

Lycurgus made the people promise to issue no change or alteration (μηδέν ἀλλάσσειν μηδὲ μετακινεῖν) in his institutions until he consulted the oracle at Delphi and returned (*Lyc.* 29.2). They promised to abide by the established polity (ἐμμενεῖν ... πολιτείᾳ; *Lyc.* 29.3). At Delphi Apollo answered that Sparta would be held in the highest honor while it kept the constitution of Lycurgus. He sent this oracle to Sparta and put an end to his own life (*Lyc.* 29.4), lest the people change his polity (μεταβάλωσι τὴν πολιτείαν; *Lyc.* 31.5). For five hundred years none of the kings made any changes (29.6), but then Agis reintroduced gold and silver, thus subverting the laws of Lycurgus (τοὺς Λυκούργου καταπολιτευσάμενος νόμους; *Lyc.* 30.1).

4. Pythagoras helped the king arrange the government of the city, with the result that many Spartan customs were mingled with the Roman ones (*Num.* 1.2). After Romulus's sudden disappearance, factionalism (στάσις) arose over the king to be appointed in his place: "for the newcomers [ἐπηλύδων] were not altogether blended with the original citizens [τοῖς πρώτοις συγκεκραμένων πολίταις]" because of their different nationalities (τῶν πατρικίων ἐν ὑποψίαις ἐκ τοῦ διαφόρου πρὸς ἀλλήλους; *Num.* 2.4; cf. 2.5–6). The senators roused the suspicion that they had changed the form of government to an oligarchy (μεθιστάντες εἰς ὀλιγαρχίαν), but both factions (ἀμφότεραι ... αἱ στάσεις) agreed that each one should appoint a king from the other (*Num.* 3.1). The Romans nominated Numa Pompilus (*Num.* 3.2–3). As Cancik observes, no other Roman comes as close to a Christian saint as does Numa, the *exemplum* of *religio* and *pietas*.[106] He forsook city existence for a life of solitude, wandering alone in the country.

---

[106] Hubert Cancik, "Reinheit und Enthaltsamkeit in der römischen Philosophie und Religion," in *Aspekte frühchristlicher Heiligenverehrung* (ed. F. von Lilienfeld; OIKONOMIA: Quellen und Studien zur orthodoxen Theologie 6; Erlangen: Universität Erlangen, Lehrstuhl für Geschichte und Theologie des christlichen Ostens an der Universität Erlangen, 1977), 10. Cancik observes (3–4), however, that celibacy was rare in Roman religion. Roman discipline was "Welt bemeisterendes, gewiss auch vergewaltigendes *exercittium*" (6), an inner-worldly asceticism that leaves no room for an other-worldly one (15). The Romans preferred examples from their own "history," not (Greek) mythological heroes. Cancik thus concludes (15) that Roman and Christian asceticism cannot be reconciled.

He even had celestial companionship: the goddess Egeria (*Num.* 4.2; 8.6; 13.1; 14.1). As Plutarch notes,

> Is it worth while, then, if we concede these [other] instances of divine favour, to disbelieve that Zaleulcus, Minos, Zoroaster, Numa, and Lycurgus, who piloted kingdoms and formulated constitutions [βασιλείας κυβερνῶσι καὶ πολιτείας διακοσμοῦσιν], had frequent audiences with the Deity? Is it not likely, rather, that the gods are in earnest when they hold converse with such men as these, in order to instruct and advise them in the highest and best way? ... However ... there is no absurdity in the other account, which is given of Lycurgus and Numa and their like, namely, that since they were managing headstrong and captious multitudes and introducing great innovations in modes of government [μεγάλας ἐπιφέροντες ταῖς πολιτείαις καινοτομίας], they pretended to get a sanction from the god, which sanction was the salvation of the very ones against whom it was contrived. (*Num.* 4.7–8; *Comp. Lyc. Num.* 1.1; 2.2)

Numa was convinced that the work of a true king is a service to God (*Num.* 6.2), so he aimed to unite and blend the citizens (ἐπὶ κοινωνίᾳ καὶ συγκράσει; *Num.* 6.4; esp. 17.1–3). As iron is softened, his goal was to change the Romans' harsh and warlike temper to greater gentleness and justice (μαλακωτέραν[107] ποιῆσαι καὶ δικαιοτέραν; *Num.* 8.1; 19.6; 20.3; *Comp. Lyc. Num.* 4.8; but see 22.7): "[H]eralding to them vague terrors from the god [ἀπαγγέλλων παρὰ τοῦ θεοῦ], strange apparitions of divine beings and threatening voices, he would subdue and humble [ἐδούλου καὶ ταπεινήν] their minds by means of superstitious fears" (*Num.* 8.3; cf. 15.1; 22.7).

Further, Numa moved March, named for Mars, from the first to the third month, "because he wished in every case that martial influences should yield precedence to civil and political" (*Num.* 19.5). The new first month, January, takes its name from Janus, the patron of civil and social order, who "is said to have lifted [changed/converted] human life out of its bestial and savage state [πολιτικὸς καὶ κοινωνικὸς ἐκ τοῦ θηριώδους καὶ ἀγρίου κέγεται μεταβαλεῖν τὴν δίαιταν]. For this reason he is represented with two faces, implying that he brought men's lives out of one sort and condition into another [ἑτέραν ἐξ ἑτέρας τῷ βίῳ περιποιήσαντα τὴν μορφὴν καὶ διάθεσιν]" (19.6). Janus had a temple at Rome, whose doors

---

[107] This is an astonishing adjective with which to describe Numa's goal for the formation of *Roman* character (but cf. 22.7). I do not find this kind of *societal* conversion discussed by Arthur Darby Nock, *Conversion: The Old and the New in Religion from Alexander the Great to Augustine of Hippo* (Oxford: Clarendon, 1933). See Eusebius, *Hist. eccl.* 1.2.22–23.

ΜΕΤΑΒΟΛΗ ΠΟΛΙΤΕΙΩΝ

were open during war but closed during peace. During the reign of Numa, the doors were closed forty-three years (i.e., war ceased; 20.1-2, 5).[108] Numa thus transformed Rome's eagerness for war into peaceful pursuits.

In all of this the character of the founder is quintessential for effecting such change, as Plutarch aptly illustrates:

> For not only was the Roman people softened and charmed by the righteousness [δικαιοσύνη] and mildness of their king, but also the cities round about, as if some cooling breeze or salubrious wind were wafted upon them from Rome, began to experience a change of temper [ἀρχὴ μεταβολῆς], and all of them were filled with longing desire to have good government, to be at peace, to till the earth, to rear their children in quiet, and to worship the gods (*Num.* 20.3).... "Blessed [Μακάριος]," indeed, is such a wise man [ὁ σώφρων] "in himself, and blessed, too, are those who hear the words of wisdom issuing from his lips" [here paraphrasing Plato, *Laws* 711e]. For possibly there is no need of any compulsion or menace in dealing with the multitude, but when they see with their own eyes a conspicuous and shining example of virtue in the life of their ruler, they will of their own accord walk in wisdom's ways, and unite with him in conforming themselves [συμμετασχηματίζονται][109] to a blameless and blessed life [μακάριον βίον] of friendship and mutual concord, attended by righteousness [δικαιοσύνης] and temperance. Such a life is the noblest end [τέλος] of all government, and he is most a king [βασιλικώτατος] who can inculcate such a life and such a disposition in his subjects. This, then, as it appears, Numa was preeminent in discerning. (*Num.* 20.3, 7-8)

When Tullus Hostilius succeeded Numa as king (*Num.* 21.1), he mocked Numa's virtues, especially his devotion to religion, asserting that it made men idle and effeminate (γυναικώδης; *Comp. Lyc. Num.* 2.2 counters this accusation). He then returned the Romans to war (πρὸς πόλεμον ἔτρεψε τοὺς πολίτας; *Num.* 22.7): "That which was the end and aim [τέλος] of Numa's government, namely, the continuance of peace and friendship between Rome and other nations, straightway vanished from the earth with him" (*Comp. Lyc. Num.* 4.6). Tullus Hostilius, however, was converted to superstition (ἀλλασσόμενος) by a disease and thus gave himself over to something far worse than the piety of his predecessor (*Num.* 22.7). The Romans increased in power after abandoning (ἐξαλλάξαντας) the institutions of Numa (*Comp. Lyc. Num.* 4.7). Nevertheless, Numa, a stranger,

---

[108] Rome was usually engaged in war, since its increasing size brought conflict with various barbarian groups, but in the time of Augustus the doors to the temple were also closed (symbolizing the Augustan *pax*). Cf. Gilbert's treatment of this theme in his essay in this volume.

[109] See 1 Cor 7:31; Phil 2:7; 3:21; Rom 12:2; 1 Pet 1:14.

changed the whole nature of the state by force of persuasion alone (πάντα πειθοῖ μεταβαλεῖν) and mastered a city that was not yet in sympathy with his views (*Comp. Lyc. Num.* 4.8). These stories clearly demonstrate that, in Plutarch's depiction, the character of the founder (here Numa and Tullus) generates changes in the lifestyle of the people.

LUKE-ACTS AND CHANGING THE CONSTITUTION

Turning now to Luke-Acts, I note six points of comparison with Plutarch: (1) Plutarch typically describes civic conflict in his *Life* of a particular founder (*Thes.* 2.2; *Rom.* 7.1; 8.6; 26.1; *Comp. Thes. Rom.* 2.1–2; *Lyc.* 5.4; *Num.* 2.4–6; 3.1); (2) a founder typically changes the constitution (*Thes.* 24.2–4; 32.1; *Comp. Thes. Rom.* 2.1; *Lyc.* 5.2, 6; 6.4–5; 7.1; 8.3; 9.1, 3; 10.1, 3; 11.1; 14–15; 18.4; 30.1; *Num.* 4.8; 20.3; 22.7; *Comp. Lyc. Num.* 1.1, 3; 2.2; 4.6, 7, 8); (3) one ideal is that the constitution does not change after the founder's death (*Lyc.* 13.1, 3; 27.3–4; 29.2–3; compare esp. Dionysius, *Ant. rom.* 7.70–72), but other traditions clearly narrate change after the founder's death (*Rom.* 27.1; *Lyc.* 6.4–5; 7.1; 30.1; *Num.* 21.1; *Comp. Lyc. Num.* 4.6–7; compare Dionysius, *Ant. rom.* 1.9.4, quoted on page 148 above); (4) civic conflict and change at the beginning—the founding—results in injury (*Lyc.* 11.1) or death for the founder (*Thes.* 29.2; *Rom.* 27.4; *Lyc.* 31.5 [suicide], but not in the case of Numa, who dies of old age); (5) ethnic diversity at the time of the founding generates civic conflict, which in turn motivates the founders to attempt to unify the city (*Thes.* 24.1; *Comp. Thes. Rom.* 4.1–2; *Num.* 6.4; esp. 17.1–3; cf. Dionysius, *Ant. rom.* 2.45.3, but not in *Lyc.*); and (6) religion becomes one means of persuading the people to accept the founder's new institutions (*Lyc.* 5.3–4; 6.1, 5; *Num.* 4.7–8; 8.3; 15.1; 22.7; *Comp. Lyc. Num.* 1.1; 2.2) or to dissuade them from changing those institutions (*Lyc.* 29.2–4; cf. Josephus, *Ant.* 4.292, 295; also 223–224, 302).

Luke-Acts similarly narrates a change in the laws of Moses that generates significant civic conflict resulting in an accusation against Jesus (Luke 23:5), the death of Stephen (Acts 6–7), and a Roman trial for Paul (Acts 21–28). One source of the conflict is clearest in Acts 10:28: Peter tells the Roman centurion Cornelius that "you yourselves know that it is unlawful for a Jew[ish follower of Jesus] to associate with or to visit a Gentile" (ἀλλοφύλῳ; a foreigner). However, then the Holy Spirit falls on all the hearers (10:44), astounding traditional believers (10:45), with the result that Peter baptizes the pagans (10:47–48). In the Lukan narrative the people of God thereby become multiethnic.

Luke's particular portrayal is fundamentally rooted in his Scripture, the Septuagint. Any consideration of the Lukan agenda must, therefore, first begin in the earlier texts. The root for foreigner (ἀλλοφυλ-) occurs 290 times in the Septuagint. Often the root is used to translate the word "Philistine," which, for the most part, carries a clear negative connotation in the biblical texts.[110] The book of Amos, however, offers an important exception to this. While Amos 1:8 prophesies that, "the remnant of the Philistines shall perish," the prophet elsewhere mentions several other kingdoms and challenges his hearers: "Go down to Gath of the Philistines. Are you better than these kingdoms?" (Amos 6:2). Most provocatively, he states: "'Are you not like the Ethiopians to me, O people of Israel?' says the Lord. 'Did I not bring Israel up from the land of Egypt and the Philistines [ἀλλοφύλους] from Caphtor?'" (Amos 9:7).[111]

The term is prominent also in Maccabean literature. King Antiochus deputizes Lysias (1 Macc 3:32), who appoints three generals. These foreigners (4:12; cf. Jdt 6:1) attack Judas Maccabeus but are defeated. The next year they attack again, and Judas prays, "Blessed are you, O Savior of Israel, who crushed the attack of the mighty warrior [Goliath] by the hand of your servant David, and gave the camp of the Philistines [ἀλλοφύλων] into the hand of Jonathan son of Saul.... Strike them down with the sword of those who love you" (1 Macc 4:30, 33). Lysias's army is then routed, and Judas rebuilds the Jerusalem altar, after which the Gentiles hear about it. One report is that the people of Ptolemais, Tyre, Sidon, and "all Galilee of the Gentiles" (πᾶσαν Γαλιλαίαν ἀλλοφύλων) gathered to annihilate Judas and his army (1 Macc 5:15). Judas, however, tears down the altars of the foreigners, burns their carved images (1 Macc 5:68; 2 Macc 10:2), and purifies the temple that they had profaned (2 Macc 10:5). It is noteworthy for our current analysis that this Maccabean viewpoint occurs in a context that is fundamentally opposed to the "adoption of foreign customs or religions" (ἀλλοφυλισμός).[112]

---

[110] Cf. the narratives about Samson (Judg 13–16), the ark (1 Sam 4–6), King Saul (1 Sam 9–19; 1 Chr 9–10), and King David (1 Sam 17–31; 1 Chr 11–18). Two texts in fact explicitly contrast *Hebrews* and *foreigners/Philistines* (1 Sam 14:21; 29:3). In terms of biblical characterization, the Philistines worship idols (1 Sam 31:9; 1 Chr 10:9; cf. Bar 6:5) and are uncircumcised (1 Sam 31:11). The Lord delivers the Philistines to Israel (1 Sam 17:46; 23:2, 4; 2 Sam 5:19–20; 1 Chr 14:10, 15; Zeph 2:5) and saves Israel from them (2 Sam 3:18; cf. Jer 47:1, 4; Pss 60:8; 108:9).

[111] Isaiah also compares Jacob with the Philistines, as both are full of diviners (2:6), and Ezekiel says the Philistines are ashamed of Jerusalem's lewd behavior.

[112] There was an increase in the adoption of foreign customs because the high priest Jason was perceived as wicked (2 Macc 4:13). The old man Eleazar chooses martyrdom rather than to allow the young to suppose that he had assimilated to a foreign religion (2 Macc 6:24). Further, Antiochus IV was punished on earth and chastised after his death for his attempts to compel Israel to become pagan (4 Macc 18:5).

I thus conclude that the Septuagint provides two fundamental options for evaluating foreigners. Historical literature (1–2 Samuel; 1 Chronicles; 1–2 and 4 Maccabees) polarizes the people of God and foreigners, who are uncircumcised worshipers of idols and who are trying to annihilate Israel. Judas prays to God to assist him in fighting foreigners just as God helped David crush Goliath (1 Macc 4:30). On the other hand, Amos (9:7), in his prophetic critique, gives another option: just as God led Israel in exodus from Egypt, so God brought foreigners from Caphtor. Both strands are imperative for understanding the Lukan direction on the issue of foreigners.

Luke radically revises the first, historical approach when retelling the story of David (Acts 2:25–31; 13:21–23, 33–37). David is not a warrior fighting with foreigners such as Goliath (1 Sam 17; 1 Macc 4:30) but rather a prophet who foresees his descendant's (i.e., Christ's) deliverance from the corruption of death and his subsequent ascension (see LXX Ps 15 [16]:8–11, cited in Acts 2:25–28; 13:35).[113] God's promise to David has brought Israel a Savior, Jesus (Acts 13:23), the messianic Son of God (13:33). This interpretation of David's role is preached by both Peter and Paul, a repetition indicating its importance to the author. This radical revision of Israel's customs generated civic disturbances in the Lukan narrative and represents a major reversal. God assisted David in killing Israel's enemies—foreigners—in the past (26x in 1 Sam 17; 1 Macc 4:30), but in Luke's narrative, at a later stage in Israel's salvation history, the Holy Spirit falls on Cornelius, a foreigner/Philistine (ἀλλόφυλος; Acts 10:28). Peter and other Jews from Jerusalem (followers of the Jew Jesus) interpret this as an event that introduces Cornelius and his household into the community of the house church.[114]

A major part of the Lukan argument rests on the premise that Mosaic, Davidic, and prophetic Scriptures (Luke 16:31; 24:44–48; Acts 13:47), as well as Jesus, prophesied God's reversal (i.e., the acceptance of all the nations). As Clare Rothschild has proposed, for Luke "the less plausible the event, the more crucial its prediction" is.[115] Prophecy thus belongs to Luke's historiographical rhetoric of persuasion. The introduction of the

---

[113] C. K. Barrett, *A Critical and Exegetical Commentary on the Acts of the Apostles* (2 vols.; ICC; Edinburgh: T&T Clark, 1994), 1:149.

[114] John O. York, *The Last Shall Be First: The Rhetoric of Reversal in Luke* (JSNTSup 46; Sheffield: Sheffield Academic Press, 1991).

[115] Clare Komoroske Rothschild, "Luke-Acts and Josephus's *Antiquitates Judaicae*: Observations of a Rhetoric of Hellenistic Historiography" (paper presented for the Luke-Acts Group at the Society of Biblical Literature Annual Meeting, Denver, Colorado, November 2001); and idem, *Luke-Acts and the Rhetoric of History: An Investigation of Early Christian Historiography* (WUNT; Tübingen: Mohr Siebeck, forthcoming).

foreigner (ἀλλόφυλος), Cornelius, and his household into the church was thereby prophesied (Isa 61:2; restated by Jesus in Luke 4:19; fulfilled by Peter's acceptance of Cornelius in Acts 10:35). This configuration functions, then, to make the argument that, despite what some Jews and Jewish Christians may think, it is a change that is not really a change.

In conclusion, the Greco-Roman and Jewish traditions surveyed here exhibit two basically different approaches to changing the constitution. One trajectory opposes any change of the founder's customs. Maccabean literature, stories about Sparta after Lycurgus's death, and, typically, Josephus take this first approach. The other option accepts historical change, only if and when the new practices are related to the founder's constitution. Literature narrating the history of Romulus and Rome, the biography/history of Numa, and Luke-Acts exhibit the second option.[116]

In terms of anthropological models, Gerd Baumann names the first approach "essentializing" discourse, which emphasizes ethnicity or religion as having some inherent, eternal core. He categorizes the second as "processual" or "instrumentalist" discourse because it emphasizes change and transformation of cultural phenomena.[117] He also observes that ethnic or religious groups with less cultural power are more likely to assert an essentialist view of ethnicity and/or religion, while dominant ethnic groups are more likely to espouse the view that both are either mutable or strategic. Cohen similarly indicates that the shifting bases of claiming Jewish identity in the Hellenistic-Roman period indicate that ethnicities and religions are cultural constructs "rhetorically employed to gain assent to the idea that they are stable and coherent even while they are being transformed."[118] Luke represents not only a group with little cultural power but also a group of pork-eating, uncircumcised Gentiles who do not rest on the Sabbath. Such radical discontinuity threatens to bring a loss of identity. So Luke must claim continuity on other grounds: the reception of foreigners such as Cornelius was prophesied, authorized by the ancient prophets Moses (no longer construed here as a founder) and Isaiah, as well as the Lukan founder, Jesus.

---

[116] The literature surveyed says little about Theseus's successors and so leaves the question open.

[117] Gerd Baumann, *The Multicultural Riddle: Rethinking National, Ethnic, and Religious Identities* (New York: Routledge, 1999), 90, as reviewed by Denise Kimber Buell, "Ethnicity and Religion in Mediterranean Antiquity and Beyond," *RelSRev* 26 (2000): 246. I drew the conclusion stated in the lead sentence of this paragraph before reading Baumann or Buell.

[118] Shaye J. D. Cohen, *The Beginnings of Jewishness: Boundaries, Varieties, Uncertainties* (Hellenistic Culture and Society 31; Berkeley and Los Angeles: University of California Press, 1999), also reviewed by Buell, "Ethnicity and Religion," 246 (quoted here).

JESUS, A FOUNDER WITHOUT A CITY OR TEMPLE?

After Alexander the Great there were attempts not only to write universal histories but also to develop ethnic cults and principles into international, universal religions. In approximately 52 B.C.E., Cicero set out a philosophical constitution with twenty-four laws of religion. Employing the Stoic understanding of "natural," he writes the following: "for these virtues originate in our natural inclination to love our fellow-men, and this is the foundation of Justice" (*Leg.* 1.15.43).[119] These laws are not only for Romans but also for all good peoples. Cicero understands his religion to be natural, reasonable, and humane, although, from a non-Roman point of view, it certainly has historical, national, and particularistic aspects. The move toward diversity is evident in that when a person attained Roman citizenship, this did not necessarily include a change of religion.[120] The Egyptian cult of Isis illustrates this same trajectory, as it developed what has been called an "exclusive universalizing" tendency[121] (Isis is the one God), which still did not deny that the One also goes by other names (Apuleius, *Metam.* 11.6). This religion is universal in thrust; Isis welcomes everyone and claims the whole person.[122]

Rome also guaranteed Jews the right to practice their ancestral religion, which included freedom from serving in the army and from appearing in court on the Sabbath (Josephus, *Ant.* 14.4, 10). Jews typically were not forced to participate in the Caesar cult but prayed for the Roman ruler in synagogues. According to 1 Macc 8, these rights began in the time of Judas, but the status of these arrangements in that time period is debated.[123] In any case, I focus here rather on the πολιτεία of the Jews *and* Christians in

---

[119] Hubert Cancik and Hildegard Cancik-Lindemaier, "*Patria—peregrina—universa:* Versuch einer Typologie der universalistischen Tendenzen in der Geschichte der römischen Religion," in *Tradition und Translation: Zum Problem der interkulturellen Übersetzbarkeit religiöser Phänomene. Festschrift für Carsten Colpe zum 65. Geburtstag* (ed. C. Elsas et al.; Berlin: de Gruyter, 1994), 66–67. On nature and the gods, cf. Cicero, *Leg.* 1.7.1.

[120] This is why so many non-Roman cults had a home in Rome. For example, the Phrygian cult of Cybele had its own rituals in Rome. See Cancik and Cancik-Lindemaier, "*Patria—peregrina—universa,*" 69.

[121] Ibid.

[122] Although, as noted with Cicero, one cannot deny a certain exclusivity even as inclusivity is emphasized, as one had to have enough money for the initiation ritual in order to join the Isis religion in the first place.

[123] See Erich S. Gruen, *The Hellenistic World and the Coming of Rome* (2 vols.; Berkeley and Los Angeles: University of California Press, 1984); and the review of this work by Emilio Gabba in *Athenaeum* 65 (1987): 205–10.

the later Greco-Roman period. One key problem for the Jews after 70 C.E. and for Luke writing late in that same century was that their respective founder and constitution did not set out laws for any city/state. There was no longer any geographical center, so they had to learn how to become a (universal) religion within a (Roman) state that had a different constitution with its own distinct laws and values.

Furthermore, as Troiani argues, the Mosaic constitution (πολιτεία) "seems to have pre-eminent ideological value in our texts [Philo, Josephus, and other Hellenistic-Jewish literature], and indicates active membership in Judaism."[124] Troiani does not present a technical, juridical discussion of the legal status of Jews in Hellenistic cities but argues that numerous texts discuss equal citizenship (ἰσοπολιτεία),[125] not citizenship in particular cities per se. As Troiani notes, earlier kings conceded "equality of political rights" (ἰσονομία) to the Jews of Asia and Libya (Josephus, *Ant.* 16.160): "The constitution [πολιτεία] went beyond the rights of citizenship in the single city; it must have also indicated the bond that united the Jews of the Greek diaspora."[126] Quoting Martin Goodman, Troiani goes on to suggest that, "like the Romans and differently from the Greeks, the Jews accepted the notion that their *politeia* was not fixed to any particular locality."[127] Jewish citizenship called for civic obedience of urban Jews in the Hellenistic world. Troiani continues by noting that Paul invites the Christian Philippians to "practice one's civic life" (πολιτεύεσθαι) in a way befitting Christ's gospel (Phil 1:27). Indeed, Eph 2:12 reminds its addressees that "once they were deprived of or alienated from the πολιτεία of Israel." In this light, it is noteworthy that Troiani focuses on the Lukan correlation with this theme: "In Luke's parable the Prodigal Son, having squandered the money inherited from his father in vice and loose living, was able to live by putting himself into the service of one of the πολῖται [co-national] of the region in an unspecified far-off land."[128] Luke was thus clearly familiar with this Hellenistic-Jewish conception. I therefore conclude that Christians adopted the Hellenistic-Jewish idea and practice of instituting a nonlocal constitution (way of life), as taught by Jesus in the Gospel of Luke.

Examples of this adoption would be the acceptance/reception of foreigners into the community (cf. the prophecy of Isa 61:2, which is reiterated by Jesus in Luke 4:19 and practiced by Peter in Acts 10:35). A

---

[124] Troiani, "ΠΟΛΙΤΕΙΑ of Israel," 15.

[125] Cf. Josephus, *Ant.* 19.281, which deals with Claudius's edict.

[126] Troiani, "ΠΟΛΙΤΕΙΑ of Israel," 18.

[127] Ibid., 18. Cf. Martin Goodman, "Jewish Proselytizing in the First Century," in *The Jews among Pagans and Christians in the Roman Empire* (ed. J. Lieu et al.; London: Routledge, 1992), 61.

[128] Troiani, "ΠΟΛΙΤΕΙΑ of Israel," 18–19, 21.

further instance would be the practice of feeding the poor (as portrayed by Jesus in Luke 14:13 and practiced in Acts 2:44–45). Another, in some tension with the last example, is the conversion of the rich householder Zacchaeus (narrated in Luke 19:1–9, repeated in the stories of Lydia and the jailer in Acts 16:11–15; 25–34). Yet another example might be leaders serving as slaves (taught by Jesus in Luke 12:37; 17:8; 22:24–27 and practiced by Paul in Acts 20:24; 21:19 [cf. 6:1–6]). Christians increasingly distanced themselves from orientation toward the holy temple in the one holy city, Jerusalem.[129] For Luke, then, Jesus founded a church that was not centered in any particular city, whether Jerusalem, Antioch, Ephesus, Athens, or Rome. However, after the conversion of the emperor Constantine, whom Eusebius legitimated, the Christian constitution reverted to one closer to the constitution of Romulus.[130] Thus, Rome gradually replaced Jerusalem for some later imperial Christians.

Conclusion: Founders, Change, and Continuity

Luke-Acts belongs to historical literature concerned with changing constitutions, literature that includes not only histories but also political biographies of founders. On the one hand, Luke-Acts represents a form of Asian historiography: God speaks Septuagintal Greek (not Attic), and Jesus teaches leaders to serve as slaves (i.e., a radical reorientation of traditional Greco-Roman values). God does not favor one ethnic group (whether Jews, Greeks, or Romans) but rather bestows benefaction on anyone who does what is deemed acceptable. The geographical movement in Luke's story (from Asia to Europe, from east to west) is thus indicative of larger ideological agendas: the Jordan River muddies the imperial Tiber.

On the other hand, Luke acculturates and Romanizes early Christianity. Like Romulus, Jesus is divinely conceived and is the Son of God. Like Numa, Jesus works miracles, feeding the multitudes. Like Romulus, Jesus' people become multiethnic. Strikingly, like Numa, who turned Rome from war to peace (and unlike Romulus), Jesus blessed the peacemakers. Both Numa and Jesus emphasized not only peace but also piety toward God and justice toward fellow humans. By their characters both individuals transformed society: Numa converted Rome, and Jesus did likewise to those he encountered in his ministry (in Acts this extends to the transformation of entire regions of imperial Rome). However, such changes generate *stasis*, which typically results in the death of the founder (e.g., the deaths of

---

[129] Cf. n. 85 above.

[130] Robert M. Grant, "Eusebius and Imperial Propaganda," in *Eusebius, Christianity and Judaism* (ed. H. W. Attridge and G. Hata; Leiden: Brill, 1992), 658–83.

ΜΕΤΑΒΟΛΗ ΠΟΛΙΤΕΙΩΝ

Romulus, Theseus, Lycurgus, and Jesus were all related to innovations they introduced). Further, both Dionysius and Luke narrate epiphanies of their founders after their deaths, and they both continue to live on in the lives of their followers.

Moreover, both Rome and the early church sent out colonists/missionaries, although the Christian missionaries from the East subverted Western, European, Roman values. These colonists/missionaries were directed by God(s) on their journeys. Some receive these emissaries, and thereby the state/religious movement grows. However, despite Romulus's and Jesus' teaching, controversy about ethnic mixing continues. Indeed, one of the primary motives Luke had in writing Luke-Acts seems to have been to persuade the church/his community to practice what Jesus taught in the first (Lukan) sermon in Nazareth: openness to strangers/foreigners. Further, both ethnic mixing and preaching the gospel in Greek (rather than Hebrew or Aramaic) promotes growth. Still, the religious movement does not assimilate totally (until centuries later under Constantine), remaining distinctive. They thus receive their own name, "Christians."

Luke-Acts concerns constitutional change brought about by Jesus' character that influences the disciples, just as Numa's character changed Rome. One stream of Israelite historiographical tradition (Ezra-Nehemiah, the Maccabean books, and Josephus) opposes ethnic mixing, but a prophetic tradition insists that God acts also among the Philistines (Amos 6:2; 9:7). Luke's characters—Jesus, Peter, and Paul—practice receiving foreigners, which generates *stasis*/riots. Luke, however, cannot concede that this changes the ancient constitution of Moses, despite the accusations made in Luke 23:2; Acts 6:11, 13–14; 21:21. Rather, long ago God revealed this coming event through the prophets, and in the present the Spirit legitimates the fulfillment of this prophecy (Acts 2:17, citing Joel 2:28–29 [LXX 3:1–2]; Acts 10:44–48; 11:12, 16–18; 15:8–9, 17, citing Amos 9:12).

I conclude this essay with a series of questions. One is related to the old historical Jesus or Paul problem. Did the historical Jesus or the historical apostles Peter or Paul introduce the practice of ethnic mixing into earliest Christianity? This practice clearly challenged an Israelite historiographical tradition but is similar to the themes in some of the ancient prophets, particularly Amos. Simultaneously, this practice also represented early Christian acculturation to Roman society, a constitutional change from priestly Mosaic to Romulus's Roman societal policies. Did Romulus (i.e., Roman society) have more influence on early Christian practice than Moses or Jesus in this respect? Centuries later when the Roman emperor Constantine converted, did not Romulus exercise a further influence on Christian practice, reintroducing a preference for war instead of peace? Does Jesus' character continue to influence church practice, or, like Numa's policies in Rome, were Jesus' policies superseded in the church? What is the relationship between the church and society reflected therein, and how can (and do) contemporary Christians legitimate their own practices? Finally, are contemporary church practices in continuity or discontinuity with the Founder?

Paul's Farewell to the Ephesian Elders and Hector's Farewell to Andromache: A Strategic Imitation of Homer's *Iliad*

Dennis R. MacDonald

Since many have undertaken to organize a narrative of the events that have been fulfilled among us, as they were handed on to us by those who from the beginning were eyewitnesses and servants of the word, it seemed good to me, having traced everything carefully from the beginning, to write them up in order for you, most excellent Theophilus, so that you may recognize the security of the information about which you have been instructed. (Luke 1:1–4)

Lukan Genre and Paul's Farewell

If one understands this prologue to Luke-Acts to mean that the author intended to write an accurate history, he or she should be astonished by its content, which bulges with events that only the most credulous could consider historically plausible. To explain this apparent discrepancy, commentators usually argue that Luke's sources were incurably naïve and that he considered it his duty to preserve these traditions as he had received them, leaving their mythological blandishments intact. This view informs most critical discussions of Luke-Acts today.

A growing number of scholars, however, have argued that Luke had no intention of writing history. Far from being a rustic, empirically challenged, Thucydides-wannabe, Luke was, among other things, a sophisticated, clever, and creative author of fiction. He created many of his stories without a scrap of tradition to inform him. If Luke were to discover that for two thousand years his readers have taken his work as a report of historical events, he might well be astonished. It is not Luke who was gullible, however, but his interpreters, including many modern critics.

In her recent book, Marianne Palmer Bonz argues that Luke-Acts is a prose epic modeled after Vergil's *Aeneid*. She maintains that "[j]ust as Vergil had created his foundational epic for the Roman people by appropriating and transforming Homer, so also did Luke create his foundational epic for the early Christian community primarily by appropriating and transforming the sacred traditions of Israel's past as narrated in the Bible of the diasporan Jewish communities, the Septuagint."[1] Luke-Acts is thus epic, not history. I think Palmer Bonz is generally on the right track, but she does not take her insight far enough. In particular, she says nearly nothing concerning the extensive echoes of the Homeric epics in Luke-Acts, echoes that might support her case for viewing Luke-Acts as a response to the *Aeneid*. In this essay I want to investigate Paul's farewell address to the Ephesian elders at Miletus in Acts 20:17–38, arguing that it represents a strategic rewriting of a famous episode in the *Iliad*.

More than in any other speech in Acts, Paul's farewell address is saturated with echoes of Paul's epistles. In fact, many interpreters think that Luke consulted several of his epistles.[2] Nonetheless, the writings of Paul alone cannot explain the form, function, and genre of the speech. Nearly all commentators on Paul's farewell address thus suppose that Luke modeled it after Jewish testaments.[3] According to the detailed treatment by Hans-Joachim Michel, Luke's account follows the testamentary form as follows: Paul summons his listeners (20:17), presents himself as an example (20:18–21, 31, 33–35), asserts his ethical integrity (20:26), announces his death (20:22–25), exhorts his listeners to moral conduct (20:28, 31, 35), prophesies future woes (20:29–30), transmits his authority to his followers (20:28), blesses them (20:32), and, finally, prays (20:36). The narrative

---

[1] Marianne Palmer Bonz, *The Past as Legacy: Luke-Acts and Ancient Epic* (Minneapolis: Fortress, 2000), 26.

[2] E.g., Lars Aejmelaeus, *Die Rezeption der Paulusbriefe in der Miletrede* [Apg 20.18–35] (Annales Academiæ Scientiarum Fennicæ B 232; Helsinki: Suomalainen Tiedeakatemia, 1987).

[3] The most important studies of the speech as a testament are Johannes Munck, "Discours d'adieu dans le Nouveau Testament et dans la littérature biblique," in *Aux sources de la tradition chrétienne: Mélanges offerts à M. Goguel* (Neuchâtel: Delachaux & Niestlé, 1950), 155–70; Otto Knoch, *Die Testamente des Petrus und Paulus: Die Sicherung der apostolischen Überlieferung in der spätneutestamentlichen Zeit* (SBS 62; Stuttgart: KBW, 1973); and William S. Kurz, "Luke 22:14–38 and Greco-Roman and Biblical Farewell Addresses," *JBL* 104 (1985): 251–68. The most thorough study of the genre of the speech is that by Hans-Joachim Michel, *Die Abschiedsrede des Paulus an die Kirche, Agp. 20,17–38: Motivgeschichte und theologische Bedeutung* (SANT 35; Munich: Kösel, 1973). On the farewell discourse in Judaism, see Eckhard von Nordheim, *Die Lehre der Alten* (2 vols.; ALGHJ 13; Leiden: Brill, 1980); and Anitra Bingham Kolenkow, "Testaments: The Literary Genre 'Testament,'" in *Early Judaism and Its Modern Interpreters* (ed. R. A. Kraft and G. W. E. Nickelsburg; Atlanta: Scholars Press, 1986), 259–67.

conclusion adheres to the pattern as well, as it ends with weeping as a gesture of final farewell (20:37).[4]

Hector's Farewell to Andromache and Ancient Imitation

No one has apparently noticed, however, that this speech finds its closest parallels not in any known Jewish testament but in Hector's famous farewell speech to Andromache. Hector decided to leave the battlefield and return to Troy to "tell the elders who speak counsel and our wives to pray to the gods" (*Il.* 6.113–115).[5] He told Hecuba, his mother, to "gather together the older women" at the temple of Athena to pray that the goddess "may have mercy" (*Il.* 6.269–276; cf. 6.296–311). He then went to the home of Paris and Helen to shame his brother into returning to battle. Helen asked Hector to linger, but he was eager to leave: "I will go home to see my own family, my beloved wife and infant son. For I do not know if ever again I shall return to them or if the gods will subdue me at the hands of the Achaeans" (*Il.* 6.365–368). Since Andromache had gone to the walls to observe the fighting, Hector then rushed to rejoin the fight. Andromache, however, ran to meet him, bringing their son Astyanax with her. Hector's final farewell thus took place not at their home but at the gate of the city.

Andromache begged him not to fight: "Come now, take pity and stay here on the wall, lest you make your son an orphan and your wife a widow." She would rather die with him than survive alone. Hector's response, which is significant for the argument that follows, is quoted here at length:

> Woman, all these things concern me, too, but I would be terribly ashamed before the Trojans and the Trojan women with trailing robes, if, like a coward, I were to shrink from the battle. My heart commands me not to, for I have learned always to be valiant and to fight on the front line with the Trojans, winning great renown both for my father and for myself. For this I know well in my mind and heart: a day will come when sacred Ilium will be destroyed—Priam and the spear-savvy people of Priam. But it is not so much the subsequent pain of the Trojans that concerns me … as yours, when some bronze-armored Achaean leads you, weeping, away and robs you of your day of freedom.… Someday someone seeing you shedding tears may say, "This is the wife of Hector, the best soldier of all the horse-taming Trojans,

---

[4] Michel, *Abschiedsrede des Paulus an die Kirche*, 68–71.

[5] All translations are my own. The use of bold italics in the parallels that follow alerts the reader to elements in the two works that are most fruitfully compared.

when they fought for Ilium." Someday someone will say this, and it will be a fresh wound for you to be deprived of such a man to stave off the day of slavery. May a heap of earth cover my corpse before I learn of your crying and your being dragged off to captivity. (*Il.* 6.441–450, 454–455, 459–465)

So saying, glorious Hector reached for his boy, but the lad immediately shrank back into the breast of his fair-belted nurse, crying, upset by the sight of his dear father, terrified when he saw the bronze and the horse-hair crest, watching it wave terribly atop the helmet. His dear father and queenly mother then laughed out loud, and immediately glorious Hector took the helmet from his head and laid it, gleaming, on the ground. Then he kissed his dear son, rocked him in his arms, and spoke a prayer to Zeus and the other gods: "Zeus and you other gods, grant that this lad, my son, may be as I am—distinguished among the Trojans, as great in strength—and may he rule Ilium with might. May someone say of him as he returns from battle, 'He is much better than his father.' After killing a foe, may he haul off the bloody spoils, and may his mother's heart rejoice." (*Il.* 6.466–481)

So saying, he placed the child in the arms of his dear wife, and she received him to her fragrant bosom, laughing as she wept. Looking at her, her husband took pity, stroked her with his hand, and addressed her by name: "My bemused lady, do not let your heart excessively grieve for me; no man will hurl me to Hades beyond my lot. I say that no man, whether cowardly or courageous, ever has escaped fate after he has been born. But go home and look after your own tasks, the loom and the distaff, and command your maidservants to pursue their work. War will concern all the men who live in Ilium, especially me." Having so said, glorious Hector took up his horse-tailed helmet, and his beloved wife went home, frequently turning back, swelling with tears. Quickly then she came to the comfortable home of man-slaying Hector and found there her many maidservants; among them all she incited wailing. So they wailed for Hector in his own house while he was still alive, for they said that he would never again return from battle, escaped from the fury and hands of the Achaeans. (*Il.* 6.482–502)

Vergil's *Aeneid* frequently echoes this famous Homeric scene. In book 2, for example, Aeneas tells Dido that during Troy's fall he was rushing off to fight when his wife Creusa met him at the threshold "holding up little Iulus [Ascanius] to his father" and begging him to take them with him (*Aen.* 2.671–678). Aeneas agreed, but Creusa was killed before she could escape, and the goddess Cybele transported her to the heavens. The Trojan pair thus had no opportunity for a proper farewell. Later, however, Creusa's ghost returns to Aeneas, allowing the poet to imitate *Iliad* 6 again. She told him that he must not grieve, for the gods had willed her death. At least she, daughter to a king and daughter-in-law to a goddess, would not suffer humiliating slavery to a Greek (*Aen.* 2.776–787).

In book 3 Aeneas recalls that his fleeing ships put into a harbor at Epirus, a land ruled by their old comrade Helenus, whom Achilles' son Neoptolemus had enslaved together with Andromache. Neoptolemus soon lost interest in her, placed her under Helenus's care, was killed, and thus left the couple a large territory. Hector's wife therefore should have been happy at last, but she could not stop grieving. Aeneas found her at Hector's cenotaph weeping and conjuring up his ghost. He asked her, "What lot has befallen you after you lost such a husband? What rather fitting fortune revisits you, Hector's Andromache?" (*Aen.* 3.317–319).[6] In her response, Andromache said that she would rather have died at Troy, like Creusa, than to have shared the bed of a Greek captor.[7] At Aeneas's departure Hector's widow appears again, bringing "gifts from the loom" for Ascanius, Aeneas's son. She recalls that her own son, Astyanax, would have been the same age had he survived the fall of Troy. Aeneas tried to console her as Hector had: "each of us in different ways is called by fate" (*Aen.* 3.494; cf. *Il.* 6.488–489).

Vergil's account of Aeneas's prayer for Ascanius clearly imitates Hector's prayer for Astyanax. Aeneas, "eager for battle ... enclosed his legs in gold, left and right. He scorns delay" (*Aen.* 12.430–431). Then, in case he does not return alive, Aeneas takes a moment to pray that his son would grow into a man like himself and his uncle Hector.

Iliad 6.472–481 and 7.1–3	*Aeneid* 12.433–435 and 438–443
Hector took **the helmet** from his head and laid it, gleaming, on the ground. Then he **kissed his dear son, rocked him in his arms,** and **spoke a prayer** to Zeus and the other gods. "Zeus and you other gods, grant that this lad, **my son**, may be **as I am—distinguished** among the Trojans, as great in **strength**—and may he rule Ilium with might. May someone say of him as he returns from battle, 'He is much better than **his father**.' After killing a foe, may he haul	He **embraced Ascanius in his arms,** lightly **kissed his cheek** through **the helmet, and said,** "**My son**, learn **courage** and true **labor from me**.... When your youth gives way to maturity, see to it that you remember [my accomplishments], and may **your father** Aeneas and your uncle **Hector** inspire your soul when you call to mind the

---

[6] This scene echoes Hector's earlier prediction in *Il.* 6.459–463.

[7] In the *Iliad*, Andromache had told Hector that she would rather die with him than survive without him (*Il.* 6.410–411).

off the bloody spoils, and may his mother's heart rejoice." … **So saying**, glorious **Hector rushed through the gates, and with him went Alexander his brother.** And in their hearts both were eager to fight and make war.	example of your kinsmen" (cf. *Aen.* 3.342–343). ***Having offered these words, he went through the gates in might,*** waving a huge spear in his hand, ***and with him,*** like a tight column, ***rushed Antheus and Mnestheus.***

Zeus did not grant Hector's request: Greek soldiers later hurled Astyanax to the earth from the walls of Troy. However, Aeneas's prayers for Ascanius would be answered; he would rule in Italy, perhaps indirectly answering Hector's prayer for Astyanax.

Hector's Farewell and Lukan Imitation

The parallels with Hector's farewell to Andromache are even more extensive in the Acts of the Apostles than in the *Aeneid*. The following list numbers motifs present in *Iliad* 6 and Acts 20 according to their order of appearance in the epic.

1. The hero states that he does not know what dangers he will face (Hector says this to Helen).
2. The hero boasts that he never shirked his duty.
3. The hero warns of disaster.
4. The hero expresses fears concerning the captivity of his loved ones.
5. The hero invokes his gods.
6. The hero prays that his successors may be like him.
7. The hero cites a comparative quotation.
8. The hero states his willingness to face his destiny with courage.
9. The hero commands his audience to attend to their tasks.

In what follows, I place *Iliad* 6 and Acts 20 side by side in parallel columns in order more readily to point out their similarities. I have followed the order of Acts 20 in the parallel presentation.

Motif 2: The Hero Boasts That He Never Shirked His Duty

Iliad 6.440–446	Acts 20:18–21
Then **he said to her**, … "But I would be terribly ashamed before	**He said to them,** "You yourselves know how I was with you the entire time from the first day that arrived in Asia—serving the Lord with all

the Trojans and the Trojan women with trailing robes, if, like a coward, **I were to shrink from the battle.** My heart commands me not to, for I have learned always **to be valiant and to fight on the front line** with the Trojans, **winning** great renown **both** for my father **and** for myself."

lowliness, tears, and testings that came to me through the plots of the Jews—that **I did not hold back anything beneficial: to preach** to you **and to teach** you **in public** and from house to house, **testifying both** to Jews **and** to Greeks about repentance toward God and faith toward our Lord Jesus."

The respective structures of Hector's and Paul's statements are strikingly similar. In both cases the hero witnesses to his courage by stating, in the first-person singular, that he never shirked his duty. Hector's danger came from Greeks; Paul's came from Jews. In both cases the hero then expands on his courage using two infinitives linked by "and" with the public location of action expressed by an adverb, followed by a nominative singular circumstantial participle in the present tense with an accusative object.

Motif 1: The Hero States That He Does Not Know What Dangers He Will Face

Iliad 6.361–362 and 367–368   Acts 20:22–23

[Hector had told Helen:]
For my heart is already impatient to assist the Trojans.... **I do not know if** ever again I shall return to them or **if the gods will subdue me at the hands of the Achaeans.**

And now, captive to the Spirit, I am on my way to Jerusalem, **not knowing what** will happen to me there, except that the Holy Spirit testifies to me in every city saying that **chains and afflictions await me.**

In each column the hero states his determination to face the dangers before him and confesses his ignorance of the future with a negated form of οἶδα. Hector suspects that the gods may subdue him; Paul expects imprisonment. Resolution to do one's duty despite awareness of the consequences is fundamental to the heroic code.

Motif 8: The Hero States His Willingness to Face His Destiny with Courage

Iliad 6.486–489   Acts 20:24

[D]o not let your heart excessively grieve for me. No man will hurl me to Hades beyond **my lot.** I say that after birth no man, whether cowardly or courageous, ever has escaped fate.

But I do not count my life of any value to myself so that I may complete **my race and the ministry that I received** from the Lord Jesus, to testify to the gospel of the grace of God.

Motif 3: The Hero Warns of Disaster

Even though Hector and Paul did not know precisely what the future held for them, they did know that they would soon die. The left-hand column contains Hector's famous line of recognition that he would not prevail: he and Troy would fall.[8] The right-hand column contains Paul's recognition that he would never again see Ephesus.

Iliad 6.447–449	Acts 20:25
For **this I know** well in my mind and heart: a day will come when **sacred Ilium** will be destroyed—Priam and the spear-savvy people of Priam.	And now **I know that** none of you will ever see my face again—you among whom I have gone about proclaiming **the kingdom.**

Here both heroes use the phrase "I know" to indicate that they are aware of the dangers ahead.

Motif 2: The Hero Boasts That He Never Shirked His Duty

Paul then reiterates his heroism, again echoing the epic.

Iliad 6.441–443	Acts 20:26–27
I would be terribly ashamed before the Trojans and the Trojan women with trailing robes, if, like a coward, **I were to shrink from** the battle.	For this reason I testify to you this day that I am pure from the blood of all, for **I did not shrink from** proclaiming the entire will of God.

Motif 9: The Hero Commands His Audience

Each speaker then switches from reasserting his courage to a command to his audience.

Iliad 6.490–493	Acts 20:28
Attend to your own tasks,	**Attend to yourselves**

---

[8] Wolfgang Schadewaldt, "Hector and Andromache," in *Homer: German Scholarship in Translation* (trans. G. M. Wright and P. V. Jones; Oxford: Clarendon, 1997), 135. See also Geoffrey S. Kirk et al., *The Iliad: A Commentary* (6 vols.; Cambridge: Cambridge University Press, 1985–93), 2:220.

the loom and the distaff,
and command your maidservants to pursue their work.
War will concern all the men who live in Ilium, especially me.

and all the flock, in which the Holy Spirit has placed you as overseers to shepherd the church of God that he rescued with his own blood.

In each column the hero gives a command in the imperative mood. The command first applies to his immediate auditor(s) and uses a reflexive; the command then extends to underlings. Hector followed his command by restating his willingness to defend the city: "War will concern all the men who live in Ilium, especially me." Similarly, Paul reminds the elders of Jesus' sacrifice on behalf of the flock. Just as Hector shed his blood trying to rescue Troy, Jesus shed his blood to rescue the church.

Motif 3: The Hero Warns of Disaster

Iliad 6.447–449

Acts 20:29–30

For ***this I know*** well in my mind and heart: ***a day will come*** when ***sacred Ilium will be destroyed***—Priam and the spear-savvy people of Priam. [Homer used wolf similes of the soldiers who would sack Troy without mercy. Hector feared the enslavement and deportation of his wife to Greece.]

I know that after my departure savage wolves will come in among you, ***not sparing the flock.*** And from your own ranks men will arise speaking perverse things to draw the disciples after them.

In both columns the hero confidently predicts future devastation using nearly identical expressions (εὖ γὰρ ἐγὼ τόδε οἶδα/ἐγὼ οἶδα ὅτι). Soon after Hector's death, Greek warriors swarmed into the city and slew the residents without mercy. Paul's warning expresses similar fears for the church.

Motif 9: The Hero Commands His Audience

Iliad 6.490 and 492–493

Acts 20:31

Attend to your own tasks....

War will concern all the men who live in Ilium, especially me.

Therefore, ***be alert,*** remembering that for three years night and day I did not cease to warn everyone with tears.

To be sure, the verbal similarities between these columns is not impressive, but in both the hero gives a command to his audience and boasts of his eagerness to perform his duty.

Motif 5: The Hero Invokes His Gods

After giving instructions to the elders, Paul launches into a prayer for them. Luke's model for this prayer seems to be Hector's prayer for Astyanax.

Iliad 6.475–478	Acts 20:32
[Hector] spoke in prayer **to Zeus and the other gods:** "**Zeus and you other gods, grant that this, my son,** may be as I am—distinguished among the Trojans, as great in strength."	And now I entrust you **to God and to the Logos** of his grace, who **has the power to build you up** and **grant you** the inheritance with all who have been made holy.

In both prayers, the hero addresses more than one divine being: "Zeus and you other gods;" "God and ... the *Logos*."

Motif 6: The Hero Prays That His Successors May Be Like Him

Iliad 6.476–478	Acts 20:33–35a
[G]rant that this lad, my son, **may be as I am**—distinguished among the Trojans, **as great in strength.**	I desired of no one silver or gold or clothing. You yourselves know that these hands ministered to my necessities and to those who were with me. **In all ways I showed you** that it is necessary to work like this to **support the weak.**

Motif 7: The Hero Cites a Comparative Quotation

Iliad 6.479–480	Acts 20:35b
May **someone say** of him as he returns from battle, **"He is much better than his father."**	Remember the words of the Lord Jesus that **he himself said, "It is more blessed to give than to receive."**

The two comparative quotations are closer in English than in Greek; even so, in both works one finds in the context of a prayer for one's descendents a quotation consisting of a single comparative statement. Hector prays that someone will say that Astyanax is an even greater warrior than his father; Luke prays that the elders will remember Jesus' words that giving is even greater than receiving.

A Strategic Imitation of Homer's Iliad   199

Clearly these parallels are substantial, but the order of shared motifs varies from the *Iliad:* 2, 1, 8, 3, 2 (again), 9, 3 (again), 9 (again), 5, 6, and 7. At first glance, this significant deviation in order might seem to militate against literary dependence, but a closer look allows one to appreciate Luke's rearrangement. Paul's speech is organized into three units: the first concerns Paul's courage (20:18–27, containing motifs 2, 1, 8, 3, and 2), the second concerns the challenges facing the elders (20:28–31, containing motifs 9, 3, and 9), and the third consists of Paul's prayer for the elders (20:32–35, containing motifs 5, 6, and 7). The three sections may be construed as a chiasm:

   A   Paul never shirked his duty to the elders, despite the danger of doing so (20:18–27).
      B   He commands the elders to be watchful because of coming disasters (20:28–31).
   A' He prays that the elders may be like him, doing their duty to others (20:32–35).

Homer inserted the prayer for Astyanax between Hector's two speeches to Andromache, while Luke put the prayer for the elders at the end of the speech. This moving of the prayer explains why motifs 5, 6, and 7 appear at the end and not toward the middle, as in the epic.

Furthermore, each of the three sections is itself a chiasm. In the first section the repetition of motif 2 provides an *inclusio*. In the second section the *inclusio* consists of the repetition of motif 9. The chiasm in the third section is made by employing the motifs in the same order as they appear in the epic and by echoing *Logos* in the reference to the *logoi* of Jesus. Here is an overview of my outline of the speech:

   A   Paul never shirked his duty to the elders, despite the danger of doing so (20:18–27).
      AA He never shirked his duty (motif 2).
         AB He did not know what the future would hold (motif 1).
         AC He did not consider his life precious (motif 8).
        AB' He did know that the elders would not see him again (motif 3).
      AA' He never shirked his duty (motif 2).
     B   Paul commands the elders to be watchful because of coming disasters (20:28–31).
      BA He commands the elders to be on guard (motif 9).
        BB He knows that wolves will come and threaten the church (motif 3).

BA' He commands the elders to be on guard, as he had been (motif 9).
A' Paul prays that the elders may be like him, doing their duty to others (20:32–35).
    A'A He invokes "God and the *Logos* of his grace" (motif 5).
    A'B He prays that the elders may be like him (motif 6).
    A'A' He reminds the elders of the "words [λόγοι] of the Lord" (motif 7).

In this larger chiasm, Paul's warnings to the elders of future dangers stand at the very center. If this treatment of the speech is correct, it would explain why the order of motifs in Acts 20 differs from their order in the epic.

Defenders of the speech as a Jewish testament are likely to argue that the parallels I have drawn to the epic likewise appear in the testament, such as the hero's defense of integrity, warnings of future disasters, readiness to die, instructions to descendants, and prayer. This is correct, but I would contend that were one to mine the entire body of Jewish testaments for parallels to Acts 20, one could not compile parallels closer than those in the Hector-Andromache scene. Defenders of the testamentary hypothesis then might object that my chiastic structure for the speech is simply a clever ploy to disguise the deviation in the sequence of shared motifs. The detection of chiasms in ancient literature is notoriously subjective, and other structural assessments of the speech in Acts are possible.

To decide the matter one needs evidence of particular items seldom found in exemplars of the genre as a whole, items that link the two texts together into a unique hermeneutical tension. The significance of distinctive traits is their capacity to cement two texts together. Furthermore, the presence of such traits distinguishes a mere echo from an allusion. Ancient authors often used such traits as flags to the reader so they could compare the text with its model. Does Acts 20:18–35 display traits distinctive to it and *Iliad* 6 and not to final testaments as a whole? I think so, and not just in the speech itself, but also in its context.

Jewish testaments characteristically take place just before the death of the patriarch, usually in his own home and on his deathbed. This is not the case either in *Iliad* 6 or in Acts 20. In fact, the settings of the two scenes share several traits foreign to the Jewish testament.

Iliad 6	Acts 20
Hector was a target of violence.	Paul was a target of violence.
Hector returned to Troy to have the elders pray to the gods.	Paul had left the Troad and summoned the elders for instruction and prayer.
Hector was eager to return to the battle despite the danger.	Paul was eager to return to Jerusalem despite the danger.

Hector's farewell to Andromache took place not at their home but at the gate. Hector would not die until days later.	Paul's farewell to the Ephesian elders took place not at their home but at Miletus. Paul would not die until years later.

The peculiar introduction to the speech in Acts 20 in fact urges the reader (perhaps even somewhat playfully) to view it as a variation of the Hector-Andromache scene.

One might suggest the same for the response of the elders after the speech. In case the reader missed the similarities between Paul and Hector, the conclusion makes it clear.

Iliad 6.466, 474–476, and 498–502	Acts 20:36–38
When he had thus said, glorious Hector reached out for the boy ... And then he **kissed his dear son, rocked him in his arms, and spoke in prayer** to Zeus.... [Andromache went home and] found there her many maidservants; **among them all** she induced **wailing.** So **they wailed** for Hector in his own house while he was still alive; **for they said that he would never again return from battle.** [Hector went back to the battle.]	And **when he had said these things,** he knelt with them all **and prayed.** There was much **weeping among them all.** They **fell on** Paul's **neck** and **kissed him, grieving** especially **because of what he had said, that they would never again see his face.** And they sent him off in the ship.

In both columns the protagonist has finished a speech and prayed. Hector hugged and kissed his son before the prayer; the elders hugged and kissed Paul after the prayer. In both columns those who heard the hero's final farewell wept at what was said: "he would never again return from battle"; "they would never again see his face." Hector will not escape "from the fury and hands of the Achaeans"; Paul will not escape the Jews who will hand him over into "the hands of the Gentiles."

CONCLUSION

How does the proposed intertextual reading contribute to understanding the text? The most obvious difference between the two scenes pertains to their depictions of heroism. Hector boasted that he never shrank from battle: he won renown for himself and his father through valor, and he prayed that his son would be a greater warrior than he ("May someone say of him as he returns from battle, 'He is much better than his father.' After killing a foe, may he haul off the bloody spoils, and may his mother's heart rejoice"). Paul, on the other hand, did not fight but provided "what was beneficial"; he "desired of no one silver or gold or clothing"; and he used his strength not to slay his opponents but to care for the weak. Unlike Hector, who wanted his son to distinguish himself in battle, Paul wanted the elders to live by the maxim, "It is more blessed to give than to receive." Hector felt bound by his fate; Paul was bound to the Holy Spirit, willing to do the will of God. Hector dismissively commanded Andromache to return home and leave the war to the men. Paul commanded the elders to take charge of their flock and to keep alert against the savage wolves that would attack it. Finally, Zeus rejected Hector's prayer for Astyanax, who would soon die in the sack of Troy. The reader of Acts, however, may assume that God and the *Logos* would strengthen the elders and grant them their inheritance, just as Paul had prayed. It thus would appear that Luke did not merely imitate the Hector-Andromache scene but emulated it to make it serve a new interpretation of heroism.

This reading of Acts 20 carries implications for understanding Acts as a whole. For example, it suggests that Luke was willing and able to create entire episodes without the benefit either of historical information or tradition apart from what he knew from his sources, in this case perhaps Paul's own letters (1 Thessalonians above all). Furthermore, we may infer that Luke's literary models, in some cases at least, were Hellenistic and not Jewish and that he expected his readers to be sufficiently conversant with Greek epic to appreciate the differences between his account and the source being imitated. To understand Acts we may have to replace historical and form-critical concerns with aesthetic and comparative literary ones, and to do this we must steep ourselves in the literature that formed the cultural competence of Luke's intended readers.

This example is but one of over thirty such parallels between Acts and classical poetry, most of which derive from the *Iliad* and the *Odyssey*, but some also from Euripides, especially the *Bacchae*. Vergil knew and transformed much of this same literature, especially the Homeric epics, often the same episodes in fact that Luke seems to have rewritten. For example, Paul's shipwreck resembles that of Odysseus in *Odyssey* 5, which also informed the shipwrecks in *Aeneid* 1. The angelic vision to Cornelius resembles the lying dream to Agamemnon, which also informed the dream of Turnus in *Aeneid* 7. Luke and Vergil also have their equivalents to the death of Elpenor, Priam's rescue of Hector's corpse, and, as we have seen, Hector's farewell to Andromache. Classical Greek poetry is the most important and perhaps also the most ignored resource for understanding early Christian narrative composition.

The analogy of the *Aeneid* is significant for understanding the genre of Luke-Acts, and not simply for the reasons cited by Palmer Bonz. Even though Vergil's epic was self-consciously fiction, it nonetheless contains much significant historical information. The poet shows care for accuracy in predictions of the founding of Rome, the Punic Wars, the Roman Civil War, and the rise of Julius Caesar and Augustus. On the other hand, he obviously knew he was creating a literary mythology. Many scholars argue that Vergil was an Epicurean, and, if so, he could hardly have thought that the gods intervened in human affairs. The truth of his narrative, however, lies in its mythical reconstruction of the past to address the ideological needs of the nascent empire.

I would say the same for Luke-Acts. Luke surely provides much credible historical information about the early church. Furthermore, he probably was less of a theological skeptic than Vergil. Even so, it would appear that Luke expected at least some of his readers to appreciate the stories not as aspiring historical reports but as fictions crafted as alternatives to those of Homer and Vergil. In other words, the truth of Luke's narrative lies in its imaginative reconstruction of the past to address the ideological needs of the nascent church.[9] If he intended to write a history, he failed, even by the standards of ancient historiography. On the other hand, if he set out to write a prose epic, he succeeded brilliantly. By insisting that Luke-Acts is history in one form or another, scholars have placed a burden on Lukan narrative that its author never intended his story to bear.

---

[9] See further, Milton Moreland's contribution in this volume.

CULTURAL DIVIDES AND DUAL REALITIES:
A GRECO-ROMAN CONTEXT FOR ACTS 14

Amy L. Wordelman

When I first began working on the Lystran episode in Acts 14, I was drawn to the text because of its setting in the interior of Asia Minor. I wanted to understand whether and in what ways the narrative shed light on the encounter between Christian, Jewish, and local religious practices in the region. My explorations, however, unexpectedly led me away from a focus on the local social-historical context of the narrative's setting to an extended exploration of the history of interpretation of the episode and eventually to an explication of the narrative's relationship to Greco-Roman literary and mythological traditions. My journey on this path commenced at the point I realized that much of the history of interpretation of Acts 14, as well as many of the historical discussions cited in those interpretations, relies upon negative cultural stereotypes related to its rural and "Eastern"/"oriental" setting. These cultural stereotypes are used to account for the Lycaonians' apparently irrational attribution of divinity to the apostles and to cast the episode as an example of an encounter with a cultural mindset wholly other than the "rational West" represented by ancient Greece and modern Europe. My task became one of identifying the long-term effects of this cultural stereotyping amidst the complexities of received traditions of interpretation and of finding ways of analyzing the substance and context of the episode that do not depend upon these traditions.[1]

Modern scholars generally manage to avoid the cultural stereotypes that sometimes skewed earlier generations' attitudes toward their historical and literary subjects. This essay, therefore, does not represent a plea to purge (so to speak) the discipline of these assumptions, because the discipline has already for the most part addressed these issues. Instead, I hope to demonstrate the value of analyzing these problematic strains in the

---

[1] This essay is based in part on Amy L. Wordelman, "The Gods Have Come Down: Images of Historical Lycaonia and the Literary Construction of Acts 14" (Ph.D. diss., Princeton University, 1994).

archives of interpretation as one means of paving the way for new insights into the narrative itself. In my experience, the process of sustained engagement with the history of interpretation can contribute to new insights in two ways. First, it helps one to identify received traditions that became standard within a context of cultural stereotyping but outlived the stereotyping because they do not carry specific markers of their origin. This essay shows how the ubiquitous references to the Baucis and Philemon myth in interpretations of Acts 14 fit this description. Second, sustained consideration of the culturally problematic elements in the archives helps us to identify gaps, confusions, flashpoints, and lines of tension in the narrative itself and between the narrative and its modern readers. These are elements that sometimes attract cultural stereotyping and suppositions of cultural superiority as solutions to problems with the narrative. These same elements still require consideration and reexamination, but in a different mode. For Acts 14, I will show how examination of the history of interpretation paves the way for new insights into the place of supernatural events and wondrous deeds in Acts, the role of etymological wordplay as a compositional technique used in the Lystran episode, and the relationship of this story to the literary portrayal of enemies of the apostles in the narrative of Acts as a whole.

In the first three sections of this essay I explore key moments in the history of interpretation of Acts 14. In the fourth I attempt to redraw the cultural map of Acts with respect to the distribution of wondrous deeds and locate the Lystran episode on that map. In the final two sections I propose the story of Lycaon of Arcadia as the mythological allusion behind the Lystran narrative and explore the interpretive implications of recognizing this allusion.

Orientalism as the "Solution" to a Problem

Early historical-critical interpreters of Acts appealed to orientalist assumptions in order to solve the problem of the Lycaonians' behavior in Acts 14. For these interpreters, preoccupied as they were with issues of historicity, the attribution of divinity to the apostles defies the canons of rational behavior, thus putting into question the historical accuracy of the account. Those most inclined to find accurate history in Acts looked for rational explanations for apparently irrational behavior, while the more skeptical sought to locate the author's inspiration for what they assumed to be an exaggerated or fictionalized account. Both camps found solutions that were dependent upon Orientalism in various forms.

This essay uses the term *Orientalism* in a somewhat more limited sense than that first introduced by Edward Said, but still in a way that owes much to his original formulation. Said uses the term to describe an imaginative "style of thought based upon an ontological and epistemological distinction" between the Orient and the Occident and a powerful system of discourse used by Europeans to dominate and hold authority over the Middle East and Asia.² This multifaceted definition of the concept includes within its scope a vastly complex array of intellectual, political, artistic, and popular forms of thought and practice that evolve over the course of several hundred years. Critics of Said suggest that he generalizes across too many centuries, regions, political contingencies, and types of historical and literary sources. In spite of these criticisms, however, the basic concept of Orientalism has proven itself a useful umbrella term for describing a varied and complex landscape of cultural attitudes, stereotypes, and power-relations predicated upon broad distinctions between East and West.³ The aspect most useful and relevant for this study is Said's characterization of Orientalism as a system of thought that creates an imaginary organic entity—the Orient—viewed as culturally uniform, eternally unchanging, inherently irrational, and in every way opposite and inferior to modern Western society.⁴ This habit of thought, which I refer to as a form of cultural stereotyping, appears frequently in the history of the interpretation of the Lystran episode.

Debates about historicity among nineteenth-century German scholars set the stage for the importation of orientalist assumptions by making the plausibility of the Lycaonians' behavior the central issue. Historical skeptics of the Tübingen school such as Eduard Zeller questioned the historicity of the episode on the basis of the implausibility of first-century Lycaonians mistaking the apostles for full-fledged gods. Such scholars argued that at most the Lycaonians would have regarded the apostles as magicians or daemons, while Acts depicts a degree of ignorance more likely in the earlier Homeric age.⁵ Their arguments do not clear the first-century Lycaonians of all irrational tendencies but instead suppose that the problem in Acts stems from attributing a degree of irrationality or ignorance greater than what could have been expected of this population. This argument becomes a mainstay of historical-critical scholarship on Acts 14 and can still be found in virtually the same form in Ernest Haenchen's commentary

---

² Edward W. Said, *Orientalism* (New York: Vintage, 1979), 2–3.

³ For recent assessments of the impact of Said's *Orientalism* on the work of historians, see the series of review essays recently published in *AHR* 105 (2000): Andrew J. Rotter, "Saidism without Said: *Orientalism* and U.S. Diplomatic History," 1205–17; Katherine E. Fleming, "*Orientalism,* the Balkans, and Balkan Historiography," 1218–33; and Kathleen Biddick, "Coming Out of Exile: Dante on the Orient(alism) Express," 1234–49.

⁴ Said, *Orientalism,* 1–28.

⁵ Eduard Zeller, *Die Apostelgeschichte nach ihrem Inhalt und Ursprung kritisch untersucht* (Stuttgart: Mäcken, 1854), 215.

on Acts.⁶ Conservative critics of the nineteenth century countered the skeptics by arguing for the plausibility of full-scale superstitious ignorance. For example, in one of the most influential nineteenth-century commentaries on Acts, Heinrich Meyer distinguished between pagan *Volksglauben* and the more rational beliefs of the ancient philosophers. He agreed with Zeller that belief in gods appearing in human form was more characteristic of the earlier Homeric age but claimed that in spite of the influence of the more rational philosophers, such folk beliefs survived into the first century and can be observed in the Lystran episode.⁷

Both skeptics and conservatives also made reference to the myth of Baucis and Philemon to support their positions. The tale, known only from the Latin poet Ovid, depicts the gods Jupiter (Zeus) and Mercury (Hermes) disguised as human beings paying a visit to the elderly Phrygian couple, Baucis and Philemon (Ovid, *Metam.* 8.612–725). The attraction of the tale for interpreters lies in its depiction of gods appearing in the form of traveling strangers, the fact that the gods in question are Zeus and Hermes traveling together, and, perhaps most importantly, that Ovid sets the tale in Phrygia (of Asia Minor), in relative close proximity to Lycaonia. The more historically skeptical, such as Zeller, used the tale to explain where the author of Acts found inspiration for the invention of the Lystran episode, while Meyer and other conservatives supposed a historical event in which the people of Lycaonia believed themselves to be experiencing an actual theophany of the sort depicted in their regional folktale. The references to the tale of Baucis and Philemon thus connect the type of irrationality depicted in the Lystran episode with a specific geographic location.

These initial arguments about plausible degrees of rationality do not necessarily depend upon assumptions about geographic, ethnic, or cultural differences. They can also be read as distinctions between rural and urban and/or educated and uneducated persons within the same sociocultural context. The references to Homer and Greek philosophers reveal the assumed context to be defined broadly as Greco-Roman. References to the tale of Baucis and Philemon, however, become the entry point through which the theme of cultural difference is introduced into scholarly discussion. The supposition that *Phrygian* means something other than Greco-Roman remains muted in the early historical-critical commentaries but soon becomes a dominant factor in interpretation as the habit of dividing the

---

⁶ Ernst Haenchen, *The Acts of the Apostles: A Commentary* (trans. B. Noble et al.; Philadelphia: Westminster, 1971), 432.

⁷ See, for example, all but the first edition of Heinrich A. W. Meyer, *Kritisch Exegetisches Handbuch über die Apostelgeschichte* (KEK 3; 4th ed.; Göttingen: Vandenhoeck & Ruprecht, 1870 [2d ed. = 1854]).

world into the rational West and the irrational East proves a popular and convenient tool for explaining the behavior of the Lycaonians, as well as for other problematic cases of supernaturalism in biblical texts.

One of the earliest examples of this phenomenon is found in the work of the French scholar Ernst Renan, who starts from the premise that the people of ancient Asia Minor were of the Orient and thus naturally prone to superstition. He describes the Lycaonians as a "credulous and wonder-loving people" who "indulged in a strange freak of imagination" and credits this superstition to an energetic "pietistic reaction" against positive philosophy in which whole regions "were as if given up to mysticism."[8] As evidence of this phenomenon in Asia Minor, he cites the Baucis and Philemon tale along with various traditions about Apollonius of Tyana and Lucian's satirical essays *Alexander the False Prophet* and the *Death of Peregrinus*. In contrast, Renan states that any educated Roman would rightly see the miracles as tricks, and even "ignorant" Romans would hardly be impressed. In the "Orient," however, "Jews and Syrians" (whom he classes together as "Semites") would look for miracles "as proof of a doctrine preached by the thaumaturgist," whereas the "heathen" populations such as the Lycaonians in Asia Minor could be expected to reach the even more superstitious conclusion that the apparent miracle indicated "the immediate revelation of a god."[9] Interestingly, Renan follows the most ardent of the historical skeptics in categorically denying the occurrence of supernatural events of any sort and in attributing to deceit or delusion the belief that such events have occurred.[10] However, unlike other historical skeptics, who also questioned the plausibility of the behavior attributed to the Lycaonians, Renan considered the readiness of the people to believe in the apostles' divinity entirely plausible and to be expected, given what he claims to be the inherently credulous nature of the inhabitants of Asia Minor.

Other commentators imported Orientalism into the discussion by drawing an analogy between the Lycaonians and various colonized peoples of the nineteenth century. For example, in one of the most influential of nineteenth-century English language commentaries, William Conybeare and John Howson compared the situation of Paul in Lystra to that of a modern British missionary in a Hindu village, where the "civilization of the conquering and governing people has hardly penetrated."[11] They

---

[8] Ernest Renan, *The History of the Origins of Christianity* (trans. I. Lockwood et al.; 7 vols.; London: Matthieson, 1889–90), 3:66.

[9] Ibid., 3:55, 59, 66–67.

[10] Ibid., 2:37, 123.

[11] William J. Conybeare and John S. Howson, *The Life and Epistles of St. Paul* (7th ed.; New York: Scribner, 1863), 185.

characterize the persistence of the Lycaonians in such "primitive superstition" as similar to the way these villages have "retained their character without alteration, notwithstanding the successive occupations by Mahomedans [sic] and English."[12] This colonial analogy assumes the same kind of persistence of ancient and primitive behavior supposed by the more conservative German critics, but it adds the variable of a presumed cultural, ethnic, or geographic difference that predisposes a certain people to persist in its superstition. In this case, the difference is seen as that between Western colonizers and Eastern subjects. The West is represented by the British and even by Muslims in India (or by analogy, the Greek-speaking apostles in Asia Minor), while Hindus (and by extension the Lycaonians) represent the quintessentially superstitious Eastern subjects. Thus, while the earliest historical-critical treatments of the Lystran episode located the superstition of the Lycaonians among the backward or uneducated of Greco-Roman culture, the orientalist impulse shifted responsibility for this superstition completely outside of the Greco-Roman sphere. Emphasis on the Phrygian setting for the Baucis and Philemon myth aided and abetted this transition.

Ramsay's Thoroughgoing Orientalism

The tendency to fuse Orientalism with the interpretation of Acts 14 reaches its most exaggerated and perhaps influential form in the work of William M. Ramsay. Ramsay, who falls squarely in the camp of those regarding the Lystran episode as a depiction of actual events in first-century Asia Minor, intertwines two types of argumentation that for the sake of convenience I will label the "material infrastructure" and the "cultural disposition" arguments, respectively. The material infrastructure arguments cite inscriptions and other material evidence suggesting that worship of deities, whom locals referred to in Greek as Zeus and Hermes, was common in the region. There is nothing especially surprising about this conclusion, and more recent studies of religion in Asia Minor have provided numerous examples of a mixture of local and Greek names for divinities throughout the region.[13] Simply saying, however, that there is nothing historically out of place about Acts 14 depicting a temple to Zeus at Lystra, or even of the

---

[12] Ibid.

[13] For a recent and thorough version of the material-infrastructure argument that presents quite a different interpretation of the Lystran episode than that presented here, see Cilliers Breytenbach, *Paulus und Barnabas in der Provinz Galatien: Studien zu Apostelgeschichte 13f.; 16,6; 18,23 und den Adressaten des Galaterbriefes* (AGJU 38; Leiden: Brill, 1996).

worship of Zeus and Hermes in tandem in this region of Asia Minor, does not address the more problematic issue of the plausibility of first-century Lycaonians preparing to worship the apostles as incarnations of Zeus and Hermes. It is with respect to this second element that Ramsay raises his cultural disposition arguments accompanied by a heavy dose of orientalist thought.

Ramsay presents as historical fact that "there was a disposition in Lystra to believe in actual theophany, or appearance of the gods on earth in human form."[14] In order to confirm the existence of this disposition in the region, he follows the lead of many before him and cites the tale of Baucis and Philemon as proof. Although Ramsay acknowledges that Ovid places the story in Phrygia and not the neighboring Lycaonia, he dismisses the significance of this geographic distinction, claiming that Phrygia and Lycaonia are virtually identical in their culture and religion.[15] He also firmly locates this disposition amidst the "indigenous pagans" who were inclined to speak their local language and not among what he assumes to be a very small number of locals, who had adopted Greek and Roman ways or had converted to Christianity.[16] Thus, from Ramsay's point of view the Lycaonians' efforts to honor Paul and Barnabas as gods testify to their adherence to a widespread cultural disposition and mythic tradition native to all of central Asia Minor. By viewing themselves as participating in a version of their own tale, the Lycaonians prove themselves to belong fully to their naturally superstitious environment. Ramsay explicitly contrasts this superstitious disposition to what might be expected from any small segment of the population open to Greek and Roman influence.

The sharp distinction between the religious sensibilities assumed for the vast majority of the indigenous population and those assumed for the few open to Greco-Roman culture reflects Ramsay's overarching interpretive framework in which Hellenism and Orientalism perpetually collide and battle in central Asia Minor. He uses the topographical difference between the western coast of Asia Minor and the inland plateau as the basis for articulating two opposing character types among the peoples of Asia Minor. He describes the plateau as vast, immobile, monotonous, subdued, melancholic, and lending itself to tales of death. In contrast, the

---

[14] William M. Ramsay, *Historical Commentary on St. Paul's Epistle to the Galatians* (New York: Putnam, 1900), 225. In his "Historical Introduction" to this commentary, Ramsay advocated the South Galatian hypothesis and thus gave a central role to the account of Paul's journey through Antioch, Iconium, and Lystra in Acts.

[15] Ibid., 226.

[16] Ibid., 225.

coasts are full of variety, life and as bright as "Greece itself."[17] He sees the plateau in a constant struggle between its native oriental spirit and the inroads of the more lively Greek spirit spread in antiquity through Roman and Christian contact, and in modern times through contact with Greek and other Europeans. He is also struck by what he terms only a "superficial" victory of the West in this ongoing battle, since people continued to speak their own languages and follow native religion in spite of Greek, Roman, Christian, and later European intervention. He even goes so far as to see the eventual conquest and conversion of the region to Islam as "the Oriental goal to which the genius of the land tended."[18]

Ramsay's historical scheme also assumes a direct line of continuity in spirit and character from antiquity to the present. A central tenet of his historical work on Asia Minor is that "the people *as they are now* offer the best introduction to the study of the people as they were in A.D. 40–60."[19] Accordingly, he uses his personal interpretation of his encounters with the inhabitants of the central regions of late nineteenth-century Turkey as a basis for constructing the character of the ancient inhabitants of the same region. It is unfortunate for both his contemporaries and his historical subjects that these characterizations reflect a full range of negative stereotypes common to the orientalist and colonial discourses of his day. He suggests, for example, that archaeologists preparing to work in central Asia Minor should equip themselves with hand tricks, children's picture books, and paper animals with which to amuse the simple-minded audiences they would find in a Turkish village.[20] He attributes what he views as a low-level of intellectual development to the "monotony" of Turkish village life. He finds an exception to this monotony in Christian villages, where, he claims, they at least raise a diversity of crops and attend to variety in food and life.[21] Ramsay also characterizes Turkish villagers as "fickle and changeable." He advises archaeologists engaging a local person as a guide to depart immediately on the expedition because, if they postpone, they are apt to find that the guide's "habitual sluggishness has resumed its sway."[22] Finally, Ramsay regards the oriental spirit of the local inhabitants as naturally submissive and marvels at what he describes as "the obedient and peaceable spirit" of Turkish refugees, who "will sit submissive to

---

[17] William M. Ramsay, *The Historical Geography of Asia Minor* (Royal Geographical Society Supplementary Papers 4; London: Murray, 1890), 23–24.

[18] Ibid., 24–25.

[19] Ramsay, *St. Paul's Epistle to the Galatians,* 234; emphasis added.

[20] William M. Ramsay, *Impressions of Turkey during Twelve Years' Wanderings* (New York: Putnam, 1897), 15, 20–21.

[21] Ibid., 21.

[22] Ibid., 77.

injustice and misery, regarding it as the will of God, where a northern race would at once rebel."[23]

Simple-minded, childish, monotonous, fickle, changeable, sluggish, obedient, peaceable, submissive—this list sums up Ramsay's attitude toward the Turks he encountered in the interior of modern Turkey. According to his own tenets of historical continuity, it also sums up his attitude toward the people of first-century Asia Minor, including the Lycaonians depicted in Acts. Ramsay saw in the Lystran episode a classic encounter between this native oriental spirit of the Anatolian plateau and the intellectually alive and vibrant Greek spirit represented by the Christian apostles. Paul and Barnabas encounter a simple-minded folk inspired by their own folktale to regard mere mortals as gods, who submissively follow their priest to make sacrifices, and then, in a final display of fickleness, turn against the very apostles they had been so anxious to honor. Ramsay interprets this ancient encounter as a type that had been going on since time immemorial. In Ramsay's words, every traveler would see "the same old conflict between the quick-witted, subtle, enterprising Greek, and the slow, dull, contented Turk."[24] For Ramsay, the Lycaonians depicted in Acts exemplified these negative stereotypes and indeed provide further proof of the region's natural tendency. In fact, for Ramsay the Lystran episode becomes an additional piece of historical evidence of this cultural disposition, which he believed is corroborated by the Baucis and Philemon myth.[25]

Learning from Cadbury

More than a half-century after Ramsay's major works, Henry J. Cadbury took a quite different approach to Acts.[26] We can see hints in Cadbury of his opposition to some of the stronger conclusions reached by Ramsay. However, he also continues to use the oriental category as a tool for classifying certain cultures. Cadbury thus provides an interesting and instructive case because, while using the category, he simultaneously adopts suppositions about cultural mixing, commonality of traits, and point

---

[23] Ibid., 112.

[24] Ramsay, *St. Paul's Epistle to the Galatians*, 33.

[25] Ramsay's historical work on Asia Minor continues to be cited today, especially on issues of the geography of ancient Asia Minor. Although the portion of his arguments based on material evidence and topography can be judged on more objective terms, we need to keep in mind that his cultural assumptions potentially skewed any conclusions he made regarding the nature of culture and religion in the region.

[26] Henry J. Cadbury, *The Book of Acts in History* (New York: Harper, 1955).

of view that defy some of the most basic assumptions originally contributing to the category's widespread use.

The oriental concept gives Cadbury trouble from the outset as he struggles to define the fifth of the five cultural strands he identifies within the narrative of Acts. He can readily name four of these: the Greek, Roman, Jewish, and Christian. Each of these strands can be relatively well-defined on the basis of ethnicity, citizenship, and/or religious adherence. However, he struggles to find a term for his fifth category that includes all cultural elements not covered by the other four. These masses of ordinary people of the eastern empire—who were not Greek, Roman, Jewish or Christian—represent a tremendous diversity of ethnic, linguistic, cultural, and religious ties. Attempting to describe this "extraneous factor in Acts," he refers to it variously as "oriental" (with the caveat that the Jewish element must also be considered oriental), as "people whom the Greek must regard as barbarians," and as "indigenous cultures" or "indigenous civilizations." He even suggests he will try discussing this element "without giving it a name" but then immediately goes on to use the term "oriental" even while trying to stress the lack of homogeneity among these populations.[27] Under the heading of this unnamed oriental, barbarian, or indigenous element in Acts, Cadbury places Philip's encounter with the Ethiopian eunuch (Acts 8:26–40), Paul's escape from Damascus (9:23–25), Paul and Barnabus in Lystra of Lycaonia (14:8–20), and Paul's shipwreck on Malta (28:1–10).[28]

In his definition of this fifth element, Cadbury characterizes Acts as providing a "double outlook" with respect to these episodes, which includes "the actual oriental elements as they existed in the ancient scene" and "the reaction of the author himself to the barbarian data in his story."[29] His reference to "actual oriental elements" leaves no doubt that he takes for granted the appropriateness and usefulness of the modern oriental category in spite of the difficulties he has in defining what attributes actually linked the inhabitants of such diverse locales as Ethiopia, Arabia, Lycaonia, and Malta. At the same time, his addition of the barbarian category as a second perspective opens the door to the possibility of reading the narrative independently of the oriental classification. Cadbury, however, does not make this shift but rather continues to use both categories as largely interchangeable references to the same set of peoples and attributes. At the same time, his discussion of these elements in Acts reveals a willingness to break down some of the most fundamental assumptions of Orientalism, especially those supposing a set of cultural

---

[27] Ibid., 11–14.
[28] Ibid., 15–27.
[29] Ibid., 14.

characteristics or dispositions wholly other than and different from the Western Greek or Roman.

For example, Cadbury's discussion of the Lystran episode assumes that the author of Acts and his Greco-Roman readers would have recognized the story as an example of an encounter with barbarians in the form of the "semi-Hellenized original stock of the tableland of Asia Minor." These barbarians speak their own language, worship local gods possibly in the form of hellenized versions of Zeus and Hermes, and interpret their situation according to the local myth of Baucis and Philemon, set "in this very neighborhood."[30] To this point his reading does not appear to be much different from many of his predecessors. We could easily substitute the term "oriental" where he uses "barbarian," and the substance of his reading would thus not differ much from Ramsay and other orientalist interpreters. However, Cadbury's reading differs significantly in that he refuses to attribute the Lycaonians' readiness to see Paul and Barnabas as gods to an oriental or barbarian disposition. Instead, he states that the "easy suggestion of divinity which the mere wonder of the cure aroused is neither particularly Greek nor barbarian but characteristic of a credulous and pre-scientific age."[31] Cadbury breaks here from the orientalist model by not identifying credulity with respect to the supernatural as inherent to any one group, and especially by leaving open the possibility that such credulity could also be present in the Greek sphere. He does not question the plausibility or realism of the Lycaonians' theophany claim but instead relativizes it by regarding such simple trust as common to all ancient and/or prescientific people.

Cadbury also departs from the orientalist model when he discusses the "fickleness" of the Lycaonians. Ramsay interpreted the end of the Lystran episode, when the Lycaonians turn against the apostles (14:19), as yet another example of typical oriental fickleness similar to his Turkish guides changing their minds and refusing to appear for his expeditions. Cadbury, on the other hand, reads the Malta and Lystra stories together as reverse illustrations of Greek assumptions about the hostility of barbarians toward strangers. The Lystran episode confirms the assumption, while the hospitality of the barbarians to shipwrecked strangers on Malta defies this "distinctively Hellenic" fear.[32] By making the Greek point of view—the fear of hostility of foreigners toward them—the object of his musings, he again defies the typical assumptions of Orientalism that locate both hostility and fearfulness in the oriental East. Cadbury's approach supposes that not only

---

[30] Ibid., 23–24.
[31] Ibid., 23.
[32] Ibid., 25–26.

fickleness but also fear and hostility may well be in the eyes of the beholder and not naturally inherent to the character of any one group.

Finally, we can see a significant departure from Ramsay's Orientalism in Cadbury's arguments against the idea that cultures and ideas have distinct frontiers. His discussion does not mention Ramsay by name, but in substance Cadbury opposes Ramsay's central idea that Asia Minor represents the frontier and battleground between the opposing cultural tendencies of East and West.[33] Instead, Cadbury presents a much more nuanced and intricate understanding of the diversity of cultures and ideas, represented by the difficulty of naming the fifth element in Acts: "some of these may be described as universally human, some as specifically ancient, while others belong to quite definite strands inside or outside the Roman Empire—Ethiopian, Arabian, Phoenician, Anatolian."[34] Where Ramsay saw a dichotomy and even battleground between the opposing cultural forces of East and West, Cadbury sees a complex mixture of common human traits and ancient habits, combined with cultural concepts and ideas unique to specific social groups. Thus, although Cadbury continues to use the term "oriental" for the purposes of classification, his understanding of the content of the category becomes so complex and multithreaded that it begins to defy its own definition and ceases to be a particularly useful term for analysis.

Cadbury thus made a key contribution to Acts scholarship by introducing the idea of analyzing the narrative in terms of images of barbarians found in the Greco-Roman culture of the author and his contemporaries. Scholars following his lead have already shown the rich potential of this approach for explicating particular cultural themes and dynamics in the narrative.[35] The tendency, however, is to replace the problematic concept of the oriental with the Greco-Roman category of the "barbarian," while assuming that both refer to the same territory on the cultural map of the ancient Mediterranean world. In the case of Acts, this means that the same episodes—most notably those of the Ethiopian eunuch, Lystra, and Malta—continue to be viewed as representative of the barbarian periphery of the Greco-Roman world, while the rest of the settings in the narrative are

---

[33] On the rarity with which Cadbury mentions other scholars by name, see Beverly R. Gaventa, "The Peril of Modernizing Henry Joel Cadbury," in *Cadbury, Knox, and Talbert: American Contributions to the Study of Acts* (ed. M. C. Parsons and J. B. Tyson; Atlanta: Scholars Press, 1992), 23.

[34] Cadbury, *Book of Acts in History*, 27.

[35] See, for example, the section on "Exotica and Orientalia" in Richard I. Pervo, *Profit with Delight: The Literary Genre of the Acts of the Apostles* (Philadelphia: Fortress, 1987), 70–72; and Clarice J. Martin, "A Chamberlain's Journey and the Challenge of Interpretation for Liberation," *Semeia* 47 (1989): 105–35.

viewed as representing the cultural mainstream. Delineating the location of the barbarian in this way inadvertently continues to impose the logic of the modern orientalist East-West divide and misses some ancient cultural dynamics invisible under this dichotomy. In the following section I reexamine Acts, arguing for an alternative cultural mapping of the narrative.

Relocating the Barbarian on the Cultural Map of Acts

A reexamination of the narrative of Acts in terms of the types of activities engaged in by the traveling apostles produces a cultural map with three separate spheres: (1) a limited barbarian sphere occupied in Acts only by the island of Malta; (2) the entire eastern empire from Macedonia through all of Asia Minor (including Lycaonia) and on to Syria, Samaria, Judea, including even the road to Gaza where Philip encounters the Ethiopian eunuch; and (3) the home territories of Greece and Rome. The key to this map lies in the distribution of supernatural marvels and persuasive speaking activities on the part of the traveling apostles.[36]

If we stay as close as possible to the terminology of the narrative itself, only the people whom Paul first encounters on the island of Malta should be described as "barbarians" (28:1–10), as the Greek term *barbaroi* appears only in this episode (28:2, 4). Although in the classical Greek period the term typically referred to all non-Greeks, its limited appearance in Acts reflects a usage more akin to the political situation of the early Roman Empire, where many non-Greeks spoke at least a little Greek. To call someone a "barbarian" meant that meaningful spoken communication could not take place, and by implication the barbarians would not be open to the persuasive message of the apostles. Although it is dangerous to attribute too much to absence in a text, it is worth noting that the Malta narrative is the only setting in Acts where an apostle performs miraculous deeds without any mention of a message being spoken or received. The barbarians begin to suggest that Paul is a god (28:6), and they bestow honors upon him at his departure (28:10), but nowhere is it implied that they hear or become believers in his message.

In most settings in the early chapters of Acts, the apostles are shown as speaking persuasively, as well as performing and experiencing wondrous

---

[36] Vernon K. Robbins uses similar mapping terminology, although for a different purpose, in "Luke-Acts: A Mixed Population Seeks a Home in the Roman Empire," in *Images of Empire* (ed. L. Alexander; JSOTSup 122; Sheffield: Sheffield Academic Press, 1991), 202–21.

deeds and signs. This depiction of the apostles starts with the activities of Peter, John, Stephen, and other apostles in Jerusalem and then spreads to the rest of Judea, Samaria, and Galilee as persecution causes the apostles to scatter throughout the region (Acts 1–8). They speak, testify, exhort, teach, and proclaim, while also healing people and experiencing other miraculous wonders and signs. As the action moves north into Syria and Cilicia, the combination of speaking and wondrous deeds continues (Acts 9–12). When Paul and Barnabas carry their message to Cyprus and the interior of Asia Minor, including Lystra, they continue both to speak and enact miraculous deeds (Acts 13–14). Even in Philippi, which Acts describes as "a leading city of Macedonia and a Roman colony" (16:12), Paul both speaks his message and casts out a spirit (16:16–18).

The depiction of Paul's activities changes, however, when he moves west from Philippi to Thessalonica, Beroea, Athens, and Corinth (Acts 17–18). As Paul arrives in territory more clearly Greek in its ancient and classical sense, mention of wondrous deeds ceases. In Thessalonica and Beroea, for instance, Paul merely argues and explains his message in the synagogue (17:1–14). In Athens he argues in the synagogue and in the marketplace (17:17). In Corinth, he settles down as a tentmaker and continues to dispute in the synagogue, proclaiming and testifying to his message (18:1–18). In each of these cases, wonders and signs are not a factor in the narrative portrayal of the apostle. Paul's power and persuasiveness arise solely from his words.

The situation changes again, however, when Paul returns to Ephesus on the west coast of Asia Minor. Although Ephesus was an ancient Greek colony, the narrative of Acts appears to understand it as sufficiently distant from Greece proper so as to again entertain miracle working by Paul. During his two-year stint Paul speaks boldly and persuasively, first in the synagogue and then in a lecture hall (19:8–10), and yet at the same time it is stressed that "God did extraordinary miracles through Paul," healing the sick and casting out evil spirits (19:11). His healing ability at Ephesus is portrayed as so powerful that even "handkerchiefs or aprons that had touched his skin" were able to cure the sick and possessed (19:12). Later, once again on the west coast of Asia Minor in Troas, Paul manages to bring the young Eutychus, who had fallen to his death from a third-story window, back to life (20:9–12). The portrayal of Paul as miracle worker extends through his sea voyage to Rome. First we have his angelic vision that makes it possible for the crew and passengers to be saved (27:21–44). Then we have his miraculous encounter with the viper in the presence of the barbarians of Malta (28:1–6). Finally, he cures the father of the "leading man of the island" and other sick people there (28:7–10). His journey is punctuated by one miraculous event after another—that is, until he arrives in Rome.

Once settled in Rome, the miracle-working aspect of Paul again disappears from the picture. He settles down in his lodgings and spends his days explaining, testifying, persuading, proclaiming, and teaching his message (28:23–31). Gone are the wonders and signs, healings and exorcisms, miraculous handkerchiefs and extraordinary visions. In Rome, as in Greece, the power of the apostle is in the persuasive word and not in the supernatural deed. Interestingly, this distribution of supernatural power is entirely geographic and not religious or ethnic. Jews in the East, such as those around the temple in Jerusalem, observe and respond to the apostles' signs and wonders. Jews in Corinth and Rome encounter a Paul who only speaks and argues.

Interpreters of the Lystran narrative have often focused on the issue of the plausibility of the behavior of the Lycaonians, as if their ready belief in the divinity of the apostles represented an anomaly, perhaps matched only by the episode on Malta. If we take seriously the distribution of all types of supernatural events and beliefs in Acts, however, the Lycaonians appear simply as one example of a much larger phenomenon of marvels and wondrous deeds. Their attribution of divinity to the apostles may be one of the more extreme forms of the phenomenon, but the difference is rather a matter of degree than of type. The more appropriate question is really why the author places supernatural events and beliefs only in the East, not why the Lycaonians seem so inclined to superstition. Why, indeed, does the narrative portray people in the East as persuaded predominantly by healing miracles and exorcisms, while argument prevails in Rome, Corinth, and Athens? Within the geographic logic of Acts the eastern sphere certainly has a sense of otherness about it, since things happen there that do not happen on Greek or Roman soil. However, this is not the otherness of the strictly barbarian, of foreigners to be feared, or the impossibility of communication. In general, people in Acts understand Greek, converse with Roman officials, and appear to live Greco-Roman lives. The East appears as a mixed realm both of the Greco-Roman world and different from Greece and Rome at the same time. I will leave for others to ponder the implications of this observation for the narrative of Acts as a whole. For the Lystran episode, however, I propose that this ambiguous and mixed status makes it possible for the author of Acts to address and even play with ancient Greek mythological traditions without having to locate those supernaturally laden and sometimes philosophically objectionable traditions on Greek soil.

Gods in Human Form as a Greek Mythological Theme

In *Profit with Delight,* Richard Pervo says that readers must be familiar with the Baucis and Philemon myth to appreciate the humor and "learned quality" of the Lystran account.[37] I contend that Pervo is right about the humorous and compositionally creative character of the episode but that he and many others have the wrong myth in mind. Deep-seated cultural assumptions, combined with the sheer persistence of received interpretive traditions, have encouraged the presumption that the mythological underpinnings of the episode must be located beyond the border of the Greco-Roman context. A strong argument can be made, however, for looking instead to the heart of the Greek mythological tradition, in general to the theme of gods disguising themselves as traveling strangers, and more specifically to mythological traditions about the transformation of Lycaon (ruler of Arcadia) into a wolf because of his inhospitable reception of Zeus in human guise. The key to this interpretation lies in the recognition of the author's use of etymological wordplay, a common, though sometimes maligned, compositional technique found especially in poetry, but in other Greek and Latin literature as well.

As we have seen, part of the attraction of the Baucis and Philemon tale as the mythological allusion behind the Lystran episode stems from its usefulness in connecting apparently irrational or superstitious behavior with a setting distant from the centers of Greco-Roman culture and influence. Especially for those looking for historicity or realism in the narrative, the Phrygian setting of the Baucis and Philemon tale, along with the setting of the Lystran episode in nearby Lycaonia, becomes the explanation for the problematic plot. However, although several generations of scholars have been quite happy to regard the fact that Ovid sets the myth in Phrygia as sufficient evidence that the story originates from, or is indicative of, religious traditions in the interior of Asia Minor, the connection of the Baucis and Philemon story with Asia Minor is really more a matter of speculation than fact. The Roman poet Ovid, writing in Latin, provides the earliest known version of the myth, making it difficult to judge how well-known the story might have been at the time Acts was composed. We also have no further clues about the geographic locales or cultural circles where the myth might have been in circulation. In Ovid's narrative, the elderly Lelex tells the story to the Athenian hero Theseus and his companions as they wait out a storm at the home of the river-god Achelous on the boundary between the regions of Acarnania and Aetolia in Greece (Ovid, *Metam.* 8.547–561). Lelex tells the tale in order to prove the legitimacy of the river-god's claims to have turned some nymphs and a young maiden into islands. One of the companions mocks the idea that the gods can "give and take away the form of things," and Lelex uses the tale to prove otherwise (8.611–623). Ovid thus puts the tale in the mouth of an elderly Greek hero

---

[37] Pervo, *Profit with Delight*, 64–65.

speaking to other Greek heroes and a Greek river-god. Whether this tale was actually ever part of local Phrygian tradition in Asia Minor is an issue that remains hidden in the shrouds of Greek heroic and mythological traditions penned by the hand of a Latin poet.[38]

On the other hand, ample literary evidence exists not only for Greek and Roman tales about gods taking on human form but also for a tradition of theological speculation and philosophical argument about whether the gods truly transform themselves or others in this way or not. Such an argument occasions the telling of the Baucis and Philemon story, and the entire *Metamorphoses* plays with the idea of these transformations in various manifestations. More important is that we find the transformation theme in Homer's *Odyssey,* at the very heart of Greek tradition. Determined to help Odysseus's son Telemachus find his father, Athena visits him disguised in the form of one of Odysseus's old friends. After receiving the sage advice of a stranger to go search for his father, Telemachus surmises that a god had been his guest. He keeps the revelation to himself as others seek information from him (Homer, *Od.* 1.96–324, 405–419). When Telemachus returns, accompanied by the beggar, who unbeknownst to everyone is actually Odysseus, he feasts with his mother's suitors in his father's house. As the unknown beggar makes his way through the hall, a member of the company throws a stool at him. The stool-thrower is cautioned by another suitor to be careful in case the beggar is a god in human disguise: "What if perchance he be some god come down from heaven? And the gods do, in the guise of strangers from afar, put on all manner of shapes, and visit the cities, beholding the violence and the righteousness of men" (Homer, *Od.* 17.484–487). Here in Homer we find the basic premise behind Acts 14: the people assume that gods "in the guise of strangers from afar" have turned up in Lystra. Because most early education through the mid-adolescent years was based on Homer, we can assume that almost anyone in the Greco-Roman world who was capable of reading Acts in Greek would also recognize the theme from Homer.[39]

---

[38] For the opposite view, see Joseph E. Fontenrose, "Philemon, Lot, and Lycaon," *University of California Publications in Classical Philology* 13 (1945): 93–120.

[39] For the prominence of Homer in the Greco-Roman world, see Ronald F. Hock, "Homer in Greco-Roman Education," in *Mimesis and Intertextuality in Antiquity and Christianity* (ed. D. R. MacDonald; Harrisburg, Pa.: Trinity Press International, 2001), 56–77; Robert Lamberton and John J. Keaney, eds., *Homer's Ancient Readers: The Hermeneutics of Greek Epic's Earliest Exegetes* (Princeton: Princeton University Press, 1992); Martin L. Clarke, *Higher Education in the Ancient World* (London: Routledge, 1971); Henri I. Marrou, *A History of Education in Antiquity* (trans. G. Lamb; New York: Sheed & Ward, 1956); and Raffaella

This very common tradition was not without its critics, most notably Plato. In the *Republic* Socrates mentions this passage from Homer as an example of the type of story that should not be permitted in the education of the future guardians of the perfect city (Plato, *Resp.* 380D–382D). His objections are theological, based on a conception of a truly good god. He argues that these stories tell falsehoods about deities, because only beings who are inferior and imperfect change their form or choose to deceive by disguise. A good and perfect god would not behave thus. At the beginning of the *Sophist,* Socrates again refers to the Homeric passage, this time in jest, as he asks whether a visiting stranger might actually be a god in disguise sent to examine his arguments (Plato, *Soph.* 216A–B). These objections reveal a tension in Greek culture between the traditional mythology and the theological arguments of the philosophers. Although interpreters of Acts 14 have tended to regard the idea of gods in human disguise as a matter of rural or barbarian thought, the tension between Homer and Plato actually reveals a peculiarly Greek theological preoccupation. The poet and the philosopher represent two sides of the Greco-Roman tradition, one side happily telling stories of gods in many forms and disguises, the other questioning the truth and validity of these popular stories.

The author of Acts handles the tension by separating the two tendencies geographically. As we saw earlier, wonders and marvels, the building blocks of mythology, occur only in the eastern empire but are excluded from the cultural centers of Greece and Rome. Thus the setting of the Lystran narrative in rural Asia Minor provides a conveniently distant location through which the author can respond indirectly to the mythological elements of the dominant culture without having to locate these elements directly on Greek or Roman soil. An educated Greco-Roman reader would have recognized both strands in Greco-Roman culture and should have been readily able to recognize Acts 14 as playing with this genre and cultural tension.[40] If the Baucis and Philemon story were well known, that may have been one of the examples that came to mind. The reader might just as readily have thought of Homer and/or Plato's objections to Homer or of any number of examples of gods disguising themselves and interacting with mortals for good or ill. Ovid alone tells three different tales of Jupiter/Zeus appearing to humans in disguise in order to test the hospitality and

---

Cribiore, *Gymnastics of the Mind: Greek Education in Hellenistic and Roman Egypt* (Princeton: Princeton University Press, 2001), esp. 140–43, 194–97, 204–5.

[40] On the supposition of a common literary culture for many segments of Greco-Roman society see F. Gerald Downing, "*A bas les Aristos:* The Relevance of Higher Literature for the Understanding of the Earliest Christian Writings," *NovT* 30 (1988): 212–30.

devotion of ordinary mortals. One is, of course, the Baucis and Philemon tale. In another tale, Jupiter, Neptune, and Mercury visit an elderly widowed farmer named Hyrieus, who gives them hospitality. In return for their good treatment, the gods grant him his wish to have a child, who eventually is transformed into the constellation Boeotian Orion (Ovid, *Fast.* 5.493–544). Like Baucis and Philemon, Hyrieus is rewarded greatly because of the hospitality he grants to these strangers—the gods disguised as humans. The third tale, the story of Lycaon, we need to consider in greater detail.

THE LYCAON TALE: AN ALLUSION THAT CREATES A DUAL REALITY

Variations on the Lycaon tale appear in numerous Greek and Latin sources, making it perhaps the most well-attested example of the genre. In Ovid's version of the tale, Jupiter (Zeus), in human disguise, wanders around Arcadia, the realm of Lycaon, encountering wickedness everywhere (Ovid, *Metam.* 1.163–167, 196–198, 209–240). When he goes to the home of Lycaon, Jupiter reveals his divinity, and the common people begin to worship him. Lycaon, however, doubts the divine identity of his visitor and decides to test him by killing him. First, however, he prepares a banquet of roasted human flesh. As soon as Lycaon serves the meat, Jupiter sends the house crashing down with a thunderbolt. Lycaon tries to run away but gradually changes into a wolf of the same savage character exhibited in his human life. The story in Ovid and other sources plays on a word association between the name Lycaon (*Lycaon* in both Greek and Latin) and *lykos* and *lupus* (the Greek and Latin terms for wolf, respectively). The human Lycaon becomes a *lykos/lupus* (wolf) upon his transformation.

Early references to the Lycaon tale can be found in fragments of Hesiod quoted by Hecataeus in the sixth century B.C.E. and by Eratosthenes in the late third or early second centuries B.C.E. In Hecataeus, Lycaon's impious sons appear to have a role in preparing the abominable meal (Hecataeus, frag 1a, 1,F.6bis,a.18).[41] In Eratosthenes, Lycaon seeks revenge against Zeus by serving him the flesh of the child Zeus fathered by seducing Lycaon's daughter Callisto (Hesiod, *Astronomy* 3). Eratosthenes continues the story by depicting Zeus throwing over the table, striking the house down with a thunderbolt, and turning Lycaon into a wolf as he runs away (Eratosthenes, *Catasterismi* 1.8R[16].1–31).[42] In

---

[41] The reference to Hecataeus, as well as the one below to Eratosthenes, were supplied by a search of TLG.

[42] It is unclear whether Eratosthenes attributes this last part to Hesiod as well. The Loeb edition of Hesiod's *Astronomy* ends the section before Zeus punishes Lycaon.

sources more contemporary to both Ovid and Acts, Nicolas of Damascus and Apollodorus (Pseudo-Apollodorus) both blame Lycaon's sons for serving Zeus human flesh, and neither author includes Lycaon's transformation into a wolf. Hyginus tells what appears to be the older version of the story in which the sons are killed by a thunderbolt and Lycaon is turned into a wolf (Hyginus, *Fabulae* 176). Pausanias also tells of Lycaon's transformation into a wolf, but in his version the transformation is occasioned by Lycaon sacrificing a baby on the Arcadian altar to Lycaean Zeus (Pausanias, *Descr.* 2.1–7). Pausanias uses the tradition as a means of discussing whether humans could be turned into gods or beasts. He argues that in the old days humans were good and could be changed into gods but that this current age is so evil that such transformations no longer happen. However, he also reports the rumor that ever since the time of Lycaon a person who makes a sacrifice to Lycaean Zeus is changed into a wolf and remains so for nine years.

The clue that this well-known story is relevant to the Lystran episode comes from the narrative detail that the people "shouted in the Lycaonian language" (Acts 14:11). The Lycaonian geographic designation has two different associations. One is, of course, an association with a region of central Asia Minor; the other concerns ancient traditions from prehistorical Arcadia. Our best evidence for this second use of the designation comes from Dionysius of Halicarnassus, who, in the process of speculating about the origins of the cities of Italy, refers to the colonists using names derived from their leaders. His account focuses on Oenotrus, son of Lycaon of Arcadia, as the leader of the Oenotrians, who, he believes, colonized the west coast of Italy many generations prior to the Trojan war (*Ant. rom.* 1.11.1–3). He later explains that these settlers, prior to colonizing Italy, had been known first as Azeians under Lycaon's father Aezeius, then as Lycaonians under Lycaon (*Ant. rom.* 1.12.1). In another place he refers to their former abode as "then called Lycaonia, and now Arcadia" (*Ant. rom.* 1.1.2). Dionysius adopts the same forms used by the author of Acts and others to refer to Lycaonia and the Lycaonians in Asia Minor (Acts 14:6, 11). Moreover, Dionysius's account identifies precedents for this pattern of naming in his historical sources, specifically noting Antiochus of Syracuse for Italus (Italians), Moreges (Morgetes), and Sicelus (Sicels, *Ant. rom.* 1.12.3), and Pherecydes of Athens for Oenotrus (Oenotrians) and Peucetius (Peucetians, *Ant. rom.* 1.13.1). Following the pattern, one moves rather easily from the ruler Lycaon to the people of Arcadia as Lycaonians. The double meaning of "Lycaonian" was so frequently assumed in late antiquity that Justinian based his decision to provide better government for the province Lycaonia in Asia Minor on its associations with the ancient settlers of Italy. Based on the identical names for the territories, Justinian appears to assume that Arcadians settled Lycaonia in Asia Minor, as well as parts of the Italian peninsula.[43]

To appreciate the mythological and literary allusions in Acts 14, it is necessary to take into account this dual meaning of "Lycaonian." The ostensive setting for the episode is Lycaonia in Asia Minor, but the theme of gods in disguise and the people's shouts in Lycaonian link the episode to the Arcadian mythological and prehistorical past. To read Acts 14 in this way assumes a Greco-Roman habit of reading that recognizes and finds meaning in plays on words, double-meanings, and etymological associations drawn between entities with similar sounding names. This form of wordplay and etymologizing has a strong precedent in Greek and Roman literature. For example, Frederick Ahl gives ample evidence for the presence of such wordplay and soundplay involving *Lycaon* and *lupus* associations, as well as many other clusters of similar-sounding words in Ovid's *Metamorphoses*. In this mode of literary composition, "if two words (or syllables) are phonetically similar, they either are conceptually related or become conceptually related."[44] James O'Hara has extensively outlined the presence of etymological wordplay in Vergil.[45] Although both Ahl and O'Hara focus on Latin sources, they trace the origin of this compositional method to classics of Greek literature, including Homer, Hesiod, the tragic poets, some of the Stoic philosophers, and especially, according to O'Hara, some of the poets associated with Alexandria, such as Callimachus and Apollonius of Rhodes.[46] The classic philosophical (and somewhat tongue-in-cheek) example is Plato's *Cratylus*.[47] As Ahl points out, this idea of reading with dual realities goes against the mainstream of classical scholarship, which tends to try to resolve ambiguities of meaning

---

[43] See Frederick M. Ahl, *Metaformations: Soundplay and Wordplay in Ovid and other Classical Poets*, (Ithaca, N.Y.: Cornell University Press, 1985), 142. For the *Novellae constitutiones of Justinian*, see Rudolfus Schoell and Wilhelm Kroll, eds., *Novellae* (vol. 3 of *Corpus Juris Civilis*; ed. W. Kroll et al.; 3 vols.; 13th ed.; Berlin: de Gruyter, 1963).

[44] Ahl, *Metaformations*, 19.

[45] James J. O'Hara, *True Names: Vergil and the Alexandrian Tradition of Etymological Wordplay* (Ann Arbor: University of Michigan Press, 1996).

[46] O'Hara (ibid., 7–42) provides an excellent summary of etymological wordplay in Greek literature. An older but still useful work is William B. Stanford, *Ambiguity in Greek Literature: Studies in Theory and Practice* (Oxford: Blackwell, 1939). For another discussion of puns and other forms of symbolic language in Acts, see Dennis Hamm, "Acts 3,1–10: The Healing of the Temple Beggar as Lucan Theology," *Bib* 67 (1986): 305–19.

[47] For an assessment of the *Cratylus*, see Timothy M. S. Baxter, *The Cratylus: Plato's Critique of Naming* (Philosophia antiqua 58; Leiden: Brill, 1992).

by determining which is the intended meaning, rather than exploring the possibility that the author creates a "texture of wordplays" or a "dual reality."[48] Reading the Lystran episode requires recognition of such a dual reality. On the one hand, Paul and Barnabas have an eventful encounter with first-century Lycaonians of Asia Minor. On the other hand, the subtext of the story, or the logic of its mythological allusions, pulls the reader not only into a different time and place but also into a mode of reading that finds meaning in its plurality and ambiguity.

What difference does it make to our reading of the Lystran episode if we take into account this dual reality and assume that knowledgeable Greco-Roman readers would have recognized the allusion to the Lycaon story? First of all, it changes the tone and increases the element of suspense in the episode. The Lycaon myths are dramatic and even gruesome. With stories of cannibalism, home- and life-destroying thunderbolts, and, of course, transformations into wolves, anything could happen. This is a very different tone from the picture of domestic bliss in the Baucis and Philemon tale. Second, Paul's speech becomes a response not to an instance of barely hellenized, peripheral, and localized religion but to the worship of Zeus and the plethora of mythology surrounding Zeus and the entire pantheon in Greek religious traditions. When Paul exhorts the Lycaonians to turn away "from these worthless things" (Acts 14:15), the reader who makes the association hears a condemnation of some of the most traditional elements of Greek religion. Third, this association with Zeus and Greek religion changes our view of the relationship of the Lystran episode to other episodes in Acts, most notably Peter's healing of a lame man in front of the Jerusalem temple (3:1–26) and Paul's speech at the Areopagus in Athens (17:16–34). The Lystran episode has parallels to each of these narratives but is often seen as the lesser and inferior of the breed because it addresses insignificant and backward local traditions rather than the power of the God of Israel or the sophistication of Greek philosophical theology. If, however, the Lystran episode cleverly and indirectly comments on the primary mythological traditions of Greece, then it must be seen as a worthy parallel to each of these episodes and part of a general effort to show the power of the God of Israel over and against the dominant religious and philosophical beliefs of the Greco-Roman world.

Finally, and most importantly, recognition of the association with the Lycaon tale helps us make sense of the ending of the episode. The contrast between the people's persistence in wanting to offer sacrifice to Paul and Barnabas and the ease with which they are persuaded to stone them has always given commentators a problem, because it defies most

---

[48] Ahl, *Metaformations*, 18.

conceptions of a logical plot. This turn of events contributes to the Lycaonians' reputation among interpreters as "fickle barbarians." However, if we take seriously the habit of reading where names are indicative of the nature or character of people and things, it is possible to make sense of this sudden turn of events and even tie this puzzling transformation into the overall framework of the narrative of Acts. To understand the puzzling ending, it is necessary to recognize that the author portrays the Lycaonians as exhibiting the wolflike character or nature indicated by their name.

The Greek term *lykophilia* ("wolf-friendship") is used to describe friendship characterized by an initial show of friendliness that quickly turns to enmity or hostility. Fragments from Menander include the saying: "Truces are but wolf-friendships."[49] Marcus Aurelius describes the genuineness and honesty of a good man using *lykophilia* as his counterexample. In comparison to the kindly and well-meaning character of a good man, "nothing is more shameful than wolf-friendship" characterized by deceit and cunning (*Meditations* 11.15). Eusebius uses the term to describe the heretic Novatus, who duplicitously pretends he does not want to be bishop, all the while persuading people to follow him. The accusations against Novatus include craftiness, duplicity, perjuries, falsehoods, unsociability, and wolflike friendship (*Hist. eccl.* 6.43.6). The term can be traced all the way back to Plato, who uses it to describe his strained relationship with his friend Dionysius. Plato claims that Dionysius put him in a tight spot, thereby producing "the wolf-friendship and absence of fellowship" between them (*Ep.* 318E). Plato also uses the example of the wolf to describe the ease with which a lover, at first in love and full of promises, reneges on those promises as soon as his appetite is satisfied and reason takes over (*Phaedr.* 241C–D). The wolf loves the lamb and then devours it; initial friendliness turns into hostility and even physical attack.

The idea that a wolf's mode of operation provides an analogy for a change in human sentiment from friendship to enmity also appears in the description of the making of a tyrant in Plato's *Republic*. Socrates argues that tyrants begin as protectors, but at some point a transformation takes place that turns them into tyrants. The starting point of this transformation occurs, according to Socrates, when the acts of the protector come to resemble the myth told about the shrine to Lycaean Zeus in Arcadia, in

---

[49] Fragments of Menander are from the following collections (source: TLG): Theodor Kock, ed., *Comicorum atticorum fragmenta* (3 vols.; Leipzig: Teubner, 1888), 3:line 833.1; August Meineke, ed., *Fragmenta comicorum graecorum* (5 vols.; Berlin: Reimer, 1841; repr., Berlin: de Gruyter, 1970), 4:line FIF.203.1; and Alfred Körte and Andreas Thierfelder, eds., *Menandri quae supersunt* (2 vols.; 2d ed.; Leipzig: Teubner, 1959), 2:line 697.1.

which the one who tastes bits of human entrails is turned into a wolf (*Resp.* 565D). "Have you not heard the story?" Socrates asks his interlocutor, and then he goes on to draw an analogy between the tale and the actions of the tyrant:

> In like manner a leader of the people who, getting control of a docile mob, does not withhold his hand from the shedding of tribal blood, but by the customary unjust accusations brings a citizen into court and assassinates him, blotting out a human life, and with unhallowed tongue and lips that have tasted kindred blood, banishes and slays and hints at the abolition of debts and the partition of lands—is it not the inevitable consequence and a decree of fate that such a one be either slain by his enemies or become a tyrant and be transformed from a man into a wolf? (*Resp.* 565E–566A)

As we saw earlier, Pausanias traces the origin of the tradition about the shrine to Lycaean Zeus to Lycaon's sacrifice of a human baby and consequent transformation into a wolf. Plato uses the analogy to depict how an initially benign leader gets a taste of power over his people, uses that power to shed the blood of one of his own people, and by that very taste is transformed into a tyrant.

When the Lycaonians turn suddenly from worship to stoning, they exhibit such wolflike character. For the reader clued into these Greek and Roman traditions—those linking sudden turns to enmity and cruelty with the character of wolves—the end of the episode would not so much surprise as fulfill the expectations implied in the name "Lycaonian." The wolf analogy also links the events of the Lystran episode to the overall theme of the persecution and rejection of the apostles in Acts. This motif is foreshadowed in the Gospel traditions in which Jesus sends the disciples out like "lambs/sheep into the midst of wolves" (Luke 10:3; Matt 10:16). In turn, the wolf allusion in the Lystran episode foreshadows Paul's speech to the Ephesian elders, where he warns "savage wolves will come in among you, not sparing the flock" (Acts 20:29). Elsewhere in this volume Dennis MacDonald enhances our understanding of this wolf simile by showing how its use in Paul's speech recalls Homer's likening of men in battle to the fury of wolves falling upon their prey.[50] As it sets up "Jews ... from

---

[50] Homer provides only one small piece of a broad and varied literary context for the Lystran episode. The allusions to deities in human disguise and comparisons to wolves are general and do not necessarily indicate direct literary dependence on any one passage in Homer. Dennis MacDonald, by contrast, seeks to demonstrate explicit literary dependence between *Iliad* 6 and Paul's farewell in Acts 20:18–35 (see his contribution to this volume).

Antioch and Iconium" (Acts 14:19) as the instigators of the Lycaonians' transformation into wolves, the Lystran episode thus draws upon a complex literary repertoire of allusions to wolves as an integral part of its portrayal of various groups of Jews and Jewish leaders as the instigators of this persecution against the apostles. Through the logic of the wolf analogy, these apparent catalysts of persecution take on the identity of wolves themselves, and the utterly Greco-Roman literary motif of evil humans being transformed into wolves becomes part of the well-documented anti-Jewish rhetoric in Acts.[51]

Once we recognize the wolf motif as part of the theme of persecution in Acts, we need to consider a final issue that we cannot resolve but is still worth pondering. Does the image of Plato's wolflike tyrant lurk behind the Lukan literary portrayal of certain Jewish leaders as those who persecute Christian apostles? The vocabulary of Acts is too varied and different from that of the *Republic* to suggest any kind of direct literary allusion or dependence. There exists, however, a striking resemblance between the actions and characteristics Plato attributes to the wolflike tyrant and those with which the narrative of Acts depicts certain groups of Jewish leaders. Plato's tyrant persuades the docile mob. Acts portrays various groups of Jews as stirring up or inciting the crowds not only in Lystra (14:19) but in Antioch of Pisidia (13:50), Iconium (14:2), Thessalonica (17:5), Beroea (17:13), and Jerusalem (6:2; 21:27). Plato's tyrant goes against his own kindred (*emphyliou*) with unjust charges. Acts depicts various Jews as accusing, handing over, or instigating the arrest of their fellow Jews—the Jewish-Christian apostles—with charges portrayed as unjust or unfounded. Peter and John are arrested "because of a good deed done" (4:1–9), and the accusations against Stephen are "secretly instigated" with "false witnesses" (6:11, 13). In Corinth Gallio refuses to accept the complaint because the charges are only "about words and names and your own law" (18:12–13), while in Jerusalem Paul is falsely accused of bringing Greeks into the temple (21:28–29). Moreover, throughout Paul's appearances before Roman officials the theme is one of charges that cannot be proved (24:1–21; 25:7, 18–19, 25). The unjust nature of the accusations is secured with King Agrippa's announcement that "this man is doing nothing to deserve death or imprisonment" (26:30–32).

---

[51] Jack T. Sanders, *The Jews in Luke-Acts* (Philadelphia: Fortress, 1987); Lloyd Gaston, "Anti-Judaism and the Passion Narrative in Luke and Acts," in *Anti-Judaism in Early Christianity* (ed. P. Richardson; 2 vols.; SCJ 2; Waterloo, Ont.: Wilfrid Laurier University Press, 1986), 1:127–53; Stephen G. Wilson, "The Jews and the Death of Jesus in Acts," in Richardson, *Anti-Judaism in Early Christianity,* 1:155–64; John G. Gager, *The Origins of Anti-Semitism: Attitudes toward Judaism in Pagan and Christian Antiquity* (New York: Oxford University Press, 1985).

The transformation of Plato's protector into a wolflike tyrant is sealed with his murderous intent to shed blood, assassinate, and blot out human life. The end of the Lystran episode portrays the crowd as incited by the "Jews ... from Antioch and Iconium" to stone Paul, drag him out of the city, and leave him there, "supposing that he was dead" (14:19; cf. 7:57–59; 21:30–31). The narrative portrays him as narrowly escaping a similar stoning in Iconium (14:5). As modern readers of Acts, accustomed to its storyline of persecution and threats of impending death, we may easily be taken in by this ready progression from opposition to murderous intent. Jewish leaders in Jerusalem are "enraged" and want to kill the apostles (5:33), Stephen is stoned to death as the unconverted Saul stands by and then continues "breathing threats and murder" (7:57–8:1; 22:20), Herod has James killed (12:1–2), Sosthenes is beaten in Corinth (18:17), and back in Jerusalem Paul is under constant threat (21:30–31; 22:22; 23:12, 21; 25:3). Behind all this lies the Lukan claim that many of the same Jewish leaders are responsible for the death of Jesus (2:23; 3:15; 5:30; 7:52; 13:28). As Acts would have us believe, those with religious power and authority, having once tasted "one bit of human entrails," turn into murderous and tyrannical wolves. Acts leaves no doubt about the identity and character of the culprits.

We can never know if the author intended these parallels to Plato's tyrant or if they are simply due to a common theme of persecution and the usefulness of the Greco-Roman wolf motif for characterizing enemies.[52] Consideration of the possibility, however, should help put the literary portrayal of those Jews in Acts who persecute Christians into sharp relief. Even in the mythology only certain very evil persons are transformed into wolves. However, in Acts the apostles encounter wolves at every turn—packs of wolves, not just an occasional evil king or supplicant at the altar of the Lycaean Zeus. Why does the author portray so much wolflike behavior? The historically inclined might say that Acts simply portrays the realities of the early Christian experience. Those who attribute more creative license to the author might point to the way sharp lines and intensity of conflict make a more suspenseful story. We could also surmise that by emphasizing Jews—and especially Jewish leaders—as

---

[52] For discussion of literary allusions to Plato in other early Christian literature, see Dennis R. MacDonald, *Christianizing Homer: The Odyssey, Plato, and the Acts of Andrew* (New York: Oxford University Press, 1994). Todd Penner's characterization (in this volume) of Acts as representing Christianity as "the model *politeia*" connects readily with the parallels between the portrait of the enemies of the apostles in Acts and the character of the tyrant who threatens the *politeia* in Plato's *Republic*. In this view, the Lycaonians and other "wolves" in Acts represent threats and opposition to the Christian *politeia*.

culprits in the persecution of the apostles, the author minimizes any impression that the Christians might be a problem to the Roman authorities. However, somewhere in the midst of the real or the imagined, we are left with a narrative that derives one piece of its forward motion from portraying enemies as deliberate and cunning foes, waiting to pounce at any opportunity and set to devour their prey. We must recognize that this portrayal of enemies in Acts is first and foremost a matter of literary composition and technique. Enemies can be real or enemies can be pure literary constructs. More often they are a mixture of the two. In the case of Acts, we can confirm little about the original historical nature of the story. We can, however, make a substantial effort to situate Acts within the literary traditions of Greece and Rome. Future scholarship would do well to probe further the extent and significance of these literary connections. Critical comparison of Acts with its literary environment has the potential to increase significantly our understanding of the techniques the author uses to convey both the positive and the more troubling aspects of his message and to enhance greatly our understanding of the range of meanings accessible to the narrative's earliest readers.[53]

---

[53] For another recent effort to contextualize Acts 14, see Dean P. Béchard, "Paul among the Rustics: The Lystran Episode (Acts 14:8–20) and Lucan Apologetic," *CBQ* 63 (2001): 84–101. Béchard suggests that the portrayal of Paul and Barnabas in Acts 14 follows a Greco-Roman literary *topos* in which an authentic sage must counter the enthusiasm of those overly impressed with his powers. Béchard finds here an apologetic element directed against charges that Christian preachers preyed upon especially gullible audiences. I find Béchard's interpretation of the apostles promising, but not his associated claim that the Lycaonians as portrayed in Acts "represent the most primitive and rustic of the world's cultures" (86). In support of this claim, he interprets Strabo as depicting the Lycaonians as "a prototypical mountain-dwelling tribe of primitive rustics" (89). However, the passages of Strabo that Béchard apparently reads as applying to the Lycaonians (*Geogr.* 12.6.5; 14.5.24) I interpret as referring instead to the inhabitants of the Taurus Mountains, which formed the southern boundary of the vast Lycaonian plateau. Strabo's descriptions of the peoples of the Taurus Mountains resemble those of others whom he characterizes as "wild" or "undomesticated" (*agrioi:* the same term used for "wild animals" and "wild fruits"). "Wild" peoples in Strabo include, among others, inhabitants of Ierne (Ireland), described as promiscuous and incestuous cannibals (1.4.3; 4.5.4); western Iberians, described as prone to warfare, unsociable, and lacking benevolence toward others (3.3.8); Scythians, described as sacrificing strangers (7.3.6); Dardanians, described as living in caves dug beneath their own dung-hills (7.5.7); and the Heptacometae (see Béchard, 89 n.17), described as living in trees or turrets and attacking passersby by leaping upon them from above (12.3.18). Absent from descriptions of these "wild" peoples are any mention of a reputation for gullibility or association with any type of religious practice whatsoever. Rather,

Conclusion

In the *Republic* Socrates asks his interlocutor "Have you not heard the tale?" (*Resp.* 565E). His partner in the dialogue replies, "I have." Most Greco-Roman readers of the Lystran episode in Acts would also have been able to answer that question in the affirmative. They would have recognized the dual reality of the episode and made the necessary etymological association between the Lycaonians and the traditions about Lycaon and wolves. For many years, however, modern interpreters of the Lystran narrative "heard" the wrong story because deep-seated assumptions about cultural differences left us listening to tales in all the wrong places. Even as we cleaned house and wiped away cobwebs of prejudice, our hearing was tuned in the wrong direction. In my own engagement with Acts, it took a sustained examination of the traditions of interpretation in order to grasp more fully the extent to which these habits of thought continue to shape our categories and assumptions. The Lystran episode may be somewhat unusual for Acts in terms of the extent to which historical-critical interpretation was shaped by Orientalism, but similar vestiges may well be at work elsewhere. It makes sense, therefore, for interpreters exploring new ways of situating Acts within its Greco-Roman literary context to give further attention to and use extra caution when the dynamics of the narrative invoke any suggestion of cultural divides, stereotypes, opposition or hostility, and especially when the narrative is governed by any kind of sustained conflict or physical violence. These are points at which cultural assumptions, literary techniques, and historical realities can readily, inadvertently, and inappropriately become fused. As interpreters, we need to understand both ancient and modern tendencies in this regard if we are to explicate and thoughtfully consider the role of such dynamics in the narrative itself and in the ways in which we interact with the text.

---

from the point of view of Strabo, religious gullibility (in the form of *deisidaimonia*) strikes the less-educated such as children, women, and illiterate men among domesticated or civilized peoples, including Greeks and Romans (see 1.2.8; 7.3.4). The Lycaonians in Acts may well appear as gullible and less-educated, but the narrative portrayal of them as engaging in such domesticated behavior as having a temple and preparing sacrifices precludes us from associating them with the "wild" peoples Strabo places on the literal and figurative edges of the inhabited world.

ROMAN PROPAGANDA AND CHRISTIAN IDENTITY IN THE WORLDVIEW OF LUKE-ACTS

Gary Gilbert

According to the book of Acts, the term *Christian* was first applied to the followers of Jesus in Antioch (Acts 11:26). The historical value of this Lukan account remains open to serious question. The brief reminiscence seems tacked on to the preceding account describing the growth of the Antiochene church.[1] For some reason, Luke inserted the detail about the term "Christian" (Χριστιανοί) at this point. Moreover, the ending *-anoi* suggests a Latin rather than a Greek-speaking environment.[2] Reports from Tacitus and Suetonius, as well as a graffito from Pompeii, equally argue for an Italian, probably Roman, origin of the term.[3] Regardless of the historical value afforded by these reports, they indicate that for approximately two or three decades those who had come to believe in Jesus as Messiah and Son of God were addressed by a variety of other names, such as brethren (ἀδελφοί), disciples (μαθηταί), or saints (ἅγιοι).[4] As Charles Barrett has pointed out, however, "these words were useless to outsiders unless it was made clear whose disciples

---

[1] Gerd Lüdemann, *Early Christianity according to the Traditions in Acts* (trans. J. Bowden; Minneapolis: Fortress, 1989), 137.

[2] This point is often made, e.g., Henry J. Cadbury, "Names for Christians and Christianity in Acts," in *The Beginnings of Christianity: The Acts of the Apostles* (ed. F. J. Foakes Jackson and K. Lake; 5 vols.; London: Macmillan, 1920–33; repr., Grand Rapids: Baker, 1979), 5:384–85. For a potential Greek origin, see Joseph B. Lightfoot, *The Apostolic Fathers* (5 vols.; repr., Peabody, Mass.: Hendrickson, 1989), 2.1:418.

[3] The term was known in Rome in the 60s C.E.; see Tacitus, *Ann.* 15.44; and Suetonius, *Nero* 16. For the graffito from Pompeii, see *CIL* 4:679; and the discussion by Erich Dinkler, "Älteste christliche Denkmäler–Bestand und Chronologie," in *Signum Crucis: Aufsätze zum Neuen Testament und zur christlichen Archäologie* (Tübingen: Mohr Siebeck, 1967), 138–41.

[4] On these two terms and several others, see Cadbury, "Names for Christians and Christianity," 375–92.

they were, in whom they believe, in whose family they were brothers."[5] The term *Christian* arose and spread as a means to differentiate this particular group of disciples or brethren from all others. Its appearance in Acts, 1 Peter, and Ignatius of Antioch, all pieces written toward the end of the first and beginning of the second centuries, reflects an interest among Christian communities to define themselves as distinct from the religious and social world in which they lived.[6] Luke's particular use of the term suggests that he, and perhaps the community to and for whom he wrote, had begun to question their relation to Jews and Judaism, as well as the broader Roman world, and as a result began to reflect on what it meant to be a Christian.[7]

Several recent studies on Luke-Acts have argued that the work, at least in part, attempts to address the question of Christian identity and to define, in a narrative manner, what it means to be a Christian. Philip Esler, drawing on the sociological work of Peter Berger and Thomas Luckmann, speaks of Luke-Acts as a work of legitimization, an attempt "to explain and justify, to 'legitimate' Christianity to his Christian contemporaries."[8] In partial agreement with Esler, Gregory Sterling envisions Luke-Acts as a form of apologetic historiography, the purpose of which was to "provide them with identity in the larger world."[9] "Luke-Acts," writes Sterling, "offered Christians a definition of Christianity as the church moved into the post-apostolic age."[10] For Marianne Palmer Bonz, who offers a comparison of Luke-Acts with classical epic traditions, (especially Vergil's *Aeneid*), Luke-Acts confers "a noble identity and an aura of destiny upon the Christian present, raising the designation 'Christian' to the level of universal human

---

[5] C. K. Barrett, *A Critical and Exegetical Commentary on the Acts of the Apostles* (2 vols.; ICC; Edinburgh: T&T Clark, 1994–98), 1:556–57.

[6] Other instances can be found in the following: Acts 26:28; 1 Pet 4:16; Ignatius, *Eph.* 11.2; *Magn.* 4; *Rom.* 3.2; Polycarp, *Phil.* 7.3.

[7] This observation does not imply that the "parting of the ways" was absolute at this time. The relations between Christians and Jews, as well as between Christianity and Judaism more generally, remain a complex issue, further complicated by their intertwining for the next couple of centuries. For one discussion of the issue, see James D. G. Dunn, *The Partings of the Ways between Christianity and Judaism and Their Significance for the Character of Christianity* (Philadelphia: Trinity Press International, 1991).

[8] Philip F. Esler, *Community and Gospel in Luke-Acts: The Social and Political Motivations of Lucan Theology* (SNTSMS 57; Cambridge: Cambridge University Press, 1987), 16.

[9] Gregory E. Sterling, *Historiography and Self-Definition: Josephos, Luke-Acts and Apologetic Historiography* (NovTSup 64; Leiden: Brill, 1992), 386.

[10] Ibid., 380.

aspiration" and in so doing functions as a "foundational epic for the newly emerging Christian community of the Greco-Roman world."[11]

Sterling and Palmer Bonz build their analysis of Luke-Acts in part through an effective comparison between Luke-Acts and contemporary literature. In so doing, they have participated in a wider discussion that locates the literary models that influenced Luke and, using this information, develops a better understanding of the work's meaning or purpose. A variety of literary features—most prominently the prefaces, speeches, and dramatic episodes—lay claim to several distinct genres.[12] The pioneering work of Henry Cadbury led numerous scholars to the conclusion that historiography exerted the primary influence on Luke-Acts and should serve as the principal lens through which to read and interpret the work. While the boundaries of historiography often prove to be permeable, many structural elements, the preface (Luke 1:1–4) and the general content among them, offer numerous parallels with various subgenres of ancient historical writings.[13] Luke, as this analysis suggests, follows in an eminent line of historians stretching back to Herodotus and Thucydides and then moving on down to Polybius, Dionysius of Halicarnassus, Diodorus Siculus, and Josephus, among others. Next to historiography, biographical texts,

---

[11] Marianne Palmer Bonz, *The Past as Legacy: Luke-Acts and Ancient Epic* (Minneapolis: Fortress, 2000), 26, 29.

[12] For general surveys, see David E. Aune, *The New Testament in Its Literary Environment* (LEC 8; Philadelphia: Westminster, 1987), 77–157; Klaus Berger, "Hellenistische Gattungen im Neuen Testament," *ANRW* 2.25.2: 1034–45; and Bruce W. Winter and Andrew D. Clarke, eds., *The Book of Acts in Its Ancient Literary Setting* (vol. 1 of *The Book of Acts in Its First Century Setting*; Grand Rapids: Eerdmans, 1993).

[13] On Luke-Acts and historiography generally, see Henry J. Cadbury, *The Making of Luke-Acts* (2d ed.; London: SPCK, 1958; repr., Peabody, Mass.: Hendrickson, 1999), 132–34; and Eckhard Plümacher, *Lukas als hellenistischer Schriftsteller: Studien zur Apostelgeschichte* (SUNT 9; Göttingen: Vandenhoeck & Ruprecht, 1972). For Acts as historical monograph, see Hans Conzelmann, *Acts of the Apostles* (ed. E. J. Epp and C. R. Matthews; trans. J. Limburg et al.; Hermeneia; Philadelphia: Fortress, 1987), xl–xli; and Martin Hengel, *Acts and the History of Earliest Christianity* (trans. J. Bowden; Philadelphia: Fortress, 1979), 36. For Acts as general or universal history, see Aune, *New Testament in Its Literary Environment*, 88–89; David Balch, "Comments on the Genre and a Political Theme of Luke-Acts: A Preliminary Comparison of Two Hellenistic Historians," *SBL Seminar Papers, 1989* (SBLSP 28; Atlanta: Scholars Press, 1989), 343. For Acts as apologetic historiography, see Sterling, *Historiography and Self-Definition*. The genre of institutional historiography has been promoted by Hubert Cancik, "The History of Culture, Religion, and Institutions in Ancient Historiography: Philological Observations concerning Luke's History," *JBL* 116 (1997): 673–95.

particularly those depicting the lives of ancient philosophers, have received careful attention.[14] Other oft-mentioned contenders for the generic locus of Luke or Acts or both are folk epic, novel, epic, or scientific monograph.[15]

While Greek and to a lesser extent Latin literature has been richly mined as Luke's model and literary inspiration, one type of discourse, political propaganda, has gone largely unnoticed. Propaganda is not a genre or even a literary style. Rather, it is best understood as a rhetorical strategy meant to communicate a particular idea or vision of the world and, with an air of transparency, to persuade the audience of its truth.[16] Propaganda seeks to provoke "conformity and stability and aims to make 'the individual participate in his society in every way.'"[17] In the methods employed in Roman antiquity, propaganda not only designates the systematic, official language and images produced by the imperial government itself but also, as Paul Zanker and others have shown, includes the discourse of mutuality and reciprocity, both verbal and visual, created in the Roman world not only by imperial mandate but also by friends and allies, both in Rome and the provinces.[18] The media for the communication of propaganda were thus diverse and interconnected. They

---

[14] Charles H. Talbert, *Literary Patterns, Theological Themes, and the Genre of Luke-Acts* (SBLMS 20; Missoula, Mont.: Scholars Press, 1974); and Loveday Alexander, "Acts and Ancient Intellectual Biography," in Winter and Clarke, *Book of Acts in Its Ancient Literary Setting*, 31–63.

[15] For Acts as folk epic, see James M. Dawsey, "Characteristics of Folk-Epic in Acts," *SBL Seminar Papers, 1989*, 317; as an ancient novel, see Richard I. Pervo, *Profit with Delight: The Literary Genre of the Acts of the Apostles* (Philadelphia: Fortress, 1987); as epic, see Palmer Bonz, *Past as Legacy;* and Dennis R. MacDonald, "Shipwrecks of Odysseus and Paul," *NTS* 45 (1999): 88–107; and as a scientific treatise, see Loveday Alexander, *The Preface to Luke's Gospel: Literary Convention and Social Context in Luke 1.1–4 and Acts 1.1* (SNTSMS 78; Cambridge: Cambridge University Press, 1993).

[16] On the use of propaganda in imperial Rome, see Jane DeRose Evans, *The Art of Persuasion: Political Propaganda from Aeneas to Brutus* (Ann Arbor: University of Michigan Press, 1992); Niels Hannestad, *Roman Art and Imperial Policy* (Jutland Archaeological Society 19; Aarhus: Aarhus University Press, 1986); and Anton Powell, ed., *Roman Poetry and Propaganda in the Age of Augustus* (London: Bristol Classical Press, 1992).

[17] Evans, *Art of Persuasion*, 2 (quoting Jacques Ellul, *Propaganda: The Formation of Men's Attitudes* [trans. K. Kellen and J. Lerner; New York: Knopf, 1965], 74–77).

[18] Paul Zanker, *The Power of Images in the Age of Augustus* (trans. A. Shapiro; Ann Arbor: University of Michigan Press, 1988); and Clifford Ando, *Imperial Ideology and Provincial Loyalty in the Roman Empire* (Classics and Contemporary Thought 6; Berkeley and Los Angeles: University of California Press, 2000).

included spectacles (e.g., processions, games, music, and costumes), architecture (e.g., sanctuaries), paintings, inscriptions, statue bases, coins, and almost any type of writing: historiography, poetry, scientific writing, or novels. It was an all-encompassing phenomenon.

Reading Luke-Acts within the context of Roman political propaganda begins from the well-established connection between that work and Roman politics. As has often been noted, Roman political figures and institutions play prominent roles in Luke-Acts. Throughout his writing, Luke draws a close comparison between Jesus and Rome. The story of Jesus' birth begins with three pieces of information: Augustus was emperor, a census took place throughout the entire world, and Quirinius served as the Roman governor of Syria (Luke 2:1–2). Likewise, Jesus' ministry commences with a notice that the events took place in the reign of the emperor Tiberius, when Pontius Pilate was governor of Judea (3:1). The prominence of Roman political officers, institutions, and ideals grows as we move into Acts. The emperor Claudius is mentioned in connection with a famine that spread throughout the whole world (Acts 11:28). The presence of Aquila and Priscilla in Corinth resulted from the order of Claudius forcing all Jews to leave Rome (18:2). Paul's journeys bring him into contact with Roman officials: Sergius Paulus in Cyprus (13:7), Gallio (18:12), and the anticipated appearance before the unnamed emperor to whom Paul has appealed (25:10; 26:32).

As we dig deeper into the Lukan terrain, we discover that these surface indicators give way to a deeper narrative structure that exhibits the richer and more profound influence of Roman political rhetoric and ideology on Luke-Acts. Three elements—the references to Jesus as savior and bringer of peace, the ascension of Jesus, and the list of nations in Acts 2—all evoke, and were likely modeled upon, rhetorical strategies frequently developed in and proliferated by Roman political propaganda. Luke, I will argue, not only adapts the rhetoric that legitimated Rome's political authority but does so in order to bolster Christian claims to universal dominion and to develop in the nascent Christian community a sense of place within the Roman world.

SAVIOR AND BRINGER OF PEACE

Various individuals in the ancient world, divine and human, bore the title of "savior."[19] The term was applied to Greek and Roman deities, heroes

---

[19] Significant treatments of the subject include Franz Dornseiff, "Σωτήρ," *PW* 2.3A.1:1211–21; Paul Wendland, "ΣΩΤΗΡ," *ZNW* 45 (1904): 335–53; H. Haerens, "ΣΩΤΗΡ et ΣΩΤΗΡΙΑ," *Studia Hellenistica* 5 (1948): 57–68; Arthur Darby Nock,

of the distant past, Hellenistic monarchs, military commanders, and local benefactors. Several notable Romans, including T. Quinctius Flamininus, Pompey, and Julius Caesar, gained such recognition. Beginning with Augustus, the title, usually *salus* in Latin or σωτήρ in Greek, became a staple designation for the Roman emperor. Indeed, few persons or even deities could compete with Augustus and his successors for being recognized as "saviors of the entire world."[20] Inscriptions from Priene, Halicarnassus and Myra praise Augustus as the "savior of the whole human race."[21] The recognition of the *princeps* as savior became a staple part of imperial honors and ideology. By the early principate, the *princeps* was the person most widely celebrated as savior; indeed, public recognition of Roman officials as savior was almost exclusively confined to the emperor himself.[22] Tiberius, Claudius, Nero, Vespasian, Domitian, and Trajan were all hailed

---

"*Soter* and *Euergetes*," in *Essays on Religion in the Ancient World* (ed. Z. Stewart; 2 vols.; Oxford: Oxford University Press, 1972), 2:720–35; Martin A. Marwood, *The Roman Cult of Salus* (British Archaeological Reports International 465; Oxford: B.A.R., 1988); Lorenz Winkler, *Salus: Vom Staatskult zur politischen Idee* (Archäologie und Geschichte 4; Heidelberg: Archäologie und Geschichte, 1995); and, most recently, Jason W. Moralee, "For Salvation's Sake (*Hyper Sôtêrias*): Ideology, Society, and Religion in the Dedications for Salvation from the Roman and Late Antique Near East, 100 BC to AD 800" (Ph.D. diss., University of California, Los Angeles, 2002).

[20] Martin P. Nilsson, *Geschichte der griechischen Religion* (3d ed.; 2 vols.; Munich: Beck, 1967–74), 2:184–85, 390–92. Various terms in addition to *savior* were used to designate the *princeps*'s universal presence and authority. Horace speaks of Augustus as "father and guardian of the human race" (*gentis humanae pater atque custos; Carm.* 1.12.49; cf. 4.15.17). The town of Pisa honored Augustus as the "guardian of the Roman empire and protector of the entire world" (*custodis imperii Romani totiusque orbis terrarum praesidis; ILS* 140.6–8). Narbo did much the same (*ILS* 112.14–16, 23–25).

[21] Fredrich Hiller von Gaertringen, ed., *Inschriften von Priene* (Berlin: Reimer, 1906), no. 105 (= *SEG* 4.490). See the translation and discussion in Frederick W. Danker, *Benefactor: Epigraphic Study of a Graeco-Roman and New Testament Semantic Field* (St. Louis: Clayton, 1982), 215–22; Charles T. Newton et al., eds., *The Collection of Ancient Greek Inscriptions in the British Museum* (4 vols.; London: British Museum, 1874–1916), 4:894; René Cagnat, ed., *Inscriptiones Graecae ad Res Romanas Pertinentes* (4 vols; Paris: Leroux, 1911–27), 3:719 (quoted in Klaus Wengst, *Pax Romana and the Peace of Jesus Christ* [trans. J. Bowden; London: SCM, 1987], 173 n. 11); and David Magie, *Roman Rule in Asia Minor to the End of the Third Century after Christ* (2 vols.; Princeton: Princeton University Press, 1950), 1:534.

[22] Glen W. Bowersock, *Augustus and the Greek East* (Oxford: Oxford University Press, 1965), 119.

as savior.[23] Hadrian, and those who followed after him, also adopted the title of savior as a formal designation.[24]

The title of savior and the related concept of salvation present a fascinating example of the intersection between religion and political ideology. It became common for priesthoods and individuals to offer vows for the salvation of the emperor (*pro salute imperatoris*/ὑπὲρ σωτηρίας σεβαστοῦ). The best documented example is the Arval Brotherhood (*Fratres Arvales*) in Rome, which, by the time of Tiberius was offering prayers for the emperor's salvation every year on January 3. Numerous individuals and cities extended similar expressions of piety and loyalty to the emperor. The salvation of the *princeps* became part of a widely disseminated imperial ideology that understood the emperor as the medium through whom imperial and local salvation was achieved.[25] The reciprocal relationship expressed through prayers for the emperor's salvation and invocations of the emperor as savior became a rhetorical and ritualized means to bring unity to the empire. People prayed for and celebrated the salvation of the emperor, who in turn provided the people themselves with the same benefit. Recognizing the *princeps* as savior became a personal sign of loyalty to him and to the imperial system he represented.[26]

The honor of savior was usually bestowed upon those who brought some tangible benefit to an individual or community. In his position as savior Augustus was understood to surpass not only everything human beings could do but also everything the gods could do. Velleius Paterculus offers his view in this regard when describing Augustus's victorious return to Rome after the defeat of Antony: "There is nothing that man can desire from the gods, nothing that the gods can grant to a man, nothing that wish can conceive or good fortune bring to pass, which Augustus on his return to the city did not bestow upon the republic, the Roman people, and the world" (Velleius Paterculus 2.89). Among the many benefactions associated with Augustus and other Roman emperors, the ability to establish peace stood out first and foremost. Velleius continues by listing off the great acts that Augustus has performed, including restoration of the laws, reestablishing the dignity of the Senate, and returning agriculture to the fields,

---

[23] See the references in PW 3.A.1:1214; cf. Pliny, *Ep.* 10.52, 102; Statius, *Silv.* 3.4.20; 4.2.14–15; and Martial 2.91.1; 5.1.7.

[24] Nock, "*Soter* and *Euergetes*," 2:727.

[25] Marwood, *Roman Cult of Salus,* 10.

[26] Like other forms of benefaction, offering prayers, sacrifices, and celebrations on behalf of the emperor were also means by which provincial elites could receive honor and status from the emperor and their local communities. On the cultural role of benefactions in the Roman world, see Paul Veyne, *Le pain et le cirque: Socio-logie historique d'un pluralisme politique* (Paris: Seuil, 1976).

respect to religion, and property rights to each citizen. Velleius places Augustus's ability to bring peace at the head of this list: "The civil wars were ended after 20 years, foreign wars suppressed, peace restored, the frenzy of arms everywhere lulled to rest" (2.89). Later he refers explicitly to the *pax Augusta:* the universality of peace "spread to the regions of the east and of the west and to the bounds of the north and of the south, preserv[ing] every corner of the world" (2.126).

Peace, *princeps,* and empire were inseparable.[27] Epictetus cites the emperor's ability to establish "profound peace" (εἰρήνη μεγάλη), where there is no war or piracy and where travel can be safely conducted from the rising of the sun to its setting (Epictetus 3.13.9). The Priene inscription mentioned above recognizes Augustus as the savior "who has made war to cease and who shall put everything in peaceful order." A variety of media, including literary texts, religious altars and shrines, inscriptions, and coins, saturated the Roman world with evocations of and tributes to the emperor as savior and testimonies of Rome's ability to establish peace.[28] The Roman Senate honored Augustus's victories in Spain and Gaul, and the peace was commemorated with the erection of the Ara Pacis in Rome (*RG* 12). Augustus advertised his role as the author of peace by recognizing this central act in the *Res Gestae* and boasting that on three occasions he shut the doors of the temple of Janus in Rome, symbolizing that peace had been achieved throughout the Roman world, a feat accomplished only twice in the entire preceding history of Rome (*RG* 13; cf. Vergil, *Aen.* 1.291–296). It is not surprising, then, that Vergil could refer to Augustus's peace as the act of a deity (Vergil, *Ecl.* 1.6–8; cf. Horace, *Carm.* 3.5.1–4).

The emphasis on peace as a salient benefit of the *imperium Romanum* continued through the first and second centuries. The doors to the temple of Janus were again shut during the reigns of Nero and Vespasian (Suetonius, *Nero* 13.2; Lucan 1.60), the latter also having erected a temple of Peace (Suetonius, *Vesp.* 9.1; Josephus, *War* 7.158; Dio Chrysostom 66.15). Aelius Aristides, writing in the middle of the second century, glorifies Rome for having established peace throughout the entire inhabited world (πᾶσα οἰκουμένη; *Or.* 97 [*Romae*]). Luke too was cognizant of the ideology that claimed an inseparable bond between peace and imperial rule. When

---

[27] Cf. Velleius Paterculus 2.131: *hanc pacem, hunc principem.*
[28] Stefan Weinstock, "*Pax* and the 'Ara Pacis,'" *JRS* 50 (1960): 44–58; Zeev Rubin, "Pax als politisches Schlagwort im alten Rom," in *Frieden und Friedenssicherung in Vergangenheit und Gegenwart* (ed. M. Schenke and K.-J. Matz; Munich: Fink, 1984), 21–40; Wengst, *Pax Romana and the Peace of Jesus Christ,* 6–54. The rhetoric of peace and concord was sometimes little more than rhetoric, as the Briton Calgacus (as represented by Tacitus) expresses with great passion (*Agr.* 30.3–31.2).

Tertullus addresses the Roman procurator Felix at Paul's trial in Jerusalem, he begins with customary words of praise, "Because of you we have long enjoyed peace" (Acts 24:2).

Given Luke's general interest in Roman politics described above, it is not surprising to find important political themes such as the term "savior" and the benefaction of peace appearing in Luke-Acts. The elements that extolled Rome's greatness and contributed to imperial unity and legitimacy, however, receive a very different hearing. Luke-Acts presents Jesus, rather than the *princeps*, as the true savior and bringer of peace. On three separate occasions Luke identifies Jesus as savior. In the first instance, the angels announce to Mary that the child born to her is the savior (Luke 2:11). In Acts, the Sanhedrin demands that Peter should cease his teaching about Jesus. Peter responds that he must obey God, who has exalted Jesus as savior (Acts 5:31). The final reference occurs in Paul's speech before the synagogue in Pisidian Antioch. In his march through Israel's history, Paul arrives at David, from whom God has brought Jesus, the savior (Acts 13:23). In addition to the specific title of savior, Luke also identifies Jesus as one who brings salvation. To the wealthy tax collector Zacchaeus, who promises to give half of his wealth to the poor and to make restitution on any fraudulent transaction, Jesus announces that salvation has come to his house (Luke 19:9). In response to a question posed by members of the high-priestly family, Peter declares, "there is salvation in no one else (but Jesus)" (Acts 4:12). According to an unnamed woman, whose possession by a spirit provides her with prophetic abilities, Paul proclaims the way of salvation (Acts 16:17).

Jesus' appearance as the unrivaled savior who alone brings salvation to all humanity presents obvious parallels with political claims for the Roman emperor. The connection is probably not coincidental. Luke's language in these instances does not rely on a preexisting source or tradition. There are no references to Jesus as savior (σωτήρ) in the Gospel of Mark (a certain source), Q, or the Gospel of Matthew, and none of these designate Jesus' presence as a medium of salvation. The Gospel of John, whose influence on Luke has been debated, employs the term only once (John 4:42). It is likely, therefore, that the identification of Jesus as savior reflects Luke's own redactional interests.

As is true in many other respects, the Septuagint, certainly known to Luke, may have influenced his application of the terms "savior" and "salvation" to Jesus. The word "savior" appears often in the Septuagint, but almost always in reference to God.[29] It is not obvious, except from the

---

[29] Deut 32:15; 1 Sam 10:19; 1 Chr 16:15; Jdt 9:11; Add Esth 15:2; Pss 23(24):5; 24(25):5; 26(27):1, 9; 61(62):2, 6; 64(65):5; 78(79):9; 94(95):1; Sir 51:1; Wis 16:7; Hab 3:18; Isa 12:2; 17:10; 25:9; 45:15, 21, 22; Bar 4:22; 1 Macc 4:30; 3 Macc 6:29,

retrospective view of later Christian theology, why Luke would have taken a divine attribute and assigned it to Jesus. The Septuagintal role (if there is one), however, does not undermine the view that Luke's selection of biblical themes and terms was influenced by contemporary political propaganda.[30] One particular narrative detail points in this direction: Luke not only identifies Jesus as savior but also classifies Jesus' major act of benefaction as the bringing of peace. In the birth narrative, Luke narrates an angelic visitation to the shepherds. After revealing that the savior has been born, the angel is immediately joined by other heavenly messengers who praise God and announce peace to those whom God favors (Luke 2:9–14). Elsewhere Luke describes Jesus as one who brings peace (Luke 1:79; Acts 10:36). The savior who brings peace finds its expression in both Roman propaganda and Luke's presentation of Jesus. With these themes, especially the manner in which they are joined in Luke-Acts, readers would likely hear an echo of Roman political ideology.[31] By identifying Jesus as savior and stressing that peace has been established through him, Luke-Acts invokes the language of imperial authority and applies it to Jesus.[32]

THE ASCENSION

Official declarations, literary reports, popular opinions, and visual displays on monuments and coins presented and mutually reinforced the

---

32; 7:16. There are a few cases, however, where *savior* does refer to biblical heroes, including the judges Othniel and Ehud, as well as Mordecai in the Greek additions to Esther (Judg 3:9, 15; Add Esth 16:13; cf. Neh 9:27). See further, Joseph A. Fitzmyer, *The Gospel according to Luke* (2 vols.; AB 28–28A; New York: Doubleday, 1981–85), 1:204–5.

[30] As Allen Brent, *The Imperial Cult and the Development of Church Order: Concepts and Images of Authority in Paganism and Early Christianity before the Age of Cyprian* (VCSup 45; Leiden: Brill, 1999), 95, has aptly argued. See also Wendland, "ΣΩTHP," 349–50. It should be noted, further, that recognizing that Luke knew the Septuagint and that the Septuagint uses the term *savior* still does not explain why Luke would have selected this particular term as a designation for Jesus in the first place.

[31] Jean-Marie André, "La Conception de l'Etat et de l'Empire dans la pensée gréco-romaine des deux premiers siècles de notre ère," *ANRW* 2.30.1: 58–60.

[32] Jesus' birth, reported to have taken place during the universal census in the time of Augustus, "presents an implicit challenge," notes Raymond Brown, "to this imperial propaganda, not by denying the imperial ideals, but by claiming that the real peace of the world was brought about by Jesus" (*The Birth of the Messiah* [New York: Doubleday, 1979], 415). Willard A. Swartley, "War and Peace in the New Testament," *ANRW* 2.26.3:2339–41, offers an interpretation of the theme of peace in Luke-Acts that rejects the connection with Roman political ideology.

common understanding that an emperor's death was followed soon thereafter by his heavenly ascent, or apotheosis.[33] Julius Caesar's own apotheosis became legendary. Shortly after his death, games were held to commemorate his military victories. On the first day of the events, a comet appeared overhead and shone for an entire week. According to later traditions, viewers understood this celestial occurrence as the manifestation of Caesar's ascension into heaven and his resultant deification.[34] Augustus realized the political value of Caesar's status as *divus* and promoted it widely, particularly through coins depicting the star of Caesar (*Caesaris astrum*).[35] At Augustus's own funeral, an eagle soared skyward, symbolizing his ascent into heaven (Dio Chrysostom 56.42.3). Depictions of apotheosis were frequently commemorated on coins showing the newest member of the heavenly retinue carried aloft on the backs of eagles or a winged genius.[36] By the time of Nero the apotheosis of the emperor had become so ingrained in Roman imagination that Seneca could use it as the basis for his satiric treatment of Claudius and his ascent into heaven.[37]

The ascent of the recently deceased emperor announced more than his translation into heaven. Roman writers not only speak about the emperor's *apotheosis* as an act of divinization, but they also tie the reports of heavenly ascent to claims of political legitimization.[38] In Cicero's account of the dream of Scipio, the reward for those who wield imperial power is everlasting life in the heavens. The older Scipio Africanus explains to his adopted grandson that "all those who have preserved, aided, or enlarged their fatherland have a special place prepared for them in the heavens, where they may enjoy an eternal life of happiness" (Cicero, *Rep.* 6.13).

---

[33] Elias Bickerman, "*Consecratio*," in *Le culte des souverains dans l'empire romain* (ed. E. J. Bickerman and W. den Boer; Entretiens sur l'antiquité classique 19; Genève: Hardt, 1973), 3–25; Mary Beard and John Henderson, "The Emperor's New Body: Ascension from Rome," in *Parchments of Gender: Deciphering Bodies in Antiquity* (ed. M. Wyke; Oxford: Clarendon, 1998), 191–219.

[34] Horace, *Carm.* 1.12.47; Vergil, *Ecl.* 9.47–49; Pliny, *Nat.* 2.93–94; Suetonius, *Jul.* 88; Dio Chrysostom 45.7.1. Cf. Stefan Weinstock, *Divus Julius* (London: Oxford University Press, 1971), 370. Ovid used the event in his description of the *apotheosis* of Romulus (*Metam.* 15.843).

[35] Lily Ross Taylor, *The Divinity of the Roman Emperor* (Middletown, Conn.: American Philological Association, 1931), 242.

[36] Bickerman, "*Consecratio*," 22.

[37] The oldest manuscript of the *Apocolocyntosis* reflects the play on the terms *apotheosis* (deification) and *apocolocyntosis* (*pumpkinification*) with the following title: *Divi Claudii* Ἀποθέωσις ... *per saturam*. See Seneca, *Apocolocyntosis* (ed. P. T. Eden; Cambridge: Cambridge University Press, 1984), 2–3.

[38] Peter White, "Julius Caesar in Augustan Rome," *Phoenix* 42 (1988): 354.

A specific connection between apotheosis and imperial rule became more pronounced during the principate. Vergil draws a particularly noteworthy connection between Augustus's imperial achievements, most especially his ability to establish peace, and his ascension into heaven. In the first book of the *Aeneid*, Zeus speaks about the future Roman leader in the following way:

> The Trojan Caesar comes to circumscribe
> Empire with Ocean, fame with heaven's stars.
> Julius his name, from Julus handed down;
> All tranquil shall you take him heavenward
> In time, laden with plunder of the East,
> And he with you shall be invoked in prayer.
> Wars at an end, harsh centuries then will soften,
> Ancient Fides and Vesta, Quirinus
> With brother Remus, will be lawgivers,
> And grim with iron frames, the Gates of War
> Will then be shut.[39]

The final lines refer to the closing of the doors to the temple of Janus, symbolizing the realization of peace. Augustus, the great builder of empire and bringer of peace, will one day occupy his place in the heavens.

In another example, Horace creates a vivid depiction of several of the mythological luminaries who ascended into heaven:

> By this virtue Pollux and the roaming Hercules
> strove and attained the fiery citadels....
> your tigers carried you, father Bacchus,
> meritorious through this virtue,
> drawing the yoke with indocile necks; by this virtue Romulus
> escaped Ascheron, drawn by the horses of Mars.

In between the mention of the heavenly residents Pollux and Hercules on the one side, and Romulus on the other, comes Augustus, who will abide with the immortals and "shall recline and drink nectar with rosy lips." The poem continues with a speech delivered by Juno. She recalls the fall of Troy and calls upon the council of the gods to allow Troy's descendants, meaning the Romans, to "hold sway in whatever region they please":

> Let the Capitol stand
> gleaming and let fierce Rome have the power

---

[39] *Aen.* 1.286–294. Translation from Robert Fitzgerald, *The Aeneid* (New York: Random House, 1983).

to dictate terms to the conquered Medes.
Feared everywhere, let her extend her name to the uttermost
shores, where the midway water
separates Europe from Africa,
where the swollen Nile irrigates the fields.[40]

Horace makes the explicit connection between Rome's destiny as ruler of the world with Augustus's ascension into heaven. The emperor's translation into heaven confirms his authority as the divinely appointed ruler of the world. Even Ovid, whose writings betray a somewhat more critical perspective of Augustus, speaks of the great accomplishments of Julius Caesar, of which none surpasses his role or position as father of Augustus.[41] The latter's status as ruler of the world is to be confirmed by Caesar's apotheosis: "By making Caesar's son [i.e., Augustus] ruler of the empire, O gods, you mightily blessed the human race. Lest he be born from mortal seed, therefore, his father had to be made a god" (Ovid, *Metam.* 15.758–761). The political implications of apotheosis are vividly portrayed on the Gemma Augustea, where Augustus, seated beside the goddess Roma, receives a crown of oak leaves from the goddess Oikoumene.[42] Ascending into heaven and being seated among the gods, in the political language of the day, marks one off as the legitimate ruler of the inhabited world.

All the canonical Gospels contain reports of Jesus' resurrection and relate stories in which Jesus appears to a variety of persons. Only Luke, however, offers a narrative depiction of Jesus' ascent into heaven (Acts 1:9–11). The Gospel concludes with a report that Jesus was carried up into heaven (Luke 24:51: ἀνεφέρετο εἰς τὸν οὐρανόν).[43] Acts opens with prefatory remarks that provide a succinct summary of the Gospel: a report of the things Jesus did and taught until the day he was lifted up (Acts 1:2:

---

[40] *Carm.* 3.3. Translation from Sidney Alexander, ed. and trans., *The Complete Odes and Satires of Horace* (Princeton: Princeton University Press, 1999).

[41] On the complex relations between Ovid and Augustus, see Karl Galinsky, *Ovid's Metamorphoses: An Introduction to the Basic Aspects* (Berkeley and Los Angeles: University of California Press, 1975), 210–61; S. Georgia Nugent, "*Tristia* 2: Ovid and Augustus," in *Between Republic and Empire: Interpretations of Augustus and His Principate* (ed. K. Raaflaub and M. Toher; Berkeley and Los Angeles: University of California Press, 1990), 239–57.

[42] Taylor, *Divinity of the Roman Emperor*, 226–27.

[43] Among the important manuscript witnesses to the Gospel of Luke, the phrase appears in $\mathfrak{P}^{75}$ among other papyri. I accept it as original, despite its omission in a few prominent manuscripts, such as Codex Sinaiticus. See Bruce Metzger, *A Textual Commentary on the Greek New Testament* (corr. ed.; London: United Bible Societies, 1975), 189–90.

ἄρχι ἧς ἡμέρας ... ἀνελήμφθη). While the ascension of Jesus clearly plays a significant role in Luke-Acts, understanding that role is admittedly a more obscure proposition.

Numerous parallels have been drawn between Luke's account of Jesus' ascension into heaven and similar contemporary Jewish, Greek, and Latin narratives. Many of the suggested parallels, however, differ considerably from the type of ascent Luke attributes to Jesus. Jesus does not make a heavenly journey and return to earth, as do figures in mystical texts; his soul is not elevated into heaven; and he does not undergo a rapture, that is, a taking up to heaven while alive (like Elijah). This last suggestion has been developed most recently by Arie Zwiep.[44] Building on the work of Gerhard Lohfink, Zwiep draws a close parallel between the ascension of Jesus in Luke-Acts and similar accounts of biblical heroes as portrayed in earlier and contemporaneous Jewish literature. While Luke may have drawn on this tradition for some narrative details, it is doubtful that he intends to have Jesus appear as a figure who experienced rapture. Unlike the figures who escape death, which is an essential component of the rapture tradition, Jesus dies and must be raised from the dead (Luke 24:46).[45] According to Zwiep, the Jewish literature portrays those who have undergone rapture as prepared to mount an imminent eschatological return. It is not clear, however, that the account of Jesus' ascension connotes this level of eschatological expectation in Luke-Acts. While two angelic-looking men explain to the disciples that Jesus will return (Acts 1:11), the event is hardly presented as imminent. Indeed, as Hans Conzelmann and others have pointed out, Luke-Acts does not seem to dwell on the imminent return of Jesus at all. Rather, Luke-Acts depicts Jesus sitting exalted at the right hand of God (Acts 2:33) and ruling from heaven (Acts 7:56).

In one respect Jesus' ascent closely mirrors the accounts of imperial ascent. Eyewitness testimony to the imperial apotheosis confirmed that the recently deceased had truly attained the honor of being seated among the deities and deserved his authority as emperor. During the early principate an eyewitness would report to the Senate that the ascent had taken place. Later it was understood that ascension took place in the sight of all.[46]

---

[44] Arie W. Zwiep, *The Ascension of the Messiah in Lukan Christology* (NovTSup 87; Leiden: Brill, 1997); idem, "*Assumptus est in caelum:* Rapture and Heavenly Exaltation in Early Judaism and Luke-Acts," *Auferstehung-Resurrection* (ed. F. Avemarie and H. Lichtenberger; WUNT 135; Tübingen: Mohr Siebeck, 2001), 323–49.

[45] Zwiep defines rapture as "a bodily translation into the 'beyond' as the conclusion of one's earthly life without the intervention of death" ("*Assumptus est in caelum,*" 331).

[46] Bickerman, "*Consecratio,*" 23.

Jesus' ascent as well took place before witnesses. At the end of the Gospel Jesus leads the eleven disciples on the road to Bethany. As he blesses them, they observe him being carried up into heaven. Furthermore, both scenarios seek to authenticate the authority of the one ascending into heaven and give legitimacy to his successors, either the next *princeps* or the disciples. The reaction to Jesus' ascension also establishes a connection with Roman ideology. After Jesus ascends, the disciples worship him (Luke 24:52). While the same cannot be said about Elijah, the scenario of Jesus' ascension does closely correspond with Roman political beliefs. Finally, this interpretation receives added support from some of the earliest readers of Luke-Acts, such as Justin Martyr, Minucius Felix, and Origen, who point out the comparison between the ascension of Jesus and the apotheosis of the Roman emperor.[47] Justin offers this comparison between the ascensions of Jesus and Roman emperors:

> And when we say also that the Word ... Jesus Christ, our teacher, was crucified and died, and rose again and ascended into heaven, we propound nothing different from what you believe.... And what of the emperors who die among yourselves, whom you deem worthy of deification, and in whose behalf you produce some one who swears he has seen the burning Caesar rise to heaven from the funeral pyre? (1 *Apol.* 21 [ANF])

This group of early Christians validates placing the account of Jesus' ascension found in Luke-Acts within the political context of its day.

List of Nations[48]

Through the military victories and diplomatic entanglements that occupied much of Roman history of the second and first centuries B.C.E., the people of Rome emerged as rulers of the world (κύριοι τῆς οἰκουμένης; e.g., Plutarch, *Life of Tiberius Gracchus* 9.5).[49] Rome's claim to mastery of the

---

[47] Justin Martyr, *1 Apol.* 21; Minucius Felix, *Oct.* 21; Origen, *Cels.* 2.68.

[48] Some of the material in this section is taken over from an earlier article: Gary Gilbert, "The List of Nations in Acts 2: Roman Propaganda and the Lukan Response," *JBL* 121 (2002): 497–529.

[49] Many writers of the first and second centuries C.E. recognized the discrepancy between rhetoric and reality in discussing the empire's boundaries and lands that existed beyond Rome's borders. See André, "Conception de l'Etat et de l'Empire," 56–58. Many Romans, including perhaps Augustus and other political and military elites, believed that the literal conquest of the entire world was within their power. See R. Moynihan, "Geographical Mythology and Roman Imperial Ideology," in *The Age of Augustus* (ed. R. Winkes; Archaeologia Transatlantica 5; Providence, R.I.: Center for Old World Archaeology and Art, Brown University, 1985), 149–62.

inhabited world, both described its political ambitions and gave legitimacy to its authority throughout the developing empire. Beginning with Augustus, Rome built a state apparatus that included official records and coinage, literary and artistic clients, and influential friends to transmit its claim. Dionysius of Halicarnassus, writing during the time of Augustus, opens his history by noting that the city of the Romans rules the entire earth (*Ant. rom.* 1.3.3). Augustan literature, particularly its poetry, played a large role in shaping and articulating the claim of universal domination as Rome's inherent destiny.[50] Vergil's *Aeneid,* the "national epic of Augustan Rome,"[51] represents a *locus classicus* for this perspective.[52] Near the opening, Jupiter utters his famous prophecy that Rome will possess an empire without end (*imperium sine fine; Aen.* 1.278–279; cf. 4.229–231; 6.782, 792–797, 851; 7.99–101; 7.258; 8.626–728).[53] Through official visual displays, such as the depiction of the *oikoumenē* on the breastplate of the Prima Porta statue of Augustus,[54] on coinage, where the goddess Roma frequently appears astride a globe (the symbol of universal domination),[55] and in public maps, Rome and its allies illustrated that "the empire had (theoretically) been

---

[50] The relation between Augustus and the poets of his day remains a complex issue. See Ronald Syme, *The Roman Revolution* (Oxford: Clarendon, 1939; repr., Oxford: Oxford University Press, 1960), 459–68; Douglas Little, "Politics in Augustan Poetry," *ANRW* 2.30.1: 254–370; Anthony J. Woodman and David West, eds., *Poetry and Politics in the Age of Augustus* (Cambridge: Cambridge University Press, 1984); Jasper Griffen, "Augustus and the Poets: *Caesar qui Cogere Posset,"* in *Caesar Augustus: Seven Aspects* (ed. F. Millar and E. Segal; Oxford: Oxford University Press, 1984), 189–218; Karl Galinsky, *Augustan Culture: An Interpretive Introduction* (Princeton: Princeton University Press, 1996), 225–79.

[51] Francis Cairns, *Virgil's Augustan Epic* (Cambridge: Cambridge University Press, 1989), 105. Cairns goes on to describe the poem as "embodying the aspirations, the pride and the self-image of the rulers of the world."

[52] Michael C. J. Putnam, *The Poetry of the Aeneid* (Cambridge: Harvard University Press, 1965), 192. R. O. A. M. Lyne, *Further Voices in Vergil's Aeneid* (Oxford: Oxford University Press, 1987), 217, has argued that the *Aeneid* is polysemous, presenting a "multiplicity of meanings," including the patriotic epic voice, but also a voice that "probes, questions, and occasionally subverts the simple Augustanism that it may appear to project." A strong refutation of this position and an analysis in support of reading the *Aeneid* as staunchly pro-Augustan comes from Hans-Peter Stahl, "The Death of Turnus: Augustan Vergil and the Political Rival," in Raaflaub and Toher, *Between Republic and Empire,* 174–211; and Galinsky, *Augustan Culture,* 246–53.

[53] Philip R. Hardie, *Virgil's Aeneid: Cosmos and Imperium* (Oxford: Oxford University Press, 1986), 293–335.

[54] Galinsky, *Augustan Culture,* 155–64.

[55] Claude Nicolet, *Space, Geography, and Politics in the Early Roman Empire* (trans. H. Leclerc; Ann Arbor: University of Michigan Press, 1991), 34–38.

expanded to the limits of the *orbis terrarum*."[56] The various efforts ensured that no one in the first century was left ignorant of Rome's "self-appointed mandate ... as world rulers."[57]

Among the various methods used to promote the ideology of universal Roman rule, the listing of nations or peoples proved to be one of the more frequent and effective. Pliny the Elder offers an example: "After having rescued the sea coast from pirates and restored to the Roman people the command of the sea, [Pompey] celebrated a triumph over Asia, Pontus, Armenia, Paphlagonia, Cappadocia, Cilicia, Syria, the Scythians, Jews, and Albanians, Iberia, the island of Crete, the Basternae, and in addition to these, over King Mithridates and Tigranes" (*Nat.* 7.98). In the new political reality of the principate, literary and visual catalogues became prominent. Writers such as Vergil, Horace, Pliny the Elder, and Josephus evoked the glory and power of the empire with their own lists of nations.[58] The passage from Ovid's *Metamorphoses* quoted above, in which the poet connects the apotheosis of Caesar with the imperial rule of Augustus, contains just such a list: "To have subdued the sea-girt Britons, to have led his victorious fleet up the seven-mouthed stream of the papyrus-bearing Nile, to have added the rebellious Numidians, Libyan, Juba, and Pontus, swelling with threats of the mighty name of Mithridates, to the sway of the people of Quirinus" (*Metam.* 15.753–756).

Seneca's satirical use of a list of nations in the imagined dirge accompanying Claudius's funeral procession—Parthians, Persians, Medes, Britons, Brigantes, and Crete—reflects how prosaic it had become to use lists of nations to express political ideals (*Apoc.* 12.3). Ethnic lists appeared not only in literary catalogues but also in epigraphic and representational forms (e.g., the *simulacra gentium*). Epigraphic lists celebrated Augustus's victory over the Alpine nations (*CIL* 5.7817; Pliny, *Nat.* 3.136–137).[59] In the *Res Gestae* Augustus tallies fifty-five geographical places conquered, pacified, added, or otherwise dominated by Rome. Visual inventories decorated the

---

[56] Ibid., 111.

[57] Zanker, *Power of Images*, 328.

[58] *Aen.* 6.780–782; Horace, *Carm.* 4.14; Pliny, *Nat.* 5.132–133; Josephus, *War* 2.358–387. Writing in the middle of the first century C.E., Curtius Rufus invokes a Hellenistic tradition in his description of the lands subdued by Alexander the Great. In the text Alexander proclaims himself master of "Caria, Lydia, Cappadocia, Phrygia, Paphlagonia, Pamphylia, the Pisidians, Cilicia, Syria, Phoenicia, Armenia, Persia, the Medes, and Parthians" (6.3.2–3). Five of these names appear in Acts 2. For examples of the earlier traditions, see the literature cited in Gerhard Schneider, *Die Apostelgeschichte* (2 vols.; HTKNT 5; Freiburg: Herder, 1980–82), 1:254 n. 94.

[59] David Braund, *Rome and the Friendly King: The Character of the Client Kingship* (London: St. Martin's, 1984); and Zanker, *Power of Images*, 297–333.

Ara Pacis, the Portico ad Nationes, and the Forum of Augustus, where inscriptions (*tituli*) listed the various regions constituting the Roman Empire (Suetonius, *Aug.* 31.8; Velleius Paterculus 2.39.2). Statues and identifying inscriptions, visual and verbal catalogues comprising well over fifty ethnic groups, decorated imperial temples in Aphrodisias and Lugdunum.[60] Following Augustus's death, images of all the *ethnē* acquired by the *princeps* were paraded through the streets of Rome (Tacitus, *Ann.* 1.8.4; Dio Chrysostom 56.34.2–3). On a much smaller scale, a sardonyx gem now housed in Paris shows Tiberius enthroned above variously costumed figures picturing nations conquered by Rome. Above Tiberius, the figure of Aeneas, seen holding a globe, reminds the viewer that the nations shown here epitomize Rome's universal authority.[61]

Embedded in the Lukan account of heavenly pyrotechnics and astonishing linguistic feats at Pentecost (Acts 2:1–42) comes a catalogue of fifteen peoples and places: Parthia, Media, Elam, Mesopotamia, Judea, Cappadocia, Pontus, Asia, Phrygia, Pamphylia, Egypt, parts of Libya (belonging to Cyrene), Rome, Crete, and Arabia. Scholars have long pondered the source of or inspiration for Luke's list.[62] The most frequently rehearsed proposals involve ancient astrological lists, lists of the Jewish Diaspora, the Table of Nations in Gen 10, and biblical prophecies such as those found in Isaiah, which refer to an eschatological ingathering of Jews from the Diaspora.[63] Each suggestion faces significant difficulties, however. More

---

[60] For Aphrodisias, see Roland Smith, "*Simulacra Gentium:* The *Ethne* from the Sebasteion at Aphrodisias," *JRS* 78 (1988): 71–77; for Lugdunum, see the reference in Strabo, *Geogr.* 4.3.2.

[61] Ando, *Imperial Ideology,* 289–90. For an image and discussion, see Adolf Furtwängler, *Die Antiken Gemmen: Geschichte der Steinschneidekunst im klassischen Altertum* (3 vols.; Amsterdam: Hakkert, 1964–65), 1:plate 60; 2:268–71.

[62] Several points speak in favor of the conclusion that this list has a traditional, pre-Lukan basis of one sort or another. The verb κατοικέω appears both in the list (Acts 2:9) and in the framing narrative (2:5, 14), but in two different senses. Second, the list interrupts a smooth, narrative flow from 2:8 to 2:11b. Finally, the names listed bear little correspondence to the geographical horizon developed in Acts. See Jacob Kremer, *Pfingstbericht und Pfingstgeschehen: Eine Exegetische Untersuchung zu Apg 2,1–13* (SBS 63/64; Stuttgart: Katholisches Bibelwerk, 1973), 142, 156; and Alexander J. M. Wedderburn, "Traditions and Redaction in Acts 2.1–13," *JSNT* 55 (1994): 44, 53. While a preexisting list probably stands behind 2:9–11, Luke had an active role in its final composition. See Ernst Haenchen, *The Acts of the Apostles: A Commentary* (trans. B. Noble et al.; Philadelphia: Westminster, 1971), 170.

[63] For the influence of astrological lists, see Stefan Weinstock, "The Geographical Catalogue in Acts 2:9–11," *JRS* 38 (1948): 43–46; J. A. Brinkman, "The Literary Background of the 'Catalogue of the Nations' (Acts 2:9–11)," *CBQ* 25 (1963): 418–27; and Johannes Thomas, "Formgesetze des Begriffs-Kataloges im N.T." *TZ* 24

helpful, I think, is to view the geographic inventory of Acts 2 as mimicking contemporary lists that celebrated Rome's position as ruler over the inhabited world.[64]

While the connection between the list of nations in Acts 2 and Roman propaganda has gone largely unexamined, I am not the first person to draw a connection between the two. Writing around the year 200 C.E., Tertullian composed an account of an ostensible debate between a Christian and a Jewish proselyte. In chapter 7, Tertullian has the Christian inquire (rhetorically) of his Jewish interlocutor whether Jesus is the Messiah about whom the prophets have spoken or whether the Jews are

---

(1968): 15–28. For the influence of lists of the Jewish Diaspora, see the passages cited in Barrett, *Acts of the Apostles,* 1:122. For the influence of Gen 10, see James M. Scott, "Luke's Geographical Horizon," in *The Book of Acts in Its Graeco-Roman Setting* (ed. D. W. J. Gill and C. H. Gempf; vol. 2 of *The Book of Acts in Its First Century Setting;* Grand Rapids: Eerdmans, 1994), 483–544; and idem, "Acts 2:9–11 as an Anticipation of the Mission to the Nations," in *The Mission of the Early Church to Jews and Gentiles* (ed. J. Ådna and H. Kvalbein; WUNT 127; Tübingen: Mohr Siebeck, 2000), 87–123. Others who have suggested the connection between Gen 10 and Acts 2 include Dean P. Béchard, *Paul outside the Walls: A Study of Luke's Socio-Geographical Universalism in Acts 14:8–20* (AnBib 143; Rome: Pontifical Biblical Institute, 2000); Heinrich J. Holtzmann, *Die Apostelgeschichte* (2d ed.; HNT 1/2; Tübingen: Mohr, 1892), 330; Michael Goulder, *Type and History in Acts* (London: SPCK, 1964), 154–58; Walter Schmithals, *Die Apostelgeschichte des Lukas* (ZBK 3.2; Zürich: TVZ, 1982), 31; and tentatively, Stephen G. Wilson, *The Gentiles and the Gentile Mission* (SNTSMS 23; Cambridge: Cambridge University Press, 1973), 126; and Philip S. Alexander, "Geography and the Bible (Early Jewish)," *ABD* 2:983. For the influence of an eschatological list, see Kremer, *Pfingstbericht und Pfingstgeschehen,* 156; Donald Juel, *Luke-Acts: The Promise of History* (Atlanta: John Knox, 1983), 58; Luke T. Johnson, *The Acts of the Apostles* (SP 5; Collegeville, Minn.: Liturgical Press, 1992), 45, 47; Rebecca Denova, *The Things Accomplished among Us: Prophetic Tradition in the Structural Pattern of Luke-Acts* (JSNTSup 141; Sheffield: Sheffield Academic Press, 1997), 173; and Jacob Jervell, *Die Apostelgeschichte* (17th ed.; KEK 3; Göttingen: Vandenhoeck & Ruprecht, 1998), 136. Werner Stenger envisions a parallel between Peter's speech in Acts 2 and Paul's speech on the Areopagus. The former addresses Jews, while the latter speaks to the entire world represented by pagans in Athens ("Beobachtungen zur sogenannten Völkerlist des Pfingstwunders [Apg 2,9–11]," *Kairos* 21 [1979]: 214). Other theories highlight the influence of Ezek 30 (George D. Kilpatrick, "A Jewish Background to Acts 2:9–11?" *JJS* 26 [1975]: 48–49); Persian inscriptions, such as the one from Behistun (Justin Taylor, "The List of the Nations in Acts 2:9–11," *RB* 106 [1999]: 408–20; and Manfred Görg, "Apg 2,9–11 in außerbiblischer Sicht," *BN* 1 [1976]: 15–18); and a document describing the conquests of Alexander the Great (Stenger, "Beobachtungen zur sogenannten Völkerlist," 206–14).

[64] For a lengthier treatment of these issues, see Gilbert, "List of Nations."

correct in thinking that the Messiah is yet to come. Tertullian's proof comes from Acts 2:

> For upon whom else have the universal nations believed, but upon the Christ who is already come? For whom have the nations believed—Parthians, Medes, Elamites, and they who inhabit Mesopotamia, Armenia, Phrygia, Cappadocia, and they who dwell in Pontus and Asia and Pamphylia, tarriers in Egypt, and the inhabitants of the region of Africa which is beyond Cyrene, Romans and proselytes, and, in Jerusalem, Jews, and all other nations. (*Adv. Jud.* 7 [ANF])

He then extends the geographic list found in Acts 2, adding,

> the Gaetulians and the manifold confines of the Moors, all the limits of the Spains and the diverse nations of the Gauls and the haunts of the Britons—inaccessible to the Romans, but subjugated to Christ—and of the Sarmatians and the Dacians and Germans and Scythians and of many remote nations and of provinces and islands many, to us unknown, and which we can scarce enumerate.

Tertullian continues by contrasting Jesus, who has received universal affirmation, with great royal figures of the past whose kingdoms were limited in geographic scope: Solomon reigned only in Judea; Darius ruled over the Babylonians and Parthians; Nebuchadnezzar held dominion from India to Ethiopia; even the kingdoms and empires of Alexander of Macedon, the Germans, Britons, Moors, and Romans were confined to their respective regions. By contrast, according to Tertullian, "Christ's name is extending everywhere, believed everywhere, worshiped by all the above enumerated nations, reigning everywhere, adored everywhere, conferred equally everywhere upon all" (*Adv. Jud.* 7). In short, Tertullian employs the Lukan catalogue in order to validate his argument that Jesus is the true ruler of the world. While the geographic catalogues produced by Rome provide the conceptual framework in which to read the list of nations from Acts 2, the message of the latter could not be more different,[65] as Luke envisions

---

[65] The individuals assembled "from every nation" (ἀπὸ παντὸς ἔθνους; Acts 2:5) serve as the proleptic marker for the inclusion of all persons in this new community (Palmer Bonz, *Past as Legacy,* 137). The same phrase is also found at the conclusion of the Gospel, where Jesus instructs his disciples that repentance and forgiveness are to be preached to "all nations" (εἰς πάντα τὰ ἔθνη; Luke 24:47). Thus inclusiveness (in spite of ethnic differences) and the lack of imperial force to bring about the *pax* differentiate this Lukan vision from its Roman counterpart. For further discussion of the Lukan peaceful alternative to the warlike stance of Rome, see David L. Balch's contribution in this volume.

the *oikoumenē* as the possession of Jesus, the church, and God, not the emperor, Rome and its pantheon.

CONCLUSION

After his defeat of Antony at Actium in 31 B.C.E., Octavian, according to Tacitus, "found the whole state exhausted by internal dissensions, and established over it a personal regime known as the principate" (*Ann.* 1.1). Whether one conceives of the political change from Republic to principate as revolutionary or merely evolutionary, change was clearly evident.[66] Many Romans deeply believed, or at least passionately feigned the belief, that the establishment of the *pax Romana* ushered in a new period of history. Other events seemed to confirm this perception. The cessation of civil war, the return of the Roman standards from Parthia, and the appointment of Augustus to new positions of power heralded the birth of a great order of the ages (*magnus ... saeclorum nascitur ordo;* Vergil, *Ecl.* 4.5).[67] The new era would be marked by the universal extension of the *imperium Romanum* (*Aen.* 6.792).[68] Augustus largely defined his own authority in terms of the well-established Republican positions of *potestas*. He held the office of consul and the traditional titles of *imperator* and *pontifex maximus*, publicly declaring that he, as the restorer of the Republic, would assume only those offices that would not be inconsistent with Roman custom (*mos*) and as befitted the first among equals.[69] As Ronald Syme once

---

[66] The image of Augustus and the Roman revolution comes from the influential work of Syme, *Roman Revolution*. The concept of an Augustan evolution comes from Galinsky, *Augustan Culture*. See also Christian Meier's chapter entitled "Augustus: Die Begründung des Monarchie als Wiederherstellung der Republik," in idem, *Die Ohnmacht des Allmächtigen Dictators Caesar: Drei biographische Skizzen* (Frankfurt: Suhrkamp, 1980), 225–87. An opposing perspective is given by Walter Eder, "Augustus and the Power of Tradition: The Augustan Principate as Binding Link between Republic and Empire," in Raaflaub and Toher, *Between Republic and Empire*, 71–122.

[67] Vergil's *Fourth Eclogue*, leaving aside the numerous highly Christianized interpretations, presents an image of the new age marked not only by restitution of stable political authority but also by a moral and spiritual revival. See Galinsky, *Augustan Culture*, 93. On the history of Christian interpretation of Vergil's *Fourth Eclogue*, see Stephen Benko, "Virgil's *Fourth Eclogue* in Christian Interpretation," *ANRW* 2.31.1:646–705.

[68] Wolfgang Kirsch, "Die Augusteische Zeit: Epochenbewusstsein und Epochenbegriff," *Klio* 67 (1985): 43–46.

[69] *RG* 6.1. On Augustus as "restorer" of the Republic, see Galinsky, *Augustan Culture*, 42–79.

noted, "By appeal to the old, Augustus justified the new; by emphasizing continuity with the past, he encouraged the hope of development in the future."[70] The effort to define and legitimize the principate was carried out in other ways, on many different levels, and in various locations. Claims of the *princeps* to be a savior and one who brings peace, reports of his ascension, and the production of lists of nations were some of the tools used to construct this new ideological edifice. Literature, architecture, inscriptions, statuary, coins, gems, and official processions saturated the Roman world with these images and ideas. The use of propaganda, by the *princeps* and his loyal supporters, aided in creating the intellectual climate needed to bolster the legitimacy of Rome's new government and its position as ruler of the world.

Like Romans and their backers, Christians were faced with a situation of trying to explain and legitimate the existence of their new community, one that to some outsiders seemed contrary to established tradition and to others included a class of humans belonging to a new superstition (Suetonius, *Nero* 16.2). Amid the various responses to this situation, Luke created "a book devoted to clarifying the Christian self-understanding."[71] He accomplished this goal in part by presenting Christians as the rightful heirs of the biblical promises and heritage of Israel.[72] However, for Luke, Christians also had to understand themselves in relation to the Roman world. Just as he does with biblical traditions, Luke mines the heritage of Rome for the language and ideas that will contribute to the formation of a Christian identity. Christians are acknowledged in Luke-Acts as those persons belonging to the true universal kingdom whose existence is expressed and authenticated through a list of nations. Their founder, Jesus, is the real savior who has brought peace to the world and whose rule has been validated through his ascension into heaven.

Recognizing the mimetic presence of Roman political propaganda in Luke-Acts prompts a final observation. Most modern studies of Luke-Acts have described the work variously as a defense of Rome, an attempt to ingratiate Rome in Christian self-identify, or an effort to declare Rome to be "politically innocent."[73] The imitation of terms and images often associated with Roman power, however, points to a different and more conflicted relationship between the Christianity represented by Luke-Acts and Rome.

---

[70] Syme, *Roman Revolution*, 521.

[71] Robert L. Maddox, *The Purpose of Luke-Acts* (ed. J. Riches; Edinburgh: T&T Clark, 1982), 181.

[72] See the recent discussions in David P. Moessner, ed., *Jesus and the Heritage of Israel: Luke's Narrative Claim upon Israel's Legacy* (Harrisburg, Pa.: Trinity Press International, 1999).

[73] Sterling, *Historiography and Self-Definition*, 386.

Unique among early Christian writings, the writer of Luke-Acts claims for Jesus and the church the same titles and achievements commonly associated with Rome: savior, bringer of peace, ascension into heaven, and ruler of the world. The language not only legitimates the community and its leaders but also deconstructs the Roman world in the process.[74] The analysis presented here would suggest that Luke-Acts generates a vigorous critique of Rome and its claims to universal authority and dominion. Through the adaptation of Roman propaganda, Luke-Acts sets up an alternative vision of universal authority—indeed, a rival to Rome's claim to be ruler of the world. Luke has co-opted and refitted the political language of his day and created an ideological confrontation between Rome and the church.[75] True possession of universal dominion lies not with Caesar but with Christ, not with Rome but with the Christians and their church. Luke-Acts has shown that "Theophilus' faith [i.e., and not *imperium romanum*] leads to the true peace, the peace of god, with salvation, victory and a new age."[76]

The claim that Luke-Acts adopts and transvalues Roman political propaganda has important parameters. It is not necessary for Luke to have read Vergil or Horace or to have set foot in the ancient city of Aphrodisias, for instance. Rome's political ideology of universal dominion spread through many channels, making it highly unlikely that Luke, or any resident of the empire, could have avoided exposure to its claims. Being familiar with the propaganda that promoted Rome's authority, Luke then applied these rhetorical strategies of power to his own religious community and to the

---

[74] See the similar argument developed by Brent, *Imperial Cult*, 125.

[75] Many resisted Rome's hegemonic claims. The two Jewish revolts represent the more visible forms of resistance. See Bowersock, *Augustus and the Greek East*, 101–11; Ramsay MacMullen, *Enemies of the Roman Order: Treason, Unrest, and Alienation in the Empire* (Cambridge: Harvard University Press, 1966); Kurt Raaflaub et al., eds., *Opposition et résistances à l'empire d'Auguste à Trajan* (Entretiens sur l'antiquité classique 33; Genève: Hardt, 1987); Kurt A. Raaflaub and Loren J. Samons, "Opposition to Augustus," in Raaflaub and Toher, *Between Republic and Empire*, 417–54. The connection between imperial rule and peace was a specific topic of contention. Tacitus offers a stirring speech of the Briton Calgacus, who states: "Stealing, butchering, and raping they call *imperium* by false names, and where they make a wasteland they call it peace" (*Agr.* 30.5). Later Christians continued the Lukan perspective through their refusal to worship the emperor and to offer vows for his *salus*. See Fergus Millar, "The Imperial Cult and the Persecutions," in Bickerman and den Boer, *Le culte des souverains*, 145–65; and Simon R. F. Price, *Rituals and Power: The Roman Imperial Cult in Asia Minor* (Cambridge: Cambridge University Press, 1984), 123–24.

[76] Brent, *Imperial Cult*, 121.

shaping of his/its narratives. Furthermore, understanding how Roman propaganda molded the narrative of Luke-Acts does not exclude other spheres of influence, whether biblical, Greek, or Roman. The argument laid out here stresses that whatever Luke gained from his knowledge of the Bible and other ancient texts, the political claims that characterize the early principate helped to shape his portrayal of Jesus and the early church.

Using the rhetorical tools that helped to establish Rome's position as a ruler of the world, Luke constructed his own claim of universal authority, namely, that the true claim to world dominion is possessed not by the *princeps* but by Jesus, who is empowered by God and not by the deities of the Roman pantheon. By echoing and repackaging various forms of Roman propaganda, Luke-Acts provides Christians with their source of legitimization and bolsters the nascent self-identification of the Christian community in the first and second centuries.

History or Story in Acts—A Middle Way? The "We" Passages, Historical Intertexture, and Oral History

Samuel Byrskog

Scholarship is a cultural phenomenon. There thus might be various subtle reasons for different scholarly emphases, including the estimation of the relationship between history and story in Acts.[1] The general attention to and use of literary patterns, narrative myths, and persuasive strategies within a particular modern society or group certainly alert its members to similar features in other societies. Furthermore, keen awareness of the past within other societies or groups makes history into a matter not easily neglected in the study of stories from distant places and times. Scholarly communities are powerful reflections and mediators of various cultural modes of thinking and acting. Postmodern discourse teaches us, if nothing else, that scholarship is deeply embedded within the relativism of our existence.[2]

Once the pluralism and culture-specific character of scholarly activity is taken seriously, an agenda of mutual dialogue and progress is in view.

---

[1] The term "history" may be employed with various nuances. Several scholars studying the narrative of Luke-Acts use insights from comparative first-century Mediterranean literature. See, e.g., Robert C. Tannehill, *The Narrative Unity of Luke-Acts: A Literary Interpretation* (2 vols.; Minneapolis: Fortress, 1986–90), 2:4–5. In this essay the term *history* is reserved for a diachronic focus that pays attention to the so-called pastness of the story, though, as we shall see, this pastness has recognizably significant social and cultural ingredients. When reference is made to an author's use of broad patterns of historical data or events, I will use the term "social" or "cultural intertexture" to designate this phenomenon.

[2] "In a post-modern world, there is no centre, no standing-place that has rights to domination, no authority that can manage or control what is to count as scholarship" (David J. A. Clines and J. Cheryl Exum, "The New Literary Criticism," in *The New Literary Criticism and the Bible* [ed. D. J. A. Clines and J. C. Exum; JSOTSup 13; Sheffield: Sheffield Academic Press, 1993], 15). As will be evidenced below, I do not share all the implications of postmodern discourses and understandings of history.

Vernon K. Robbins has developed such an agenda.³ His interdisciplinary approach seeks to establish a coherent framework and conceptual forum for relating each scholarly work to a broader spectrum of analysis and interpretation. This method has potential for bridging the cultural gap between various groups of scholars. Among many other things, the sociorhetorical model seeks to modify traditional historical criticism's attention to the history behind the texts.

Most of the papers in this present volume were presented at two Society of Biblical Literature International Meetings located in major European cities (Rome and Berlin). Several of them represent, with various emphases, a tendency to read the book of Acts within ancient literary and narrative settings, being part of an influential scholarly paradigm of research.⁴ The history behind the text is here of little interest. Modern European scholarship is not, to the same extent, a part of this trend. For instance, while Hans Conzelmann's and Ernst Haenchen's old commentaries are widely employed in the present discussion, it is rarely taken seriously that Jacob Jervell's commentary—in all essentials—distances itself from Haenchen's commentary, which it is intended to replace.⁵ Other commentaries, in yet other European languages, share Jervell's reluctance to abandon or minimize the historical dimension of Acts.⁶

---

³ Vernon K. Robbins, *Exploring the Texture of Texts: A Guide to Socio-Rhetorical Interpretation* (Valley Forge, Pa.: Trinity Press International, 1996); idem, *The Tapestry of Early Christian Discourse: Rhetoric, Society and Ideology* (London: Routledge, 1996). Robbins has developed his approach further in later publications.

⁴ F. Scott Spencer traces this trend back to Charles Talbert's work and role as chairman of the Luke-Acts Seminar in the Society of Biblical Literature ("Acts and Modern Literary Approaches," in *The Book of Acts in Its Ancient Literary Setting* [ed. B. W. Winter and A. D. Clarke; vol. 1 of *The Book of Acts in Its First Century Setting*; Grand Rapids: Eerdmans, 1993], 388). For an extensive, recent study along these lines, see Marianne Palmer Bonz, *The Past as Legacy: Luke-Acts and Ancient Epic* (Minneapolis: Fortress, 2000). According to Palmer Bonz, the Lukan prologue has nothing to do with the author's historical aims but is intended to show his desire to write "in a manner worthy of Greco-Roman literary style" (130), which is the Roman epic as represented, above all, in Vergil's *Aeneid*. For a discussion of the shifts in Acts research, see Joseph Tyson's essay in this volume.

⁵ Jacob Jervell, *Die Apostelgeschichte* (17th ed.; KEK 3; Göttingen: Vandenhoeck & Ruprecht, 1998). Joseph Tyson puts Conzelmann's and Haenchen's works in proper perspective by comparing them with Jervell's studies (*Luke, Judaism, and the Scholars: Critical Approaches to Luke-Acts* [Columbia: University of South Carolina Press, 1999], 66–109).

⁶ See the leading commentaries in Swedish by Edvin Larsson, *Apostlagärningarna* (3 vols.; Kommentar till Nya testamentet 5A–C; Stockholm: EFS-förlaget,

History or Story in Acts—A Middle Way?

In this essay I seek to present a model of historical interpretation that avoids the scholarly antithesis between history and story, offering some suggestions for understanding the complex synthesis of diachronic and synchronic elements in Acts as exemplified by the "we" passages. In order to do so, after studying the diachronic elements of the "we" passages, I will relate Robbins's notion of a text as a tapestry to another model of inquiry, namely, that of oral history. The reason for relating the two models has to do partly with the way in which sociorhetorical criticism challenges traditional historical criticism and partly with the way in which oral history redefines history and history writing by its profound attention to the oral medium of communication. I have previously explained and employed the oral history approach more extensively,[7] but not with regard to Acts and not with a basis in the notion of the text as a tapestry. All in all, this is not another study of the history behind the text of Acts but an attempt to think hermeneutically about history, to comprehend how the past is interpreted and narrativized. By relating to Robbins's well-known model and discussing its possible implication for historical investigation along the lines of oral history, I hope to clarify my position to those who understand it as nothing else but a naive turn from story to history.[8]

HISTORY IN THE STORY: THE "WE" PASSAGES OF ACTS

In order to provide a context for reflections concerning the text as a tapestry and oral history, I will begin by investigating the understanding of history reflected in the author's use of sources in Acts. The question of sources in Acts is indeed an old one. It is to some extent the point where the recent trend to focus on the literary and narrative dimension of the writing confronts other attempts to reckon with the history behind the narrative. While most scholars agree that the author used sources in Acts, just as he did in the Gospel, it is difficult to find a consensus on the nature and

---

1983–96); and Evald Lövestam, *Apostlagärningarna* (Tolkning av Nya testamentet 5; Stockholm: Verbum, 1988).

[7] Samuel Byrskog, *Story as History—History as Story: The Gospel Tradition in the Context of Ancient Oral History* (WUNT 123; Tübingen: Mohr Siebeck, 2000; repr., Leiden: Brill, 2002).

[8] See especially Christopher R. Matthews, review of Samuel Byrskog, *Story as History—History as Story*, *JBL* 121 (2002): 175–77. Other reviewers have been more appreciative, most extensively Peter M. Head, "The Role of Eyewitnesses in the Formation of the Gospel Tradition: A Review Article of Samuel Byrskog, *Story as History—History as Story*," *TynBul* 52 (2001): 275–94; and, most forcefully, Craig A. Evans, review of Samuel Byrskog, *Story as History—History as Story*, *BibInt* 9 (2001): 422–24.

extent of these sources.⁹ Scholars with an interest in the history behind the narrative seem content to identify the authorship, provenance, and wording of the material used by the author, thus neglecting to appreciate that history is mostly available in terms of sociorhetorical discourses and constantly entering into new narrative configurations. Scholars focusing on the literary and narrative dimension of Acts often resign in their attempts to identify sources. Stressing, rather, the unity of style, they seek ways to integrate the sources within the rhetoric of the narrative. This focus has resulted in a failure to appreciate that the literary and narrative rhetoric is essentially persuasive precisely as a rhetoric that makes visible its diachronic elements, as the author seems to indicate in the prologue of the Gospel.[10]

Luke's narrator makes visible a diachronic dimension in Acts in several subtle ways, such as in the sense for details, the way of framing speeches, the use of doublets, the Semitisms, perhaps even the focus on hospitality and lodging.[11] It is by no means certain that the author actually used sources on all these occasions—if he did he clearly put his own stylistic and narrative characteristic on them—but he apparently used the narrator to give that impression. Each of these items could be investigated in view of its function to provide the story with an intrinsic diachronic character. The sudden appearance and disappearance of the first-person plural is probably the most remarkable historicizing technique. Since the so-called "we" passages continue to attract the attention of scholars,[12] I will use them as a case study for the issue at hand. As is well known, the passages are found in 16:10–17; 20:5–15; 21:1–18; 27:1–29; and 28:1–16.[13] Scholars isolate them somewhat variously,[14] but the verbs put in the first-person

---

[9] Jacques Dupont concluded long ago that "despite the most careful and detailed research, it has not been possible to define any of the sources used by the author of Acts in a way which will meet with widespread agreement among the critics" (*The Sources of Acts: The Present Position* [London: Darton, Longman & Todd, 1964], 87). This situation has not changed.

[10] Even Quintilian, being eager to persuade the judge by almost any means, realizes the exceptional rhetorical value of information "derived from the knowledge of fact and precedent" (*Inst.* 10.1.34). See further, Byrskog, *Story as History*, 203–13.

[11] See Ben Witherington, *The Acts of the Apostles: A Socio-Rhetorical Commentary* (Grand Rapids: Eerdmans, 1998), 165–67.

[12] See the recent discussion by Alexander J. M. Wedderburn, "The 'We'-Passages in Acts: On the Horns of a Dilemma," *ZNW* 93 (2002): 78–98, which refers to the most significant previous investigations.

[13] With most scholars, I regard the "we" reading in 11:28 as secondary: "as we were gathered."

[14] I am following the division of Stanley E. Porter, *The Paul of Acts: Essays in Literary Criticism, Rhetoric, and Theology* (WUNT 115; Tübingen: Mohr Siebeck,

plural and the pronoun occur almost exclusively in these portions of the writing.[15]

These passages contain a number of peculiar features that give the hearers/readers pause. First, and most evidently, the "we" sections appear irregularly, often suddenly, and most end abruptly. On three occasions the pronoun "we" is explicitly put out in front of the verb (20:6, 13; 21:7), but not at the beginning of the sections. All attempts to isolate them therefore become somewhat arbitrary. The episode in 16:10 forms a transition from the pericope concerning Paul's vision of the man of Macedonia (16:6–9) to the passage concerning the conversion of Lydia (16:11–15), and the first-person plural verb ἐζητήσαμεν seems to be occasioned only by the intention to cross over from Troas to Macedonia. Furthermore, 16:17, with its peculiar reference to "Paul and us," is closely connected with the abrupt change to the third-person account about Paul and Silas that follows. Similarly, the "we" of 20:5 is entirely unexpected in view of its function within an account of Paul's travels to Macedonia and Greece (20:1–6) and occasioned by the purpose of meeting up with Paul and his group in Troas; after 20:15 the "we" disappears and is followed by a brief account of what Paul himself had decided concerning the travels. The first-person plural occurs again in 21:1, after Paul's speech and the narrator's comments in 20:17–38. Here the "we" section is introduced at the beginning of a new episode, though it links closely with the preceding section through the initial "when we had parted from them." It ends, however, as abruptly as the other instances. While the narrator includes an indication that Paul went to visit James "with us" (21:18), he afterwards focuses entirely on a third-person account about Paul. In 27:1 the "we" passage is again introduced at the beginning of a new episode, but in 27:29 it ends with a blunt reference to the fear "that we might run on the rocks," being followed by a third-person account of both Paul's encouraging advice to the soldiers and other people

---

1999; repr., Peabody, Mass.: Hendrickson, 2001), 28–33. Notice, however, the use of "we" in 27:37. Porter understands it as a trivial use of an inclusive first-person plural. Others see it as a sign that 27:1–28:16 forms one unit. As will be evident below, I am not convinced by Porter's attempt to reconstruct a continuous, independent source.

[15] In 16:10–17 the verbs are found in 16:10, 11, 12, 13, 16, and "us" (ἡμᾶς/ἡμῖν/ἡμῶν) in 16:15, 16, 17; in 20:5–15 the verbs are found in 20:6, 7, 8, 13, 15, and "us" in 20:5, 14; in 21:1–18 the verbs are found in 21:1, 2, 3, 4, 5, 6, 7, 8, 10, 12, 14, 15, 16, 17, and "us" in 21:5, 11, 16, 17, 18; in 27:1–29 the verbs are found in 27:1, 2, 3, 4, 5, 7, 8, 15, 16, 18, 27, 29, and "us" in 27:2, 6, 7, 20; in 28:1–16 the verbs are found in 28:1, 10, 11, 12, 13, 14, 16, and "us" in 28:2, 7, 10, 15. The reading "where they were meeting" in 20:8 is secondary; the "we" in 27:26 is within Paul's speech.

on the ship and the shipwreck itself (27:30–43). Finally, in 28:1 the narrator gives the impression that "we" had been present all the time during the preceding event. Only on this occasion does the "we" section end at a logical point in the narrative development: "when we came into Rome." The repeated occurrence of the "we" evidently has its own impenetrable logic. The hearers/readers must have been bewildered at this irregular and seemingly arbitrary appearance and disappearance of the first-person plural.

Second, and linked to the previous observation, one is struck by the tendency not to identify who is included in the "we" group. To be sure, there have been different proposals,[16] but they are all more or less conjectural because the narrator has no interest in informing the hearers/readers about the identity of the "we." One learns merely that "we" were regarded as servants of the Most High God and preachers of a way of salvation (16:17) and that, at one point, some disciples from Caesarea (21:16) and Aristarchus (27:2) joined the "we" group.[17] On the surface of the narrative, the "we," it seems, can be two or more persons, including Paul, but only Paul is important as a single individual while the rest, including the narrator, simply give the impression of having been anonymously present on certain occasions.

Third, the "we" sections are sometimes interrupted by short passages where the narrative turns into a third-person singular account about Paul: his concern for the man who fell asleep (20:9–12), his discussion concerning the dangers of sailing from Fair Havens to Phoenix (27:9–14), his rebuke for not following his advice and his comfort to the people with him at sea (27:21–26), and his confrontation with the inhabitants of Malta as a viper fastened itself onto his hand (28:3–6).[18] As it appears, the "we" group is present on these occasions but fades strangely into the background only to reappear again, as if its members served as historical witnesses to Paul's words and deeds.

---

[16] Besides Paul, primarily Silas and Timothy come into view, but the two were already with Paul in the narrative before the appearance of the "we." Cf. Hans Conzelmann, *Acts of the Apostles* (ed. E. J. Epp and C. R. Matthews; trans. J. Limburg et al.; Hermeneia; Philadelphia: Fortress, 1987), xxxix. Jürgen Wehnert argues strongly for Silas and regards him as the author of the "we" source (*Die Wir-Passagen der Apostelgeschichte: Ein lukanisches Stilmittel aus jüdischer Tradition* [GTA 40; Göttingen: Vandenhoeck & Ruprecht, 1989]). For a valid critique, see Claus-Jürgen Thornton, *Der Zeuge des Zeugen: Lukas als Historiker der Paulusreisen* (WUNT 56; Tübingen: Mohr Siebeck, 1991), 114–16. The people mentioned in 20:4 are distinguished from the "we" group in 20:5–6.

[17] For Aristarchus, see 19:29; 20:4. He is also mentioned in Col 4:10 and Phlm 24.

[18] For scholars who regard 20:5–21:29 and 27:1–28:16 as two units of "we" sections, 20:17–38 and 27:30–44 present extensive interruptions of the "we" accounts.

Fourth, the "we" passages are intersected with a number of seemingly unnecessary details. The geographical specificity is evident in the frequent reference to a number of stopping places, but also in additional comments such as that Philippi was a leading city of the district of Macedonia and a Roman colony (16:12); that Lydia was from Thyatira (16:14); that Agabus, whom the narrator had already introduced (11:28), was a prophet from Judea (21:10); that Mnason was from Cyprus (21:16); that the ship that was to take them to Italy came from Adramytium (27:2); that Aristarchus, whom the narrator had already identified (19:29; 20:4), was from Macedonia (27:2); that the ship found in Myra came from Alexandria (27:6); that Fair Havens was located near the city of Lasea (27:8); and that the ship with the Twin Brother as its figurehead was from Alexandria (27:11).[19] This geographical specificity is coupled with numerous other details, such as, most evidently, the mention of minor chronological items (16:13; 20:6, 7, 15; 21:1, 4, 7, 10, 18; 27:27; 28:11, 12, 13, 14), that there were many lamps in the room upstairs (20:8), and that the violent wind was called the northeaster (27:14). These details are present in an unusual measure in the "we" passages, sometimes with rather extreme specificity,[20] and cannot be reduced to an evident and consistent narrative or literary pattern.[21] Precisely, then, as seemingly ad hoc pieces of information within passages in first-person plural, they provide, whether historically accurate or not, the narrative with a realistic stamp. This observation strengthens the impression of a diachronic dimension in the story and presents a conceptual bridge between the *now* of the narrator and the *then* of Paul.

---

[19] Conzelmann claims that the "addition of unimportant stopping places along the way can be explained on purely literary grounds" (*Acts of the Apostles*, xl). However, one must take into account that the geographical specificity extends further than to the mere mention of stopping places.

[20] Colin Hemer and Porter call attention to 16:11–12, claiming that its level of detail is not elsewhere provided in Acts (Colin J. Hemer, *The Book of Acts in the Setting of Hellenistic History* [ed. C. H. Gempf; WUNT 49; Tübingen: Mohr Siebeck, 1989; repr., Winona Lake, Ind.: Eisenbrauns, 1990)], 346–47; Porter, *Paul of Acts*, 36). Cf. Dietrich-Alex Koch's observation regarding the greater detail of 20:5–21:8 as compared to 18:18–22a ("Kollektenbericht, 'Wir'-Bericht und Itinerar: Neue Überlegungen zu einem alten Problem," *NTS* 45 [1999]: 367–90, esp. 370–72). Koch's source-critical conclusions are not mandatory. See the critique by Wedderburn, "The 'We'-Passages in Acts," 90–92.

[21] Jacob Jervell states: "There is a wealth of details in these sections compared to other parts of Acts, even details with no significance for his account" ("The Future of the Past: Luke's Vision of Salvation History and Its Bearing on His Writing of History," in *History, Literature, and Society in the Book of Acts* [ed. B. Witherington; Cambridge: Cambridge University Press, 1996], 117). So also Jervell, *Apostelgeschichte*, 63.

Finally, one should not underestimate the peculiarities of literary style. While Adolf von Harnack strongly influenced scholarship by his insistence that, apart from the use of the first-person plural, the literary style of the "we" passages resembles the rest of Acts, Stanley Porter calls attention to the disproportionately high number of *hapax legomena* in the "we" passages, that is, words that are not to be found in Luke or other parts of Acts.[22] His estimation differs slightly from von Harnack's, who counted 111 *hapax legomena*, but it points rather strikingly to a weakness in von Harnack's hypothesis and puts into question the attempts to minimize all the specific characteristics of the "we" sections. Statistical method is indeed tricky, and stylistic data are open to different explanations. Porter uses his observation to argue that the author of Acts used a source that was not his own. While these peculiarities are manifestly linked to typical Lukan features of syntax, one must at least recognize that here the narrator subtly and occasionally gives the hearers/readers the impression that he narrates things that the author had learned from others, thus further *historicizing* the account of Paul.

What are we to make of these five features? Why did the author, through his narrator, choose to present the "we" sections in this fashion? One may seek a literary, or narrative, answer. I have already suggested that Luke thereby gave the story an intrinsic diachronic character, full of details and vividness, which give the impression of a story based on history.[23] By presenting a narrator who speaks in first-person plural, the author himself appears, albeit vaguely, as present in the arena of history. Clearly, from a narrative point of view, the author is included among the "we," and that is sufficient; no further naming or numbering of participants is necessary. The "we" are, within the narrative of Acts, historical witnesses to the details and vividness of Paul's words and deeds.[24] I stress that this is a narrative answer. The large amount of details is in itself no sign that the author in fact used sources, as is often assumed, because this can be found in narratives that are clearly fictional.[25] So, to begin with, each feature of the "we" passages adds cumulatively to the intrinsic pastness of the story and places the hearers/readers within a colorful retrospective discourse about Paul.

---

[22] Porter, *Paul of Acts*, 35–37; he includes all the references to von Harnack's studies.

[23] Polybius, for instance, misses the vividness of facts in Timaeus's writing, "as this can only be produced by the personal experience of the authors" (12.25h.4).

[24] Dennis R. MacDonald denies this function of the first-person plural, arguing that it flags these passages as imitations of the *Odyssey* ("The Shipwrecks of Odysseus and Paul," *NTS* 45 [1999]: 88–107). See also his contribution in this volume. For a critique, however, see Wedderburn, "The 'We'-Passages in Acts," 92–93.

[25] Byrskog, *Story as History*, 202.

Looking at the matter somewhat closer, however, it becomes evident that the literary or narrative answer needs to be supplemented.[26] Why employ the technique of the irregular and seemingly arbitrary use of "we"? The intrinsic pastness of the story, which we may refer to as the "diachronic rhetoric" of the narrative, is conveyed subtly and strangely, almost by accident, and is not supported by any consistent literary or narrative convention. Whatever intertextual parallels there might be to the first-person account,[27] they were evidently not a common way to provide the narrative with an intrinsic dimension of pastness and historical presence. The historians, who were most eager to persuade the hearers/readers by reference to things in the past, do not employ it to prove that their writings are based on personal observation and experience.[28] They are usually much more explicit and direct about such matters.[29] In addition, the presence of the "we" sections is, as we have seen, far from logical in the narrative and not signaled in a consistent and clear manner. So, granting that the author of Acts wanted to write/speak about the past and give the story an intrinsic diachronic dimension, why then this technique of impenetrable logic? Moreover, why the slight contradiction between the narrative inclusion of the author in the "we" and the occasional peculiarities of style? On the one hand, one receives the impression that the author wished to tell Theophilus of things he had seen and heard himself, while on the other hand, it seems that he sometimes used a terminology that was not his own. As we know so well from redactional studies of the Gospel,[30] the author was usually not shy to put his own stamp on the writing.

The most reasonable explanation is that the "we" sections are not endlessly fiction of fictions but the result of a complex process of reorealization and narrativization of an extrafictional past reality. This is how I prefer to express what scholars usually call "use of sources." Just as in the prologue of the Gospel, wherein the author, as we will see, presents himself as an oral historian, in the "we" sections he conveys the impression that he relied

---

[26] Luke T. Johnson accurately writes that a narrative "can be significantly shaped by an author's imagination and still report substantial historical information" (*The Acts of the Apostles* [SP 5; Collegeville, Minn.: Liturgical Press, 1992], 7). Presumably there is something in the writing that validates this view.

[27] Porter (*Paul of Acts*, 12–24); and Wedderburn ("The 'We'-Passages in Acts," 81–84) critically survey the most influential proposals.

[28] Thornton, *Zeuge des Zeugen*, 150–97, 199, 360–67.

[29] See Byrskog, *Story as History*, 48–65, 154–57.

[30] Ben Witherington is thus right to study the editing of the Gospel of Luke in order to perceive better the author's redactional activity in Acts ("Editing the Good News: Some Synoptic Lessons for the Study of Acts," in Witherington, *History, Literature, and Society*, 324–47).

on information from people who had been involved.³¹ As a hearer/reader of the "we" section, one learns not only that he had been there as a witness (that he was his own source) but also that he was a witness among one or several other witnesses whose stories he had heard and partly integrated into his own reminiscences and narrative. In this sense, as a subtle authorial message to Theophilus, the extrafictional past—history—is present in the story of the narrative.

This explanation of the diachronic elements in the "we" passages of Acts is far from claiming that we can identify the sources at the author's disposal. Rather, it is indicative of a communication about the past in a context where sources were not regarded as semantic entities unto themselves. Several scholars envision a written "we" source; some think it was oral. The matter is probably more complicated in the end. The synthesis of historical and narrative elements in the "we" sections of Acts seems to reflect a situation where the sources were never objectified entities to be reproduced passively but were constantly reoralized and integrated into participatory, living sociorhetorical discourses about the past.³² For the author of Acts, the past was thus not systematically explored and exposed but narratively exploited; it was not passively re-presented, but narratively represented.

The "Oral Text"

What are we to make of this complex interaction between the past and the present in the "we" sections of Acts? What does it say about the text of

---

³¹ Daniel Marguerat points out that the "I" of Luke 1 is extradiegetic, while the "we" of the "we" passages is intradiegetic, thus arguing that the use of "we" is a narrative device (*The First Christian Historian: Writing the "Acts of the Apostles"* [SNTSMS 121; Cambridge: Cambridge University Press, 2002], 24–25). If this authorial "I," as Marguerat puts it, "overhangs the story" (24), it does have a certain intradiegetic function that calls for a way of relating the "we" passages to the extradiegetic claims of the preface.

³² This supports, in my view, Wedderburn's recent proposal that the "we" passages reflect the activity of a Pauline school and come—probably orally—from a pupil who had accompanied Paul on some of his travels. The author of Acts was himself, according to Wedderburn, a pupil of that pupil ("The 'We'-Passages in Acts," 94–98). It is in such contexts of participation that sources remain socially and rhetorically relevant discourses. Wedderburn neglects, however, to consider the narrative effects of the inclusion of the "we" passages in Acts, with the author thus being included in the "we." The school context has also been brought to the fore, though from a different angle, by Loveday Alexander in "Acts and Ancient Intellectual Biography," in Winter and Clarke, *Book of Acts in Its Ancient Literary Setting*, 31–63.

Acts itself? What does it say about the notion of history? What are the perspectives from which we may analyze and comprehend it?

Granting that this understanding of the diachronic rhetoric of the "we" passages is correct and to some extent indicative of larger portions of Acts, we may bring our inquiry one step further by reflecting on what kind of text provides such a dialectic between history and story. A fundamental aspect of Robbins's sociorhetorical program is the suggestion that a text has textures. Just as these textures are not limited to the inner dynamics of the story, so the texts are not merely windows through which one looks at the outside world. The text is both a discourse with mind and body, exposing the language border of its internal fiction, and a social product, possession, and tool.[33] The image used to bring out the implication of this suggestion is that of a tapestry. The textures are a result of webs (cf. Latin *texere*, "to weave") of signification or meaning and meaning effects, which communicate differently according to the different angles—textures—from which one approaches the text. Robbins's use of the image of a tapestry is deeply rooted in the ancient Greek and Roman understanding of a text as a web. In their book entitled *The Craft of Zeus,* John Scheid and Jesper Svenbro show in some detail how the metaphor of weaving was employed for different things in the ancient Greek and Roman world, including those that had to do with linguistic weaving.[34] A writing belonged to what was handmade; it was *Handwerk* in a concrete sense. It was therefore but a short step to think of it as some kind of weaving.

Quintilian is the first author to use the Latin words *textus* and *textum,* and he does so in a manner that implies that the very syntax of an expression is thought of in terms of weaving: "just as the value of a thought varies according to the words that express it, so that of words varies according to the arrangement that joins them, whether in the fabric or at the end of complete sentences" (*Inst.* 9.4.13). Having previously compared a verbal discourse to the secret power in musical rhythms and modes, Quintilian now implies that the semantic value of words depends on their place *in textu,* in the fabric of the phrase.

Looking briefly into the Platonic background of this ancient idea of syntax, we discover that there is more to it than the mere arrangement of words. While in the *Statesman* Plato introduces the image of something

---

[33] Robbins, *Tapestry of Early Christian Discourse,* 19.

[34] John Scheid and Jesper Svenbro, *The Craft of Zeus: Myths of Weaving and Fabric* (Revealing Antiquity 9; Cambridge: Harvard University Press, 1996). See also Margaret E. Dean's discussion of sociorhetorical criticism in "Textured Criticism," *JSNT* 70 (1998): 79–91, esp. 80; and Samuel Byrskog, "Talet, minnet och skriften: Evangelietraditionen och den antika informationsteknologin," *SEÅ* 66 (2001): 139–50, esp. 140–41.

that is intertwined (συμπλοκή) to describe the weaving process on a phonological level as children learn to spell by reading aloud (*Pol.* 277d–278b), in the *Sophist* he uses the same metaphor of weaving on a syntactical level. Isolated nouns, the Stranger points out to Theaetetus, do not form a discourse (λόγος) unless one mixes some verbs with them: "Then harmony is established and, instantly, the first joining [συμπλοκή] made into a discourse [λόγος]" (*Soph.* 262c). Just as one combines written letters with vocal sounds on a phonological level and thus learns to spell, only in this way, by weaving together verbs and nouns—two items that the Stranger considers to be contraries—is it possible to make meaningful constructions on a syntactical level.

How does that weaving come about? Where, or through what activity, does it emerge? The answer is the audible reading, the oral medium of communication. Scheid and Svenbro illustrate the union of writing and reading by reference to Phaedrus and the manuscript of Lysias's discourse that he carries with him. When Phaedrus, the lover of Lysias, reads the writing aloud, he plays the role of the beloved, because one of the Greek models of written communication defines the writer as a metaphorical lover.[35] Socrates' seemingly casual comment that Phaedrus carries Lysias's writing "under the cloak" and, by so doing, makes Lysias present (Plato, *Phaedr.* 228d–e), implies that the writer and the reader are intimately united under the same fabric. For the Greeks, "to go under the same cloak" was an expression of sexual union. Hence, the writing is the warp, and the reader's voice is the woof; together they form the web. The writing is not the text; the text is not a web of written signs; rather, the text is the harmonious unification of the author's writing and the reader's voice. Scheid and Svenbro draw out the implication of this insight: "Once the reading is over, the fabric will unravel into the written warp and the vocal woof—so that the warp can be used in other weavings, in other readings,"[36] thereby, we may add, creating new webs of signification or meaning and meaning effects.

Along similar lines Robbins notes, "To be what it truly is, a text must be read, which may mean 'read aloud.'"[37] This remark is significant. Texts are rhetorical entities and as such they are part of an oral matrix of communication. Acts was composed and heard/read for the first time within a rhetorical culture in which writing and speaking interrelated closely.[38]

---

[35] Cf. Jesper Svenbro, *Phrasikleia: An Anthropology of Reading in Ancient Greece* (Myth and Poetics; Ithaca, N.Y.: Cornell University Press, 1988), 189–98.

[36] Scheid and Svenbro, *Craft of Zeus*, 126.

[37] Robbins, *Tapestry of Early Christian Discourse*, 19.

[38] I am aware of the need to distinguish between various forms of orality. Such classifications exist; here I am alluding to Robbins's own way of speaking of the

Texts were, in a sense, oral texts. Though the Platonic view was modified and altered throughout the centuries, this ancient understanding of a text adds a significant aspect to the tapestry of Acts. It shows that the oral/aural dimension of the writing was not something that was added to the text but an essential part of what actually constituted the text to begin with. Its essentially oral character provides a culture-specific, media-based justification for regarding it as a social as well as rhetorical entity, because oral texts are part of both reality and fiction. If sociorhetorical interpretation regards the text of Acts as a social product, possession, and tool, its appreciation of the text as rhetoric opens up the vast domain of the ancient oral/aural technologies of communication and integrates it within its very conception of a text. As Werner Kelber reminds us, rhetoric is essentially an outgrowth of a media world dominated by speaking; it has a profoundly oral disposition, as language, mind, and body are synergistic forces that negotiate knowledge and perception.[39] Today there is a growing awareness of the multifaceted interpretative potentials of the oral medium,[40] thus adding a significant dimension to the influential rhetorical analyses of biblical texts.

---

rhetorical culture of the first century Mediterranean world. I am skeptical of chronological models of classification and would rather focus on culture-specific factors that may or may not transcend specific periods of time. For an excellent account of the defining categories of orality, see Øivind Andersen, "Oral Tradition," in *Jesus and the Oral Gospel Tradition* (ed. H. Wansbrough; JSNTSup 64; Sheffield: Sheffield Academic Press, 1991), 9–58.

[39] Werner H. Kelber, "Modalities of Communication, Cognition, and Physiology of Perception: Orality, Rhetoric, Scribality," *Semeia* 65 (1994): 193–216. See also the challenge to the rhetorical study of the Pauline letters by Pieter J. Botha, "The Verbal Art of the Pauline Letters: Rhetoric, Performance and Presence," in *Rhetoric and the New Testament: Essays from the 1992 Heidelberg Conference* (ed. S. E. Porter and T. H. Olbricht; JSNTSup 90; Sheffield: Sheffield Academic Press, 1993), 409–28.

[40] For an informative survey of some influential studies, see Martin S. Jaffee, "Oral Culture in Scriptural Religion: Some Exploratory Studies," *RelSRev* 24 (1998): 223–30. For some more recent contributions, see John D. Harvey, *Listening to the Text: Oral Patterning in Paul's Letters* (Grand Rapids: Baker, 1998); Casey W. Davis, *Oral Biblical Criticism: The Influence of the Principles of Orality on the Literary Structure of Paul's Epistle to the Philippians* (JSNTSup 172; Sheffield: Sheffield Academic Press, 1999); Richard A. Horsley and Jonathan A. Draper, *Whoever Hears You Hears Me: Prophets, Performance, and Tradition in Q* (Harrisburg, Pa.: Trinity Press International, 1999); and Richard A. Horsley, *Hearing the Whole Story: The Politics of Plot in Mark's Gospel* (Louisville: Westminster John Knox, 2001).

The Diachronic Dimension of the "Oral Text"

Acts is a writing about the past, regardless of how we define its genre.[41] The text has, as we have seen, an intrinsic historical intertexture. However, what happens to this historical dimension once we take seriously that Acts resides within a profoundly oral setting stimulating the creation of a complex interactive web of the written and the oral media of communication? What happens when this kind of ancient writing is approached as a source about the history of Paul and early Christianity? Is it at all possible to "unpick" the textual web of writing and speaking and enter the diachronic path leading to historical events? Granting that Acts was composed and heard/read within the ancient matrix of oral texts briefly depicted above, with the subtle interaction between what was written and what was read aloud, one is easily led to conclude that it represents the reality of the storyteller and conveys an entirely fictionalized account of the past. Influential scholarship is indeed moving in this direction.

There is much truth in this conclusion. The events of history are fictionalized as soon as they enter the minds of people,[42] thus ultimately betraying the interests and values of eyewitnesses, historians, and storytellers.[43] However, in my understanding this conclusion is one-sided, and the "we" passages do not easily yield to such a view, as we have seen. A basic—sometimes hidden—assumption in this kind of thinking is that the oral medium, with its inherent pragmatic force of persuasion, is itself devoid of a real sense of pastness. It lives in the present time of performance, producing its own fictions. In accordance with his thesis of oral transmission as a process of social identification and preventive censorship, Kelber endorses the view that "a tradition that cannot overcome the social threshold to communal reception is doomed to extinction. Loss and discontinuity no less than growth and continuity dictate the realities of oral life."[44] An important corollary to this view is that the oral medium exhibits

---

[41] The question of the factual accuracy of Acts is irrelevant to generic classification. See David E. Aune, *The New Testament in Its Literary Environment* (LEC 8; Philadelphia: Westminster, 1987), 80.

[42] I am using *events of history* in a broad sense, including what happened, who was involved, and where and when the events occurred. All these aspects are immediately fictionalized in the sense that they become part of a person's framework of interpretation.

[43] See Byrskog, *Story as History*, 145–98, and below.

[44] Werner H. Kelber, *The Oral and the Written Gospel: The Hermeneutics of Speaking and Writing in the Synoptic Tradition, Mark, Paul, and Q* (Philadelphia: Fortress, 1983; repr., Bloomington: Indiana University Press, 1997), 29.

no real interest in the past: "It is only with writing that a true sense of pastness is possible."[45] Kelber does not work with Acts, but, as it seems, he relies on Jack Goody's and Ian Watt's influential article from 1968, where the functional theory of homeostasis was introduced.[46] There exists, according to this theory, a complete congruence between an oral society or group and its traditions; the permanent written record is necessary in order truly to appreciate the pastness of the past.[47]

Several social anthropologists and ethnologists would avoid making such radical statements today;[48] even Goody himself is not, it seems, as extreme in his later publications.[49] Some scholars, most significantly Ruth Finnegan,[50] stress the culture-specific character of each occurrence of orality, implying that while the preservative consciousness of transmission might be missing in one culture, it might be quite strong in another.[51] What

---

[45] Ibid., 209.

[46] Jack Goody and Ian Watt, "The Consequences of Literacy," in *Literacy in Traditional Societies* (ed. J. Goody; Cambridge: Cambridge University Press, 1968), 27–68.

[47] "The pastness of the past, then, depends upon a historical sensibility which can hardly begin to operate without permanent written records" (Ibid., 34).

[48] Meinhard Schuster, a professor of ethnology, remarks: "Das Schreibenkönnen und das Geschichtehaben werden also in einer aus der europäischen Wissenschaftstradition leicht verständlichen Verwechslung von Geschichte mit dem Umfang und der Zuverlässigkeit ihrer Dokumentation ursächlich und funktional miteinander verknüpft" ("Zur Konstruktion von Geschichte in Kulturen ohne Schrift," in *Vergangenheit in mündlicher Überlieferung* [ed. J. von Ungern-Sternberg and H. Reinau; Colloquium Rauricum 1; Stuttgart: Teubner, 1988], 57).

[49] See Jack Goody, *The Interface between the Written and the Oral* (Studies in Literature, Family, Culture and the State; Cambridge: Cambridge University Press, 1987), 174–82. Already in the first presentation of the theory, Goody and Watt expressed some cautious remarks, as for instance the following: "Formalized patterns of speech, recital under ritual conditions, the use of drums and other musical instruments, the employment of professional remembrancers—all such factors may shield at least part of the content of memory from the transmuting influence of the immediate pressures of the present" ("Consequences of Literacy," 31).

[50] Most of Ruth Finnegan's experiences and insights are reflected in *Oral Traditions and the Verbal Arts: A Guide to Research Practices* (ASA Research Methods in Social Anthropology; London: Routledge, 1992). Note the following statement: "Complementing the long tradition of classification and generalisation there is now a counter-trend towards exploring people's own views and artistry rather than analysing through outsiders' categories" (26).

[51] Even Goody admits this: "I do not wish for a moment to deny that in nonliterate cultures some standardized oral forms are memorized in exact form" (*Interface,* 176). However, he considers this practice to be a rare phenomenon.

is, after all, "a true sense of pastness"? Is it to be equated with a sense of historical truth—fact against fiction? In that case, it is noteworthy that the genre definition of a predominantly oral culture can depend precisely on the issue of fact or fiction. Jan Vansina tells of genres in Rwanda where *ibitéekerezo* differs from the narrative *umugani* in that the one is supposed to be ancient fact and the other is fiction.[52] It is therefore inadequate to argue that each generation of an oral culture generates its own past or to claim that the traditions of origin do not represent a true sense of pastness. The archaisms in an oral tradition are signs that there hardly exists a total homeostatic and functional congruence between an oral group and its traditions.[53] Vansina is indeed critical of the theory of homeostasis.[54] It is one thing to say that personal or societal present-day concerns always interact with the historical intentionality of an oral account, as Vansina does, and another to claim that only writing makes possible a true sense of pastness, as Kelber does. An oral tradition can very well be regarded as a kind of a "historiology" of the past, an account of how people have interpreted their history.[55] In this sense the tradition may indeed reflect a real sense of pastness.

As far as Greek antiquity is concerned, Wolfgang Rösler argues that the ancient consciousness of fictivity was conditioned by the existence of literacy, because oral cultures have no notion of private reading or genre and thus no conception of fiction.[56] However, we have just seen that a predominantly oral culture might indeed have notions of genre. Furthermore, private reading was a rare thing even in settings where a significant amount of literacy can be assumed.[57] There are, moreover, ancient pieces

---

[52] Jan Vansina, *Oral Tradition as History* (Madison: University of Wisconsin Press, 1985), 83. Elsewhere Vansina goes so far as to claim that "for every functional type of written source in Europe one can find an equivalent oral source in Africa" ("Once Upon a Time: Oral Traditions as History in Africa," *Dædalus* 100 [1971]: 442–68, esp. 443).

[53] Walter J. Ong realizes that archaisms do survive, but only, he asserts, through their current use (*Orality and Literacy: The Technologizing of the Word* [New Accents; London: Routledge, 1982], 47). Still, the current use of an archaism cannot be used as an argument for an extreme functional theory concerning traditions, since the current use must in that case relate to a current meaning, which is not always the case. See the discussion of survivals or cultural lag in Åke Hultkrantz, *Metodvägar inom den jämförande religionsforskningen* (Stockholm: Esselte Studium, 1973), 108–9.

[54] Vansina, *Oral Tradition*, 120–23.

[55] Ibid., 196.

[56] Wolfgang Rösler, "Die Entdeckung der Fiktionalität in der Antike," *Poetica* 12 (1980): 283–319.

[57] The reference to Bishop Ambrose's private reading in Augustine, *Conf.* 6.3, is most well known. A. K. Gavrilov has pointed out that this reading was considered

of information that cannot be disposed of all that easily. The problems inherent in Rösler's attitude toward concepts of truth and fiction in oral cultures become evident in some utterances of the early Greek singers. For example, Odysseus says to the bard Demodocus, "You sing of the fate of the Achaeans most excellently, how much the Achaeans did and suffered and how much they toiled, as if you had been present yourself or heard it from someone else" (*Od.* 8.489–491).[58] The Muses of Olympus or Helicon sing for the shepherding Hesiod thus: "We know how to speak many false things like real things, and we know, when we wish, to utter true things" (*Theog.* 27–28).[59] While ancient fiction certainly must be measured by categories beyond the modern notions of true and false (as Rösler rightly reminds us), one cannot escape the impression that the singers of antiquity were somewhat aware of the extent to which poetry represents what they perceived as true reality.[60] Not everything sung was considered true, as one would expect if there were no notion of fictional elements at all, yet not everything was considered false, as one would expect if poetry were to be measured solely by its function of representing reality. Even in predominantly oral cultures a subtle awareness of questions concerning what is true and what is false might indeed occur. As Wolfgang Kullmann insists, "Evidently the 'oral society' is after all not as homogenous as is claimed."[61]

---

an obstacle precisely because Ambrose read privately in the presence of others ("Techniques of Reading in Classical Antiquity," *CQ* 91 NS 47 [1997]: 56–73). Similarly Carsten Burfeind, "Wen hörte Philippus? Leises Lesen und lautes Vorlesen in der Antike," *ZNW* 93 (2002): 138–45, esp. 139.

[58] Joachim Latacz comments: "Die Reputation des oral poet bemißt sich also nach dem Autentizitätsgrad seiner Darstellung. Unter Autentizitätsgrad ist dabei nicht nur objektive Faktenwiedergabe verstanden, sondern darüber hinaus auch 'stimmige' Wiedergabe der Fakten*wirkung*" ("Zu Umfang und Art der Vergangenheitsbewahrung in der mündlichen Überlieferungsphase des griechischen Heldenepos," in von Ungern-Sternberg and Reinau, *Vergangenheit*, 168).

[59] Wolfgang Kullmann states, "Auch wenn es den Begriff Fiktion nicht gibt, ist doch klar, daß von Hesiod nicht alles so geglaubt wird, wie es im Epos erzählt wird" ("Der Übergang von der Mündlichkeit zur Schriftlichkeit im frühgriechischen Epos," in *Logos und Buchstabe: Mündlichkeit und Schriftlichkeit im Judentum und Christentum der Antike* [ed. G. Sellin and F. Vouga; TANZ 20; Tübingen: Francke, 1997], 73).

[60] There were, of course, various notions of truth, as especially *Theog.* 27–28 shows, with its interplay between ἔτυμα (corresponding to reality) and ἀληθέα (corresponding to what is revealed). For this distinction, see Michèle Simondon, *La mémoire et l'oubli dans la pensée grecque jusqu'à la fin du Ve siècle avant J.-C.* (Paris: Belles Lettres, 1982), 112–15.

[61] Wolfgang Kullmann, "'Oral Tradition/Oral History' und die frühgriechische Epik," in von Ungern-Sternberg and Reinau, *Vergangenheit*, 189: "Offenbar ist die 'oral society' doch nicht so homogen wie proklamiert."

Acts was not produced and heard/read in a purely oral culture but within a setting promoting the kind of interactive rhetorical mode of communication outlined above. My point thus far is twofold, being based on a certain understanding of what constitutes a text: (1) all texts, even those composed in a writing such as Acts, had an inherent oral dimension that surfaced in the oral performance of the writing; (2) the oral dimension of a text such as Acts does not preclude a sense of history but points toward an environment where the past reality and the present fiction—history and story—interact in textual compositions and performances.

We can bring this inquiry one step further by asking how a literate person aiming to tell a story about the past claimed to have knowledge about that past. In the writings of the ancient historians we confront their strong preference for eyewitness testimony and oral tradition as a means of gaining information concerning the past over and against written material.[62] Polybius's critique of Timaeus is one example among many. According to Polybius (12.25d.1), Timaeus made a great mistake in considering his access to written material in Athens as a sufficient qualification to write history. After explaining the three parts of πραγματικὴ ἱστορία in 12.25e.1–2 (the study and collation of written sources, *autopsia,* and political experience), Polybius ranks the first one as of limited value to anyone writing contemporary history. It is "absolutely foolish," he says (12.25e.7), to rely only upon the mastery of written material, as Timaeus apparently did. He was too "bookish" (12.25h.3). "From these considerations," Polybius concludes, "each one would evidently agree that the study of written sources is [only] a third part of history and stands in the third place" (12.25i.2). The reason is simple: isolation from the practical realities follows from too strong a focus on written sources. If not combined with eyewitness testimony and oral tradition, the reliance upon written sources gives a one-sided and distorted picture of past realities. According to Polybius, writing does not give a true sense of pastness, as eyewitness testimony and oral tradition might do.

Hence, there is no reason to let history go just because the text of Acts is a complex, interactive web of written and oral communication. The historians of antiquity betray a keen sense of pastness, and they were well capable of writing and employing written sources. However, despite all that, their primary means of relating to the past—becoming contemporaneous with it—was not the written medium but the various, interrelated oral/aural modalities of seeing, speaking, and hearing. Such a consistent pattern of developing a sense of history would certainly be surprising were the oral sources themselves totally devoid of a genuine retrospective

---

[62] The historians present the best comparative material simply because they are most explicit about the way they related to the past and sought out information.

dimension. The various forms of oral performance and communication, as it thus appears, are not inherently opposed to history in its pastness. Rather, the oral legacy is the matrix of living not merely in the present but between the past and the present. The textual web of the written and the spoken word in Acts cannot therefore be stripped of its genuinely diachronic dimension without losing some of the colorful threads that hold it together.

The Oral History Approach

While biblical scholars have employed ancient and modern rhetoric to produce several helpful models for analyzing and comprehending the multifaceted character of oral and written communication, only rarely has sufficient methodological attention been given to the diachronic dimension of the oral genre.[63] However, social anthropologists and historians have developed an approach that takes seriously the historical dimension of orality and have provided a conceptual framework for understanding its subtle interplay between past and present. The embryo of this so-called oral history approach emerged as a reaction against the influential views of Leopold von Ranke and his school of thought. Georg Iggers, one of the leading experts on European historiography, illustrates the criticism leveled against the Rankean conception of historical science by a new generation of historians who sought to incorporate methods of various social sciences into historical study.[64] The two world wars added to this tendency by narrowing the scope of research to immediate objectives and alerting the historians to the complex nature of sources and interpretation. The wars caused scholars to question the objective, impartial ideal of the segregated professional. The Oral History Association's declaration traces the origin of oral history as a method of historical documentation back to 1948, when the historian Allan Nevins began

---

[63] See Byrskog, "Talet, minnet och skriften," 139–50, where I critique Kelber's and John Dominic Crossan's notions of orality. Crossan's view of how memory functioned in antiquity is based on a strange and one-sided selection of evidence (144–47). Cf. the section entitled "Memory and Orality" in John D. Crossan, *The Birth of Christianity: Discovering What Happened in the Years Immediately after the Execution of Jesus* (San Francisco: HarperSanFrancisco, 1998), 47–93.

[64] Georg G. Iggers, "The Crisis of the Rankean Paradigm in the Nineteenth Century," in *Leopold von Ranke and the Shaping of the Historical Discipline* (ed. G. Iggers and J. M. Powell; Syracuse: Syracuse University Press, 1990), 170–79. Iggers develops this discussion more fully in his *Historiography in the Twentieth Century: From Scientific Objectivity to the Postmodern Challenge* (Hanover, N.H.: Wesleyan University Press, 1997), 23–94.

recording the memoirs of significant American individuals. The Second World War saw the rise of a wide use of oral history in other countries as well. As Iggers argues, "World War II appears to have been followed by a clearer caesura in European historiography than World War I."[65] He is referring to the new interest in empirical social sciences among historians. The development of the last decades shows that oral history now belongs firmly within the domain of historiography,[66] with natural interdisciplinary connections to other fields. It has its own associations, journals, conferences, and the like.[67]

Oral history also has its own ideology, understanding that the modern historian's task is different from that of many professional historians of earlier generations. With the publication of *The Voice of the Past* in 1978, Paul Thompson presented the first comprehensive introduction to oral history. The thoroughly revised editions from 1988 and 2000 constitute the most influential discussion of its theory and practice.[68] "Oral evidence," Thompson writes, "by transforming the 'objects' of study into 'subjects,' makes for a history which is not just richer, more vivid, and heart-rending, but truer."[69] Oral history brings new insights into what we may perceive as true or false, fact or fiction, in history. Its social dimension is thus central to Thompson's approach.[70] To treat oral sources simply as documents ignores the special value that they have as subjective, spoken testimony. More specifically, what we have in these sources are not the so-called facts but the social perception of facts; in effect, we receive social meaning through these sources.

The distinctiveness of oral evidence, with its social implication for concepts such as true or false, fact or fiction, results from a variety of factors. The most obvious one, of course, is that it presents itself in an oral form. This quality makes it, to some extent, more reliable than written documents, according to Thompson. The historian senses the social clues

---

[65] Georg G. Iggers, *New Directions in European Historiography* (Middletown, Conn.: Wesleyan University Press, 1975), 31.

[66] Martin Schaffner, a professor of history, concludes: "Innerhalb der Geschichtswissenschaft läßt sich somit ein ganzes Spektrum von Arbeitsmöglichkeiten mit Oral History ausmachen" ("Plädoyer für Oral History," in von Ungern-Sternberg and Reinau, *Vergangenheit*, 348).

[67] Excerpts of the most influential writings by scholars in the field have been collected by Robert Perks and Alistair Thomson, eds., *The Oral History Reader* (London: Routledge, 1998).

[68] Paul Thompson, *The Voice of the Past: Oral History* (3d ed.; New York: Oxford University Press, 2000).

[69] Ibid., 117.

[70] Ibid., 118–72.

of the speaker: the nuances of uncertainty, the humor, the pretense, or the dialectic of what has been said; the former can, if necessary, challenge the latter immediately.

The evidence of oral history is distinctive also because it is retrospective over a longer span of time. This characteristic brings the role of memory into focus. Remembering the past is a complex process of selection and discarding, with durable traces established by a chemical process. However, what is essential in oral history is the recognition that the memory process depends largely upon individual comprehension and interest. This implies that the memorizer, the informant, is of vital importance as a social and psychological being, because, as Thompson develops, memory is always subjective.[71] We may reach to the history behind the oral story by taking seriously the informant's own feelings about the past. Such attention to the uniqueness of each eyewitness account presents, of course, a problem for the historian and needs to be coupled with a sense of its representativeness by a careful method of strategic sampling. It is precisely both the uniqueness and the representativeness of each life story that is one of the deepest lessons of oral history.

In what sense then, according to Thompson, can we speak of true or false, reliable or unreliable, with respect to oral sources? The query itself might be an improper one, because it gives wrong alternatives. Thompson urges the historian "to appreciate the complexity with which reality and myth, 'objective' and 'subjective,' are inextricably mixed in all human perception of the world, both individual and collective."[72] The historian always needs to sense how a question is answered from another person's perspective. The misunderstanding comes when one attempts to see patterns from another angle, from the long-range experience of several generations rather than from that of a single lifecycle. Quoting from Alessandro Portelli's article on the peculiarities of oral history,[73] Thompson argues that so-called false and untrue statements—errors—sometimes reveal more than factually accurate accounts; the credibility of oral sources is one that takes into account not only facts but also imagination and symbolism.[74] What people imagined happened may be as crucial to history as what did happen. The oral historian is concerned with both, because the oral story and the oral history behind that story are inseparably linked.

---

[71] Ibid., 173–89.
[72] Ibid., 156–57.
[73] Alessandro Portelli, "What Makes Oral History Different," in Perks and Thomson, *Oral History Reader*, 63–74.
[74] Thompson, *Voice of the Past*, 161.

Are we then in the end left with an inextricable mixture of fact and fiction, with no means of reaching beyond subjective, imaginary, and symbolic perceptions of the world? This is not necessarily so. The discipline of oral history is not to be confused with an array of theories that denies that genuine knowledge about the past is possible. Oral history becomes oral tradition as the accounts are handed down by word of mouth to later generations; the transmission entails that this tradition, while being subject to changes and suppression, cannot be seen merely as evidence of the present. As Thompson argues (with reference to Vansina), Goody and Watt's theory of homeostasis is exaggerated as a general dogma of the relationship between a society and its tradition, because social changes often leave older variations and archaisms intact, and suppressed items usually leave traces.[75] The story, one might say, is not merely a mirror of the present time of the narrative or a window to the author's time and situation; it reveals a historical, diachronic intertexture, being a flickering reflection of what happened before history became story.

We are also not left with a mere reproduction of the oral sources, according to Thompson. A complete absence of the wider historical perspectives of an experienced historian "will lead to the creation of one-dimensional historical myths rather than to a deeper social understanding."[76] In the chapter entitled "Interpretation: The Making of History," Thompson sets out to explain more fully how to make history from oral sources.[77] The historian is faced with the choice of putting together oral history through a single life-story narrative (which might be full of significant memories), through a collection of eyewitness accounts around a theme, or through a cross-analysis with ensuing arguments; sometimes a combination of all three is preferable. In addition, the sources have to be evaluated in view of their subjective biases. One assesses the internal consistency of the interview, cross-checks with other sources, and places the evidence in a wider social context. The historian examines the interview as a genre that imposes its own conventions and constraints on the speakers and thus looks at it as both a form of discourse and of testimony.

The basic ideology of oral history is thus a move from below; it represents a fundamental concern to liberate the oral evidence of witnesses of every variety from the powerful structures of professional paradigms. The oral historian is not in essence someone who holds a monopoly over interpretation but, in the words of Ronald J. Grele, is "someone who cares

---

[75] Ibid., 170.
[76] Ibid., 211–12.
[77] Ibid., 265–308.

about the pastness of the past ... [and] ... involves members of the public in the creation of their own history."[78]

The oral-history approach redefines how history is written and learned in a way that comes close to the basic concerns of sociorhetorical interpretation.[79] It reminds us of Herodotus's own realization: the bare facts of history are inextricably embedded within various forms of discourses about the past. Moreover, since these retrospective discourses are oral, they are also social and rhetorical. The truth of history resides in a matrix where the present and the past interact through various social and rhetorical mechanisms. By focusing on the actors of history themselves, oral history takes seriously the social aspects of any attempt to communicate something about the past. By being profoundly attentive to the oral dimension of communication, it provides an agenda for appreciating the rhetorical aspects of stories about the past. The two aspects are closely intertwined because the rhetorical features usually depend upon the social circumstances of the informant. Oral texts are sociorhetorical texts. To the extent that sociorhetorical criticism is regarded as a forum for meaningful dialogue between practices of interpretation that are often separated from one another, the oral history approach holds promise for modifying the historical-critical paradigm in a way that makes such a dialogue constructive.[80]

A MIDDLE WAY

My intention in this essay was to present a model of historical interpretation that avoids the scholarly antithesis between history and story and to bring out some suggestions for understanding the synthesis of diachronic and synchronic elements in Acts. I have used the "we" passages as a case study, arguing that they exhibit an intrinsic diachronic character

---

[78] Ronald J. Grele, *Envelopes of Sound: The Art of Oral History* (2d ed.; Chicago: Precedent, 1985), vii–viii.

[79] In Robbins's sociorhetorical mode of analysis and interpretation, historical intertexture "challenges traditional historical criticism on its own turf" (Robbins, *Tapestry of Early Christian Discourse,* 120).

[80] This is a critique not only of some historical-critical dogmas but also of some recent efforts toward alternative methodological and hermeneutical theories and practices. I am skeptical of many of the critiques against historical studies that have been brought out in recent years because they rarely define the points of debate and often neglect to relate constructively to previous paradigms of research. If a scholar working with ordinary philological and historical methods is to define her or his way of proceeding, one finds in fact numerous points of agreement. See, e.g., Martin Hengel, "Problems of a History of Earliest Christianity," *Bib* 78 (1997): 131–44, esp. 132–36, 143–44.

indicative of a source that was reoralized and integrated into sociorhetorical discourses. I have suggested that such features should be analyzed within the sociocultural framework of interaction between past and present in oral texts and that they can be adequately comprehended within the theoretical framework of oral history as related to the notion of a text's sociorhetorical intertexture. Just as a modern writing of history integrates the social and rhetorical dimensions of interviews and oral reports into its textual web, so the "we" passages in Acts reflect a process of reoralization and narrativization of the past and make the writing persuasive by providing it with a forceful diachronic rhetoric.

In conclusion, it might be important to place the Lukan synthesis within a broader context. When the author of Luke-Acts set out to explain his compositional enterprise in the prologue of the Gospel (Luke 1:1–4), his stated ambition is not far from that of an oral historian. He wished to create another story (διήγησις) concerning things of the past that had been fulfilled among him and his contemporaries (τῶν πεπληροφορημένων ἐν ἡμῖν πραγμάτων). This programmatic statement of interaction between a coherent story and the history of the past attaches a significant role to the oral medium of communication (καθὼς παρέδοσαν ἡμῖν), to eyewitnesses who had been or became actively involved in the events themselves (οἱ ἀπ' ἀρχῆς αὐτόπται καὶ ὑπηρέται γενόμενοι τοῦ λόγου), and to the means by which the author had been investigating or following everything closely (παρηκολουθηκότι ἄνωθεν πᾶσιν ἀκριβῶς).[81] One should not, in my view, empty the prologue's significance by referring to its conventional character, because conventional formulae and modes of expression might indeed serve an author's specific idea of certain matters and reflect the actual course of events. Whatever opinion we hold on pre-Lukan sources and traditions, the author evidently holds a view that is close to central concerns of the oral-history approach and that seems to agree with the complex synthesis of diachronic and synchronic elements in the "we" passages.

The prologue shares in a larger cultural discourse about how to relate to the past. The pre-Socratic philosopher Heraclitus once said that "eyes are surer witnesses than ears,"[82] and several ancient historians were emphatic

---

[81] I cannot here discuss all the ramifications of these expressions. The standard work is Loveday Alexander, *The Preface to Luke's Gospel: Literary Convention and Social Context in Luke 1.1–4 and Acts 1.1* (SNTSMS 78; Cambridge: Cambridge University Press, 1993). See also the contributions in David P. Moessner, ed., *Jesus and the Heritage of Israel: Luke's Narrative Claim upon Israel's Legacy* (Harrisburg, Pa.: Trinity Press International, 1999), 9–123.

[82] Hermann Diels and Walther Kranz, eds., *Die Fragmente der Vorsokratiker: Griechisch und Deutsch* (6th ed.; 2 vols.; Zürich: Weidmann, 1992 [=1951–52]), 22B frag. 101a. Also in Charles H. Kahn, *The Art and Thought of Heraclitus* (Cambridge:

on the value of eyewitness testimony.⁸³ Just like Herodotus, Thucydides, and Polybius, these writers might refer to it as an essential means of historical inquiry, being aware of the need for careful interrogation and critical judgment; or, just like Ephorus, Theopompus, and other historians influenced by the rhetorical tradition of Isocrates, they might employ it as a means of winning the confidence of the audience.⁸⁴ There emerges in all this an unresolved tension between the desire to reach back to the past and the various social and rhetorical interests of the eyewitness as well as the authors of the writings. Past history becomes present in the form of mental and verbal discourses; it is, in a sense, a social product, possession, and tool. The author of Luke-Acts and the ancient historians reveal that cultural discourses about the past, whether from an eyewitness or a writing historian, were essentially retrospective sociorhetorical discourses.

It is essential to realize that interpretation is part and parcel of the notion of oral history and *autopsia*. The very moment of observation itself is a moment of interpretation.⁸⁵ It is not by accident, then, that οἶδα, "I know," essentially means "I have seen." Heraclitus, who was the first to speak of the value of personal observation, realized that "eyes and ears are poor witnesses for human beings having barbarian souls,"⁸⁶ indicating that direct vision and hearing need the rational thought of the educated soul.⁸⁷ Plato and Aristotle elaborate this philosophical understanding of sight.⁸⁸ Eyewitnesses were thus as much interpreters as they were observers.

As modern oral historians know so well, the interview situation further develops the inextricable blend of the events of the past on the one hand and interpretative frameworks of the people involved on the other. Polybius, who was critical of sensational kinds of history writing and was committed to historical truth, is perfectly aware that each historian has a

---

Cambridge University Press, 1979), frag. 15. A similar view is expressed elsewhere by Heraclitus: "Whatever [comes from] sight, hearing, learning from experience: this I prefer" (Diels and Kranz, *Fragmente der Vorsokratiker*, 22B frag. 55; see also Kahn, *Art and Thought of Heraclitus*, frag. 14).

⁸³ Heraclitus's statement is actually known to us from Polybius. Criticizing Timaeus for neglecting *autopsia*, Polybius quotes it in 12.27.1 under Heraclitus's name.

⁸⁴ For references, see Byrskog, *Story as History*, 48–65, 93–99, 214–23.

⁸⁵ Kelber has written an appreciative review of my position but wonders if we, according to my view, ought not "to believe in innocent eyes, ears, and pens after all" (*JR* 82 [2002]: 271). I answer with an emphatic no, adding that interpretation—we sometimes call it faith—is not necessarily opposed to history in its pastness.

⁸⁶ Diels and Kranz, *Fragmente der Vorsokratiker*, 22B frg. 107.

⁸⁷ So Kahn, *Art and Thought of Heraclitus*, 107.

⁸⁸ Byrskog, *Story as History*, 146–49.

case to argue. Therefore, as he describes how the interrogation of an eyewitness is to proceed, he focuses on the historian's active role in the process.[89] "The inquirer," he says, "contributes to the narrative no less than the informants" (12.28a.9). Thereby he implies that the inquirer must guide the memory of the eyewitness; this guiding is done by persons with viewpoints formed by their own personal experiences and who do not let the informant merely drift along at the mercy of a train of associations.[90] The inquirer's interpretative frame of mind becomes a significant factor as soon as she or he tries to reach back to the past.

The potentials of the Lukan prologue lie within a profound rethinking of the larger historical intertexture as it relates to the early Christian use of sources and tradition, as well as to redaction and composition as some kind of narrative performance. Robbins speaks of "recitation composition," focusing on how an ancient writer perceived an antecedent oral or written text as a performance and how a new performance perpetuated as much or as little verbatim wording as was congenial to the writer.[91] By contrast, I have employed here the notion of reoralization as defined by Margaret A. Mills,[92] which in this context describes the perpetual return to oral currency in early Christian texts. These labels cover partly different things, but both can be used as a means to understand various aspects of the growth and development of early Christian tradition. Whatever label or combination of labels we prefer, it is clear that the Lukan prologue, being a substantial introduction to the Lukan fiction as well as a social product, possession, and tool, integrates the historical intertexture within the fiction

---

[89] See Guido Schepens, "Some Aspects of Source Theory in Greek Historiography," *Ancient Society* 6 (1975): 257–74, esp. 262–65.

[90] For the sense of this passage, see Frank W. Walbank, *A Historical Commentary on Polybius* (3 vols.; Oxford: Clarendon, 1957–79), 2:412; idem, *Polybius* (Sather Classical Lectures 42; Berkeley and Los Angeles: University of California Press, 1972), 74 n. 30.

[91] Vernon K. Robbins, "Writing as a Rhetorical Act in Plutarch and the Gospels," in *Persuasive Artistry: Studies in New Testament Rhetoric in Honor of George A. Kennedy* (ed. D. F. Watson; JSNTSup 50; Sheffield: Sheffield Academic Press, 1991), 142–68; idem, "Oral, Rhetorical, and Literary Cultures: A Response," *Semeia* 65 (1994): 75–91.

[92] Margaret A. Mills, "Domains of Folkloristic Concern: The Interpretation of Scriptures," in *Text and Tradition: The Hebrew Bible and Folklore* (ed. S. Niditch; SemeiaSt; Atlanta: Scholars Press, 1990), 231–41. I have made use of this approach previously in Samuel Byrskog, *Jesus the Only Teacher: Didactic Authority and Transmission in Ancient Israel, Ancient Judaism and the Matthean Community* (ConBNT 24; Stockholm: Almqvist & Wiksell, 1994), 341–49; and idem, *Story as History*, 16, 138–44, 254–55, 301.

of the narrative, thus betraying an explicit sensitivity to the diachronic dimension of the story. Regardless of whether the Gospel and Acts were conceived from the start as a single work,[93] which I tend to believe,[94] the beginning of Acts presents itself as a continuation of the story begun in the Gospel. Hence, the two-volume writing, which eventually emerges as a coherent διήγησις about the past, was for the author deeply embedded within the matrix of the social circumstances of people seeking to pursue certain interests by reference to what had happened.

Perhaps there is thus a middle way between Acts as story and as history. As a close study of the "we" passages indicates, and as the notion of the oral text and the oral-history approach suggests, it is essential that scholars exploring the literary and narrative dimension of Acts avoid the pitfall of methodological purism. This essay suggests that instead of aiming only to establish coherent patterns of synchrony within the writing, scholars working with a writing such as Acts also need to pay full attention to its literary and narrative irregularities and oddities. By the same token, scholars seeking out the history behind the writing will not appreciate the complexities of how the past is communicated unless they take seriously the dynamic process of reoralization and narrativization, realizing that the sources are sociorhetorical entities entering into Acts as new narrative configurations. As it seems, we need both history and story in order to appreciate fully the colorful threads of the textual tapestry we call the book of Acts.

---

[93] See Loveday Alexander, "The Preface to Acts and the Historians," in Witherington, *History, Literature, and Society*, 73–103; and idem, "Reading Luke-Acts from Back to Front," in *The Unity of Luke-Acts* (ed. J. Verheyden; BETL 142; Leuven: Leuven University Press, 1999), 419–46.

[94] See Byrskog, *Story as History*, 228–29.

The Jerusalem Community in Acts: Mythmaking and the Sociorhetorical Functions of a Lukan Setting

Milton Moreland

The book of Acts is a powerful and successful story of Christian origins. Its persuasive power is best illustrated in the simple fact that for nearly two millennia it has been considered to be a true account of the spread of earliest Christianity from Jerusalem to the rest of the world.[1] Christianity, however, did not begin in Jerusalem. At the very least, knowing what we do about the diversity of earliest Christianity, it is reasonable to claim that, at the end of the first century, many expressions of this movement would not have automatically traced their individual communities' etiologies back to the city of Jerusalem.[2] Like so much of the content of Luke-Acts, the choice of Jerusalem as the setting at the opening of Acts demonstrates Lukan intentionality.[3] The author could have selected Capernaum in

---

[1] Ron Cameron, "Alternative Beginnings—Different Ends: Eusebius, Thomas and the Construction of Christian Origins," in *Religious Propaganda and Missionary Competition in the New Testament World: Essays Honoring Dieter Georgi* (ed. L. Bormann et al.; NovTSup 74; Leiden: Brill, 1994), 501–25.

[2] This observation was made earlier by Frederick J. Foakes-Jackson and Kirsopp Lake, editors of the monumental study on Luke-Acts, *The Beginnings of Christianity* (1920–33). They concluded that Luke-Acts was clearly not acceptable to all Christian communities. Thus, their task was to find a community that could reasonably have had an affinity for Luke's theology and story of the past. They were well aware that Mark, Matthew, and Paul, for example, did not agree with Luke-Acts; it was difficult, therefore, to imagine these texts arising in the same type of Christian community. Their thesis supports the idea that Luke-Acts was a product of a specific community with specific reasons for constructing the past in the fashion it was in the two volumes. In particular, see Frederick J. Foakes-Jackson and Kirsopp Lake, "The Internal Evidence of Acts," in *The Beginnings of Christianity: The Acts of the Apostles* (ed. F. J. Foakes-Jackson and K. Lake; 5 vols; London: Macmillan, 1920–33; repr., Grand Rapids: Baker, 1979), 2:121–204, esp. 196–99.

[3] Following scholarly convention, I use the name "Luke" throughout this essay for the anonymous author of Luke-Acts, holding to the ancient tradition of

Galilee, Antioch, Damascus, or any number of other places as his key location for Christian beginnings, but he clearly and purposely chose Jerusalem. Knowing about this intentional selection should prompt us to formulate a set of questions regarding the intentions of the writer, both as an author who was writing for a particular community of early Christians in the process of social formation and as one who understood the rhetorical power of ancient literary production. For instance, we may query why Luke was interested in creating an idealized narrative picture of a Christian community in Jerusalem in the first place. What did the author gain by creating this story and linking his early Christian group to the setting of Jerusalem? What social function did this literary production have for what was probably a predominantly Gentile community of readers/hearers? Why did Luke's story of origins end at least thirty years prior to its date of authorship?

In the history of scholarship on Luke-Acts there are numerous answers to these and other questions related to the gap between the narrative world and the actual world of Luke. In an earlier work, I attempted to analyze many of these explanations and contributed what might be classified as a sociorhetorical approach to the topic. With particular interest in Luke's narrative and ideological use of Jerusalem, I illustrated the extent to which Jerusalem was tied to his ideological *topoi* of virtuous living, righteousness, and kingship; his narrative scheme of promise and fulfillment; his idea of the persecuted prophet; his eschatological outlook; and his general desire to link his community to the Jewish epic.[4] Drawing from and expanding on that foundation, this present study is interested in the ways literary and sociological comparisons of Acts with other Greco-Roman texts and communities help explain why Luke's story, particularly his focus on Jerusalem as the center of Christian origins in the beginning of Acts, may have made sense to an audience of Gentile and Jewish Christians at the end of the first century. Furthermore, my current focus is on the social functions that narrative etiologies such as Acts accomplish in new religious movements.

This essay is divided into three sections. First, the goals and achievements of comparing Acts to other ancient literature is assessed briefly in order to illustrate the need to focus more attention on the equally important task of relating the function of Acts to other mythmaking enterprises occurring in contemporaneous early Roman groups. The second section explores several avenues that might lead to a more socially coherent, interdisciplinary approach to Acts. This approach involves strategies for thinking

---

attribution without linking this figure to any person known from other early Christian texts.

[4] Milton Moreland, "Jerusalem Imagined: Rethinking Earliest Christian Claims to the Hebrew Epic" (Ph.D. diss., Claremont Graduate University, 1999).

about Acts as part of the mythmaking process that occurs in the course of social formation. In the third and final section, I examine briefly the first six chapters of Acts through the comparative lenses of rhetorical strategies and sociological formation processes in order to explain more fully Luke's choice of Jerusalem as the focus of his literary etiological project.

ACTS AND OTHER ANCIENT LITERARY PRODUCTIONS

The social and the rhetorical components of sociorhetorical criticism are similar to the principle of the compound, achromatic lens in the field of optics. The social lens of anthropological and sociological analysis and postmodern criticism is combined with the rhetorical lens of literary, redaction, and narrative criticisms in order to produce a clearer picture of an ancient text and community. In many respects, the quest to understand the genre of Acts fits well with this sociorhetorical enterprise. Comparing Acts to other ancient literary projects, especially ancient historiography, has resulted in a better understanding of both the rhetorical components of the text and the social setting in which it was written and received. Already at the beginning of the twentieth century we can observe a scholarly interest in the process of comparing Acts to Greek and Jewish historiography. Following the methods of Henry J. Cadbury and Martin Dibelius, comparing Acts to other ancient literary productions has become a standard practice for New Testament scholars interested in the style, content, purpose, social-historical setting, and genre of the Lukan narrative. This tendency to compare Acts with other ancient texts is interesting and worthy of reflection in order to understand the successes and the shortcomings of the method.

Literary comparisons have been helpful for several reasons. They have clarified, for instance, that Acts is not unique. Comparing Acts to works of historiography, biography, *apologia,* ancient novels, or Greco-Roman epics has illustrated that the author was engaged in something quite ordinary and understandable within his sociocultural context. Acts fits rather well within the parameters of typical ancient literary production. Additionally, these comparisons have shown the extent to which the author was familiar with the literature and rhetorical techniques of his era.[5] Even if one

---

[5] Recent surveys of scholarship on the genre of Luke and Acts include Todd Penner, "In Praise of Christian Origins: Stephen and the Hellenists in Lukan Apologetic Historiography" (Ph.D. diss., Emory University, 2000), 1–13; Richard I. Pervo, "Israel's Heritage and Claims upon the Genre(s) of Luke and Acts: The Problems of a History," in *Jesus and the Heritage of Israel: Luke's Narrative Claim upon Israel's Legacy* (ed. D. P. Moessner; Harrisburg, Pa.: Trinity Press International, 1999), 127–43; and Christoph Heil, "Arius Didymus and Luke-Acts," *NovT* 42 (2000): 358–93. For my purposes, the recent articles of Hubert Cancik and Walter Wilson

concludes, as I do, that no genre category perfectly fits Acts, it has become quite clear that the author of Acts could employ elements from a number of ancient literary categories.[6] The data accumulated from the many recent studies of Luke's genre make it apparent that the author used common themes, dramatic episodes, rhetorical strategies, characterizations, type-scenes, and other narrative devices, as would be expected of someone who was educated in the late first century and who was familiar with common types of Greco-Roman literature. Furthermore, as a practical result of these comparisons, scholars have not only observed many things about the text that may have gone unnoticed by earlier readers (including some explanations for seemingly enigmatic elements), but they have also been able to provide rhetorical and narrative analyses of the text that have led scholars to ask new questions about why the author wrote the way that he did. Todd Penner has summarized the result of the comparisons as follows:

> Appropriate and accurate comparison of the material in Acts with similar types of literature sharing the same literary, social and cultural context can illuminate texts that often seem opaque to the modern reader. Or, if the texts are clear at one level, such comparison may help elucidate aspects of authorial intention or particular features of a writer's work that otherwise might go unnoticed. Even particular themes, which may seem rather banal within the larger structure of an early Christian text, may be enlivened in their comparison with similar themes in contemporary

---

are also worth noting due to their interest in comparing Acts to institutional or community histories. See Hubert Cancik, "The History of Culture, Religion, and Institutions in Ancient Historiography: Philological Observations Concerning Luke's History," *JBL* 116 (1997): 673–95; and Walter T. Wilson, "Urban Legends: Acts 10:1–11:18 and the Strategies of Greco-Roman Foundation Narratives," *JBL* 120 (2001): 77–99.

[6] In general, I agree with the following assessment: "[Luke's] readers were not particular about the niceties [of genre classifications], and it is not outrageous to suspect that he was an author who regarded models as bridges that might be burned once their purposes had been fulfilled" (Richard I. Pervo, "Must Luke and Acts Belong to the Same Genre?" in *SBL Seminar Papers, 1989* [SBLSP 26; Atlanta: Scholars Press, 1989], 311). One difficulty with the modern quest for Luke's ancient genre is the problematic quality of grouping the ancient texts into categories that would have made sense to the ancient reader. Heil has recently observed that "the comparison of Luke-Acts with 'the historiography of philosophy' shows a typical dilemma of Form Criticism. If the net is cast widely and if a broad basis of texts is chosen, the number of parallels with Luke-Acts grows. If only one ancient text is compared with Luke-Acts, the formal parallels will be few (but possibly instructive nevertheless), and the discrepancies receive more attention" (Heil, "Arius Didymus and Luke-Acts," 360).

writers, highlighting elements and patterns that were important for the writer but have escaped our notice.[7]

Similarly, Marianne Palmer Bonz has stated, "genre is fundamental to interpretation. Genre provides the initial key to understanding what an author actually means by what he has written."[8] Thus, one of the primary results of literary comparisons has been to describe authorial intention and the possible ways that an ancient audience would have heard and interpreted the text.

Besides clarifying reasons why an ancient author such as Luke would have used a particular style or incorporated various episodes into his narrative, literary comparisons on a more general level have functioned to explain the potential purposes of the whole Lukan project. These comparisons have shown that Greco-Roman biographies, novels, and histories were written in order to achieve several different (not necessarily incompatible) goals. Their reasons for remembering, reinterpreting, and creating events from the past in their literary activities include reaffirmation and validation of a group or person (heritage, precedence, continuity, legitimization, as well as adoration and even deification); providing group identity (giving meaning, purpose, and value to life); guidance through models (moral instruction); enrichment (knowledge, entertainment, artistic creation); and escape from present realities. The past could also be recounted or created for negative reasons, such as to deny the validity of a group or to show the problems with the past in order to press for a different path in the future.[9] Clearly, several of these reasons dovetail with ancient sociopolitical motivations for literary production.[10] Authors related

---

[7] Penner, "In Praise of Christian Origins," 107.

[8] Marianne Palmer Bonz, *The Past as Legacy: Luke-Acts and Ancient Epic* (Minneapolis: Fortress, 2000), 183. Similarly, Walter Wilson describes one of the primary outcomes of comparing Luke to urban foundation narratives as follows: "Comparative analysis of these literary themes and strategies helps illumine both the expectations Greco-Roman readers would have had for stories about communal origins and how Luke interacts with these expectations in recognizable though creative ways" (Wilson, "Urban Legends," 98).

[9] The terminology for this list is derived from David Lowenthal, *The Past Is a Foreign Country* (Cambridge: Cambridge University Press, 1985), 35–73.

[10] See the study of ancient political rhetoric in Jane DeRose Evans, *The Art of Persuasion: Political Propaganda from Aeneas to Brutus* (Ann Arbor: University of Michigan Press, 1992). On ancient epic as being politically motivated, see Nicholas M. Horsfall, "Virgil, History and the Roman Tradition," *Prudentia* 8 (1976): 73–89; Page duBois, *History, Rhetorical Description and the Epic: From Homer to Spenser* (Cambridge: Brewer, 1982), 28–51; and David Quint, *Epic and Empire: Politics and*

to or writing for dominant groups created stories of the past that legitimized their present power structures.[11] Professional authors under the auspices of the empire wrote most Greco-Roman histories, epics, and biographies.[12] Wealthy sponsors of this Greco-Roman literature considered flattery and malice to be of particular concern, both equally distorting the perceived goals of their literary investments.[13] Similarly, Arnaldo Momigliano characterized the desire for biography among Greek and Roman kings and politicians as "an instrument of self assertion and self defense."[14] The idea

---

Generic Form from Virgil to Milton (Princeton: Princeton University Press, 1993), 21–96.

[11] On the poet-patron relationship that is central to the discussion of motivation and method of Greco-Roman historiography, see Peter White, "*Amicitia* and the Profession of Poetry in Early Imperial Rome," *JRS* 68 (1978): 50–66; idem, "Positions for Poets in Early Imperial Rome," in *Literary and Artistic Patronage in Ancient Rome* (ed. B. Gold; Austin: University of Texas Press, 1982), 50–66; Gordon Williams, "Phases in Political Patronage of Literature in Rome," in Gold, *Literary and Artistic Patronage*, 3–27; and Richard P. Saller, *Personal Patronage under the Early Empire* (Cambridge: Cambridge University Press, 1982).

[12] On the ancient historians' use of history as national or ethnic propaganda, see Charles W. Fornara, *The Nature of History in Ancient Greece and Rome* (Berkeley and Los Angeles: University of California Press, 1983). Useful studies of propaganda in Herodotus and Thucydides are Virginia J. Hunter, *Past and Process in Herodotus and Thucydides* (Princeton: Princeton University Press, 1982); idem, *Thucydides: The Artful Reporter* (Toronto: University of Toronto Press, 1993). Outside of Greece, the major propagandistic historians of whom we know are Hecataeus of Abdera, whose *History of Egypt* was the model for Manetho's *History of Egypt,* and Berossus, who produced the *History of Babylonia.* Edith Hall's informative study of the Greek literature outside of the generically defined histories is also useful in pointing out the propaganda of the Greeks. See Edith Hall, *Inventing the Barbarian: Greek Self-Definition through Tragedy* (New York: Oxford University Press, 1991). Within the Roman tradition, Livy is a good example of a propagandistic, patriotic historian. See further, Thomas A. Dorey, ed., *Livy* (London: Routledge, 1971).

[13] In the treatise *How to Write History,* Lucian stresses the importance of seeking the truth in a useful way, while admitting that most of the contemporary histories are full of flattery and exaggeration. Timothy P. Wiseman's studies of Greco-Roman histories describe a number of similar reasons motivating historical composition in the ancient world (*Clio's Cosmetics: Three Studies in Greco-Roman Literature* [Leicester: Leicester University Press, 1979]). On the Roman nobles' claims of descent from mythological heroes, see Timothy P. Wiseman, "Legendary Genealogies in Late Republican Rome," *Greece and Rome* 21 (1974): 153–63.

[14] Arnaldo Momigliano, *The Development of Greek Biography* (exp. ed.; Cambridge: Harvard University Press, 1993), 103. A statement by Josephus related to this point is worth noting: "Many have written the history of Nero. Some have been favourable to him, careless of the truth because he benefited them. Others, out of

that histories were written to stimulate patriotism is closely related to this idea. The second-century B.C.E. historian Asellio, preserved only in fragments, argued that histories should "make men readier to defend their country and avoid wrong-doing."[15] Many of the comparable literary projects from the Greco-Roman world were conceived by competing political and social groups that wished to legitimize their efforts.[16]

Regarding the way that literature was used for moral instruction, the fact that many Greco-Roman authors wrote in order to illustrate virtue has become a valuable reference point for scholars interested in Acts. Richard Buxton has shown that one of the primary functions of writing about the past was to provide moral instruction, a phenomenon summed up in the term *paradeigmata* (i.e., the exemplars to be followed).[17] The connection between rhetoric and historiography is important in this regard. Those who wrote history were trained as rhetoricians.[18] The forensic, deliberative, and epideictic types of rhetoric (the three categories given by Aristotle) were all useful to the historian, who had to find the appropriate styles and arguments for many different situations and audiences. In order to stress the

---

hatred and hostility towards him, have behaved like shameless drunkards in their lies, and deserve condemnation for it. I am not surprised at those who have lied about Nero, since even in their accounts of events before his time they have not preserved the truth of history" (*Ant.* 20.154–55).

[15] Quoted by Timothy P. Wiseman in "Practice and Theory in Roman Historiography," *History* 66 (1981): 379.

[16] The sociopolitically motivated, rhetorically written accounts of history from the Greco-Roman world suggest a clear correspondence with the motivations of many Jewish authors of the same period. For instance, 1 Maccabees is a defense of the Hasmonean dynasty, and, more generally, Josephus's *Antiquities of the Jews* is a history that defends the traditions and heritage of the Jews. On Josephus's idea of historiography, especially as it is revealed in his *Against Apion,* see Shaye J. D. Cohen, "History and Historiography in the *Against Apion* of Josephus," *History and Theory* 27 (1988): 1–11. Besides the Maccabean literature and Josephus, other propagandistic Jewish historians were Artapanus, Eupolemus, and Pseudo-Eupolemus. On the extent to which they created and defended the Jewish traditions, see Erich S. Gruen, *Heritage and Hellenism: The Reinvention of Jewish Tradition* (Hellenistic Culture and Society 30; Berkeley and Los Angeles: University of California Press, 1998), esp. 137–60.

[17] Richard Buxton, *Imaginary Greece: The Contexts of Mythology* (Cambridge: Cambridge University Press, 1994), esp. 169–81.

[18] The connection between classical education, centered on rhetoric, and historiography is well illustrated by Anthony J. Woodman, *Rhetoric in Classical Historiography: Four Studies* (London: Croom Helm, 1988); and Kenneth S. Sacks, "Rhetoric and Speeches in Hellenistic Historiography," *Athenaeum* 64 (1986): 383–95.

cultural values of the Greco-Roman world through glorifying, eulogizing, shaming, or refuting their characters, the historians used the skills learned in their rhetorical training.[19] As James Luce observed, "History ... can lead to moral improvement; it was on its way to becoming 'philosophy teaching by examples,' which was a popular definition in the Roman period."[20] For scholars interested in the Lukan corpus, two of the most obvious examples of writing literature in order to teach virtue are the second-century B.C.E. historian Polybius,[21] and Plutarch, who is roughly contemporary with Luke (ca. 45–125 C.E.).[22]

In order to illustrate how the development of the theme of virtuous living was important to Luke, several observations by Halvor Moxnes are worth mentioning. Moxnes observes that one of the major images of Jesus and the apostles in Luke's story is their presentation as benefactors or patrons.[23] Luke stresses the virtuous qualities of his protagonists as these

---

[19] On the moral purposes of Greco-Roman literature, see T. James Luce, *The Greek Historians* (London: Routledge, 1997), 113–15. The following summary by Stanley F. Bonner (*Education in Ancient Rome: From the Elder Cato to the Younger Pliny* [Berkeley and Los Angeles: University of California Press, 1977], 87) is informative: "No less important to the orator was that part of the philosophical territory which formed the province of ethics. In every branch of his art, whether he was delivering a panegyric or an invective, or urging or deprecating some political measure, or justifying a client's action, or establishing or defaming a man's character, or maintaining the principle of equity—in all this, the orator had to have moral arguments at his command. He must be prepared to speak on virtue and vice, on right and wrong; he must, as the occasion demands, have something to say on piety and patriotics, on duty neglected or fulfilled, on the manifold effects of human emotions."

[20] Luce, *Greek Historians*, 116.

[21] See the analysis of Arthur M. Eckstein, *Moral Vision in the Histories of Polybius* (Berkeley and Los Angeles: University of California Press, 1994); and the comparison of Polybius and Luke in Garry W. Trompf, *The Idea of Historical Recurrence in Western Thought: From Antiquity to the Reformation* (Berkeley and Los Angeles: University of California Press, 1979).

[22] On Plutarch as a historian, see Alan Wardman, *Plutarch's Lives* (Berkeley and Los Angeles: University of California Press, 1974); and Christopher P. Jones, *Plutarch and Rome* (Oxford: Oxford University Press, 1971). More particularly, on Plutarch's literary picture of Alexander, see the detailed introduction in James R. Hamilton, *Plutarch: Alexander; A Commentary* (Oxford: Clarendon, 1969), xiii–lxix; and Vernon K. Robbins, "Laudation Stories in the Gospel of Luke and Plutarch's *Alexander*," *SBL Seminar Papers, 1981* (SBLSP 20; Chico, Calif.: Scholars Press), 293–308.

[23] Halvor Moxnes, *The Economy of the Kingdom: Social Conflict and Economic Relations in Luke's Gospel* (Philadelphia: Fortress, 1988); and idem, "Patron-Client

were defined and understood in a society based on the patron-client relationship. On the other hand, according to Moxnes, Luke developed a characterization of the Pharisees that illustrated the abuse of power that was possible in the patronage system. Thus, Luke's picture of first-century Palestine was built upon the value system that his Greco-Roman audience understood, thereby producing a value-laden message.

Finally, one might ask if comparing Acts to other literature from the Greco-Roman era can help clarify the issue of whether or not Acts is historically reliable. Richard Pervo has suggested that "[o]ne can learn very little about the accuracy of a text from its implicit or explicit genre."[24] Regardless of whether Acts is situated within the genre of historiography, novel, epic, or biography, I agree with his conclusion: we learn very little about its historical reliability as a result of such positioning. None of the authors writing in any of the ancient genre categories would consider our modern concept of historical fact to be an important criterion. One might expect that the category of historiography was an exception, but as Penner has illustrated in his comparison of Acts to Greco-Roman *historia*, by categorizing Acts as ancient historiography we have moved no closer to discovering the hard-core facts of earliest Christian history.[25] It is not possible to identify certain elements in Luke's text as historical and others as part of Luke's theological interests. The modern "distinction between Luke the historian and Luke the theologian" is just that, modern. Penner states, "in Luke's literary environment there is no separation between historian and theologian ... [and] it is very difficult, if not impossible, to move

---

Relations and the New Community in Luke-Acts," in *The Social World of Luke-Acts: Models for Interpretation* (ed. J. Neyrey; Peabody, Mass.: Hendrickson, 1991), 241–68. See also Richard Rohrbaugh, "The Pre-industrial City in Luke-Acts: Urban Social Relations," in Neyrey, *Social World of Luke-Acts*, 125–50, who expresses a similar concern with respect to the patronage system. The motif of honor and shame in Luke-Acts has been aptly illustrated by Bruce Malina and Jerome Neyrey, "Honor and Shame in Luke-Acts: Pivotal Values of the Mediterranean World," in Neyrey, *Social World of Luke-Acts*, 25–65. Additionally, on the topic of virtues in Luke-Acts, see Marie-Eloise Rosenblatt, "Under Interrogation: Paul as Witness in Juridical Contexts in Acts and the Implied Spirituality for Luke's Community" (Ph.D. diss., Graduate Theological Union, 1987); Vernon K. Robbins, "Socio-Rhetorical Criticism: Mary, Elizabeth and the Magnificat as a Test Case," in *The New Literary Criticism and the New Testament* (ed. E. V. McKnight and E. Struthers Malbon; Valley Forge, Pa.: Trinity Press International, 1994), 164–209; John York, *The Last Shall Be First: The Rhetoric of Reversal in Luke* (JSNTSup 46; Sheffield: Sheffield Academic Press, 1991); and Penner, "In Praise of Christian Origins," 445–572.

[24] Pervo, "Israel's Heritage," 129.

[25] Penner, "In Praise of Christian Origins," particularly ch. 3: "Writing Hellenistic History: Identity, Rhetoric, and the Persuasive Narrative," 192–386

beyond the framework, order, characterization, and style of the narrative to a concrete bedrock of assured reliable and verifiable data. The very understanding and practice of writing history in Luke's day would seem to bear this out."[26]

Histories, epics, biographies, and novels were written for many reasons, but it is quite clear that the goal of providing a historically reliable account (in the modern sense) was not an ancient objective. Erich Gruen has recently observed this emphasis in the Jewish literature of the period.[27] The extent to which Jewish historians in the Greco-Roman world invented, adapted, molded, and embellished the Jewish tradition corresponds to what has been observed in the literary productions of authors such as Polybius and Plutarch. In view of these recent studies, I would contend that, when considering the historical accuracy of Acts, the burden of proof is on those who claim Luke intended to provide his readers with the brute facts of earliest Christian history.

While this brief summary of the positive conclusions derived from the growing corpus of literary comparisons does not do justice to the details of the discussion, it should be sufficient to show the general trail that has been blazed in the genre debate. These comparisons have led to a greater critical appreciation of Luke's style, content choices, characterizations, purposes in writing, depiction of moral themes, and interest (or lack thereof) in actually presenting a historically reliable story.

However, the hard work of comparing Acts to other ancient literature can only take us so far along the path of understanding all the reasons that the story was written. One of the potential shortfalls of the genre debate is the lack of attention directed to the social formation processes in which the author of Luke-Acts was a participant. One (unfortunate) possibility when considering the genre of Acts is that scholars begin to imagine the author as a man of leisure, a literary figure who had the ability to take it upon himself to write out the origins of the Christian religion. Clearly the author of Acts was in some respects a literary figure: he was well educated, possessed significant literary skill, and had the financial security that afforded time to write. However, comparing Luke to figures such as Vergil, Plutarch, Polybius, or Cicero may have the (unintentional) effect of dulling the scholar's attentiveness to the real sociopolitical differences between the Roman professional author and an author who was deeply entrenched in the messy work of community formation through mythmaking. In other words, as a member of a new religious movement—an early Roman cult—a Christian author such as Luke was in an inherently different

---

[26] Ibid., 582, 202.
[27] Gruen, *Heritage and Hellenism,* 137–88.

situation—sociologically and politically—from that of Vergil or Cicero. At stake for Luke, then, were concerns different from those of the authors of the dominant culture, who wrote about the founding of a city, the fighting of a war, the history of an ethnic group, the history of philosophy, political history, or the biography of a historical figure. While the study of the similarities between the content and style of comparable Greco-Roman literature and Luke are no doubt informative, the essential sociopolitical and religious differences must not be obscured or forgotten.

THE MYTHMAKING PROCESS IN SOCIAL FORMATION

ACTS IN COMPARATIVE PERSPECTIVE

Rather than assuming Luke to have been a historian writing for a widespread, unspecified audience of Christians, it is more likely that Acts was written as an etiology for a particular community with specific social, economic, and political concerns. Luke was associated with a specific group that espoused a very particular type of Christianity. My basic premise is that at the time Acts was written there was no unified Christian phenomenon in existence for which the author could have been writing. Thus, it is anachronistic to assume that Luke made a general apology for Christianity such as Josephus made for Judaism. Acts could be considered apologetic, but only for a particular expression of Christianity. Not until the end of the second century, when it was taken up by Irenaeus as a way to counter gnostic tendencies in some forms of Christianity, do we have significant evidence that the story of Acts was favorably received by a wider Christian audience.[28] As is becoming increasingly acknowledged by scholars of Christian origins, we cannot simply reconstruct the context of Luke's literary project by interjecting it into the picture of Christian origins that Luke himself created.[29] Luke's desire to picture Christianity as a unitary movement, his characterizations of the early Christian leaders, his settings, and his descriptions of Christian groups stemming from Jerusalem should not routinely be used as the backdrop for assessing the narrative of Acts.

As has become clear within the burgeoning area of sociorhetorical criticism, in order to develop a complete picture of the Lukan setting and purpose, scholars need to include nonliterary comparisons in their data pool. Thus, an interest in sociological and anthropological correspondences between the social, political, and economic dynamics of early

---

[28] See Ernst Haenchen, *The Acts of the Apostles: A Commentary* (trans. B. Noble et al.; Philadelphia: Westminster, 1971), 9; and Cameron, "Alternative Beginnings."

[29] As Christopher Mount has recently demonstrated in *Pauline Christianity: Luke-Acts and the Legacy of Paul* (NovTSup 104; Leiden: Brill, 2002).

Christian groups and other Roman religious movements, schools, and voluntary associations is important for the process of describing the context and purpose of Acts. Additionally, comparisons with groups from similar sociopolitical and religious backgrounds from periods other than the Greco-Roman should also be considered.[30] In this light, Acts should be compared with other types of social histories that allow communities to explore and create etiologies. While the genre debate is defined primarily by its interest in literary style and content in order to discern what the author intended for the reader or how the reader might have interpreted the text, the additional interest in community formation and mythmaking forces us to expand the horizons to include detailed questions about what the potential social aims and consequences of the literary project were for the author and original audience (as well as subsequent audiences).

In my earlier study, I examined over forty-five different scholarly proposals from the past 150 years for the authorial setting of Luke-Acts.[31] Clearly this endeavor is alive and well. Many of these studies have already begun the process of accounting for the social function of the text. Since the seminal work of Philip Esler, *Community and Gospel in Luke-Acts*,[32] and the innovative studies collected by Jerome Neyrey in *The Social World of Luke-Acts*, scholars are more accustomed to thinking about Acts as fulfilling a social function for a community.[33] For instance, in his recent

---

[30] For several informative studies of how minority ethnic and religious groups in the modern world appeal to history in ways that are similar to that found in Acts, see Elizabeth Tonkin, Maryon McDonald, and Malcolm Chapman, eds., *History and Ethnicity* (ASA Monographs 27; London: Routledge, 1989). Also see Maryon McDonald, *"We Are Not French!" Language, Culture, and Identity in Brittany* (London: Routledge, 1989), who offers a detailed study of the use of the past to construct an identity in modern Brittany. Other studies of the creation of the past by oppressed or minority groups that I have found informative include Janet Hoskins, *The Play of Time: Kodi Perspectives on Calendars, History, and Exchange* (Berkeley and Los Angeles: University of California Press, 1993); A. M. Alonso, "The Effects of Truth: Re-presentations of the Past and the Imagining of Community," *Journal of Historical Sociology* 1 (1988): 33–57; Michael Herzfeld, *Ours Once More: Folklore, Ideology, and the Making of Modern Greece* (Austin: University of Texas Press, 1982); and idem, *A Place in History: Social and Monumental Time in a Cretan Town* (Princeton: Princeton University Press, 1991).

[31] Moreland, "Jerusalem Imagined," 30–126.

[32] Philip F. Esler, *Community and Gospel in Luke-Acts: The Social and Political Motivations of Lucan Theology* (SNTSMS 57; Cambridge: Cambridge University Press, 1987).

[33] In distinction from my current proposal, many of the studies in Neyrey, *Social World of Luke-Acts,* were concerned with showing the extent to which Luke's text

exemplary article in which Acts 10–11 is compared to Greco-Roman urban foundation narratives, Walter Wilson suggests that Luke and his readers would have recognized the similarities between his "literary themes and strategies" and those of other "stories about communal origins." He thus concludes,

> The similarities ... point to a shared context of cultural phenomena and the literary representation of those phenomena that could be pressed into the service of communal self-definition and apologetic. Inasmuch as Luke, like other "native" historians, participates in this context, we have further evidence of how he has Hellenized the traditions of his group's origins, shaping them in accordance with Greco-Roman conventions of storytelling in order to dramatize his movement's distinctive place in the Greco-Roman world.[34]

In order to add to this line of reasoning, I will clarify in what follows why Luke's project makes sense as part of the processes of social formation. In these preliminary reflections I suggest two areas of research that might benefit our study: (1) a continued consideration of the idea of myth as a social process; and (2) the use of recent studies of social and community formation in order to suggest a reasonable social setting for the original audience of Luke-Acts.

DEFINING MYTH AND MYTHMAKING

Of the many definitions of myth available to the modern scholar, a description by Bruce Lincoln is worth noting: "By whatever appellation they may assume, [myths] are the stories through which groups accomplish the task of sociocultural reproduction by inscribing their values and sense of shared identity on those who are their members-in-the-making so that they will come to know and remember just who they are and just where

---

can be *interpreted* better when the modern reader has an understanding of the "common, recurrent patterns of conceptualizing, perceiving, and behaving" in the Roman world. As Neyrey states in the preface to the volume, "Our goal, then, is to propose culturally appropriate scenarios for interpreting the Lukan narrative, to see and understand historical particulars within a more encompassing social framework" (xiii). In this essay I am not necessarily proposing better interpretative models for the narrative (i.e., honor-shame systems, theories of ancient personality); rather, my interest is more general: to investigate social and literary comparisons as a means of understanding the *social function* of the Lukan literary project. In this regard, the article by Vernon K. Robbins, "The Social Location of the Implied Author of Luke-Acts," in Neyrey, *Social World of Luke-Acts*, 305–32, is of greatest interest.

[34] Wilson, "Urban Legends," 98–99.

they belong."³⁵ The mythmaking process is the way that groups make sense of their current situation, since providing links from the past to the present is part of a community's inscription practice. In this way, the past is framed so as to explain the present situation. In the process, the so-called members-in-the-making learn their values and identity. Thinking of myth in this way also helps to point out the fluctuating nature of mythology. Myths are not static; they must shift as the composition and values of the group shifts. In a similar vein, Russell McCutcheon has recently observed three qualities of myth that are helpful for this current discussion of Acts:

> (1) ... myths are not special (or "sacred") but ordinary human means of fashioning and authorizing their lived-in and believed-in "worlds," (2) ... myth as an ordinary rhetorical device in social construction and maintenance makes *this* rather than *that* social identity possible in the first place and (3) ... a people's use of the label "myth" reflects, expresses, explores and legitimizes their own self-image.³⁶

Mythmaking is thus the constant social process of fashioning the ordinary into the extraordinary; we observe it in the "powerful instances where active processes have dressed up what might otherwise be mundane and forgettable historical moments as extraordinary ones."³⁷ In the process of mythmaking, a group takes the common symbols, figures, storylines, and the like and makes them important and meaningful explanations for the group's self perception and values. As such, myths are intentionally complex; they are inherently about the group, although on the surface they are about something completely different. For example, stories such as those told in Acts—etiological myths—can appear to be about the actual origins of the community. However, what we learn from a study of comparative mythology (as defined above) is that we should expect a gap between the group's setting and the narrative world it creates. Myths are not stories that perfectly reflect a group's social circumstances; rather, the disparity or gap is part of their force.³⁸ Myths

---

³⁵ Bruce Lincoln, "Mythic Narrative and Cultural Diversity in American Society," in *Myth and Method* (ed. L. L. Patton and W. Doniger; Charlottesville: University Press of Virginia, 1996), 167–68.

³⁶ Russell McCutcheon, "Myth," in *Guide to the Study of Religion* (ed. W. Braun and R. T. McCutcheon; London: Cassell, 2000), 200 (emphasis original).

³⁷ Ibid., 202.

³⁸ On the idea of the gap, see Jonathan Z. Smith, "Good News Is No News: Aretalogy and Gospel," in *Map Is Not Territory: Studies in the History of Religions* (SJLA 23; Leiden: Brill, 1978; repr., Chicago: University of Chicago Press, 1993), 206; idem, "The Bare Facts of Ritual," in *Imagining Religion: From Babylon to Jonestown*

should be understood as a group strategy for mediating and applying certain cultural symbols in order that this new application, though not a perfect fit, will make the community's experience understandable.

With these succinct comments about mythmaking in mind, several questions that might arise concerning the Lukan project can be summarized: How does one go about making the connection between the Lukan story and the Lukan community? Why would a group/author at the end of the first century be interested in investing a great deal of mental energy in the task of imagining and narrating the events that occurred approximately fifty years before in Jerusalem? Why is the story not concerned with narrating the events of the approximately thirty years that had passed since the time of Peter and Paul? An analysis of Acts within the parameters of mythmaking might help clarify these complex elements in the Lukan corpus. While not promising any definitive answers, I will attempt to follow up on these questions in the final section of this essay.

SOCIAL AND COMMUNITY FORMATION IN THE ROMAN CONTEXT

Turning now to examine the types of social formation that can be imagined for the Lukan setting, one might begin by asking what the social components of a new religious movement in the late first century would have been. If we can identify certain prevalent elements or patterns that appeared in the process of community formation in the Roman world, we should be able to compare what we find in Luke-Acts to that material in order to suggest the extent to which the Lukan literary project can be understood as mythmaking in the process of community formation. While scholars interested in Luke's genre compare the text to other ancient literary productions, scholars interested in Luke's social setting can compare the text to other mythmaking enterprises in ancient religious communities. In the following probes, two general points will be considered: (1) social and religious dislocation was a precursor to new types of social formation in the Roman world, and (2) Roman political and social control impacted all new groups. This list could be expanded, but as a preliminary illustration these two points should be sufficient.

Fortunately, for the purposes of comparison, it is quite clear that members of early Christian groups were not the only people experimenting with new types of community formation. With the publication of the collected essays entitled *Voluntary Associations in the Graeco-Roman World*, scholars of early Christianity have a new database of information about

---

(Chicago: University of Chicago Press, 1982), 53–65, esp. 56; and Jan Vansina, *Oral Tradition as History* (Madison: University of Wisconsin Press, 1985), 120–23.

Roman group formation.³⁹ Of the many intriguing observations in the essays, several stand out as particularly relevant to the study of Luke's community. Regarding the profusion of associations and groups in the early Roman period, John Kloppenborg notes,

> The reasons for the growth of such associations are not especially difficult to grasp. The ties that bound a citizen to the polis were weakened by the relative ease of travel and by the diminished influence that local inhabitants had over their own affairs. Significant dislocations of persons resulted from the establishment of trading conventicles in foreign territories, from the slave markets, and from the Roman practice of settling veterans in cities near the frontiers. Each of these forces separated individuals and groups from their *patriae* and created the need for social arrangements that would replace the older structures of the family, the deme, the tribe, and the polis.⁴⁰

Social dislocation thus appears as a major factor in the establishment and proliferation of voluntary associations in the Roman world,⁴¹ a context that makes sense when considering early Christian group formations. As Burton Mack has observed, during this period of rapid social change early Christian communities were struggling, along with many other voluntary associations, "to cultivate a social vision of human community in the face of a world held together only by the armies and political interests of the Roman imperium."⁴² Luke's desire to link his community so integrally with the traditions of the Hebrew epic makes sense within a social world where past loyalties and social structures had come into question.

---

³⁹ John S. Kloppenborg and Stephen G. Wilson, eds., *Voluntary Associations in the Graeco-Roman World* (New York: Routledge, 1996). The work of Richard S. Ascough is also informative regarding the types of social formations that early Christian communities were modeled upon: the synagogue, the philosophical school, the ancient mystery cult, and the voluntary association (*What Are They Saying about the Formation of the Pauline Churches?* [New York: Paulist, 1998]), as are the observations of Wayne Meeks regarding the formation of the *ekklēsia* (*The First Urban Christians* [New Haven: Yale University Press, 1983], 74–110).

⁴⁰ John S. Kloppenborg, "*Collegia and Thiasoi:* Issues in Function, Taxonomy and Membership," in Kloppenborg and Wilson, *Voluntary Associations,* 17–18.

⁴¹ On the use of the term *voluntary associations,* see Stephen G. Wilson, "Voluntary Associations: An Overview," in Kloppenborg and Wilson, *Voluntary Associations,* 1–15; and Sandra Walker-Ramisch, "Graeco-Roman Voluntary Associations and the Damascus Document: A Sociological Analysis," in Kloppenborg and Wilson, *Voluntary Associations,* 128–45, esp. 131–32.

⁴² Burton L. Mack, *The Christian Myth: Origins, Logic, and Legacy* (New York: Continuum, 2001), 125.

In a recent article, "The Heroic Past in a Hellenistic Present," Susan Alcock provides an interesting comparative analysis in her study of ancient cults that venerated the Homeric heroes in the small cities of the Mediterranean region. She observes that the Homeric heroes did not fade away under the shroud of the myriad other myths that were available in the Hellenistic world. In a period that was often chaotic, filled with cultures uniting in ways previously not imagined, including significant moments of political and economic turmoil, "[g]enealogy provided that longed-for sense of local history and identity, and the heroic age anchored that thread of time."[43] The Homeric heroes offered "a sense of origin and identity" for groups that may have been threatened by the idea of empire.[44] That some early Christian groups desired to link up with the heroes of the Hebrew epic is a clear parallel case of a similar socially formative mythmaking process.

Additionally, on the topic of social dislocation, it is helpful to draw attention to a recent essay by Jonathan Z. Smith, "Here, There, and Anywhere," dealing with religions in the late antique Mediterranean world. Smith categorizes ancient religions into three types, utilizing the "form of a topography": (1) the "here" of domestic religion, located primarily in the home and in burial sites; (2) the "there" of public civic and state religions, largely based in temple constructions; and (3) the "anywhere" of a rich diversity of religious formations that occupy an interstitial space between these other two loci, including a variety of religious entrepreneurs and ranging from groups we term "associations" to activities we label "magic."[45]

It is during the Hellenistic and early Roman periods that "religions of 'anywhere' rise to relative prominence, although the religions of 'here' and 'there' continue, often in revised forms."[46] As translocal associations, not tied to a particular site, state, or temple, Christian groups in the early Roman

---

[43] Susan E. Alcock, "The Heroic Past in a Hellenistic Present," in *Hellenistic Constructs: Essays in Culture, History, and Historiography* (ed. P. Cartledge et al.; Hellenistic Culture and Society 26; Berkeley and Los Angeles: University of California Press, 1997), 34.

[44] Ibid., 33. See also Rosalind Thomas, *Oral Tradition and Written Record in Classical Athens* (Cambridge Studies in Oral and Literate Culture 18; Cambridge: Cambridge University Press, 1989), esp. 173–95, who comments on the Greek desire to link up with the heroic genealogies rather than with a real family genealogy.

[45] Jonathan Z. Smith, "Here, There, and Anywhere" (paper presented at the conference "Prayer, Magic and the Stars in the Ancient and Late Antique World," University of Washington, Department of Near Eastern Languages and Civilization, 3–5 March 2000), 4. This essay will be published as "Here, There, and Anywhere," in *Prayer, Magic and the Stars in the Ancient and Late Antique World* (ed. S. Noegel et al.; Magic in History; University Park: Pennsylvania State University Press, 2003).

[46] Ibid., 14 (page references are to the unpublished paper).

imperial period fit well within the category of "anywhere." These associations attempted to replace the important functions of the now-inaccessible domestic religions (the "here") by "adapting elements more characteristic of the religions of 'there.'" Of the many significant details Smith describes, one stands out as especially relevant to this study: part of the sociological function of these associations was the restoration of a family unit (fictive kinship group) in the midst of social dislocation. These associations developed new notions of the homeplace by forming a new social location for the group members. Despite the fact that members of the new fictive kinship group addressed one another as "brothers" and "sisters," "this apparent egalitarianism stands in notable contrast to the hierarchical ordering of members, bearing an often bewildering diversity of titles, some of which echo those in the highly organized bureaucracy of the religions of 'there.'"[47] Finally, Smith notes that as part of the social formation process, rules and rituals for the members were established as contractual markers of group identity.

As a result of these comments there appears to be a clear need for scholars of Christian origins to examine our data (the texts) for examples of how the early Christian communities responded to the social dislocation prevalent in the Roman Empire. For example, Luke's interest in church offices, his claims on the ancient sacred city of Jerusalem (see below), his interest in virtuous conduct, and his concern to elaborate on the rules and rituals involved in group membership all can be understood as part of an agenda for group formation.

Wendy Cotter provides another important component of the social formation process that needs to be considered when thinking about the Lukan community: "the very real dangers in belonging to an unrecognized society during the imperial period." As we seek to understand the early Christian groups, Cotter observes the need to incorporate "the clear evidence of Roman prohibition of such societies and the constant threat of their sudden investigation and dissolution."[48] Social formation was not undemanding or risk free. New religious movements would certainly have been politically dubious and therefore carefully monitored.

Among scholars of Luke-Acts there is already a well-established tradition of considering what these stories reveal about the author's political context. Similarly, there is a long list of works that consider the relationship between Jews and Gentiles in the Lukan community. Many studies have concluded that Luke's interest in linking his group with Judaism was

---

[47] Ibid., 19. Similarly, Meeks, *First Urban Christians,* 84–103.

[48] Wendy Cotter, "The *Collegia* and Roman Law: State Restrictions on Voluntary Associations, 64 BCE–200 CE," in Kloppenborg and Wilson, *Voluntary Associations,* 88.

an attempt to gain political advantage in the eyes of the Romans.[49] It has often been noted that Luke was intentionally portraying Christianity as a virtuous religion in order to dispel concerns that his group would cause trouble for Roman politicians.[50] In keeping with Cotter's observations, it seems likely that these lines of inquiry will continue to benefit those scholars interested in discussing Luke's community.

It makes sense at this point to step back and to consider Acts through the joint lenses of rhetoric and mythmaking in the service of social formation. Luke's choice of writing his etiology in a format that contains elements from the Roman genre of historiography fits perfectly with the sociopolitical need to portray his group as being praiseworthy for their superior values.[51] That Luke was compelled to do so at the end of the first century suggests something interesting about the setting of Luke's social formation project. Luke's project reveals the imagination, experimentation, and intellectual labor that were necessary for the success of a socially and politically questionable group in the empire.[52] When Luke's literary project is placed within the framework of the goals related to Smith's category "anywhere," it is interesting to note how many of Luke's mythic features can be explained as social information intended to meet the real needs of his community. Like all mythmaking, his information is not direct; the gap between the narrative and the real world has to be bridged, although viewing Acts through the lens of community formation may help explain this gap. These brief remarks concerning Luke's project set in the context of the basic components of group formation in the Roman world are preliminary, yet my hope is that they will encourage more discussion of Acts as a text that can be understood as a social process and product.

ACTS AS A TYPE OF ROMAN MYTHMAKING: THE EXAMPLE OF THE JERUSALEM COMMUNITY IN ACTS 1–6

I now return to my opening remarks regarding Luke's choice of Jerusalem as the center of his etiological project and his interest in presenting

---

[49] Joseph B. Tyson, ed., *Luke-Acts and the Jewish People: Eight Critical Perspectives* (Minneapolis: Augsburg, 1988), remains a valuable starting point for gaining access to the variety of perspectives on this issue.

[50] Stephen G. Wilson, *Related Strangers: Jews and Christians 70–170 C.E.* (Minneapolis: Fortress, 1995), 67–71, offers helpful observations and reviews of relevant scholarship on this issue.

[51] The terminology and suggestion are based on the conclusions of Penner, "In Praise of Christian Origins," 577.

[52] On the ideas of experimentation and intellectual labor in the social formation process, see Burton Mack, *Who Wrote the New Testament? The Making of the Christian Myth* (San Francisco: HarperSanFrancisco, 1995), 11, 19–41.

the group there as developing in a context of unsurpassed virtue and honor. By considering Acts to be a text that derived from a new religious association within the cultural context of the social disorientation inherent in the Roman Empire, there are several reasons that can be proposed for why Luke pictured the group the way he did and why Jerusalem was so important to him as the setting for a large section of his etiology. While not intended to be exhaustive, by considering Luke's literary and rhetorical style, his ideological interests, and his involvement in the intellectual and practical labor of social formation, the following points suggest how our lenses of rhetoric and social formation can work in tandem to reconstruct several of the goals of Lukan narrative argumentation. The purpose is to demonstrate the extent to which Luke's description of the Jerusalem community reflects his literary, rhetorical, and ideological themes, being fashioned in concert with his late first-century or early second-century sociopolitical setting.

I begin with Luke's treatment of the transition of the followers of Jesus from Galileans to residents of Jerusalem and the ways in which this new setting provided the author with the opportunity to conceive of an extraordinary beginning point for Christianity. While the Gospels of Matthew and John shifted the setting of their stories back to Galilee after their resurrection narratives, Luke retained the setting of Jerusalem. Luke was not interested in the precise mechanism of this transition; he simply implies that Jesus' Galilean followers were suddenly residents of the city.[53] It is quite clear that for the purposes of his story Luke was committed to picturing the disciples in the context of Jerusalem without interruption. Having accomplished this unencumbered shift in settings, and following upon the first events subsequent to the departure of Jesus in Luke's narrative, the author now establishes the body of people constituting the charter members of the Jerusalem group. Building on the final theme of Peter's address related to apostleship (Acts 1:15–22), and in conjunction with Luke's story of the appointment of Matthias (1:23–26), Luke provided his audience with an indication of the original organization of the community. The selection of Matthias—clearly dependent on divine providence—is described as well managed and methodical. These clear interests in leadership roles fit positively with late first- and early second-century Christian interests in church offices and hierarchy as exemplified in the *Didache*. According to Luke, apostles were the first chosen leaders; their credibility stemmed both from being with Jesus and from being in

---

[53] One should note that while this transition provides good literary flow, the idea that a large group of Galileans could have so easily moved to Jerusalem is historically improbable.

Jerusalem. In line with other early Christian circles, it is likely that the author believed that his community was legitimized through and gained authority by being connected with these apostles.

Luke was also concerned to show that the origins of the religion were in the context of the public domain. Building upon this narrative image of the able and competent leadership of these apostles, the author continued the idea that was previously stressed in Luke 24:18 by now suggesting in Acts 1:19 that everyone in Jerusalem knew what was taking place concerning the events of Jesus' death and the actions of his followers. The group was recognized and initially accepted—even by the Jewish residents of Jerusalem. Luke stressed that Christianity was not a secret society that developed in private; everyone in the capital of Palestine saw the movement's birth (see Acts 26:26). The rejection of the group in that city, according to Luke's portrayal, was only a result of nonvirtuous Jewish leaders in Jerusalem (Acts 4:1, 5–6), who unjustly sought the group's destruction.

In this regard, Luke pictured the Jerusalem group growing and facing opposition from within the temple. Luke also developed scenes that spoke to his community about the pressures that arose from within as the group tried to maintain their virtuous lifestyle (Acts 5:1–11; 6:1–6). Regarding the need for this group to persevere, Luke elaborated upon three themes in Acts 3–7: (1) the growing tensions with the temple; (2) the ability of the faithful to overcome the persecution and hold to their values; and (3) the inevitable ethnic and/or religious divisions within the Jerusalem group. The relationship of the group to the temple reached its high point in Acts 2:46: "they spent much time together in the temple." Following Peter's speech in the temple in 3:11–26, however, the above-mentioned escalation of conflict with the temple authorities began (4:1–2). This conflict allowed Luke to stress the second theme: the group's leaders were bold in speech (3:13, 29), and, after praying and being filled with the Holy Spirit, the group members also became emboldened (3:31). Although persecuted (4:3; 5:18), the bold apostles were either miraculously rescued (5:19) or saved by the witness of a wise Pharisee (5:33–40).[54] Whether or not Luke's community was actually facing persecution remains in doubt, yet it appears clear that with these stories the author was interested in clarifying and establishing boundaries and constructing membership codes and rituals for his late first-century community. In the Lukan community, the ideal member was one who was virtuous, faithful, and able to overcome persecution, just like the members of the ideal Jerusalem group.

---

[54] The witness of Gamaliel also fits the Lukan theme of pious Jews realizing the validity of the Christian claims and reminds the reader of the trials of Jesus, where Pilate and Herod claimed Jesus was innocent.

By picturing the Christians in confrontation with the Jewish temple authorities, Luke was able to stress both the links his group had to the ancient religion and the idea that even the Jewish leaders had recognized the significance of Jesus' followers (Acts 4:16-18). The conception that Jerusalem was the setting for the organization of this first Christian community was significant to the author because it established his ability to construct a story that directly compared the leaders of Christianity to the Jewish temple leaders. Throughout the first section of Acts Luke took every opportunity to stress both the connection of Christianity to the ancient Jewish traditions and setting as well as the superiority of the new leaders (the apostles) over the old (the temple priests and Jerusalem leaders).

As to the remarkable makeup of the group in Jerusalem and their exemplary virtue, the narrative provides an initial picture of the group's solidarity and their values by reference to the idea that the whole group was staying together in an upstairs room (Acts 1:13; cf. Luke 22:12). This image is bolstered by a description of their major preoccupation: "all these were constantly devoting themselves to prayer" (1:14). The community's values continue to be illustrated in the following chapters of Acts. For example, because the group was situated in Jerusalem, Luke was able to claim that the early Christian founders were extremely pious in their practice of the Jewish faith (2:46: "they spent much time together in the temple"; 3:1: "Peter and John were going up to the temple at the hour of prayer"). As Richard Cassidy has observed, there is additional attention paid to the community's care for the sick and the poor, their use of material possessions, their opposition to injustice and corruption, their inclusion of oppressed groups (esp. women and Samaritans), and their rejection of violence.[55] The fact that this description represents an idealized community portrait, comparable to ancient Greco-Roman descriptions of the model state or the ideal of friendship in the philosophical schools, has been observed in several recent studies.[56] Furthermore, by establishing the presence of women

---

[55] Richard J. Cassidy, *Society and Politics in the Acts of the Apostles* (Maryknoll, N.Y.: Orbis, 1987), 21–38. Also note the important suggestions of David L. Balch regarding Luke's use of "the social-political theme of rich and poor" in comparison to its use by other ancient historians ("Rich and Poor, Proud and Humble in Luke-Acts," in *The Social World of the First Christians: Essays in Honor of Wayne Meeks* [ed. L. M. White and O. L. Yarbrough; Minneapolis: Fortress, 1995], 214–33).

[56] David L. Mealand, "Community of Goods and Utopian Allusions in Acts II–IV," *JTS* 28 (1977): 96–99; Alan C. Mitchell, "The Social Function of Friendship in Acts 2:44–47 and 4:32–37," *JBL* 111 (1992): 255–72; Luke T. Johnson, *The Literary Function of Possessions in Luke-Acts* (SBLDS 39; Missoula, Mont.: Scholars Press, 1979), 1–5; idem, *The Acts of the Apostles,* (SP 5; Collegeville, Minn.: Liturgical

in the group of followers in Jerusalem, Luke continued to develop the theme of inclusiveness that was already established in the Gospel. Luke's interest in Greco-Roman values illustrates both that his group was deeply entrenched in the culture of the day and that Luke was interested in defending Christianity as a viable, trustworthy institution.

Our two lenses together recommend that Luke's portrayal of the earliest Christians in Jerusalem as virtuous was not only in keeping with the typical theme of Roman historiography but also a basic survival tactic for a new religious movement under the gaze of Roman officials. By claiming that the origin of his community was within the sphere of the Jewish temple in Jerusalem, that the group was exceptionally pious, and that even the Jewish leaders recognized their power (Acts 4:16), Luke was legitimizing the foundation of his group. The effectiveness of his narrative was partially dependent on his ability to claim that the Jewish leaders had in fact acknowledged the group's origins and that the group was persecuted only because of deceit and "false witnesses" (6:11–14), not because they deserved punishment. This story works best in the setting of Jerusalem; only by placing the story in the Jewish holy city could the author construct a narrative that clearly explained the positive link to Judaism as well as the reason the group was forced to move from that region.

The story of the early Christians being rejected by the temple authorities and eventually by the residents of the city also fits well with the idea of kingdom/kingship, which is a significant Lukan ideological *topos* (e.g., Acts 1:3: Jesus was "speaking about the kingdom of God"; 1:6: "they asked him, 'Lord, is this the time when you will restore the kingdom to Israel?'" NRSV).[57] For instance, in light of the way Luke understood Jerusalem, the possibility exists that he was working with the idea of Jesus as a king with Jerusalem as his royal city. Considering the fact that Jerusalem was destroyed by the time Luke wrote, it is tempting to speculate that Luke might have been influenced by the popular Hellenistic concept of the king as benefactor. This concept could have helped Luke explain to his audience why Christians were rejected in the city and why Jerusalem was eventually destroyed: cities that did not honor their king for his benevolence were condemned. Within the Greco-Roman world the notion that a

---

Press, 1992), 62; S. Scott Bartchy, "Community of Goods in Acts: Idealization or Social Reality?" in *The Future of Early Christianity: Essays in Honor of Helmut Koester* (ed. B. A. Pearson; Minneapolis: Fortress, 1991), 309–18; and Jacques Dupont, *The Salvation of the Gentiles* (trans. J. Keating; New York: Paulist, 1979), 85–102.

[57] The scholarly interest in Acts 1:6 has produced an abundance of interpretations. I have surveyed several of the key positions in Moreland, "Jerusalem Imagined," 109–20.

city would suffer enormous consequences if it were to kill a king—and then persecute the king's supporters—would have resonated with readers of Acts.[58] In the case of Jerusalem, Luke may well have been setting the stage at the very beginning of his second volume for his audience to appreciate why Jerusalem had to be abandoned and replaced by Rome by the end of Acts.

Luke's use of the persecuted prophet motif and the idea of promise-fulfillment (both of which are well-discussed themes in recent scholarship) are also integrally tied to the story of the rejection of the early Christians by the Jewish leaders in Jerusalem. In the opening chapters of Acts, Jerusalem and its inhabitants were once again promised salvation, but Jerusalem ended up killing the promised prophet/king and persecuting his servants. By beginning the story of Acts in Jerusalem, Luke established a setting wherein his narrative theme could easily be developed toward its logical conclusion.

Alongside the themes related to rejection and destruction, Luke also wished to stress that the early Christians experienced great success in the city. The setting of Jerusalem was crucial to Luke's narrative portrayal of thousands of converts to Christianity from among the most pious Jews (Acts 2:41, 47; 6:7; 21:20). The parallels in the opening of Acts with the opening chapters of his first volume indicate that Luke continued to picture a partially receptive element among the most pious Jews of the city ("a great many of the priests became obedient to the faith" [6:7]; "they are all zealous for the law" [21:20 NRSV]). As in his story of Jesus, Luke suggested that the conflict with the unrepentant Jewish leaders escalated as the group's members preached and did miracles in the city (4:1-2, 5-6; 5:17, 21, 24, 26, 27, 33; 7:1, 54). The dispersion in Acts 8:1 represented the culmination of this growing conflict. Prior to this dispersion, however, and as part of Luke's mythmaking in the service of social formation, the notion that Christianity was immediately well received in Jerusalem by thousands of Jews was no doubt of political significance. With this story in hand, Luke's late first-century community was able to relate to the initially favorable response by the Jerusalem residents and visitors; this was a valuable tool for a community that was attempting to establish itself as a valid religious movement.

If Luke were writing from one of the large urban centers of the Mediterranean, such as Rome, Ephesus, or possibly even Antioch—all

---

[58] See Klaus Bringmann, "The King as Benefactor: Some Remarks on Ideal Kingship in the Age of Hellenism," in *Images and Ideologies: Self-Definition in the Hellenistic World* (ed. A. Bulloch et al.; Hellenistic Culture and Society 12; Berkeley and Los Angeles: University of California Press, 1993), 7–24.

reoccurring suggestions over the past century—his ability to claim that Christianity derived from Jerusalem could have had political consequences, since Jerusalem was one of the few cities of early Roman Palestine that people all around the Mediterranean would have readily recognized. Claiming Capernaum or Nazareth as the fountainhead of one's community would not have been nearly as impressive.[59] Claiming Jerusalem would have conjured ideas of ancient religion and ritual. Claiming that the temple authorities in Jerusalem respected, even feared, the leaders of this Christian movement would have proved a strong argument in favor of the positive origins of this religion.

Since we know of early Christian groups that were not interested in linking their communities to Jerusalem, Luke may also have intended his construction of Christian origins to establish the prominence of his group over other early Christian communities. By portraying Jerusalem as having such a prominent role in his etiology, Luke may have been positioning his community as the most valid expression of Christianity. If Luke's community was located in Rome, this account may have been intended to show the supremacy of that community due to its direct connection with Paul (and the Jerusalem church). This is, of course, one of the ways Eusebius applied this story as he wrote his *Ecclesiastical History* two centuries later. Similarly, a setting such as Ephesus could explain both Luke's strong interest in the story of Paul and the need of Luke's community to establish itself as a viable religion in a rapidly developing Roman city.[60]

Conclusion

In this essay I have observed that recent studies of Luke's genre categories and literary patterns have helped to demonstrate the extent to which Acts fits within the confines of ancient literary productions. Acts is neither unique nor abnormal in this respect. The author of Acts followed many of

---

[59] One might consider here too the exotic flavor of a city such as Jerusalem—a far-off place—in the imaginations of Greco-Roman readers. On this novelistic emphasis, see further Saundra Schwartz's contribution in this volume.

[60] The Ephesian setting has also been suggested because of details seemingly available to Luke about Paul's activities there (Acts 18:24–20:1; cf. 20:17–38). Luke also highlighted Ephesus as the city to which Paul was emotionally attached (see esp. 20:36–38). The significant set of articles collected in the volume edited by Helmut Koester provides a valuable starting point for reevaluating Ephesus as Luke's setting (see esp. Helmut Koester, "Ephesos in Early Christian Literature," in *Ephesos Metropolis of Asia: An Interdisciplinary Approach to Its Archaeology, Religion, and Culture* [ed. H. Koester; Valley Forge, Pa.: Trinity Press International, 1995], 119–40).

the rhetorical conventions of his age as he wrote this story of the origins of his group. Then, by describing Acts as a type of mythmaking that typically occurs in the process of community formation, I further pressed the modern reader to think about Acts in comparison with other etiological projects from antiquity. I argued that when ideas about group formation and mythmaking are brought to bear on the Lukan project, scholars will be better equipped to think about Luke's story within a Greco-Roman social milieu where people were experimenting with innovative notions of community in the midst of a rapidly changing sociopolitical setting. I suggested that studies of the function of mythology in groups and an examination of the types of community formation that were prevalent in the ancient Roman world would lead to more nuanced ways of understanding the purpose of Acts within the late first-century context of at least one group of Christians.

Finally, by way of example, I proposed several ways that one might better understand the role that Luke's portrait of the followers of Jesus within the setting of Jerusalem had in the context of the author's rhetorical, theological, social, and/or ideological objectives. Within the narrative of the opening chapters of Acts, the idea of Jerusalem as the setting for the activities of the "earliest" Christians is firmly established. This emphasis was found to be explicable as a valuable, pragmatic, and paradigmatic part of Luke's literary and ideological agenda. The author's interest in depicting an ideal, virtuous group that was both accepted and eventually rejected by the Jewish leaders of the temple was shown to fit well with the needs of a religious association that was struggling to gain acceptance in the Roman Empire. While this study remains preliminary, my hope is that it will draw more attention to the need for a well-developed, interdisciplinary approach to Acts as an ancient social and rhetorical literary project.

GENDER AND GENRE: ACTS IN/OF INTERPRETATION
Caroline Vander Stichele

Even at the beginning of the twenty first century, masculinity retains the invisibility of the norm: the paradigmatic human being is usually assumed to be male. Women must be mentioned explicitly to be present at all.[1]

The leading focus of this concluding essay will be on assessing how a reflection on gender could contribute to the discussions taking place in this collection. As I will show, a gender-critical analysis proves to be not only complementary but also central to the concerns raised throughout this volume. Rather than discussing this issue in more general terms, however, in what follows I will start from observations made by the contributors themselves. To begin, I will look at how they deal with issues of gender as they feature in the book of Acts. Next, I will analyze how gender relates to the discussion about the genre of Acts in this volume. Finally, I will broaden the perspective to the sociorhetorical and cultural contexts of research on Acts itself.

GENDERING ACTS

Studies on gender initially focused on the role of women, but in the past decade a shift has taken place from feminist and women studies to the more broadly defined field of gender studies, which not only includes examination of the roles of women (and men) but also explicitly addresses the construction of male as well as female identity reflected in the texts under discussion.[2] Reflection on gender issues in Acts in this broader sense

---

[1] Mary Rose D'Angelo, "The **ANHP** Question in Luke-Acts: Imperial Masculinity and the Deployment of Women in the Early Second Century," in *A Feminist Companion to Luke* (ed. A.-J. Levine with M. Blickenstaff; FCNTECW 3; Sheffield: Sheffield Academic Press, 2002), 44.

[2] Relevant in this respect are the following recent studies on masculinity in antiquity: Maud W. Gleason, *Making Men: Sophists and Self-Presentation in Ancient Rome* (Princeton: Princeton University Press, 1995); Erik Gunderson, *Staging*

is still largely absent in current scholarship, which so far has mostly focused on the role of women. As feminist scholars have pointed out, women are less prominent in Acts and their roles are more restricted than in Luke's Gospel.[3] The so-called gender pairs offer a good illustration of this difference between Luke and Acts.[4] What is meant here is the phenomenon of paired stories in the Gospel of Luke, where one narrative about a male is paired with another similar story about a female character.[5] As noted by Turid Karlsen Seim, this phenomenon is largely absent from Acts.[6] This does not imply that no pairing takes place at all but rather that the pairs take on a different form in Acts, insofar as either individuals or groups are mentioned in gender-inclusive expressions.[7] Apart from these

---

Masculinity: The Rhetoric of Performance in the Roman World (Ann Arbor: University of Michigan Press, 2000); Virginia Burrus, *"Begotten, Not Made": Conceiving Manhood in Late Antiquity* (Stanford, Calif.: Stanford University Press, 2000); and Matthew Kuefler, *The Manly Eunuch: Masculinity, Gender Ambiguity, and Christian Ideology in Late Antiquity* (Chicago: University of Chicago Press, 2001).

[3] See, e.g., Mary Rose D'Angelo, "Women in Luke-Acts: A Redactional View," *JBL* 109 (1990): 442–45; idem, "(Re)Presentations of Women in the Gospel of Matthew and Luke-Acts," in *Women and Christian Origins* (ed. R. S. Kraemer and M. R. D'Angelo; New York: Oxford University Press, 1999), 181–87; Turid Karlsen Seim, *The Double Message: Patterns of Gender in Luke and Acts* (Nashville: Abingdon, 1994), 3; and Clarice J. Martin, "The Acts of the Apostles," in *Searching the Scriptures: A Feminist Commentary* (ed. E. Schüssler Fiorenza; New York: Crossroad, 1994), 771–76.

[4] For a discussion of the material in question, see D'Angelo, "Women in Luke-Acts," 445–48; idem, "(Re)Presentations of Women," 181–84; and Seim, *Double Message*, 11–24. Luke's tendency toward conciseness and avoidance of parallel scenes in the Gospel, as noted by Mikeal Parsons ("Luke and the *Progymnasmata*: A Preliminary Investigation into the Preliminary Exercises," 54–55, in this volume), clearly does not apply to these gender pairs, because Luke deliberately includes or creates material here in order to provide parallel scenes.

[5] See the examples in Seim, *Double Message*, 14–15. See also D'Angelo, "Women in Luke-Acts," 444–46.

[6] Seim, *Double Message*, 17–18.

[7] D'Angelo ("Women in Luke-Acts," 445) describes the phenomenon in Acts as "either the names of couples or the *merismus* 'both men and women.'" This definition gives an accurate picture of the difference between Luke and Acts but may be too narrow in that it does not cover all instances. On the one hand, the term *couples* suggests married couples, which excludes, for instance, Agrippa and Bernice, who is his sister (25:13, 23), as well as Dionysius and Damaris (17:34). On the other hand, the expression ἄνδρες τε καὶ γυναῖκες (5:14; 8:3, 12; 9:2; 22:4) does not cover the expression οἱ ἅγιοι καὶ αἱ χῆραι (9:41), which may also serve as a gendered group description, as Seim suggests (*Double Message*, 19). Shelly Matthews (*First Converts: Rich Pagan Women and the Rhetoric of Mission in Early Judaism*

pairs there are also five stories in which specific women play a distinctive role: Sapphira (5:1–11), Tabitha (9:36–43), Mary the mother of John, Rhoda (12:12–17), Lydia (16:11–40), and Priscilla (18:1–11, 18–28).[8] Some of these texts are also mentioned in this volume. Milton Moreland, for instance, refers to the presence of women in the community at the beginning of Acts, and Saundra Schwartz makes note of Sapphira, Drusilla, and Bernice in her discussion of the trial scenes in Acts. In what follows, I will discuss their analysis of these texts.

In the second part of his article, where he interprets Acts as a type of Roman mythmaking, Moreland sets out "to demonstrate the extent to which Luke's description of the Jerusalem community reflects his literary, rhetorical, and ideological themes, being fashioned in concert with his late first-century or early second-century sociopolitical setting."[9] As Moreland observes, Luke offers a highly idealized presentation of the community in the opening chapters of Acts. Its members are depicted as virtuous and pious, and, in line with his Gospel, Luke also stresses the presence of women followers (Acts 1:14). The writer also takes a clear interest in the organization of the nascent community and its apostolic leadership, as the story about the replacement of Judas by Matthias in Acts 1:26 indicates. Moreland mentions Matthias in relation to the issue of leadership and notes the presence of women in order to illustrate the inclusive character of the Jerusalem community. Gender, however, plays a role in *both* cases, since maleness is listed by Peter as one of the selection criteria for the new apostle (Acts 1:21–22). Women may well be included in the community, but they are efficiently excluded when it comes to assuming leadership roles in that very same community. This difference in status within the community can in fact already be noticed in Acts 1:14, where the presence of women is signaled, but men are mentioned first and identified by name. The only exception here is Mary, who is identified as the mother of Jesus,

---

and Christianity [Contraversions; Stanford, Calif.: Stanford University Press, 2001], 54) points out that most of these gender-inclusive expressions occur in the chapters preceding Paul's Gentile mission, but there are also three occasions during Paul's travels where prominent Gentile women are mentioned in conjunction with men (13:50; 17:4, 12).

[8] Gail O'Day, "Acts," in *The Women's Bible Commentary* (ed. C. A. Newsom and S. H. Ringe; Louisville: Westminster John Knox, 1992), 306. Cf. Jane Schaberg, "Luke," in Newsom and Ringe, *Women's Bible Commentary*, 280. Other female figures mentioned by name in Acts are Mary the mother of Jesus (1:14), Candace (8:27), Damaris (17:34), Artemis (19:23–41), Drusilla (24:24), and Bernice (25:13, 23).

[9] Milton Moreland, "The Jerusalem Community in Acts: Mythmaking and the Sociorhetorical Functions of a Lukan Setting," 304, in this volume.

but her presence seems mostly symbolic in establishing a link with the Lukan Gospel, since she plays no role whatsoever in the rest of Acts.

Moreland further argues that the picture of the Jerusalem community in Acts is informed by Luke's ideological framework, but he overlooks the connection between this framework and the limited role women are allowed to play in Luke's sociopolitical agenda. As Seim observes, "When women in Acts are excluded from becoming apostles or from being leaders in other ways, this is a consequence of Luke's restricted and special concept of apostleship and acceptance of the public sphere as a man's world. So the public act of witness has to be carried out by men."[10] D'Angelo's analysis of the use of ἀνήρ in Acts points in the same direction. Luke does not want his message compromised by its messengers. It therefore has to be delivered by "ambassadors suitable for the public and civic forum."[11] As one of the Twelve, this is also the representative role Matthias is supposed to perform.

Apart from being the ones to deliver the message, men also appear as its primary recipients. In the first chapter of Acts, the apostles who witness Jesus' ascension are addressed by two men (ἄνδρες δύο) as ἄνδρες Γαλιλαῖοι (1:11), and when Peter addresses the assembly in 1:16 he similarly calls his audience ἄνδρες ἀδελφοί.[12] The reference to women in 1:14 is thus framed by these references to men. Gender is thus already an issue even before women enter the scene in Acts. They may well be included, but from the very beginning their place in the community is carefully delineated. If Acts 1 is in some sense programmatic for the rest of the book, the selection of Matthias is indeed telling and indicates the shape of things to come. According to Moreland, "Luke's interest in church offices, his claims on the ancient sacred city of Jerusalem..., his interest in virtuous conduct, and his concern to elaborate on the rules and rituals involved in group membership all can be understood as part of an agenda for group formation."[13] That agenda, however, is gendered from the start, and this bears consequences for the roles that group members are allowed to play in what follows.

---

[10] Seim, *Double Message*, 162.

[11] D'Angelo, "ANHP Question in Luke-Acts," 52.

[12] D'Angelo notes that ἄνδρες ἀδελφοί is the most frequently used address in Acts ("ANHP Question in Luke-Acts," 55). The addition of ἄνδρες to ἀδελφοί makes it harder to interpret this address in a gender-inclusive way than the ἀδελφοί used by Paul to address his audience in his letters. The NRSV blends this problem out by translating ἄνδρες ἀδελφοί in Acts 1:16 with "friends," although it mentions the literal translation in a footnote. See also *The New Testament and Psalms: An Inclusive Version* (ed. V. R. Gold et al.; New York: Oxford University Press, 1995).

[13] Moreland, "Jerusalem Community in Acts," 302.

In a similar vein, Schwartz mentions the presence of three women in her discussion of the trial scenes in Acts. She does not analyze their role but makes some interesting observations in the first part of her essay with respect to the role of women in the Greek novels, which make it possible to draw some conclusions for Acts as well. First of all, she notes that the courtroom scene in general takes the form of a contest between two opponents, the expected outcome being the victory of one over the other.[14] She further observes that ancient rhetorical treatises categorize arguments using terminology from athletic competition. The connection established between the verbal competition in the courtroom and the physical rivalry in athletics is interesting, as it reveals the underlying presumption that in both cases the contestants are male. Trials and sports take place in the public sphere, which is the arena par excellence for the formation and display of masculinity. This feature is by and large affirmed by other observations in Schwartz's contribution. In the novels, crimes of passion such as adultery and seduction are the most common ones, but the defendant in the trial scenes in most cases is the male protagonist of the novel. As Schwartz observes, "The female protagonists are more likely to assume a passive role, as the objects over which men contend in the trials. They are involved in trials insofar as their safety or marital status gives rise to legal actions."[15]

A very different picture emerges when we turn to Acts. Schwartz observes that, as far as the nature of the crimes is concerned, "The crimes of passion in the Greek novels (murder, adultery) are replaced by crimes against religion (blasphemy, teaching against the law of the temple, profaning the temple, introduction of an alien religion) or against the state (disturbing the peace, claiming that there is a king other than Caesar)."[16] Apart from this difference, similarities can be noted as well, especially when it comes to the function of these trials in their larger narrative setting. Schwartz contends in her conclusion that the trials serve an ideological agenda. That agenda may well be different in the case of Acts and the ancient novels, but what they have in common in terms of their ideology is at least the perception of the public sphere—where the courtroom is situated—as a male-gendered space. Men dominate the courtroom scenes in the novels, and even more so in Acts, where women hardly play a role at all. Still, there are three scenes in Acts in which women do appear, even if not all of them qualify as trial scenes in the strict sense as defined by Schwartz.

---

[14] Saundra Schwartz, "The Trial Scene in the Greek Novels and in Acts," 110, in this volume.
[15] Ibid., 113 n. 35.
[16] Ibid., 117.

The first case is the story of Ananias and Sapphira (Acts 5:1–11). As Schwartz notes, the interval between the trial of Peter and John in Acts 4:1–22 and the trial of the apostles in 5:12–42 "creates an opportunity for the narrative to juxtapose an alternative model of justice. This is the scene in Acts 5 when Peter confronts Ananias and his wife Sapphira about withholding part of their donation to the church."[17] Sapphira and Ananias both appear as defendants, but the public character of the occasion is indeed unclear. The only other character involved in this scene is Peter in the role of accuser. The parallelism between the meeting with Ananias (5:2b–6) and the meeting with Sapphira (5:7–11) in terms of both structure and content is, however, apparent: both stand accused, are considered guilty, die on the spot, and are buried by the same young men.[18] They undergo an identical fate, even though they may not be guilty of exactly the same thing. Ananias is accused of lying and deceiving, while Sapphira is accused of consent (and therefore complicity). According to Ivoni Richter Reimer, this difference is meaningful and should be understood against the background of the power structures within patriarchal marriage. It reveals that Sapphira's role in the decision-making process has been different from that of Ananias. He has executed the decision; she gave her consent.[19]

In the second text, Drusilla is mentioned with her husband Felix (24:24). She is introduced as both his wife and a Jewish woman (τῇ ἰδίᾳ γυναικὶ οὔσῃ Ἰουδαίᾳ). Here Felix appears in his capacity as judge with Paul as the defendant. This meeting seems to have a more private character, since no one else is present. According to Schwartz, Drusilla is introduced here to highlight the informal character of the setting, but a different explanation is possible as well. The fact that Luke explicitly mentions that Drusilla is Jewish may be intended to explain why this meeting occurs in the first place: she wants to hear Paul, a Jewish follower of the way (24:14), and Felix has created an opportunity for her to do so.[20] As

---

[17] Ibid., 120.

[18] O' Day, "Acts," 309; Seim, *Double Message*, 78. According to Martin, "Sapphira is depicted as neither a subordinate nor a passive (but complicit) observer—she is fully a participatory agent in the sale and the distribution of the funds" ("Acts of the Apostles," 779).

[19] Ivoni Richter Reimer, *Women in the Acts of the Apostles: A Feminist Liberation Perspective* (trans. L. M. Maloney; Minneapolis: Fortress, 1995), 1–29.

[20] Ibid., 257. According to D'Angelo, "Luke presents the procurator Felix as accompanied by his Jewish wife Drusilla (24.24), as Trajan and Hadrian were accompanied by Plotina and Sabina on campaign" ("ANHP Question in Luke-Acts," 66), but this does not explain why Luke notes that Drusilla is Jewish (cf. Josephus, *Ant*. 20.143, who similarly mentions Drusilla's Jewish heritage).

Schwartz further notes, "In this alternative rhetorical space, Paul discusses an alternate form of justice with the judge (Acts 24:25)."[21] The result is that in talking about justice (περὶ δικαιοσύνης), self-control (ἐγκρατείας), and the coming judgment (τοῦ κρίματος τοῦ μέλλοντος), Paul effectively reverses the situation. No longer he himself but Felix and Drusilla now stand on trial, a situation to which Felix responds with fear.

The third case is again a hearing, but different from the previous two scenes in that it is clearly a public event. Paul now appears before King Agrippa, who arrived with Bernice the day before to welcome Festus at Caesarea (25:13). Although Bernice is the sister and not the wife of Agrippa, Luke introduces them as a pair and does not specify their relationship.[22] Her presence is explicitly mentioned when the beginning of the hearing is described: "So on the next day Agrippa and Bernice came with great pomp, and they entered the audience hall with the military tribunes and the prominent men of the city" (25:23 NRSV). She is again mentioned at the end of the meeting (26:30). Although Bernice does not play a role in the hearing, the fact that Luke mentions her three times gives prominence to her presence.[23]

What Drusilla and Bernice have in common is that they are "present, though silent, at the apologies of Paul."[24] Both elements are significant. In hearing Paul, these upper-class women may well "play a role in legitimizing the new religion."[25] In being silent, they conform to Luke's depiction of women as recipients of his message. The only woman allowed to speak in these trial scenes is Sapphira, but only in order to reveal her complicity (i.e., her speaking clearly has a narrative function). In all three cases, however, the women are wealthy and identified by name. All three are also mentioned together with a male relative, husband, or brother and are presented in subordinate roles. Drusilla and Bernice may appear in public, but their roles are restricted to accompanying men in the latter's public functions. In the end, the representation of women in Acts may reveal more about Luke's agenda and his audience—more about the male discourse in the service of which they are put to use—than about the women in question themselves.[26] To achieve a fuller grasp of the roles both women and men play in his story, then, it is important to take into account their

---

[21] Schwartz, "Trial Scene," 130.

[22] The information that Bernice is Agrippa's sister is from Josephus, *Ant.* 20.145.

[23] In her overview of the trial scenes, Schwartz only mentions Bernice insofar as she is one of the spectators ("Trial Scene," 137, table 2, no. 14).

[24] D'Angelo, "ANHP Question in Luke-Acts," 63.

[25] Matthews, *First Converts,* 62.

[26] Ibid., 6.

rhetorical function in the larger sociocultural ethos established and promoted by Luke.[27]

Genre and Gender

In her 1929 University of Würzburg dissertation, Rosa Söder presented a comparative analysis of the apocryphal Acts and the ancient novels.[28] As she pointed out in the introduction, the comparison itself was not new. Already in 1902 Ernst von Dobschütz had suggested that the apocryphal Acts were in fact Christian novels, modeled on the Greek ones. Others after him had made similar suggestions and offered alternative proposals,[29] but a more systematic analysis of the novelistic character of the apocryphal Acts had, as of yet, not been undertaken. This is precisely what Söder set out to do in her study. Following Friedrich Pfister, she distinguished five motifs that can be considered essential for the novel in Greek literature: the travel motif, the aretalogical motif, the teratological motif, the tendentious motif (religious, philosophical, political, and ethical), and the erotic motif (represented in its most developed form in the sophistic novel).[30] Her analysis was guided by the following questions: Are these five motifs also present in the apocryphal Acts, implying that they belong to the same ancient novelistic genre? Can any relations be found between the apocryphal Acts and a specific type of novel, resulting in a closer relationship with that type of novel? Are there other motifs present in the apocryphal Acts, for which parallels can be found also in ancient novels?[31] After analyzing the material with these questions in mind, she came to the following conclusion: the apocryphal Acts cannot

---

[27] For an analysis of Paul along these same lines, see also Todd Penner and Caroline Vander Stichele, "Unveiling Paul: Gendering *Ēthos* in 1 Corinthians 11:2–16," in *Rhetoric, Ethic and Moral Persuasion in Biblical Discourse* (ed. T. H. Olbricht and A. Eriksson; Harrisburg, Pa: T&T Clark, forthcoming).

[28] Rosa Söder, *Die apokryphen Apostelgeschichten und die romanhafte Literatur der Antike* (Stuttgart: Kohlhammer, 1932; repr., Darmstadt: Wissenschaftliche Buchgesellschaft, 1969).

[29] Richard Reitzenstein, for instance, considered it more likely that the aretalogies of prophets and philosophers provided the literary model for the apocryphal Acts. See Richard Reitzenstein, *Hellenistische Wundererzählungen* (Leipzig: Teubner, 1906), 55.

[30] Friedrich Pfister, *Die Religion der Griechen und Römer, mit einer Einführung in die vergleichende Religionswissenschaft: Darstellung und Literaturbericht (1918–29/30)* (Jahresbericht über die Fortschritte der klassischen Altertumswissenschaft 229, supplementary vol.; Leipzig: Reisland, 1930), 150.

[31] Söder, *Die apokryphen Apostelgeschichten*, 5–6.

be considered novels in the sense of the Greek novels, and they themselves do not all belong to the same genre. Rather, they are folkloristic tales for the masses and not, as the novel, meant for the educated elite. They are intended to provide education through entertainment, which does not exclude the possibility that the writers made use of the literary tools they learned in school. Such tools are used in the Greek novels as well, but this should not be taken as an indication that they have influenced the apocryphal Acts or that these texts should be considered a continuation of the novel, because the tools themselves are definitely older than the novel and have been used before in historiography and even earlier in epic literature.[32]

This concise overview of Söder's work is worth noting in this context because it throws a different light on the genre discussion in this volume. To begin with, it clearly illustrates continuity between past scholarship and the current debate: the *Umwelt* has not lost its importance or fascination. As already noted in the introduction to this volume, the focus on the Greco-Roman world is reminiscent of a *Religionsgeschichtliche* approach in this respect.[33] However, there is more, for although the issue of their relationship with the canonical Acts is not explicitly raised, several remarks in Söder's book reveal the underlying presumption that the apocryphal Acts are mostly fictitious in nature, while the canonical Acts is firmly based on fact. The apocryphal Acts cannot make such a claim to historicity and have remained, therefore, outside of the canon. Söder further explains this observation in a footnote: "The few historical reminiscences are completely overgrown by legends, in contradistinction to the canonical Acts. Between these and the apocryphal Acts exists a relationship similar to the one between the Alexander history and the Alexander novel."[34] The comparison with the novels, then, is strictly limited to the apocryphal Acts and does not really affect the discussion about the genre of the canonical book.[35] Söder's

---

[32] Ibid., 216.

[33] Todd Penner, "Contextualizing Acts," 18, in this volume.

[34] Söder, *Die apokryphen Apostelgeschichten*, 6 n. 2 (my translation). This precise issue has been reevaluated by contemporary scholars, see esp. Christine M. Thomas, *The Acts of Peter, Gospel Literature, and the Ancient Novel: Rewriting the Past* (New York: Oxford University Press, 2003).

[35] It is interesting in this light to look at the recent remarks by Rosemary M. Dowsett, who begins her commentary on Acts with the following observation: "If Acts were a novel, it would be a blockbuster thriller. It has all the ingredients of a gripping tale: intrigue and suspense; dramatic escapes; exotic travel; the extraordinary and the bizarre rubbing shoulders with the mundane; and the ultimate triumph, against all odds, of the heroes and heroines of the piece. Of course, Acts

work, therefore, stays well within the theologically defined boundaries of the discipline at that time.

Compared with the research in this volume, the contrast is obvious. The focus of the genre debate has clearly shifted over the past seventy years from the apocryphal to the canonical Acts, and the sharp distinction between the two has been deconstructed even further. The purely historiographical character of Acts, still an unshakeable certainty in Söder's work, has now become a point of serious contention. As the essays in this volume demonstrate, other genres are now considered alongside the novel. Here another similarity with Söder's analysis of the apocryphal Acts can be noted. Rather than thinking in terms of mutually exclusive categories, there seems to be a growing appreciation for the complexity of the relationship with other bodies of literature in the same time period. The quest for the one genre that explains everything is gradually being replaced by the idea of complexity, or, as Moreland states, "no genre category perfectly fits Acts, [and] it has become quite clear that the author of Acts could employ elements from a number of ancient literary categories."[36] A similar appreciation of the complexity of Acts is also present in Samuel Byrskog's contribution, as he seeks "to present a model of historical interpretation that avoids the scholarly antithesis between history and story, offering some suggestions for understanding the complex synthesis of diachronic and synchronic elements in Acts."[37]

Further reflection may well be necessary here. As Byrskog notes, for instance, "the writing is the warp, and the reader's voice is the woof; together they form the web."[38] Reading Acts from a different perspective will no doubt create new webs of signification and thus new meanings as well. When Acts is read from the perspective of the rhetorical handbooks, different observations will come to mind than when compared with the *Iliad,* ancient novels, or Plutarch's *Lives.* While the idea that the reader/interpreter is involved in the process of signification is not itself new, it does allow us to raise some intriguing hermeneutical questions with respect to the genre discussion. To what extent, for instance, does the interest of the researcher play a role in the preference for a particular

---

isn't a novel—it is an extraordinary, remarkably accurate historical record" ("Acts of the Apostles," in *The IVP Women's Bible Commentary* [ed. C. Clark Kroeger and M. J. Evans; Downers Grove, Ill.: InterVarsity Press, 2002], 606).

[36] Moreland, "Jerusalem Community," 288.

[37] Samuel Byrskog, "History or Story in Acts—A Middle Way? The 'We' Passages, Historical Intertexture, and Oral History," 259, in this volume.

[38] Ibid., 268.

approach/genre? What factors shape that interest?[39] And to what extent is the preference for a particular genre for/approach to Acts also gendered and why? This latter question is worth exploring here in more detail.

Far from suggesting that there exists a great divide between female and male scholars in this respect or that gender is the only decisive element in individual assessments of genre, one can perceive an intriguing tendency when it comes to defining the genre of Acts. Female scholars are well represented among those who explore venues other than the traditional historiographical paradigm. The essays of Schwartz and Wordelman in this volume provide excellent examples. Schwartz explores more specifically the parallels between the Greek novels and Acts, while Wordelman focuses on Greco-Roman literary and mythological traditions underlying Acts 14. In a larger framework, it is worth observing that female scholars seem to take a greater interest in the narrative parallels from novels,[40] epic,[41] and myth[42] than in historiography.[43] Söder's work can be considered prototypical here as well. So how does one explain this preference for other genres? Are genres and the process of genre selection somehow and to some degree gendered? And does that explain why male and female readers take a differing interest in and approach to this matter?[44]

---

[39] As already noted in the case of Söder, but also in the introduction to this volume (Penner, "Contextualizing Acts," 11–12]), when Acts is considered an important (and also normative) source of information about the first Christian communities, there may be a theological interest at stake in safeguarding its historical character. Such an interest, however, is not the privilege of the defender of its historicity; it can just as well play a role in explicitly denying the historicity of Acts.

[40] See Saundra Schwartz, "Courtroom Scenes in the Ancient Greek Novels" (Ph.D. diss., Columbia University, 1998); Susan Marie Praeder, "Luke-Acts and the Ancient Novel," in *SBL Seminar Papers, 1981* (SBLSP 20; Chico, Calif.: Scholars Press, 1981), 269–92; and Stephen P. Schierling and Marla J. Schierling, "The Influence of the Ancient Romances on the Acts of the Apostles," *ClassBul* 54 (1978): 81–88.

[41] Marianne Palmer Bonz, *The Past as Legacy: Luke-Acts and Ancient Epic* (Minneapolis: Fortress, 2000).

[42] Amy L. Wordelman, "The Gods Have Come Down: Images of Historical Lycaonia and the Literary Construction of Acts 14" (Ph.D. diss., Princeton University, 1994).

[43] For a critical engagement of the assessment of Acts as historiography, see Loveday Alexander, "Fact, Fiction and the Genre of Acts," *NTS* 44 (1998): 380–99.

[44] There are undoubtedly cultural factors that also need to be considered in this context. A further exploration of the intersection of gender and larger cultural trends and perspectives with respect to certain genre choices and approaches would be instructive.

Questions about the gendered nature of writings are usually raised in connection with authorship rather than audience. In the case of Acts, the author is presumed to be male,[45] while his audience is usually defined in religious terms (Jewish/Gentile, Christian/non-Christian) or in terms of socio-economic class/rank, rather than gender. Further, in this volume at least, the issue of the genre of Acts is generally understood to be related to the author's purpose and sociocultural context, while suggestions concerning his audience focus on the reader's appreciation of the content rather than the genre of Luke's work.[46] Joseph Tyson summarizes the prevailing view in the essays as follows: "[The essays] take seriously the fact that Luke-Acts was written in Greek by an author who presupposed an audience that spoke and read the Greek language and had a wide familiarity with epic literature, an ability to hear echoes from well-known texts, and an appreciation for a carefully presented argument."[47]

However, Luke's choice when it comes to genre may have been determined at least as much by the audience he had in mind as by his personal preferences and agendas. It is at this juncture, in my perception, that the connection between genre and gender comes into play. This connection can be discovered when one takes into consideration the particular setting of the genres in question. It is here also that gender and class intersect.[48] If the public sphere of the *polis* is dominated by Greek, freeborn, educated male

---

[45] Most early Christian writers are presumed to be males, although in some cases female authorship has been suggested for both canonical and apocryphal writings. Priscilla was put forward as the author of Hebrews by Adolf von Harnack ("*Probabilia* über die Adresse und den Verfasser des Hebräerbriefes," ZNW 1 [1900]: 16–41) and more recently by Ruth Hoppin (*Priscilla's Letter: Finding the Author of the Epistle to the Hebrews* [San Francisco: International Scholars Publications, 1997]). There is a substantive discussion of the issues related to female authorship in antiquity in Mary R. Lefkowitz, "Did Ancient Women Write Novels?" in *"Women Like This": New Perspectives on Jewish Women in the Greco-Roman World* (ed. A.-J. Levine; SBLEJL 1; Atlanta: Scholars Press, 1991), 199–219; and Ross Shepherd Kraemer, "Women's Authorship of Jewish and Christian Literature in the Greco-Roman Period," in Levine, *"Women Like This,"* 221–42.

[46] E.g., Dennis R. MacDonald, who states that Luke "expected his readers to be sufficiently conversant with Greek epic to appreciate the differences between his account and the source being imitated" ("Paul's Farewell to the Ephesian Elders and Hector's Farewell to Andromache: A Strategic Imitation of Homer's *Iliad*," 202, in this volume).

[47] Joseph B. Tyson, "From History to Rhetoric and Back: Assessing New Trends in Acts Studies," 37, in this volume.

[48] For a discussion of the "multiplicative interdependence of gender, race, and class stratification" in the Greek *polis*, see Elisabeth Schüssler Fiorenza, *But She Said: Feminist Practices of Biblical Interpretation* (Boston: Beacon, 1992), 114–18.

citizens, then both public speech and writing related to that sphere can be expected to be dominated by higher-class males, both at the delivering and receiving end of the spectrum. In this case, the intended audience will link up with the author, who, in speaking and/or writing, has his fellow (male) citizens in view. Even if the author is not consciously excluding others, these citizens will constitute his target audience. Genres, then, such as historiography, political biographies, philosophy, and rhetoric, which by their nature have the public sphere of the *polis* as their primary location, can therefore be expected to be male gendered.[49] Novels, however, meant as entertainment[50] for the educated classes and belonging to the private sphere of the home, may have had a broader audience in view, including women.[51] This mixed-gender status of the novels on the level of their audience, as well as the presence of female protagonists on the level of their content, may well

---

[49] This observation is illustrated well by David Balch's and Todd Penner's contributions in this volume related to the civic discourse of Acts, where it becomes readily apparent that the political discourse of the Greeks and Romans is so completely male-focused that it excludes, to a large degree, any significant female presence and participation.

[50] Kate Cooper, however, argues that the novels were more than just entertainment; they also contained an ideological agenda: "We see here a harnessing of desire—the hero's desire and the reader's desire—to a moral: at the tale's end, the marriage feast must be celebrated, and the work of maintaining and renewing the city must begin" (*The Virgin and the Bride: Idealized Womanhood in Late Antiquity* [Cambridge: Harvard University Press, 1996], 24). Worth noting are the comments by Judith Perkins, *The Suffering Self: Pain and Narrative Representation in the Early Christian Era* (New York: Routledge, 1995), who argues that "Christian discourse challenged the discourse of power being constructed in other texts of the period" (115). See also the recent study by Katharine Haynes, *Fashioning the Feminine in the Greek Novel* (New York: Routledge, 2003), who draws out strong ideological connections for the Greek novel.

[51] Both the class and gender of the audience of the Greek novels are a point of discussion. According to Pervo, "These works were evidently composed to meet the leisure needs of citizen groups in the cities of the Hellenistic and imperial east. These persons were the beneficiaries of general education, open in many cases to women" (Richard I. Pervo, *Profit with Delight: The Literary Genre of the Acts of the Apostles* [Philadelphia: Fortress, 1987], 84). See also Renate Johne, "Women in the Ancient Novel," in *The Novel in the Ancient World* (ed. G. Schmeling; rev. ed.; MnSup 159; Leiden: Brill, 2003), 151–207, who focuses on upper-class female readership of the novels. That the Greek novels were meant for a female audience has earlier been used as an argument to discredit the genre: "If cultural decadence was discounted as an explanation for the romances' imputed literary failings, the next best theory was that the intended readership was female" (Cooper, *Virgin and the Bride*, 23). Cooper herself thinks that the Greek novels were rather meant for a male audience.

explain the fact that, compared with other genres, the ancient novel has attracted so much interest among female scholars in our own time.[52]

How does this discussion of the gendered nature of genre affect the study of Acts? A first observation is that if Luke had a mixed audience in mind, this can be expected to have influenced also the choices he made with respect to genre. He may have used different genres in order to appeal to different audiences, including women.[53] The exclusive focus on one particular genre or setting rules out the possibility that elements of other genres and settings may be functioning in Acts as well and that deliberate (rather than just unintentional) multivalency may be operative in Acts as a result.[54] It is therefore important to use strategies of multiple readings from different places and viewpoints.

Second, if genre is not gender neutral, neither is scholarship. The fact that male and female scholars seem, at least at one level, to be drawn to different types of literature bears further reflection.[55] It also raises more

---

[52] This interest is not limited to the Greek novels but also includes Jewish and Christian literature attributed to this genre. See, e.g., Melissa Aubin, "Reversing Romance? *The Acts of Thecla* and the Ancient Novel," in *Ancient Fiction and Early Christian Narrative* (ed. R. F. Hock et al.; SBLSymS 6; Atlanta: Scholars Press, 1998), 257–72; Angela Standhartinger, *Das Frauenbild im Judentum der Hellenistischen Zeit: Ein Beitrag anhand von Joseph und Aseneth* (AGJU 26; Leiden: Brill, 1995); idem, "Joseph und Aseneth: Vollkommene Braut oder himmlische Prophetin," in *Kompendium Feministische Bibelauslegung* (ed. L. Schottroff and M.-T. Wacker; 2d ed.; Gütersloh: Kaiser, 1999), 459–64; and Ross Shepard Kraemer, *When Aseneth Met Joseph: A Late Antique Tale of the Biblical Patriarch and His Egyptian Wife, Reconsidered* (New York: Oxford University Press, 1998).

[53] The idea that Acts draws on a mix of genres is also suggested by Moreland, "Jerusalem Community in Acts," 288; and Penner, "Contextualizing Acts," 15.

[54] Mark D. Given, *Paul's True Rhetoric: Ambiguity, Cunning and Deception in Greece and Rome* (ESEC 7; Harrisburg, Pa: Trinity Press International, 2001), has developed such an approach to Luke's portrayal of Paul in Acts.

[55] In an earlier article I have argued, along similar lines, that there is a pronounced gendered nature to the assessment of the authenticity of Paul's prohibition against women speaking in the assembly: male scholars tend to view 1 Cor 14:33b–35 as a later interpolation, while female scholars consider it to be authentically Pauline (Caroline Vander Stichele, "Is Silence Golden? Paul and Women's Speech in Corinth," *LS* 20 [1995], 241–53). One can draw out this observation further in terms of methodology as well. It would be interesting, for instance, to compare the study of the trial scenes in Schwartz's essay in this volume with the most recent assessment by Heike Omerzu, *Der Prozess des Paulus: Eine exegetische und rechtshistorische Untersuchung der Apostelgeschichte* (BZNW 115; Berlin: de Gruyter, 2002). Worth noting is the proper sphere deemed suitable for comparison in the study of the trials. Moreover, the respective bibliographies reflect the difference in interests as well.

fundamental hermeneutical questions. To what extent do we construct the world in which we situate Acts in our own image? Similar observations can also be made for class issues. What does it mean to reconstruct Luke's audience in terms of an educated elite? Tyson already pointed to the tendency to situate Luke's work "at the topmost rung of the literary ladder"[56] rather than as *Kleinliteratur*, reflecting an image of Luke that comes (maybe suspiciously) close to that of a contemporary scholar. Far from discrediting scholarship, I think addressing these issues rather increases its relevance and potential as a (self- and ideology-) critical discourse.

Culture in Context

If Söder's study illustrates that the discussion of genre is gendered, it similarly demonstrates that it is firmly rooted in Western, historical-critical discourse and that larger cultural interests are clearly informing this discussion.[57] In this respect, another observation already made by Tyson in his contribution to this volume deserves to be repeated here as well: the focus of most essays is decidedly on the Greco-Roman world. As he notes, the result thereof is that "we now seem to be neglecting the other major context in which Christianity arose and in which the author of Acts appears to have a great interest: the Jewish context."[58] Given the importance of "things Jewish" to Luke, this "constitutes a serious deficiency."[59] I share this concern and would like to expand on Tyson's analysis, because I do not think the problem is merely one of content or the solution only a matter of paying more attention to the place of Jews and Judaism in Acts.

First of all, I wonder if the shift to the Greco-Roman world, noted by Tyson and acknowledged by Penner in the introduction to this volume,[60] is not the consequence of a more secular, literary approach to Acts and if the exploration of different genres cannot be seen as the result of leaving behind a theologically motivated historiographical approach to the text. In such an approach the normative and historical significance of Acts are interconnected in that the normativity of Acts depends on its presumed historicity—form and content are thus firmly linked. With a literary approach to Acts, however, this link is at risk of being severed. When only

---

[56] Tyson, "From History to Rhetoric and Back," 37.

[57] In his introduction, Penner similarly stresses the importance of the realization of the "culturedness of our own approaches" and observes that the "quest to dispense with the history behind the text ... is ... to be situated emphatically within a North American context" ("Contextualizing Acts," 17).

[58] Tyson, "From History to Rhetoric and Back," 38.

[59] Ibid., 39.

[60] Penner, "Contextualizing Acts," 19–20.

literary genres from the Greco-Roman world are used as models to categorize texts, its form becomes secularized. At first glance this procedure may give the impression of being merely descriptive, but upon closer inspection more may be going on. In focusing on the Greco-Roman world a firm link is established between Christian discourse and Greco-Roman culture, especially the acclaimed literary canon of that culture. In the process, however, Judaism tends to be reduced to a matter of content rather than context and thus is deprived of its materiality. Without critical reflection on these implications, one runs the risk of simply reinscribing dominant culture(s), not just ancient culture, but also contemporary Western culture.

At this juncture, Wordelman's analysis of the cultural stereotypes operative in the interpretation of Acts 14 and her reexamination of the text are illuminating.[61] As she notes, it is not enough to scrutinize previous scholarship for its shortcomings and biases in order to avoid the pitfalls of the past. If past scholarship did not escape serving ideological agendas, the same can be assumed for the present. Rather than failing to observe this phenomenon altogether or only paying lip service to this principle, one should address this issue as Wordelman does. In her conclusion she observes that there are

> points at which cultural assumptions, literary techniques, and historical realities can readily, inadvertently, and inappropriately become fused. As interpreters, we need to understand both ancient and modern tendencies in this regard if we are to explicate and thoughtfully consider the role of such dynamics in the narrative itself and in the ways in which we interact with the text.[62]

As Wordelman's analysis of Acts 14 also demonstrates, postcolonialism can help Western scholars to analyze and to reflect critically on their own cultural prejudices (including their reliance on the Greco-Roman world narrowly and exclusively defined) in drawing their attention to the presence of colonial discourse on the level of the biblical text, of interpretation, and of the guild. On the level of the biblical text, this reflection can make scholars more aware of the colonial and imperial ideology embedded in that text (in this case Acts), as well as of the concomitant marginalization of the subaltern other thereby taking place. On the level of interpretation,

---

[61] For a short description as well as a positive appreciation of her doctoral dissertation, see Vernon K. Robbins, *The Tapestry of Early Christian Discourse: Rhetoric, Society and Ideology* (London: Routledge, 1996), 201–7.

[62] Wordelman, "Cultural Divides and Dual Realities: A Greco-Roman Context for Acts 14," 232, in this volume.

it can reveal where such ideologies are reproduced or legitimated in subsequent interpretations of these texts. On the level of the guild, it can show where scholarly interests are implicated. This type of analysis can, for instance, be done by studying "the involvement and incorporation of European and American institutional processes which facilitated, legitimatized and perpetuated such inequalities."[63] In this respect, Kwok Pui-lan notes that, while the cultural imperialism of Christian missionaries has been heavily criticized, the role academic discourse has played in supporting such imperialism has largely escaped notice.[64]

In this perspective, the ideological character of a concept or category such as the Greco-Roman world with its focus on the Western part of the ancient world, while neglecting other parts of that world (especially Africa and Asia), becomes more readily apparent. It makes one aware that a certain selection has taken place, a choice to focus on the historical winners. However, a closer look reveals that the principle of selectivity, applied *ad extra* in this case, is further reproduced in distinctions *ad intra,* more specifically in the subsequent focus on specific historical times and bodies of literature within the Greco-Roman world itself. As Judith Hallett notes, the established Loeb Classical Library can serve as a particular example of a literary canon that purports to include everything that is important in Greek and Latin literature and thus can be considered "classical." However,

> efforts at designating works of literature as "classical," as canonical, often do not clearly separate the assessment of these literary works from the assessment of the cultural circumstances—the time, the place, and political environment—in which these works are produced, or even from the definition of the cultural circumstances in which literary works are produced as constituting a major historical "period."[65]

In other words, the "classical" is most often the conventional, with much being left off the map in the process of selection.

Despite the fact that such canonicity and selectivity are unavoidable, I agree with Hallett that it is important to rethink our literary canons and to revisit criteria traditionally utilized to construct them in the first place.

---

[63] Rasiah S. Sugirtharajah, "Postcolonial Theory and Biblical Studies," in *Fair Play: Diversity and Conflicts in Early Christianity: Essays in Honour of Heikki Räisänen* (ed. I. Dunderberg et al.; NovTSup 103; Leiden: Brill, 2002), 549.

[64] Kwok Pui-lan, *Introducing Asian Feminist Theology* (IFT 4; Sheffield: Sheffield Academic Press, 2000), 44.

[65] Judith P. Hallett, "Feminist Theory, Historical Periods, Literary Canons, and the Study of Greco-Roman Antiquity," in *Feminist Theory and the Classics* (ed. N. S. Rabinowitz and A. Richlin; New York: Routledge, 1993), 45.

Hallett herself does so in order to retrieve the role and representation of women. Although I subscribe to that agenda, I would broaden the perspective here to all others marginalized in dominant cultural discourses—ancient and modern. In Western discourse not only women but also Jews appear as particular others of the universal subject, which is presumed to be Christian and male.[66] Postcolonialism in turn has further exposed the interconnections between colonialism, sexism, and anti-Judaism and added colonized groups to this list of *others*. These categories may prove to be helpful tools for the analysis of existing structures, but binary oppositions at work in such distinctions are also in need of deconstruction.[67]

These and no doubt other issues as well deserve more attention and systematic reflection, but it would be wrong to blame sociorhetorical criticism for not sharing those concerns. To the contrary, it is part and parcel of a sociorhetorical approach to do so. Tyson already states in his essay that "[s]ociorhetorical criticism goes beyond an interest in the rhetorical strategies of the text and examines the social context within which the text was written."[68] This observation is indeed the case, but as an integrated approach to interpretation this method claims more than that. According to Vernon Robbins, "one of the goals of socio-rhetorical criticism is to nurture a broad-based interpretive analytics rather than simply to introduce another specialty into New Testament interpretation."[69] As such, it also explicitly addresses issues such as the interpreter's location and ideology as well as the ideological texture of early Christian discourse, which includes ideology in texts, in authoritative traditions of interpretation, in intellectual discourse, and in individuals and groups.[70] Moreover, sociorhetorical criticism also explores the interconnection between the original ideology of an ancient text and the subsequent ideologies of readers, examining the power of ideologies to reproduce and reinscribe themselves on one another.

---

[66] See Daniel Boyarin, *A Radical Jew: Paul and the Politics of Identity* (Berkeley and Los Angeles: University of California Press, 1994), 17.

[67] See also Pui-lan, *Introducing Asian Feminist Theology*, 62.

[68] Tyson, "From History to Rhetoric and Back," 33.

[69] Robbins, *Tapestry of Early Christian Discourse*, 13.

[70] See ibid., 192–236, for a more extensive presentation of ideological texture. A similar plea for a reconceptualization of biblical studies in rhetorical terms can also be found in Elisabeth Schüssler Fiorenza's work. She argues that "not detached value-neutrality but an explicit articulation of one's rhetorical strategies, interested perspectives, ethical criteria, theoretical frameworks, religious presuppositions, and sociopolitical locations for critical public discussion are appropriate in such a rhetorical paradigm of biblical scholarship" (*Rhetoric and Ethic: The Politics of Biblical Studies* [Minneapolis: Fortress, 1999], 27).

The essays in this volume tackle these (and related) issues in different ways and to varying degrees, offering as many interpretations of Acts as they engage in acts of interpretation. While they do take the Greco-Roman world as their point of departure, they also have the potential to lead us beyond the Greco-Roman world as we currently know and understand it. Future scholarship on Acts has much to look forward to in terms of exploring and mapping this (as of yet) unknown territory, but the essays in this volume provide some first steps toward this new cartography of both the ancient world and our own.

BIBLIOGRAPHY OF PRIMARY SOURCES

Achilles Tatius. *Leucippe and Clitophon*. Edited by E. Vilborg. Studia Graeca et Latina Gothoburgensia 1. Stockholm: Almqvist & Wiksell, 1955.
Aphthonius of Antioch. *Aphthonii Progymnasmata*. Edited by H. Rabe. Rhetores Graeci 10. Leipzig: Teubner, 1926.
———. "The *Progymnasmata* of Aphthonius in Translation." Translated by R. E. Nadeau. *Speech Monographs* 19 (1952): 264–85.
Aristotle. *Posterior Analytics. Topica*. Translated by H. Tredennick and E. S. Forster. LCL. Cambridge: Harvard University Press, 1960.
Aristotle, Longinus, and Demetrius. *Poetics. On the Sublime. On Style.* Translated by S. Halliwell, W. H. Fyfe, and D. C. Innes. LCL. Cambridge: Harvard University Press, 1995.
Arius Didymus. *Arius Didymus: Epitome of Stoic Ethics*. Edited and translated by A. J. Pomeroy. SBLTT 44. Atlanta: Scholars Press, 1999.
Augustine, *Confessions*. Translated by W. Watts. 2 vols. LCL. Cambridge: Harvard University Press, 1912.
Cagnat, René, ed. *Inscriptiones Graecae ad Res Romanas Pertinentes*. 4 vols. Paris: Leroux, 1911–27.
Chariton. *Callirhoe*. Translated by G. P. Goold. LCL. Cambridge: Harvard University Press, 1995.
Cicero. Translated by C. W. Keyes et al. 29 vols. LCL. Cambridge: Cambridge University Press, 1913–2001.
Diels, Hermann, and Walther Kranz, eds. *Die Fragmente der Vorsokratiker: Griechisch und Deutsch*. 2 vols. 6th ed. Zürich: Weidmann, 1992.
Diodorus Siculus. *Library of History*. Translated by C. H. Oldfather et al. 12 vols. LCL. Cambridge: Harvard University Press, 1933-1967.
Dionysius of Halicarnassus. *Critical Essays*. Translated by S. Usher. 2 vols. LCL. Cambridge: Harvard University Press, 1974–85.
———. *Denys d'Halicarnasse: Antiquités Romaines*. Translated by V. Fromentin. Paris: Belles Lettres, 1998.
———. *Roman Antiquities*. Translated by E. Cary and E. Spelman. 7 vols. LCL. Cambridge: Harvard University Press, 1937–50.
Evelyn-White, Hugh G., trans. *Hesiod, the Homeric Hymns and Homerica*. LCL. Cambridge: Harvard University Press, 1914.
Gaertringen, Hiller von, ed. *Inschriften von Priene*. Berlin: Reimer, 1906.

Gold, Victor R., et al., eds. *The New Testament and Psalms: An Inclusive Version*. New York: Oxford University Press, 1995.
Heliodorus. *Les Éthiopiques (Théagène et Chariclé)*. Edited by R. M. Rattenbury and T. W. Lumb. Translated by J. Maillon. 3 vols. Paris: Budé, 1935–43.
Hermogenes of Tarsus. *Hermogenes Opera*. Edited by H. Rabe. Rhetores Graeci 6. Leipzig: Teubner, 1913.
Hock, Ronald F., and Edward N. O'Neil, eds. and trans. *The Chreia and Ancient Rhetoric: Classroom Exercises*. SBLWGRW 2. Atlanta: Society of Biblical Literature, 2002.
———. *The* Progymnasmata. Vol. 1 of *The Chreia in Ancient Rhetoric*. SBLTT 27. Atlanta: Scholars Press, 1986.
Holladay, Carl R., ed and trans. *Fragments from Hellenistic Jewish Authors*. 4 vols. SBLTT 20, 30, 39, 40. Atlanta: Scholars Press, 1983–96.
Homer. *The Odyssey*. Translated by A. T. Murray and G. E. Dimock. 2 vols. LCL. Cambridge: Harvard University Press, 1919.
Horace. *The Complete Odes and Satires of Horace*. Edited and translated by S. Alexander. Princeton: Princeton University Press, 1999.
Isocrates. Translated by G. Norlin and L. R. Van Hook. 3 vols. LCL. Cambridge: Harvard University Press, 1928–45.
John of Sardis. *Ioannis Sardiani Commentarium in Aphthonii Progymnasmata*. Edited by H. Rabe. RG 15. Leipzig: Teubner, 1928.
Josephus. Translated by H. St. J. Thackeray et al. 13 vols. LCL. Cambridge: Harvard University Press, 1926–67.
———. *Judean Antiquities 1–4: Translation and Commentary*. Edited and translated by L. H. Feldman. Vol. 3 of *Flavius Josephus: Translation and Commentary*. Edited by S. Mason. Leiden: Brill, 2000.
Justinian. *Novellae [constitutiones]*. Edited by R. Schoell and W. Kroll. Vol. 3 of *Corpus Juris Civilis*. Edited by W. Kroll et al. 13th ed. 3 vols. Berlin: de Gruyter, 1963.
Kennedy, George A., ed. and trans. *Progymnasmata: Greek Textbooks of Prose Composition and Rhetoric*. SBLWGRW. Atlanta: Society of Biblical Literature, 2003.
Kock, Theodor, ed. *Comicorum atticorum fragmenta*. 3 vols. Leipzig: Teubner, 1888.
Libanius. *Imaginary Speeches*. Edited and translated by D. A. Russell. London: Duckworth, 1996.
Lightfoot, Joseph B., ed. and trans. *The Apostolic Fathers*. 5 vols. Repr., Peabody, Mass.: Hendrickson, 1989.
Livy. *History of Rome*. Translated by B. O. Foster et al. 14 vols. LCL. Cambridge: Harvard University Press, 1919–59.
Longus. *Daphnis and Chloe*. Edited by M. D. Reeve. Leipzig: Teubner, 1982.

Lucian. Translated by A. M. Harmon et al. 8 vols. LCL. Cambridge: Harvard University Press, 1913–67.

Marcus Aurelius. *Meditations.* Translated by C. R. Haines. LCL. Cambridge: Harvard University Press, 1916.

Matsen, Patricia P., Philip Rollinson, and Marion Sousa, eds. and trans. *Readings from Classical Rhetoric.* Carbondale: Southern Illinois University Press, 1990.

Meineke, August, ed. *Fragmenta comicorum graecorum.* 5 vols. Berlin: Reimer, 1841. Repr., Berlin: de Gruyter, 1970.

Menander. *Menandri quae supersunt.* Edited by A. Körte and A. Thierfelder. 2d ed. 2 vols. Leipzig: Teubner, 1959.

Newton, Charles T., Edward L. Hicks, and Gustav Hirschfeld, eds. *The Collection of Ancient Greek Inscriptions in the British Museum.* 4 vols. London: British Museum, 1874–1916.

Nicolaus of Myra. *Nicolai Progymnasmata.* Edited by J. Felten. Rhetores Graeci 11. Leipzig: Teubner, 1913.

Origen. *Contra Celsum.* Translated by H. Chadwick. Cambridge: Cambridge University Press, 1953.

Ovid. Translated by G. Showerman et al. 6 vols. LCL. Cambridge: Harvard University Press, 1914–31.

Persius. *The Satires of Persius.* Translated by W. Barr. Liverpool: Cairns, 1987.

Plato. Translated by H. N. Fowler et al. 12 vols. LCL. Cambridge: Harvard University Press, 1914–35.

Pliny the Elder. *Natural History.* Translated by H. Rackham, W. H. S. Jones, and D. E. Eichholz. 10 vols. LCL. Cambridge: Harvard University Press, 1938–63.

Plutarch. *Moralia.* Translated by F. C. Babbitt et al. 16 vols. LCL. Cambridge: Harvard University Press, 1927–76.

———. *Parallel Lives.* Translated by B. Perrin. 11 vols. LCL. Cambridge: Harvard University Press, 1914–26.

———. *Plutarco, Le Vite di Lucurgo e di Numa.* Edited by M. Manfredini and L. Piccarilli. 2d ed. Milan: Mondadori, 1990.

———. *Plutarco, Le Vite di Teseo e di Romolo.* Edited by C. Ampolo and M. Manfredini. Milan: Mondadori, 1988.

Polybius. *The Histories.* Translated by W. R. Paton. 6 vols. LCL. Cambridge: Harvard University Press, 1922–27.

Quintilian. *Institutio Oratoria.* Translated by H. E. Butler. 4 vols. LCL. Cambridge: Harvard University Press, 1920–22.

Radicke, Jan, ed. *Imperial and Undated Authors.* Fascicle 7 of vol. 4A of *Biography.* 8 fascicles. *FGH* 4A/7. Leiden: Brill, 1999.

Reardon, Bryan P., ed. *Collected Ancient Greek Novels.* Berkeley and Los Angeles: University of California Press, 1989.

Scott, Walter, ed and trans. *Hermetica: the Ancient Greek and Latin Writings Which Contain Religious or Philosophic Teachings Ascribed to Hermes Trismegistus*. London: Dawsons, 1968.
Seneca. *Apocolocyntosis*. Edited by P. T. Eden. Cambridge: Cambridge University Press, 1984.
Seneca. *Epistles*. Translated by R. M. Gummere. 3 vols. LCL. Cambridge: Harvard University Press, 1917–25.
Spengel, Leonhard von, ed. *Rhetores Graeci*. 3 vols. Leipzig: Teubner, 1854–56.
Stephens, Susan A., and John J. Winkler, eds. *Ancient Greek Novels: The Fragments*. Princeton: Princeton University Press, 1995.
Strabo. *Geography*. Translated by H. L. Jones. 8 vols. LCL. Cambridge: Harvard University Press, 1917–32.
Theon. *Aelius Théon: Progymnasmata*. Edited and translated by M. Patillon and G. Bolognesi. Paris: Belles Lettres, 1997.
———. "The *Progymnasmata* of Theon: A New Text with Translation and Commentary." Edited and translated by J. R. Butts. Ph.D. diss., Claremont Graduate School, 1986.
Thucydides. Translated by C. F. Smith. 4 vols. LCL. Cambridge: Harvard University Press, 1919–23.
Velleius Paterculus. *Compendium of Roman History. Res Gestae Divi Augusti*. Translated by F. W. Shipley. LCL. Cambridge: Harvard University Press, 1924.
Vergil. *The Aeneid*. Translated by R. Fitzgerald. New York: Random House, 1983.
Xenophon. *Scripta Minora: Memorabilia and Oeconomicus. Symposium and Apologia*. Translated by E. C. Marchant and O. J. Todd. LCL. Cambridge: Harvard University Press, 1968.
Xenophon of Ephesus. *Les Éphésiaques ou le Roman d'Habrocomes et d'Anthia*. Edited and translated by G. Dalmeyda. Paris: Belles Lettres, 1926.

Bibliography of Modern Authors

Aejmelaeus, Lars. *Die Rezeption der Paulusbriefe in der Miletrede [Apg 20.18–35]*. Annales Academiæ Scientiarum Fennicæ B 232. Helsinki: Suomalainen Tiedeakatemia, 1987.

Ahl, Frederick M. *Metaformations: Soundplay and Wordplay in Ovid and Other Classical Poets*. Ithaca, N.Y.: Cornell University Press, 1985.

Alcock, Susan E. "The Heroic Past in a Hellenistic Present." Pages 20–34 in *Hellenistic Constructs: Essays in Culture, History, and Historiography*. Edited by P. Cartledge, P. Garnsey, and E. Gruen. Hellenistic Culture and Society 26. Berkeley and Los Angeles: University of California Press, 1997.

Alexander, Loveday. "Acts and Ancient Intellectual Biography." Pages 31–63 in *The Book of Acts in Its Ancient Literary Setting*. Edited by B. W. Winter and A. D. Clarke. Vol. 1 of *The Book of Acts in Its First Century Setting*. Grand Rapids: Eerdmans, 1993.

———. "The Acts of the Apostles as an Apologetic Text." Pages 15–44 in *Apologetics in the Roman Empire: Pagans, Jews, and Christians*. Edited by M. Edwards et al. New York: Oxford University Press, 1999.

———. "Fact, Fiction and the Genre of Acts." *NTS* 44 (1998): 380–99.

———. "Formal Elements and Genre: Which Greco-Roman Prologues Most Closely Parallel the Lukan Prologues?" Pages 9–26 in *Luke and the Heritage of Israel: Luke's Narrative Claim upon Israel's Legacy*. Edited by D. P. Moessner. Harrisburg, Pa.: Trinity Press International, 1999.

———. "'In Journeying Often': Voyaging in the Acts of the Apostles and in Greek Romance." Pages 380–99 in *Luke's Literary Achievement: Collected Essays*. Edited by C. M. Tuckett. JSNTSup 116. Sheffield: Sheffield Academic Press, 1995.

———. "Marathon or Jericho? Reading Acts in Dialogue with Biblical and Greek Historiography." Pages 92–125 in *Auguries: The Jubilee Volume of the Sheffield Department of Biblical Studies*. Edited by D. J. A. Clines and S. D. Moore. JSOTSup 269. Sheffield: Sheffield Academic Press, 1998.

———. "Narrative Maps: Reflections on the Toponymy of Acts." Pages 17–57 in *The Bible in Human Society: Essays in Honour of John Rogerson*.

Edited by M. D. Carroll R., D. J. A. Clines, and P. R. Davies. JSOTSup 200. Sheffield: Sheffield Academic Press, 1995.

———. "The Preface to Acts and the Historians." Pages 73–103 in *History, Literature, and Society in the Book of Acts*. Edited by B. Witherington. Cambridge: Cambridge University Press, 1996.

———. *The Preface to Luke's Gospel: Literary Convention and Social Context in Luke 1.1–4 and Acts 1.1*. SNTSMS 78. Cambridge: Cambridge University Press, 1993.

———. "Reading Luke-Acts from Back to Front." Pages 419–46 in *The Unity of Luke-Acts*. Edited by J. Verheyden. BETL 142. Leuven: Leuven University Press, 1999.

Alexander, Philip S. "Geography and the Bible (Early Jewish)." *ABD* 2: 977–88.

Allen, O. Wesley. *The Death of Herod: The Narrative and Theological Function of Retribution in Luke-Acts*. SBLDS 158. Atlanta: Scholars Press, 1997.

Alonso, A. M. "The Effects of Truth: Re-Presentations of the Past and the Imagining of Community." *Journal of Historical Sociology* 1 (1988): 33–57.

Alonso-Núñez, J. M. "The Emergence of Universal Historiography from the Fourth to the Second Centuries BC." Pages 173–92 in *Purposes of History: Studies in Greek Historiography from the Fourth to the Second Centuries BC*. Edited by H. Verdin et al. Studia Hellenistica 30. Leuven: n.p., 1990.

Andersen, Øivind. "Oral Tradition." Pages 9–58 in *Jesus and the Oral Gospel Tradition*. Edited by H. Wansbrough. JSNTSup 64. Sheffield: Sheffield Academic Press, 1991.

Ando, Clifford. *Imperial Ideology and Provincial Loyalty in the Roman Empire*. Classics and Contemporary Thought 6. Berkeley and Los Angeles: University of California Press, 2000.

André, Jean-Marie. "La Conception de l'Etat et de l'Empire dans la penseé gréco-romaine des deux premiers siècles de notre ère." *ANRW* 2.30.1: 3–73.

Arnold, Bill. "Luke's Characterizing Use of the Old Testament in the Book of Acts." Pages 300–323 in *History, Literature and Society in the Book of Acts*. Edited by B. Witherington. Cambridge: Cambridge University Press, 1996.

Ascough, Richard S. "Narrative Technique and Generic Designation: Crowd Scenes in Luke-Acts and in Chariton." *CBQ* 58 (1996): 69–82.

———. *What Are They Saying about the Formation of the Pauline Churches?* New York: Paulist, 1998.

Attridge, Harold W. *The Interpretation of Biblical History in the* Antiquitates Judaicae *of Flavius Josephus*. HDR 7. Missoula, Mont.: Scholars Press, 1976.

Aubin, Melissa. "Reversing Romance? *The Acts of Thecla* and the Ancient Novel." Pages 257–72 in *Ancient Fiction and Early Christian Narrative*. Edited by R. F. Hock, J. Bradley Chance, and J. Perkins. SBLSymS 6. Atlanta: Scholars Press, 1998.

Auerbach, Erich. *Mimesis: The Representation of Reality in Western Literature*. Translated by W. R. Trask. Princeton: Princeton University Press, 1953.

Aune, David E. "Luke 1:1–4: Historical or Scientific Prooimion?" Pages 138–48 in *Paul, Luke and the Graeco-Roman World: Essays in Honour of Alexander J. M. Wedderburn*. Edited by A. Christophersen et al. JSNTSup 217. Sheffield: Sheffield Academic Press, 2003.

———. *The New Testament in Its Literary Environment*. LEC 8. Philadelphia: Westminster, 1987.

Bachmann, Michael. "Die Stephanusepisode [Apg 6,1–8,3]: Ihre Bedeutung für die lukanische Sicht des Jerusalemischen Tempels und des Judentums." Pages in 545–62 in *The Unity of Luke–Acts*. Edited by J. Verheyden. BETL 142. Leuven: Leuven University Press, 1999.

Bagnall, Roger S. *Egypt in Late Antiquity*. Princeton: Princeton University Press, 1993.

Bal, Mieke. *Narratology: Introduction to the Theory of Narrative*. 2d ed. Toronto: University of Toronto Press, 1997.

Balch, David L. "ἀκριβῶς ... γράψαι (Luke 1:3): To Write the *Full* History of God's Receiving All Nations." Pages 229–50 in *Jesus and the Heritage of Israel: Luke's Narrative Claim upon Israel's Legacy*. Edited by D. P. Moessner. Harrisburg, Pa.: Trinity Press International, 1999.

———. "Attitudes toward Foreigners in 2 Maccabees, Eupolemus, Esther, Aristeas, and Luke-Acts." Pages 22–47 in *The Early Church in Its Context: Essays in Honor of Everett Ferguson*. Edited by A. J. Malherbe et al. NovTSup 90. Leiden: Brill, 1998.

———. "Commentary on Luke." *Eerdmans Commentary on the Bible*. Grand Rapids: Eerdmans, forthcoming.

———. "Comments on the Genre and a Political Theme of Luke-Acts: A Preliminary Comparison of Two Hellenistic Historians." Pages 343–61 in *SBL Seminar Papers*, 1989. SBLSP 28. Atlanta: Scholars Press, 1989.

———. "Paul in Acts: '... You Teach All the Jews ... to Forsake Moses, Telling Them Not to ... Observe the Customs' (Act. 21,21)." Pages 11–23 in *Panchaia: Festschrift für Klaus Thraede*. Edited by M. Wacht. JAC Ergänzungsband 22. Münster: Aschendorff, 1995.

———. "Paul's Portrait of Christ Crucified (Gal 3:1) in Light of Paintings and Sculptures of Suffering and Death in Pompeiian and Roman Houses." In *Early Christian Families in Context: A Cross-Disciplinary Dialogue*. Edited by D. L. Balch and C. Osiek. Grand Rapids: Eerdmans, 2003.

———. "Political Friendship in the Historian Dionysius of Halicarnassus, *Roman Antiquities*." Pages 123–44 in *Greco-Roman Perspectives on Friendship*. Edited by J. T. Fitzgerald. SBLRBS 34. Atlanta: Scholars Press, 1997.

———. "Rich and Poor, Proud and Humble in Luke-Acts." Pages 214–33 in *The Social World of the First Christians: Essays in Honor of Wayne Meeks*. Edited by L. M. White and O. L. Yarbrough. Minneapolis: Fortress, 1995.

Baldwin, Charles S. *Medieval Rhetoric and Poetic (to 1400) Interpreted from Representative Works*. New York: Macmillan, 1928.

Balsdon, John P. V. D. "Dionysius on Romulus: A Political Pamphlet?" *JRS* 61 (1971): 18–27.

———. *Romans and Aliens*. Chapel Hill: University of North Carolina Press, 1979.

Bar-Kochva, Bezalel. *Pseudo-Hecataeus, "On the Jews": Legitimizing the Jewish Diaspora*. Berkeley and Los Angeles: University of California Press, 1996.

Barclay, John M. G. "Judaism in Roman Dress: Josephus' Tactics in the *Contra Apionem*." Pages 231–45 in *Internationales Josephus-Kolloquium Aarhus 1999*. Edited by J. U. Kalms. MJS 6. Münster: LIT, 2000.

Barrett, C. K. *A Critical and Exegetical Commentary on the Acts of the Apostles*. 2 vols. ICC. Edinburgh: T&T Clark, 1994–98.

Bartchy, S. Scott. "Community of Goods in Acts: Idealization or Social Reality?" Pages 309–18 in *The Future of Early Christianity: Essays in Honor of Helmut Koester*. Edited by B. A. Pearson. Minneapolis: Fortress, 1991.

Bartlett, John R. *Jews in the Hellenistic World: Josephus, Aristeas, The Sibylline Oracles, Eupolemus*. Cambridge Commentaries on Writings of the Jewish and Christian World, 200 BC to AD 200. Cambridge: Cambridge University Press, 1985.

Bartsch, Shadi. *Decoding the Ancient Novel: The Reader and the Role of Description in Heliodorus and Achilles Tatius*. Princeton: Princeton University Press, 1989.

Baslez, Marie-Françoise. "De l'histoire au roman: la Perse de Chariton." Pages 311–42 in *Le monde du roman grec*. Edited by M. Baslez, P. Hoffman, and M. Trédé. Paris: l'École normale supérieure, 1992.

Batstone, William W. "The Antithesis of Virtue: Sallust's *Synkrisis* and the Crisis of the Late Republic." *CA* 7 (1988): 1–29.

Bauckham, Richard. "The *Acts of Paul* as a Sequel to Acts." Pages 105–52 in *The Book of Acts in Its Ancient Literary Setting*. Edited by B. W. Winter and A. D. Clarke. Vol. 1 of *The Book of Acts in Its First Century Setting*. Grand Rapids: Eerdmans, 1993.

———. "James and Gentiles (Acts 15.13–21)." Pages 154–84 in *History, Literature and Society in the Book of Acts*. Edited by B. Witherington. Cambridge: Cambridge University Press, 1996.

———. *Jude and the Relatives of Jesus in the Early Church*. Edinburgh: T&T Clark, 1990.

———. "Kerygmatic Summaries in the Speeches of Acts." Pages 185–217 in *History, Literature and Society in the Book of Acts*. Edited by B. Witherington. Cambridge: Cambridge University Press, 1996.

Baumann, Gerd. *The Multicultural Riddle: Rethinking National, Ethnic, and Religious Identities*. New York: Routledge, 1999.

Baur, Ferdinand Christian. *Paul, the Apostle of Jesus Christ, His Life and Work, His Epistles and His Doctrine: A Contribution to a Critical History of Primitive Christianity*. Translated by A. Menzies. 2 vols. London: Williams & Norgate, 1876.

———. *The Church History of the First Three Centuries*. Translated by A. Menzies. 3 vols. London: Williams & Norgate, 1878.

Baxter, Timothy M. S. *The Cratylus: Plato's Critique of Naming*. Philosophia antiqua 58. Leiden: Brill, 1992.

Beard, Mary, and John Henderson. "The Emperor's New Body: Ascension from Rome." Pages 191–219 in *Parchments of Gender: Deciphering Bodies in Antiquity*. Edited by M. Wyke. Oxford: Clarendon, 1998.

Beavis, Mary Ann. "Ancient Slavery as an Interpretive Context for the New Testament Servant Parables with Special Reference to the Unjust Steward (Luke 16:1–8)." *JBL* 111 (1992): 37–54.

———. "Parable and Fable: Synoptic Parables and Greco-Roman Fables Compared." *CBQ* 52 (1990): 473–98.

Béchard, Dean P. "Paul among the Rustics: The Lystran Episode (Acts 14:8–20) and Lucan Apologetic." *CBQ* 63 (2001): 84–101.

———. *Paul outside the Walls: A Study of Luke's Socio-Geographical Universalism in Acts 14:8–20*. AnBib 143. Rome: Pontifical Biblical Institute, 2000.

Benko, Stephen. "Virgil's Fourth Eclogue in Christian Interpretation." *ANRW* 2.31.1:646–705.

Berger, Klaus. "Hellenistische Gattungen im Neuen Testament." *ANRW* 2.25.2:1031–432.

Berry, D. H., and Malcolm Heath. "Oratory and Rhetoric." Pages 393–420 in *Handbook of Classical Rhetoric in the Hellenistic Period 330 B.C.–A.D. 400*. Edited by S. E. Porter. Leiden: Brill, 1997.

Betz, Hans Dieter. *Galatians: A Commentary on Paul's Letter to the Churches in Galatia*. Hermeneia. Philadelphia: Fortress, 1979.

———. "Gottmensch II: Griechisch-römische Antike u. Urchristentum." *RAC* 12 (1983): 234–312.

Bickerman, Elias J. "*Consecratio.*" Pages 3–25 in *Le culte des souverains dans l'empire romain.* Edited by E. J. Bickerman and W. den Boer. Entretiens sur l'antiquité classique 19. Genève: Hardt, 1973.

Biddick, Kathleen. "Coming Out of Exile: Dante on the Orient(alism) Express." *AHR* 105 (2000): 1234–49.

Black, C. Clifton. "The Rhetorical Form of the Hellenistic Jewish and Early Christian Sermon: A Response to Lawrence Wills." *HTR* 81 (1988): 1–8.

Blomberg, Craig L. *Interpreting the Parables.* Downers Grove, Ill.: InterVarsity Press, 1990.

———. "The Law in Luke-Acts." *JSNT* 22 (1984): 53–80.

Bloomer, W. Martin. *Latinity and Literary Society at Rome.* Philadelphia: University of Pennsylvania Press, 1997.

Blue, Brad. "The Influence of Jewish Worship on Luke's Presentation of the Early Church." Pages 473–97 in *Witness to the Gospel: The Theology of Acts.* Edited by I. H. Marshall and D. Peterson. Grand Rapids: Eerdmans, 1998.

Blumenfeld, Bruno. *The Political Paul: Justice, Democracy and Kingship in a Hellenistic Framework.* JSNTSup 210. Sheffield: Sheffield Academic Press, 2002.

Blundell, Mary W. "*Ēthos* and *Dianoia* Reconsidered." Pages 155–75 in *Essays on Aristotle's Poetics.* Edited by A. O. Rorty. Princeton: Princeton University Press, 1992.

Bonner, Stanley F. *Education in Ancient Rome: From the Elder Cato to the Younger Pliny.* Berkeley and Los Angeles: University of California Press, 1977.

———. *Roman Declamations in the Late Republic and Early Empire.* Berkeley and Los Angeles: University of California Press, 1949.

Bonz, Marianne Palmer. See Palmer Bonz, Marianne.

Bosworth, A. B. *From Arrian to Alexander: Studies in Historical Interpretation.* New York: Oxford University Press, 1988.

Botha, Pieter J. J. "The Verbal Art of the Pauline Letters: Rhetoric, Performance and Presence." Pages 409–28 in *Rhetoric and the New Testament: Essays from the 1992 Heidelberg Conference.* Edited by S. E. Porter and T. H. Olbricht. JSNTSup 90. Sheffield: Sheffield Academic Press, 1993.

Bowersock, Glen W. *Augustus and the Greek East.* Oxford: Oxford University Press, 1965.

———. *Fiction as History: Nero to Julian.* Sather Classical Lectures 58. Berkeley and Los Angeles: University of California Press, 1994.

———. "Historical Problems in Late Republican and Augustan Classicism." Pages 57–75 in *Le Classicisme à Rome aux 1ers Siècles avant et après J.-C.* Edited by H. Flashar. Entretiens sur l'antiquité classique 25. Geneva: Hardt, 1979.

Bowie, Ewen L., and Stephen J. Harrison. "The Romance of the Novel." *JRS* 83 (1993): 159–78.
Boyarin, Daniel. *A Radical Jew: Paul and the Politics of Identity*. Berkeley and Los Angeles: University of California Press, 1994.
Braun, Willi. *Feasting and Social Rhetoric in Luke 14*. SNTSMS 85. Cambridge: Cambridge University Press, 1995.
Braund, David. *Rome and the Friendly King: The Character of the Client Kingship*. London: St. Martin's, 1984.
Brawley, Robert. "Abrahamic Covenant Traditions and the Characterization of God in Luke-Acts." Pages 109–32 in *The Unity of Luke-Acts*. Edited by J. Verheyden. BETL 142. Leuven: Leuven University Press, 1999.

———. *Text to Text Pours Forth Speech: Voices of Scripture in Luke-Acts*. Bloomington: Indiana University Press, 1995.
Brehm, Harold A. "Vindicating the Rejected One: Stephen's Speech as Critique of the Jewish Leaders." Pages 266–99 in *Early Christian Interpretation of the Scriptures of Israel: Investigations and Proposals*. Edited by C. A. Evans and J. A. Sanders. JSNTSup 148. SSEJC 5. Sheffield: Sheffield Academic Press, 1997.
Bremmer, Jan N., and Nicholas M. Horsfall. *Roman Myth and Mythography*. University of London, Institute of Classical Studies Bulletin Supplement 52. London: Institute of Classical Studies, 1987.
Brenk, Frederick E. "An Imperial Heritage: The Religious Spirit of Plutarch of Chaironeia." *ANRW* 2.36.1:248–349.
Brent, Allen. *The Imperial Cult and the Development of Church Order: Concepts and Images of Authority in Paganism and Early Christianity before the Age of Cyprian*. VCSup 45. Leiden: Brill, 1999.

———. "Luke-Acts and the Imperial Cult in Asia Minor." *JTS* 48 (1997): 111–38.
Breytenbach, Cilliers. *Paulus und Barnabas in der Provinz Galatien: Studien zu Apostelgeschichte 13f.; 16,6; 18,23 und den Adressaten des Galaterbriefes*. AGJU 38. Leiden: Brill, 1996.
Bringmann, Klaus. "The King as Benefactor: Some Remarks on Ideal Kingship in the Age of Hellenism." Pages 7–24 in *Images and Ideologies: Self-Definition in the Hellenistic World*. Edited by A. Bulloch et al. Helenistic Culture and Society 12. Berkeley and Los Angeles: University of California Press, 1993.
Brinkman, J. A. "The Literary Background of the 'Catalogue of the Nations' (Acts 2:9–11)." *CBQ* 25 (1963): 418–27.
Brodie, Thomas L. "Luke the Literary Interpreter: Luke-Acts as a Systematic Rewriting and Updating of the Elijah-Elisha Narrative in 1 and 2 Kings." Ph.D. diss., Pontifical University of St. Thomas Aquinas [Rome], 1981.

———. "Luke's Redesigning of Paul: Corinthian Division and Reconciliation (1 Corinthians 1–5) as One Component of Jerusalem Unity (Acts 1–5)." *IBS* 17 (1995): 98–128.

———. "Towards Tracing the Gospels' Literary Indebtedness to the Epistles." Pages 104–16 in *Mimesis and Intertextuality in Antiquity and Christianity*. Edited by D. R. MacDonald. Harrisburg, Pa.: Trinity Press International, 2001.
Brown, Raymond E. *The Birth of the Messiah*. New York: Doubleday, 1979.
———. *The Gospel According to John*. 2 vols. AB 29–29A. New York: Doubleday, 1966–70.
Bruce, F. F. "The Acts of the Apostles: Historical Record or Theological Reconstruction." *ANRW* 2.25.3:2569–603.
———. *The Book of Acts*. Rev. ed. NICNT. Grand Rapids: Eerdmans, 1988.
Buell, Denise Kimber. "Ethnicity and Religion in Mediterranean Antiquity and Beyond." *RelSRev* 26 (2000): 243–49.
Bultmann, Rudolf. "New Testament and Mythology." Pages 1–44 in vol. 1 of *Kerygma and Myth: A Theological Debate*. Edited by H. W. Bartsch. Translated by R. H. Fuller. 2 vols. London: SPCK, 1953.
Burchard, Christoph. *Der dreizehnte Zeuge: Traditions- und kompositionsgeschichtliche Untersuchungen zu Lukas' Darstellung der Frühzeit des Paulus*. FRLANT 103. Göttingen: Vandenhoeck & Ruprecht, 1970.
Burfeind, Carsten. "Wen hörte Philippus? Leises Lesen und lautes Vorlesen in der Antike." *ZNW* 93 (2002): 138–45.
Burridge, Richard A. *What Are the Gospels? A Comparison with Graeco-Roman Biography*. SNTSMS 70. Cambridge: Cambridge University Press, 1992.
Burrus, Virginia. *"Begotten, Not Made": Conceiving Manhood in Late Antiquity*. Stanford, Calif.: Stanford University Press, 2000.
Butts, James R. "The *Progymnasmata* of Theon: A New Text with Translation and Commentary." Ph.D. diss., Claremont Graduate School, 1986.
Buxton, Richard. *Imaginary Greece: The Contexts of Mythology*. Cambridge: Cambridge University Press, 1994.
Byrskog, Samuel. *Jesus the Only Teacher: Didactic Authority and Transmission in Ancient Israel, Ancient Judaism and the Matthean Community*. ConBNT 24. Stockholm: Almqvist & Wiksell, 1994.
———. *Story as History—History as Story: The Gospel Tradition in the Context of Ancient Oral History*. WUNT 123. Tübingen: Mohr Siebeck, 2000. Repr., Leiden: Brill, 2002.
———. "Talet, minnet och skriften: Evangelietraditionen och den antika informationsteknologin." *SEÅ* 66 (2001): 139–50.
Cadbury, Henry J. *The Book of Acts in History*. New York: Harper, 1955.
———. "Four Features of Lucan Style." Pages 87–102 in *Studies in Luke-Acts*. Edited by L. E. Keck and J. L. Martyn. Nashville: Abingdon, 1966.
———. *The Making of Luke-Acts*. 2d ed. London: SPCK, 1958. Repr., Peabody, Mass.: Hendrickson, 1999.

———. "Names for Christians and Christianity in Acts." Pages 384–85 in vol. 5 of *The Beginnings of Christianity: The Acts of the Apostles*. Edited by F. J. Foakes Jackson and K. Lake. 5 vols. London: Macmillan, 1920–33. Repr., Grand Rapids: Baker, 1979.

———. "The Speeches in Acts." Pages 402–27 in vol. 5 of *The Beginnings of Christianity: The Acts of the Apostles*. Edited by F. J. Foakes Jackson and K. Lake. 5 vols. London: Macmillan, 1920–33. Repr., Grand Rapids: Baker, 1979.

———. *The Style and Literary Method of Luke*. Cambridge: Harvard University Press, 1920.

Cairns, Francis. *Virgil's Augustan Epic*. Cambridge: Cambridge University Press, 1989.

Calame, Claude. "The Rhetoric of *Muthos* and *Logos:* Forms of Figurative Discourse." Pages 119–43 in *From Myth to Reason? Studies in the Development of Greek Thought*. Edited by R. Buxton. New York: Oxford University Press, 1999.

Cameron, Ron. "Alternate Beginnings—Different Ends: Eusebius, Thomas, and the Construction of Christian Origins." Pages 501–25 in *Religious Propaganda and Missionary Competition in the New Testament World: Essays Honoring Dieter Georgi*. Edited by L. Borman, K. Del Tredici, and A. Standhartinger. NovTSup 74. Leiden: Brill, 1994.

Cancik, Hubert. "The History of Culture, Religion, and Institutions in Ancient Historiography: Philological Observations Concerning Luke's History." *JBL* 116 (1997): 673–95.

———. "Reinheit und Enthaltsamkeit in der römischen Philosophie und Religion." Pages 1–15 and 126–42 in *Aspekte frühchristlicher Heiligenverehrung*. Edited by F. von Lilienfeld. OIKONOMIA: Quellen und Studien zur orthodoxen Theologie 6. Erlangen: Lehrstuhl für Geschichte und Theologie des christlichen Ostens an der Universität Erlangen, 1977.

Cancik, Hubert, and Hildegard Cancik-Lindemaier. "*Patria—peregrina—universa:* Versuch einer Typologie der univeralistischen Tendenzen in der Geschichte der römischen Religion." Pages 64–74 in *Tradition und Translation: Zum Problem der interkulturellen Übersetzbarkeit religiöser Phänomene. Festschrift für Carsten Colpe zum 65. Geburtstag*. Edited by C. Elsas et al. Berlin: de Gruyter, 1994.

Capper, Brian. "The Palestinian Context of Community of Goods." Pages 323–56 in *The Book of Acts in Its Palestinian Setting*. Edited by R. Bauckham. Vol. 4 of *The Book of Acts in Its First Century Setting*. Grand Rapids: Eerdmans, 1995.

———. "Reciprocity and the Ethic of Acts." Pages 499–518 in *Witness to the Gospel: The Theology of Acts*. Edited by I. H. Marshall and D. Peterson. Grand Rapids: Eerdmans, 1998.

Carandini, Andrea, and Rosanna Cappelli. *Roma: Romolo, Remo e la fondazione della città*. Exhibition, Rome; Museo Nationale Romano. 28 June–29 October 2000. Milan: Electa, 2000.
Cassidy, Richard J. *Society and Politics in the Acts of the Apostles*. Maryknoll, N.Y.: Orbis, 1987.
Centrone, Bruno. "Platonism and Pythagoreanism in the Early Empire." Pages 559–84 in *The Cambridge History of Greek and Roman Political Thought*. Edited by C. Rowe and M. Schofield. Cambridge: Cambridge University Press, 2000.
Clark, Andrew C. *Parallel Lives: The Relation of Paul to the Apostles in the Lucan Perspective*. Carlisle: Paternoster, 2001.
———. "The Role of the Apostles." Pages 169–90 in *Witness to the Gospel: The Theology of Acts*. Edited by I. H. Marshall and D. Peterson. Grand Rapids: Eerdmans, 1998.
Clark, Donald L. *Rhetoric in Greco-Roman Education*. New York: Columbia University Press, 1957.
Clarke, Martin L. *Higher Education in the Ancient World*. London: Routledge, 1971.
Clines, David J. A., and J. Cheryl Exum. "The New Literary Criticism." Pages 11–25 in *The New Literary Criticism and the Bible*. Edited by D. J. A. Clines and J. C. Exum. JSOTSup 13. Sheffield: Sheffield Academic Press, 1993.
Cohen, Shaye J. D. *The Beginnings of Jewishness: Boundaries, Varieties, Uncertainties*. Hellenistic Culture and Society 31. Berkeley and Los Angeles: University of California Press, 1999.
———. "History and Historiography in the *Against Apion* of Josephus." *History and Theory* 27 (1988): 1–11.
Colin, Jean. *Les villes libres de l'Orient gréco-romain et l'envoi au supplice par acclamations populaires*. Collections Latomus 82. Brussels-Berchem: Latomus, 1965.
Connolly, Joy. "Mastering Corruption: Constructions of Identity in Roman Oratory." Pages 130–51 in *Women and Slaves in Greco-Roman Culture*. Edited by S. R. Joshel and S. Murnaghan. London: Routledge, 1998.
Connors, Catherine. "Field and Forum: Culture and Agriculture in Roman Rhetoric." Pages 71–89 in *Roman Eloquence: Rhetoric in Society and Literature*. Edited by W. J. Dominik. New York: Routledge, 1997.
Conte, Gian Biagio. *Genres and Readers: Lucretius, Love Elegy, Pliny's Encyclopedia*. Translated by G. W. Most. Baltimore: Johns Hopkins University Press, 1994.
Conybeare, William J., and John S. Howson. *The Life and Epistles of St. Paul*. 7th ed. New York: Scribner, 1863.
Conzelmann, Hans. *The Acts of the Apostles*. Edited by E. J. Epp and C. R. Matthews. Translated by J. Limburg, A. T. Kraabel, and D. H. Juel. Hermeneia. Philadelphia: Fortress, 1987.

———. "The Address of Paul on the Areopagus." Pages 217–30 in *Studies in Luke-Acts: Essays Presented in Honor of Paul Schubert*. Edited by L. E. Keck and J. L. Martyn. Nashville: Abingdon, 1966.

———. *The Theology of St. Luke*. Translated by G. Buswell. New York: Harper & Row, 1961.

Cooper, Kate. *The Virgin and the Bride: Idealized Womanhood in Late Antiquity*. Cambridge: Harvard University Press, 1996.

Corbeill, Anthony. "Political Movement: Walking and Ideology in Republican Rome." Pages 182–215 in *The Roman Gaze: Vision, Power, and the Body*. Edited by D. Fredrick. Baltimore: Johns Hopkins University Press, 2002.

Cotter, Wendy. "The Collegia and Roman Law: State Restrictions on Voluntary Associations, 64 B.C.E.–200 C.E." Pages 74–89 in *Voluntary Associations in the Graeco-Roman World*. Edited by J. S. Kloppenborg and S. G. Wilson. London: Routledge, 1996.

Cribiore, Raffaela. *Gymnastics of the Mind: Greek Education in Hellenistic and Roman Egypt*. Princeton: Princeton University Press, 2001.

Crossan, John Dominic. *The Birth of Christianity: Discovering What Happened in the Years Immediately after the Execution of Jesus*. San Francisco: HarperSanFrancisco, 1998.

Csapo, Eric, and William J. Slater. *The Context of Ancient Drama*. Ann Arbor: University of Michigan Press, 1995.

Culpepper, R. Alan. "Luke." *NIB* 9:1–490.

Dahl, Nils A. "The Story of Abraham in Luke-Acts." Pages 139–58 in *Studies in Luke-Acts*. Edited by L. E. Keck and J. L. Martyn. Nashville: Abingdon, 1966.

D'Angelo, Mary Rose. "The **ANHP** Question in Luke-Acts: Imperial Masculinity and the Deployment of Women in the Early Second Century." Pages 44–69 in *A Feminist Companion to Luke*. Edited by A.-J. Levine, with M. Blickenstaff. FCNTECW 3. Sheffield: Sheffield Academic Press, 2002.

———. "(Re)Presentations of Women in the Gospel of Matthew and Luke-Acts." Pages 171–95 in *Women and Christian Origins*. Edited by R. S. Kraemer and M. R. D'Angelo. New York: Oxford University Press, 1999.

———. "Women in Luke-Acts: A Redactional View." *JBL* 109 (1990): 441–61.

Danker, Frederick W. *Benefactor: Epigraphic Study of a Graeco-Roman and New Testament Semantic Field*. St. Louis: Clayton, 1982.

Darr, John A. *Herod the Fox: Audience Criticism and Lukan Characterization*. JSNTSup 163. Sheffield: Sheffield Academic Press, 1998.

———. "Irenic or Ironic? Another Look at Gamaliel before the Sanhedrin (Acts 5:33–42)." Pages 121–39 in *Literary Studies in Luke-Acts: Essays in Honor of Joseph B. Tyson*. Edited by R. P. Thompson and T. E. Phillips. Macon, Ga.: Mercer University Press, 1998.

Davis, Casey Wane. *Oral Biblical Criticism: The Influence of the Principles of Orality on the Literary Structure of Paul's Epistle to the Philippians.* JSNTSup 172. Sheffield: Sheffield Academic Press, 1999.

Dawsey, James M. "Characteristics of Folk-Epic in Acts." Pages 317–25 in *SBL Seminar Papers, 1989.* SBLSP 28. Atlanta: Scholars Press, 1989.

Dean, Margaret E. "Textured Criticism." *JSNT* 70 (1998): 79–91.

Deissmann, Adolf. *Light from the Ancient East: The New Testament Illustrated by Recently Discovered Texts of the Graeco-Roman World.* Translated by L. R. M. Strachan. London: Hodder & Stoughton, 1910.

Delling, Gerhard. "Philons Enkomion auf Augustus." *Klio* 54 (1972): 171–92.

Denaux, Albert. "The Theme of Divine Visits and Human (In)Hospitality in Luke-Acts: Its Old Testament and Graeco-Roman Antecedents." Pages 255–79 in *The Unity of Luke-Acts.* Edited by J. Verheyden. BETL 142. Leuven: Leuven University Press, 1999.

Denova, Rebecca. *The Things Accomplished among Us: Prophetic Tradition in the Structural Pattern of Luke-Acts.* JSNTSup 141. Sheffield: Sheffield Academic Press, 1997.

Dibelius, Martin. *Studies in the Acts of the Apostles.* Edited by H. Greeven. Translated by M. Ling. London: SCM, 1956.

Dihle, Albrecht. *Die Entstehung der historischen Biographie.* Sitzungsberichte der Heidelberger Academie der Wissenschaften, Philosophisch-historische Klasse 3. Heidelberg: Universitätsverlag, 1987.

———. "Der Beginn des Attizismus." *Antike und Abendland* 23 (1977): 162–77.

Dinkler, Erich. "Älteste christliche Denkmäler–Bestand und Chronologie." Pages 134–78 in *Signum Crucis: Aufsätze zum Neuen Testament und zur christlichen Archäologie.* Tübingen: Mohr Siebeck, 1967.

Dodd, Charles H. *Parables of the Kingdom.* Rev. ed. New York: Scribner, 1961.

Dorey, Thomas A., ed. *Livy.* London: Routledge, 1971.

Dormeyer, Detlev. "*Stasis*-Vorwürfe gegen Juden und Christen und Rechtsbrüche in Prozessverfahren gegen sie nach Josephus' *Bellum Judaicum* und Mk 15,1–20 parr." Pages 63–78 in *Internationales Josephus-Kolloquium Aarhus 1999.* Edited by J. U. Kalms. MJS 6. Münster: LIT, 2000.

Dornseiff, Franz. "Σωτήρ." *PW* 2.3A.1:1211–21.

Dougherty, Carol. *The Poetics of Colonization: From City to Text in Archaic Greece.* New York: Oxford University Press, 1993.

Downing, F. Gerald. "*A bas les Aristos:* The Relevance of Higher Literature for the Understanding of the Earliest Christian Writings." *NovT* 30 (1988): 212–30.

Dowsett, Rosemary M. "Acts of the Apostles." Pages 606–27 in *The IVP Women's Bible Commentary.* Edited by C. Clark Kroeger and M. J. Evans. Downers Grove, Ill.: InterVarsity Press, 2002.

duBois, Page. *History, Rhetorical Description and the Epic: From Homer to Spenser.* Cambridge: Brewer, 1982.

Duff, Timothy E. *Plutarch's Lives: Exploring Virtue and Vice.* New York: Oxford University Press, 1999.

Dunn, James D. G. *The Partings of the Ways between Christianity and Judaism and Their Significance for the Character of Christianity.* Philadelphia: Trinity Press International, 1991.

Dupont, Jacques. *The Salvation of the Gentiles: Studies in the Acts of the Apostles.* Translated by J. Keating. New York: Paulist, 1979.

———. *The Sources of Acts: The Present Position.* London: Darton, Longman & Todd, 1964.

Easton, Burton S. "The Purpose of Acts." Pages 33–118 in *Early Christianity: The Purpose of Acts and Other Papers.* Edited by F. C. Grant. Greenwich: Seabury, 1954.

Eckstein, Arthur M. *Moral Vision in the Histories of Polybius.* Berkeley and Los Angeles: University of California Press, 1994.

Eder, Walter. "Augustus and the Power of Tradition: The Augustan Principate as Binding Link between Republic and Empire." Pages 71–122 in *Between Republic and Empire: Interpretations of Augustus and His Principate.* Edited by K. A. Raaflaub and M. Toher. Berkeley and Los Angeles: University of California Press, 1990.

Edwards, Douglas R. "Defining the Web of Power in Asia Minor." *JAAR* 57 (1994): 699–718.

———. "Pleasurable Reading or Symbols of Power? Religious Themes and Social Context in Chariton." Pages 31–46 in *Ancient Fiction and Early Christian Narrative.* Edited by R. F. Hock, J. B. Chance, and J. Perkins. SBLSymS 6. Atlanta: Scholars Press, 1998.

———. *Religion and Power: Pagans, Jews, and Christians in the Greek East.* New York: Oxford University Press, 1996.

Ellul, Jacques. *Propaganda: The Formation of Men's Attitudes.* Translated by K. Kellen and J. Lerner. New York: Knopf, 1965.

Engberg-Pedersen, Troels. "The Hellenistic Öffentlichkeit: Philosophy as a Social Force in the Greco-Roman Empire." Pages 15–37 in *Recruitment, Conquest, and Conflict: Strategies in Judaism, Early Christianity, and the Greco-Roman World.* Edited by P. Borgen, V. K. Robbins, and D. B. Gowler. ESEC 6. Atlanta: Scholars Press, 1998.

Esler, Philip F. *Community and Gospel in Luke-Acts: The Social and Political Motivations of Lucan Theology.* SNTSMS 57. Cambridge: Cambridge University Press, 1987.

Evans, Craig A. "Luke and the Rewritten Bible: Aspects of Lukan Hagiography." Pages 170–201 in *The Pseudepigrapha and Early Biblical Interpretation.* Edited by J. H. Charlesworth and C. A. Evans. JSPSup 14. SSEJC 2. Sheffield: Sheffield Academic Press, 1993.

———. Review of S. Byrskog, *Story as History—History as Story*. *BibInt* 9 (2001): 422–24.

Evans, Craig A., and James A. Sanders. *Luke and Scripture: The Function of Sacred Tradition in Luke-Acts*. Minneapolis: Fortress, 1993.

Evans, Jane DeRose. *The Art of Persuasion: Political Propaganda from Aeneas to Brutus*. Ann Arbor: University of Michigan Press, 1992.

Farmer, William R. "Notes on a Literary and Form-Critical Analysis of Some of the Synoptic Material Peculiar to Luke." *NTS* 8 (1961–62): 301–16.

Fearghail, Fearghus Ó. *The Introduction to Luke-Acts: A Study of the Role of Lk 1,1–4,44 in the Composition of Luke's Two-Volume Work*. AnBib 126. Rome: Pontifical Biblical Institute, 1991.

Fears, J. Rufus. "The Cult of Jupiter and Roman Imperial Ideology." *ANRW* 2.17.1:3–141.

Feldman, Louis H. "David." Pages 537–69 in *Josephus's Interpretation of the Bible*. Hellenistic Culture and Society 27. Berkeley and Los Angeles: University of California Press, 1998.

———. "Josephus' Biblical Paraphrase as a Commentary on Contemporary Issues." Pages 124–210 in *The Interpretation of Scripture in Early Judaism and Christianity: Studies in Language and Tradition*. Edited by C. A. Evans. JSPSup 33. SSEJC 7. Sheffield: Sheffield Academic Press, 2000.

———. "Moses." Pages 374–442 in *Josephus's Interpretation of the Bible*. Hellenistic Culture and Society 27. Berkeley and Los Angeles: University of California Press, 1998.

———. *Studies in Josephus' Rewritten Bible*. JSJSup 58. Leiden: Brill, 1998.

Finnegan, Ruth. *Oral Traditions and the Verbal Arts: A Guide to Research Practices*. ASA Research Methods in Social Anthropology. London: Routledge, 1992.

Fitzmyer, Joseph A. *The Gospel according to Luke*. 2 vols. AB 28–28A. New York: Doubleday, 1981–85.

Fleming, Katherine E. "Orientalism, the Balkans, and Balkan Historiography." *AHR* 105 (2000): 1218–33.

Foakes Jackson, Frederick J., and Kirsopp Lake, eds. *The Beginnings of Christianity*. 5 vols. London: Macmillan, 1920–33. Repr., Grand Rapids: Baker, 1979.

Fontenrose, Joseph E. "Philemon, Lot, and Lycaon." *University of California Publications in Classical Philology* 13 (1945): 93–120.

Fornara, Charles W. *The Nature of History in Ancient Greece and Rome*. Berkeley and Los Angeles: University of California Press, 1983.

Foucault, Michel. "What Is an Author?" Pages 101–20 in *The Foucault Reader*. Edited by P. Rabinow. New York: Pantheon, 1984.

Fredriksen, Paula. *Jesus of Nazareth, King of the Jews: A Jewish Life and the Emergence of Christianity*. New York: Knopf, 1999.

Fuks, Alexander. *Social Conflict in Ancient Greece*. Edited by M. Stern and M. Amit. Leiden: Brill, 1984.
Funk, Robert. *Poetics of Biblical Narrative*. Sonoma, Calif.: Polebridge, 1988.
Furtwängler, Adolf. *Die Antiken Gemmen: Geschichte der Steinschneidekunst im klassischen Altertum*. 3 vols. Amsterdam: Hakkert, 1964–65.
Gabba, Emilio. *Dionysius and the History of Archaic Rome*. Sather Classical Lectures 56. Berkeley and Los Angeles: University of California Press, 1991.
———. "Political and Cultural Aspects of the Classicistic Revival in the Augustan Age." *CA* 1 (1982): 43–65.
———. Review of Erich S. Gruen, *The Hellenistic World and the Coming of Rome*. *Athenaeum* 65 (1987): 205–10.
———. "True History and False History in Classical Antiquity." *JRS* 71 (1981): 50–62.
Gadamer, Hans Georg. *Truth and Method*. Translated by J. Weinsheimer and D. G. Marshall. 2d ed. New York: Continuum, 1993.
Gager, John G. *The Origins of Anti-Semitism: Attitudes Toward Judaism in Pagan and Christian Antiquity*. New York: Oxford University Press, 1985.
Galinsky, Karl. *Augustan Culture: An Interpretive Introduction*. Princeton: Princeton University Press, 1996.
———. *Ovid's Metamorphoses: An Introduction to the Basic Aspects*. Berkeley and Los Angeles: University of California Press, 1975.
Gaston, Lloyd. "Anti-Judaism and the Passion Narrative in Luke and Acts." Pages 127–153 in vol. 1 of *Anti-Judaism in Early Christianity*. Edited by P. Richardson, with D. Granskou. 2 vols. SCJ 2. Waterloo, Ont.: Wilfrid Laurier University Press, 1986.
Gaventa, Beverly R. "The Peril of Modernizing Henry Joel Cadbury." Pages 7–26 in *Cadbury, Knox, and Talbert: American Contributions to the Study of Acts*. Edited by M. C. Parsons and J. B. Tyson. Atlanta: Scholars Press, 1992.
Gavrilov, A. K. "Techniques of Reading in Classical Antiquity," *CQ* 91 NS 47 (1997): 56–73.
Gerber, Christine. *Ein Bild des Judentums für Nichtjuden von Flavius Josephus: Untersuchungen zu seiner Schrift Contra Apionem*. AGJU 40. Leiden: Brill, 1997.
Gilbert, Gary. "The List of Nations in Acts 2: Roman Propaganda and the Lukan Response." *JBL* 121 (2002): 497–529.
Gill, Christopher, and Timothy P. Wiseman, eds. *Lies and Fiction in the Ancient World*. Exeter: University of Exeter Press, 1993.
Given, Mark D. *Paul's True Rhetoric: Ambiguity, Cunning and Deception in Greece and Rome*. ESEC 7. Harrisburg, Pa: Trinity Press International, 2001.

Glaser, Konrad. "Numa." *PW* 17:1242–52.
Gleason, Maud. *Making Men: Sophists and Self-Presentation in Ancient Rome*. Princeton: Princeton University Press, 1995.
Goldhill, Simon. Review of George A. Kennedy, *A New History of Classical Rhetoric;* Glen W. Bowersock, *Fiction as History: Nero to Julian;* Maud A. Gleason, *Making Men: Sophists and Self-Presentation in Ancient Rome;* and John Poulakos, *Sophistical Rhetoric in Classical Greece*. *BMCR* 6 (1995): 350–63.
Goodman, Martin. "Jewish Proselytizing in the First Century." Pages 53–78 in *The Jews among Pagans and Christians in the Roman Empire*. Edited by J. Lieu, J. North, and T. Rajak. London: Routledge, 1992.
Goody, Jack. *The Interface between the Written and the Oral*. Studies in Literature, Family, Culture and the State. Cambridge: Cambridge University Press, 1987.
Goody, Jack, and Ian Watt. "The Consequences of Literacy." Pages 27–68 in *Literacy in Traditional Societies*. Edited by J. Goody. Cambridge: Cambridge University Press, 1968.
Görg, Manfred. "Apg 2,9–11 in außerbiblischer Sicht." *BN* 1 (1976): 15–18.
Goulder, Michael. *Type and History in Acts*. London: SPCK, 1964.
Grant, Robert M. "Eusebius and Imperial Propaganda." Pages 658–83 in *Eusebius, Christianity and Judaism*. Edited by H. W. Attridge and G. Hata. Leiden: Brill, 1992.
Gray, Vivienne J. "Xenophon and Isocrates." Pages 142–54 in *The Cambridge History of Greek and Roman Political Thought*. Edited by C. Rowe and M. Schofield. Cambridge: Cambridge University Press, 2000.
Green, Joel B. *The Gospel of Luke*. Grand Rapids: Eerdmans, 1997.
———. "Salvation to the End of the Earth: God as Saviour in the Acts of the Apostles." Pages 83–106 in *Witness to the Gospel: The Theology of Acts*. Edited by I. H. Marshall and D. Peterson. Grand Rapids: Eerdmans, 1998.
Grele, Ronald J. *Envelopes of Sound: The Art of Oral History*. 2d ed. Chicago: Precedent, 1985.
Griffen, Jasper. "Augustus and the Poets: *Caesar qui Cogere Posset*." Pages 189–218 in *Caesar Augustus: Seven Aspects*. Edited by F. Millar and E. Segal. Oxford: Oxford University Press, 1984.
Griffin, Miriam. "Seneca and Pliny." Pages 532–58 in *The Cambridge History of Greek and Roman Political Thought*. Edited by C. Rowe and M. Schofield. Cambridge: Cambridge University Press, 2000.
Gruen, Erich S. *The Hellenistic World and the Coming of Rome*. 2 vols. Berkeley and Los Angeles: University of California Press, 1984.
———. *Heritage and Hellenism: The Reinvention of Jewish Tradition*. Hellenistic Culture and Society 30. Berkeley and Los Angeles: University of California Press, 1998.

Gunderson, Erik. *Staging Masculinity: The Rhetoric of Performance in the Roman World.* Ann Arbor: University of Michigan Press, 2000.
Haenchen, Ernst. *The Acts of the Apostles: A Commentary.* Translated by B. Noble et al. Philadelphia: Westminster, 1971.
Haerens, H. "ΣΩTHP et ΣΩTHPIA." *Studia Hellenistica* 5 (1948): 57–68.
Hahm, David E. "Kings and Constitutions: Hellenistic Theories." Pages 457–76 in *The Cambridge History of Greek and Roman Political Thought.* Edited by C. Rowe and M. Schofield. Cambridge: Cambridge University Press, 2000.
Hall, Edith. *Inventing the Barbarian: Greek Self-Definition through Tragedy.* New York: Oxford University Press, 1991.
Hall, Robert G. *Revealed Histories: Techniques for Ancient Jewish and Christian Historiography.* JSPSup 6. Sheffield: Sheffield Academic Press, 1991.
Hallett, Judith P. "Feminist Theory, Historical Periods, Literary Canons, and the Study of Greco-Roman Antiquity." Pages 44–72 in *Feminist Theory and the Classics.* Edited by N. S. Rabinowitz and A. Richlin. New York: Routledge, 1993.
Hamilton, James R. *Plutarch; Alexander: A Commentary.* Oxford: Clarendon, 1969.
Hamm, Dennis. "Acts 3,1–10: The Healing of the Temple Beggar as Lucan Theology." *Bib* 67 (1986): 305–19.
Hannestad, Niels. *Roman Art and Imperial Policy.* Jutland Archaeological Society 19. Aarhus: Aarhus University Press, 1986.
Hardie, Philip R. *Virgil's* Aeneid: *Cosmos and Imperium.* Oxford: Oxford University Press, 1986.
Harnack, Adolf von. *Luke the Physician: The Author of the Third Gospel and the Acts of the Apostles.* Translated by J. R. Wilkinson. New Testament Studies 1. London: Williams & Norgate, 1908.
———. "Probabilia über die Adresse und den Verfasser des Hebräerbriefes." *ZNW* 1 (1900): 16–41.
Harvey, John D. *Listening to the Text: Oral Patterning in Paul's Letters.* Grand Rapids: Baker, 1998.
Haynes, Katharine. *Fashioning the Feminine in the Greek Novel.* New York: Routledge, 2003.
Head, Peter M. "The Role of Eyewitnesses in the Formation of the Gospel Tradition." Review of Samuel Byrskog, *Story as History—History as Story. TynBul* 52 (2001): 275–94.
Heil, Christoph. "Arius Didymus and Luke-Acts." *NovT* 42 (2000): 358–93.
Hellerman, Joseph H. *The Ancient Church as Family.* Minneapolis: Fortress, 2001.
Hemer, Colin J. *The Book of Acts in the Setting of Hellenistic History.* Edited by C. H. Gempf. WUNT 49. Tübingen: Mohr Siebeck, 1989. Repr., Winona Lake, Ind.: Eisenbrauns, 1990.

Hengel, Martin. *Acts and the History of Earliest Christianity*. Translated by J. Bowden. Philadelphia: Fortress, 1979.

———. "Problems of a History of Earliest Christianity." *Bib* 78 (1997): 131–44.

Henten, Jan Willem van, and Ra'anan Abusch. "The Depiction of Jews as Typhonians and Josephus' Strategy of Refutation in *Contra Apionem*." Pages 271–309 in *Josephus' Contra Apionem: Studies in Its Character and Context*. Edited by L. H. Feldman and J. R. Levison. AGJU 34. Leiden: Brill, 1996.

Hernández Lara, Carlos. "Rhetorical Aspects of Chariton of Aphrodisias." *Giornale italiano di filologia* 42 (1990): 267–74.

Herzfeld, Michael. *Ours Once More: Folklore, Ideology, and the Making of Modern Greece*. Austin: University of Texas Press, 1982.

———. *A Place in History: Social and Monumental Time in a Cretan Town*. Princeton: Princeton University Press, 1991.

Hidber, Thomas. *Das klassizistische Manifest des Dionys von Halikarnass: Die Praefatio zu De oratoribus veteribus. Einleitung, Übersetzung, Kommentar*. Beiträge zur Altertumskunde 70. Stuttgart: Teubner, 1996.

Hilgert, Earle. "Speeches in Acts and Hellenistic Canons of Historiography and Rhetoric." Pages 83–109 in *Good News in History: Essays in Honor of Bo Reicke*. Edited by E. L. Miller. Atlanta: Scholars Press, 1993.

Hill, Craig C. "Acts 6.1–8.4: Division or Diversity?" Pages 129–53 in *History, Literature and Society in the Book of Acts*. Edited by B. Witherington. Cambridge: Cambridge University Press, 1996.

———. *Hellenists and Hebrews: Reappraising Division within the Early Church*. Minneapolis: Fortress, 1992.

Hobart, William K. *The Medical Language of St. Luke*. Dublin: Figgis, 1882.

Hock, Ronald F. "Homer in Greco-Roman Education." Pages 56–77 in *Mimesis and Intertextuality in Antiquity and Christianity*. Edited by D. R. MacDonald. Harrisburg, Pa.: Trinity Press International, 2001.

Hock, Ronald F., J. Bradley Chance, and Judith Perkins, eds. *Ancient Fiction and Early Christian Narrative*. SBLSymS 6. Atlanta: Scholars Press, 1998.

Hogan, Derek. "Paul's Defense: A Comparison of the Forensic Speeches in Acts, *Callirhoe*, and *Leucippe and Clitophon*." *PRSt* 29 (2002): 73–87.

Holtzmann, Heinrich J. *Die Apostelgeschichte*. 2d ed. HNT 1/2. Tübingen: Mohr, 1892.

Honoré, A. M. "A Statistical Study of the Synoptic Problem." *NovT* 10 (1968): 95–147.

Hopkins, Keith. "Past Alternative." Review of Glen W. Bowersock, *Fiction as History: Nero to Julian. The Times Literary Supplement* (16 February 1996): 29.

Hoppin, Ruth. *Priscilla's Letter: Finding the Author of the Epistle to the Hebrews*. San Francisco: International Scholars Publications, 1997.

Hornblower, Simon. *Thucydides.* London: Duckworth, 1987.
Horsfall, Nicholas M. "Virgil, History and the Roman Tradition." *Prudentia* 8 (1976): 73–89.
Horsley, G. H. R. "Speeches and Dialogue in Acts." *NTS* 32 (1986): 609–14.
Horsley, Richard A. *Hearing the Whole Story: The Politics of Plot in Mark's Gospel.* Louisville: Westminster John Knox, 2001.
Horsley, Richard A., and Jonathan A. Draper. *Whoever Hears You Hears Me: Prophets, Performance, and Tradition in Q.* Harrisburg, Pa.: Trinity Press International, 1999.
Hoskins, Janet. *The Play of Time: Kodi Perspectives on Calendars, History, and Exchange.* Berkeley and Los Angeles: University of California Press, 1993.
Hultkrantz, Åke. *Metodvägar inom den jämförande religionsforskningen.* Stockholm: Esselte Studium, 1973.
Hunter, Virginia J. *Past and Process in Herodotus and Thucydides.* Princeton: Princeton University Press, 1982.
———. *Thucydides: The Artful Reporter.* Toronto: University of Toronto Press, 1993.
Iggers, Georg G. *New Directions in European Historiography.* Middletown, Conn.: Wesleyan University Press, 1975.
———. "The Crisis of the Rankean Paradigm in the Nineteenth Century." Pages 170–79 in *Leopold von Ranke and the Shaping of the Historical Discipline.* Edited by G. G. Iggers and J. M. Powell. Syracuse: Syracuse University Press, 1990.
———. *Historiography in the Twentieth Century: From Scientific Objectivity to the Postmodern Challenge.* Hanover, N.H.: Wesleyan University Press, 1997.
Jacoby, Felix. *Atthis: The Local Legends of Ancient Athens.* Oxford: Clarendon, 1949.
Jaffee, Martin S. "Oral Culture in Scriptural Religion: Some Exploratory Studies." *RelSRev* 24 (1998): 223–30.
Jeremias, Joachim. *The Parables of Jesus.* Translated by S. H. Hooke. 2d ed. New York: Scribner, 1972.
Jervell, Jacob. *Die Apostelgeschichte.* 17th ed. KEK 3. Göttingen: Vandenhoeck & Ruprecht, 1998.
———. "The Future of the Past: Luke's Vision of Salvation History and Its Bearing on His Writing of History." Pages 104–26 in *History, Literature and Society in the Book of Acts.* Edited by B. Witherington. Cambridge: Cambridge University Press, 1996.
Jeska, Joachim. *Die Geschichte Israels in der Sicht des Lukas: Apg 7,2b–53 und 13,17–25 im Kontext antik-jüdischer Summarien der Geschichte Israels.* FRLANT 195. Göttingen: Vandenhoeck & Ruprecht, 2001.

Johne, Renate. "Women in the Ancient Novel." Pages 151–207 in *The Novel in the Ancient World*. Edited by G. Schmeling. Rev. ed. MnSup 159. Leiden: Brill, 2003.

Johnson, Luke T. *The Acts of the Apostles*. SP 5. Collegeville, Minn.: Liturgical Press, 1992.

———. *The Literary Function of Possessions in Luke-Acts*. SBLDS 39. Missoula, Mont.: Scholars Press, 1979.

———. *Septuagintal Midrash in the Speeches of Acts*. Milwaukee: Marquette University Press, 2002.

Jones, Arnold H. M. *The Greek City from Alexander to Justinian*. Oxford: Clarendon, 1940.

Jones, Christopher P. "Le personnalité de Chariton." Pages 161–67 in *Le monde du roman grec*. Edited by M. Baslez, P. Hoffman, and M. Trédé. Paris: l'École normale supérieure, 1992.

———. *Plutarch and Rome*. Oxford: Oxford University Press, 1971.

Juel, Donald. *Luke-Acts: The Promise of History*. Atlanta: John Knox, 1983.

———. "Social Dimensions of Exegesis: The Use of Psalm 16 in Acts 2." *CBQ* 43 (1981): 543–56.

Kahn, Charles H. *The Art and Thought of Heraclitus*. Cambridge: Cambridge University Press, 1979.

Kaster, Robert A. "Controlling Reason: Declamation in Rhetorical Education at Rome." Pages 317–37 in *Education in Greek and Roman Antiquity*. Edited by Y. L. Too. Leiden: Brill, 2001.

Keith, A. M. *Engendering Rome: Women in Latin Epic*. Roman Literature and Its Contexts. Cambridge: Cambridge University Press, 2000.

Kelber, Werner H. "Modalities of Communication, Cognition, and Physiology of Perception: Orality, Rhetoric, Scribality." *Semeia* 65 (1994): 193–216.

———. *The Oral and the Written Gospel: The Hermeneutics of Speaking and Writing in the Synoptic Tradition, Mark, Paul, and Q*. Philadelphia: Fortress, 1983. Repr., Bloomington: Indiana University Press, 1997.

———. Review of S. Byrskog, *Story as History—History as Story*. *JR* 82 (2002): 270–71.

Kelly, Shawn. *Racializing Jesus: Race, Ideology and the Formation of Biblical Scholarship*. New York: Routledge, 2002.

Kennedy, George A. *New Testament Interpretation through Rhetorical Criticism*. Chapel Hill: University of North Carolina Press, 1984.

Kilpatrick, George D. "A Jewish Background to Acts 2:9–11?" *JJS* 26 (1975): 48–49.

Kirk, Geoffrey S., et al. *The Iliad: A Commentary*. 6 vols. Cambridge: Cambridge University Press, 1985–93.

Kirsch, Wolfgang. "Die Augusteische Zeit: Epochenbewusstsein und Epochenbegriff." *Klio* 67 (1985): 43–55.

Klauck, Hans-Josef. *The Religious Context of Early Christianity: A Guide to Graeco-Roman Religions*. Translated by B. McNeil. Edinburgh: T&T Clark, 2000.

Kloppenborg, John S. "*Collegia* and *Thiasoi:* Issues in Function, Taxonomy and Membership." Pages 16–30 in *Voluntary Associations in the Graeco-Roman World*. Edited by J. S. Kloppenborg and S. G. Wilson. London: Routledge, 1996.

Kloppenborg, John S., and Stephen G. Wilson, eds. *Voluntary Associations in the Graeco-Roman World*. New York: Routledge, 1996.

Knoch, Otto. *Die "Testamente" des Petrus und Paulus: Die Sicherung der apostolischen Überlieferung in der spätneutestamentlichen Zeit*. SBS 62. Stuttgart: KBW, 1973.

Koch, Dietrich-Alex. "Kollektenbericht, '*Wir*'-Bericht und Itinerar: Neue (?) Überlegungen zu einem alten Problem." *NTS* 45 (1999): 367–90.

Koester, Helmut. "Ephesos in Early Christian Literature." Pages 119–40 in *Ephesos Metropolis of Asia: An Interdisciplinary Approach to Its Archaeology, Religion, and Culture*. Edited by H. Koester. Valley Forge, Pa.: Trinity Press International, 1995.

Kolenkow, Anitra Bingham. "Testaments: The Literary Genre 'Testament.'" Pages 259–67 in *Early Judaism and Its Modern Interpreters*. Edited by R. A. Kraft and G. W. E. Nickelsburg. Atlanta: Scholars Press, 1986.

Konstan, David. "The Invention of Fiction." Pages 3–17 in *Ancient Fiction and Early Christian Narrative*. Edited by R. F. Hock, J. B. Chance, and J. Perkins. SBLSymS 6. Atlanta: Scholars Press, 1998.

———. *Sexual Symmetry: Love in the Ancient Greek Novel and Related Genres*. Princeton: Princeton University Press, 1994.

Kraemer, Ross Shepard. "Women's Authorship of Jewish and Christian Literature in the Greco-Roman Period." Pages 221–42 in *"Women Like This": New Perspectives on Jewish Women in the Greco-Roman World*. Edited by A.-J. Levine. SLBEJL 1. Atlanta: Scholars Press, 1991.

———. *When Aseneth Met Joseph: A Late Antique Tale of the Biblical Patriarch and His Egyptian Wife, Reconsidered*. New York: Oxford University Press, 1998.

Kremer, Jacob. *Pfingstbericht und Pfingstgeschehen: Eine Exegetische Untersuchung zu Apg 2,1–13*. SBS 63/64. Stuttgart: Katholisches Bibelwerk, 1973.

Kuefler, Matthew. *The Manly Eunuch: Masculinity, Gender Ambiguity, and Christian Ideology in Late Antiquity*. Chicago: University of Chicago Press, 2001.

Kullmann, Wolfgang. "'Oral Tradition/Oral History' und die frühgriechische Epik." Pages 184–96 in *Vergangenheit in mündlicher Überlieferung*. Edited by J. von Ungern-Sternberg and H. Reinau. Colloquium Rauricum 1. Stuttgart: Teubner, 1988.

———. "Der Übergang von der Mündlichkeit zur Schriftlichkeit im frühgriechischen Epos." Pages 55–75 in *Logos und Buchstabe: Mündlichkeit und Schriftlichkeit im Judentum und Christentum der Antike*. Edited by G. Sellin and F. Vouga. TANZ 20. Tübingen: Francke, 1997.

Kurz, William S. "Luke 22:14–38 and Greco-Roman and Biblical Farewell Addresses." *JBL* 104 (1985): 251–68.

———. "Narrative Models in Luke-Acts." Pages 171–89 in *Greeks, Romans, and Christians: Essays in Honor of Abraham J. Malherbe*. Edited by D. L. Balch et al. Minneapolis: Fortress, 1990.

Lamberton, Robert, and John J. Keaney, eds. *Homer's Ancient Readers: The Hermeneutics of Greek Epic's Earliest Exegetes*. Princeton: Princeton University Press, 1992.

Larsson, Edvin. *Apostlagärningarna*. 3 vols. Kommentar till Nya testamentet 5A–C. Stockholm: EFS-förlaget, 1983–96.

Latacz, Joachim. "Zu Umfang und Art der Vergangenheitsbewahrung in der mündlichen Überlieferungsphase des griechischen Heldenepos." Pages 153–83 in *Vergangenheit in mündlicher Überlieferung*. Edited by J. von Ungern-Sternberg and H. Reinau. Colloquium Rauricum 1. Stuttgart: Teubner, 1988.

Lefkowitz, Mary R. "Did Ancient Women Write Novels?" Pages 199–219 in *"Women Like This": New Perspectives on Jewish Women in the Greco-Roman World*. Edited by A.-J. Levine. SLBEJL 1. Atlanta: Scholars Press, 1991.

Leppä, Heikki. "Luke's Critical Use of Galatians." Ph.D. diss., University of Helsinki, 2002.

Levinskaya, Irina. *The Book of Acts in Its Diaspora Setting*. Vol. 5 of *The Book of Acts in Its First Century Setting*. Grand Rapids: Eerdmans, 1996.

Linafelt, Todd, ed. *A Shadow of Glory: Reading the New Testament after the Holocaust*. New York: Routledge, 2002.

Lincoln, Bruce. "Mythic Narrative and Cultural Diversity in American Society." Pages 163–76 in *Myth and Method*. Edited by L. L. Patton and W. Doniger. Charlottesville: University Press of Virginia, 1996.

Lintott, Andrew. "The Theory of the Mixed Constitution at Rome." Pages 70–85 in *Philosophia Togata II: Plato and Aristotle at Rome*. Edited by J. Barnes and M. Griffin. New York: Oxford University Press, 1997.

Little, Douglas. "Politics in Augustan Poetry." *ANRW* 2.30.1:254–370.

Luomanen, Petri, ed. *Luke-Acts: Scandinavian Perspectives*. Publications of the Finnish Exegetical Society 54. Göttingen: Vandenhoeck & Ruprecht, 1991.

Lövestam, Evald. *Apostlagärningarna*. Tolkning av Nya testamentet 5. Stockholm: Verbum, 1988.

Lowenthal, David. *The Past Is a Foreign Country*. Cambridge: Cambridge University Press, 1985.

Luce, T. James. *The Greek Historians*. London: Routledge, 1997.
Lüdemann, Gerd. *Early Christianity according to the Traditions in Acts*. Translated by J. Bowden. Minneapolis: Fortress, 1989.
Lyne, R. O. A. M. *Further Voices in Vergil's Aeneid*. Oxford: Oxford University Press, 1987.
MacDonald, Dennis R. *Christianizing Homer: The Odyssey, Plato, and the Acts of Andrew*. New York: Oxford University Press, 1994.
———. *The Homeric Epics and the Gospel of Mark*. New Haven: Yale University Press, 2000.
———. "The Shipwrecks of Odysseus and Paul." *NTS* 45 (1999): 88–107.
———, ed. *Mimesis and Intertextuality. Studies in Antiquity and Christianity*. Harrisburg, Pa.: Trinity Press International, 2001.
Mack, Burton L. *The Christian Myth: Origins, Logic, and Legacy*. New York: Continuum, 2001.
———. *Rhetoric and the New Testament*. GBS. Minneapolis: Fortress, 1990.
———. *Who Wrote the New Testament? The Making of the Christian Myth*. San Francisco: HarperSanFrancisco, 1995.
Mack, Burton L., and Vernon K. Robbins. *Patterns of Persuasion in the Gospels*. Sonoma, Calif.: Polebridge, 1989.
MacMullen, Ramsay. *Enemies of the Roman Order: Treason, Unrest, and Alienation in the Empire*. Cambridge: Harvard University Press, 1966.
Maddox, Robert L. *The Purpose of Luke-Acts*. Edited by J. Riches. Edinburgh: T&T Clark, 1982.
Mader, Gottfried. *Josephus and the Politics of Historiography: Apologetic and Impression Management in the* Bellum Judaicum. MnSup 205. Leiden: Brill, 2000.
Magie, David. *Roman Rule in Asia Minor to the End of the Third Century after Christ*. 2 vols. Princeton: Princeton University Press, 1950.
Malina, Bruce, and Jerome Neyrey. "Honor and Shame in Luke-Acts: Pivotal Values of the Mediterranean World." Pages 25–65 in *The Social World of Luke-Acts: Models for Interpretation*. Edited by J. H. Neyrey. Peabody, Mass.: Hendrickson, 1991.
Marguerat, Daniel. *The First Christian Historian: Writing the "Acts of the Apostles."* Translated by K. McKinney, G. J. Laughery, and R. Bauckham. SNTSMS 121. Cambridge: Cambridge University Press, 2002.
———. "Luc-Actes: Une Unité à Construire." Pages 57–81 in *The Unity of Luke-Acts*. Edited by J. Verheyden. BETL 142. Leuven: Leuven University Press, 1999.
Marincola, John. *Authority and Tradition in Ancient Historiography*. Cambridge: Cambridge University Press, 1997.
Marrou, Henri I. *A History of Education in Antiquity*. Translated by G. Lamb. London: Sheed & Ward, 1956.

Marshall I. Howard, and David Peterson, eds. *Witness to the Gospel: The Theology of Acts*. Grand Rapids: Eerdmans, 1998.

Martin, Clarice J. "The Acts of the Apostles." Pages 763–99 in *Searching the Scriptures: A Feminist Commentary*. Edited by E. Schüssler Fiorenza. New York: Crossroad, 1994.

―――. "A Chamberlain's Journey and the Challenge of Interpretation for Liberation." *Semeia* 47 (1989): 105–35.

Marwood, Martin A. *The Roman Cult of Salus*. British Archaeological Reports [BAR] International Series 465. Oxford: B.A.R., 1988.

Matthews, Christopher R. Review of S. Byrskog, *Story as History—History as Story*. *JBL* 121 (2002): 175–77.

Matthews, Shelly. *First Converts: Rich Pagan Women and the Rhetoric of Mission in Early Judaism and Christianity*. Contraversions. Stanford, Calif.: Stanford University Press, 2001.

Mattill, A. J., Jr. "The Purpose of Acts: Schneckenburger Reconsidered." Pages 108–22 in *Apostolic History and the Gospel: Biblical and Historical Essays Presented to F. F. Bruce on His Sixtieth Birthday*. Edited by W. W. Gasque and R. P. Martin. Grand Rapids: Eerdmans, 1970.

Mayer, Edgar. *Die Reiseerzählung des Lukas (Lk 9,51–19:10): Entscheidung in der Wüste*. Europäische Hochschulschriften 23, Theologie 554. Frankfurt: Lang, 1996.

McCutcheon, Russell. "Myth." Pages 190–208 in *Guide to the Study of Religion*. Edited by W. Braun and R. T. McCutcheon. London: Cassell, 2000.

McDonald, Maryon. *"We Are Not French!" Language, Culture, and Identity in Brittany*. London: Routledge, 1989.

McDonald, William A. *The Political Meeting Places of the Greeks*. Baltimore: Johns Hopkins University Press, 1943.

McKenzie, Steven L., and Stephen R. Haynes, eds. *To Each Its Own Meaning: An Introduction to Biblical Criticisms and Their Application*. Rev. ed. Louisville: Westminster John Knox, 1999.

Mealand, David L. "Community of Goods and Utopian Allusions in Acts II–IV." *JTS* 28 (1977): 96–99.

Meeks, Wayne. *The First Urban Christians*. New Haven: Yale University Press, 1983.

Meier, Christian. *Die Ohnmacht des Allmächtigen Dictators Caesar: Drei biographische Skizzen*. Frankfurt: Suhrkamp, 1980.

Merkelbach, Reinhold. *Isis regina—Zeus Sarapis: Die griechisch-ägyptische Religion nach den Quellen dargestellt*. Stuttgart: Teubner, 1995.

Metzger, Bruce M. "Ancient Astrological Geography and Acts 2:9–11." Pages 123–33 in *Apostolic History and the Gospel: Biblical and Historical Essays Presented to F. F. Bruce on His Sixtieth Birthday*. Edited by W. W. Gasque and R. P. Martin. Grand Rapids: Eerdmans, 1970.

———. *A Textual Commentary on the Greek New Testament.* Corrected ed. London: United Bible Societies, 1975.
Meyer, Heinrich A. W. *Kritisch Exegetisches Handbuch über die Apostelgeschichte.* 4th ed. KEK 3. Göttingen: Vandenhoeck & Ruprecht, 1870.
Meynet, Roland. *L'Évangile selon saint Luc: Analyse rhétorique.* 2 vols. Paris: Cerf, 1988.
Michel, Hans-Joachim. *Die Abschiedsrede des Paulus an die Kirche, Agp. 20,17–38: Motivgeschichte und theologische Bedeutung.* SANT 35. Munich: Kösel, 1973.
Millar, Fergus. "The Imperial Cult and the Persecutions." Pages 145–65 in *Le culte des souverains dans l'Empire Romain.* Edited by W. den Boer. Entretiens sur l'antiquité classique 19. Genève: Hardt, 1973.
Mills, Margaret A. "Domains of Folkloristic Concern: The Interpretation of Scriptures." Pages 231–41 in *Text and Tradition: The Hebrew Bible and Folklore.* Edited by S. Niditch. SemeiaSt. Atlanta: Scholars Press, 1990.
Mitchell, Alan C. "'Greet the Friends By Name': New Testament Evidence for the Greco-Roman *Topos* on Friendship." Pages 225–62 in *Greco-Roman Perspectives on Friendship.* Edited by J. T. Fitzgerald. SBLRBS 34. Atlanta: Scholars Press, 1997.
———. "The Social Function of Friendship in Acts 2:44–47 and 4:32–37." *JBL* 111 (1992): 255–72.
Moessner, David P. "The Appeal and Power of Poetics (Luke 1:1–4): Luke's Superior Credentials (παρηκολουθηκότι), Narrative Sequence (καθεξῆς), and Firmness of Understanding (ἡ ἀσφάλεια) for the Reader." Pages 84–123 in *Jesus and the Heritage of Israel: Luke's Narrative Claim upon Israel's Legacy.* Edited by D. P. Moessner. Harrisburg, Pa.: Trinity Press International, 1999.
———. "Dionysius's Narrative 'Arrangement' (οἰκονομία) as the Hermeneutical Key to Luke's Re-Vision of the 'Many.'" Pages 149–64 in *Paul, Luke and the Graeco-Roman World: Essays in Honour of Alexander J. M. Wedderburn.* Edited by A. Christophersen et al. JSNTSup 217. Sheffield: Sheffield Academic Press, 2002.
———. "'Eyewitnesses,' 'Informed Contemporaries,' and 'Unknowing Inquirers:' Josephus' Criteria for Authentic Historiography and the Meaning of ΠΑΡΑΚΟΛΟΥΘΕΩ." *NovT* 38 (1996): 105–22.
———. *Lord of the Banquet: The Literary and Theological Significance of the Lukan Travel Narrative.* Minneapolis: Fortress, 1989. Repr., Harrisburg, Pa.: Trinity Press International, 1998.
———. "The Lukan Prologues in the Light of Ancient Narrative Hermeneutics: Παρηκολουθηκότι and the Credentialed Author." Pages 399–417 in *The Unity of Luke-Acts.* Edited by J. Verheyden. BETL 142. Leuven: Leuven University Press, 1999.

———. "The 'Script' of the Scriptures in the Acts of the Apostles: Suffering as God's 'Plan' (Βουλή) for the 'Release of Sins.'" Pages 218–50 in *History, Literature, and Society in the Book of Acts*. Edited by B. Witherington. Cambridge: Cambridge University Press, 1996.

———. "Two Lords 'at the Right Hand'? The Psalms and an Intertextual Reading of Peter's Pentecost Speech (Acts 2:14–36)." Pages 215–32 in *Literary Studies in Luke-Acts: Essays in Honor of Joseph B. Tyson*. Edited by R. P. Thompson and T. E. Phillips. Macon, Ga.: Mercer University Press, 1998.

———, ed. *Jesus and the Heritage of Israel: Luke's Narrative Claim upon Israel's Legacy*. Harrisburg, Pa.: Trinity Press International, 1999.

Moessner, David P., and David L. Tiede. "Conclusion: 'And Some Were Persuaded...'" Pages 358–68 in *Jesus and the Heritage of Israel: Luke's Narrative Claim upon Israel's Legacy*. Edited by D. P. Moessner. Harrisburg, Pa.: Trinity Press International, 1999.

Momigliano, Arnaldo. *The Development of Greek Biography*. Enlarged ed. Cambridge: Harvard University Press, 1993.

Moore, Stephen D. *God's Beauty Parlor and Other Queer Spaces in and around the Bible*. Stanford, Calif.: Stanford University Press, 2001.

Moralee, Jason W. "For Salvation's Sake (*Hyper Sôtêrias*): Ideology, Society, and Religion in the Dedications for Salvation from the Roman and Late Antique Near East, 100 BC to AD 800." Ph.D. diss., University of California, Los Angeles, 2002.

Moreland, Milton. "Jerusalem Imagined: Rethinking Earliest Christian Claims to the Hebrew Epic." Ph.D. diss., Claremont Graduate University, 1999.

Morgan, John R. "The Story of Knemon in Heliodoros' *Aithiopika*." *JHS* 109 (1989): 99–113.

———. "Make-Believe and Make Believe: The Fictionality of the Greek Novels." Pages 175–229 in *Lies and Fiction in the Ancient World*. Edited by C. Gill and T. P. Wiseman. Exeter: University of Exeter Press, 1993.

Morgenthaler, Robert. *Lukas und Quintilian: Rhetorik als Erzählkunst*. Zürich: Gotthelf, 1993.

Mount, Christopher. *Pauline Christianity: Luke-Acts and the Legacy of Paul*. NovTSup 104. Leiden: Brill, 2002.

Moxnes, Halvor. *The Economy of the Kingdom: Social Conflict and Economic Relations in Luke's Gospel*. Philadelphia: Fortress, 1988.

———. "Patron-Client Relations and the New Community in Luke-Acts." Pages 241–68 in *The Social World of Luke-Acts: Models for Interpretation*. Edited by J. H. Neyrey. Peabody, Mass.: Hendrickson, 1991.

Moynihan, R. "Geographical Mythology and Roman Imperial Ideology." Pages 149–62 in *The Age of Augustus*. Edited by R. Winkes. Archaeologia

Transatlantica 5. Providence, R.I.: Center for Old World Archaeology and Art, Brown University, 1985.
Muilenburg, James. "Form Criticism and Beyond." *JBL* 88 (1969): 1–18.
Munck, Johannes. "Discours d'adieu dans le Nouveau Testament et dans la littérature biblique." Pages 155–70 in *Aux sources de la tradition chrétienne: Mélanges offerts à M. Goguel*. Neuchâtel: Delachaux & Niestlé, 1950.
Neudorfer, Heinz-Werner. "The Speech of Stephen." Pages 275–94 in *Witness to the Gospel: The Theology of Acts*. Edited by I. H. Marshall and D. Peterson. Grand Rapids: Eerdmans, 1998.
Neyrey, Jerome H. "The Forensic Defense Speech and Paul's Trial Speeches in Acts 22–26: Form and Function." Pages 210–24 in *Luke-Acts: New Perspectives from the Society of Biblical Literature Seminar*. Edited by C. H. Talbert. New York: Crossroad, 1984.
———. "Luke's Social Location of Paul: Cultural Anthropology and the Status of Paul in Acts." Pages 251–79 in *History, Literature, and Society in the Book of Acts*. Edited by B. Witherington. Cambridge: Cambridge University Press, 1996.
———, ed. *The Social World of Luke-Acts: Models for Interpretation*. Peabody, Mass.: Hendrickson, 1991.
Nicolet, Claude. *Space, Geography, and Politics in the Early Roman Empire*. Translated by H. Leclerc. Ann Arbor: University of Michigan Press, 1991.
Nilsson, Martin P. *Geschichte der griechischen Religion*. 3d ed. 2 vols. Munich: Beck, 1974.
———. "Political Propaganda in Sixth Century Athens." Pages 743–48 in vol. 2 of *Studies Presented to David Moore Robinson on His Seventieth Birthday*. 2 vols. St. Louis: Washington University, 1951–53.
Nock, Arthur Darby. *Conversion: The Old and the New in Religion from Alexander the Great to Augustine of Hippo*. Oxford: Clarendon, 1933.
———. "*Soter* and *Euergetes*." Pages 720–35 in vol. 2 of *Essays on Religion in the Ancient World*. Edited by Z. Stewart. 2 vols. Oxford: Oxford University Press, 1972.
Noè, Eralda. "Ricerche su Dionigi d'Alicarnasso: la prima stasis a Roma e l'episodio di Coriolano." Pages 21–116 in *Ricerche di storiografia greca di età romana*. Edited by C. Letta, E. Noè, and L. Troiani. Biblioteca di studi antichi 22. Vol. 1 of *Ricerche di storiografia antica*. 2 vols. Pisa: Giardini, 1979–80.
Nolland, John. "Salvation-History and Eschatology." Pages 63–81 in *Witness to the Gospel: The Theology of Acts*. Edited by I. H. Marshall and D. Peterson. Grand Rapids: Eerdmans, 1998.
Nordheim, Eckhard von. *Die Lehre der Alten*. 2 vols. ALGHJ 13. Leiden: Brill, 1980.

North, Helen F. "Canons and Hierarchies of the Cardinal Virtues in Greek and Latin Literature." Pages 165–83 in *The Classical Tradition: Literary and Historical Studies in Honor of Harry Caplan*. Edited by L. Wallach. Ithaca, N.Y.: Cornell University Press, 1966.

Nugent, S. Georgia. "*Tristia* 2: Ovid and Augustus." Pages 239–57 in *Between Republic and Empire: Interpretations of Augustus and His Principate*. Edited by K. Raaflaub and M. Toher. Berkeley and Los Angeles: University of California Press, 1990.

Ober, Josiah. "The Orators." Pages 130–41 in *The Cambridge History of Greek and Roman Political Thought*. Edited by C. Rowe and M. Schofield. Cambridge: Cambridge University Press, 2000.

O'Day, Gail. "Acts." Pages 305–12 in *The Women's Bible Commentary*. Edited by C. A. Newsom and S. H. Ringe. Louisville: Westminster John Knox, 1992.

O'Hara, James J. *True Names: Vergil and the Alexandrian Tradition of Etymological Wordplay*. Ann Arbor: University of Michigan Press, 1996.

Oldenhage, Tania. *Parables for Our Time: Rereading New Testament Scholarship after the Holocaust*. New York: Oxford University Press, 2002.

Omerzu, Heike. *Der Prozess des Paulus: Eine exegetische und rechtshistorische Untersuchung der Apostelgeschichte*. BZNW 115. Berlin: de Gruyter, 2002.

Ong, Walter J. *Orality and Literacy: The Technologizing of the Word*. New Accents. London: Routledge, 1982.

Orentzel, Anne E. "Declamation in the Age of Pliny," *ClassBul* 54 (1978): 65–68.

Osiek, Carolyn, and David L. Balch. *Families in the New Testament World: Households and House Churches*. Louisville: Westminster John Knox, 1997.

O'Sullivan, James N. *Xenophon of Ephesus: His Compositional Technique and the Birth of the Novel*. Berlin: de Gruyter, 1995.

O'Toole, Robert. *Acts 26, The Christological Climax of Paul's Defense Speech (Ac22,1–26,32)*. AnBib 78. Rome: Pontifical Biblical Institute, 1978.

Palmer Bonz, Marianne. *The Past as Legacy: Luke-Acts and Ancient Epic*. Minneapolis: Fortress, 2000.

Palmer, Darryl W. "Acts and the Ancient Historical Monograph." Pages 1–29 in *The Book of Acts in Its Ancient Literary Setting*. Edited by B. W. Winter and A. D. Clarke. Vol. 1 of *The Book of Acts in Its First Century Setting*. Grand Rapids: Eerdmans, 1993.

Parsons, Mikeal C. *Luke: Storyteller, Interpreter, and Evangelist*. Peabody, Mass.: Hendrickson, forthcoming.

Parsons, Mikeal C., and Richard I. Pervo. *Rethinking the Unity of Luke and Acts*. Minneapolis: Fortress, 1993.

Pelling, Christopher. *Literary Texts and the Greek Historian*. New York: Routledge, 2000.

———. *Plutarch, Life of Antony*. Cambridge: Cambridge University Press, 1988.

Penner, Todd. "Early Christian Heroes and Lukan Narrative: Stephen and the Hellenists in Ancient Historiographical Perspective." In *Persuasion and Performance: Rhetoric and Reality in Early Christian Discourses*. Edited by W. Braun. SCJ. Waterloo, Ont.: Wilfrid Laurier University Press, forthcoming.

———. "Narrative as Persuasion: Epideictic Rhetoric and Scribal Amplification in the Stephen Episode in Acts." Pages 352–67 in *SBL Seminar Papers, 1996*. SBLSP 35. Atlanta: Scholars Press, 1996.

———. "In Praise of Christian Origins: Stephen and the Hellenists in Lukan Apologetic Historiography." Ph.D. diss., Emory University, 2000.

Penner, Todd, and Caroline Vander Stichele. "Unveiling Paul: Gendering Ēthos in 1 Corinthians 11:2–16." In *Rhetoric, Ethic and Moral Persuasion in Biblical Discourse*. Edited by T. H. Olbricht and A. Eriksson. Harrisburg, Pa.: T&T Clark, forthcoming.

Perkins, Judith. "Social Geography in the Apocryphal Acts of the Apostles." Pages 118–31 in *Space in the Ancient Novel*. Edited by M. Paschalis and S. Frangoulidis. Ancient Narrative, Supplementum 1. Groningen: Barkhuis, 2002.

———. *The Suffering Self: Pain and Narrative Representation in the Early Christian Era*. New York: Routledge, 1995.

Perks, Robert, and Alistair Thomson, eds. *The Oral History Reader*. London: Routledge, 1998.

Pervo, Richard I. "Dating Acts." Paper presented at the semiannual meeting of the Acts Seminar. Westar Institute. Santa Rosa, Calif., 19 October 2002.

———. "Israel's Heritage and Claims upon the Genre(s) of Luke and Acts: The Problems of a History." Pages 127–43 in *Jesus and the Heritage of Israel: Luke's Narrative Claim upon Israel's Legacy*. Edited by D. P. Moessner. Harrisburg, Pa.: Trinity Press International, 1999.

———. "Must Luke and Acts Belong to the Same Genre?" Pages 309–16 in *SBL Seminar Papers, 1989*. SBLSP 26. Atlanta: Scholars Press, 1989.

———. *Profit with Delight: The Literary Genre of the Acts of the Apostles*. Philadelphia: Fortress, 1987.

Peterson, David. "The Motif of Fulfillment and the Purpose of Luke-Acts." Pages 83–104 in *The Book of Acts in Its Ancient Literary Setting*. Edited by B. W. Winter and A. D. Clarke. Vol. 1 of *The Book of Acts in Its First Century Setting*. Grand Rapids: Eerdmans, 1993.

———. "The Worship of the New Community." Pages 373–95 in *Witness to the Gospel: The Theology of Acts*. Edited by I. H. Marshall and D. Peterson. Grand Rapids: Eerdmans, 1998.

Pfister, Friedrich. *Die Religion der Griechen und Römer, mit einer Einführung in die vergleichende Religionswissenschaft: Darstellung und Literaturbericht (1918–29/30)*. Jahresbericht über die Fortschritte der klassischen Altertumswissenschaft 229. Supplementary vol. Leipzig: Reisland, 1930.

Plümacher, Eckhard. "Die Apostelgeschichte als historische Monographie." Pages 457–66 in *Les Actes des Apôtres: Traditions, rédaction, théologie*. Edited by J. Kremer. BETL 48. Leuven: Leuven University Press, 1979.

———. *Lukas als hellenistischer Schriftsteller: Studien zur Apostelgeschichte*. SUNT 9. Göttingen: Vandenhoeck & Ruprecht, 1972.

———. "The Mission Speeches in Acts and Dionysius of Halicarnassus." Pages 251–66 in *Jesus and the Heritage of Israel: Luke's Narrative Claim upon Israel's Legacy*. Edited by D. P. Moessner. Harrisburg, Pa.: Trinity Press International, 1999.

Portelli, Alessandro. "What Makes Oral History Different." Pages 63–74 in *The Oral History Reader*. Edited by R. Perks and A. Thomson. London: Routledge, 1998.

Porter, Stanley E. *The Paul of Acts: Essays in Literary Criticism, Rhetoric, and Theology*. WUNT 115. Tübingen: Mohr Siebeck, 1999. Repr., Peabody, Mass.: Hendrickson, 2001.

———. "Thucydides 1.22.1 and Speeches in Acts: Is There a Thucydidean View?" *NovT* 32 (1990): 121–42.

Porter, Stanley E., and Dennis L. Stamps, eds. *The Rhetorical Interpretation of Scripture: Essays from the 1996 Malibu Conference*. JSNTSup 180. Sheffield: Sheffield Academic Press, 1999.

Potter, David S. *Literary Texts and the Roman Historian*. New York: Routledge, 1999.

Powell, Anton, ed. *Roman Poetry and Propaganda in the Age of Augustus*. London: Bristol Classical Press, 1992.

Powell, Mark A. *What Are They Saying about Acts?* New York: Paulist, 1992.

Praeder, Susan M. "Luke-Acts and the Ancient Novel." Pages 269–92 in *SBL Seminar Papers, 1981*. SBLSP 20. Chico, Calif.: Scholars Press, 1981.

Price, Robert M. *The Widow Traditions in Luke-Acts: A Feminist-Critical Scrutiny*. SBLDS 155. Atlanta: Scholars Press, 1997.

Price, Simon R. F. *Rituals and Power: The Roman Imperial Cult in Asia Minor*. Cambridge: Cambridge University Press, 1984.

Pui-lan, Kwok. *Introducing Asian Feminist Theology*. IFT 4. Sheffield: Sheffield Academic Press, 2000.

Putnam, Michael C. J. *The Poetry of the Aeneid*. Cambridge: Harvard University Press, 1965.

Quint, David. *Epic and Empire: Politics and Generic Form from Virgil to Milton*. Princeton: Princeton University Press, 1993.

Raaflaub, Kurt A., Adalberto Giovannini, and Denis van Berchem, eds. *Opposition et résistances à l'empire d'Auguste à Trajan.* Entretiens sur l'antiquité classique 33. Genève: Hardt, 1987.
Raaflaub, Kurt A., and Loren J. Samons. "Opposition to Augustus." Pages 417–54 in *Between Republic and Empire: Interpretations of Augustus and His Principate.* Edited by K. A. Raaflaub and M. Toher. Berkeley and Los Angeles: University of California Press, 1990.
Rajak, Tessa. "The *Against Apion* and the Continuities in Josephus's Political Thought." Pages 222–46 in *Understanding Josephus: Seven Perspectives.* Edited by S. Mason. JSPSup 32. Sheffield: Sheffield Academic Press, 1998.
———. "Josephus." Pages 585–96 in *The Cambridge History of Greek and Roman Political Thought.* Edited by C. Rowe and M. Schofield. Cambridge: Cambridge University Press, 2000.
Ramsay, William M. *Historical Commentary on St. Paul's Epistle to the Galatians.* New York: Putnam, 1900.
———. *The Historical Geography of Asia Minor.* Royal Geographical Society Supplementary Papers 4. London: Murray, 1890.
———. *Impressions of Turkey during Twelve Years' Wanderings.* New York: Putnam, 1897.
Raubitschek, Antony E. "The Speech of the Athenians at Sparta." Pages 32–48 in *The Speeches in Thucydides.* Edited by P. A. Stadter. Chapel Hill: University of North Carolina Press, 1973.
Reardon, Bryan P. "Chariton: Chaereas and Callirhoe." Pages 17–124 in *Collected Ancient Greek Novels.* Edited by B. P. Reardon. Berkeley and Los Angeles: University of California Press, 1989.
———. *The Form of Greek Romance.* Princeton: Princeton University Press, 1991.
———, ed. *Collected Ancient Greek Novels.* Berkeley and Los Angeles: University of California Press, 1989.
Reimer, Ivoni Richter. *Women in the Acts of the Apostles: A Feminist Liberation Perspective.* Translated by L. M. Maloney. Minneapolis: Fortress, 1995.
Reitzenstein, Richard. *Hellenistische Wundererzählungen.* Leipzig: Teubner, 1906.
Renan, Ernest. *The History of the Origins of Christianity.* Translated by I. Lockwood et al. 7 vols. London: Mathieson, 1889–90.
Richard, Earl J. *Acts 6–8:4: The Author's Method of Composition.* SBLDS 41. Missoula, Mont.: Scholars Press, 1978.
Richlin, Amy. "Gender and Rhetoric: Producing Manhood in the Schools." Pages 90–110 in *Roman Eloquence: Rhetoric in Society and Literature.* Edited by W. J. Dominik. London: Routledge, 1997.
Robbins, Vernon K. "The Claims of the Prologues and Greco-Roman Rhetoric: The Prefaces to Luke and Acts in Light of Greco-Roman Rhetorical Strategies." Pages 63–83 in *Jesus and the Heritage of Israel: Luke's*

Narrative Claim upon Israel's Legacy. Edited by D. P. Moessner. Harrisburg, Pa.: Trinity Press International, 1999.

———. "From Enthymeme to Theology in Luke 11:1–13." Pages 191–214 in *Literary Studies in Luke-Acts: Essays in Honor of Joseph B. Tyson.* Edited by R. P. Thompson and T. E. Phillips. Macon, Ga.: Mercer University Press, 1998.

———. *Exploring the Texture of Texts: A Guide to Socio-Rhetorical Interpretation.* Valley Forge, Pa.: Trinity Press International, 1996.

———. "Introduction: Using Rhetorical Discussions of the Chreia to Interpret Pronouncement Stories." *Semeia* 64 (1994): vii–xvii.

———. "Laudation Stories in the Gospel of Luke and Plutarch's Alexander." Pages 293–308 in *SBL Seminar Papers, 1981.* SBLSP 20. Chico, Calif.: Scholars Press, 1981.

———. "Luke-Acts: A Mixed Population Seeks a Home in the Roman Empire." Pages 202–221 in *Images of Empire.* Edited by L. Alexander. JSOTSup 122. Sheffield: Sheffield Academic Press, 1991.

———. "Narrative in Ancient Rhetoric and Rhetoric in Ancient Narrative." Pages 169–84 in *SBL Seminar Papers, 1996.* SBLSP 35. Atlanta: Scholars Press, 1996.

———. "Oral, Rhetorical, and Literary Cultures: A Response." *Semeia* 65 (1994): 75–91.

———. "Prefaces in Greco-Roman Biographies and Luke-Acts." Pages 193–207 in vol. 2 of *SBL Seminar Papers, 1978.* 2 vols. SBLSP 14. Missoula, Mont.: Scholars Press, 1978.

———. "Progymnastic Rhetorical Composition and Pre-Gospel Traditions: A New Approach." Pages 111–47 in *The Synoptic Gospels: Source Criticism and the New Literary Criticism.* Edited by C. Focant. BETL 110. Leuven: Leuven University Press, 1993.

———. "The Social Location of the Implied Author of Luke-Acts." Pages 305–32 in *The Social World of Luke-Acts: Models for Interpretation.* Edited by J. H. Neyrey. Peabody, Mass.: Hendrickson, 1991.

———. "Socio-Rhetorical Criticism: Mary, Elizabeth and the Magnificat as a Test Case." Pages 164–209 in *The New Literary Criticism and the New Testament.* Edited by E. V. McKnight and E. S. Malbon. Valley Forge, Pa.: Trinity Press International, 1994.

———. *The Tapestry of Early Christian Discourse: Rhetoric, Society and Ideology.* London: Routledge, 1996.

———. "The Woman Who Touched Jesus' Garments: Socio-Rhetorical Analysis of the Synoptic Accounts." *NTS* 33 (1987): 502–15.

———. "Writing as a Rhetorical Act in Plutarch and the Gospels." Pages 142–68 in *Persuasive Artistry: Studies in New Testament Rhetoric in Honor of George A. Kennedy.* Edited by D. F. Watson. JSNTSup 50. Sheffield: Sheffield Academic Press, 1991.

Rohrbaugh, Richard. "The Pre-industrial City in Luke-Acts: Urban Social Relations." Pages 125–50 in *The Social World of Luke-Acts: Models for Interpretation*. Edited by J. H. Neyrey. Peabody, Mass.: Hendrickson, 1991.

Rosenblatt, Marie-Eloise. "Under Interrogation: Paul as Witness in Juridical Contexts in Acts and the Implied Spirituality for Luke's Community." Ph.D. diss., Graduate Theological Union, 1987.

Rösler, Wolfgang. "Die Entdeckung der Fiktionalität in der Antike." *Poetica* 12 (1980): 283–319.

Rosner, Brian S. "Acts and Biblical History." Pages 65–82 in *The Book of Acts in Its Ancient Literary Setting*. Edited by B. W. Winter and A. D. Clarke. Vol. 1 of *The Book of Acts in Its First Century Setting*. Grand Rapids: Eerdmans, 1993.

Rothschild, Clare Komoroske. "Luke-Acts and Josephus's *Antiquitates Judaicae:* Observations of a Rhetoric of Hellenistic Historiography." Paper presented for the Luke-Acts Group at the Society of Biblical Literature Annual Meeting. Denver, November 2001.

———. *Luke-Acts and the Rhetoric of History: An Investigation of Early Christian Historiography*. WUNT. Tübingen: Mohr Siebeck, forthcoming.

Rotter, Andrew J. "Saidism without Said: *Orientalism* and U.S. Diplomatic History." *AHR* 105 (2000): 1205–17.

Roueché, Charlotte. "Acclamations in the Later Roman Empire: New Evidence from Aphrodisias." *JRS* 74 (1984): 181–99.

Rowe, Christopher. "Aristotelian Constitutions." Pages 366–89 in *The Cambridge History of Greek and Roman Political Thought*. Edited by C. Rowe and M. Schofield. Cambridge: Cambridge University Press, 2000.

Rubin, Zeev. "Pax als politisches Schlagwort im alten Rom." Pages 21–40 in *Frieden und Friedenssicherung in Vergangenheit und Gegenwart*. Edited by M. Schenke and K.-J. Matz. Munich: Fink, 1984.

Ruiz Montero, Consuelo. "Aspects of the Vocabulary of Chariton of Aphrodisias." *CQ* 41 (1991): 484–89.

Rusam, Dietrich. *Das Alte Testament bei Lukas*. BZNW 112. Berlin: de Gruyter, 2003.

Russell, Donald A. *Greek Declamation*. Cambridge: Cambridge University Press, 1983.

Ryffel, Heinrich. *ΜΕΤΑΒΟΛΗ ΠΟΛΙΤΕΙΩΝ: Der Wandel der Staatsverfassungen*. New York: Arno, 1973.

Sacks, Kenneth S. "Rhetoric and Speeches in Hellenistic Historiography." *Athenaeum* 64 (1986): 383–95.

Said, Edward. *Orientalism*. New York: Vintage, 1979.

Saïd, Suzanne. "Les langues du roman grec." Pages 169–86 in *Le monde du roman grec*. Edited by M. F. Baslez, P. Hoffman, and M. Trédé. Paris: l'École normale supérieure, 1992.

———. "Rural Society in the Greek Novel, or The Country Seen from the Town." Pages 83–107 in *Oxford Readings in the Greek Novel*. Edited by S. Swain. New York: Oxford University Press, 1999.
Saller, Richard P. *Personal Patronage under the Early Empire*. Cambridge: Cambridge University Press, 1982.
Sanders, Ed P. *The Tendencies of the Synoptic Tradition*. SNTSMS 9. Cambridge: Cambridge University Press, 1969.
Sanders, Jack T. *The Jews in Luke-Acts*. Philadelphia: Fortress, 1987.
Sanders, James A. *Canon and Community: A Guide to Canonical Criticism*. Philadelphia: Fortress, 1984.
———. *From Sacred Story to Sacred Text: Canon as Paradigm*. Philadelphia: Fortress, 1987.
Satterthwaite, Philip E. "Acts against the Background of Classical Rhetoric." Pages 337–79 in *The Book of Acts in Its Ancient Literary Setting*. Edited by B. W. Winter and A. D. Clarke. Vol. 1 of *The Book of Acts in Its First Century Setting*. Grand Rapids: Eerdmans, 1993.
Schaberg, Jane. "Luke." Pages 275–92 in *The Women's Bible Commentary*. Edited by C. A. Newsom and S. H. Ringe. Louisville: Westminster John Knox, 1992.
Schadewaldt, Wolfgang. "Hector and Andromache." Pages 124–42 in *Homer: German Scholarship in Translation*. Translated by G. M. Wright and P. V. Jones. Oxford: Clarendon, 1997.
Schaffner, Martin. "Plädoyer für Oral History." Pages 343–48 in *Vergangenheit in mündlicher Überlieferung*. Edited by J. von Ungern-Sternberg and H. Reinau. Colloquium Rauricum 1. Stuttgart: Teubner, 1988.
Schefold, Karl. "Kleisthenes." *MH* 3 (1946): 59–93.
———. *Der religiöse Gehalt der antiken Kunst und die Offenbarung*. Kulturgeschichte der Antiken Welt 78. Mainz: Zabern, 1998.
Scheid, John, and Jesper Svenbro. *The Craft of Zeus: Myths of Weaving and Fabric*. Revealing Antiquity 9. Cambridge: Harvard University Press, 1996.
Schepens, Guido. "Some Aspects of Source Theory in Greek Historiography." *Ancient Society* 6 (1975): 257–74.
Schierling, Stephen P., and Marla J. Schierling. "The Influence of the Ancient Romances on the Acts of the Apostles." *ClassBul* 54 (1978): 81–88.
Schmeling, Gareth L. *Chariton*. Twayne's World Authors Series 295. New York: Twayne, 1974.
Schmidt, Daryl D. "The Historiography of Acts: Deuteronomistic or Hellenistic?" Pages 417–27 in *SBL Seminar Papers, 1985*. SBLSP 24. Atlanta: Scholars Press, 1985.
———. "Rhetorical Influences and Genre: Luke's Preface and the Rhetoric of Hellenistic Historiography." Pages 27–60 in *Jesus and the Heritage of Israel: Luke's Narrative Claim upon Israel's Legacy*. Edited by D. P. Moessner. Harrisburg, Pa.: Trinity Press International, 1999.

Schmidt, Karl Ludwig. *The Place of the Gospels in the General History of Literature*. Translated by B. R. McCane. Columbia: University of South Carolina Press, 2002.

Schmithals, Walter. *Die Apostelgeschichte des Lukas*. ZBK 3/2. Zürich: TVZ, 1982.

Schneckenburger, Matthias. *Über den Zweck der Apostelgeschichte*. Bern: Fischer, 1841.

Schneider, Gerhard. *Die Apostelgeschichte*. 2 vols. HTKNT 5. Freiburg: Herder, 1980–82.

Schultze, Clemence Elizabeth. "Dionysius of Halicarnassus and His Audience." Pages 121–41 in *Past Perspectives: Studies in Greek and Roman Historical Writing*. Edited by I. S. Moxon et al. Cambridge: Cambridge University Press, 1986.

———. "Dionysius of Halicarnassus as a Historian: An Investigation of His Aims and Methods in the Antiquitates Romanae." Ph.D. diss., Oxford University, 1980.

Schüssler Fiorenza, Elisabeth. *But She Said: Feminist Practices of Biblical Interpretation*. Boston: Beacon, 1992.

———. *Rhetoric and Ethic: The Politics of Biblical Studies*. Minneapolis: Fortress, 1999.

Schuster, Meinhard. "Zur Konstruktion von Geschichte in Kulturen ohne Schrift." Pages 57–71 in *Vergangenheit in mündlicher Überlieferung*. Edited by J. von Ungern-Sternberg and H. Reinau. Colloquium Rauricum 1. Stuttgart: Teubner, 1988.

Schwartz, Daniel. "The Accusation and the Accusers at Philippi (Acts 16,20–21)." *Bib* 65 (1984): 357–63.

Schwartz, Saundra. "Clitophon the *Moichos:* Achilles Tatius and the Trial Scene in the Greek Novel." *Ancient Narrative* 1 (2000–2001): 93–113.

———. "Courtroom Scenes in the Ancient Greek Novels." Ph.D. diss., Columbia University, 1998.

———. "Rome in the Greek Novel? Images and Ideas of Empire in Chariton's Persia." *Arethusa* 36 (2003): 375–94.

Scott, Brandon B., and Margaret E. Dean. "A Sound Mapping of the Sermon on the Mount." Pages 311–78 in *Treasures New and Old: Contributions to Matthean Studies*. Edited by D. R. Baur and M. A. Powell. SBLSymS 1. Atlanta: Scholars Press, 1996.

Scott, James M. "Acts 2:9–11 as an Anticipation of the Mission to the Nations." Pages 87–123 in *The Mission of the Early Church to Jews and Gentiles*. Edited by J. Ådna and H. Kvalbein. WUNT 127. Tübingen: Mohr Siebeck, 2000.

———. "Luke's Geographical Horizon." Pages 483–544 in *The Book of Acts in Its Graeco-Roman Setting*. Edited by D. W. J. Gill and C. H. Gempf.

Vol. 2 of *The Book of Acts in Its First Century Setting*. Grand Rapids: Eerdmans, 1994.

Scullard, Howard H. *From the Gracchi to Nero: A History of Rome 133 BC to AD 68*. 5th ed. London: Routledge, 1982.

Seeley, David. *Deconstructing the New Testament*. BibInt 5. Leiden: Brill, 1994.

Seim, Turid Karlsen. *The Double Message: Patterns of Gender in Luke and Acts*. Nashville: Abingdon, 1994.

Sherwin-White, A. N. *The Roman Citizenship*. Oxford: Clarendon, 1939.

———. *Roman Society and Roman Law in the New Testament*. Oxford: Clarendon, 1963.

Simondon, Michèle. *La mémoire et l'oubli dans la pensée grecque jusqu'à la fin du Ve siècle avant J.-C.* Paris: Belles Lettres, 1982.

Smith, Jonathan Z. *Drudgery Divine: On the Comparison of Early Christianities and the Religions of Late Antiquity*. Chicago: University of Chicago Press, 1990.

———. "Good News Is No News: Aretalogy and Gospel." Pages 190–207 in idem, *Map Is Not Territory: Studies in the History of Religions*. SJLA 23. Leiden: Brill, 1978. Repr., Chicago: University of Chicago Press, 1993.

———. "Here, There, and Anywhere." Paper presented at the conference "Prayer, Magic and the Stars in the Ancient and Late Antique World." University of Washington, Department of Near Eastern Languages and Civilization, Seattle, Washington, 3–5 March 2000.

———. "Here, There, and Anywhere." In *Prayer, Magic and the Stars in the Ancient and Late Antique World*. Edited by S. Noegel, J. Walker, and B. Wheeler. Magic in History. University Park: Pennsylvania State University Press, 2003.

———. *Imagining Religion: From Babylon to Jonestown*. Chicago: University of Chicago Press, 1982.

Smith, Roland. "*Simulacra Gentium:* The *Ethne* from the Sebasteion at Aphrodisias." *JRS* 78 (1988): 50–77.

Soards, Marion L. "The Speeches in Acts in Relation to Other Pertinent Ancient Literature." *ETL* 70 (1994): 65–90.

———. *The Speeches in Acts: Their Content, Context, and Concerns*. Louisville: Westminster John Knox, 1994.

Söder, Rosa. *Die apokryphen Apostelgeschichten und die romanhafte Literatur der Antike*. Stuttgart: Kohlhammer, 1932. Repr., Darmstadt: Wissenschaftliche Buchgesellschaft, 1969.

Soulen, Richard N., and R. Kendall Soulen. *Handbook of Biblical Criticism*. 3d ed. Louisville: Westminster John Knox, 2001.

Spencer, F. Scott. "Acts and Modern Literary Approaches." Pages 381–414 in *The Book of Acts in Its Ancient Literary Setting*. Edited by B. W.

Winter and A. D. Clarke. Vol. 1 of *The Book of Acts in First Century Setting*. Grand Rapids: Eerdmans, 1993.

Squires, John T. *The Plan of God in Luke-Acts*. SNTSMS 76. Cambridge: Cambridge University Press, 1993.

Stahl, Hans-Peter. "The Death of Turnus: Augustan Vergil and the Political Rival." Pages 174–211 in *Between Republic and Empire: Interpretations of Augustus and His Principate*. Edited by K. A. Raaflaub and M. Toher. Berkeley and Los Angeles: University of California Press, 1990.

Standhartinger, Angela. *Das Frauenbild im Judentum der Hellenistischen Zeit: Ein Beitrag anhand von Joseph und Aseneth*. AGJU 26. Leiden: Brill, 1995.

———. "Joseph und Aseneth: Vollkommene Braut oder himmlische Prophetin." Pages 459–64 in *Kompendium Feministische Bibelauslegung*. Edited by L. Schottroff and M.-T. Wacker. 2d ed. Gütersloh: Kaiser, 1999.

Stanford, William B. *Ambiguity in Greek Literature: Studies in Theory and Practice*. Oxford: Blackwell, 1939.

Starr, Raymond J. "Reading Aloud: *Lectores* and Roman Reading." *CJ* 86 (1990–91): 337–43.

Stenger, Werner. "Beobachtungen zur sogenannten Völkerlist des Pfingstwunders [Apg 2,9–11]." *Kairos* 21 (1979): 206–14.

Stenschke, Christoph. "The Need for Salvation." Pages 125–44 in *Witness to the Gospel: The Theology of Acts*. Edited by I. H. Marshall and D. Peterson. Grand Rapids: Eerdmans, 1998.

Sterling, Gregory E. "'Athletes of Virtue': An Analysis of the Summaries in Acts (2:41–47; 4:32–35; 5:12–16)." *JBL* 113 (1994): 679–96.

———. *Historiography and Self-Definition: Josephus, Luke-Acts and Apologetic Historiography*. NovTSup 64. Leiden: Brill, 1992.

———. "'Opening the Scriptures': The Legitimation of the Jewish Diaspora and the Early Christian Mission." Pages 199–225 in *Jesus and the Heritage of Israel: Luke's Narrative Claim upon Israel's Legacy*. Edited by D. P. Moessner. Harrisburg, Pa.: Trinity Press International, 1999.

Stewart, Roberta. *Public Office in Early Rome: Ritual Procedure and Political Practice*. Ann Arbor: University of Michigan Press, 1998.

Strecker, Georg. *Theology of the New Testament*. Translated by M. E. Boring. Louisville: Westminster John Knox, 2000.

Sugirtharajah, Rasiah S. "Postcolonial Theory and Biblical Studies." Pages 541–52 in *Fair Play: Diversity and Conflicts in Early Christianity: Essays in Honour of Heikki Räisänen*. Edited by I. Dunderberg, C. M. Tuckett, and K. Syreeni. NovTSup 103. Leiden: Brill, 2002.

Sussman, Lewis A. *The Declamations of Calpurnius Flaccus*. MnSup 133. Leiden: Brill, 1994.

Svenbro, Jesper. *Phrasikleia: An Anthropology of Reading in Ancient Greece*. Myth and Poetics. Ithaca, N.Y.: Cornell University Press, 1988.

Swain, Simon. *Hellenism and Empire: Language, Classicism, and Power in the Greek World, A.D. 50–250*. New York: Oxford University Press, 1996.

———. Review of G. W. Bowersock, *Fiction as History*. *JRS* 86 (1996): 216–17.

Swartley, Willard A. "War and Peace in the New Testament." *ANRW* 2.26.3: 2298–408.

Syme, Ronald. *The Roman Revolution*. Oxford: Clarendon, 1939. Repr., Oxford: Oxford University Press, 1960.

Talbert, Charles H. "The Acts of the Apostles: Monograph or Bios?" Pages 58–72 in *History, Literature, and Society in the Book of Acts*. Edited by B. Witherington. Cambridge: Cambridge University Press, 1996.

———. *Literary Patterns, Theological Themes, and the Genre of Luke-Acts*. SBLMS 20. Missoula, Mont.: Scholars Press, 1974.

———. *Luke and the Gnostics: An Examination of the Lucan Purpose*. Nashville: Abingdon, 1966.

———. *Reading Luke: A Literary and Theological Commentary on the Third Gospel*. New York: Crossroad, 1982.

Talbert, Charles H., and John H. Hayes. "A Theology of Sea Storms in Luke-Acts." Pages 321–36 in *SBL Seminar Papers, 1995*. SBLSP 34. Atlanta: Scholars Press, 1995.

Tannehill, Robert C. *The Narrative Unity of Luke-Acts: A Literary Interpretation*. 2 vols. Minneapolis: Fortress, 1986–90.

Taylor, Justin. "The List of the Nations in Acts 2:9–11." *RB* 106 (1999): 408–20.

Taylor, Lily Ross. *The Divinity of the Roman Emperor*. Middletown, Conn.: American Philological Association, 1931.

Taylor, Robert O. P. *Groundwork for the Gospels, with Some Collected Papers*. Oxford: Blackwell, 1946.

Thomas, Christine M. *The Acts of Peter, Gospel Literature, and the Ancient Novel: Rewriting the Past*. New York: Oxford University Press, 2003.

Thomas, Johannes. "Formgesetze des Begriffs-Kataloges im N.T." *TZ* 24 (1968): 15–28.

Thomas, Rosalind. *Oral Tradition and Written Record in Classical Athens*. Cambridge Studies in Oral and Literate Culture 18. Cambridge: Cambridge University Press, 1989.

Thompson, Paul. *The Voice of the Past: Oral History*. 3d ed. Oxford: Oxford University Press, 2000.

Thompson, Richard P., and Thomas E. Phillips, eds. *Literary Studies in Luke-Acts: Essays in Honor of Joseph B. Tyson*. Macon, Ga.: Mercer University Press, 1998.

Thornton, Claus-Jürgen. *Der Zeuge des Zeugen: Lukas als Historiker der Paulusreisen.* WUNT 56. Tübingen: Mohr Siebeck, 1991.
Tinh, Tran Tam. "Sarapis and Isis." Pages 101–17 and 207–10 in *Self-Definition in the Greco-Roman World.* Vol. 3 of *Jewish and Christian Self-Definition.* Edited by B. F. Meyer and E. P. Sanders. Philadelphia: Fortress, 1982.
Toher, Mark. "Augustus and the Evolution of Roman Historiography." Pages 139–54 in *Between Republic and Empire: Interpretations of Augustus and His Principate.* Edited by K. A. Raaflaub and M. Toher. Berkeley and Los Angeles: University of California Press, 1990.
Tomson, Peter J. "Gamaliel's Counsel and the Apologetic Strategy of Luke-Acts." Pages 585–604 in *The Unity of Luke-Acts.* Edited by J. Verheyden. BETL 142. Leuven: Leuven University Press, 1999.
Tonkin, Elizabeth, Maryon McDonald, and Malcolm Chapman, eds. *History and Ethnicity.* ASA Monographs 27. New York: Routledge, 1989.
Too, Yun Lee. *The Idea of Ancient Literary Criticism.* New York: Oxford University Press, 1998.
Townsend, John T. "The Date of Luke-Acts." Pages 47–62 in *Luke-Acts: New Perspectives from the Society of Biblical Literature Seminar.* Edited by C. H. Talbert. New York: Crossroad, 1984.
Trites, Allison A. "The Importance of Legal Scenes and Language in the Book of Acts." *NovT* 16 (1974): 278–84.
Troiani, Lucio. "The ΠΟΛΙΤΕΙΑ of Israel in the Graeco-Roman Age." Pages 11–22 in *Josephus and the History of the Greco-Roman Period: Essays in Memory of Morton Smith.* Edited by F. Parente and J. Sievers. StPB 41. Leiden: Brill, 1994.
Trompf, Garry W. *Early Christian Historiography: Narratives of Retributive Justice.* New York: Continuum, 2000.
———. *The Idea of Historical Recurrence in Western Thought: From Antiquity to the Reformation.* Berkeley and Los Angeles: University of California Press, 1979.
Tuckett, Christopher M., ed. *Luke's Literary Achievement: Collected Essays.* JSNTSup 116. Sheffield: Sheffield Academic Press, 1995.
Tyson, Joseph B. "The Date of Acts: A Reconsideration." Paper presented at the semiannual meeting of the Acts Seminar. Westar Institute. Santa Rosa, Calif., 19 October 2002.
———. *Luke, Judaism, and the Scholars: Critical Approaches to Luke-Acts.* Columbia: University of South Carolina Press, 1999.
———, ed. *Luke-Acts and the Jewish People: Eight Critical Perspectives.* Minneapolis: Augsburg, 1988.
Unnik, Willem C. van. "Josephus' Account of the Story of Israel's Sin with Alien Women in the Country of Midian (Num. 25.1ff.)." Pages 241–61

in *Travels in the World of the Old Testament: Studies Presented to Professor M. A. Beek.* SSN 16. Assen: Van Gorcum, 1974.

———. "Luke's Second Book and the Rules of Hellenistic Historiography." Pages 37–60 in *Les Actes des Apôtres: Traditions, rédaction, théologie.* Edited by J. Kremer. BETL 48. Leuven: Leuven University Press, 1979.

Vander Stichele, Caroline. "Is Silence Golden? Paul and Women's Speech in Corinth." *LS* 20 (1995): 241–53.

Vansina, Jan. "Once Upon a Time: Oral Traditions as History in Africa." *Dædalus* 100 (1971): 442–68.

———. *Oral Tradition as History.* Madison: University of Wisconsin Press, 1985.

Veltman, Fred. "The Defense Speeches of Paul in Acts." Pages 243–56 in *Perspectives on Luke-Acts.* Edited by C. H. Talbert. Macon, Ga.: Mercer University Press, 1978.

Verheyden, Joseph. "The Unity of Luke-Acts: What Are We Up To?" Pages 3–56 in *The Unity of Luke-Acts.* Edited by J. Verheyden. BETL 142. Leuven: Leuven University Press, 1999.

———, ed. *The Unity of Luke-Acts.* BETL 142. Leuven: Leuven University Press, 1999.

Veyne, Paul. *Le pain et le cirque: sociologie historique d'un pluralisme politique.* Paris: Seuil, 1976.

Vielhauer, Philip. "On the 'Paulinism' of Acts." Pages 33–50 in *Studies in Luke-Acts.* Edited by L. E. Keck and J. L. Martyn. Nashville: Abingdon, 1966.

Vilborg, Ebbe. *Achilles Tatius: Leucippe and Clitophon: A Commentary.* Studia Graeca et Latina Gothoburgensia 15. Stockholm: Almqvist & Wiksell, 1962.

Vinson, Richard B. "A Comparative Study of Enthymemes in the Synoptic Gospels." Pages 119–41 in *Persuasive Artistry: Studies in New Testament Rhetoric in Honor of George A. Kennedy.* Edited by D. F. Watson. JSNTSup 50. Sheffield: Sheffield Academic Press, 1991.

Walbank, Frank W. *A Historical Commentary on Polybius.* 3 vols. Oxford: Clarendon, 1957–79.

———. *Polybius.* Sather Classical Lectures 42. Berkeley and Los Angeles: University of California Press, 1972.

Walker-Ramisch, Sandra. "Graeco-Roman Voluntary Associations and the Damascus Document: A Sociological Analysis." Pages 128–45 in *Voluntary Associations in the Graeco-Roman World.* Edited by J. S. Kloppenborg and S. G. Wilson. London: Routledge, 1996.

Walker, William O. "Acts and the Pauline Corpus Revisited: Peter's Speech at the Jerusalem Conference." Pages 77–86 in *Literary Studies in Luke-Acts: Essays in Honor of Joseph B. Tyson.* Edited by R. P. Thompson and T. E. Phillips. Macon, Ga.: Mercer University Press, 1998.

Wallace, Robert W. "Aristotelian Politeiai and *Athenaion Politeia* 4." Pages 269–86 in *Nomodeiktes: Greek Studies in Honor of Martin Oswald*. Edited by R. M. Rosen and J. Farrell. Ann Arbor: University of Michigan Press, 1993.
Wallace-Hadrill, Andrew. "*Civilis Princeps:* Between Citizen and King." *JRS* 72 (1982): 32–48.
Wardman, Alan. *Plutarch's Lives*. Berkeley and Los Angeles: University of California Press, 1974.
Watson, Duane F. "Paul's Speech to the Ephesian Elders (Acts 20.17–38): Epideictic Rhetoric of Farewell." Pages 184–208 in *Persuasive Artistry: Studies in New Testament Rhetoric in Honor of George A. Kennedy*. Edited by D. F. Watson. JSNTSup 50. Sheffield: Sheffield Academic Press, 1990.
———, ed. *Persuasive Artistry: Studies in New Testament Rhetoric in Honor of George A. Kennedy*. JSNTSup 50. Sheffield: Sheffield Academic Press, 1991.
Watson, Duane F., and Alan J. Hauser, eds. *Rhetorical Criticism of the Bible: A Comprehensive Bibliography with Notes on History and Method*. BibInt 4. Leiden: Brill, 1994.
Webb, Ruth. "The *Progymnasmata* as Practice." Pages 289–316 in *Education in Greek and Roman Antiquity*. Edited by Y. L. Too. Leiden: Brill, 2001.
Wedderburn, Alexander J. M. "Traditions and Redaction in Acts 2.1–13." *JSNT* 55 (1994): 27–54.
———. "The 'We'-Passages in Acts: On the Horns of a Dilemma." *ZNW* 93 (2002): 78–98.
Wehnert, Jürgen. *Die Wir-Passagen der Apostelgeschichte: Ein lukanisches Stilmittel aus jüdischer Tradition*. GTA 40. Göttingen: Vandenhoeck & Ruprecht, 1989.
Weinstock, Stefan. *Divus Julius*. London: Oxford University Press, 1971.
———. "The Geographical Catalogue in Acts 2:9–11." *JRS* 38 (1948): 43–46.
———. "*Pax* and the 'Ara Pacis.'" *JRS* 50 (1960): 44–58.
Wendland, Paul. *Die Hellenistisch-Römische Kultur in ihren Beziehungen zu Judentum und Christentum*. HNT 1/2. Tübingen: Mohr, 1912.
———. "ΣΩΤΗΡ." *ZNW* 45 (1904): 335–53.
Wengst, Klaus. *Pax Romana and the Peace of Jesus Christ*. Translated by J. Bowden. London: SCM, 1987.
White, Peter. "*Amicitia* and the Profession of Poetry in Early Imperial Rome." *JRS* 68 (1978): 50–66.
———. "Julius Caesar in Augustan Rome." *Phoenix* 42 (1988): 334–56.
———. "Positions for Poets in Early Imperial Rome." Pages 50–66 in *Literary and Artistic Patronage in Ancient Rome*. Edited by B. Gold. Austin: University of Texas Press, 1982.

Whitmarsh, Tim. *Greek Literature and the Roman Empire: The Politics of Imitation.* New York: Oxford University Press, 2001.

Wiens, Delbert L. *Stephen's Sermon and the Structure of Luke-Acts.* N. Richland Hills, Tex.: BIBAL, 1995.

Wilckens, Ulrich. "Kerygma und Evangelium bei Lukas (Beobachtungen zu Acta 10 34–43)." *ZNW* 49 (1958): 223–37.

———. *Die Missionsreden der Apostelgeschichte: Form- und Traditionsgeschichtliche Untersuchungen.* 3d ed. WMANT 5. Neukirchen-Vluyn: Neukirchener, 1974.

Wilcox, Max. "A Foreward to the Study of the Speeches in Acts." Page 206–25 in vol. 1 of *Christianity, Judaism and other Greco-Roman Cults: Studies for Morton Smith at Sixty.* Edited by J. Neusner. 4 vols. SJLA 12. Leiden: Brill, 1975.

Williams, Gordon. "Phases in Political Patronage of Literature in Rome." Pages 3–27 in *Literary and Artistic Patronage in Ancient Rome.* Edited by B. Gold. Austin: University of Texas Press, 1982.

Wilson, Stephen G. *The Gentiles and the Gentile Mission in Luke-Acts.* SNTSMS 23. Cambridge: Cambridge University Press, 1973.

———. "The Jews and the Death of Jesus in Acts." Pages 155–164 in vol. 1 of *Anti-Judaism in Early Christianity.* Edited by P. Richardson, with D. Granskou. 2 vols. SCJ 2. Waterloo, Ont.: Wilfrid Laurier University Press, 1986.

———. *Luke and the Law.* SNTSMS 50. Cambridge: Cambridge University Press, 1983.

———. *Related Strangers: Jews and Christians 70–170 C.E.* Minneapolis: Fortress, 1995.

———. "Voluntary Associations: An Overview." Pages 1–15 in *Voluntary Associations in the Graeco-Roman World.* Edited by J. S. Kloppenborg and S. G. Wilson. London: Routledge, 1996.

Wilson, Walter T. "Urban Legends: Acts 10:1–11:18 and the Strategies of Greco-Roman Foundation Narratives." *JBL* 120 (2001): 77–99.

Wink, Walter. *The Bible in Human Transformation: Toward a New Paradigm for Biblical Study.* Philadelphia: Fortress, 1973.

Winkler, John J. "The Mendacity of Kalasiris and the Narrative Strategy of Heliodoros' *Aithiopika*." *YCS* 27 (1982): 93–158.

———. *Auctor and Actor: A Narratological Reading of Apuleius's The Golden Ass.* Berkeley and Los Angeles: University of California Press, 1985.

Winkler, Lorenz. *Salus: Vom Staatskult zur politischen Idee.* Archäologie und Geschichte 4. Heidelberg: Archäologie und Geschichte, 1995.

Winter, Bruce W. "The Importance of the *Captatio Benevolentiae* in the Speeches of Tertullus and Paul in Acts 24:1–21." *JTS* 42 (1991): 505–31.

———. "Official Proceedings and the Forensic Speeches in Acts 24–26." Pages 305–36 in *The Book of Acts in Its Ancient Literary Setting*. Edited by B. W. Winter and A. D. Clarke. Vol. 1 of *The Book of Acts in Its First Century Setting*. Grand Rapids: Eerdmans, 1993.

———, ed. *The Book of Acts in Its First Century Setting*. 5 vols. Grand Rapids: Eerdmans, 1993–96.

Winter, Bruce W., and Andrew D. Clarke, eds. *The Book of Acts in Its Ancient Literary Setting*. Vol. 1 of *The Book of Acts in Its First Century Setting*. Grand Rapids: Eerdmans, 1993.

Winter, Sara C. "Παρρησία in Acts." Pages 185–202 in *Friendship, Flattery, and Frankness of Speech: Studies on Friendship in the New Testament World*. Edited by J. T. Fitzgerald. NovTSup 82. Leiden: Brill, 1996.

Wiseman, Timothy P. *Clio's Cosmetics: Three Studies in Greco-Roman Literature*. Leicester: Leicester University Press, 1979.

———. "Legendary Genealogies in Late Republican Rome." *Greece and Rome* 21 (1974): 153–63.

———. "Practice and Theory in Roman Historiography." *History* 66 (1981): 375–93.

Witherington, Ben. *The Acts of the Apostles: A Socio-Rhetorical Commentary*. Grand Rapids: Eerdmans, 1998.

———. Addendum to W. James McCoy, "In the Shadow of Thucydides." Pages 23–32 in *History, Literature and Society in the Book of Acts*. Edited by B. Witherington. Cambridge: Cambridge University Press, 1996.

———. "Editing the Good News: Some Synoptic Lessons for the Study of Acts." Pages 324–47 in *History, Literature, and Society in the Book of Acts*. Edited by B. Witherington. Cambridge: Cambridge University Press, 1996.

———. "Finding Its Niche: The Historical and Rhetorical Species of Acts." Pages 67–97 in *SBL Seminar Papers, 1996*. SBLSP 35. Atlanta: Scholars Press, 1996.

———. ed. *History, Literature, and Society in the Book of Acts*. Cambridge: Cambridge University Press, 1996.

Woodman, Anthony J. *Rhetoric in Classical Historiography: Four Studies*. London: Croom Helm, 1988.

Woodman, Anthony J., and David West, eds. *Poetry and Politics in the Age of Augustus*. Cambridge: Cambridge University Press, 1984.

Wordelman, Amy L. "The Gods Have Come Down: Images of Historical Lycaonia and the Literary Construction of Acts 14." Ph.D. diss., Princeton University, 1994.

Wuellner, Wilhelm H. "The Rhetorical Genre of Jesus' Sermon in Luke 12.1–13.9." Pages 93–118 in *Persuasive Artistry: Studies in New Testament*

Rhetoric in Honor of George A. Kennedy. Edited by D. F. Watson. Sheffield: Sheffield Academic Press, 1991.

York, John. *The Last Shall Be First: The Rhetoric of Reversal in Luke.* JSNTSup 46. Sheffield: Sheffield Academic Press, 1991.

Zanker, Paul. *The Power of Images in the Age of Augustus.* Translated by A. Shapiro. Ann Arbor: University of Michigan Press, 1988.

Zeller, Eduard. *Die Apostelgeschichte nach ihrem Inhalt und Ursprung kritisch untersucht.* Stuttgart: Mäcken, 1854.

Zintzen, Clemens. "Geister (Dämonen): c. Hellenistische und kaiserzeitliche Philosophie." *RAC* 9 (1976): 640–68.

Zweck, Dean. "The *Exordium* of the Areopagus Speech, Acts 17.22, 23." *NTS* (1989): 94–103.

Zwiep, Arie. *The Ascension of the Messiah in Lukan Christology.* NovTSup 87. Leiden: Brill, 1997.

———. "Assumptus est in caelum: Rapture and Heavenly Exaltation in Early Judaism and Luke-Acts." Pages 323–49 in *Auferstehung-Resurrection* Edited by F. Avemarie and H. Lichtenberger. WUNT 135. Tübingen: Mohr Siebeck, 2001.

Index of Primary Sources

Hebrew Scriptures

Genesis
10	250

Exodus
23:7	93

Numbers
25:1–15	169

Deuteronomy
32:15	241

Judges
3:9	242
3:15	242
13–16	181

1 Samuel
4–6	181
9–19	181
10:19	241
14:21	181
17	182
17–31	181
17:46	181
23:2	181
23:4	181
29:23	181
31:9	181

2 Samuel
3:18	181
5:19–20	181

1 Chronicles
9–10	181
10:9	181
11–18	181
14:10	181
14:15	181
16:15	241

Ezra
10:3	140
10:9–15	140
10:18–44	140

Nehemiah
9:27	242
9:32	140
13:1	140
13:3	140
13:23	140
13:25	140
13:28	140
13:30	140

Psalms (parenthetical references are to English versification)
15(16):8–11	182
16	97
23(24):5	241
24(25):5	241
26(27):1	241
26(27):9	241
60:8	181
61(62):2	241
61(62):6	241
64(65):5	241
78(79):9	241
94(95):1	241
105(106):32–36	170
105(106):35	140
108:9	181

110:1	97	**Daniel**		
		2:43		140
Isaiah				
12:2	241	**Joel**		
17:10	241	2:28–29 (3:1–2)		187
25:9	241			
45:15	241	**Amos**		
45:21	241	1:8		181
45:22	241	6:2		181, 187
58:6	161	9:7		181–82, 187
61:1	165	9:11–12		100
61:1–2	165	9:12		187
61:2	158, 161, 165, 183, 185			
		Habakkuk		
Jeremiah		3:18		241
47:1	181			
47:4	181	**Zephaniah**		
		2:5		181

NEW TESTAMENT

Matthew		2:9–14	242
5:3	165	2:11	241
10:16	228	3:1	237
11:5	165	3:6	152
27:45	161	3:13	165
		3:23	154
Mark		3:38	156
1:16–20	55	4:14	158
6:1–6	54	4:16–30	55
14:39	54	4:18–19	165
15:33	161	4:18–21	158
		4:19	158, 183, 185
Luke		4:22	156
1–2	152	4:23–27	158
1:1–4	189, 235, 280	4:24	165
1:2	154	4:26–27	152
1:3	52	5:1–11	55
1:5	154	5:13	158
1:10	60	6:37–38	49
1:21	60	7:36–50	55
1:26–38	156	8:1	52
1:32	55	8:40	165
1:35	156	9:5	165
1:68	60	9:10–17	156
1:79	242	9:48	165
2:1–2	154, 237	9:51	162

Index of Primary Sources 381

9:51–19:27	159	22:24–27	186
9:53	165	22:24–30	153
10:3	228	22:47	159
10:5	159, 163	23	160
10:8	165	23:1	159
10:10	165	23:2	187
10:38	165	23:5	140, 158, 160, 180
11:1–13	49	23:44	161
11:2–4	49	24:18	305
11:4	49	24:30	162
11:5–8	49	24:31	161
11:9–10	49	24:39	162
12:27	166	24:41–43	162
12:37	153, 186	24:44–48	182
13:19	166	24:46	246
14:13	186	24:47	154, 162, 163, 252
14:24	153	24:51	162, 245
15	59	24:52	247
15:11	59		
15:11–32	59	**John**	
15:12	59	4:42	241
15:13	59	21:1–14	55
15:18	59		
15:19	59	**Acts**	
15:20	59	1	314
15:21	59	1–8	218
15:22	59	1–12	153
15:24	59	1:1	154
15:25	59	1:2	245
15:27	59	1:3	307
15:28	59	1:4	39
15:30	59	1:6	39, 307
16:1–8	50	1:9	162
16:8–9	50	1:9–10	162
16:8–13	50	1:9–11	245
16:10–12	50	1:11	246, 314
16:13	50	1:13	306
16:31	182	1:14	306, 313–14
17:8	186	1:15–22	304
18:17	165	1:15–23	96
19:1–9	186	1:16	314
19:6	165	1:21–22	313
19:9	241	1:22	154
19:19	163	1:23–26	304
19:47	158	1:26	313
22:12	306	2	90, 102, 168, 249, 251–52
22:19	159	2:1–4	97

2:1–42	250	4:16–18	306
2:4	171	5:1–11	305, 313, 316
2:5	250, 252	5:1–42	136
2:8	250	5:2	121
2:8–11	171	5:2b–6	316
2:9	250	5:7–11	316
2:9–11	152	5:12–42	316
2:11	250	5:14	312
2:14	250	5:17	308
2:17	187	5:18	305
2:23	230	5:19	305
2:25–28	182	5:21	308
2:25–31	182	5:22–25	121
2:31	97	5:24	308
2:33	246	5:26	308
2:34–35	97	5:27	308
2:36	97	5:28	120
2:38	90	5:30	230
2:38–40	90	5:31	241
2:41	92, 165, 308	5:33	308
2:42	90	5:33–40	305
2:43–47	90	5:36–37	163
2:44–45	186	6	99, 168
2:46	163, 305–6	6–7	89, 160, 180
2:47	90, 93, 308	6:1	96
2:67–68	121	6:1–6	96, 186, 305
3–7	305	6:1–8:4	6
3:1	306	6:2	229
3:1–26	226	6:3	95
3:11–26	305	6:5	95
3:13	305	6:7	166, 308
3:15	230	6:7–15	83
3:24	52	6:8–7:1	136
3:29	305	6:11	84, 140, 149, 163, 187, 229
3:31	305	6:11–14	307
4–5	123	6:13	229
4:1	305	6:13–14	140, 149, 163, 187
4:1–2	305, 308	6:14	84
4:1–9	229	6:15	121
4:1–22	136	7	83–84
4:2	119	7:1	308
4:3	125, 305	7:2	59
4:5	121	7:6	59
4:5–6	305, 308	7:7	59
4:12	241	7:9	59
4:13	120	7:17	59, 166
4:16	307	7:20	59

Index of Primary Sources

Reference	Pages
7:25	59
7:32	59
7:35	59
7:37	59
7:40	59
7:42	59
7:43	59
7:45	59
7:46	59
7:52	230
7:54	84, 308
7:55–56	121
7:56	59, 246
7:57–59	230
7:57–8:1	230
8:1	84, 93, 163
8:3	93, 163, 312
8:12	312
8:26–40	214
8:27	313
9–12	218
9:1	60
9:2	312
9:5	60
9:10	60
9:11	60
9:13	60
9:17	60
9:19	60
9:23–25	214
9:25	60
9:26	60
9:27	60
9:28	60
9:31	60, 163
9:35	60
9:36–43	313
9:42	60
10	52, 165, 168
10–11	89, 297
10–15	150
10:1–11:18	158
10:28	140, 180, 182
10:34–35	26, 153
10:35	152, 165, 183, 185
10:36	242
10:37	154
10:43	152
10:44	171
10:44–48	187
10:45	180
10:47–48	180
11	53
11–28	260
11:1	165
11:4	52
11:5–17	99
11:12	187
11:14	163
11:15	154
11:16–18	187
11:18	26
11:26	170, 233
11:28	237, 263
12	60
12:1–2	230
12:1–25	122, 136
12:2	60
12:5	60
12:12–17	313
12:21	123
12:22	60, 96
12:23	60
12:24	60, 166
13–14	218
13:1	60
13:1–3	163
13:7	237
13:21–23	182
13:23	182, 241
13:28	230
13:33	182
13:33–37	182
13:35	182
13:39	26
13:47	182
13:50	229, 313
14	205–7, 210, 221, 225, 231, 321, 326
14:2	229
14:4	163
14:5	230
14:6	224
14:8–20	214

14:11	224	17:12	313
14:14	163	17:13	229
14:15	156, 226	17:16–34	136, 226
14:17	94	17:17	218
14:19	215, 229–30	17:19	125
15	99–100	17:23	58
15:2	154, 160	17:24	58
15:3	163	17:25	94
15:4–30	96	17:26	168
15:8–9	187	17:27	58
15:11	26	17:28–29	156
15:13–21	99	17:29	58
15:14	60	17:30	58
15:16–17	100	17:34	312, 313
15:17	187	18:1–11	313
15:41	163	18:1–18	218
16–19	124	18:2	237
16:4	263	18:8	163
16:5	163	18:12	125, 237
16:6–9	261	18:12–13	229
16:6–10	152	18:12–17	136
16:10	261	18:14	165
16:10–17	260	18:17	230
16:11	241, 261	18:18–28	313
16:11–12	263	18:23	52
16:11–15	186, 261	18:24–20:1	309
16:11–40	312	19:8–9	167
16:12	218, 261, 263	19:8–10	218
16:12–13	125	19:10	167
16:13	261, 263	19:11	218
16:15	261	19:12	218
16:16	261	19:17	167
16:16–18	218	19:20	166–67
16:16–40	136	19:23–41	313
16:17	261–62	19:23–20:1	136
16:19–20	125	19:29	262–63
16:25–34	186	19:30	96
16:31	125, 163	19:33	96
17	102	19:40	160
17–18	218	20	194, 200, 202
17:1–14	218	20:1–6	261
17:4	313	20:4	262–63
17:5	96, 229	20:5	261
17:5–9	136	20:5–6	262
17:6	125	20:5–15	260
17:7	165	20:5–21:29	262
17:11	165	20:6	261, 263

20:7	261, 263	21:17–26	27
20:8	261, 263	21:18	261, 263
20:9–12	218, 262	21:18–26	96
20:13	261	21:19	186
20:14	261	21:20	308
20:15	261, 263	21:21	139–40, 149, 163, 187
20:17	190	21:24	160
20:17–38	35, 190, 261–62, 309	21:27	229
20:18–21	190, 194	21:27–30	125
20:18–27	199	21:27–22:30	136
20:18–35	200, 228	21:28–29	229
20:20	163	21:30–31	230
20:22–23	195	22	60
20:22–25	190	22–26	130
20:24	186, 195	22:4	312
20:25	196	22:20	230
20:26	190	22:22	230
20:26–27	196	22:30–23:11	136
20:28	163, 190, 196	23:6	27, 129
20:28–31	199	23:7	160
20:29	228	23:8	27
20:29–30	190, 197	23:10	160
20:31	190, 197	23:11	131
20:32	190, 198	23:12	230
20:32–35	190, 198–99	23:21	230
20:35	35, 190, 198	24:1	129
20:36	190	24:1–21	229
20:36–38	201, 309	24:1–23	136
20:37	191	24:2	241
21–26	26, 117	24:5	160
21–28	139, 180	24:24	313, 316
21:1	261, 263	24:25	130, 317
21:1–18	260	25:1–12	136
21:2	261	25:3	230
21:3	261	25:7	130, 229
21:4	261, 263	25:10	237
21:5	261	25:13	312, 313, 317
21:6	261	25:13–26:3	136
21:7	261, 263	25:18–19	229
21:8	261	25:23	312, 313, 317
21:10	261, 263	25:25	229
21:11	261	26	60
21:12	261	26:1–23	130
21:14	261	26:5	27
21:15	261	26:6	58
21:16	261–63	26:8	58
21:17	165, 261	26:17	163

26:18	58	28:12	261, 263
26:20	58	28:13	261, 263
26:22	58	28:14	261, 263
26:24	130	28:15	60, 261
26:26	305	28:16	261
26:28	234	28:23	60
26:29	58	28:23–31	219
26:30	317	28:28	39
26:30–32	229	28:30	165
26:32	237	28:31	60
27:1	261		
27:1–29	260–61	**Romans**	
27:1–28:16	261–62	12:2	179
27:2	261–63		
27:3	261	**1 Corinthians**	
27:4	261	7:31	179
27:5	261	14:33b–35	324
27:6	261, 263		
27:7	261	**Galatians**	
27:8	261, 263	2:1–10	100
27:9–14	262	3:28	152–53
27:11	263		
27:14	263	**Ephesians**	
27:15	261	2:12	185
27:16	261	4:4–6	168
27:18	261		
27:20	261	**Philippians**	
27:21–26	262	1:27	185
27:21–44	218	2:7	179
27:26	261	3:21	179
27:27	261, 263		
27:29	261	**Colossians**	
27:30–43	262	4:10	262
27:30–44	262		
27:33–43	262	**Philemon**	
27:37	261	24	262
28:1	261–62		
28:1–10	214, 217	**1 Peter**	
28:1–16	218, 260	1:14	179
28:2	217, 261	4:16	234
28:3–6	262		
28:4	217		
28:6	60, 217		
28:7	261		
28:7–10	218		
28:10	217, 261		
28:11	261, 263		

Index of Primary Sources

ANCIENT JEWISH AND CHRISTIAN SOURCES

Additions to Esther
15:2	241
16:13	242

Augustine, *Confessions*
6.3	272

Baruch
4:22	241
6:5	181

Eusebius, *Historia ecclesiastica*
1.2.22–23	178
6.43.6	227

Ignatius, *To the Ephesians*
11.2	234

Ignatius, *To the Magnesians*
4	234

Ignatius, *To the Romans*
3.2	234

Josephus, *Contra Apionem*
2.145–146	91
2.154	94
2.225–231	94
2.259	94
2.273	94

Josephus, *Antiquitates judaicae*
1.10	148
1.13	148
4.102–158	168
4.129–130	169
4.131	169
4.133	169
4.137–140	169
4.140	169
4.146	169
4.148	140
4.148–149	169
4.149	169
4.153	140, 169
4.159	140, 169
4.200–201	168
4.223–224	148, 180
4.292	148, 180
4.295	148, 180
4.302	148, 180
4.326	161
6.31–67	146
6.39	148
6.83–85	148
6.90	148
6.92	148
6.262–268	148
14.4	184
14.10	184
16.160	185
20.143	316
20.144	317

Josephus, *Bellum judaicum*
2.358–387	249
4.618	162
7.158	240

Judith
6:1	181
9:11	241

Justin, *1 Apology*
21	247

1 Maccabees
1–4	166
3:32	181
4:12	181
4:30	181–82, 241
4:33	181
5:15	181
5:68	181
8	184

2 Maccabees
4–7	166
4:13	181
6–7	160, 168

6:24	181	Origen, *Contra Celsum*		
10:2	181	2.68		247
10:5	181			
14:3	140	Philo, *Legatio ad Gaium*		
3 Maccabees		18		162
6:29	241	231		162
6:32	241			
7:16	242	Polycarp, *To the Philippians*		
		7.3		162
4 Maccabees				
18:5	181	**Sirach**		
		51:1		241
Martyrdom of Pionius				
22	122	Tertullian, *Against the Jews*		
		7		252
Martyrdom of Polycarp				
16	122	**Wisdom**		
		16:7		241
Minucius Felix, *Octavius*				
21	247			

GREEK AND LATIN AUTHORS

Achilles Tatius, *Leucippe and Clitophon*		Apuleius, *Metamorphoses*		
		11.6		184
7.7–16	134	Aristotle, *Poetica*		
8.1.4	128	1450A		80
8.7–15	134	1457A		57
Aelius Aristides, *Orationes*		Aristotle, *Politica*		
97	240	2.3.9–11		94
		2.3.11		94
***Antheia* fragments**		2.6		94
1	110	2.6.21		95
2.15–16	110	3.5.1–4		94
		3.11.11		96
Aphthonius, *Progymnasmata*		3.12.1		96
2	76			
14	100	Aristotle, *Rhetorica*		
		1.1.10		123
Appian, *Bella civilia*		1.7.27		57
2.148	162	2.23.2		57
		3.9.9		57
Appian, *Historia romana*				
12.48	151	Aristotle, *Topica*		
12.61–62	151	3.1.6–12		83

Index of Primary Sources

Arius Didymus, fragments
11b	77

Arrian, *Anabasis of Alexander*
1.11.5	152
1.16.7	152
2.7.4–6	152
3.15.2–3	152
3.23.8	152
4.4.2	152

Asellio, fragment 291

(Marcus) Aurelius, *Meditations*
11.15	227

Cassius Dio, *Roman History*
48.30.1	151

Chariton, *Chaereas and Callirhoe*
1.4–6	134
3.4	134
4.2–3	126
4.6.5–6	120
5.4–9	134
5.4.5–7	114
5.4.7	121
5.10–6.2	134
6.1.8–12	120
6.3	120

Cicero, *Epistulae ad Atticum*
12.6	152

Cicero, *De inventione rhetorica*
1.21.29–30	55–56
1.28	53

Cicero, *De legibus*
1.1.15	74
1.15.43	184
1.2.5	73
1.3.1	144
1.7.1	184
2.7–22	168
2.26	89

Cicero, *De officiis*
1.85–86	95
1.86	93
1.89	93
1.142	93
1.153–159	93

Cicero, *De oratore*
2.36	73

Cicero, *De republica*
2.47	94
6.13	243

Corpus Hermeticum
16.1–2	172

Curtius Rufus, *The History of Alexander*
6.3.2–3	249

Demosthenes, *De Corona*
169–173	127

Dio Chrysostom, *Orationes*
45.7.1	243
56.34.2–3	250
56.42.3	243
66.15	240

Diodorus Siculus, *Library of History*
1.2.2	78
1.2.5–6	78
13.24.2	92
13.24.4–5	93
13.25.2–3	93
15.1.1	75
31.15.1	75

Diogenes Laertius, *De clarorum philosophorum vitis*
7.100	93
7.189	152

Dionysius, *De antiquis oratoribus*
1	152
1–3	150

Index of Primary Sources

Dionysius, *Antiquitates romanae*

1.1.2	224	1.33.4	150, 158, 171
1.1.3	75	1.34.2	167
1.4.2	150	1.34.4	158
1.4.3	151	1.34.5	163
1.5.1	145	1.38.2	158
1.5.2	145	1.39.4	158
1.6.4	145	1.40.1	156
1.7.3	157	1.40.3	156
1.7.4	145	1.40.3–6	158
1.8	145	1.41.1	150, 167
1.8.1–2	146	1.42.2	150
1.8.2	159	1.44.2	158
1.8.3	146–47, 164	1.45.2	170
1.9.2	167	1.50.3	164, 171
1.9.3	170	1.52.3	171
1.9.4	148, 164, 180	1.53.1	170
1.10.2	167, 170	1.55.1	163
1.10.3	162	1.57.4	163–64
1.11.1–3	224	1.58.2	163, 167
1.11.3	165	1.58.4	167
1.12.1	224	1.59.1	167
1.12.3	224	1.59.4	163
1.13.1	224	1.59.5	163, 165, 167
1.16.1	162	1.60.1	167
1.16.2	162, 165	1.60.1–3	167
1.16.3	164	1.61.1–3	156
1.19.3	167	1.62.2	156
1.20.1	163–64	1.63.2	164–65
1.20.3	171	1.64.2	167
1.21.1–2	158	1.64.4	165
1.23.1	165	1.65.1	170
1.24.2	159	1.66.1	163
1.25.2	170	1.66.2	164–65
1.25.3	158	1.67–69	158
1.26.1	170	1.67.1	163
1.27.3	162	1.71.3	158
1.29.3	171	1.72.1	154
1.3.1	165	1.73.2	164, 167
1.3.3	248	1.74–75	154
1.3.4	165	1.76–2.56	143
1.30.2	171	1.76.3	158
1.30.3	170	1.77.1–2	155
1.31.2	159	1.77.3	146, 155
1.31.3	163, 165	1.79.8	158
1.32.5	158	1.79.9	163
1.33.1–3	158	1.79.10	154
		1.79.11	158

Index of Primary Sources

1.80.4	154	2.19.3	158
1.85.1–2	159	2.20.1	146
1.85.2	159, 162	2.21.1	146
1.85.4	167	2.23.2	158
1.86	163	2.23.4	158
1.86.1	159	2.23.5	158
1.87.4	159	2.23.6	158
1.89.1	154	2.25.7	158
1.89.2	167	2.26–27	158
1.89.3	158, 167, 171	2.27.3	154
1.89.3–4	158, 167, 170–71	2.28.1	157–58
1.89.4	150, 158, 171	2.30.1	147
1.90.1	167, 171	2.30.2	167
1.90.2	147	2.32.2	165
2.1.1	162	2.34.3	158
2.2.2	167, 170	2.34.4	158
2.2.3	156	2.35.4	162
2.3.1	157	2.35.5	162
2.3.2	159	2.36.2	162, 164–65
2.3.4	159	2.45.3	180
2.3.5	147	2.46.2	170
2.3.7	147	2.46.3	167
2.4.1	147, 157	2.47.1	165
2.5.1	163	2.49.1	170
2.6–29	157	2.49.3	162
2.6.1	158	2.49.4	159
2.6.2	158	2.50.1	165
2.6.3	158	2.50.5	162
2.6.4	146, 159	2.55.6	161
2.7.1	147	2.56.2–3	161
2.7.2	147	2.56.3	159, 161
2.9.1	159–60	2.56.6	146, 161
2.10.4	148	2.57–76	143, 149
2.11.2	154–55	2.57.3	159
2.11.2–3	148	2.58.1	159
2.12.4	158	2.60.4	157
2.14.3	158	2.60.6	157
2.14.4	147	2.61.1	157
2.15	158	2.62.5	165
2.15–17	165	2.63.1	154
2.15.3	166	2.63.3	146, 159
2.17.1–3	166	2.63.3–4	162
2.17.3	150	2.65.4	158
2.18–22	158	2.66	158
2.18.2	154	2.72.14–18	158
2.19.2	158	2.74.4	158
2.19.2–5	148	3.1–35	143

392   Index of Primary Sources

3.36–45	143	**Heliodorus,** *An Ethiopian Tale*	
3.46–73	143	1.9–14	134
4.1.2–2.3	156	1.13.1	114
4.2.2	156	1.14–17	134
4.2.3–4	156	2.8–9	134
4.6.6	156	4.17–21	134
4.24	169	8.8–15	134
4.41–85	143, 146	8.9.13	122
4.63	147	8.9.15	122
4.73–74	149	10.9–17	134
5.56	147	10.34–38	134
5.74.2–3	148		
6.22–92	146, 149, 170	**Heraclitus, fragments**	
6.74.3	148	14	281
6.92–8.62	146	15	281
7.65.5	95	55	281
7.66	147	107	281
7.66.3	148		
7.70–72	180	**Hermogenes,** *Progymnasmata*	
7.70.5	148	4.9–15	51
7.72.2	148		
7.72.4	148	**Herodotus,** *Histories*	
8.5.4	148	1.58.4	165
8.30.4	148		
10.51.3	148	**Hesiod,** *Astronomy*	
10.55.3	148	3	223

Dionysius, *De Isocrates*
11.4	146

Hesiod, *Theogonia*
27–28	273

Dionysius, *De Lysia*
16.1–3	146

Homer, *Ilias*
6	35, 192, 194, 200, 228
6.113–15	191

Dionysius, *De Thucydide*
37–42	81

6.269–276	191
6.296–311	191
6.361–362	195

Epictetus, *Dissertationes*
1.6.40	92, 94
3.1.27–35	75
3.13.9	140

6.365–368	191
6.367–368	195
6.410–411	193
6.440–446	194
6.441–443	196

Eratosthenes, *Catasterismi*
1.8R[16].1–31	223

6.441–450	192
6.447–449	196–97
6.454–455	192

Hecataeus, *Historical Fragments*
1a, 1F.6bis,a.18	223

6.459–463	193
6.459–465	192
6.466	201

6.466–481	192	**Libanius, *Orationes***	
6.472–481	193	22	85
6.474–476	201	39	85
6.475–478	198	**Livy, *Ab urbe condita libri***	
6.476–478	198	Preface 9	77
6.479–480	198	1.16	162
6.482–502	192	1.16.7	159
6.486–489	195		
6.488–489	193	**Longus, *Daphnis and Chloe***	
6.490	197	2.12–19	134
6.490–493	196		
6.492–493	197	**Lucan, *Bellum civile***	
6.498–502	201	1.60	240
7.123	193		
		Lucian, *Historia*	
Homer, *Odyssea*		8–9	74
1.96–324	221	37	77
1.405–419	221	38	74
8.489–491	273	41	74
11.631	157	55	76
17.484–487	221	61	74
Horace, *Carmina*		**Martial, *Epigrams***	
1.12.47	243	2.91.1	239
1.12.49	238	5.1.7	239
3.3	245		
3.5.1–4	240	**Menander, fragments**	
4.14	249	3:line 833.1	227
4.15.17	238	4:line FIF203.1	227
		2:line 267.1	227
Hyginus, Fabulae			
176	224	**Nicolaus, *Progymnasmata***	
		4.18–19	61
Inscriptions			
CIL 5.7817	249	**Ovid, *Fasti***	
ILS 112.14–18	238	5.493–544	223
ILS 112.23–25	238		
ILS 140.6–8	238	**Ovid, *Metamorphoses***	
		1.163–167	223
Isocrates, *Nicocles*		1.196–198	223
2.48–49	76	1.209–240	223
2.50–52	76	8.547–561	220
		8.611–623	220
Isocrates, *Panegyricus*		8.612–725	208
158	150	15.753–756	249
		15.758–761	245
		15.843	243

394 Index of Primary Sources

Pausanius, *Graeciae description*
2.1–7   224

Petronius, *Satyrica*
108–109   110

Photius, *Bibliotheca*
166[112a]   110
94[74b-24-30]   110

Plato, *Epistulae*
318E   227

Plato, *Phaedrus*
241C–D   227
228D–E   268

Plato, *Politicus*
277D–278B   268

Plato, *Respublica*
380D–382D   222
565D   228
565E   232
565E–566A   228

Plato, *Sophista*
216A–B   222
262C   268

Plato, *Symposium*
209C–E   95

Pliny the Elder, *Naturalis historia*
2.18–19   162
2.93–94   243
3.136–137   249
5.132–133   249
7.98   249

Pliny the Younger, *Epistulae*
10.52   239
10.102   239

Pliny the Younger, *Panegyricus*
11.1–3   162
35.4   162

Plutarch, *Ad principem ineruditum*
781A   92
781E   94

Plutarch, *Alexander*
1.1   144

Plutarch, *Antonius*
2   151

Plutarch, *Comparatio Lycurgi et Numae*
1.1   163–64, 176, 178, 180
1.3   176, 180
2.2   176, 178–80
2.5   155
3.3   176
3.5   176
4.6   179–80
4.6–7   162, 180
4.7   166, 179–80
4.8   178, 180

Plutarch, *Comparatio Thesei et Romuli*
2.1   175, 180
2.1–2   175, 180
4.1   168
4.1–2   180
6.3–4   167
6.5   155, 163

Plutarch, *Lycurgus*
1.1   161, 164
1.1–3   155
1.4   156
3.5   164
4.3   164
4.5–6   164
5.2   175, 180
5.3   156, 175–76
5.4   176, 180
5.6   176, 180
6.1   163, 176
6.4   176
6.4–5   158, 162, 180
6.5   163, 176

Index of Primary Sources

7.1	176, 180	1.2	177
7.3	155	1.3	167
8.3	176, 180	1.4	155
9.1	176, 180	2.1	155, 161
9.3	176, 180	2.3	162
10.1	176, 180	2.4	177
10.3	176, 180	2.4–6	180
11.1	161, 176, 180	2.5–6	177
11.3	176	3.1	177, 180
11.14–15	180	3.2–3	177
13.1	158, 176, 180	3.4	155
13.3	158, 176, 180	3.6	163
13.5	158	4	163
13.6	163, 176	4.2	178
14–15	176	4.7–8	178
14.1	158	4.8	180
14.4	158	5.1	155
15.1	158	5.2	166
15.3	158	5.3	155
18.4	158, 176, 180	5.4	158
19.1	158	5.5	158, 166
19.3	158	6.2	163, 178
20	158	6.4	178, 180
21	158	7.2–3	163
23.2	163, 176	8.1	159, 178
27.1	158	8.2	166
27.3	164, 176	8.3	166, 178
27.3–4	180	8.3–10	163
27.4	158, 177	8.6	178
28	158	9.6	178
29.2	164, 177	10.2	163
29.2–3	158, 180	12.1	158
29.2–4	180	13.1	163, 178
29.3	177	14.1	158, 178
29.4	158, 161, 177	15.1	158, 165, 178
29.4–5	164	15.4–5	163
29.5	164	17.1–3	167–68, 170, 178
29.6	158, 177	19.5	178
30.1	158, 162, 164, 177, 180	19.6	178
30.5	158	20.1–2	179
31.2	158	20.3	178–80
31.3	156	20.5	179
31.4	161	20.7–8	179
31.5	158, 164, 177, 180	21.1	162, 179–80
		21.4	155
Plutarch, *Numa*		22.1	161
1.1	155	22.2	158

22.4	158	27.1	158, 175, 180
22.6	161	27.3	155
22.7	162, 178–80	27.3–8	161
		27.4	180

Plutarch, *Quomodo adulator ab amico internoscatur*

		28.6–8	162
		29.3	167
56	75	29.7	155
61	77		
66	75	**Plutarch, *Theseus***	
		1.2	144
Plutarch, *Romulus*		1.4–5	144
1.1	164	2.1	155
1.1–2	170	2.2	161, 168, 175, 180
1.3	165	3.3–4	163
2.3–4.3	155	6.1–2	155
4.2	156	6.6	164
7.1	165, 180	6.26–28	164
7.5–6	155	7.4	155
8.6	180	8.7	155
8.7	155	12.1	155
9.2	167	13.3	167
9.3	165	18.1	155
9.7	163	20.2	156–57
11.1	158, 167	24.1	168, 180
12.1	155	24.2	175
12.4–6	155	24.2–4	175, 180
12.5	155–56	24.3	175
13.1	158	25.2	163
13.3	158	28.2	161
14.1	163	29.2	175, 180
14.2	167	30.4	164
14.6	167	32.1	175, 180
15.3	171	33.1	165
15.5	155	35.4	161
16.2	165	35.5	162
16.5	166	36.2	165
19.1	163	36.3	156
19.1–3	164		
19.7	167	**Plutarch, *Tiberius Gracchus***	
20.1	166	9.5	247
20.4	167		
21.1	167	**Polybius, *Histories***	
21.2	163	1.1.2	77
22.3	158	2.37.8	165
24.1	163	2.39.11	165
25.1	166	2.56.7–10	74
26.1	175, 180	2.56.11	77

3.48.8–9	74	**Seneca, *Apocolocyntosis***	
5.10.1	165	1.1–2	162
6.43.2	165	12.3	249
10.2.8–13	95	**Seneca, *Epistulae***	
12.25b.1–4	74, 77	114.2–3	88, 148
12.25d.1	274		
12.25e.1–2	274	**Statius, *Silvae***	
12.25e.6–7	77	3.4.20	239
12.25e.7	274	4.2.14–15	239
12.25g.2–3	77		
12.25h.3	274	**Strabo, *Geographica***	
12.25h.4	264	1.2.8	232
12.25i.2	274	1.4.3	231
12.25i.6	77	2.6.3	74
12.25i.9	74	3.3.8	231
12.27.1	281	4.5.4	231
12.28a.9	282	7.3.4	232
15.36.1–7	74	7.3.6	231
15.36.8	74	7.5.7	231
		12.3.18	231
Quintilian, *Institutio oratoria*		12.6.5	231
2.4.41	85	14.5.24	231
2.10.2	86		
4.2.32	55–56	**Suetonius, *De vita Caesarum***	
4.2.83	52	***Divus Augustus***	
9.1.34	57	31.8	250
9.3.27	57, 61	100.4	162
9.3.28	57	***Divus Julius***	
9.3.37	57	88	243
9.4.13	267	***Nero***	
10.1.34	260	13.2	240
		16	233
Res Gestae Divi Augusti		16.2	254
12	240	***Divus Vespasianus***	
13	240	9.1	240
Rhetorica ad Alexandrum		**Tacitus, *Agricola***	
30.1–4	55	30.3–31.2	240
30.28–31	52	30.5	255
84.17–18	53	33–34	143
Rhetorica ad Herennium		**Tacitus, *Annales***	
1.9.15	52	1.1	253
1.14	53	1.8.4	250
4.22.30–31	57	3.65	77
		15.44	233

Index of Primary Sources

Theon, *Progymnasmata*

1.15–16	47
1.40–42	68
1.47–48	68
2.138–143	68
2.145–149	75
10	83
12	100
60.3–4	51
60.3–11	51
60.4	53
60.5	51
60.6	53
62.10–64.25	53
64.1	54
67.4	53
69	61
70.3	53
70.6	53
70.12	53
70.24–30	45
72.28	50
74.24–25	60
74.24–35	57
75.28–31	50
76.31–35	53
76.35–77.9	55
77.15	53
78.16–17	51
79.20–22	51
79.21–24	53
79.28–29	55
80.17	53
80.26–29	51
81.2	53
81.7	53
81.8–10	53
83.15–19	53
83.25	53
83.25–84.10	53
83.31	53
84.5–17	53
84.17–18	53
84.19–24	55
85.29–31	56
86.9–87.13	52
87.13	51
87.23	53
91.15	53
96.19–20	48
97.11–99	48
99.34–100.3	48
101.4–5	48
101.10–103.2	57
121.2	53
122.30	53
123.1	53

Thucydides, *History of the Peloponnesian War*

1.22.2–4	74
2.43.3	77

Velleius Paterculus, *History*

2.39.2	250
2.89	239–40
2.126	240
2.131	240

Vergil, *Aeneis*

1.278–279	248
1.286–294	244
1.291–296	240
2.671–678	192
2.776–787	193
3.313–319	193
3.342–343	194
3.494	193
4.229–231	248
6.780–782	249
6.782	248
6.792	253
6.792–797	248
6.851	248
7.99–101	248
7.258	248
8.626–728	248
12.430–431	193
12.433–435	193
12.438–443	193

Vergil, *Eclogues*

1.6–8	240
4.5	253

9.47–49	243	6.3–4	95
		10.4	95
Xenophon, *Hellenica*		10.7	95
2.3.32	160		
Xenophon, *Respublica Lacedaemo-*		**Xenophon of Ephesus, *An Ephesian***	
niorum		***Tale***	
5.2	95	2.5–10	126
5.5	95	3.12–4.4	134

Index of Modern Authors

Abusch, Ra'anan 91
Aejmelaeus, Lars 190
Ahl, Frederick M. 225–26
Alcock, Susan E. 301
Alexander, Loveday 4–5, 8, 16, 35–37, 67, 71, 80, 82, 105–6, 142, 236, 266, 280, 283, 321
Alexander, Philip S. 251
Alexander, Sidney 245
Allen, O. Wesley 94
Alonso, A. M. 296
Alonso-Núñez, J. M. 145, 172
Ampolo, Carmine 145, 156
Andersen, Øivind 269
Ando, Clifford 127, 236, 250
André, Jean-Marie 242, 247
Arnold, Bill 5
Ascough, Richard S. 118, 300
Attridge, Harold W. 81
Aubin, Melissa 324
Auerbach, Erich 65–66
Aune, David E. 67, 142, 235, 270
Bachmann, Michael 8
Bagnall, Roger S. 173
Bal, Mieke 111
Balch, David L. 8, 34–35, 67, 76, 79, 88–89, 95, 97, 99, 139, 145, 149, 151, 153, 159, 166, 168–70, 235, 252, 306, 322
Baldwin, Charles S. 45
Balsdon, John P. V. D. 148, 157, 168
Barclay, John M. G. 91
Bar-Kochva, Bezalel 154
Barrett, Charles K. 83, 182, 234, 251
Bartchy, S. Scott 307
Bartlett, John R. 169
Bartsch, Shadi 115
Baslez, Marie-Françoise 107
Batstone, William W. 83
Bauckham, Richard 4–5, 100
Baumann, Gerd 183
Baur, Ferdinand Christian 27
Baxter, Timothy M. S. 225
Beard, Mary 243
Beavis, Mary Ann 50
Béchard, Dean P. 94, 231, 251
Benko, Stephen 253
Berger, Klaus 48, 235
Berry, D. H. 85, 87
Betz, Hans Dieter 31, 157
Bickerman, Elias J. 243, 246
Biddick, Kathleen 207
Black, C. Clifton 43
Blomberg, Craig L. 50, 119
Bloomer, W. Martin 87
Blue, Brad 7
Blumenfeld, Bruno 103
Blundell, Mary W. 80
Bolognesi, Giancarlo 46
Bonner, Stanley F. 44, 84, 292
Bosworth, A. B. 81
Botha, Pieter J. J. 269
Bowersock, Glen W. 86, 106, 108, 122–23, 152, 238, 255
Bowie, Ewen L. 106
Boyarin, Daniel 328
Braun, Willi 44, 48, 153
Braund, David 249
Brawley, Robert 8, 20
Brehm, Harold A. 83
Bremmer, Jan N. 155
Brenk, Frederick E. 155
Brent, Allen 88–89, 96, 99, 102, 242, 255
Breytenbach, Cilliers 210
Bringmann, Klaus 308

Index of Modern Authors

Brinkman, J. A. 250
Brodie, Thomas L. 66, 100
Brown, Raymond E. 55, 242
Bruce, Frederick F. 1, 73
Buell, Denise Kimber 183
Bultmann, Rudolf 156
Burchard, Christoph 83
Burfeind, Carsten 273
Burridge, Richard A. 142–43
Burrus, Virginia 312
Butts, James R. 45–47, 68, 100
Buxton, Richard 291
Byrskog, Samuel 32, 76, 81, 259–60, 264–65, 267, 270, 275, 281–83, 320
Cadbury, Henry J. 28–29, 54, 79, 213–16, 233, 235
Cagnat, René 238
Cairns, Francis 248
Calame, Claude 76
Cameron, Ron 77, 285
Cancik, Hubert 67, 170, 177, 184, 235, 287–88
Cancik-Lindemaier, H. 184
Cappelli, Rosanna 155
Capper, Brian 7
Carandini, Andrea 155
Cassidy, Richard J. 306
Centrone, Bruno 92
Chance, J. Bradley 105
Chapman, Malcolm 296
Clark, Andrew C. 4, 6, 83, 235
Clark, Donald L. 44
Clarke, Martin L. 221
Clines, David J. A. 257
Cohen, Shaye J. D. 183, 291
Colin, Jean 108, 127
Connolly, Joy 85, 87, 101
Connors, Catherine 152
Conte, Gian Biagio 15
Conybeare, William J. 209–10
Conzelmann, Hans 125, 129, 235, 262–63
Cooper, Kate 323
Corbeill, Anthony 75
Cotter, Wendy 302
Cribiore, Raffaela 68, 85, 222
Crossan, John Dominic 275

Csapo, Eric 127
Culpepper, R. Alan 55
Dahl, Nils A. 7, 89
D'Angelo, Mary Rose 89, 311–12, 314, 316–17
Danker, Frederick W. 238
Darr, John A. 93–94
Davis, Casey Wane 269
Dawsey, James M. 236
Dean, Margaret E. 69, 267
Deissmann, Adolf 66
Delling, Gerhard 163
Denaux, Albert 9
Denova, Rebecca 251
Dibelius, Martin 79–80, 82
Diels, Hermann 280–81
Dihle, Albrecht 152
Dinkler, Erich 233
Dodd, Charles H. 50
Dorey, Thomas A. 290
Dormeyer, Detlev 140, 159
Dornseiff, Franz 237
Dougherty, Carol 159
Downing, F. Gerald 222
Dowsett, Rosemary M. 319
Draper, Jonathan A. 269
duBois, Page 289
Duff, Timothy E. 83, 144
Dunn, James D. G. 234
Dupont, Jacques 90, 260, 307
Easton, Burton S. 71
Eckstein, Arthur M. 292
Eden, P. T. 243
Eder, Walter 253
Edwards, Douglas R. 90, 107–8
Ellul, Jacques 236
Engberg-Pedersen, Troels 103
Esler, Philip F. 2, 234, 296
Evans, Craig A. 20, 67, 259
Evans, Jane DeRose 236, 289
Exum, J. Cheryl 257
Farmer, William R. 48
Fearghail, Fearghus Ó 67
Fears, J. Rufus 96
Feldman, Louis H. 141, 157, 161, 169–70
Finnegan, Ruth 271

Fitzgerald, Robert	244	Hall, Edith	290
Fitzmyer, Joseph A.	50, 55, 156, 242	Hall, Robert G.	83
Fleming, Katherine E.	207	Hallett, Judith P.	327
Foakes Jackson, Frederick J.	3, 28, 285	Hamilton, James R.	292
Fontenrose, Joseph E.	221	Hamm, Dennis	225
Fornara, Charles W.	73, 81, 290	Hannestad, Niels	236
Foucault, Michel	16	Hardie, Philip R.	248
Fredriksen, Paula	1	Harnack, Adolf von	29, 322
Fromentin, V.	145–46	Harrison, Stephen J.	106
Fuks, Alexander	99	Harvey, John D.	269
Funk, Robert	60	Hauser, Alan J.	46
Furtwängler, Adolf	250	Hayes, John H.	164
Gabba, Emilio	146, 150–51, 157, 166, 184	Haynes, Katharine	323
		Haynes, Stephen R.	25
Gadamer, Hans Georg	11	Head, Peter M.	259
Gaertringen, Fredrich H. von	238	Heath, Malcolm	45, 85, 87
Gager, John G.	229	Heil, Christoph	287–88
Galinsky, Karl	245, 248, 253	Hellerman, Joseph H.	170
Gaston, Lloyd	229	Hemer, Colin J.	73, 108, 263
Gaventa, Beverly R.	216	Henderson, John	243
Gavrilov, A. K.	272	Hengel, Martin	235, 279
Gerber, Christine	91	Henten, Jan Willem van	91
Gilbert, Gary	34, 71, 89–90, 92, 101, 247, 251	Hernández Lara, Carlos	107
		Herzfeld, Michael	296
Gill, Christopher	106	Hidber, Thomas	146, 150–52, 171
Given, Mark D.	324	Hilgert, Earle	80
Glaser, Konrad	159	Hill, Craig C.	6, 83
Gleason, Maud	76, 300	Hobart, William K.	29
Gold, V. R.	314	Hock, Ronald F.	48, 68, 105, 221
Goldhill, Simon	106	Hogan, Derek	43
Goodman, Martin	185	Holladay, Carl R.	154
Goody, Jack	271	Holtzmann, Heinrich J.	251
Goold, G.P.	107	Honoré, A. M.	54
Görg, Manfred	251	Hopkins, Keith	106
Goulder, Michael	251	Hoppin, Ruth	322
Grant, Robert M.	186	Hornblower, Simon	81
Gray, Vivienne J.	95	Horsfall, Nicholas M.	155, 289
Green, Joel B.	6, 59	Horsley, G. H. R.	81
Grele, Ronald J.	279	Horsley, Richard A.	269
Griffen, Jasper	248	Hoskins, Janet	296
Griffin, Miriam	92, 248	Howson, John S.	209–10
Gruen, Erich S.	184, 291, 294	Hultkrantz, Åke	272
Gunderson, Erik	75–76, 311	Hunter, Virginia J.	290
Haenchen, Ernst	42, 83, 97, 208, 250, 295	Iggers, Georg G.	275–76
		Jacoby, Felix	146
Haerens, H.	237	Jaffee, Martin S.	269
Hahm, David E.	95–96	Jeremias, Joachim	59

Index of Modern Authors

Jervell, Jacob	73, 82, 251, 258, 263
Jeska, Joachim	83
Johne, Renate	323
Johnson, Luke T.	20, 80, 251, 265, 306
Jones, Arnold H. M.	108
Jones, Christopher P.	107, 292
Juel, Donald	251
Kahn, Charles H.	280–81
Kaster, Robert A.	84, 87, 99
Keaney, John J.	221
Keith, A. M.	76
Kelber, Werner H.	269–71, 281
Kelly, Shawn	12
Kennedy, George A.	31–32, 39, 43, 45–46, 61, 68, 83
Kilpatrick, George D.	251
Kirk, Geoffrey	196
Kirsch, Wolfgang	253
Klauck, Hans-Josef	162
Kloppenborg, John S.	300
Knoch, Otto	190
Koch, Dietrich-Alex	263
Kock, Theodor	227
Koester, Helmut	309
Kolenkow, Anitra Bingham	190
Konstan, David	106, 109
Körte, Alfred	227
Kraemer, Ross Shepard	322, 324
Kranz, Walther	280–81
Kremer, Jacob	250–51
Kroll, Wilhelm	225
Kuefler, Matthew	312
Kullmann, Wolfgang	273
Kurz, William S.	88, 190
Lake, Kirsopp	3, 28, 285
Lamberton, Robert	221
Larsson, Edvin	258
Latacz, Joachim	273
Lefkowitz, Mary R.	322
Leppä, Heikki	100
Levinskaya, Irina	4, 6
Lightfoot, Joseph B.	233
Linafelt, Todd	13
Lincoln, Bruce	298
Lintott, Andrew	95
Little, Douglas	248
Lövestam, Evald	259
Lowenthal, David	289
Luce, T. James	292
Lüdemann, Gerd	233
Luomanen, Petri	9
Lyne, R. O. A. M.	248
MacDonald, Dennis R.	35, 228, 230, 236, 264, 322
Mack, Burton L.	48, 300, 303
MacMullen, Ramsay	255
Maddox, Robert L.	71, 254
Mader, Gottfried	99
Magie, David	238
Malina, Bruce	293
Manfredini, Mario	145, 156
Marguerat, Daniel	14, 83, 266
Marincola, John	75
Marrou, Henri I.	221
Marshall I. Howard	6
Martin, Clarice J.	216, 312, 316
Marwood, Martin A.	238–39
Matthews, Christopher R.	259
Matthews, Shelly	312, 317
Mattill, A. J., Jr.	26
Mayer, Edgar	164
McCutcheon, Russell	298
McDonald, Maryon	296
McDonald, William A.	127
McKenzie, Steven L.	25
Mealand, David L.	306
Meeks, Wayne	300, 302
Meier, Christian	253
Meineke, August	227
Merkelbach, Reinhold	172–73
Metzger, Bruce M.	90, 245
Meyer, Heinrich A.	208
Meynet, Roland	48
Michel, Hans-Joachim	190–91
Millar, Fergus	255
Mills, Margaret A.	282
Mitchell, Alan C.	90, 306
Moessner, David P.	5, 7–8, 20, 79–80, 97, 164, 254, 280
Momigliano, Arnaldo	290
Moore, Stephen D.	70
Moralee, Jason W.	238
Moreland, Milton	34, 36, 39–40, 69, 77, 190, 286, 296, 307, 313–14, 320, 324

Morgan, John R. 106, 113
Morgenthaler, Robert 43, 67
Mount, Christopher 295
Moxnes, Halvor 292
Moynihan, R. 247
Muilenburg, James 31
Munck, Johannes 190
Nadeau, Ray E. 45
Neudorfer, Heinz-Werner 6
Newton, Charles T. 238
Neyrey, Jerome H. 2, 5–6, 43, 130, 293, 296
Nicolet, Claude 248–49
Nilsson, Martin P. 157, 238
Nock, Arthur Darby 178, 237, 239
Noé, Eralda 146
Nolland, John 6
Nordheim, Eckhard von 190
North, Helen F. 91
Nugent, S. Georgia 245
Ober, Josiah 87
O'Day, Gail 313, 316
O'Hara, James J. 225
Oldenhage, Tania 13
Omerzu, Heike 324
O'Neil, Edward N. 48, 68
Ong, Walter J. 272
Orentzel, Anne E. 86
Osiek, Carolyn 153, 170
O'Sullivan, James N. 108
O'Toole, Robert 58
Palmer, Darryl W 67
Palmer Bonz, Marianne 36, 39, 66, 77, 190, 235–36, 252, 258, 289, 321
Parsons, Mikeal C 8, 33, 47, 68, 312
Patillon, Michel 46
Pelling, Christopher 69, 78, 81, 151
Penner, Todd 32–34, 70, 72–73, 80, 82–83, 88–89, 97, 111, 146, 169, 230, 287, 289, 293, 303, 318–19, 321–22, 324–25
Perkins, Judith 105, 113, 323
Perks, Robert 276
Pervo, Richard I. 1, 8, 38, 40, 66, 105, 118, 123, 127, 160, 216, 220, 236, 287–88, 293–94, 323
Peterson, David 4, 6–7

Pfister, Friedrich 318
Phillips, Thomas E. 9
Piccarilli, Luigi 145
Plümacher, Eckhard 67, 72, 80, 235
Portelli, Alessandro 277
Porter, Stanley E. 32, 81, 139, 260, 263–65
Potter, David S. 86
Powell, Anton 236
Powell, Mark A. 10
Praeder, Susan M. 66, 105, 321
Price, Robert M. 97
Price, Simon R. F. 255
Pui-lan, Kwok 327–28
Putnam, Michael C. J. 248
Quint, David 289
Raaflaub, Kurt A. 255
Radicke, Jan 142
Rajak, Tessa 99, 141, 170
Ramsay, William M. 211–13
Raubitschek, Antony E. 81
Reardon, Bryan P. 69, 107
Reimer, Ivoni Richter 316
Reitzenstein, Richard 318
Renan, Ernest 209
Richard, Earl J. 12
Richlin, Amy 76
Robbins, Vernon K. 3, 8, 33, 48–49, 51, 67–68, 217, 258, 267–68, 279, 282, 292–93, 297, 326, 328
Rohrbach, Richard 293
Rosenblatt, Marie-Eloise 293
Rösler, Wolfgang 272
Rosner, Brian S. 67
Rothschild, Clare Komoroske 182
Rotter, Andrew J. 207
Roueché, Charlotte 127
Rowe, Christopher 92, 94
Rubin, Zeev 240
Ruiz Montero, Consuelo 107
Rusam, Dietrich 20
Russell, Donald A. 84–85, 98, 110–11, 116, 130
Ryffel, Heinrich 140, 146, 160
Sacks, Kenneth S. 81, 291
Said, Edward 207
Saïd, Suzanne 109, 119

Index of Modern Authors

Saller, Richard P.	290	Standhartinger, Angela	324
Samons, Loren J.	255	Stanford, William B.	225
Sanders, E. P.	54–55	Starr, Raymond J.	109
Sanders, Jack T.	229	Stenger, Werner	251
Sanders, James A.	20, 156	Stenschke, Christoph	6
Sandy, Gerald N.	110	Stephens, Susan A.	110
Satterthwaite, Philip E.	4, 43–44, 67	Sterling, Gregory E.	67, 73, 84, 89, 91, 145–46, 234–35, 254
Schaberg, Jane	313		
Schadewaldt, Wolfgang	196	Stewart, Roberta	96
Schaffner, Martin	276	Strecker, Georg	140
Schefold, Karl	157	Sugirtharajah, Rasiah S.	327
Scheid, John	267–68	Sussman, Lewis A.	87
Schepens, Guido	282	Svenbro, Jesper	267–68
Schierling, Marla J.	105, 321	Swain, Simon	106, 109, 131
Schierling, Stephen P.	105, 321	Swartley, Willard A.	242
Schmeling, Gareth L.	108	Syme, Ronald	248, 253–54
Schmidt, Daryl D.	8, 67, 79	Talbert, Charles H.	5–6, 66, 71, 119, 142, 164, 236
Schmidt, Karl Ludwig	29, 38		
Schmithals, Walter	251	Tannehill, Robert C.	9, 52, 118–22, 124, 257
Schneckenburger, Matthias	26, 71		
Schneider, Gerhard	249	Taylor, Justin	251
Schoell, Rudolfus	225	Taylor, Lily Ross	243, 245
Schultze, Clemence Elizabeth	146–49	Taylor, Robert O. P.	44
Schüssler Fiorenza, Elisabeth	322, 328	Thierfelder, Andreas	227
Schuster, Meinhard	271	Thomas, Christine M.	319
Schwartz, Daniel	124, 126	Thomas, Johannes	250
Schwartz, Saundra	34, 105, 309, 315–17, 321, 324	Thomas, Rosalind	301
		Thompson, Paul	276–78
Scott, Brandon B.	69	Thompson, Richard P.	9
Scott, James M.	90, 251	Thomson, Alistair	276
Scott, Walter	172	Thornton, Claus-Jürgen	73, 262, 265
Scullard, Howard H.	168	Tiede, David L.	7, 20
Seeley, David	70	Tinh, Tran Tam	171–72
Seim, Turid Karlsen	312–13, 316	Toher, Mark	146, 255
Sherwin-White, Adrian N.	124, 127, 168	Tomson, Peter J.	8
Simondon, Michèle	273	Tonkin, Elizabeth	296
Slater, William J.	127	Too, Yun Lee	77–78
Smith, Jonathan Z.	18, 173, 298, 301–2	Townsend, John T.	108
Smith, Roland	250	Trites, Allison A.	118, 129
Soards, Marion L.	43, 80, 83	Troiani, Lucio	168, 185
Söder, Rosa	318–19	Trompf, Garry W.	70, 292
Soulen, R. Kendall	25	Tuckett, Christopher M.	9
Soulen, Richard N.	25	Tyson, Joseph B.	20, 39–40, 258, 303, 322, 325, 328
Spencer, F. Scott	4, 258		
Squires, John T.	163	Unnik, Willem C. van	72, 169
Stahl, Hans-Peter	248	Vander Stichele, Caroline	70, 88, 318, 324
Stamps, Dennis L.	32		

Vansina, Jan	272, 299	Wiens, Delbert L.	84
Veltman, Fred	43	Wilckens, Ulrich	80, 169
Verheyden, Joseph	8, 10	Wilcox, Max	79
Veyne, Paul	239	Williams, Gordon	290
Vielhauer, Philip	100	Wilson, Stephen G.	119, 229, 251, 300, 303
Vinson, Richard B.	48		
Walbank, Frank W.	282	Wilson, Walter T.	89, 92, 159, 163, 287–89, 297
Walker, William O.	100		
Walker-Ramisch, Sandra	300	Wink, Walter	24
Wallace, Robert W.	94	Winkler, John J.	110, 115
Wallace-Hadrill, Andrew	93	Winkler, Lorenz	238
Wardman, Alan	292	Winter, Bruce W.	3–4, 6, 31, 43, 235
Watson, Duane F.	32, 43, 46	Winter, Sara C.	96
Watt, Ian	271	Wiseman, Timothy P.	106, 290–91
Webb, Ruth	68	Witherington, Ben	4–6, 73, 260, 265
Wedderburn, Alexander J. M.	250, 260, 263–66	Woodman, Anthony J.	248, 291
		Wordelman, Amy L.	39, 205, 321, 326
Wehnert, Jürgen	262	Wuellner, Wilhelm H.	48
Weinstock, Stefan	240, 243, 250	York, John	182, 293
Wendland, Paul	79, 237, 242	Zanker, Paul	88, 236, 249
Wengst, Klaus	240	Zeller, Eduard	207
West, David	248	Zintzen, Clemens	155
White, Peter	243, 290	Zweck, Dean	43
Whitmarsh, Tim	76	Zwiep, Arie	246

Contributors

David L. Balch is Professor of New Testament at Brite Divinity School, Fort Worth, Texas.

Samuel Byrskog is Professor in the Department of Religious Studies at Göteborg University, Sweden, and Adjunct Professor at Stockholm School of Theology, Sweden.

Gary Gilbert is Assistant Professor of Religious Studies at Claremont McKenna College, Claremont, California.

Dennis R. MacDonald is John Wesley Professor of New Testament at Claremont School of Theology and Director of the Institute for Antiquity and Christianity and Professor of Religion at Claremont Graduate University, Claremont, California.

Milton Moreland is Assistant Professor of Religion at Rhodes College, Memphis, Tennessee.

Mikeal C. Parsons is Professor and Macon Chair of Religion at Baylor University, Waco, Texas.

Todd Penner is Assistant Professor of Religion at Austin College, Sherman, Texas.

Saundra Schwartz is Assistant Professor of History and Humanities at Hawaii Pacific University, Honolulu, Hawaii.

Joseph B. Tyson is Professor Emeritus of Religious Studies at Southern Methodist University, Dallas, Texas.

Caroline Vander Stichele is Universitair Docent in Religious Studies at the University of Amsterdam, The Netherlands.

Amy L. Wordelman is Associate Director, Five College Center for the Study of World Languages, at Five Colleges, Incorporated, Amherst, Massachusetts.

www.ingramcontent.com/pod-product-compliance
Lightning Source LLC
Chambersburg PA
CBHW020636300426
44112CB00007B/134